Collectibles
PRICE GUIDE 2003

Collectibles

PRICE GUIDE 2003

Judith Miller

DK PUBLISHING

LONDON, NEW YORK, MUNICH,
MELBOURNE, DELHI

A joint production of DORLING KINDERSLEY
and THE PRICE GUIDE COMPANY

THE PRICE GUIDE COMPANY LIMITED

Publisher Judith Miller

Collectibles Specialist Mark Hill

Publishing Manager Julie Brooke

Editor Carolyn Wilmot

Assistant Editors Megan Watson, Sara Sturgess

Editorial Assistants Emily Crane, Sonya Harvey, Sarah Wainwright

Design and DTP Tim Scrivens, TJ Graphics

Digital Image Coordinator Cara Miller

Advertising Julian Ellison

Photographers Graham Rae, Bruce Boyajian, John McKenzie, Mike Molloy, Byron Slater, Elizabeth Field, Dave Pincott, Jeremy Larkin

Indexer Hilary Bird

Workflow Consultant Edward MacDermott

Business Advisor Nick Croydon

DORLING KINDERSLEY LIMITED

Category Publisher Jackie Douglas

Managing Art Editor Heather M^{C}Carry

Managing Editor Julie Oughton

DTP Designer Mike Grigoletti

Senior Designer Mandy Earey

Jacket Designer Nicola Powling

Jacket Editor Beth Apple

Production Controller Joanna Bull

Production Manager Sarah Coltman

First American Edition, 2003
00 01 02 03 04 05 10 9 8 7 6 5 4 3 2 1

Published in the United States by
DK Publishing, Inc.,
375 Hudson Street,
New York, NY 10014

The Price Guide Company (UK) Ltd
Studio 21, Waterside
44-48 Wharf Road
London N1 7UX
info@thepriceguidecompany.com

A Cataloging-in-Publication record for this book is available from the Library of Congress
ISBN 0-7894-9303-9
Printed and bound in Germany by GGP Media GmbH

See our complete product line at
www.dk.com

CONTENTS

Contents

WELCOME TO THE FIRST OF MY ANNUAL PRICE GUIDES TO COLLECTIBLES, published in association with DORLING KINDERSLEY. The market for collectibles has grown enormously in recent years and, having been part of its growth, I can understand how hard it can be to spot the reason why two seemingly similar pieces can have such different values. One of the most important things I learned early on is to look at an object. Not just a cursory glance, but a really good look. What shape is it? What color is it? What is the design or pattern like?

This is why a full-color, professionally illustrated guide is imperative. So much of what we all use to discern values is taken from the appearance of the object in front of us. This is one of the main reasons for our Closer Look features.

We can never hope to cover all collectible areas thoroughly in one book. For me, that's one of the most exciting attractions. By producing an annual guide, we hope to show you the enormous breadth of what is available over the years, but also to help you to learn more by showing you the most useful thing – the object itself – in full color with descriptive caption, price range and code showing you where the item was sold.

Judith Miller.

List of consultants

Americana

Wes Cowan
Cowans Historic Americana,
673 Wilmer Avenue,
Cincinnati, Ohio 45226

Automobilia

Tony Wraight
Finesse Fine Art,
Empool Cottage, West Knighton,
Dorset DT2 8PE, UK

Ceramics

David Rago
Craftsman Auctions,
333 North Main Street,
Lambertville,
New Jersey 08530

Judith Miller
The Price Guide Company (UK) Ltd

Commemoratives

John Pym
Hope and Glory,
131a Kensington Church Street,
London W8 7LP, UK

Computer Games

Hugo Lee Jones
electroniccollectables@hotmail.com

Costume Jewelry

John Wainwright
Vista 2000 Ltd

Steven Miners
Cristobal,
26 Church Street,
London NW8 8EP, UK

Dolls

Sidney Jeffrey
www.mydollydearest.com

Glass

Dudley Brown
James D. Julia Auctioneers Inc.,
P.O. Box 830,
Fairfield, Maine 04937

Militaria

Roy Butler
Wallis and Wallis,
West Street Auction Galleries,
Lewes, East Sussex BN7 2NJ, UK

Optical, Plastics and Scientific Instruments

Mark Hill
The Price Guide Company (UK) Ltd

Pens

Alexander Crum-Ewing
Author of *The Fountain Pen – A Collector's Companion*
alexander@crumewing.fsnet.co.uk

Space Memorabilia

Victoria Campbell
Aurora Galleries International
30 Hackamore Lane, Suite 2,
Bell Canyon, California 91307

Toys

James Bridges

Glenn Butler
Wallis and Wallis,
West Street Auction Galleries,
Lewes, East Sussex BN7 2NJ, UK

Category Heading
Indicates the general category as listed in the Table of Contents on pp.5–6.

The Object
All collectibles are shown in full color, which is a vital aid to identification and valuation.

The Caption
Describes the item and can include the maker, model, year of manufacture, size and condition.

The Price Guide
All prices are shown in ranges and give you a 'ball park' figure close to what you should expect to pay for a similar item. The great joy of collectibles is that there is not a recommended retail price. The price given is not necessarily that which a dealer will pay you. As a general rule, expect to receive approximately 30% less. When selling, pay attention to the dealer or auction house specialist to understand why this may be, and consider that they have to run a business as well as make a living. When buying, listen again. Condition, market forces, and location of the place of sale will all affect a price.

The Source Code
The image is credited to its source with a code. Use the 'Key to Illustrations' on pp.576–579 to check it against.

Find out more...
To help you seek further information, these boxes list websites, books, and museums where you can find out more.

Page Tab
Shows the first letter of the general category heading – for easy reference when using the book.

Subcategory Heading
Indicates the subcategory of the main category heading, and shows the general contents of the page.

Historical information
Provides background information on the designer, factory or make of the piece or style in question.

A Closer Look at...
Here, we highlight particularly interesting items or show identifying features, pointing out rare or desirable qualities.

TINS

- The period from the 1860s to the 1930s is considered to be the 'golden age' of tins. Tins economically, practically and decoratively housed many perishable products from biscuits to tea and tobacco. The biscuit manufacturers Huntley & Palmers are the best-known name, but desirable tins were also made by Jacob's, Crawford of Edinburgh, Fry's and Macfarlane Lang & Co.

- Novelty shapes, such as carriages, boats and books, are highly sought after. Most had realistic rich external decoration and some had moving parts such as wheels.

- Tins that advertise products are popular, partly as they illustrate the evolution of graphic advertising from the late 19th to the mid 20th centuries. Commemorative tins can cross into other collecting areas, such as royal memorabilia.

- Avoid tins that have rust, dents, scratches, splits or missing parts, such as wheels or catches. Always buy in the best condition possible but near mint or mint condition tins (when found) will command an extremely high premium. Look inside and outside for damage.

- Never wash lithograph printed tins in water as this will damage the printed surface and the underlying tin considerably.

- Keep tins away from bright sunlight, which will bleach colors.

A Huntley & Palmers 'Literature' biscuit tin, in the form of eight finely embossed books with marble edges, titled on the spines: "History of England", "Pilgrim's Progress", "Burns", "Pickwick Papers", "Robinson Crusoe", "Gulliver's Travels", "Self Help" and "Shakespeare", bound together with a simulated leather strap and buckle, bookmark pull-tab missing.

These highly popular 'trompe l'oeil' tins were a best seller in their period, with different spines showing different ranges of books.

c1901

$70-100   **DN**

A Carr and Co 'Art Box' biscuit tin, of square aluminium construction pressed with a formalized Art Nouveau design of flower heads, impressed "Rd.No.709075" with maker's initials N.C.J. for N.C.

c1924

$60-100   **DN**

An early to mid-20thC William Crawford & Sons Ltd biscuit tin caddy.

6in (15.5cm) wide

$80-120   **SS**

A Huntley & Palmers biscuit tin.
c1868   *8.5in (21.5cm) high*

$400-600   **DH**

A Huntley & Palmers 'Bookstand' tin.
c1905   *6.25in (16cm) high*

$180-220   **DH**

A Huntley & Palmers 'Creel' biscuit tin, in the shape of an angler's fishing basket with belt loops, small handle, hinged lid, and small catch, marked "Regd. No. 486204" near base on back.
c1907

$150-200   **DN**

A William Crawford & Sons 'Lucie Attwell's Fairy House' money box biscuit tin, in the shape of a mushroom printed around the stem with typical Attwell characters, the domed roof with coin slot, some rusting, dent in roof, also another small circular money box tin in the form of a clock, the dial with the inscription "Save Time & Money" and the alphabet around the perimeter.

$200-250   **DN**

A Huntley & Palmers 'Maplewood Casket' biscuit tin, in the form of an octagonal veneered wood casket with inlaid stringing around edges, the hinged lid with a central oval hunting scene, with an inscription on the base including "No.4813".

1926-27

$60-100   **DN**

A Crawford's 'Sundial' tin.

c1926   *9.5in (24cm) high*

$180-220   **DH**

A pair of Huntley & Palmers 'Worcester Vase' biscuit tins, of tapered octagonal shape with removable necks forming the lids, marked "H.B. and S. Ltd. Reading" beneath the bases.

c1934

$150-200   **DN**

A Macfarlane Lang 'Wonderland Cottage' tin money box.

c1930   5.25in (13.5cm) high

$80-120   **DH**

A Huntley & Palmers 'Ginger Nuts' tin.

c1930   1.5in (4cm) wide

$40-60   **DH**

A J. Lyons biscuit tin, to commemorate the silver jubilee of King George V and Queen Mary.

c1935   10in (25.5cm) wide

$30-50   **DH**

A Peek Frean biscuit box tin.

c1950   2.25in (5.75cm) wide

$30-40   **DH**

A W. & R. Jacob & Co Ltd 'Coronation Coach' biscuit tin, in the form of the royal coach with tinplate wheels, the removable roof with crown-shaped knop.

c1936

$150-200   **DN**

A Carr & Company Ltd biscuit tin, to commemorate the coronation of Queen Elizabeth II.

1953   11.35in (29cm) high

$30-40   **DH**

A Cadbury's Dairy Milk Chocolate money box tin, in the shape of a milk churn with removable lid, the coin slot near the top of one side.

$30-40   **DN**

A 'Tatjana Needles' record needles tin.

c1910   *1.5in (4cm) wide*

$70-100   **DH**

A 'Herald Tango' record needles tin.

c1910   *1.5in (4cm) wide*

$80-120   **DH**

A 1920s HMV 'His Masters Voice, Loud Tone' record needles tin.

1.5in (4cm) wide

$10-15   **DH**

A Sem record needles tin.

1.5in (4cm) wide

$80-120   **DH**

A rare Art Nouveau olive oil tin, with inscription "A. Bennasser, Marcca registrada Mallorca".

c1905   *6in (15cm) high*

$200-300   **DH**

A Rowntree & Co Ltd tin, to commemorate the coronation of King George V and Queen Mary.

1902   *5in (12.5cm) wide*

$20-30   **DH**

A 'Three British Queens' tin, in the form of a brass-bound carved wood casket, the surfaces embossed with Queen Mary's royal initials "R" and "M.I."

$30-40   **DN**

FIND OUT MORE...

Museum of Reading, Blagrave Street, Reading, RG1 1QH, England, www.readingmuseum.org.uk . This museum houses a display of over 300 tins made for Reading-based biscuit maker, Huntley & Palmers.

'Biscuit Tins 1868-1939: The Art of Decorative Packaging', by M.J. Franklin, New Cavendish Books, U.S.A.

'Decorative Printed Tins: The Golden Age of Printed Tin Packaging', by David Griffith, Studio Vista, 1996.

A Queen Mary's Troops Christmas tin.

1914   *5in (13cm) wide*

$30-50   **MB**

A J. S. Fry & Sons tin, to commemorate the silver jubilee of King George V and Queen Mary.

1935   *7.5in (19cm) wide*

$30-40   **DH**

A tin, showing George VI, Queen Elizabeth, and Princesses Elizabeth and Margaret.

5.25in (13.5cm) wide

$30-40 DH

A Mazawatte 'Old Folks at Home' tea tin.

3.75in (9.5cm) wide

$30-40 DH

A Matabele Tobacco tin.

3in (8cm) high

$320-280 DH

A Prince of Wales Cigarettes tin.
c1900 *3in (7.5cm) wide*

$300-400 DH

A Gaiety Girl Straight Cut Cigarettes tin.

3in (7.5cm) high

$300-500 DH

A Macdonalds Cut Golden Bar 'Kitty Brand' tin, Glasgow.

4in (10cm) high

$100-150 DH

A 1950s Salvation Army Collection tin, with inscription 'Where there's need there's The Salvation Army' with key, remains of paper label to base.

5in (12.5cm) high

$30-40 DH

A rare Johnson & Gluckstein Ltd 'King Rufus Cigarettes' tin.
c1950

$700-1,000 DH

A 1930s John Player & Sons 'Players Navy Cut' tin, with printed paper label.

2.25in (5.5cm) diam

$15-20 DH

A SPG Medical Missions collecting tin, in the shape of a medicine bottle, with inscription 'Society for the Propagation of the Gospel in Foreign Parts'.

c1910 *6.25in (16cm) high*

$15-25 DH

A Cunard Line tin.

c1920 *3.25in (8.5cm) wide*

$300-500 DH

- Card signs, also known as 'standees', were made as counter top displays for use in shops and department stores, using brightly colored and stylish period designs to attract customers' attention.
- Usually more affordable than posters advertising the same product, collectors can build collections comparatively inexpensively.
- Card signs are smaller and easier to display and store than posters.
- They often had the same or similar artwork as the poster version of the same product by familiar poster artists, so collectors can still follow the changing fashions and styles of advertising through the ages.

A Salamander Brandy card sign.

15.75in (40cm) high

$180-225   DO

An Ovaltine card sign, 'Drink Delicious Ovaltine & Face the Winter with a Smile'.

14.5in (37cm) high

$70-100   DO

A Dubonnet card sign, 'Donne de l'appetit pour deux'.

14.5in (36.5cm) high

$70-100   DO

A Symons Devonshire Cider card sign.

13in (33cm) wide

$50-80   DO

An Edmondson's Toffee card sign.

18in (45.5cm) high

$50-80   DO

A Marquise Slumber & Setting Net card sign, 'In all Hair Pastel Shades, Made in England'.

12.5in (32cm) high

$50-80   DO

A Crème Mouson card sign, 'Agissant en Profondeur.'

12in (30.5cm) high

$70-100   DO

A Drocourt card sign, 'Desserts de la favorite desserts du roi'.

15.75in (40cm) high

$30-40   DO

A Pitralon card sign.

16.5in (42cm) high

$30-50   DO

A Meridian card sign, 'The Perfect Fabric for Sensitive Skins'.

9.5in (24cm) high

$5-8   DO

A Radiator Glace de Lingue card sign.

15.75in (40cm) high

$80-120   **DO**

A Japlac card sign, 'For Magic Colour Laquer Paint'.

14.25in (36cm) high

$50-80   **DO**

A Maëstro card sign.

17.25in (43.5cm) high

$70-100   **DO**

A Charles Roberson & Co. card sign.

17.75in (45cm) high

$60-100   **DO**

A Nuit à l'Arlequin card sign, Paris.

14in (35.5cm) high

$60-100   **DO**

A Jager Krüllschnitt Cruwell Tabak card sign.

15in (38cm) high

$50-80   **DO**

An Anggoer Obat Serravallo card sign.

11.5in (29.5cm) high

$50-80   **DO**

An Anggoer Obat Serravallo card sign.

16.25in (41cm) high

$50-80   **DO**

A 1930s Ashtead Potters Guinness ashtray, "Guinness is Good for You".
4.25in (11cm) diam

$60-100   **DH**

FIND OUT MORE...
www.guinntiques.com

A Guinness poster, "See the Animals at Edinburgh Zoo".
30in (76cm) high

$300-500   **DO**

A pair of 20thC novelty Guinness pottery salt and pepper shakers, each in the form of a pint of Guinness.
2in (5cm) high

$100-150   **J&H**

A Guinness rubber toucan advertising figure.
1950s   *6.75in (17cm) high*

$180-220   **DH**

GUINNESS MEMORABILIA

- Guinness advertising started in 1928, with the famous toucan character by the artist John Gilroy (1898-1985) being introduced in 1935.
- The slogan 'Guinness is good for you' was thought up by the advertising company S.H. Benson Ltd., who employed Gilroy and worked with Guinness from 1928.
- In the 1950s, Carlton Ware were commissioned to make advertising ceramics for Guinness and produced a sought-after range of designs.
- Since the late 1920s a huge range of items have been produced and Guinness has become a collecting subject all of its own.
- Collectors should beware that many reproductions of ceramic Guinness memorabilia exist, especially the flying toucan wall ornaments. Although these are collectable, values should be much lower than for the originals.

A late 1940s Guinness blue and white plate, "My Goodness My Guinness".
6.75in (17.5cm) diam

$50-80   **DH**

A 1950s Guinness paper cup, "Guinness is good for you".
4.5in (11.5cm) high

$10-15   **DH**

A set of six 1950s Guinness buttons, "Guinness is Good for You".
Box 6.25in (16cm)

$80-120   **DH**

A Guinness pocket calendar, "My Goodness My Guinness".
1959   *3.5in (9cm) high*

$30-50   **DH**

A Carlton Ware Guinness penguin table lamp, holding a plaque inscribed "Draught Guinness", the figure with original fitting and shade.
6.75in (17cm) high

$700-1,000   **BAR**

A pair of Coca-Cola advertising trays, each pictures a woman outdoors with a glass of Coke, with minimal overall wear.

c1917   6in (15cm) high

$500-600   **HA**

Two Coca-Cola advertising trays, featuring a golf scene and drive-in restaurant, with light age wear.

1927   13in (33cm) long

$850-950   **HA**

Three 1920s advertising tin trays, including two Coca-Cola painted trays each of a woman drinking Coke, one tray with blemish at bottom right corner, also includes a Hires tray with portrait of a woman.

1920s   13in (33cm) long

$850-950   **HA**

Three Coco-Cola enamel signs, of three decades, two German and one Dutch.

$220-280   **TK**

A large enameled tin sign button, made in Canada, paint on the edge restored.

48in (122cm) diam

$200-300   **TK**

A department store restaurant advertising display banana split.

$30-40   **BCAC**

A department store restaurant advertising display of a slice of cake on a plate.

$25-35   **BCAC**

A department store restaurant advertising display chocolate cake.

$35-45   **BCAC**

A Kentucky Fried Chicken Colonel Saunders advertising figure, with nodding head

$100-300   **Koz**

A Warner Brothers Superman IV cardboard advertising placard, in the form of a cut-out figure of Christopher Reeve, some minor damage, written inscription for Cannon Cinema, Reading, England.

c1987   71.75in (182cm) high

$45-55   **DN**

A 1960s Sony boy advertising toy.

$200-400   **Koz**

A Rockwood Milk Chocolate advertising model cow.

$200-300   **BCAC**

A watch trade sign, original paint.

38.5in (72cm) long

$1,200-1,600   **BCAC**

A locksmith's trade sign.

Such metal trade signs were made to hang outside a tradesman's shop and advertised their products or services very clearly, through the use of a related motif. They fell out of use during the 20thC, and were replaced with signs bearing the brand or name of the shop. Condition, particularly of the finish or paint, is often very poor due to damage and wear caused by birds and the weather. Nevertheless, they make very decorative features.

39in (99cm) wide

$1,200-1,800   **BCAC**

A 19thC painted tin country store dispenser, inscribed "American Can Company" and "70", nice original finish, some dents.

12.5in (31.5cm) high

$350-450   **TWC**

A rare store window advertisement for a man's truss.

c1930

$180-220   **BCAC**

A 1950s Aspro medicine dispenser/self-serve automatic machine.

$120-180   **DH**

A Mayo's tobacco advertising sign, large painted canvas banner, with light overall wear.

c1910   *47in (119.5cm) long*

$120-180   **HA**

Two Lorillard snuff jars, including an amber glass jar, lacking cork, with Maccoboy Snuff paper label, and an amber glass jar with Maccoboy Snuff paper label, retaining original cork.

c1900 Tallest 4.5in (11.5cm) high

$500-600   **HA**

A lithographed metal store advertising display, for Flamemaster Asbestos Wicking.

c1925   *13in (33cm) high*

$25-35   **TWC**

A Planters Peanuts counter top display jar, with raised lettering and Mr Peanut characters, glass lid may not be original.

12in (30.5cm) high

$40-60   **TWC**

A "Boye" lithographed tin general store needle dispenser display, in very nice working condition, retains some of the original needle tubes.

16in (40.5cm) diam

$100-200   **TWC**

A quantity of 1920s/30s Player's Cigarettes cards, includes a set of cricketers, tennis group, uniforms of the Territorial Army group, Speedway Riders group, and actors group, also includes five original cigarette boxes.

$50-60   **HA**

PHOTOGRAPHS

- Scarce photographic images of well-known historical personalities and those showing native American Indians in unusual or traditional settings are very popular and desirable. The better known the personality or composition and subject matter, the higher the price.
- There are many different types of photograph, many of which took considerable time to develop. Tintypes were inexpensive photographs on tin, taken and developed quickly.
- As well as composition, condition is important. If out of their cases, the image can be scratched and worn which reduces value. Cleaning and restoration should only be undertaken by a professional.

A late 19thC sixth-plate tintype of a cavalryman, holding a Starr revolver, in a full composition case.

$400-500 CHAA

A late 19thC sixth-plate tintype of a Civil War African-American enlisted man, in a black gutta percha case, with minor corner damage.

$500-600 CHAA

A late 19thC quarter-plate tintype of two non-commissioned officers, standing behind a 34-star flag, in full composition case.

$750-850 CHAA

A late 19thC quarter-plate ruby ambrotype of a mounted Union cavalry officer, brandishing his saber against the backdrop of an unidentified stone building, remounted in an earlier daguerreotype mat and retainer, in a full composition case.

$1,400-1,600 CHAA

A carte-de-visite of armed Private John K. Messmore, 99th OVI, anonymous, with period pencil identification on verso.

Messmore, of Company D, enlisted in June 1862 and transferred to the Veteran Reserve Corps in October 1864, finally mustering out in June 1865. Raised in Lima, Ohio, the 99th OVI marched to Perryville and was baptized by fire at Stones' River. The regiment participated in the Tullahoma campaign followed by Chickamauga, then Atlanta with the 23rd Corps.

$350-450 CHAA

A carte-de-visite of General George Custer, from a negative by Mora, on light blue mount, possibly a copy print.

$500-600 CHAA

A cabinet card of William Tecumseh Sherman, as Major General, by Sarony, signed in verso and dated 1889, with an additional personal inscription on verso, signed and dated March, 11, 1889.

$1,000-1,500 CHAA

A carte-de-visite of Major T. S. Osborn, 1st New York Light Artillary, by "Hart's Gallery, Watertown, NY" and signed "T.W. Osborn Col." in his hand on verso.

Osborn originally commanded Battery D, 1st NYLA before promotion to Major in March 1863. Subsequently, he was Chief of 11th Corps artillery at Gettysburg and later O. O. Howard's 4th Corps artillery during the Atlanta campaign. Osborn is cited frequently in the Offical Records.

$1,000-1,200 | **CHAA**

An albumen print of American Horse, unsigned but -attributed to C. M. Bell, mounted with Rookwood typed strip label and handstamp on verso.

This image was purchased from the Rookwood Pottery files.

$1,200-1,800 | **CHAA**

An albumen print of Ponca chief Standing Buffalo, unsigned but attributed to C. M. Bell, mounted on larger board, with Rookwood Pottery typed strip label and handstamp on verso.

Bell was a long-time Washington photographer who captured images of visiting American Indian delegation members. Purchased from the Rookwood Pottery when the studio ws moved in the 1960s; probably originally purchased from the Bureau of American Ethology.

7.5in (19cm) high

$1,500-2,000 | **CHAA**

An albumen cabinet card with two images of Rain-In-The-Face, on W. E. Hook orange stock, slight surface soil.

This Sioux chief supposedly killed General Custer.

$260-300 | **CHAA**

An albumen print of an Ogallak Sioux woman, mounted on larger board, with Rookwood Pottery typed strip label and handstamp verso, three small glue spots on print to left; mount with surface dirt.

The original negative was probably taken by Alexander Gardner, during a visit of a treaty delegation in 1872; printed later by the Bureau of American Ethology. Purchased from the Rookwood Pottery.

7.5in (19cm) high

$300-400 | **CHAA**

An albumen print of a Yankton chief, mounted on larger board, titled in negative "L(ower) Yanktonai 2", with Rookwood Pottery handstamp on verso, printed from an original cracked negative; mount with edge chips or tears, none affecting image.

The neagative for this print is probably by Alexander Gardner and was taken when the chief was part of a treaty delegation in Washington in 1872. It is likely it was printed later by the Bureau of American Ethology. Purchased from the Rookwood Pottery.

7.5in (19cm) high

$2,000-2,500 | **CHAA**

An albumen print of Ponca chief Hairy Bear, unsigned but attributed to C. M. Bell, mounted on larger board, with Rookwood Pottery typed strip label and handstamp on verso.

Purchased from the Rookwood Pottery files.

7in (18cm) high

$2,500-3,000 | **CHAA**

A carte-de-visite of an Indian holding a bow, by the Jackson Brothers, on mount, with crayon ID "Long Tail" on verso, card stock with stain. 1868-70

$150-200 | **CHAA**

A carte-de-visite of Winnebago Indian, Little Man, by Joel Whitney of St. Paul, with discoloration in several places along margin that appears to be in original negative.

$300-400 | **CHAA**

A cabinet card of a Wild West performer, possibly Texas Ben, unsigned but possibly by Julius Wendt, trimmed at bottom of mount.

$100-150 | **CHAA**

An albumen cabinet card of an Ute squaw with papoose, by Charles R. Savage of Salt Lake, titled in negative "Indian Cradle Ute Tribe", and with inked inscription on verso "Chief Wooly Head's Wife and Child".

$400-500   CHAA

A cabinet card of Wild West performers Texas Ben and Texas Annie, with imprint of Julius Wendt, of New York, faint pencilled inscription on verso "Compliments of Texas Ben and Texas Annie, Dallas, TEX" that may not be original.

$400-500   CHAA

A cabinet-sized silver gelatin print of a Wild West woman, anonymous, mounted on larger grey card stock, upper left corner of mount broken.
c1910

$250-350   CHAA

An albumen carte-de-visite of Jefferson Davis, with Anthony backmark, adhesive stain where photo was attached to card.

$120-180   CHAA

A small tintype of Abraham Lincoln, mounted in a carte-de-visite sized card with lithographed frames, some toning.

Card 4in (10cm) high

$550-650   CHAA

An albumen print of a Civil War tinclad, probably the "Judge Torrence", anonymous, mounted on larger board, mount with slight surface soil, tiny tack holes in corners.

7.25in (18.5cm) wide

$500-600   CHAA

A quarter-plate tintype of Mark Twain's steamboat Arago, anonymous, image dark, with bends, and scratches.

Like many inland-water steamers, the Arago was built at Brownsville, Pennsylvania, leaving in March 1860 on her first trip, to St. Louis. From there she formed part of the St. Louis, Arkansas River and Vicksburg Line. On July 31, 1860, the Arago left St. Louis for Vicksburg, with Samuel Clemens standing pilot watch, with J.W. Hood acting as his partner. George Sloan was the boat's master, and principal owner. Returning to Cairo on August 11th, the packet left the following day for New Orleans, and returned to St. Louis on August 31. It was during the trip from New Orleans to St. Louis that Clemens penned "The Pilot's Memoranda" that he and Hood published on August 31st. This image of the Arago was likely taken not long after the outbreak of the war, as attested by the iron railing around the lower part of the pilothouse. Initially placed here to fend off shot and cannonballs, this light armoring eventually gave way to the famous "tinclads" of the "Brown-water Navy".

An albumen print of a Civil War ironclad ship, on the Mississippi, with the bluffs of Vicksburg or Natchez in the distance, the letters "S" and "X" visible on her stacks, mounted on larger board, mount with tiny tack holes in corners.

7.5in (19cm) wide

$900-1,000   CHAA

$1,800-2,200   CHAA

A pair of unusual Benjamin Harrison campaign ribbons, comprising a ribbon with affixed shield carved in mother-of-pearl, together with a small flag affixed to an unusual bar with photographic portrait.

Three Benjamin Harrison campaign ribbons, including one with an affixed celluloid portrait, an example from Lancaster, PA and another from Yonkers' "Business Men's Protection Club" with unusual name bar.

A McKinley-Hobart campaign ribbon, issued by the "Cloak and Suit Trade," with solid brass and celluloid bar at top.

$150-250	CHAA

$150-250	CHAA

$350-450	CHAA

A Grand Army of the Republic delegates badge, from the Philadelphia encampment, gilded brass with white metal and enamel on a ribbon, in original paste-board box.

These badges were given to delegates who attended the 33rd GAR encampment, or convention, held in Philadelphia, in 1890. It features the Liberty Bell, Independence Hall and the PA state seal.

A Garfield-Arthur cardboard campaign badge, with portraits of Garfield and Arthur, attached to red ribbon with black lettering, "For President, J.A. Garfield. For Vice President, C.A. Arthur", some scattered light soiling.

A Cleveland-Hendrix campaign shell badge, with jugate albumen photo in a brass shell pin, with ribbon.

Image 1in (2.5cm) diam

4.75in (12cm) long

5in (12.5cm) long

$500-600	CHAA

$350-450	CHAA

$550-650	CHAA

A Grover Cleveland silk ribbon, with sepia photo of Cleveland applied to frame in a gilt banner which reads, "Cleveland Our President", some wear to bottom of gilt image.

A pair of James Blaine campaign ribbons, comprising a Sullivan/Fischer ribbon, with illustration of a campaign banner in support of Blaine and Logan in 1884 by the Utica Continentals, a club in Upstate New York, and a reception ribbon for an 1886 visit by Blaine to Altoona, PA.

A large Horatio Seymour campaign stickpin, with ferrotype portrait in beveled frame.

A Horatio Seymour ferro stickpin, in brass shell with red enamel surround, minor streak on face.

7in (18cm) long

1in (2.5cm) diam

0.75in (2cm) diam

$180-220	CHAA

$550-650	CHAA

$180-220	CHAA

$180-220	CHAA

A rare McKinley tin tab badge, die-cut lithographed shield with McKinley in the center, with a few spots of rust along the edge.

4in (10cm) wide

$500-600 CHAA

A rare cotton Henry Clay Texas campaign flag, with the added names of Houston and Stockton below Clay and Frelinghuysen, colors bright, minor scattered browning, small piece missing at far right.

The added names refer to Sam Houston and probably Robert Stockton, both of whom figured in the "Texas Question." Houston's role in the struggle for Texas's independence is clear, but Stockton's merits further mention and provides clues to the origins of this textile. Richard Stockton (1817-1836) was a member of the Stockton lineage of New Jersey. After the death of his father, he moved first to Virginia (1823), and then to Nagadoches, Texas. Along with other Easterners, he joined the Texas Volunteer Auxiliary Corps in December of 1835. He was sent to San Antonio de Bexar with Crockett and was killed in the battle of the Alamo on March 6, 1836. The juxtaposition of two Texas heroes' names – one from a New Jersey family – suggests the flag was meant to appeal to potential New Jersey voters who supported annexation, and is testimony to Clay's hesitancy over the matter which led directly to Polk's election.

61in (155cm) wide

$16,000-18,000 CHAA

A Benjamin Harrison campaign poster, "The Nation Redeemed! Protection the National Policy. Hurrah! Harrison Electors 233. Cleveland 168. Congress Republican. VICTORY!", some restoration.

28in (71cm) high

$550-650 CHAA

A Lincoln-Hamilton campaign flag, with 33 stars in the field of blue and attached to a wooden stick, small hole from top near the field of stars and a larger hole in the same strip of linen, only slightly faded.

1860   11.5in (29cm) wide

$7,500-8,500 CHAA

A McKinley-Roosevelt campaign parade umbrella, with portraits of the candidates on two sides, fading to the flag design and several fabric stains and large holes at the top where the umbrella is attached to the frame.

$180-220 CHAA

An 1856 Presidential candidates campaign poster, issued as a supplement for the NYC newspaper "Brother Jonathan" and given as a "memento of the Christmas Holidays" with central column of advertising messages from the publisher.

34in (86.5cm) high

$550-650 CHAA

A Benjamin Harrison silk campaign hankerchief.

1888   18in (45.5cm) wide

$130-150 CHAA

A Roosevelt and Fairbanks campaign banner, faded and showing light staining throughout.

1904

$350-450 CHAA

A Blain and Logan campaign parade helmet, canvas over heavy cardboard, with hatband reading "Blaine and Logan", lacks plume and break across top.

$350-450 CHAA

A Lincoln satirical cartoon, showing Lincoln and Davis in a tug-of-war with a map of the United States, caption reads: "The True Issue or 'That's Whats the Matter'", framed and glazed.

9in (23cm) wide

$400-450   **CHAA**

An early George Washington printed felt portrait, based on the painting by Gilbert Stuart. minor pile loss in upper right corner, colors still bright, framed and glazed with old Staton's Galleries, Phil., label retained on verso.

c1810-20 21in (53.5cm) high

$650-750   **CHAA**

A George Washington "Forget Me Not" pin box, with hand-colored glass lid adorned by a portrait of Washington with a mirror recessed in the inside lid, and a glass panel on the bottom with a heart-shaped valentine sentiment.

3.75in (9.5cm) high

$650-750   **CHAA**

A group of Andrew Jackson "Hard Time" tokens, showing expected age and dark patina.

These 'substitute' coins date from the financial panic of 1837-8, and were made to ridicule the Administration by mimicking the gold and silver currency of the day.

$250-350   **CHAA**

A pamphlet debating the 12th Amendment, "Mr. Tracy's Speech in the Senate of the United States, Friday, December 2, 1803, 8vo pamphlet bound with red silk ribbon, lacks final page of the original 24.

In the wake of the Jefferson-Burr election debacle of 1800, an amendment to the Constitution was proposed to prevent a reoccurrence. It called for separate balloting for the offices of president and Vice-President. Uriah Tracy, a Federalist Senator from Connecticut who succeeded Jonathan Trumbull, voices his opposition to the bill, fearing it would prevent the most qualified men from being elected. His "nay" vote is recorded on the last page of the pamphlet.

1803

$250-350   **CHAA**

A handmade 34-star American flag, with machine-sewn stripes and hand-sewn stars, some repairs, shows signs of use.

The canton (the blue square) sits on red rather than white, which may be intentional as this flag became official in July 1861 with the admission of Kansas to the Union, and several months after the first battle of the civil war at Ft. Sumter. The official 34-star flag had rows of stars in 7-7-6-7-7 pattern, whilst this one has five rows of six stars with the remaining four at the bottom.

41.5in (105.5cm) wide

$3,000-4,000   **CHAA**

Folk Art

A Pennsylvania German rainbow quilt, excellent condition.

c1910

$900-1,100   **BCAC**

A Pennsylvania quilt, appliquéd.

c1870

$1,200-1,800   **BCAC**

A folkart marquetry plaque of William McKinkley, unsigned, in fancy inlay frame.

14in (35.5cm) high

$300-350   **CHAA**

A Pennsylvania German Scherenschnitte of two birds, in tiger maple frame.

Motif 4.75in (12cm) square

$100-150   **BCAC**

A framed bookmark, possibly a Valentine's gift, from Governor Hubbard's house in Augusta, Maine, motto reads: "J. Hubbard keep thy heart with all diligence".

c1840   *12in (30.5cm) long*

$875-975   **RAA**

A pack basket, Adirondack NY, woven from red oak splints, double-wrapped rim, runners on base for reinforcement, leather strap around top.

c1840   *20in (51cm) high*

$570-650   **RAA**

A pack basket, painted red oak splints, double-wrapped rim, runners on base for reinforcement, leather strap around top.

c1840   *17in (43cm) high*

$850-950   **RAA**

A blue and natural splint basket, with handle.

These baskets were tourist souvenirs.

$260-300   **RAA**

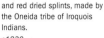

A miniature basket, natural and red dried splints, made by the Oneida tribe of Iroquois Indians.

c1830

$260-300   **RAA**

A piece of calligraphy, pen and ink on woven paper, "Youth is to precipitate" and featuring an American eagle and shield, drawn by Sanford Yeoman of Columbia, New York City.

1824   *9.5in (24cm) high*

$570-650   **RAA**

A ballot box, NY state, cast iron frame, painted pine box rotates and tumbles, probably used by a fraternal organization.

c1910   *11in (28cm) high*

$260-300   **RAA**

A rare and unusual 19thC doll of a farmer.

Provenance: The Abbey Aldrich Rockefeller Folk Art Collection, Williamsburg VA.

29in (73.5cm) high

$2,200-2,800   **BCAC**

A folky painted 'Indian' on a stand.

39in (99cm) high

$1,200-1,800   **BCAC**

TRADE CATALOGS

- Trade catalogs are highly collectible as they act as excellent, original reference guides to what a company produced, helping collectors to date pieces.
- However, dates should not be relied on for total accuracy as a piece may have been produced for years before or after it appeared in the catalog.
- Original prices, different sizes or formats available and entire product ranges can be seen. They also act as first hand references to decorative styles of the period.
- Condition is important, but as they are paper items, many have not survived in good condition. Some foxing and wear is acceptable as they are important as reference sources, rather than as an aesthetic object.

An 1890s Robert Mitchell Furniture Company household furniture trade catalog, folio in horizontal format, over 144 pages, printed paper wraps, lithographed illustrations.

$180-220   **CHAA**

An Anderson Furniture Co. trade catalog, titled "Our Perpetual Catalogue", from the Anderson Furniture Co., Ltd., Woodstock, Ontario, Canada.

1900

$500-600   **CHAA**

An Indiana Furniture Company, Connersville, IN, trade catalog, dated January 1905, illustrating "Sideboards, Buffets and Odd Dressers," 48 pages.

1905

$250-350   **CHAA**

An 1870s Mitchell, Vance & Co trade catalog, comprising 57 loose plates of chromolithographs.

$3,500-4,500   **CHAA**

A Galloway Pottery Co. trade catalog No. 29, 52 pages.

$80-120   **CHAA**

A rare Civil War regulation 8 frock coat of Lt. Josiah Meigs Hubbard, 11th Kansas Cavalry, together with sword belt and intact hangers. Lacking all but two of the original buttons, the coat shows considerable wear from use.

Josiah Meigs Hubbard, of Middletown, Connecticut, was an early Kansas Free-Soiler, an original member of the New Haven Colony and Beecher Rifle Company. He was a founder of the town of Wabaunsee, Kansas, and was serving as Judge of the Wabaunsee County Probate when he enlisted as a 1st Lieutenant in Company K, 11th Kansas Infantry in September 1862. He saw action in Arkansas, Kansas and Missouri. Hubbard returned to the family farm in Middletown in 1865 and, except for the occasional reunion in Kansas, remained there until his death in 1909. For the last 45 years of his life he was a gentleman-farmer engaged in civic pursuits. He was elected to county office and later to the Connecticut General Assembly serving also as Commissioner and Trustee on numerous State, institutional and academic boards. His descendants still reside near Middletown.

$6,000-8,000   CHAA

A United Confederate Veterans kepi, with tarred leather bill and canvas liner, traces of old paper label on inside, repaired and sweat stained.

$250-350   CHAA

A Civil War era decorated snare drum, with paint-decorated spread-winged eagle holding a ribbon banner with "Reg. U.S. Infantry", some paint loss.
17in (43cm) high

$1,500-2,000   CHAA

An anti-slavery meeting broadside, probably New England, announcing a fair to be held in conjunction with a local anti-slavery meeting to raise funds for the anti-slavery cause. *c1840s-50s 16in (40.5cm) wide*

$1,800-2,200   CHAA

Two steel bookends, made from track from the first railroad to Skagway; engraved on other side edge "Made in Skagway Alaska by J.D. True".
3.75in (9.5cm) high

$180-220   CHAA

An 1840s slave bill of sale, large 8vo, one page receipt for the sale of Juliet, "about twenty two years age....sound in mind and body, a slave for life..." signed "B.H. Dockery & Co."

$180-220   CHAA

An Allender patent counterfeit gold coin detector, with pans marked for $10, 20, 5, 2.5 and 1 gold dollars, marked "Patent Pending", lacks counter weight.
1851-53

$180-220   CHAA

A half-sheet Buffalo Bill's Wild West Show advertising poster, featuring Chief Iron Tail, printed by The Enquirer Job Printing Co., Cincinnati, OH, recently restored and linen-backed.
28in (71cm) high

$6,000-8,000   CHAA

A Buffalo Bill's Wild West Show farewell tour program, 36 pages in chromolithographed paper wraps, published by L.M. Southern & Co., NY & Cincinnati, and printed by Chas. O. Ebel, Cincinnati.

$150-250   CHAA

A relic from Commodore Perry's flag ship, USS Niagara, comprising a large piece of oak and an iron spike, with label reading; "Part of the - Brig - U.S.S. Niagara. Flagship of Commodore Perry U.S.N. Battle of Lake Erie 1813..." and in ink "H.H. Murphy -- Erie, Pa."

$1,400-1,800   CHAA

A section of TransAtlantic telegraph cable, together with the original certification issued by Tiffany's, lacks brass plate with Tiffany identification from center of cable section.

$250-350   CHAA

DUCK DECOYS

- Duck decoys originate in America before pioneering settlers arrived, with Native Americans binding together reeds and sticks to make models of ducks. By the mid 1800s, a small but widespread industry creating wooden decoy ducks had grown, including factories such as the 'Mason Decoy Factory' in Michigan.

- The aim of decoys is to attract live ducks to land near them so that they are within hunting range. Decoys are often arranged in groups called 'rigs' with decoys in different but natural poses including preening, sleeping or feeding. This would fool live ducks into thinking the area was safe, so that they would join the dummy ducks.

- Large scale production continued through the late 19th century and up until the 1920s when the threat of extinction of some birds led to the outlawing of commercial bird hunting. This led to a decline in demand for decoys by hunters, but collectors of folk art and those who appreciate the forms of these models have meant that production has continued, albeit on a smaller basis.

- Decoys are hotly collected today by a growing number of enthusiasts, with specialist auctions devoted to them. The market is divided into regions, each with their own carvers and styles based on indigenous birds.

- Collectors look out for 19th century examples, particularly those by noted makers such as Obediah Verity, William Bowman and Elmer Crowell, although many of these fetch extremely high prices when offered for sale. Noted makers of the 20th century include the Ward brothers.

- Signatures on a decoy are not necessarily the maker and often relate to the owner. Collectors should look out for decoys in as good condition as possible. Some of the more naïve versions can be highly attractive folk art pieces.

A drake duck decoy, from New Jersey, hollow construction, glass eyes, old gunning paint.

13in (33cm) long

$320-380   BCAC

A widgeon drake duck decoy, maker unknown, from California, very old original paint, gunning wear.

11in (28cm) long

$250-350   BCAC

A drake canvasback duck decoy, maker unknown, from Susquehana Flats, Havre de Grace, Maryland, very early, worn gunning paint, cast iron keel weight.

c1900   14in (36cm) long

$200-300   BCAC

A duck decoy, one of a pair of white wing scoters, from New England, old gunning paint, tack eyes, branded by gunman.

c1930

$250-350   BCAC

A pintail drake duck decoy, early and very primitive, original paint with gunning wear.

16.5in (42cm) long

$100-150   BCAC

A Goldeneye drake decoy duck, maker unknown, very primitive, tack eyes, very old gunning paint.

13in (33cm) long

$180-220   BCAC

A black duck decoy, made by Raoul Pilon, Quebec, all original scratch painting, turned head.

c1930   15.75in (40cm) long

$300-400   BCAC

A eider drake duck decoy, original gunning paint, maker unknown, unusual size.

13in (33cm) long

$200-250   BCAC

A Mallard duck decoy, cork, sleeping head construction, original paint, maker unknown.

12.25in (31cm) long

$100-170   BCAC

A Canada goose decoy, hollow construction, Delaware River style, original paint with gunning wear.

20in (51cm) long

$600-700   BCAC

A green-winged teal duck decoy, by George 'Coot' Ganton, Bridgeton, New Jersey, all original, glass eyes, unique swimming head position.

13.25in (33.5cm) long

$100-140   BCAC

A Canada goose decoy, hollow construction, Delaware River style, original paint with gunning wear.

22.75in (58cm) long

$600-700   BCAC

A Canada goose decoy, made by Nick Calvese and John Egel, Delaware River, Trenton, New Jersey area, all original, hollow construction, tack eyes, swimming head position, gunning wear.

$500-700   **BCAC**

A Canada goose decoy, by Jay Parker of Parkertown New Jersey, early paint, unusual swimming head position.
c1920

$650-750   **BCAC**

A yellowlegs decoy, made by Ken Kirby, South Carolina, carved and painted in the style of Harry Y. Shounds, all original, glass eyes.

A peep or sandling decoy, metal bill and tack eyes.

7in (18cm) long

A curlew decoy, by Ken Kirby, South Carolina, all original, largely carved in the Bowman style, carved wing, glass eyes.

A yellowlegs decoy, by Bruce Bieber, New Jersey Shore, all original, turned head in preening position, painted eyes.

$100-140   **BCAC**   **$100-140**   **BCAC**   **$100-170**   **BCAC**   **$100-140**   **BCAC**

A curlew decoy, made by Bill Sachse, all original, in gunning/feeding position.

$100-170   **BCAC**

FIND OUT MORE...

The Havre de Grace Decoy Museum, 215 Giles Street, Havre de Grace, MD 21078, USA.

William F. Mackey Jnr, 'American Bird Decoys', published by E.P. Dutton & Co. 1965.

A spotted salamander fish decoy, from Wisconsin, all original.

A spotted salamander fish decoy, from Minnesota, all original, glass eyes.

$50-80   **BCAC**   **$70-90**   **BCAC**

A rainbow trout fish decoy, hand-carved and painted, tin fins, tack eyes.

Fish decoys were used for much the same purposes as duck decoys – to attract fish when hunting. Attached to a 'jiggling stick' they could be jerked about underwater to fool other fish, such as pike, into coming close to them where they would be caught.

19.75in (50cm) long

$100-150   **BCAC**

A salamander fish decoy, from Wisconsin, all original.

Brightly colored salamander decoys were used to attract fish.

$50-80   **BCAC**

ANTIQUITIES

- An antiquity is the physical remains or a relic from Ancient times and usually originates from the Middle or Far East and some Mediterranean countries. Considering the age of the pieces, the antiquities market is very accessible, with many affordable prices. However, smaller pieces such as ushabti, amulets and jewellery, previously at the lower end of the market, now command higher prices.

- Many of the pieces available to the collector will be domestic in original use and will have been made in large quantities, such as oil lamps, vessels, or jewellery.

- Weapons are also commonly found and affordable. Luristan, in Western Iran, has become noted for its engraved bronze weapons, which are deemed sophisticated.

- Over the past ten years, the antiquities trade has been riddled with high profile stories involving looting of sites and fakes. Although this is not unusual, and has occurred for as long as the trade has existed, always buy from a reputable dealer or auction house who will be happy to demonstrate their expertise and probity.

- Despite its fragility, much Roman glass has survived and with its delicate colouring, makes a superb collection. In most cases, long periods of burial have altered the surface of the glass making uniquely and beautifully coloured pieces that have inspired designers such as Louis Comfort Tiffany and Christopher Dresser.

- Size, period and subject matter will affect value. Also look closely at the quality of manufacture and condition. Learn how to recognise styles and characters and motifs such as the gods which are depicted frequently.

Amulets

An Egyptian faience amulet, depicting Horus as a hawk.

c400 BC   *1.5in (3.5cm) high*

$100-150   AnA

A Egyptian blue faience amulet, depicting Horus with Solar disc.

c400 BC   *1in (2.5cm) high*

$150-200   AnA

An Egyptian faience amulet, of a papyrus scroll.

c400 BC   *2in (5cm) high*

$70-100   AnA

An Egyptian faience amulet, depicting the Eye of Horus.

c400 BC   *1in (2.5cm) high*

$70-100   AnA

An Egyptian steatite scarab amulet, with pharonic cartouche.

0.5in (1.5cm) long

$100-150   AnA

An Egyptian faience heart scarab amulet.

c400 BC   *1in (2.5cm) long*

$100-150   AnA

An Egyptian faience amulet, depicting a jackal-headed Anubis.

c400 BC   *1.75in (4.5cm) high*

$150-200   AnA

An Egyptian steatite scaraboid, with pattern and hieroglyph.

1.25in (3cm) long

$100-150   AnA

A large Egyptian heart scarab.

2.5in (6cm) wide

$300-450   AnA

An Egyptian faience amulet, depicting Thoth, Ibis-headed god.

2in (5cm) high

$500-600   AnA

Ushabti

An Egyptian faience amulet, of a Djed column, backbone of Isis.
c400 BC   *1.5in (4cm) high*

$70-100   **AnA**

An Egyptian faience amulet, depicting Bes standing.
c400 BC   *2in (2.5cm) high*

$70-100   **AnA**

An Egyptian New Kingdom faience ushabti, the mummiform figure with arms crossed over the abdomen, wearing a tripartite wig, the details in black glaze, including a single line of hieroglyphic text.
1200-1085 BC   *5in (12.8cm) h*

$400-450   **SI**

An Egyptian 22nd Dynasty faience ushabti, with black hair.
5in (13cm) high

$700-1,000   **AnA**

A Late Period Egyptian faience ushabti, depicted mummiform, wearing a striated tripartite wig and curved false beard, the arms crossed over the chest holding hoes, a seed bag over the left shoulder, inscribed with nine lines of hieroglyphic text.
664-525 BC   *8in (21cm) high*

$2,000-3,000   **SI**

A Late Period Egyptian faience ushabti, depicted mummiform, wearing a tripartite wig and a false beard, inscribed with hieroglyphic text.
664-525 BC   *4.7in (12cm) high*

$150-200   **SI**

A Late Period Egyptian faience ushabti, depicted mummiform, wearing a tripartite wig and a false beard, inscribed with hieroglyphic text.
664-525 BC   *4in (10.2cm) high*

$200-250   **SI**

A Late Period Egyptian faience ushabti, depicted mummiform, wearing a tripartite wig and a false beard, inscribed with hieroglyphic text.
664-525 BC   *4in (10.2cm) high*

$300-400   **SI**

Two Late Period Egyptian white and turquoise faience ushabtis, depicted mummiform, wearing tripartite wigs and false beards.
664-525 BC   *3in (7.6cm) high*

$200-250   **SI**

An Egyptian faience ushabti.
c400 BC   *4in (10cm) high*

$100-150   **AnA**

An Egyptian faience ushabti.
c400 BC   *4.5in (11cm) high*

$300-400   **AnA**

An Egyptian 26th Dynasty ushabti.
c400 BC   *5.25in (13.5cm) high*

$800-1,000   **AnA**

A B C D E F G H I J K L M N O P Q R S T U V W XYZ

Jewelry

An Egyptian faience ushabti.
c200 BC   2.75in (7cm) high

$70-100   **AnA**

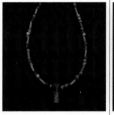

An Egyptian necklace.
c1800 BC   ?in (40cm) long

$80-120   **AnA**

An Egyptian necklace, with blue faience beads and amulets.
c500 BC   14in (36cm) long

$1,500-2,000   **AnA**

An Egyptian necklace, with gold and blue faience amulets.
18in (46cm) long

$2,200-2,800   **AnA**

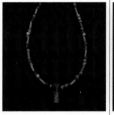

A Late Period Egyptian necklace, with faience beads and amulets, including mummy ring, cylindrical beads and a turquoise amulet.
305-30 BC

$300-400   **SI**

A Late Period Egyptian faience necklace, composed of mummy ring and cylindrical beads in numerous colours.
305-30 BC

$450-550   **SI**

A Late Period Egyptian necklace, composed of mummy ring and cylindrical beads and a turquoise amulet.
305-30 BC

$300-400   **SI**

A Late Period Egyptian necklace, composed of mummy ring and cylindrical beads and a turquoise amulet.
305-30 BC

$300-400   **SI**

A Pre-Dynasty Egyptian ovoid vase, with wavy line decoration in brown.
4in (10.5cm) high

$500-600   **AnA**

A Pre-Dynastic alabaster dish, probably for cosmetic use.
c3000 BC 4.5in (11.5cm) high

$300-400   **AnA**

An Egyptian Abydos ware jug in terracotta.
c3000 BC 7.75in (20cm) high

$300-400   **AnA**

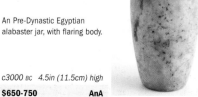

An Pre-Dynastic Egyptian alabaster jar, with flaring body.
c3000 BC   4.5in (11.5cm) high

$650-750   **AnA**

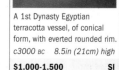

A 1st Dynasty Egyptian terracotta vessel, of conical form, with everted rounded rim.
c3000 BC   8.5in (21cm) high

$1,000-1,500   **SI**

A Late Period Egyptian mask.

c500 BC   5.5in (14cm) high

$700-1,000   **AnA**

A Late Period Egyptian gilt wood figure of a sphinx, on a rectangular plinth, wearing a short wig.

730-16 BC 2.2in (5.7cm) long

$650-750   **SI**

A Late Period Egyptian wood sarcophagus mask, wearing a tripartite wig.

730-16 BC 21in (53.3cm) high

$7,000-10,000   **SI**

A Greek/Egyptian figure, carved from animal bone.

6.25in (16cm) high

$300-400   **AnA**

A Late Period Egyptian turquoise glass fragment, of circular form and molded with a lion head.

730-16 BC 1.5in (3.5cm) diam

$350-450   **SI**

An Egyptian mosaic glass fragment, with opaque black inlay and floral decoration.

3rdC BC - AD 1stC   2.5in (4cm) wide

$300-400   **SI**

A Roman Period Egyptian faience bead mummy mask, composed of numerous ring beads.

AD 1st-2ndC 7.2in (18.4cm) high

$550-650   **SI**

An Egyptian frog-type terracotta oil lamp.

3.5in (9cm) wide

$80-120   **AnA**

Roman

A Roman translucent iridescent glass jar, with two handles and dimpled body.

AD c200   3.5in (9cm) high

$550-650   **AnA**

A Roman translucent blue glass double ungentarium, with handles at side, highly iridescent.

AD c200   4in (10.5cm) high

$500-600   **AnA**

A Roman translucent green glass flask, with handle and wheel cut lines to the body.

AD 1st-2ndC 4in (10cm) high

$800-1,000   **AnA**

A Roman translucent iridescent glass flask, with everted rim.

AD c300 4.75in (12cm) high

$350-450   **AnA**

A Roman translucent iridescent green glass beaker, with applied blue glass discs.

AD c300   4in (10.5cm) high

$550-650   **AnA**

Three Roman greenish-amber glass bottles, with broad pyriform bodies, flaring neck and rim; one pear shaped with cylindrical neck, from Egypt.

AD 3rd-4thC Lg 3in (7.6cm) high

$400-500   **SI**

Two Roman green glass bottles, one of globular form with a waisted neck, the other of pear shape with an elongated neck and a C-form handle.
AD c200-300   *Larger 5in (12.8cm) high*

$300-400   **SI**

A Roman single-handled translucent glass flask.
AD 400-500 2.75in (7cm) high

$300-400   **AnA**

A emerald green glass ungentarium or 'tear bottle'.
4.75in (12cm) high

$300-400   **AnA**

Oil lamps

A Roman terracotta oil lamp, with a pair of rhytons.
AD 1stC   4in (10cm) long

$1,000-1,200   **AnA**

A Roman terracotta oil lamp, with Pegasus flying.
AD 1stC   4.75in (12cm) long

$800-1,000   **AnA**

A Roman terracotta oil lamp.
AD 1stC   4.5in (11.5cm) long

$70-100   **AnA**

A Roman amber glass ungentarium or 'tear bottle,' with good iridescence.
3.5in (9cm) high

$300-400   **AnA**

A Roman oil lamp, in North African red ware, with profile bust of an Emperor.
AD c300   5in (12.5cm) long

$180-220   **AnA**

A Roman oil lamp, in African red ware, with chi-rho symbol.
AD c400   6in (15cm) long

$180-220   **AnA**

A Roman terracotta oil lamp, with female mark.
AD c200   4in (10.5cm) long

$300-400   **AnA**

A Roman terracotta mask.

AD c200   5in (13cm) long

$500-600   **AnA**

A large Roman patinated bronze appliqué bust, depicting Pan.
AD c200   3.5in (8.5cm) high

$2,000-3,000   **AnA**

A Roman bronze knife or dagger handle, in the form of a statue of the God Mars.
AD c200   4.25in (11cm) high

$2,500-3,500   **AnA**

A bronze knife handle, in the form of the head and shoulders of the Goddess Minerva.
AD c200   3.5in (9cm) high

$800-1,200   **AnA**

A Roman provincial marble head of a female.

AD c300   3in (7.5cm) high

$500-600   **AnA**

A Byzantine silver finial, in the form of an eagle with wings closed.

2in (5.5cm) high

$800-1,000   **AnA**

A bronze mount, in the form of a bust of Alexander The Great, personified as Hercules with lion's skin drapery.

3.75in (9.5cm) high

$1,800-2,200   **AnA**

A bronze applique, depicting a running cherubic figure.

1.5in (4cm) long

$100-150   **AnA**

Jewelry

A large bronze brooch, inlaid with enamel.

AD c200   2.75in (7cm) diam

$650-750   **AnA**

A pair of Roman gold earrings, with applied bosses.

AD c200   1in (2.5cm) long

$200-300   **AnA**

A Roman bronze key ring.

AD c200   1in (2.5cm) high

$70-100   **AnA**

A bronze brooch, with four animal heads.

AD c300   1.75in (4.5cm) high

$100-150   **AnA**

A Roman British trumpet-type brooch or fibula.

Fibula were used as fasteners to hold clothing together and come in a variety of shapes and sizes and designs.

2.75in (7cm) high

$70-100   **AnA**

A Roman bronze phallic amuletic pendant.

1in (3cm) high

$100-150   **AnA**

A Roman bronze gilt ring, with plain glass intaglio.

1in (3cm) wide

$150-200   **AnA**

BYZANTINE JEWELRY

■ Although Byzantine jewelry can be seen to represent a continuation of the Roman tradition, by the 4th century its own principles and styles are evident. Throughout the Byzantine Empire jewelry was valued by high-ranking officials at the court. Their signet rings were decorated with complicated monograms and jewelry became a sign of economic prosperity. Jewelry was also used for ceremonial purposes and objects include crosses, censers, rings, and buckles for ecclesiastical garments and they are often set with semi-precious stones.

A Byzantine cross, with setting.

AD 6th-7thC   1.5in (4cm) high

$80-120   **AnA**

A Byzantine bronze reliquary cross, with incised figures of Jesus and Mary.

AD c900   4in (10.5cm) long

$650-750   **AnA**

A Byzantine cross, with figure of Christ.

AD c1000   1.5in (4cm) high

$100-150   **AnA**

FIND OUT MORE...

Trade in Illicit Antiquities: The Destruction of the World's Heritage, by Neil Brodie, Jennifer Doole and Colin Renfrew, published by McDonald Institute for Archaeological Research, 2001.

The Art and Architecture of Ancient Egypt, by William Stevenson Smith et al, published by Yale University Press Pelican History of Art, 1999.

The Cambridge History of Ancient China, by Michael Loewe and Edward L. Shaughnessy, published by Cambridge University Press, 1999.

A Roman bronze medical/cosmetic instrument.
4.25in (11cm) long

$100-150   **AnA**

A Roman bronze medical/cosmetic instrument.
5.5in (14cm) long

$100-150   **AnA**

A Roman bronze medical/cosmetic instrument.
4.75in (12cm) long

$100-150   **AnA**

A Roman bronze medical/cosmetic instrument.
6.25in (16cm) long

$100-150   **AnA**

A Roman bronze medical scalpel.

3.25in (8.5cm) long

$100-150   **AnA**

A Roman North African red ware wine flagon.

AD c200   6in (15cm) high

$200-250   **AnA**

An Old Babylonian haematite cylinder seal, with presentation scene and cuneiform inscription.

c3000 BC   0.75in (2cm) long

$300-400   **AnA**

CYLINDER SEALS

■ Cylinder seals are small (2-6cm) cylinder-shaped stones carved with a decorative engraved design. The cylinder was rolled over wet clay to mark or identify clay tablets, envelopes, ceramics and bricks. The seals were used as a signature, confirmation of receipt, or to mark building blocks. Inscriptions are mostly carved in reverse, so they leave a positive image on the clay with figures standing out, although some are directly carved and leave a negative imprint.

A Sumerian black stone cylinder seal bead, with animal freize.

c3000 BC   0.75in (2cm) long

$200-300   **AnA**

A Sumerian stone stamp seal bead, in the form of a lion's head.

c3000 BC   0.75in (2cm) long

$550-650   **AnA**

A Sumerian white stone amulet, in the form of a male head.

c3000 BC   0.75in (2cm) long

$350-450   **AnA**

An Old Babylonian cylinder seal blue bead, with presentation scene in lapis lazuli.

c1700 BC   0.5in (1.5cm)

$250-350   **AnA**

An Old Babylonian haematite cylinder seal blue bead, with presentation scene.

c1700 BC   0.75in (2cm) long

$250-350   **AnA**

A pair of Mesopotamian solid gold hoop earrings.

c1000 BC   0.5in (1.5cm) diam

$250-350   **AnA**

A Luristan bronze bangle, with animal headed terminals.

c1000 BC   3.5in (9cm) diam

$80-120   **AnA**

Vases

An Luristan bronze bowl.

c8thC BC   6in (15cm) diam

$200-300   **AnA**

A Trans-Jordon terracotta Amphoriskos, with line decoration.

c3000 BC   3in (8cm) high

$50-80   **AnA**

An early Bronze Age Trans-Jordon red burnished jar.

c3000 BC   8.25in (21cm) high

$150-200   **AnA**

An Early Bronze Age Trans-Jordan jar, in burnished red ware.

c3000 BC   4.25in (11cm) high

$350-450   **AnA**

A Sumerian alabaster bowl, with flared sides.

c3000 BC   7.75in (20cm) diam

$650-750   **AnA**

A Mesopotamian terracotta fertility figure, with bird-like features.

2000-1000 BC 6.25in (16cm) long

$200-300   **AnA**

A cuneiform nail of Gudea, King of Lagash.

c2000 BC   4.25in (11cm) long

$200-300   **AnA**

- Due to the enormous variety, collectors should focus on building a collection of a specific area, such as political figures or movie stars, although it can be fun to build a collection in a book based on first hand meetings, such as autograph signing events, or by mail.

- Many very famous people, who could not cope with the enormous amounts of requests, used their assistants and secretaries to sign autographs, so beware.

- Personal dedications, unless that person is also notable or connected to the star in some way, often make an autograph less desirable on the open market.

- Authenticity is vital. If you did not obtain the autograph yourself in person, ensure that the seller is reputable. Look closely at condition too, as tears, fading and other damage affect value and desirability.

- Signed letters and documents can have a historical importance depending on their date and content, increasing the value of the autograph alone. Such documents that actually relate to the reason why the person is famous will be more attractive to collectors.

- Collectors should avoid fads and buy autographs of personal or long-lived public interest. Autographs from people who captured the public imagination on an enduring basis, or who are renowned for their life or an event, are always likely to be sought after by more people, ensuring a strong and consistent value.

ABBA, four matching album pages signed in blue and black inks by each of the members of this enduring pop band, Bjorn adding the band's name to his signature, mounted together with a photograph of the Swedish popular music artists in their prime.

$600-1,000 FA

Woody Allen, a white album page with a clear signature in pencil, with a faint pencil dedication to Stanley.

$120-180 FA

Gillian Anderson, a 10x8 still of Anderson as "The X-Files" "Dana Scully", signed across the lower right corner of the image in bold blue ink.

10in (25.5cm) high

$120-180 FA

Ursula Andress, a 10x8 photograph of Andress, clearly signed in blue ink across the image.

10in (25.5cm) high

$150-200 FA

Jennifer Aniston, a white card signed in bold blue ink by this popular actress, mounted together with a photograph.

$120-180 FA

Brigitte Bardot, an attractive postcard-size photograph of Bardot in her prime, signed across a lower portion of the image in bold black ink.

$180-220 FA

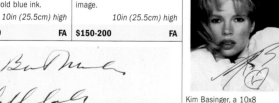

Tallulah Bankhead, a strong fountain pen signature, in black ink on an off-white album page, mounted together with a black and white photograph, folded, otherwise in fine condition.

$180-220 FA

Kim Basinger, a 10x8 photograph, signed across a lower portion of the image in bold blue ink, with trademark heart to the end of the signature.

10in (25.5cm) high

$120-180 FA

P.T. Barnum, a lined white page with a fountain pen inscription in black ink which reads 'Truly Yours P.T. Barnum. American Museum New York Feb 4th 1865. To Simmon W. Stone', in fine general condition with single fold and very light smudging, neither of which effect the signature itself.

This legendary U.S. showman (1810-91) was famed for his flamboyant and innovative publicity built upon his central philosophy that 'there's a sucker born every minute'. In 1871, after a varied career as a promoter, Barnum continued the success of his New York 'museum' by taking to the road with 'The Greatest Show on Earth' comprising a circus, menagerie and an exhibition of freaks including 'General Tom Thumb' all conveyed from city to city by 100 railroad cars.

4.75in (12cm) wide

$1,000-1,500   FA

John Betjeman, a white page signed in bold green ink, mounted together with a photograph of Betjeman who succeeded Cecil Day-Lewis as Poet Laureate in 1972.

$180-220   FA

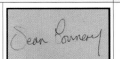

The Bee Gees, three matching white cards signed in blue ink by Maurice, Barry and Robin Gibb, mounted together with a photograph of the band.

$350-450   FA

Dirk Bogarde, a white page signed and inscribed with "Best Wishes" in blue fountain pen ink by one of Britain's most prolific and respected actors.

$150-200   FA

Enid Blyton, a postcard featuring a color illustration of "The Six Cousins" and a facsimile signature from the author, on the reverse is a printed letter of thanks for a donation to a children's home at the close of which is a genuine signature from Blyton in blue ink, beside the printed message Blyton has also added a handwritten line "What a good idea to have a toffee raffle!", with post cancellation stamp dated January 6, 1957, with a heavy fold across the card.

$450-550   FA

Two James Bond related signatures, including individual clipped autograph album pages, signed Sean Connery and Gert Frobe, matted with a black and white image of Bond (Sean Connery) and Auric Goldfinger (Gert Frobe) playing golf, from "Goldfinger".

16in (41cm) wide

$450-550   CO

Ten James Bond "You Only Live Twice" related signatures, including ten individual clipped signatures of Sean Connery (James Bond), Bernard Lee (M), Lois Maxwell (Miss Moneypenny), Desmond Llewelyn (Q), Charles Gray (Henderson), Karin Dor (Helga Brandt), Donald Pleasence (Ernst Stavro Blofeld), Cubby Broccoli (producer), John Barry (composer), and Roald Dahl (screenplay), matted with small reproduction color poster.

23in (58cm) high

$700-1,000   CO

Lloyd Bridges, a pale blue album page featuring a vintage fountain pen signature in blue ink mounted together with a photograph of the stage and screen actor.

$120-180   FA

Pierce Brosnan, a 10x8 photograph of Brosnan posing as James Bond with a large signature in bold blue ink along the right hand edge of the image.

10in (25.5cm) high

$150-200   FA

Leonardo di Caprio, a white card signed in bold blue ink, sold together with a colour photograph.

$120-180   FA

Barbara Cartland, a black and white photograph of the late romantic novelist, signed in her customary pink ink across the upper left corner of the image.

5.75in (14.5cm)

$60-100   FA

Agatha Christie, a pink page signed in black ink.

$600-1,000   FA

Winston Churchill, a clear signature in black ink on an off-white page, mounted, framed and glazed, with a portrait photograph.

$1,800-2,200   FA

Winston Churchill, a photograph signed and dated "Winston Churchill 1947", in blue ink, mounted, framed and glazed.

13in (33cm) high

$2,200-2,800   CO

Arthur C. Clark, a magazine photograph of the science fiction writer, signed and dated "22nd June 98" across a lighter portion of the image in bold black ink.

9in (23cm) high

$150-200   FA

Montgomery Clift, a vintage, unposed snapshot of a young Clift in a suit and tie walking along a street, signed across a lighter portion of the image in black fountain pen ink, with some creasing which does not affect the signature.

4.25in (10.5cm) high

$1,200-1,800   FA

George Clooney, a white card signed in blue ink, mounted together with a head-and-shoulders length, color photograph of the popular actor.

$70-100   FA

Noel Coward, a clear signature in blue ink on an off-white page, mounted together with a photograph of the celebrated wit, playwright and actor.

$220-280   FA

Charles Darwin, a clear signature in black ink on an off-white page clipped from the close of a letter, mounted, framed, glazed, with a portrait.

$3,000-4,000   FA

Doris Day, a 10x8 studio photograph clearly signed by the great Oscar-winning American actress and singer in bold black ink across a lighter portion.

10in (25.5cm)

$120-180   FA

William Frederick Cody, "Buffalo Bill", a handwritten letter in black ink over two sides of a sheet of "Buffalo Bill and the 101 Ranch Shows" headed stationery, dated 12th October 1916.

£2,000-2,500   FA

David Duchovny, a white album page signed in black ink, mounted together with a photograph of the actor best known as "Fox Mulder" in "The X Files".

$100-150   FA

Clint Eastwood, a 10x8 photograph signed in bold blue ink.

10in (25.5cm) high

$150-200   FA

Britt Ekland, a white album page signed in blue ink.

$70-100 FA

Duke Ellington, a green album page dedicated to Linda, signed in blue ink by the great jazz musician and composer.

$300-500 FA

Douglas Fairbanks Jnr, a white page signed in blue ink by Fairbanks, the swash-buckling star of "The Prisoner of Zenda" and "Gunga Din".

$100-150 FA

Ella Fitzgerald, a white page signed "Sincerely Ella Fitzgerald" in blue ink mounted together with a photograph of the legendary jazz singer in her prime.

$320-380 FA

Errol Flynn, a hand-tinted publicity card of Errol Flynn and Olivia De Havilland in "The Adventures Of Robin Hood", signed "Hi, Errol Flynn" in black ink.

9in (23cm) high

$1,800-2,200 FA

Errol Flynn, an off-white album page signed and dedicated in black ink to Audrey, mounted together with a photograph of Flynn as he appeared in the 1935 swash-buckling adventure "Captain Blood".

$600-1,000 FA

Greta Garbo, a publicity photograph signed Greta Garbo in pencil, with additional printed signature, mounted, framed and glazed.

13in (33cm)

$700-1,000 FA

Jean Paul Gaultier, a hand-drawn sketch of a face in bold black ink on a white page, by the celebrated French fashion designer Jean-Paul Gaultier, signed and dated 98 by Gaultier below the sketch also in bold black ink.

9.75in (25cm)

$300-500 FA

Cary Grant, a yellow album page with a strong, clear signature in blue ink from Grant. Mounted, framed and glazed together with a photograph of this unique British actor.

$1,000-1,500 FA

William Randolph Hearst, American newspaper owner and inspiration for the Orson Welles movie classic "Citizen Kane". A clear signature in black ink on an off-white album page. Mounted, framed and glazed together with a photograph of Hearst.

$1,000-1,500 FA

Ernest Hemingway, an envelope signed 'From E. Hemingway' in the return address (in Cuba), addressed in Hemingway's hand to a gentleman in Copenhagen, Denmark, postmarked 31st December 1946. With two file holes not affecting the text or signature and some smudging affecting the 'g' and 'w' of Hemingway, a good example of a rare and sought-after signature, mounted, framed and glazed together with a photograph of the celebrated author best known for works such as "A Farewell to Arms", 1929 and "For Whom the Bell Tolls", 1940.

$3,000-4,000 FA

Alfred Hitchcock, a copy of the 1967 publication "Hitchcock" by Francis Truffaut. The book which documents Hitchcock's life and works through the form of interview transcripts is signed and dedicated to Harry Wilkinson by Hitchcock across one of the opening pages in black ink, Hitchcock has added his trademark self-caricature above the signature, also in black ink.

$2,200-2,800 FA

David Hockney, a 10x8, (landscape), half-length, black and white photograph of the Bradford-born British artist associated with the Pop Art movement from his earliest work. Signed at the base of the image in bold blue ink. Mounted framed and glazed.

$400-600 FA

Bob Hope, a white card signed in bold blue ink by the veteran comedian. Mounted together with a half-length, color photograph of Hope in his prime.

$180-220 FA

Rock Hudson, a pale pink album page dedicated to Esther and signed in blue ink by Rock Hudson. With an undedicated signature in blue ink from American stage star Dolores Gray.

$220-280 FA

George Lucas, A white card signed in black ink. Mounted together with a photograph of the creator of 'Star Wars'.

$180-220 FA

Shirley Maclaine, A white card clearly signed in black ink by this unique, Academy Award-winning actress. Mounted together with a photograph.

$150-200 FA

Elle MacPherson, a white card signed with her first name only in bold blue ink. Mounted together with a photograph of the Australian supermodel.

$150-200 FA

Marilyn Monroe, a United Airlines DC-7 postcard, signed and dedicated on the reverse "To Judy Love & Kisses Marilyn Monroe", in blue ballpoint pen, matted together with a color image of the actress.

16 x 12in (41 x 30cm)

$4,000-6,000 CO

Marilyn Monroe, a check drawn on the 'Bankers Trust Company' New York dated the 11th August 1961, made payable for the sum of one hundred and twenty seven pounds and ninety cents to a May Reis. Signed in blue ink by Monroe, the check is stamped as paid and has perforation holes which do not affect the signature. An excellent example of a highly sought -after signature, mounted framed and glazed together with a photograph of the goddess of the silver screen.

$6,000-10,000 FA

Dudley Moore, an off-white card signed and inscribed in blue ink, 'With best wishes from Dudley Moore' by the late British actor and comedian.

$150-200 FA

Kate Moss, a white card signed in bold black ink mounted together with a photograph of the British supermodel.

$120-180 FA

Yours sincerely,

Stirling Moss.

Stirling Moss, a typed letter on a single side of a sheet of personalized stationery, the letter dated 4th May 1971, with folds to fit an envelope which do not affect the signature.

$180-220 FA

Ivor Novello, a clear signature in black ink on the back of a check dated 20th February 1950 made payable to Novello for the sum of one pound and eleven shillings from Esme Percy, popular British stage and screen actress of the 1930's and 1940's, appearing in movies such as Hitchcock's 1930 classic "Murder". Mounted together with a photograph of Novello.

$100-150 FA

Al Pacino, a white card signed in bold blue ink by the famous Hollywood actor, star of movies such as "Scarface" and "The Godfather". Mounted with a photograph.

$150-200 FA

Brad Pitt, a white card signed in bold blue ink by Pitt mounted together with a photograph of the popular actor.

$150-200   FA

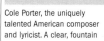

Cole Porter, the uniquely talented American composer and lyricist. A clear, fountain pen signature in blue ink on a pale green page.

$1,000-1,500   FA

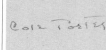

J. K. Rowling, a hardback copy of the 1998 publication "Harry Potter and the Chamber of Secrets" signed on the title page in black ink by author J.K. Rowling. In fine condition, a good example of a rare and extremely sought after signature on one her most popular publications.

$1,500-2,000   FA

Nick Park, a white cotton handkerchief embroidered with a picture of Gromit the dog. Above, is an original drawing in bold black ink, of Wallace by the duo's Oscar winning creator Nick Park. Also signed by Park in black ink.

$800-1,200   FA

Charles Schultz, a lined white index card (approx. 8.5x13cm) featuring a small original drawing of Snoopy in blue ink by his much admired creator. Clearly signed in same pen to the right of the sketch as 'Charles M. Schultz'.

$1,800-2,200   FA

Steven Spielberg, a white card signed in black ink, mounted together with a photograph of the massively successful movie director.

$150-200   FA

Jerry Seinfeld, a 10x8, almost full length color photograph of actor and comedian Jerry Seinfeld jumping to reach a microphone. Signed across the lower right corner of the image in bold blue ink.

$150-200   FA

Peter Sellers, a mounted pale yellow card featuring a large fountain pen signature, dedicated to Terry, in blue ink from the great British comedian. A sought after signature.

$320-380   FA

Frank Sinatra, a yellow album page signed in blue ink by the great singer and movie star. Mounted, framed and glazed together with a black and white head-and-shoulders length photograph of Sinatra.

$1,200-1,800   FA

Quentin Tarantino, a white card signed in black ink by the celebrated director, producer, screenwriter and actor, mounted with a photograph.

$150-200   FA

Star Trek, a collection of seven individual album pages signed by major Star Trek cast members: Shatner, Takei, Nicholls, Kelly, Koenig, Doohan and Nimoy (signed "Live Long and Prosper!"). Mounted, framed and glazed together with a cast photograph.

$1,000-1,500   FA

Mother Teresa, a postcard size, head and shoulders length, black and white photograph, signed and inscribed "God Bless You, M Teresa MC", in blue ink below the image.

$1,000-1,500   FA

John Travolta, a white card signed in bold black ink, together with a photograph.

$180-220   FA

CAR MASCOTS

- Car mascots were made to be screwed on top of car radiators. There are three main categories. Accessory mascots forms include animals, good luck symbols, figures and characters. Manufacturer mascots were mascots used by car manufacturers to adorn their cars, eg; Rolls Royce's 'Spirit of Ecstasy'. Finally, advertising mascots were used by parts manufacturers to advertise their products, such as Mr Bibendum, used by tyre maker Michelin.

- Although ships have long had figureheads to guide the ship onwards safely, the first car mascot is reputed to have been used by legendary car enthusiast Lord Montagu of Beaulieu on his 1899 Daimler.

- Most early mascots are accessory mascots with devils, elves and lucky horseshoes being popular forms. Many were satirical or whimsical in inspiration, or meant to bring good fortune. Characters such as Disney's Mickey Mouse are later extensions of these whimsical feelings.

- Many mascots represent and evoke certain attributes such as speed, usually portrayed by flying birds or nymphs. Lions represented strength. Postures are often heroic and 'point' forwards 'conquering' the oncoming roads.

- Early mascots are usually made from brass or bronze. More 'fragile' die cast mascots made from zinc and magnesium alloys came later, but the majority are made from long-lived metals. Glass was also used, with the most famous maker being Lalique. Other names who used glass to look for are Red Ashay and Sabino of Paris, which are generally less expensive than Lalique examples.

- Maker's marks are important, look for Souest, Ashay, Bazin, Finnigans and A & E Lejeune (AEL). Unmarked examples showing excellent modelling, detailing and a good pose will also be desirable.

- Details should be crisp with original plating. Replating and over-polishing removes original patination and will reduce value and desirability. Some of the die-cast mascots used a 'fragile' metallo bronze, which shows fatigue after 80 years. This should be minimal on the best examples. Clearly, fragile glass mascots should not show chips or cracks.

- Good quality, early mascots fetch very high prices today. Some of the more common types from the 1920s can be found for under $200, but attention is now turning to mascots from the 1940s and 1950s. Reproductions are common, which are usually heavier and less finely detailed than originals.

A rare 'Emily' car mascot, by Rolls-Royce Ltd.

$450-500 TK

A rare 'Femme-chauve-souris' mascot, by E. Famin, finished in heavy bronze, signed.

1922 5.5in (14cm) high

$2,500-3,500 FFA

A winged goddess car mascot, created by Ch. Soudant, finished in silvered bronze with Susse Fres. foundry markings.

Known under the name 'Prouesse', when originally retailed in France. An extremely rare mascot and the most impressive version of the two sizes produced. Used as an accessory mascot for the Rubay Automobile from 1922-1924 only.

1922-1924 7in (18cm) long

$7,000-10,000 FFA

A butterfly girl car mascot, by Red Ashay, in satin finish glass. This figure is one of five designs registered by Red Ashay between April 1928 and April 1931.

7.5in (19cm) high

$4,000-6,000 FFA

A winged nude Egyptian car mascot, by Coudray, signed to base "S. Coudray", marked "9" to rear on base.

1910 9.5in (24.5cm) wide

$12,000-18,000 FFA

A rare Icarus car mascot, by Colin George, silvered bronze, with foundry stampings from Cotenot & Lelièvre, cartouche and numbers to the rear of the base, also signed Colin George to side of lower drape.

c1925   *6in (15cm) high*

$2,500-3,500   **FFA**

A nude riding a broomstick car mascot, created by Franz Bergman, Austria, heavy bronze with original enamel highlight, signed "NamGreb", Bergman backwards.

This is one of the few mascots Bergman created and is unrecorded.

c1910   *20.5in (52.5cm) high*

$4,000-6,000   **FFA**

A 'Sirène' car mascot, by George Colin, silver-plated French nickel bronze, on original marble base, signed "G. Colin", foundry mark for Cotenot & Lelièvre and "2348" and "10" on the side.

This piece was marketed by Hermes in 1922-1925 and was awarded a medal by L'Auto in 1922.

1922-25   *7in (18cm) high*

$12,000-18,000   **FFA**

An Art Deco car mascot, by Varnier, silvered bronze, with period cap.

Two sizes were originally produced, this is the largest of them.

c1920   *6in (15.5cm) high*

$7,000-9,000   **FFA**

A glass Chrysis car mascot, by Red Ashay.

c1928   *7in (18cm) high*

$12,000-18,000   **FFA**

A glass Speed Head car mascot, by Red Ashay.

Based on Lalique's 'Victoire' design.

1929   *5in (13cm) high*

$4,000-6,000   **FFA**

A fine glass racing driver car mascot, by Red Ashay, mounted on filtered radiator cap with a propellor that rotates, turning the colored filters within it.

c1930   *5.5in (14cm)*

$7,000-10,000   **FFA**

A Gregoire 'Archer Egyptienne' car mascot, by M. Guiraud Riviere, bronze, with full base markings, signature, date and "Depose French" stamp.

1918-1924 6.75in (17cm) high

$7,000-10,000   **FFA**

A rare Nostradamus car mascot, by A. Loir, heavy bronze.

c1920   *8.5in (22cm) high*

$5,000-8,000   **FFA**

An 'amour frileux' car mascot, by F. Bazin, heavy silvered bronze, signed 'F. Bazin'.

This design is usually seen as a deskpiece rather than a car mascot.

c1920   *6in (15cm) high*

$3,500-4,500   **FFA**

An American Indian car mascot, attributed to Frederick Bazin.

c1920

$7,000-10,000   **FFA**

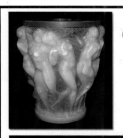

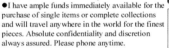
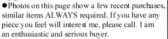

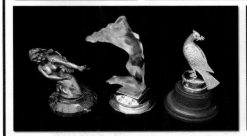

A harlequin resting on a moon car mascot, by Mady, silvered bronze, signed.

c1920   4.75in (12cm) high

$7,000-9,000   FFA

A rare 'The Kid' car mascot, by Jean Verschneider, heavy nickel bronze with ivory face, deciptimg Jackie Coogan, signed "J. Verschneider" on base with "The Kid" logo to the front, small chip to side of nose.

Car mascots with ivory faces are very rare.

1925   6in (15cm) high

$12,000-18,000   FFA

A racing driver car mascot, sculpted and designed by Boccazzi, in silver-plated bronze.

c1920

$7,000-10,000   FFA

A rare satin glass female charioteer car mascot, by Red Ashay, mounted on original radiator cap.

Lalique made a similar mascot called 'Cinq Cheveaux' exclusively for Citroen and Red Ashay decided to incorporate a charioteer into their own design and made it three dimensional, based around five galloping horses pulling a chariot, created in semi Art Deco form.

c1928   6.75in (17.cm) wide

$10,000-15,000   FFA

A bird car mascot, by Bouraine, heavy bronze with ivory beak, signed with foundry stamping, age cracks to ivory.

PROVENANCE: This mascot came directly from the Bouraine family.

7.5in (19cm) high

$7,000-10,000   FFA

An Hispano Suiza car mascot, by Frederick Bazin, silvered bronze on a marble base.

c1919   9in (22cm) high

$4,000-6,000   FFA

An eagle car mascot, by Casimir Brau, nickel bronze, signed.

c1925   8.25in (21cm) high

$2,500-3,500   FFA

A 'Coq Gaulois' car mascot, signed by Charles Paillet, gilded bronze on original French radiator cap.

1920-24 6.75in (17.5cm) high

$2,500-3,500   FFA

An Art Deco horse car mascot, by Casimir Brau, heavy silvered bronze.

This is the larger and rarer of the two sizes produced. It was retailed by Hermes and featured in their 1925 catalogue.

A hare and tortoise car mascot, signed C. Seul, cast in bronze with integral cap, dated.

1911   5in (13cm) high

$3,500-4,500   FFA

A 1920s hare car mascot, by Henri Payen, two-tone bronze.

5.5in (14cm) high

$4,000-6,000   FFA

A hare on tortoise car mascot, by Petrilly, heavy silvered bronze, signed in base, with full base inscription.

c1920 6.75in (17.5cm) high

$4,000-6,000   FFA

1925   8.25in (21cm) long

$4,000-6,000   FFA

A horse's head car mascot, by Bregeon, silvered bronze, signed.

c1925   *4.75in (12cm) high*

$2,500-3,500   **FFA**

A Peugeot lion car mascot, by R. Baudichon, signed on the base.

1923   *7.25in (18.5cm) long*

$2,500-3,500   **FFA**

A butterfly car mascot, by Frederick Bazin, silvered bronze mounted on original French radiator cap, signed 'Bazin'.

c1920   *5in (13cm) high*

$2,500-3,500   **FFA**

A cat on the moon car mascot, by Etienne Mercier, mounted in period French radiator cap, signed on base.

This is an unrecorded variation, the cat usually sits on the base of the moon.

c1925   *4.75in (12cm) high*

$7,000-10,000   **FFA**

A 'La Sagesse' car mascot, created by A. Delm, depicting the three wise monkeys.

$10,000-15,000   **FFA**

A 1930s 'Mickey Mouse' car mascot, by Desmo, finished in bronze.

4.5in (11.5cm) high

$7,000-10,000   **FFA**

A late 1920s bronze Mickey Mouse car mascot, marked "Reproduced by Consent of Walter. E. Disney".

$12,000-18,000   **FFA**

A 'Felix the Cat' car mascot, produced by A. E. Le Jeune, heavy nickel bronze, with copyright stamp.

c1926   *6in (15.5cm) high*

$2,500-3,500   **FFA**

A 'chat botte' car mascot, by Antoine Bofill, with Bofill signature and "MAM" foundry stamp.

$10,000-15,000   **FFA**

A Bibendum 'Scrutant L'Horizon' car mascot, by Ets Generes, Paris, heavily silvered metallo bronze, marked "Generes et Cie" and "Made in France" under the base and "Michelin Cable" on the tyre.

4.5in (11.5cm) high

$8,000-12,000   **FFA**

A devil car mascot, by Gelas, two-tone gilt on bronze highlighted with silver, signed on base.

c1920   *4.5in (11.5cm) high*

$12,000-18,000   **FFA**

A racing Renault car mascot, sculpted by Verecke and produced exclusively for Garage Ponthieu, mounted on an original Renault radiator cap.

c1925   *5.25in (13.5cm) long*

$7,000-10,000   **FFA**

A 1920s Junior Racing Drivers' Club radiator badge, by the Birmingham Medal Company, mounted on an old racing car piston.

7.5in (19cm) high

$1,500-2,500   **FFA**

A rare pair of 1920s Carl Zeiss nickel plated fork-mounted head lamps.

These lamps are rare as they are fork mounted – the vast majority of Zeiss lamps had pillar mountings. These were made specifically for use on the Speed 6 Bentley.

12in (30.5cm) diam

$8,000-12,000   FFA

A pair of Lucas P100 lamps, restored.

1932-35

$3,500-4,500   FFA

A pair of Lucas QK596 hazard lamps.

Reproductions are common at present, and buyers should be aware that they are being passed off as original.

$7,000-9,000   FFA

A pair of Lucas sidelamps, restored.
c1910

$1,500-2,500   FFA

A pair of 1930s Lucas long windtone trumpet horns, restored.

$1,200-1,800   FFA

A pair of Lucas P100DB "bullseye" head lamps, restored.
1928-32

$7,000-9,000   FFA

A pair of Lucas R100 lamps, restored.

1938-39

$2,500-3,500   FFA

A rare pair of Zeiss spotlamps, restored.

Carl Zeiss of Jena, Germany is a renowned optical company that also made camera lenses and cameras, microscopes and binoculars.

1929

$8,000-12,000   FFA

A pair of Lucas sidelamps, restored.
c1910

$1,500-2,500   FFA

A pair of Lucas ST44/N rear lamps, restored.
1928-38

$2,000-3,000   FFA

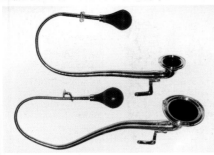

Two "boa constrictor" car horns.
1910-20

Smaller $1,500-2,500, Larger $2,000-3,000 FFA

An early car radio, for General Motors, with loudspeakers and five valve-set for medium and short wave reception.

$45-55 TK

A 1920s WMF inkwell and pen rest, in the form of a racing car.

$7,000-9,000 FFA

A driving school demonstration model, with working engine, lights and steering mechanism.

51in (130cm) long

$450-550 TK

An NBC (National Benzole Company Ltd) Lubricants oil can.

$40-50 DH

A tobacco box, in the form of racing car driver with turned-up collar and goggles.
c1909

$1,500-2,500 FFA

A 1930s tinplate Rolls Royce model, in box.

$2,000-3,000 FFA

A Studebaker Carriages Trade Catalog, with lithographed illustrations and printed paper wraps, minor soiling on cover.
1899

$250-300 CHAA

A CLOSER LOOK AT A BRONZE SCULPTURE

This fine sculpture was produced in 1928 to celebrate the racing achievements of the Czechoslovakian Elizabeth Junek in the Targa Florio race in 1927.

Lady drivers were very unusual at this time. Junek's peformance was considered the best to date in terms of speed and endurance.

The sculpture is very well modeled, capturing the speed of the car as it emerges from under a horseshoe archway.

It was produced in a limited edition and is signed by the sculptor, Vincenzo Cavaglieri on the rear.

A bronze sculpture of a Bugatti racing through a horseshoe bridge.
Provenance: Ex Raymond E. Holland Automotive Art Collection.

1928

$10,000-15,000 FFA

The Modern Motorcar Magazine, with Maurice Beck on cover, produced by Shell.
1937   13.5in (34.5cm) high

$45-55 DH

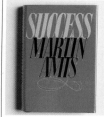

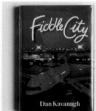

Amis, Kingsley, "I Like It Here", first edition published by Gollancz, London, spine slightly darkened.
1958

$60-100   **PB**

Amis, Martin, "Success", first edition of the author's third book and signed on the title page, published by Jonathan Cape.
1978

$300-400   **PB**

Amis, Martin, "The Rachel Papers", first edition published by Jonathan Cape, minor spotting to some pages, slightly creased on back panel and spine, price clipped.
1973

$700-800   **PB**

Ballard, J.G. "The Disaster Area", first edition, published by Jonathan Cape, scattered foxing to edges, small red ink marks on front free endpaper and a few red scribbles on rear endpapers, spine faded and extremities rubbed.
1967

$50-80   **PB**

MODERN FIRST EDITIONS

- First editions represent the original version of the book and are widely collected. Some later editions are collected but these must have important additional material. Be careful that the book is a true first edition and not a later reprint or a book club version.
- Condition is vital when considering collecting – the most sought-after books are in as fine condition as the day they were sold.
- The presence of the original dust cover is highly important – values of the same book with and without the dust wrapper will usually vary widely.
- Creases and tears to the dust cover must also be considered and can affect value. A mint copy of a first edition may command a very large premium.
- Any notes, inscriptions and dedications will usually devalue a book – exceptions being if an inscription relates to or is by a famous previous owner or if the book is signed by the author.
- First editions of popular books that captured the public's imagination will generally be desirable. This includes Ian Fleming's James Bond, Agatha Christie's detective stories and J.K. Rowling's Harry Potter stories. A first edition of "The Philosopher's Stone", signed by J.K. Rowling, fetched $19,500.

Barber, Willetta Ann and Schabelitz, R.F "Murder Enters the Picture", first edition, published by Doubleday Crime Club, Garden City, NY, edges worn and chipped, back panel faded.
1942

$60-90   **PB**

Barnes, Julian (as Dan Kavanagh), "Fiddle City", first edition, published by Jonathan Cape, London, the second of the Duffy detective novels.
1981

$120-180   **PB**

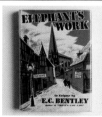

Bentley, E.C., "Elephant's Work", first US edition, published by Knopf, New York, back panel slightly dusty.
1950

$50-80   **PB**

Berkeley, Anthony, "Not to be Taken", first edition, published by Hodder & Stoughton, London, published in the US by Doubleday as "A Puzzle in Poison", pale blue boards a little faded in places, very slightly cocked, top edge a trifle dusty with some faint foxing, short tears at spine, neatly repaired at foot, spine and back panel slightly darkened, a scarce book, especially in the dust jacket.
1938

$800-1,200   **PB**

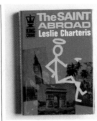

De Bernières, Louis, "Captain Corelli's Mandolin", first edition, published by Secker & Warburg, London, signed by the author on the title page, first issue white boards, usual tanning to edges, vertical crease to inner rear flap.

1994

$600-1,000　　PB

De Bernières, Louis, "The Troublesome Offspring of Cardinal Guzman", first edition, published by Secker & Warburg, London, signed and dated by the author on the title page, usual faint browning to page edges.

1992

$300-400　　PB

Burton, Miles (John Rhode), "The Cat Jumps", first edition, published by Collins Crime Club, light vertical crease to front free endpaper, spine slightly bumped, spine darkened, slight wear to top edge.

1946

$180-220　　PB

Charteris, Leslie, "The Saint Abroad", first edition, published by Hodder & Stoughton, London.

1970

$200-250　　PB

Christie, Agatha, "Destination Unknown", first edition, published by Collins Crime Club, London, margins of pages slightly browned, spine slightly rubbed, back panel dusty and faintly browning, price clipped.

1954

$50-80　　PB

Christie, Agatha, "4.50 from Paddington", first edition, published by Collins Crime Club, London, top edge slightly browned, some internal foxing, spine slightly darkened and one small closed tear at spine.

1957

$50-80　　PB

Christie, Agatha, "Ordeal by Innocence", first edition, published by Collins Crime Club, London, spine very slightly bumped and faint offsetting to endpapers, small stain to top edge, back panel slightly soiled with small closed tear, slight wear to spine.

1958

$50-80　　PB

Cornwell, Bernard, "Sharpe's Gold", first edition, published by Collins, London, signed by the author on the title page, edges slightly dusty, head of spine very slightly rubbed, inner flaps very faintly spotted.

1981

$320-380　　PB

Cumberland, Marten, "The Man Who Covered Mirrors", first edition, published by Doubleday Crime Club, Garden City, NY, pages browned, spine and edges very slightly rubbed.

1949

$40-60　　PB

Derleth, August, "In Re: Sherlock Holmes", The Adventures of Solar Pons, first US edition, published by Mycroft and Moran, Sauk City, the first hardcover collection of Derleth's Sherlock Holmes pastiches, spine and edges slightly browned, back panel dusty and price clipped.

1945

$120-180　　PB

Dexter, Colin, "The Secret Annexe 3", first edition, published by Macmillan, London, signed by the author on the title page, edges of pages sunning slightly, with minimal sunning to top edge.

1986

$400-600　　PB

Dexter, Colin, "Last Seen Wearing", first edition, published by Macmillan, London, the second Inspector Morse novel, usual faint tanning to pages.

1976

$1,000-1,500　　PB

Donleavy, J.P., "A Singular Man", first US edition, published by Atlantic-Little, Brown, Boston, precedes the UK edition, author's second novel, slight fading to boards, slight wear to top edge.

1963

$30-50   PB

Douglas, Norman, "Birds and Beasts of the Greek Anthology", first US edition, published by Jonathan Cape and Harrison Smith, New York, two small, closed tears and top of spine chipped and worn.

1929

$40-60   PB

Douglas, Norman, "In the Beginning", first US edition, published by John Day, New York, original white spine and decorated paper boards, fore-edge and tail uncut, half title page has a tiny nick to edge, very faint offsetting to endpapers.

1928

$100-150   PB

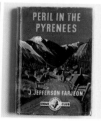

Farjeon, J. Jefferson, "Peril in the Pyrenees", first edition, published by Collins Crime Club, London, edges foxed, two small closed tears, extremities slightly worn.

1946

$80-120   PB

Faulks, Sebastian, "A Trick of the Light", first edition, published by Bodley Head, London, very slight wear to top edge.

1984

$600-1,000   PB

Fleming, Ian, "From Russia with Love", first edition, published by Jonathan Cape, London, extremities and spine slightly rubbed and chipped, back panel slightly soiled, price clipped.

1957

$500-800   PB

Greene, Graham, "A Sense of Reality", first edition, published by Bodley Head, London, price clipped.

1963

$80-120   PB

Gribble, Leonard R., "The Grand Modena Murder", first edition, published by Doubleday Crime Club, Garden City, New York, the third Inspector Slade Detective Story, slight foxing to fore-edge, slight wear at spine, a scarce title.

1931

$200-250   PB

Grierson, Edward, "A Crime of One's Own", first edition, published by Chatto & Windus, London, slight rubbing and browning to edges and spine with one small closed tear, from the library of Peter Apap Bologna with his bookplate on the front pastedown.

1967

$40-60   PB

Harris, Robert, "Fatherland", first edition, published by Hutchinson, London, signed by author on the title page, slightly sunned and very slight wear to top edge.

1992

$220-280   PB

Highsmith, Patricia, "This Sweet Sickness", first UK edition, published by Heinemann, London, previous owner's neat ink inscription on front free endpaper, edges and preliminaries slightly foxed, spine and edges of dust jacket sunned, very slight wear to top edge, back panel dusty.

1961

$50-80   PB

Highsmith, Patricia, "The Blunderer", first UK edition, published by Cresset, London, worn at extremities, back panel dusty.

Highsmith is well known for her homicidal character Tom Ripley who appeared in a series of books starting with "The Talented Mr Ripley".

1956

$200-300   PB

Irish, William (Woolrich, Cornell), "The Dancing Detective", first edition, published by Lippincott, Philadelphia, spine slightly bumped, tanning to edges of pages, extremities worn, head and foot of spine chipped with slight creases to head of front panel.

1946

$300-400 | **PB**

Irish, William (Woolrich, Cornell), "Somebody on the Phone", first edition, published by Lippincott, New York, top edge very faintly tanned and head of spine very slightly bumped, back panel slightly dusty with faint foxing on the outer edge, a scarce title.

1940

$1,000-1,500 | **PB**

James, P.D., "The Skull Beneath the Skin", first edition, published by Faber & Faber, London, signed by the author on the title page.

1982

$80-120 | **PB**

Lees-Milne, James, "Midway on the Waves", first edition, published by Chatto & Windus, London, fourth volume of the author's diaries, covering his work for the National Trust in 1948 and 1949.

1985

$30-50 | **PB**

Leon, Donna, "Death in a Strange Country" first edition, published by Chapmans, London, the author's second novel.

1993

$150-200 | **PB**

Marsh, Ngaio, "Died in the Wool", first edition, published by Collins Crime Club, London, owner's tiny inscription on front free endpaper, edges tanned, back panel darned.

1945

$120-180 | **PB**

Melville, James, "The Wages of Zen", first edition, published by Secker & Warburg, London, signed by the author on the title page, Melville's first novel featuring Inspector Otani, price clipped by the publisher with price sticker on the flap, it appears to have offset onto the front free endpaper leaving a faint mark.

1979

$70-100 | **PB**

Mortimer, John, "Charade", first edition, published by Bodley Head, London, the first book from the creator of Rumpole of the Bailey, a review copy with the publisher's slip laid in, top edge very slightly darkened and rubbed.

1947

$200-250 | **PB**

Murdoch, Iris, "The Italian Girl", first edition, published by Chatto & Windus, London, back panel dusty.

1964

$60-100 | **PB**

O'Brian, Patrick, "The Fortune of War", first edition, published by Collins, London, the sixth Jack Aubrey novel, spine very slightly faded.

1979

$300-400 | **PB**

O'Brian, Patrick, "H.M.S. Surprise", first edition, published by Collins, London, the third book in the Jack Aubrey series, very slight browning to top edge and spine slightly faded with one very small closed tear.

1973

$500-800 | **PB**

Paretsky, Sara, "Indemnity Only", first edition, published by Gollancz, London.

1982

$150-200 | **PB**

Peake, Mervyn, "Shapes and Sounds", first edition, published by Chatto & Windus, London, dust jacket designed by the author, fore and top edges foxed, spine tanned, lower covers slightly foxed and worn at edges.

1941

$300-400   **PB**

Peters, Ellis, "The Sanctuary Sparrow: The Seventh Chronicle of Brother Cadfael", first edition, published by Macmillan, London.

1983

$220-280   **PB**

Powell, Anthony, "Books do Furnish a Room", first edition, published by Heinemann, London, tenth in series "A Dance to the Music of Time".

1971

$80-120   **PB**

Rankin, Ian, "The Black Book", first edition, published by Orion, London, the fifth Inspector Rebus novel, signed by the author on the title page, an unpriced export copy.

1993

$200-250   **PB**

FIND OUT MORE...

www.abebooks.com

www.biblion.com

Antiquarian Booksellers'
Association www.aba.org.uk

Antiquarian Booksellers'
Association of America
www.abaa.org

Rankin, Ian, "Westwind", first edition, published by Barrie & Jenkins, London, inscribed by the author on the title page with his hangman sketch, as new.

1990

$400-600   **PB**

Rendell, Ruth, "No More Dying Then", first edition, published by Hutchinson, London.

1971

$320-380   **PB**

Rendell, Ruth, "A Sleeping Life", first edition, published by Macmillan, London.

1978

$100-150   **PB**

Rendell, Ruth, "Shake Hands for Ever", first edition, published by Hutchinson, London, slight eraser marks on the front free endpaper, a trifle worn at corners and spine.

1975

$150-200   **PB**

Rowling, J.K., "Harry Potter and the Chamber of Secrets", first edition, published by Bloomsbury, London, one corner and spine very slightly bumped.

1998

$3,000-4,000   **PB**

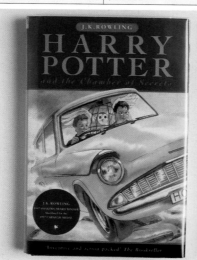

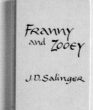

Salinger, J.D., "Franny and Zooey", first edition, published by Heinemann, London, white areas slightly dusty, spine sunned to blue with some very faint loss of color at head and foot, one small closed tear on back panel.

1962

$80-120   **PB**

Seymour, Gerald, "Harry's Game", first edition, published by Collins, London, the author's first book.

1975

$180-220 PB

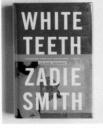

Smith, Zadie, "White Teeth" first edition, published by Hamish Hamilton, London, signed by the author on the title page, as new.

2000

$180-220 PB

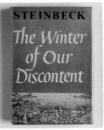

Steinbeck, John, "Winter of our Discontent", first edition, published by Viking, New York, lightly sunned.

1961

$200-250 PB

Swift, Graham, "Waterland", first edition, published by Heinemann, London, nominated for the Booker Prize, as new.

1983

$180-220 PB

Vickers, Roy, "Murdering Mr Velfrage", first edition, published by Faber, London, corners and spine chipped, spine darkened.

1950

$50-80 PB

Walters, Minette, "The Ice House", first edition, published by Macmillan, London, the author's first novel.

1992

$800-1,200 PB

Walters, Minette, "The Sculptress", first edition, published by Macmillan, London, signed and dated by the author on the title page, the author's second book, very faint tanning to edges of pages.

1993

$100-150 PB

Waugh, Evelyn, "Brideshead Revisited", first edition, published by Chapman & Hall, London, boards slightly faded, spine and corners bumped and edges foxed, rather soiled, worn and chipped at the corners and spine but reinforced and presentable.

1945

$600-1,000 PB

Waugh, Evelyn, "Black Mischief", first edition, published by Chapman & Hall, London, slight stain to fore-edge, chipped and creased at head of spine but without loss to title, slight soiling and spine darkened, scarce in the dust jacket.

1932

$500-800 PB

Wilson, A.N., "The Sweets of Pimlico", first edition, published by Secker & Warburg, London, the author's first book.

1977

$320-380 PB

Wingfield, R.D., "Night Frost", first edition, published by Constable, London, as new.

1992

$400-600 PB

Winterson, Jeanette, "Sexing the Cherry", first edition, published by Bloomsbury, London, presentation copy signed by the author on the title page, as new.

1989

$120-180 PB

Attwell, Mabie Lucie, "Lucie Atwell's A B C Pop-up Book", Dean, illustrated glazed boards with simple pop-ups, color illustrations throughout, very good condition.

1960

$40-60   **Bib**

Awdry, The Rev. W., "The Little Old Engine – Railway Series No. 14", Edmund Ward, illustrations by John T. Kenney.

1959

$80-120   **Bib**

Awdry, The Rev. W., "Very Old Engines - Railway Series No. 20", Edmund Ward, illustrations by Gunvor and Peter Edwards.

1965

$100-150   **Bib**

Barker, C.M., "Flower Fairies of the Summer", Blackie, with dust jacket, clean with little loss to head and tail of spine.

c1940

$70-100   **Bib**

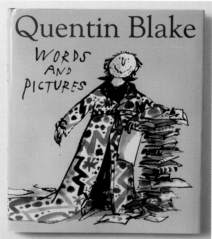

Blake, Quentin, "Words and Pictures", Chris Beetles Ltd, features pictures from 20 years of publication, signed, with very slight bumped spine, color illustrations, large format.

2000

$50-80   **Bib**

Blyton, Enid, "The Secret Seven", The Brockhampton Press Ltd, first edition with illustrations by George Brook.

1949

$120-180   **Bib**

Blyton, Enid, "You Funny Little Noddy", Sampson Low, Marston & Co., first edition.

1955

$30-50   **Bib**

Briggs, Raymond, "Father Christmas Goes on Holiday", Sir Joseph Causton & Sons, first edition.

1975

$50-80   **Bib**

Browning, Robert, "The Pied Piper of Hamelin", Routledge & Sons, with illustrations by Kate Greenaway.

$200-300 Bib

Dickens, Charles, "The Magic Fishbone", Fredrick Warne & Co. Ltd, first published 1868, illustrations by F. D. Bedford.

$50-80 Bib

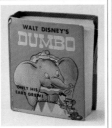

Disney, Walt, "Dumbo, Only His Ears Grew – The Better Little Books", Whitman Publishing, based on the motion picture, illustrated in black and white and with moving picture effect in the corner, with slight chipping at spine.

1941

$200-300 Bib

FIND OUT MORE...
George Edwards Library, EH Shepard Archive, University of Surrey GU2 7XH, England.

National Center for Children's Illustrated Literature: www.nccil.org

De Brunhoff, Jean, "The Story of Babar, The Little Elephant", Methuen, with a preface by A.A. Milne.
1934

$200-250 Bib

Crompton, Richmal, "William and the Witch", George Newnes Ltd, London, first edition with color illustrations by Thomas Henry and Henry Ford, bumped at edges and corners, good green cloth boards.
1964

$120-180 Bib

Milne, A. A., "Winnie The Pooh" and "The House at Pooh Corner", Methuen, first edition, with decorations by E.H. Shepard.
1926

$5,000-7,000 Bib

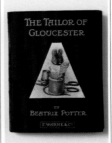

Johns, Captain W.E., "Biggles Sets a Trap", Hodder and Stoughton, first edition with black and white illustrations by Stead, bumped at top and bottom, very good condition.
1962

$70-100   Bib

Norton, Mary, "The Borrowers Aloft", Dent, first edition of the second Borrowers book, illustrations by Diana Stanley, rubbed edges, inscription on front end paper.
1961

$50-80   Bib

Potter, Beatrix, "The Tailor of Gloucester", Warne & Co., first edition.
1903

$300-500   Bib

Ransome, Arthur, "Swallows and Amazons", Jonathan Cape.
1953

$270-330   Bib

Potter, Beatrix, "The Tale of Piggling Bland", Warne & Co., first edition with paper-covered boards, lettered in maroon, with pictorial onlay to upper cover, pictorial noticeboard endpapers, 15 color plates and many line drawings, ownership inscription on half title and front blank, with modern box.
1913

$300-550   Bib

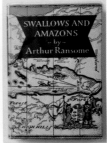

Seuss, Dr., "How The Grinch Stole Christmas", NY Random House, first edition, a scarce book with illustrations by the author.
1957

$1,200-1,800   Bib

Tolkien, J.R.R., "The Hobbit," Allen & Unwin, third edition, seventh impression, illustrations by the author.

Thanks to Peter Jackson's recent films of The Lord Of The Rings, Tolkien books have seen an immense popular revival that extends far beyond devoted collectors and Tolkien fans. Condition is vital and collectors' or first edition copies of The Lord Of The Rings with dust jackets in fine condition have fetched prices exceeding tens of thousands of dollars at auction.

1972   **$220-280**   Bib

Tourtel, Mary, "Rupert, Little Bear, More Stories", Sampson Low, Marston & Co.
1939

$800-1,300   Bib

Uttley, Alison, "Moldy Warp The Mole", Collins, first edition with illustrations by Margaret Tempest.
1940

$50-80   Bib

CAMERAS

EARLY CAMERAS

Most 19th century cameras had wooden bodies and
brass fitments. Photography began to spread from
c1840, with most cameras from this date being
made in box-like forms using a 'wet plate' process
involving glass plates with a film of light-sensitive
chemicals. These cameras, dating from the 1840s-
c.1880s are highly desirable. Bellows were
introduced c1851.

- In 1864, attempts were made to develop a
photographic plate that could be made in advance
and taken to the field 'dry'. At first, these plates took
longer to develop, but after experiments by many
photographers, George Eastman set up the
'Eastman Dry Plate Company' (which eventually
became 'Kodak') in 1880, producing such plates on
a commercial scale.

A 19thC mahogany Lancaster
International quarter plate
camera, with rare blue bellows
and rotary shutter.

$550-650   ColC

A 19thC mahogany Lancaster
Extra Special quarter plate
camera, with see-saw shutter.

$600-700   ColC

- These plates were used in mahogany and brass
'folding' cameras with leather or fabric bellows
which were still available up to the first decades of
the 20th century. The back panel held a ground
glass screen to check composition and a frame for
holding the wooden plate holders.

A 19thC mahogany Lancaster
Imperial Instantograph quarter
plate camera.

$500-600   ColC

A mahogany Lizars Challenge
quarter plate camera, needs
restoration.
c1905

$150-250   TK

- A large number of dry plate folding cameras
survive today. Collectors should look for examples
with manufactures' names, especially Sanderson,
Watson and Lancaster.

- They are often contained in leather bags containing
shutters, lenses and other accoutrements such as
cloths and wooden plate holders. Cameras
accompanied by a range of accessories are likely to
be more desirable.

A 19thC mahogany London
Stereoscopic Co. quarter plate
camera, with Waterhouse stop
and rectilinear lens.

$500-600   ColC

A mahogany J. F. Shew & Co.
Eclipse quarter plate camera,
shutter does not work.
c1890

$200-300   TK

A 19thC fiddle-back mahogany
Sanderson quarter plate
camera.

$650-750   ColC

A CLOSER LOOK AT A SANDERSON QUARTER PLATE CAMERA

The system used moving
arms to allow the lens board
to move more freely than
before with a full range of
rise, fall, swing and tilt.

The arms and board could be
fixed in place with screws.

The photographer can
monitor the composition via
the glass panel at the back
of the camera.

This example is for use in
tropical climates.Teak is
naturally resistant to insects
and the bellows were also
treated to deter attack.

A teak Sanderson tropical quarter plate camera, with Ross lens.

Sanderson cameras were innovative due to the way the lens board is mounted. Frederick
Sanderson, an architect, needed a way to photograph buildings and the simple 'rising front' panel
cameras of the time were not enough.

c1910

$600-700   ColC

A 19thC mahogany Watson
tailboard half plate camera,
with stereo sliding frame.
c1890

$650-750   ColC

CAMERAS

LEICA CAMERAS

- Leica cameras are made by the optical company Leitz, based at Wetzlar in Germany. There are other factories, such as at Solms, also in Germany.

- The Leica was developed by the technician Oscar Barnack in 1913 and used compact 35mm cine film. Barnack's original prototype, known as the 'UR Leica', was launched in 1925 after brief testing of 31 hand-made prototypes known as 'Nullserie' cameras.

- The first Leicas (the Leica I(a) models) had non-interchangeable, fixed lenses and caught on quickly as they were small, light, easy to use, well built and used the high quality optics that Leitz were known for.

- Interchangeable lenses were introduced in 1930. These were screw fit, a system that did not change until the introduction of the 'M' series of cameras in 1954, which used a bayonet mounting.

- Today, Leicas are hotly collected all over the world. The accessories and lenses, usually contained in recognisable red card boxes, are also collected. Rare lenses and accessories can fetch very high prices. Many of these cameras are still useable today.

- All Leica cameras bear a serial number which allows precise dating to a year and also identification of a model, using tables found in specialist books. The model IIIa is perhaps the most common and fetches lower prices than other models.

- Condition is vital with Leica cameras. Collectors look for examples in as close to mint condition as possible. Scratches, scuffs and dents, modifications and damage to the mechanism all affect value seriously. Both the chrome plating and the black painted finish can show damage.

- Collectors particularly look for Leica cameras with unusual variations, such as those with different finishes, like an imitation 'sharkskin' covering to the body. Unusual engravings are very popular, and include those made for military purposes such as for the German Air Force, (engraved 'Luftwaffe Eigentum' – Luftwaffe Property), those used by Leitz for display (engraved Leitz Eigentum – Leitz Property) and other engravings such as 'Monté en Sarre'.

A Leica IA, with Elmar 3.5/50mm lens.

1930

$700-800   TK

A Leica Model C.

This was the first Leitz camera produced with an interchangable lens.

c1931

$500-600   ColC

A black Leica II, with nickel Elmar 3.5/50mm lens.

1932

$450-550   TK

A Leica IA near focus model, with Elmar 3.5/50mm lens, close focus to 1.5 feet, top and base plate restored professionally, with lens cap and camera case.

1929

$1,000-1,500   TK

A Leica IF converted from a IC, with Elmar 3.5/50mm lens, black dial.

1950

$600-700   TK

A black Leica II camera, Leitz, with nickel Elmar lens.

1928

$550-650   TK

A chrome Leica II, with nickel Elmar lens.

1939

$450-550   TK

A black Leica III, synchronized later with nickel Hektor 2.5/50mm lens, coated, no number, maker's case.

c1933

$600-700   TK

Leica
D.R.P.
Ernst Leitz
Wetzlar
Germany
Monté en Sarre

A Leica IIIa, with rare sharkskin body and Summitar lens, engraved "Monté en Sarre", accessory shoe and some screws replaced, flash synchronization below shoe, certificate for service warranty.

Due to heavy tax duty, Leica licensed Saropitco in St Ingbert, Saare to produce Leicas for the French market from 1949 to 1951. These cameras were marked "Monté en Saare".

1949

$4,000-4,500   TK

A Leica IIIa, with Elmar lens, flange "0" standardized.

1939

| $350-450 | | TK |

A Leica IIIf, factory converted from a 3C.

c1948

| $450-550 | | ColC |

A Leica IIIa, with Summar 2/50mm lens, rewind knob damaged, with case.

1939

| $400-500 | | TK |

A Leica IIIc, with Summaron 3.5/3.5 cm lens.

1949

| $550-650 | | TK |

FIND OUT MORE...

Dennis Laney, 'Leica Pocket Book', published by Hove Collectors Books, 1996.

Dennis Laney, 'Leica Collectors' Guide', published by Hove Collectors Books, 1992.

A Leica IIIb, with collapsible Summitar 2/5 cm lens, with "Leica" engraved in red, shutter needs help, with case.

1948

| $450-550 | | TK |

A Leica CL, with Summicron-C 2/40, lens hood, cap and maker's case.

1973-74

| $500-600 | | TK |

A Leica M2, with Summilux 1.4/50 lens, with self timer, protection film on base plate and lens cap.

1960

| $1,000-1,500 | | TK |

A Leica M3 body, single wind, with body cap.

1957

| $500-600 | | TK |

A black Leica M3 body, speed dial, accessory shoe and base plate probably restored, with body cap.

1961

| $1,800-2,200 | | TK |

A Leica M4, with Summaron 3.5/3.5 lens, filter and lens cap.

1970-71

| $1,000-1,500 | | TK |

A black Leica M6 body, as new, boxed.

1996

| $1,200-1,800 | | TK |

An American Al-Vista panoramic camera, with clockwork mechanism.

Standard cameras usually have an angle of view of 40-50 degrees, but the lens on a panoramic camera swivels by clockwork from pointing to the left to pointing to the right, enabling a wider 'panorama' image to be taken, without need for the camera itself to be moved.

c1903

$650-750 ColC

An Anscoflex III, plastic body with twin lenses and flash, and with case and instructions.

c1958

$35-45 ColC

A Bolsey B2 35mm camera, made in the USA.

c1950

$30-40 ColC

An Italian Bilora Radix 35mm camera in tin, for 24x24 on rapid cassettes.

Collectors should look for the box for this camera as its presence can raise the value of the camera from $20-30.

1947-51

$90-100 OACC

A Butcher's Reflex carbine 120 film camera, with case.

c1925 10.5in (26.5cm) high

$120-180 OACC

A Canon L1, with Canon 1.8/50mm lens, lens cap and instruction manual.

1957

$550-650 TK

A 1960s Russian Cmena rapid load camera.

$15-20 ColC

A chrome Canon P body, made in Japan, No. 728.655, chrome curtains not smooth, shutter runs well.

1958

$250-300 TK

A chrome Canon VL body, made in Japan, signs of use but no damage, metallic curtains not completely smooth but shutter runs reliably.

1958

$250-300 TK

A 1960s Fed 2 35mm camera, made in the USSR.

$50-60 ColC

A 1950s Franke Solida 120 camera, with Schneider Radiana lens.

$45-55 ColC

A Russian Hapyucc 16mm SLR camera, with removeable prism.

Early, white models were designed for use medical use.

1964

$300-400 ColC

A German Goerz press-type camera, with Anchutz shutter.

If the mechanism is damaged, the value is greatly reduced. The Anschutz type camera was developed in 1896 and has four struts supporting the panel containing the lens. These can be collapsed allowing the camera to become flat.

c1910

$100-150   ColC

A Houghtons Ltd Ensign Reflex Model B SLR camera, focal plane shutter does not work.

1930

$100-150   TK

A teak Houghton Butcher Ensign Special Reflex tropical camera, brass bound with crown Russian leather bellows and viewing hood, FP shutter 15-1000.

c1935

$650-750   OACC

A Russian Kiev IIIA, in working order.

This is a copy of a Contax camera. The Russians copied many Western styles and designs under their own name, the majority are of comparatively low value.

c1967

$70-90   ColC

A Kodak Folding 4A camera.

This is the early version with a mahogany frame, the later versions have a metal frame.

1909

$350-450   ColC

A brown No. 1A Pocket Kodak.

Brown is scarcer than the more common black version, which is worth about £20.

c1930

$70-100   ColC

A Bakelite Kodak Baby Box Brownie camera, with box.

This example comes with its box, which adds value to the camera. Hundreds of thousands of Box Brownies were made with the majority having comparatively minimal values. The Box Brownie was designed by Frank Brownell for George Eastman (owner of the Eastman Kodak Co. of Rochester, New York) in 1900 and underwent design changes until the 1930s when it was phased out, although the name remained for some time afterwards, being used on similarly inexpensive and widely sold cameras. Named to draw on the popularity of 'brownie' characters by a well-known illustrator, it was aimed at the young and those who wanted to take photographs simply and inexpensively.

c1935

$20-25   OACC

A Kodak Flash Brownie, with Bakelite body.

c1946

$20-25   ColC

A silver and cream 'Jersey' Kodak Brownie, with Bakelite body.

This model was launched as a prototype in Jersey in black and in this rare cream version. It was not a popular camera and was not available for general release.

c1955

$200-300   ColC

A Kodak Retina IIIc.

This model was produced in the Stuttgart factory, which was originally owned by Nagel.

c1957

$200-250   ColC

A Kodak Brownie Bullseye, with Bakelite body, made in the USA.

1958

$20-25   ColC

A Kodak Pony II.

c1959

$10-15   ColC

A Kodak Retinette 1B.

c1963

$20-25   ColC

A Kodak Instant, with original bag and papers.

Due to copyright infringement, Kodak was forced to withdraw this model at a huge cost.

c1979

$12-18   ColC

A Russian Leitz Leningrad 35mm camera, with spring-motor drive, with Leica mount.

c1960

$100-150   OACC

A Mamiya 6, with correct Olympus lens.

c1951

$100-150   ColC

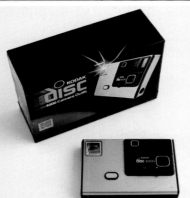

A Kodak Disc 4000, near mint and boxed.

The fashion for disc format cameras first hit manufacturers during the mid 1980s, spurred on by this model, Kodak's first. It was not successful and the format did not last. This was also the first mass produced camera with an aspheric lens.

c1985

$20-30   ColC

A Mec 16 SB camera.

This was the first camera to feature TTL (through the lens light metering), despite Pentax advertsing that they had achieved this first.

c1960

$80-120   ColC

A CLOSER LOOK AT A MECAFLEX 35MM CAMERA

Although heavy, the Mecaflex has a compact size and clean lines when the top panel is closed. When flipped up, the top panel reveals a waist level view finder with magnifier, a lever film winding mechanism, a shutter release and the film rewind knob.

It has interchangeable lenses and allowed 50 exposures on 24mm x 24mm format film.

A Metz Mecaflex 35mm camera.

The Mecaflex, produced in the 1950s by Metz, was released in 1953 and was based on a prototype dating from 1947 designed by Heinz Kilfitt. It was not commercially successful and is now very rare.

c1953

$1,200-1,800   ColC

A Micro Precision Products Microflex twin lens reflex camera, with Micronar 3.5/77.5 lens, with lens cap, case and instruction manual.

1959

$250-300   TK

A German Minnigraph 35mm camera, with single speed shutter.

This is considered the first 35mm camera produced in Europe.

c1915

$1,200-1,800   ColC

A Minolta 'A' 35mm camera, with coupled rangefinder, Chiyoda Kogaku shutter and 3.5 Chiyoko Rokkor lens.

c1956

$90-100   OACC

A Minolta 110 zoom SLR camera.

This was the first Single Lens Reflex camera for 110 film.

c1976

$40-60   OACC

A Nikon 'S' 35mm camera.

This was the second model that Nikon produced.

c1952

$700-900   ColC

A Nikon SP camera.

This was the last model made by Nikon before they launched the 'F' series.

1957-63

$1,500-2,000 ColC

A Nikon F photomic camera, with 50mm 1.4 lens.

The Nikon F was the first 35mm SLR (single lens reflex) camera that could take a motor drive.

c1965

$300-400   ColC

A Nikon F Photomic FTN, made in Japan.

1968

$350-450   TK

An Olympus Pen F half frame 35mm SLR camera, new rotary focal plane shutter synched to 1/500, lever codes shutter on first stroke, advances film on second.

c1965

$100-150 OACC

A silver Corfield Periflex I SLR camera, with periscope-finder, camera case.

The Periflex incorporated a small inverted periscope that was lowered into the film plane. This allowed the user to to see a very small part of the image about to be taken and then focus very finely. The periscope was drawn up and the optical viewfinder used to check composition before the shutter was released.

1955

$150-250 TK

A 1930s English Perma Special, with Bakelite body and gravity driven shutter.

$200-300 ColC

A Polaroid Miniportrait, made in Japan.

c1980

$120-180 ColC

A German Robot 1 camera, with Tessar 2.8 lens and spring motor drive.

The Robot used the first practical automatic film advance. The large knob on the top plate was wound, tensing a spring. Every time the shutter was released, the spring automatically advanced the film onwards.

c1936

$200-300 ColC

A Reflex-Kovelle camera, made by Kochmann, single lens reflex for 12 exposures on 120 film.

c1935

$70-100 OACC

A Franke & Heidecke Rolleicord I.

The Rollei TLR (Twin Lens Reflex) cameras were made by the German company Franke & Heidecke and their introduction was considered a great innovation.

Founded in 1920, Franke & Heidecke initially made stereoscopic cameras. The TLR was based on this model and was the first compact TLR camera. The photographer looked down onto the image which was composed through one lens, and the second was used to take the picture.

The first Rollei TLR camera was released in 1928 and took 117 film which was advanced with a knob. However the film format was changed shortly afterwards to 127 making those that hold the original film format scarce. Crank-wound mechanisms, introduced to deal with the new film format, became standard.

Rolleiflex cameras are still produced today. Collectors look for classic models and models with color variations and rare lenses.

c1935

$180-220 TK

A grey Franke & Heidecke Rolleiflex T camera, excellent condition, with case.

1958

$300-400   **TK**

A Franke & Heidecke Rolleicord V b, with Xenar 3.5/75 lens Synchro-Compur X, shutter closes slowly, with lens cap.

1966

$250-300   **TK**

An early German Rollei 35 camera, shutter and light meter are working.

1967

$250-300   **TK**

A 1980s Chinese Seagull 35mm camera.

A copy of a Super Ikonta.

$70-100   **ColC**

A Russian 'Sputnick' stereoscopic camera, with viewer.

Without a viewer, this camera would be worth less. Condition is very important with this model as the Bakelite is often cracked. Stereoscopic cameras used two lenses a small distance from each other on the same plane to take two slightly different images of the same view. When these apparently identical images are viewed side by side in the viewer, the eye is tricked into seeing the image almost in '3D'. The third lens is the viewing lens, used to compose the image. Stereography had its heyday in the late 19th century, and although it largely died out by the turn of the century, it was still catered for by a very few manufacturers even as late as mid 20th century.

c1957

$200-300   **ColC**

A Thornton-Pickard Junior Special Ruby Reflex, SLR with focusing screen back and canvas bag.

1926

$150-200   **TK**

A Voigtländer Bergheil camera, with four part roll film back and cassettes, cased.

1925

$100-150   **TK**

A Voigtländer Vitessa II camera, with Color-Skopar 3.5/50 lens.

1955

$150-200   **TK**

A 1960s Voitlander Bessa II Rangefinder, with Color Heliar lens.

$550-650   **ColC**

A Voigtländer Bessa II, with Apo-Lanthar lens, with masks for 4.5 x 6cm and leather case.

The inclusion of the rare Apo-Lanthar lens on this model make it more desirable and valuable than similar models with different lenses.

1955

$2,500-3,000   **TK**

A Yashica 'J' 35mm camera.

c1962

$20-25   **ColC**

A Yashica Electro 35.

c1962

$30-40   **ColC**

A Zeiss Colibri camera.

As the 127 film used in this camera is no longer produced, the value has dropped recently as they cannot be used.

1930-35

$200-300   ColC

A 1930s Zeiss Ikarette 120 camera, with adjustable 10.5cm f4.5 Tessar lens.

$70-100   ColC

A Baby Ikonta 'Ikomat', with rare 3.5 Tessar lens.

This camera usually comes with a Novar lens.

c1935

$200-300   ColC

A 1930s Zeiss Adoro teak, nickel-plate and leather tropical camera.

$650-750   ColC

A Zeiss Ikon Contax II, with two lenses, shutter does not work correctly.

1936

$250-300   TK

An early Zeiss Ikon Contax III, with Sonnar 2/5cm lens, light meter does not work.

1936

$250-300   TK

A Zeiss Contaflex 35mm camera, with twin lens relex.

This was the first camera with a built-in light meter. If the shutter does not function or the meter is inoperative, the value will be lower.

c1936

$1,000-1,500   ColC

A Zeiss Ikon Contax II a, with Zeiss-Opton Sonnar 1.5/50 lens, lens a bit stained.

1952

$250-300   TK

A 1950s Ikonta 521, with Novar lens.

$45-55   ColC

A Zeiss Ikon Contarex I, with Planar 2/50 lens, lens hood and case.

1960-1967

$400-500   TK

A Zorki 35mm camera, made in the USSR.

c1974

$40-60   ColC

A 1930s Bell & Howell Filmo 16mm camera, with textured brown finish.

$40-60   ColC

A 1960s triple lens Bolex 8mm cine camera.

$100-150   ColC

A 1960s Bolex B8L 8mm cine camera, with seven speeds, two rotating lenses and TTL.

$40-60   ColC

A French Emel 8mm cine camera, with three lenses, two later. *1938-39*

$120-180   ColC

A 1930s Ensign "Auto Kinecam" 16mm cine camera, with Taylor-Hobson lens and triple turrets to hold three lenses.

$100-150   ColC

A 1930s Ensign "Auto Kinecam" 16mm cine camera, with hand-cranked mechanism.

$120-180   ColC

A 1930s Siemens 16mm camera, with rare sliding turrets and three Schneider lenses.

$350-450   ColC

A 1960s brown Goerz Wien 16mm Minicord, with twin lenses and case.

$350-450   ColC

A 1930s Midas combined 9.5mm camera and projector, with Taylor-Hobson lens, lacks film magazine.

$70-100   ColC

A Zeiss 16mm Moviecon cine camera.

c1937

$200-300   ColC

A French Stylophot miniature camera.

c1955

$200-300   **ColC**

A silver-plated brass Kombi combined camera and graphoscope, by Alfred Kemper, USA.

c1893   *2in (5cm) long*

$250-350   **ColC**

A Minox BL subminiature camera, with feet dial, case and chain.

These Minox subminiature cameras were popularised as spy cameras after they appeared in a James Bond film, where Bond used a similar camera to photograph plans.

c1973

$350-450   **TK**

A Newman & Guardia London Special B Detective plate camera, with Zeiss Protar convertible lens.

This camera has a pneumatic action rather than an oil shutter and due to this unusual feature it was one of the cameras that Herbert Ponting took to the Antarctic with Scott's famous expedition in 1903 as the air was more reliable than oil at cold temperatures.

c1909

$350-450   **ColC**

A brown Bakelite Coronet Midget subminiature camera, with case.

This miniature camera came in a rainbow of Bakelite colors including mottled green and blue. These brighter colors fetch higher prices than the brown and black versions.

1936

$150-200   **TK**

An R. J. Beck's Frena No. 0 Memorandum detective box magazine camera, with original box.

1901

$150-250   **TK**

A Japanese Echo 8 novelty 'spy' camera, shaped as a Zippo lighter and usable as a lighter and camera.

c1954

$800-1,200   **ColC**

A 1970s 'button-hole' spy camera.

$700-1,000   **ColC**

A bronze Stirn 'button-hole' spy camera.

This camera was developed by A.D. Gray c1885-6. In July 1886, Carl P. Stirn of Berlin acquired the rights and patented the design across Europe. It was produced at a time when concealed and hidden cameras were very popular, being hidden in plain boxes or even handbags. This camera was worn under a waistcoat, with the lens protruding through a buttonhole. It was triggered by pulling on the loop on the bottom.

1886-1892

$1,200-1,800   **ColC**

A B C D E F G H I J K L M N O P Q R S T U V W XYZ

CANES

CANES

- Decorated canes first became popular during the 16th century but reached the apex of their popularity during the Victorian and Edwardian periods, primarily amongst the bourgeoisie and upper classes. Canes had largely gone out of fashion by the end of the First World War.

- A gentleman could have many canes, for either day or evening use. As well as a functional use, for support, the materials and quality of workmanship displayed the owner's wealth and social standing.

- Shafts are usually made from wood and may be carved or inlaid. Woods used include mahogany, fruitwoods and teak. Handles, or the round 'pommels', are most commonly found in carved wood or ivory. Precious metal covered handles are also common, which can be tooled or set with jewels.

- The metal tip often found at the other end is known as a 'ferrule' and is often missing. Although this will affect value slightly, it will not reduce it as much as other damage.

- Some canes have holes or 'eyelets' at the top of the shaft, under the handle and collar, which held a wrist cord.

- Most canes found will date from the mid-19th to the early 20th century and fall into three main categories – decorative, folk art and 'gadget'.

- Folk Art canes often use a whimsical or highly personal subject matter that was important to the carver or owner. Condition, subject and quality of carving, choice of wood and patina are important factors in determining the value of these pieces.

- Walking sticks made by sailors often use stacked shark vertebrae for the shaft and may have a handle carved from a type of ivory known as 'marine' or 'morse' ivory which is a very tight form taken from a walrus tusk.

- Materials and the level and quality of ornamentation and carving are the most important factors that affect values. Condition is important, with damage to carving, missing settings and cracks reducing value. Makers' marks are important, but not essential as many fine and valuable canes are not marked. Age is also important, with more modern sticks holding lower values.

A carved walrus ivory cane in the form of a lobster, mounted on an ebonized tapered hardwood shaft, ivory has very tight crack.

2in (5cm) high

$800-1,200   **CHAA**

A carved ivory figural cane, in the form of a running greyhound, with the collar decorated with scroll work borders, marked "Sterling", mounted on a briar wood shaft, slight chips on ears.

5in (12.5cm) high

$350-450   **CHAA**

A carved walrus ivory cane, in the form of a horse's head with glass eyes and gold-plated band decorated with floral designs, on a tapering malacca shaft.

1.5in (4cm) high

$550-650   **CHAA**

A carved ivory cane, in the form of a lizard climbing a branch, mounted on a black palm shaft with gold-plated collar.

3.25in (8.5cm) high

$800-1,200   **CHAA**

A carved stag antler cane, in the form of a greyhound with inset glass eyes and coin silver collar, unmarked.

4in (10cm) high

$180-220   **CHAA**

A carved cane, in the form of a dragon's head, with red rhinestone eyes, mounted on an ebonized black palm shaft with brass collar, ebonized finish worn.

$400-500   **CHAA**

A carved antler cane, in the form of two horses' heads, with wide gold-filled collar engraved "F.A.F." on an ebonized hardwood shaft.

2.25in (5.5cm) high

$800-1,200   **CHAA**

A carved walrus ivory cane, in the form of a Turk's head knot, mounted on a hardwood shaft, one inch vertical crack.

2.5in (6.5cm) high

$450-550   **CHAA**

A turned walrus ivory cane, with three inset silver wire bands, silver disk on top engraved "John Clapp / 1866" with Masonic compass in the center and silver band engraved "Warwick, R.I.", very small drying crack on top.

1.75in (4.5cm) high

$1,000-1,500   CHAA

An ivory knobbed cane, with coin silver collar and stepped malacca shaft.

2in (5cm) high

$550-650   CHAA

A carved bone cane, with a lotus nut "knob" on a long bone handle, with wide nickel band joining the handle to the shaft, several small areas of bone loss, one leaf missing.

5.25in (13.5cm) high

$300-400   CHAA

A folk art one-piece carved hardwood cane, with root knob in the form of a human skull with a snake entwined in the eye sockets.

The skull is a popular 'memento mori' motif, acting as a reminder of ultimate death for all.

2in (5cm) high

$600-700   CHAA

A folk art two-piece carved cane, with burl knob in the form of a man's head, with two braids forming U-shaped loops and a winged cherub's head carved at the back, mounted on a tapered hardwood shaft, some chipping.

2.5in (6.5cm) high

$750-850   CHAA

A primitive one-piece carved rosewood cane, the handle in the form of a clenched fist handle with inlaid brass and ivory dots at the cuff.

The clenched fist is a popular motif for cane pommels.

$90-100   CHAA

A carved hazelwood cane, in the form of an otter's head.

$180-220   MM

A one-piece carved hardwood crook-handled cane, the handle in the form of a bust labelled "George V", also marked "Klam" and "S.N."

3.5in (9cm) high

$450-550   CHAA

A one-piece carved cane, the handle in the form of a hound's head, faded.

4.5in (11.5cm) high

$400-500   CHAA

A carved horn figural cane, in the form frigate bird's head, with a brass collar and tapered ebony shaft.

1.5in (4cm) high

$450-550   CHAA

An L-shaped cane, the metal handle in the form of bamboo on a birchwood shaft, a few dents.

2.5in (6.5cm) high

$250-350   CHAA

An L-shaped cane, with unmarked silver snake's head mounted in on a tapered exotic hardwood shaft.

2in (5cm) long

$250-350   CHAA

A silver knobbed cane, decorated with Japanese-style relief bamboo plants, with engraving plate, mounted in a tapered malacca shaft.

1.75in (4.5cm) high

$300-400   CHAA

A French silver knobbed cane, with hallmark for "LB" and other marks, shaft stamped "Beitalle".

1.75in (4.5cm) high

$220-280   CHAA

A Victorian gold knobbed presentation cane, with bright-cut floral and scroll decoration, on an ebony shaft.

2.75in (7cm) high

$300-400   CHAA

An Edwardian gold-plated presentation cane, with bright-cut scrollwork decoration, engraved "W.L.Griffin From J.H. Herald & Family 1-18-24", mounted on a tapered ebony shaft, light wear to top of plate.

$150-200 CHAA

A Victorian gold-filled knobbed cane, with scroll and floral decoration and presentation engraving panel, mounted in an ebonized hardwood shaft.

2in (5cm) high

$180-220 CHAA

A cast bronze figural cane, in the form of a bust of Hercules with a lion's skin draped over his shoulders, mounted on a tapered hardwood shaft.

3.5in (9cm) high

$250-300 CHAA

An L-shaped agate handled cane, with engraved gold-plated collar, mounted on a tapered American walnut shaft.

$350-450 CHAA

A Meissen-handled figural cane, with tau-shaped handle in the form of woman's bust, the body of handle decorated with a landscape with a courting couple and other vignettes, mounted on a tapered malacca shaft.

'Tau' is the name for the distinctively shaped handle which curves down at the back and up at the front.

3in (7.5cm) high

$1,200-1,800 CHAA

Gadget Canes

- As the cane's shaft is long and, like the handle, wide enough to hold items internally, many canes were made with specific uses or built-in gentleman's accessories – these are known as 'gadget' or 'system' canes.
- The simplest and most common have handles that unscrew to reveal items concealed in the shaft, such as drinking, smoking or writing accessories, but the variety of gadgets is huge, including camera tripods that use a split shaft as the stand, telescopes and even seats.
- On occasion, canes were also used as much for defence as for support and were adapted into sword sticks or gun canes with concealed weapons. Collectors should understand that some countries restrict the import or export of these pieces, and it is generally illegal to carry one in public.
- Most gadget canes date from the 1870s until the early 20th century, and must be intact. Ingenious or unusual designs and skilled workmanship are good indicators of high value pieces.

A 62 caliber percussion gun cane, with threaded round barrel and under hammer mechanism, woodworm damage to grip, paint worn, light surface rust, hammer repaired and missing barrel plug.

35in (89cm) long

$300-400 CHAA

An unmarked 52 caliber percussion gun cane, two-piece burled walnut grip, the barrel segment with threaded front to attach barrel, cocking spur broken off, missing barrel plug.

37in (94cm) long

$400-500 CHAA

A 9mm percussion gun cane, probably European, of all steel construction with L-shaped tubular handle, tapered barrel and pull-tab-cocking mechanism, light surface rust, does not appear to function.

$250-300 CHAA

A malacca sword cane, with turned hardwood knob, nickel collar and double-edged steel blade.

36in (91.5cm) long

$250-300 CHAA

A dagger cane, with blued steel blade and carved horn handle in the form of a hoof mounted on an ebonized hardwood shaft.

35.25in (89.5cm) long

$450-550 CHAA

FIND OUT MORE...

Catherine Dike, 'Walking Sticks', published by Shire Publications, 1992.

Catherine Dike, 'Cane Curiosa: From Gun to Gadget', published by Les Editions de L'Amateur, Paris & C. Dike Publications, 1983.

Jeffrey Snyder, 'Canes: From the Seventeenth to the Twentieth Century', Schiffer Publishing, 1997.

A horn cigarette and match safe cane, with silver-mounted tau-shaped handle containing cigarette compartment and match holder and striker, mounted on a stepped, tapered bamboo shaft.

Handle 4.25in (10.5cm) long

$750-850 | **CHAA**

A chrome-plated brass gadget cane, with stamped floral decoration, the hinged lid opening to reveal a cigarette compartment and a retractable candle holder, mounted on a tapered hardwood shaft.

Handle 4in (10cm) high

$550-650 | **CHAA**

A brass monocular spy-glass cane, probably English, mounted on a tapered ebonized hardwood shaft with a brass ferrule.

36in (91.5cm) high

$300-400 | **CHAA**

A gadget cane, the black-finished wooden knob in the form of a wind-activated siren/alarm with nickel mounts, mounted on a tapered hardwood shaft.

Knob 1.5in (4cm) high

$350-450 | **CHAA**

A horse measuring cane, the carved root knob pulls up to reveal a marked maplewood measuring stick with spirit level, mounted on a bamboo shaft.

36.25in (92cm) high

$180-220 | **CHAA**

A novelty figural gadget cane, the Britannia silver knob in the form of a man's head, with a threaded collar mounted on a bamboo shaft, a small button on the shaft forces water from the reservoir in the shaft out through the mouth of the figure.

Knob 2.5in (6.5cm) high

$250-300 | **CHAA**

BLUE AND WHITE

A Ridgway Angus Seats series plate, showing a view of Lumley Castle, Durham.

c1820   7.25in (18.5cm) diam

$200-250   **SN**

A 'Cowman' pattern plate, maker unknown.

c1820   9.75in (25cm) diam

$220-280   **SN**

A Spode 'The Lion in Love' pattern soup plate, from the Aesop's Fables series.

c1830   9.75in (25cm) diam

$300-500   **SN**

- Blue and white patterns were first used by the Chinese during the Ming Dynasty where designs were hand-painted. The invention of under-glaze transfer printing in the late 18th century saw a massive expansion of blue and white ware. Here, a design was transferred to a warm copper plate using a cobalt (blue) oil and ink mix over which paper was pressed firmly, transferring the now reversed design to paper. This was then pressed onto the surface of the ceramic which was then fired and glazed and fired again.

- Plates, chargers and platters are desirable and highly collected as they are easily displayed and show off the pattern as much as possible. Collectors often concentrate on collecting one type of item, such as jugs.

- The type of pattern affects the value and desirability of the piece. The 'Willow' pattern is held as the most popular design, followed by 'Asiatic Pheasants' and 'Italian'.

- Restoration will affect value. Be careful with restored pieces which should be dipped in water only briefly to clean them. Do not use metal sprung grips to hang the plates as the grips can damage the plate's rim.

A Copeland and Garratt 'Death of the Bear' pattern plate.

With its sad subject matter, this pattern is considered the most common of the 'Indian Sporting' series introduced by Spode in 1820.

1833-1847   9.75in (25cm) diam

$320-400   **SN**

A Wedgwood Botanical series plate.

c1810   8in (20.5cm) diam

$220-280   **SN**

A Riley 'Dromedary' pattern plate.

1802-1828 10in (25cm) diam

$220-280   **SN**

A Spode 'Long Eliza' pattern plate.

c1815

$180-220   **SN**

A Minton Monk's Rock series soup plate, with watermill scene.

c1810   9.25in (23.5cm) diam

$200-300   **SN**

A Goodwin, Bridgewood & Orton 'Oriental Flower Garden' pattern plate.

1827-1829   7in (18cm) diam

$120-180   **SN**

An 1820s 'Russian Palace' pattern plate, maker unknown.

10in (26cm) diam

$220-280   **SN**

A 'Wild Rose' pattern dessert plate, maker unknown.

c1820   10in (26cm) diam

$220-280   **SN**

A Job Ridgway 'Curling Palm' pattern supper section dish.

1802-1808　　　　　*12.25in (31cm) wide*

$200-300　　　　　　　　　　**SN**

An 1820s Minton 'Filigree' pattern dessert dish.

8.25in (21cm) diam

$270-330　　　　　　　　　　**SN**

A Burleigh teapot stand.

c1900　　6.25in (16cm) diam

$80-120　　　　　　　　　　**SN**

A 'Ponterotto' pattern tureen stand, attributed to Rogers.

1815-1842　8.25in (21cm) w

$180-220　　　　　　　　　　**SN**

A Rogers 'Camel' pattern plate.

c1815　　7.75in (20cm) wide

$300-350　　　　　　　　　　**SN**

An 1820s 'Family & Mule' pattern tureen stand, maker unknown.

17in (43cm) wide

$300-500　　　　　　　　　　**SN**

An 1820s Minton 'Filigree' pattern platter.

15in (38.5cm) wide

$300-500　　　　　　　　　　**SN**

An 1820s Rogers 'Greek Statue' pattern basket stand.

$300-500　　　　　　　　　　**SN**

A Copeland 'British Flowers' pattern drainer.

c1850　　12.25in (31cm) wide

$400-600　　　　　　　　　　**SN**

An 1830s Maddock Sedders 'Fairy Villas' pattern drainer.

15in (38cm) wide

$300-500　　　　　　　　　　**SN**

A Copeland and Garratt broth bowl.

c1833-1847

$300-500　　　　　　　　　　**SN**

An 1820s 'India Flowers' pattern pickle set.

11in (28cm) wide

$700-1,000　　　　　　　　　　**SN**

An 1820s 'Gleaners' pattern tea bowl and saucer, maker unknown.

Gleaners were poor farm workers or peasants who, after the harvest had been collected, scoured the fields for remaining corn to take home.

2in (5cm) high

$300-350 **SN**

A Copeland and Garratt 'Italian' pattern covered jar.

The 'Italian' pattern can also be found on Spode pieces, since Spode introduced it in 1816. From 1833, the pattern was used by Copeland and Garrett who bought the Spode pottery and continued to produce it. Between 1870 and 1970, Copeland ware carried a mark identifying the date of manufacture. The letter is the first letter of the month of manufacture and the two numbers represent the year. The Spode name was reintroduced in the 1970s.

c1833-1847 3.25in (8.5cm) h

$320-380 **SN**

An invalid's feeding cup, maker unknown.

The form of this cup allowed the invalid to drink while lying down.

2.75in (7cm) high

$200-250 **SN**

A Copeland 'Camilla' pattern sauce tureen, stand and ladle.

c1900 *6.75in (17cm) high*

$300-500 **SN**

A treacle jar, with fox-hunting scene, maker unknown.

c1850 *6in (15cm) high*

$400-600 **SN**

An 1820s mug, with Regency scene, maker unknown.

3in (7.5cm) high

$180-220 **SN**

A Minton 'Floral Vases' pattern mug.

c1825 *3.5in (9cm) high*

$300-400 **SN**

An 'Elephant' pattern child's chamber pot.

c1820 *3in (8cm) high*

$300-500 **SN**

A William Ridgway 'Oriental' pattern child's chamber pot.

1834-1854 *5in (12.5cm) high*

$300-500 **SN**

An Adams 'Bird and Basket' pattern loving cup.

c1900 *4.25in (11cm) high*

$300-400 **SN**

An 'Asiatic Pheasants' pattern sauce boat, maker unknown.

c1860 *4.25in (11cm) high*

$180-220 **SN**

A B C D E F G H I J K L M N O P Q R S T U V W XYZ

A 'Woodman' pattern jug, maker unknown.

c1830   *8.5in (22cm) high*

$300-500   **SN**

A Wedgwood 'Ferrara' pattern jug.

c1900   *5.5in (14cm) high*

$200-300   **SN**

A Riley 'Dromedary' pattern sauce boat.

c1815   *2.25in (6cm) high*

$300-500   **SN**

A child's teapot, maker unknown.

c1815   *3.5in (9cm) high*

$320-380   **SN**

An 1820s Leeds Pottery coffee pot.

$300-500   **SN**

An Adams 'Bird and Basket' pattern tea caddy.

c1900   *5.5in (14cm) high*

$300-400   **SN**

A Minton 'Sicilian' pattern soup ladle.

c1830   *11.75in (30cm) long*

$180-220   **SN**

FIND OUT MORE...

R.K. Henrywood & A.W. Coysh, 'Dictionary of Blue & White Printed Pottery' 1780-1880 (Vols 1 & 2), published by Antique Collectors' Club, Woodbridge, 1982 & 1989.

R. Copeland, 'Transfer Printed Pottery', published by Shire Books, Princes Risborough, UK. 1999.

The Spode Museum & Visitors' Centre, Church Street, Stoke-on-Trent, ST4 1BX, UK.

An 1830s Davenport 'Muleteer' pattern pepper pot.

4.75in (12cm) high

$220-280   **SN**

A pair of 'Willow' pattern ladles, maker unknown.

The 'Willow Pattern' was first introduced by Thomas Minton for the Caughley factory. It tells the story of a rich man's daughter who falls in love with her father's assistant. The father disapproves of the relationship and bans the assistant from the house, forcing the lovers to elope. When they are found, the assistant is killed. The daughter sets fire to the house, dying in the flames. They reunite in death as two birds, seen at the top of the design. The eponymous willow symbolises sadness.

c1830   *7in (18cm) long*

$100-150 each   **SN**

A 'Fitzhugh' pattern chestnut basket, possibly Spode.

c1800   *7.5in (19cm) wide*

$320-380   **SN**

An Adams 'Tendril' pattern egg stand.

c1810   *6in (15cm) high*

$300-500   **SN**

An 1870s Minton Hollins & Co scenic tile.

6.25in (16cm) wide

$70-100   **SN**

A Carlton ware yellow glazed fruit bowl.

1930s

$15-25 **AS&S**

CARLTON WARE

- Tradename used on china and earthenware from 1890 onwards by Wiltshaw & Robinson Ltd of the 'Carlton Works', Stoke, England.
- Crested souvenir ware may bear the name 'Crown China'.
- The name became 'Carlton Ware Ltd' in 1958.
- During the 1920s and 1930s the factory produced colorful geometric designs that are highly sought after, as are pieces made for Guinness in the 1950s.
- The richly decorated and colored pieces with enameled decoration on a dark glaze were inspired by the success of Wedgwood's lusterwares.
- A key style is chinoiserie with rich enameled decoration including banded ornamentation. It was inspired by Oriental ceramics.
- Key chinoiserie motifs are birds, plant and tree forms, flowers and butterflies.
- Numerous manufacturers now make limited edition pieces under license.

An unusual Carlton ware comical dog, decorated in black and white with a brown collar.

6in (15cm) high

$120-180 **PSA**

A Carlton ware "Egyptian Fan" vase.

7.5in (19cm) high

$1,500-2,000 **RH**

A Carlton ware "Barge" pattern bowl.

10in (25.5cm) diam

$400-600 **RH**

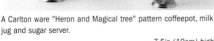

A Carlton ware "Heron and Magical tree" pattern coffeepot, milk jug and sugar server.

7.5in (19cm) high

$600-800 **RH**

A CLOSER LOOK AT CARLTON WARE

This wall charger is a large size which can be displayed easily with great visual impact.

There is no wear to the pattern, Carlton ware pieces were functional objects.

This rare pattern sums up the period well, with bold, bright colors and distinctive designs and is thus popular. The pattern and decoration is also highly typical of Carlton ware.

A 1930s Carlton ware "springtime" dish.

6.75in (17cm) wide

$100-150 **RH**

A Carlton ware "lily pink" cruet set.

1.5in (4cm) high

$150-200 **RH**

A 1930s Carlton ware "Floral Comets" wall charger.

12.5in (32cm) diam

$1,500-2,500 **RH**

A Carlton ware "Castle" pattern wall charger.

12.5in (32cm) diam

$600-1,000 **RH**

Two Carlton Walking Ware mugs, hand-painted, unnamed designer.

1970s *Left: 5in (12cm) high Right: 3.25in (8.5cm) high*

$50-80 each **FFM**

A Carlton ware crimped edged dish, "Rouge Royale" design.

9.5in (24cm) diam

$100-150 **OACC**

A Carlton ware "dog rose" teapot.

5in (12.5cm) high

$220-280 **RH**

A Carlton ware "dog rose" tea cup and saucer.

3in (7.5cm) high

$50-80 **RH**

An 'Old Charley' small character jug, no. D5527, glaze fault.

$30-40 **PSA**

A Carlton ware box, "Rouge Royale" design.

5.5in (14cm) long

$100-150 **OACC**

A Carlton ware vase, of octagonal section with chinoiserie reserves in black against a red/orange ground, gilt wear to rim.

9in (22.5cm) high

$100-150 **FRE**

A Carlton ware luster bowl, of deep form with everted rim and ring base, mottled orange glaze with reserves of frolicking children silhouetted against a blue sky, gilt highlights, a few scrapes to the glaze.

9in (22.5cm) diam

$200-300 **FRE**

Four pieces of Carlton ware, including two octagonal trays, with painted fruit/floral motifs, chip to rim on both, a covered square box with embossed and painted oak trees on square blue ground, a few nicks, and a dish of similar oak tree pattern in the shape of an oak leaf.

$100-150 **FRE**

A Royal Winton 'Chintz Orient' trio.
c1954   *Cup 2.75in (7cm) high*

$70-100   **RH**

A Royal 'Winton Chintz Somerset' trio.
c1933   *Cup 2.75in (7cm) high*

$100-150   **RH**

A Wade Chintz 'Butterfly' trio.
c1955   *Cup 2.75in (7cm) high*

$100-150   **RH**

A Shelley Chintz 'Marguerite' teacup and saucer.
c1945   *2.5in (6.5cm) high*

$80-120   **RH**

CHINTZWARE

- Chintzware is inspired by the bright and colorful floral patterns found on cotton fabrics imported from India from the late 16th century. Found on tea sets and dressing sets, it is viewed as quintessentially English. Chintzware has seen two 'golden ages' – the 1920s and the 1950s.

- Over 200 patterns are known and popular manufacturers are Royal Winton, Lord Nelson Ware Ltd, James Kent Ltd, Shelley, Wade and Crown Ducal. Royal Winton is considered to be the first manufacturer to produce Chintz and the 'Marguerite' pattern, incorporating white daisies, yellow flowers and bluebells on a beige ground, was the first pattern designed.

- Designs are not hand-painted but applied by lithographic transfer. Here the pattern is applied to paper which is stuck to the ceramic and removed, leaving the pattern, before firing. Joins are usually invisible, but those that show joins are either devalued or considered more individual due to this error, depending on the collector.

- Familiarize yourself with the intricate patterns very carefully as some patterns appear the same but are different in minute and subtle ways. This is especially important when building up a set in one pattern. Some factories also used different pattern names for the same pattern.

- Collectors usually either collect one or a number of patterns or selected items such as jugs or plates which show patterns off to their best advantage.

- Examine pieces for signs of restoration, such as chips. Be aware of modern versions, which are not as desirable.

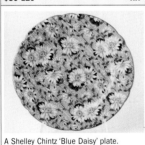

A Shelley Chintz 'Blue Daisy' plate.
c1948   *7in (17.5cm) diam*

$30-50   **RH**

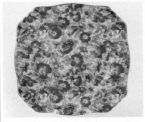

A Royal Winton Chintz 'Royalty' pattern plate.
c1936   *6in (15cm) diam*

$40-60   **RH**

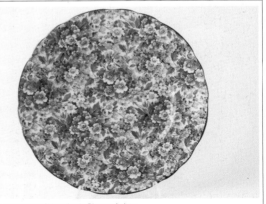

A 1930s James Kent Chintz 'Apple Blossom' plate.

8.75in (22cm) diam

$50-80   **RH**

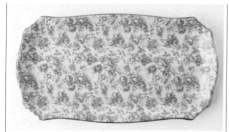

A Royal Winton Chintz 'English Rose' pattern tray.

c1951   *11.5in (29cm) wide*

$150-200   **RH**

A Grimwades Royal Winton 'Paisley' part tea service, comprising teapot, two cups, three saucers, five side plates and one cake plate.

$30-50 (service)   **AS&S**

A 1920s double-lipped vase with early 'Chintz' decoration, print and enamel, maker and designer unknown.

       4.5in (11cm) high

$15-25   **FFM**

A Royal Winton Chintz tea set for one, decorated in the 'Evesham' pattern, comprising teapot, cup, saucer, side plate, sugar bowl and jug.

$250-300   **PSA**

· FIND OUT MORE...

Muriel M. Miller, 'Collecting Royal Winton Chintz', Wallace Homestead Book Co, 1996.

Susan Scott, 'Chintz: The Charlton Standard Catalogue' (3rd edition), Charlton International Inc, 1997.

A Royal Winton Chintz 'Hazel' three-bar toast rack.

c1934   *4.5in (11.5cm) long*

$180-225   **RH**

A 1950s Royal Winton Chintz 'Kew' pattern five-bar toast rack.

       7in (18cm) long

$180-225   **RH**

A 1920s Grimwades Chintz candlestick.

The Grimwade brothers owned the Royal Winton company and their name can often be found along with Royal Winton marks on the base of Chintz pieces. The Grimwades also devised a new lithographic transfer process using flexible paper to transfer the pattern to the ceramic surface. This allowed them to decorate ridged surfaces like this candlestick. The delicate paper used to do this previously was prone to tearing..

       10.25in (26cm) high

A late 1940s Royal Winton Chintz lamp base.

       9.5in (24cm) high

$200-300   **RH**

A Crown Clarence Chintz 'Briar Rose' biscuit barrel.

c1935   *6.5in (16cm) high*

$70-100   **RH**

$100-150   **RH**

CLARICE CLIFF (1899-1972)

- She joined A.J.Wilkinson Ltd. Near Burslem, Staffordshire in 1916.
- In 1920, the firm acquired Newport Pottery and gave Cliff a studio there.
- Cliff and her decorators hand-painted biscuit-fired wares with brightly colored enamels over a 'honey' glaze.
- She visited the Paris Exposition in 1925 and was influenced by Cubism and Art Deco.
- In 1928 the highly successful 'Bizarre' range was launched.
- Cliff designed over 500 shapes and 2000 patterns.
- Value is determined by shape, pattern, size, rarity and condition.
- There are fakes – so beware poor quality painting, smudged design, washed-out colors and a thick, un-even glaze.

A Clarice Cliff 'Autumn' pattern beehive honey pot.

4in (10cm)

$320-380 **GorL**

A Clarice Cliff 'Blue Chintz' pattern lotus jug, with abstract flowers in pastel colours, single strap handle.

This was an extremely popular pattern and was also produced in an orange colorway. The one to look out for is the rare 'Green Chintz'.

1932-33 12in (29.5cm) diam

$1,500-2,000 **FRE**

A Clarice Cliff 'Apples' pattern lotus jug, with single applied strap handle and ribbed body, with hand-painted decoration of apples, leaves and lines between yellow banding.
1931-32 11.5in (29cm) high

$3,500-4,500 **FRE**

A rare Clarice Cliff 'Carpet' pattern cup and saucer.

Cliff copied this pattern from an illustration in a magazine of a carpet designed by Da Silva Bruhn.

c1930 2.25in (6cm) high

$800-1,200 **SCG**

A Clarice Cliff 'Broth' pattern large bowl, decorated with sunrays and bubbles in green, black, red and blue.

This pattern was originally called 'Fantasque 105', which, due to its success, was given the name 'Broth'. Bowls tend to be less popular with collectors, unless the pattern is very rare, as they do not show the pattern as well, nor are they as easy to display as chargers, jugs and vases.

1929-30 8.5in (21.5cm) diam

$650-750 **FRE**

A Clarice Cliff Biarritz 'Coral Firs' pattern plate.

c1935 7in (18cm) wide

$200-250 **RH**

A 1930s Clarice Cliff 'Cowslip' basket.

13.5in (34cm) high

$1,000-1,500   **RH**

A Clarice Cliff 'Crocus' pattern beehive honey pot.

3.75in (9.5cm)

$220-280   **GorL**

A Clarice Cliff 'Diamonds' pattern jardinière, with geometric decoration in blue, purple and orange, scrapes to rim.

1929-30   9.5in (24cm) diam

$1,500-2,000   **FRE**

A Clarice Cliff 'Crocus' pattern bowl.

$220-280   **GorL**

A Clarice Cliff 'Crocus' pattern octagonal fruit bowl.

9in (23cm)

$350-400   **GorL**

A Clarice Cliff 'Delicia Citrus' pattern Athens shape tea cup and saucer.

The colorway of this pattern to really look out for is the rare version where the fruit has a silver and gold luster finish.

c1932   cup 2.5in (6cm) high

$300-500   **RH**

A Clarice Cliff 'Gayday' pattern cream jug and matching cup and saucer.

1930-34

$150-200   **GorL**

A Clarice Cliff 'Crocus' pattern conical sugar sifter.

5.75in (14.5cm)

$120-180   **GorL**

A Clarice Cliff Citrus 'Delicia' pattern flower ring.

1932-34   7in (18cm) diam

$400-600   **SCG**

A Clarice Cliff 'Etna' pattern vase, of squat form with ribbed body, hand-painted with stylized mountainous landscape.

6.75in (17cm) diam

$7,000-10,000   **FRE**

A Clarice Cliff 'Gayday' pattern vase, of lobed bulbous form with colorful daisies between yellow and brown bands.

1930-34   8in (20.5cm) high

$1,500-2,000   **FRE**

A Clarice Cliff 'Gibraltar' pattern milk jug, decorated with sailboats on a lake, mountains and clouds in pink, blue, yellow and green.

1931-35 4.25in (10.5cm) high

$700-1,000   **FRE**

A Clarice Cliff 'Honolulu' pattern side plate.

1933-34   *7in (18cm) diam*

$300-400   **GorL**

A Clarice Cliff 'Rudyard' pattern ribbed, tapered, cylindrical vase, shape 6028.

This is the blue and green version of Honolulu, named after Rudyard, near Stoke.

1933-34   *7in (18cm)*

$1,000-1,500   **GorL**

Nine pieces of Clarice Cliff 'Lightning' pattern, including two tea cups, a creamer and six plates, some wear to plates.

1929-30   7in (17.5cm) diam

$3,000-4,000 (set)   **FRE**

A Clarice Cliff 'Melons' pattern bowl.

6in (15cm) diam

$450-650   **RH**

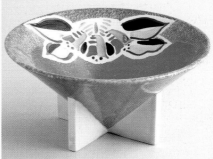

A Clarice Cliff 'Oranges and Lemons' pattern plate.

1931-32   9.5in diam

$1,500-2,000   **SCG**

A Clarice Cliff 'Rhodanthe' pattern bowl.

This pattern took over from 'Crocus' as the best-selling design. It was produced by the etching technique.

1934-39   9in (22.5cm) diam

$350-450   **RH**

A Clarice Cliff 'Nuage' pattern conical bowl.

c1932   *7.5in (19cm) diam*

$1,000-1,500   **SCG**

A Clarice Cliff 'Solomon's Seal' cup and saucer, with solid triangular handle.

This pattern was named after the flower and was produced with a printed outline, which was then hand-colored. This method lacked the spontaneity of the best Cliff designs, it was not a commercial success and the process was discontinued.

c1930

$270-330   **GorL**

A CLOSER LOOK AT CLARICE CLIFF

Collectors look for bold, geometric patterns.

The enamel paint was applied relatively thickly, leaving behind visible brush strokes, although by this period they were slightly less dominant.

Lotus jugs are popular because they show the pattern clearly – you get a lot of pattern for your money.

This piece is in perfect condition, with no scratches or rubbing on the enamels.

This piece is made more desirable because it epitomises the designs and style of Clarice Cliff.

A Clarice Cliff 'Sliced Circle' pattern lotus jug, with single strap handle and slightly ribbed body, decorated in an abstract circles pattern in orange, blue, green and yellow.
1929-30   *11.5in (29cm) high*

$8,000-12,000   **FRE**

A Clarice Cliff 'Sunray' pattern bowl, decorated with bright, vibrant abstract decoration.
1929-30 4.5in (11.5cm) diam

$700-1,000   **FRE**

A Clarice Cliff 'Sunrise' pattern cream pitcher, with reverse painting in green, orange, blue and brown, 2in (5cm) hairline crack at rim near handle, 1in (2.5cm) crack at rim.
3.75in (9.5cm) high

$350-400   **FRE**

A Clarice Cliff 'Tennis' pattern conical creamer, with stylized geometric design.
c1931   *4in (10cm) high*

$1,800-2,200   **FRE**

A Clarice Cliff 'Tennis' pattern 24 piece dessert service, including seven cups, nine saucers (two are not tennis pattern, one of these is repaired) one totally repaired, tiny chips to two, seven dessert plates, two with wear and one serving plate.
c1931   *serving dish 9in (22.5cm)*

$6,000-10,000   **FRE**

A Clarice Cliff 'Tulips' pattern vase, of spherical form on footring, with stylized trees and tulips against a yellow cloudy sky, restored.

Many of the elements of this pattern have been taken from earlier designs. The fact that it is painted in pastel shades tells us it is a later date.

1934-35   *6in (15.5cm)*

$1,000-1,500   **FRE**

A Clarice Cliff 'Woodland' pattern milk jug, with colorful abstract landscape.
4.25in (10.5cm) high

$350-400   **FRE**

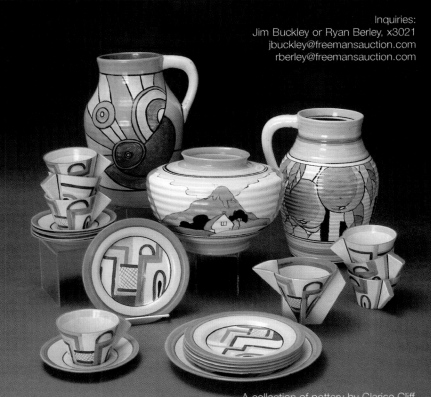

A Clarice Cliff 'Woodland' pattern bowl, decorated with colorful flowers and trees in an abstract landscape, scrapes to interior, 1.25in hairline crack to rim.

7in (17.5cm) diam

$220-280 **FRE**

A Clarice Cliff 'Shape 362' vase, with colorful geometric and triangular design with blue borders.

7.75in (19.5cm)

$700-1,000 **GorL**

A Clarice Cliff conical banded jug.

1930s *7in (17.5cm) high*

$270-330 **RH**

An extremely rare pair of Clarice Cliff 'Bizarre' bookends, each modeled with a kneeling North American Indian chief, with turquoise loin cloth and mocassins and long sand-colored feathered headdress with orange tips, "Bizarre Wilkinson Limited" marks.

6in (15cm)

$5,000-7,000 **GorL**

A Clarice Cliff cocoa pot.

1930s *6in (15cm) high*

$400-600 **RH**

A Clarice Cliff 'Chahar' wall mask, of a lady with an elaborate Egyptian headdress, the highly modeled mask has hand-painted details.

These masks, or wall medallions, as the factory called them, were produced from 1933. This mask was produced in small quantities and hence is desirable.

11in (28cm) high

$1,800-2,200 **FRE**

A 1930s Clarice Cliff 'Bizarre' pattern egg cup stand, modeled with a figure of a duckling, together with two egg cups.

$300-500 **GorL**

A Clarice Cliff Royal Staffordshire dish, of ovoid form with twin black ribbon handles and ivy chain decoration.

14in (35.5cm) high

$220-280 **FRE**

A Susie Cooper for Grays lemonade jug.
c1928   *7.25in (18.5cm) high*

$400-600   **SCG**

A Susie Cooper 'Cubist' pattern jug.
c1929   *4.75in (12cm) high*

$400-600   **SCG**

A Susie Cooper 'Moon and Mountain' pattern jug.
c1928   *7.5in (12cm) high*

$400-600   **SCG**

A Susie Cooper for Grays cup and saucer.
c1929   *Saucer 5.5in (14cm) diam*

$320-380   **SCG**

A Susie Cooper 'Geometric' pattern plate.
c1929

$800-1,200   **SCG**

A Susie Cooper for Grays 'Quadrupeds' pattern plate.
c1929   *8.75in (22.5cm) diam*

$320-380   **SCG**

Susie Cooper part coffee service, yellow decoration with black dot border, comprising coffee pot, six cups, six saucers, sugar bowl and jug, one cup badly damaged.
1930s

$150-200   **AS&S**

A Susie Cooper hand-painted coffee pot.
c1930   *6in (15.5cm) high*

$320-380   **SCG**

A Susie Cooper jug.
c1930   *5in (12.5cm) high*

$400-600   **SCG**

A B C D E F G H I J K L M N O P Q R S T U V W XYZ

CERAMICS

SUSIE COOPER (1902-1995)

- After abandoning her intended career in fashion, Cooper joined A.E. Gray & Co. in the Staffordshire Potteries, England, in 1922 as a paintress. She was soon promoted, becoming a designer.
- In 1929 she set up her own company which decorated locally made white-ware blanks.
- In 1931 she moved production to the famous 'Crown Works', part of Woods & Sons.
- By 1932 she was designing her first shapes and adopted the famous Leaping Deer mark. The rounded and traditional 'Kestrel', 'Curlew' and 'Wren' shapes produced at this time are very collectable.
- Highly desirable decoration includes hand-painted or lithographed brightly colored geometric shapes or polka dots. These are typical of the Art Deco period and were all produced before 1939.
- Post-War production is less brightly colored and is inspired by organic and plant-like designs.
- In 1950 Cooper acquired a bone china manufacturer and began producing dinnerware, but these pieces are less desirable to collectors.
- Reproductions can be found. Examples include The Bradford Exchange which reproduced Cooper's geometric design plates in 1999, and Wedgwood, which re-released the Kestrel breakfast sets in 1987.
- Fakes are often found – primarily the miniature tea sets – check for irregular and fuzzy marks.

A Susie Cooper hand-painted 'Geometric' pattern cookie barrel.

c1930   *5in (12.5cm) high*

$1,000-1,300   **SCG**

A Susie Cooper cup and saucer.

c1931   *4.25in (11cm) diam*

$220-280   **SCG**

A Susie Cooper 'Studio Range' pink vase.

1932-1934   *7.75in (20cm) high*

$220-280   **SCG**

A Susie Cooper 'Studio Range' green fruit plate.

1932-34   *7in (18.5cm) diam*

$60-100   **SCG**

A Susie Cooper stylized floral trefoil dish.

c1932   *8.5in (21.5cm)*

$180-230   **SCG**

A Susie Cooper hand-painted floral plate.

c1932   *7.75in (20cm) diam*

$60-100   **SCG**

A Susie Cooper ladle.

c1932   *7.75in (20cm) long*

$100-150   **SCG**

A Susie Cooper 'Graduated Black Bands' pattern plate.

c1932   *5.25in (13.5cm) diam*

$30-50   **SCG**

A Susie Cooper 'Plaid' pattern fruit bowl.
c1933   *9.5in (24cm) diam*

$320-380   **SCG**

A Susie Cooper 'Tea for Two' set.
c1932   *4.75in (12cm) high*

$400-600   **SCG**

A Susie Cooper 'Galleon' pattern plate.
This pattern is rare.
c1933   *11in (28cm) diam*

$500-700   **SCG**

A Susie Cooper 'Noah's Arc' divided dish.
c1933   *7.75in (20cm) diam*

$320-380   **SCG**

A Susie Cooper 'Skier' mug.
1933-1934   *3.75in (9.5cm) high*

$320-380   **SCG**

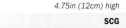

A Susie Cooper 'Guardsman' plate.
This is one of the rarest Nursery Ware patterns.
c1933   *6.25in (16cm)*

$270-330   **SCG**

A Susie Cooper stylized floral gravy boat.
c1934   *3in (8cm) high*

$80-120   **SCG**

A Susie Cooper 'Modernist' pattern kestrel
shape tureen, made for the Dorland Hall
exhibition.
c1934   *10.25in (26cm) wide*

$150-200   **SCG**

A Susie Cooper Kestrel shape 'Dresden
Spray' pattern tea set.
c1935   *Teapot 4.75in (12cm) high*

$500-700   **SCG**

A Susie Cooper hand-painted bowl with
stylized leaves.
c1936   *9.75in (25cm) diam*

$300-500   **SCG**

A Susie Cooper hand-painted fruit plate.
c1936   *11in (28cm) diam*

$320-380   **SCG**

A Susie Cooper 'Angel Fish' table center.
c1936   *10.75in (27.5cm) high*

$1,800-2,200   **SCG**

A Susie Cooper 'Crayon' pattern stylized floral plate.
c1937   *8.5in (22cm) diam*

$80-120   **SCG**

A Susie Cooper 'Turkey and Chicken' plate, with hand-painted outline on lithograph.
c1937   *17.75in (45cm) high*

$500-700   **SCG**

A Susie Cooper 'Scraffito Crescents' pattern breakfast tea set.
c1937   *Teapot 4.75in (12cm) high*

$700-1,000   **SCG**

A Susie Cooper 'Scraffito Chicken' pattern television cup and saucer, made for the American market.
c1938   *7in (18cm) long*

$100-150   **SCG**

A Susie Cooper 'Starburst' wall-charger.
c1938   *12in (30.5cm) diam*

$270-330   **SCG**

A Susie Cooper Pottery 'Chinese Fern' pattern plate, hand-painted.
c1947   *25cm diam*

$40-60   **FFM**

A Susie Cooper Falcon shape 'Asterix' pattern coffee set.
c1938   *Coffee pot 7.5in (19cm) high*

$500-700   **SCG**

A Susie Cooper Falcon shape 'Green Feather' pattern coffee set.
c1942   *Coffee pot 7.5in (19cm) high*

$400-600   **SCG**

An Alcock bone china cup and saucer.
c1838

$80-120   MH

A John Aynsley cup and saucer.
c1900

$50-80   MH

A William Alsager Adderley cup and saucer, with blue ground, pattern no. 5165.
c1910-20

$50-80   MH

A John Aynsley cup and saucer, decorated with pink roses.
c1900

$80-120   MH

A John Aynsley cup and saucer, decorated with green leaves and daisies.
c1930-40

$50-80   MH

A Bishop & Stonier cup and saucer.
c1900

$50-80   MH

A Brown-Westhead & Moore cup and saucer.

$80-120   MH

A Brown-Westhead & Moore cup and saucer.
c1900

$50-80   MH

A Coalport cup and saucer.
c1940

$40-60   MH

A Coalport porcelain cup and saucer.
c1830

$80-120   MH

A fine Coalport porcelain cup and saucer.
c1850

$200-250   MH

A Coalport cup and saucer.
c1840

$50-80   MH

A Coalport plate, cup and saucer, pattern no. 4562.
c1920

$60-100   MH

A Collingwood plate, cup and saucer, pattern no. 775.
c1900

$70-100   MH

A Crown Derby porcelain cup and saucer.
c1949

$50-80   MH

A Crown Derby cup and saucer, pattern no. 2451.
c1914

$50-80   MH

A Crown Ducal plate, cup and saucer.
1930s

$30-50   MH

A Crown Staffordshire cup, saucer and plate.
c1906

$80-120   MH

A Henry Daniels cup and saucer.
c1825

$120-180   MH

A Daniels Savoy-shape cup and saucer, painted with scenes, pattern no. 450.
c1840

$200-250   MH

A Daniels cup and saucer.
c1850

$120-180   MH

A Davenport cup and saucer, pattern no. 356.

c1860

$120-180   **MH**

A Crown Derby porcelain plate, cup and saucer.

c1880

$100-150   **MH**

A Royal Doulton cup, saucer and plate, pattern no. 2588.

$50-80   **MH**

A Doulton Lambeth stoneware cup and saucer, applied with graduated rows of florets picked out in pale brown and deep-blue borders.

Cup 3.25in (8cm) high

$70-100   **DN**

A Hilditch cup and saucer.

c1830-35

$120-180   **MH**

A Hilditch & Hopwood cup and saucer.

c1844

$100-150   **MH**

A Hilditch cup and saucer.

c1845

$70-100   **MH**

A George Jones cup and saucer, decorated with roses.

c1900-20

$40-60   **MH**

A George Jones plate, cup and saucer.

c1909

$50-80   **MH**

A C.J. Mason cup and saucer.

c1835-45

$80-120   **MH**

A C.J. Mason cup and saucer.

c1835-45

$100-150   **MH**

A B **C** D E F G H I J K L M N O P Q R S T U V W XYZ

A Meyer & Sherratt (Melba china) plate, cup and saucer.
c1935-41

$40-60 MH

A Minton cup and saucer.
c1910

$80-120 MH

A Minton cup and saucer.
c1863

$50-80 MH

A Minton cup and saucer, with butterfly handle, pattern no. G599.
c1860

$200-250 MH

A Nautilus plate, cup and saucer.
c1896

$100-150 MH

An Osbourne cup and saucer, decorated with pansies.
1940s

$50-80 MH

A Paragon plate, cup and saucer, pattern no. 11.
c1930

$40-60 MH

An RH & SL Plant plate, cup and saucer.
c1930

$50-80 MH

An A.G. Richardson cup and saucer, pattern no.439.
c1928

$30-50 MH

A John Ridgway cup and saucer.
c1850

$80-120   **MH**

A John Rose Coalport cup and saucer.
c1815

$300-400   **MH**

A Royal Albert cup and saucer, decorated
with roses, pattern no. 1341.

$35-45   **MH**

A Ridgway 'London-shape' cup and saucer.
c1820

$150-200   **MH**

A Shelley pale blue 'Vogue' shape trio.

Cup 2.5in (6.5cm) high

$200-250   **RH**

A Queen Ann Shelley 'Sunset and Trees'
trio.

$120-180   **MH**

A Shelley cup and saucer.

$50-80   **MH**

A Spode cup and saucer.

c1827-30

$180-220   **MH**

A B C D E F G H I J K L M N O P Q R S T U V W XYZ

A Spode porcelain cup and saucer.
c1815

$320-380 MH

A Spode cup and saucer, with 'Imari' pattern, pattern no. 471.
c1820

$200-250 MH

A 'Vogue' shape "Horn of Flowers" trio.
Cup 2.5in (6.5cm) high

$500-800 RH

A Thomas Wild (Royal Albert) plate, cup and saucer.
c1940

$40-60 MH

A Wileman & Co. plate, cup and saucer.
c1890

$120-180 RH

A Wileman & Co. cup and saucer.
c1897

$70-100 MH

A Wileman & Co. plate, cup and saucer.
c1890

$70-100 MH

A Grainger Worcester porcelain cup and saucer.
c1835

$200-300 MH

Lambeth

A massive pair of Doulton Lambeth stoneware vases, decorated by Hannah Barlow, each of shouldered ovoid form incised with a frieze of ponies within bands of incised and applied leaf and flowerhead motifs, the cylindrical neck and convex rim similarly decorated, the glazes in shades of blue and green, impressed marks and incised initials.

c1885   *18.5in (47cm) high*

$5,000-7,000   **L&T**

A Doulton Lambeth stoneware 'seaweed' vase, by George Tinworth, of ovoid form and decorated with meandering horizontal bands of beaded aquatic foliage applied with florets and picked out in blue against a streaky amber-colored ground, impressed factory marks, dated and with "GT" monogram on side, restored on base.

1875   *11in (27.5cm) high*

$400-600   **DN**

A Doulton Lambeth stoneware jardinière, in 'Natural Foliage' design of brown oak leaves on a mottled amber ground.

7in (18cm) high

$100-150   **BAR**

A Doulton footwarmer, registration date 1892.

c1892   *9.5in (24cm) wide*

$100-150   **BS**

A Doulton Lambeth silver-mounted stoneware pitcher, various incised and impressed marks, tapering cylindrical vessel incised with leafage between beaded borders, strap handle with scale decoration and a silver rim, together with another Doulton Lambeth globular gold-swirl ground three-handled footed vase.

1878-79   *Highest 9.5in (24cm) high*

$320-380   **SI**

A Doulton Lambeth stoneware ewer, by Eliza Simmance, the oviform body having a cut-out shaped neck and foliate handle, carved with scrolling foliage and incised with florets picked out in pale greens and browns against dark green within a beaded panel, the neck and base in streaked amber, factory marks and "ES" monogram, numbered "203", some glaze losses and small repair on neck.

9in (23cm) high

$270-330   **DN**

An early Doulton Lambeth stoneware ewer, by Arthur Barlow, of oviform with tapering neck and loop handle, simply decorated with blue and dark brown foliage against a greyish ground, oval factory mark, dated and with "ABB" monogram.

This piece was purchased from the Doulton Reserve Collection at Phillips Auctioneers in London, November 1999.

1874   *10.5in (26cm) high*

$800-1,000   **DN**

A pair of early Doulton Lambeth stoneware candlesticks, by Frank A. Butler, oval factory marks and with "FAB" monogram, some restoration to bases.

10in (25.5cm) high

$500-700   **DN**

A Royal Doulton Series Ware jug, 'The Pickwick Papers', in low relief by C.J. Noke.

$180-220   **DN**

A B **C** D E F G H I J K L M N O P Q R S T U V W XYZ

CERAMICS

A Doulton Burslem 'Holbeinware' oviform vase, painted by W. Hodkinson, in naturalistic colors with a sunset scene of cattle drinking from a stream and flanked on the banks by trees, factory marks and signed on side "W. Hodkinson", restored.

12.25in (31cm) high

$150-200   **DN**

A stoneware cachepot, probably Doulton Lambeth, modelled with six reserves of differing animal portraits in relief within scroll frames on a brown ground, unmarked except incised "WH" monogram.

6.5in (16.5cm) high

$270-330   **BAR**

A pair of large Royal Doulton vases, each of baluster form with cobalt glazed body, floral reserves, celadon neck and leaf-decorated everted rim, stamped marks.

16.5in (42cm) high

$1,000-1,500   **FRE**

A pair of Royal Doulton vases, each with bulbous body molded with floral panels against a cobalt ground, tapering neck with floral collar and flat evereted rim, stamped marks.

15.25in (38.5cm) high

$500-700   **FRE**

A pair of Royal Doulton vases, with floral panels.

9in (23cm)

$220-280   **GorL**

A pair of Royal Doulton stoneware vases, each of a footed ovoid form with tall baluster necks, decorated in tube-line with floral panels and painted in green, blue and brown glazes, impressed and incised marks.

15.35in (39cm) high

$400-600   **L&T**

A pair of Royal Doulton stoneware vases, each of shouldered ovoid form, painted in colors with wisteria on an olive ground, impressed and incised marks.

10.75in (27cm) high

$400-600   **L&T**

A Royal Doulton stoneware tobacco jar and cover, painted in colors with a landscape on mottled blue ground.

4.75in (12cm) high

$300-500   **L&T**

A pair of Royal Doulton vases, of tapered cylindrical form with heart-shape motifs, on marmalade grounds, one badly damaged.

7in (18cm)

$220-280   **GorL**

A Royal Doulton stoneware twin-handled oviform vase, by Mark V. Marshall, factory marks, initialled "M.V.M" numbered "269" and with date code.

1906   *12.25in (31cm) high*

$500-700   **DN**

1 A pair of Royal Doulton Lambeth stoneware vases, each of baluster shape, tube-line decorated with clematis pendant from the shoulders and picked out in naturalistic colors, factory marks and "BN" for Bessie Newberry.

13in (32.5cm) high

$400-600 **DN**

2 A Royal Doulton Lambeth stoneware oviform vase, decorated around the shoulders in naturalistic colors with grapes and vine leaves, against an off-white and beige ground and another Doulton stoneware vase, similarly decorated with grapes, leaves and blossom, both with impressed factory marks.

Largest 7in (18cm) high

$300-400 **DN**

3 A pair of Royal Doulton stoneware vases, each painted in colors around the slightly swollen shoulders with stylised flowers and leaves against greeny-grey ground with an area of mottled purple and mauve below, impressed factory marks.

9in (22.5cm) high

$220-280 **DN**

A Royal Doulton ovoid vase, with Slater's patent panels.

8in (20.5cm)

$150-200 **GorL**

A Royal Doulton jardinière, with wavy rim and floral palmette panels.

9in (23cm)

$220-280 **GorL**

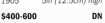

A Royal Doulton stoneware tobacco jar and cover, made to commemorate the Centenary of Nelson's death, bearing inscription "England expects that every man will do his duty", impressed factory marks.

1905 *5in (12.5cm) high*

$400-600 **DN**

1 A Royal Doulton Lambeth stoneware baluster vase, painted around the shoulders with square-edged flowers in mauve flanked by olive-green foliage above a band of vertical black lines, impressed factory marks on base.

10.75in (27cm) high

$300-500 **DN**

2 A Royal Doulton Lambeth stoneware oviform vase, tube-line decorated with three groups of narcissi with white petals and blue centers, having green foliage against a streaky greyish ground, impressed factory marks.

6.75in (17cm) high

$270-330 **DN**

3 A Royal Doulton Lambeth stoneware vase, decorated by Eliza Simmance, of slender oviform with a cup-shaped neck and painted highly stylised Art Nouveau tulips, buds and foliage in mauve, olive green and deeper green against a milky pinkish-grey ground, impressed factory marks and incised "ES" monogram, numbered "349" and date code for 1910, flaw on base glazed over.

1910 *14in (35.5cm) high*

$700-1,000 **DN**

4 A Royal Doulton Lambeth stoneware jardinière, decorated by Eliza Simmance, of compressed globular shape, painted around the shoulders with a trellis and thorny branches of roses in milky-pink and olive-green tones against a shaded pale blue ground, impressed factory marks, incised "ES" monogram, numbered "323" and date code.

1916 *6.5in (16cm) high*

$500-700 **DN**

5 A Doulton Lambeth stoneware oviform jug, decorated by Edith Lupton, carved with scrolling panels of stylized foliage in blues and brown, flanking oval panels delicately painted in pate-sur-pate technique with scrolling foliage and florets against a greeny-brown ground, factory marks with initials "EDL" numbered "422" and dated.

1883 *9in (22.5cm) high*

$700-1,000 **DN**

6 A Royal Doulton Lambeth stoneware globular vase, decorated by Margaret Thompson, in naturalistic colors with blossom and foliage against an apple-green and streaked blue glaze, impressed factory marks and "MET" artist's monogram.

5.25in (13cm) high

$180-220 **DN**

CERAMICS

A Royal Doulton silver-mounted whisky bottle, with Art Nouveau buds on a dark blue ground.

9.5in (24cm)

$180-220 GorL

A Royal Doulton Brangwyn Ware 'Harvest' pattern jug, of oviform with strap handle painted in colors with wheatsheaves, fruit and foliage against a shaded ground, factory marks on base, date code and marked "D 6120".

1940 7.5in (19cm) high

$120-180 DN

A set of eight 20thC Royal Doulton luncheon plates, purple printed factory mark, retailed by Tiffany & Co., each printed in green, brown, black and gilt with a border of stylized flowers round a central rosette and vine.

9in (23cm) diam

$150-200 SI

Figures

PEGGY DAVIES

- Davies worked as a freelance designer on a contract basis with Doulton, producing her first model in 1946.
- Her first figures were girls and figures in contemporary dress and styles, but she went on to produce a diverse range of figures including dancers, historical characters and studies of children.
- Davies was responsible for around 250 figure designs during her 40 year career with Doulton.

A Royal Doulton figure, 'Town Crier', HN2119, by Peggy Davies.

1953-1976 8in (20.5cm) high

$270-330 DN

A Royal Doulton figure, 'Sweet Dream', designed by Peggy Davies, introduced 1971.

5in (12.5cm) high

$180-220 OACC

A Royal Doulton figure, 'Noelle', HN2179, by Peggy Davies.

1957-1967 7in (17.5cm) high

$220-280 DN

A Royal Doulton figure, 'Teenager' HN 2203, by Peggy Davies.

1957-1962 7.5in (18.5cm) h

$150-200 DN

A Royal Doulton figure, 'Maureen', HN1770, by Leslie Harradine.

1936-1959 7.75in (19.5cm) h

$180-220 DN

A rare Royal Doulton figure, 'All a blooming', by Leslie Harradine, this figure has not been given an HN number but is a color variant of HN1466.

c1931 6.25in (16cm) high

$1,500-2,000 DN

A Royal Doulton figure, 'Lily', HN 1798, by Leslie Harradine.

1936-1971 5in (13cm) high

$80-120 DN

LESLIE HARRADINE

- Harradine worked for Doulton's Lambeth factory from 1902-1912 before leaving for Canada. He returned to work as a freelance designer, releasing his first figure in 1920.
- Over the next 30 years, he sent at least one model per month to be produced, including stylishly dressed ladies and excellent studies of Dickens' characters. His work dominated 1930s' production, particularly fashionably dressed ladies and notable stars of the time. Harradine retired in 1956.

A Royal Doulton figure, 'Susanna' (HN 1288), by Leslie Harradine.

1928-36   6in (15cm) high

$1,200-1,800   DN

A Royal Doulton figure, 'Windflower' HN 1763, by Leslie Harradine, date code for 1937.

1937   8in (18cm) high

$300-500   DN

A Royal Doulton figure, 'The Orange Lady', HN1759, by Leslie Harradine.

1936-1975   8.75in (22cm) h

$220-280   DN

A Royal Doulton figure, 'Harlequinade' HN 585, by Leslie Harradine, repaired at neck.

1923-38   6.75in (17cm) high

$600-1,000   DN

A Leslie Johnson hand-painted figure, modelled as a young woman wearing a mauve bonnet tied with a green ribbon, a scarlet jacket painted with roses and other flowers and a pink skirt, painted with roses, signed "Leslie Johnson" on base.

Johnson was a decorator at Royal Doulton so it is conceivable that this is by the same artist but on his own account.

10.25in (26cm) high

$80-120   DN

A Royal Doulton figure, 'Cobbler' HN 1706, by C.J. Noke.

1935-69   8in (20.5cm) high

$120-180   DN

A Royal Doulton Ships' Figureheads series 'Benmore Full Rigged Ship' figure number 614 in a limited edition of 950.

1870-1924 10.5in (27cm) high

$300-500   OACC

C.J. NOKE

- Previously a modeler at the Worcester factory, joined Doulton in 1889 and during his later career, was influenced by the early work of Harradine.
- Preferring to work on figures, he released his first figural design in 1892 after modelling vases.
- He led a revival of Staffordshire style figurines, along with a team of artists, launching the range in 1912.
- Noke retired in 1941.

A large Royal Doulton flambé 'Tiger'.

13in (33cm) long

$400-600   PSA

A Royal Doulton flambé 'Rhinoceros', seated and rearing his head, with red flambé glaze and a veined bluish-orange glaze to base.

9in (22.5cm) high

$1,000-1,500 **FRE**

A Royal Doulton flambé sculpture 'Gift Of Life', of a mare and her foal seated on a circular base, under a red flambé glaze.

1987-1996 9.5in (24cm) high

$700-1,000 **FRE**

A 20thC Royal Doulton model of a cat, with white fur and bright yellow eyes, factory marks on base, numbered "2539".

5in (12.5cm) high

$80-120 **DN**

Three 20thC Royal Doulton model, Bunnykins 'Grandpa's Story' DB14, by Walter Hayward, a Bunnykins 'Busy Needles' DB10 and a 'Mr Bunnykins 'Autumn Days', by Walter Hayward.

Largest 4.25in (10.5cm) high

$270-330 **DN**

A Royal Doulton 101 Dalmations series 'Cruella De Vil' DM1, with box.

$70-100 **PSA**

A Royal Doulton 101 Dalmations series 'Pongo' DM6, with box.

$40-60 **PSA**

A Royal Doulton 101 Dalmations series 'Perdita' DM7, with box.

$15-20 **PSA**

A Royal Doulton The Winnie the Pooh collection 'Christopher Robin and Pooh' WP10, with 70th anniversary backstamp.

$20-30 **PSA**

A Royal Doulton 101 Dalmations series 'Penny', 'Roly', and 'Lucky', all with box, nos. DM2, DM4 and DM8 respectively.

$50-80 **PSA**

A Royal Doulton 101 Dalmations series 'Patch, Roly and Freckles' DM5 tableau, limited edition number 273 of 3500, boxed with plinth.

$120-180 **PSA**

A Royal Doulton Snowmen series 'Snowball' money box.

$30-40 **PSA**

A Royal Doulton 'Grumpy's Bathtime' SW20, with box, number 2009.

$40-60 **PSA**

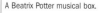

A Beatrix Potter musical box.

$40-60 **PSA**

A B.B. Craig alkaline swirl face jug, in two-tone gray, with blue eyes, under a glossy glaze, stamped "BB CRAIG/VALE N.C."

7in (18cm) high

$700-800 **CR**

A B.B. Craig devil's face jug, covered in a brown and cream swirled glaze, stamped "B.B. CRAIG/VALE, N.C."

9in (23cm) high

$180-220 **CR**

A B.B. Craig double-face jug, covered in a brown, white and indigo swirled glaze, signed "B.B.C." on both sides.

12in (30.5cm) high

$450-550 **CR**

An unusual B.B. Craig swirl face wall pocket, in green, cobalt and ivory with blue eyes, under a glossy glaze, stamped "BBC".

7.5in (19cm) high

$550-650 **CR**

A B.B. Craig face jug, of swirled brown, green and white clays, stamped mark, small chip to base and burst bubble to back.

9in (23cm) high

$350-450 **CR**

A B.B. Craig jug, with snake wrapped around swirled clay base, stamped mark.

8.25in (21cm) high

$350-450 **CR**

A Steve Abee, Lenoir, N.C., bearded face jug, with oozing white eyes and pointed nose, incised mark.

9in (23cm) high

$350-450 **CR**

A Louis Brown face jug, Arden N.C., covered in a mottled umber and ivory glaze, incised "Brown's Pottery/Arden/N.C./Louis Brown/70 yrs old".

15in (38cm) high

$250-350 **CR**

A Dwayne Craig face jug, covered in a speckled brown glaze, signed "Dwayne Craig".

8in (20cm) high

$450-550 **CR**

A Dwayne Craig face jug, with cobalt, black and orange decoration against a tan ground, signed "Dwayne Craig" in script.

12in (30.5cm) high

$450-550   **CR**

A Walter Fleming double-face jug, covered in a green alkaline glaze on front, and brown glaze on back, stamped "WALTER FLEMING" twice.

15in (38cm) high

$750-850   **CR**

A Walter Fleming three-face totem jar, with handle, covered in a mottled dark brown glossy glaze, stamped "WALTER FLEMING".

20in (51cm) high

$450-550   **CR**

A tall J. Flowers stoneware jug, with large applied dragon, covered in pink, blue and green dripping glaze, incised "J. Flowers/1997".

1997   14in (35.5cm) high

$500-600   **CR**

An A. G. Meaders face jug, incised with expressive eyebrows and eyelashes, and covered in a dripping glossy green glaze, large bruise to one ear, incised in script "A.G. Meaders 1990".

1990   12in (30.5cm) high

$450-550   **CR**

An Albert Hodge devil's face jug, with terracotta eyes, hand signed "Albert Hodge" on reverse 11 times, signature to bottom.

10.5in (26.5cm) high

$600-700   **CR**

A Charles Lisk two-handled face jar, with cobalt blue drips, hand signed and stamped twice.

14.5in (37cm) high

$500-600   **CR**

An A.V. Smith face jug, covered in a candy apple red glaze, with bulging blue eyes, signed "AV SMITH".

11.5in (29.5cm) high

$500-600   **CR**

A Lanier Meaders stoneware face jug, with misshapen face and seven teeth, covered in a dripping green glaze, incised in script "Lanier Meaders".

c1990   11.5in (29.5cm) high

$1,600-2,000   **CR**

FULPER

- In 1814, Samuel Hill began producing utilitarian wares in Flemington, New Jersey, for sale in the surrounding area.
- One of his employees, Abraham Fulper (1815-1881) became Hill's partner in 1847, and took over the running of the company when Hill died. The company changed its name a number of times and became the Fulper Pottery Company in 1899 when Fulper's grandson William took over.
- In 1909 the pottery introduced its first art pottery line, Vasekraft. From 1910 the company began producing artistic wares under the direction of German ceramic engineer Martin Stangl and William Fulper. It produced matt glazed vessels in Japanese or Arts and Crafts form. Stangl became vice president of the company in 1924.
- Production moved from Flemington to Trenton following a fire in 1929 and a year later Stangl purchased the pottery. In 1955, the company changed its name to Stangl Pottery, but by 1978, Stangl Pottery ceased trading.
- The large table lamps and artist-signed lusterware are the most highly sought-after pieces.

A Fulper bulbous vase, covered in a café-au-lait glaze, ink racetrack mark.

7.5in (19cm) high

$400-500   **CR**

A Fulper Colonial Ware ribbed pitcher covered in a mottled caramel glaze, ink racetrack mark.

5.25in (13.5cm) high

$55-65   **CR**

A Fulper squat urn, with buttressed handles covered in a cat's-eye flambé glaze, ink racetrack mark, bruise to one handle.

8in (20cm) high

$200-250   **CR**

A Fulper squat urn, with angular handles covered in a copperdust crystalline glaze, incised racetrack mark.

5in (12.5cm) high

$200-250   **CR**

A Fulper Roman urn, with scrolled handles covered in a mirror black and copper dust crystalline glaze, paper label, invisible restoration to one handle and to chip at base.

15in (38cm) high

$800-900   **CR**

A Fulper bullet vase, covered in a frothy elephant's breath and mahogany flambé glaze, ink racetrack mark, chip to rim, and small grinding chip.

7in (18cm) high

$350-450   **CR**

A Fulper buttressed vase, covered in a fine leopard skin crystalline glaze, ink racetrack mark, minor nick and short, tight line inside rim.

8.25in (21cm) high

$1,000-1,500   **CR**

A Fulper bulbous urn, covered in a mission verde glaze, raised racetrack mark.

10.25in (26cm) high

$650-750   **CR**

A Fulper lamp, covered in a pale green glaze and decorated with an applied rose, small ink racetrack mark, restored chip to one petal.

6.5in (16.5cm) high

$150-200   **CR**

A Fulper ovoid bud vase, covered in a fine frothy pale green to beige flambé, ink racetrack mark.

9.25in (23.5cm) high

$300-350   **CR**

A rare Fulper collared urn, with two angular handles, covered in a sheer olive green crystalline glaze, raised racetrack mark, horizontal crack to body near base.

9.25in (23.5cm) high

$500-600   **CR**

A Fulper squat bowl, with two scrolled handles covered in a turquoise and green crystalline glaze, ink racetrack mark.

8in (20.5cm) high

$150-200   **CR**

A Fulper faceted vase, with embossed rim covered in a blue and gray mottled matte glaze, rectangular ink mark and Vasekraft paper label.

4.5in (11.5cm) high

$350-450   **CR**

A Fulper bulbous vase, with flaring rim and embossed prunts to the shoulder, covered in a frothy blue crystalline glaze, incised racetrack mark.

7in (17.5cm) high

$300-350   **CR**

A fine Fulper bulbous vase, covered in a rich blue crystalline flambé glaze, small grinding chip.

7.75in (19.5cm) high

$350-450   **CR**

A large Fulper footed centerbowl, with cut-out flaring foot, covered in a Chinese blue crystalline flambé glaze, impressed mark, re-glued foot, hairline to rim, and several burst glaze bubbles to interior.

17in (43cm) diam

$220-280   **CR**

A Fulper ovoid vase, covered in Chinese blue flambé glaze, ink racetrack mark.

10in (25.5cm) high

$550-650   **CR**

A tall Fulper classically shaped vase, covered in a famille rose glaze, raised racetrack mark.

12in (30.5cm) high

$800-1,000   **CR**

A Fulper bulbous urn, with collared rim, covered in a moss-to-rose flambé glaze, ink racetrack mark, grinding chip.

8in (20cm) high

$250-350   **CR**

A fine Fulper gourd-shaped vase, incised racetrack mark.

6.5in (16.5cm) high

$350-450   **CR**

Two Fulper figural flower frogs, of a boy and girl, both marked, glaze smudge and a few nicks to base of the boy.

5.5in (14cm) high

$300-350   **CR**

A rare Fulper duck, covered in a fine green and blue flambé glaze, impressed "Fulper", small tight line to base.

9in (23cm) wide

$2,200-2,800   **CR**

HUMMEL

- Franz Detleff Goebel and his son, William Goebel founded the Goebel Company in 1871, in Bavaria. The company introduced the first Goebel porcelain figures in 1890. By 1933, there was an extensive line of porcelain figures. Later pieces were influenced by the artist Sister Maria Innocentia Hummel, a member of the Sisters of the Third Order of St. Francis, at the Convent of Siessen. In 1934, Franz Goebel wrote a letter to her proposing that Goebel artists translate her two-dimensional drawings into three-dimensional figurines. She eventually agreed and in 1935 the factory introduced the first Hummel figures based on these designs, many of which are still in production.

- Early Hummel pieces generally command the highest prices. Figures from the 1930s and 1940s bear a 'V' mark surmounted by a large bumble-bee in blue. On later pieces the bee sits within the 'V'.

A 1940s Hummel figure, "Weary Wanderer", restored.

6in (15cm) high

$100-150 OACC

A Hummel figure, "Sister", small restoration to hair.

5.5in (14cm) high

$100-150 OACC

A Hummel figure, "Mother's Darling".

1940-56   6in (15cm) high

$100-150 OACC

A Hummel Club figure, "Forever Yours", first issue 1996/7.

4in (10cm) high

$70-100 OACC

A Hummel figure, "For Mother", dated.

1963   5in (12.5cm) high

$70-100 PSA

A Hummel ashtray, "Joyful", withdrawn in December 1984.

$70-100 OACC

A Hummel Club figure, "Garden Treasures", membership year 1998/99.

3.5in (9cm) high

$50-80 OACC

A Hummel figure, "Merry Wanderer".

4in (10cm) high

$70-100 OACC

A Hummel figure, "Meditation".

4.5in (11cm) high

$50-80 OACC

A Hummel figure, "Cuddles", dated.

1997   3.5in (9cm) high

$50-80 OACC

A Hummel figure, "My best friend", first issue 1998.

3.5in (9cm) high

$50-80 OACC

A German Hummel-style figure, modelled as a boy with an umbrella, black painted marks to base.

$10-15 PSA

CERAMICS

LENOX

- Walter Scott Lenox (1859-1920) was born in Trenton, New Jersey in 1859.
- In 1875 he started an apprenticeship with Ott & Brewer and later worked for Willetts as well as studying with local painter and sculptor Isaac Broome. He eventually became art director at Ott & Brewer.
- In the second half of the 19th century, Irish workers brought the formula for the thin Belleek porcelain to Lenox. The factory used it to produce a wide range of decorated and undecorated wares to a very high standard. The early painted pieces are considered some the highest quality American porcelain ever produced.
- Together with Jonathan Coxon, superintendent of Ott & Brewer, Lenox started the Ceramic Art Company in 1889 and by 1894 had bought out Coxon. From 1906 the company traded as Lenox, Inc.
- Lenox, Inc is one of the few Trenton-based ceramics manufacturers still in production today and it is the tableware of choice at the White House.

An early Lenox covered jar, hand-painted with an ermine-clad lady, with gilded border, unmarked, nick to finial.

8in (20cm) high

$300-400 CR

A rare transitional Lenox/Ceramic Art Company hand-painted urn, decorated by D. Campana, with a portrait of a young girl , purple "CAC/Lenox" stamp, and artist signature.

c1905 10in (25.5cm) high

$950-1,100 CR

A transitional Ceramic Art Company/Lenox baluster vase, painted by H. Nosek, with an 18thC lady, green CAC/Lenox stamp, artist signed.

c1905 10.5in (26.5cm) high

$2,000-3,000 CR

A transitional Ceramic Art Company/Lenox vase, painted by H. Nosek, in the Classical style with a maiden, green CAC/Lenox stamp, artist signed.

c1905 10in (25.5cm) high

$2,000-2,500 CR

A rare transitional Lenox/Ceramic Art Company bulbous vase, decorated by A. Boullemier, artist signed only, restoration.

c1905 13.5in (34.5cm) high

$850-950 CR

A rare transitional Lenox/Ceramic Art Company bulbous vase, decorated by A. Boullemier, artist signed and Tiffany mark, restoration.

c1905 13.5in (34.5cm) high

$850-950 CR

A transitional Ceramic Art Company/Lenox pear-shaped vase, painted with tea roses, and gilded with wreaths and blue dots on an ivory ground, green CAC/Lenox stamp.

c1905 8in (20.5cm) high

$400-500 CR

A rare Lenox three-piece tea set, each piece faceted, with gilded handles, hand-painted with pink roses over a green body, green Lenox stamps.

c1910 Teapot 9.5in (24cm) high

$550-650 CR

A Lenox Belleek urn, decorated by E. Orrison, china-painted with chrysanthemums on a green ground, green ink stamp, artist signed and dated, bruise and repair to chip at base, a few minor flecks.

1912 12in (30.5cm) high

$450-550 CR

Nine 1920s Lenox service plates, each hand-painted by William Morley, with a different bird, acid-etched gilding borders monogrammed "HWS", green Lenox stamps, bird names, "X8"/C23, W.H. Morley".

8in (20.5cm) diam

$1,700-2,000 | **CR**

A large transitional CAC/Lenox bulbous vase, hand-painted by William Morley, green CAC/Lenox stamp, artist signed, small nick to side.

14.5in (37cm) high

$1,700-2,000 | **CR**

A large transitional CAC/Lenox cylindrical vase, hand-painted by William Morley, green CAC/Lenox stamp, artist signed, small nick to side.

15.5in (39.5cm) high

$1,700-2,000 | **CR**

A rare set of twelve Lenox service plates, painted by William Morley, each with a different orchid, surrounded by gilt border, green Lenox stamp, artist signed, "1830/0-63A".

pre-1932 | *10.5in (26.5cm) diam*

$2,800-3,200 | **CR**

A pair of Lenox bookends, with the bust of a man and woman, green ink stamp.

9in (23cm) high

$250-350 | **CR**

A rare Lenox figurine, "The Reader," done in the Meissen style with a lady in 18thC dress with a book on her lap, green "Lenox/USA" stamp.

5.5in (14cm) high

$550-650 | **CR**

A rare Lenox figurine of a little girl in pink dress, sitting on a block, green "Lenox/USA stamp", restoration to bow in her hair.

3.75in (9.5cm) high

$400-450 | **CR**

A rare Lenox figurine of a little girl in blue dress, sitting on a block, green "Lenox/USA stamp".

3.75in (9.5cm) high

$350-450 | **CR**

A rare Lenox figurine of a ballerina, in white tutu, hand-painted with roses, green "Lenox/USA" stamp.

6in (15.5cm) high

$800-900 | **CR**

A rare Lenox figurine of a ballerina, in pink tutu, hand-painted with roses, green "Lenox/USA" stamp".

6in (15.5cm) high

$850-950 | **CR**

MARBLEHEAD

- Marblehead Pottery, of Marblehead MA, was started by Dr. Herbert J. Hall in 1904. It was initially used as therapy for his patients and Hall employed Arthur Baggs to run it.

- In 1908, Hall separated the pottery from the sanatorium and Baggs ran it as a commercial operation, with the profits going to the hospital. The pottery was always small, with a maximum of six people working there at any time.

- With the exception of wares such as tiles and bookends, all Marblehead pots are hand thrown. Wares fall into two main types: decorated and undecorated. Typical decorated pieces have simple geometric or stylised floral designs, although animals and birds are also found. The most common undecorated glaze color is blue, but green, gray, brown, pink and yellow are also found.

A Marblehead squat vessel, covered in a speckled blue matte glaze, impressed ship mark, some very light abrasion around rim.

4.5in (11.5cm) diam

$180-220 CR

A Marblehead squat vessel, covered in a smooth dark blue matte glaze, impressed ship mark.

4.25in (10.5cm) diam

$550-650 CR

A Marblehead vase, covered in dark blue speckled matte glaze, ship stamp, tiny fleck to inner rim.

3.5in (9cm) high

$500-600 CR

A Marblehead spherical hanging basket, with three hanging handles covered in blue matte glaze, unmarked.

6in (15.5cm) diam

$180-220 CR

A Marblehead ovoid vase, covered in a smooth matte lavender glaze, impressed ship mark, a couple of minor burst bubbles.

5.25in (13.5cm) high

$450-500 CR

A Marblehead spherical vase, covered in a speckled pink matte glaze, impressed ship mark.

5in (12.5cm) diam

$350-450 CR

Two Marblehead vessels, one pear-shaped, covered in a speckled gray matte glaze, the other squat covered in speckled dark green, impressed ship mark.

Tallest 5.5in (14cm) high

$250-350 CR

Two Marblehead vessels, comprising a small ovoid vase covered in a smooth matte blue glaze and a spherical vessel covered in a pale lavender matte glaze, both marked, latter has paper label.

Largest 4.5in (11.5cm) high

$450-550 CR

A Marblehead bulbous vase, covered in a speckled brown matte glaze, impressed ship mark.

4.25in (11cm) diam

$1,000-1,200 CR

MASON'S IRONSTONE

- Miles Mason founded the Mason porcelain works in 1802 in Lane Delph, Staffordshire, England. The factory produced a hybrid hard paste porcelain, using both English and Chinese designs. In 1813 Mason passed the business to his sons, George and Charles James Mason. Charles James introduced the Patent Ironstone China, for which the company has become renowned.

- Ironstone China is a hard white earthenware, slightly transparent but very strong. It is made by adding ironstone slag to the porcelain mix, and is dense and durable. The strength of the china meant it could withstand heat and so it was popular for dinner services. Other wares include large vases and fireplaces. The pieces were most commonly decorated in Oriental patterns in bold colours, with flower and bird motifs.

- In 1848 Charles James Mason went bankrupt and subsequent Mason shapes and patterns have been produced under many company banners including George Ashworth & Brothers and, since 1973, the Wedgwood Group.

A pair of Mason's Patent Ironstone China tea plates, enamelled in colours with a table and vase pattern, single-line impressed marks, one also with brown-printed crown and drape mark.

1813-25   *7.25in (18.5cm) diam*

$120-180   **DN**

A Mason's Ironstone china footbath jug, glue-filled firing crack to body.

1820-40   12in (30.5cm) high

$2,500-3,000   **DN**

A Mason's Ironstone 'Imari' two-handled vase, of octagonal section with flared neck and foot, applied with two gilt serpent handles, impressed mark.

c1825   8in (20cm) high

$400-500   **DN**

1 An English ironstone octagonal jug, of Fenton-type shape with molded dragon's head upper terminal to the handle, decorated with a typical Japan pattern, unmarked except for red-painted pattern number 7322.

1825-50   *6.25in (16cm) high*

$350-450   **DN**

2 An English ironstone drainer, possibly Mason's, decorated with a typical Japan pattern, unmarked, hair crack from centre hole, together with a small Mason's Ironstone dish with combed base and a different Japan pattern, printed crown and drape mark, small area of restoration to rim.

c1820-30   *Largest 13.25in (33.5cm) wide*

$350-450   **DN**

A Mason's Ironstone 'Blue Pheasants' pattern vegetable tureen and cover.

c1825   9.5in (24cm) wide

$150-200   **DN**

A mid-19thC Jonathan Lowe Chetham Stone China 'Amherst Japan' pattern ewer and basin, with oriental buildings and flowering shrubs, together with a similar ovoid two-handled pot pourri vase and pierced cover.

Basin 14.5in (37cm) diam

$600-700   **DN**

A Mason's Ironstone octagonal sauce tureen.

c1830 Stand 8in (20cm) long

$200-250   **DN**

A Mason's Ironstone scent bottle and stopper, of globular form, gilt with floral sprays beneath broad gilt rims, on a dark blue ground, restoration to the rim.

c1830   4.75in (12cm) high

$250-350   **DN**

A Midwinter Fashion shape 'Alpine Pink' pattern plate, unnamed designer, transfer-printed.

This pattern was also produced in blue.

c1960   6in (15.5cm) diam

$6-9   FFM

A Midwinter Stylecraft shape 'Blue Domino' pattern sugar bowl, designed by Jessie Tait, hand-painted.

The blue version is rarer than the 'Red Domino' pattern.

c1954   2.25in (6cm) high

$15-25   FFM

A Midwinter Fashion shape 'Cannes' pattern plate, by Sir Hugh Casson, with printed and enameled decoration.

This is a later version of the 1954 'Riviera' pattern.

c1960   8.5in (22cm) diam

$20-30   FFM

A Midwinter Fashion shape 'Capri' pattern TV cup and plate, designed by Jessie Tait, with printed and enameled decoration.

This was also produced as the 'Bolero' pattern using different colors.

1955 Plate 8.5in (22cm) diam

$50-80   FFM

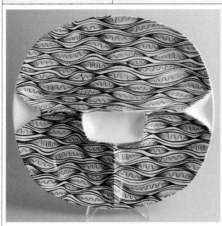

A Midwinter Fashion shape 'Caribbean' pattern buffet or TV plate, with recessed area in one corner for cup, designed by Jessie Tait, with printed and enameled decoration.

c1955   12.25in (31cm) diam

$100-150   FFM

MIDWINTER

- Founded in 1910 in Burslem, Stoke-on-Trent, England, by William Robinson Midwinter.
- Early production was of standard tea sets and dinnerware with typical Art Deco patterns and shapes.
- Midwinter excelled at producing nurseryware with printed images by William Heath Robinson. These are now highly sought after and valuable.
- Roy Midwinter (the founder's son) joined in 1946 and proceeded to revolutionize British tableware with his innovative designs. During the 1950s, factory output was immense with many different designs.
- Aimed at a younger market, pieces could be bought separately and had multiple uses. Shapes were squared off and patterns often came from up-and-coming designers of the time, including Sir Terence Conran, who designed the colorful 'Plant Life' and the 'Nature Study' patterns, Sir Hugh Casson and Jessie Tait.
- The first range in February 1953 was 'Stylecraft', which was followed in 1955 by the 'Fashion' range.
- 1957 saw the release of Midwinter's 'Melanex' range – a break-resistant material made from melamine.
- Collectors should look for pieces that sum up the design fads of the time – in terms of shape, design and coloring.
- Condition is important as these were functional pieces and often show signs of wear or damage through use, which affects value.

A Midwinter Fashion shape 'Cassandra' pattern plate, unnamed designer, transfer-printed.

c1957   9.5in (24.5cm) diam

$10-12   FFM

A Midwinter Fashion shape 'Cassandra' pattern salt and pepper pots, unnamed designer, transfer-printed.

c1957   2.75in (7cm) high

$15-25   FFM

A Midwinter Fine shape 'Cherry Tree' pattern coffee set, designed by Nigel Wylde, transfer-printed.

c1966   Pot 7.75in (20cm) high

$50-80   FFM

A Midwinter Fashion shape 'Cherokee' pattern trio, designed by Jessie Tait, hand-painted.

c1957 *Plate 6in (15.5cm) diam*

$40-60 **FFM**

A late 1950s Midwinter Fashion shape 'Contemporary' pattern meat plate, unnamed designer, transfer-printed.

13.75in (35cm) diam

$30-40 **FFM**

A Midwinter Stylecraft shape 'Cottage Ivy' pattern milk jug, designed by Jessie Tait, hand-painted.

c1953 *2.25in (5.5cm) high*

$20-30 **FFM**

A Midwinter Stonehenge 'Day' pattern trio set, possibly by Eve Midwinter, transfer-printed.

1970s 6.75in (17.5cm) diam

$20-30 **FFM**

A Midwinter Stylecraft shape 'Domino Variant' pattern trio set, designed by Jessie Tait, hand-painted.

This variation is rarer than the 'Red Domino' pattern.

c1954 *16in (15.5cm) diam*

$30-50 **FFM**

A hand-painted Midwinter Stylecraft shape 'Fantasy' pattern plate, designed by Jessie Tait.

c1953 *8.5in (22cm) diam*

$30-40 **FFM**

A hand-painted Midwinter Fashion shape 'Festival' pattern dinner plate, designed by Jessie Tait.

c1955 8.75in (22.5cm) diam

$30-50 **FFM**

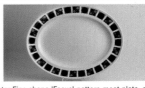

A Midwinter Fine shape 'Focus' pattern meat plate, designed by Barbara Brown, transfer-printed.

c1954 *15.5in (39.5cm) diam*

$20-30 **FFM**

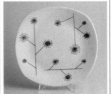

A hand-painted Midwinter Fashion shape 'Festival' pattern egg cup, designed by Jessie Tait.

c1955 *1.75in (4.5cm) high*

$30-40 **FFM**

A Midwinter Fashion shape 'Flower Mist' pattern plate, designed by Jessie Tait, with printed and enameled decoration.

c1956 *8.5in (22cm) diam*

$40-60 **FFM**

A Midwinter Fashion shape 'Happy Valley' pattern plate, designed by Jessie Tait, with printed and enameled decoration.

c1959 *6in (15.5cm) diam*

$15-18 **FFM**

A Midwinter Stylecraft shape 'Homeweave' pattern trio set, designed by Jessie Tait, hand-painted.

This is the rare version with colored holloware.

c1960 *Plate 6in (15.5cm) diam*

$30-50 **FFM**

A Midwinter Fashion shape coffee pot with later version of 'Happy Valley' pattern, designed by Jessie Tait, blue transfer-printed decoration on white glaze.

c1961   8.5in (22cm) high

$40-60   **FFM**

A Midwinter Fashion shape 'Magic Moments' pattern plate, designed by Jessie Tait, hand-painted.

c1956   6in (15.5cm) diam

$30-40   **FFM**

A Midwinter Fashion shape 'Marguerite' pattern coffee set, unnamed designer, transfer-printed.

This pattern was also made in yellow.

c1958   Coffee pot 9.75in (20cm) high

$50-80   **FFM**

A Midwinter Fashion shape 'Melody' pattern trio set, unnamed designer, transfer-printed.

c1958   6in (15.5cm) diam

$50-80   **FFM**

A Midwinter Stylecraft shape unusual 'Mimosa' pattern trio set, unnamed designer, transfer-printed.

c1953   6in (15.5cm) diam

$20-30   **FFM**

A Midwinter Fashion shape 'Monaco' pattern plate, designed by Jessie Tait, transfer-printed.

c1956   8.5in (22cm) diam

$15-25   **FFM**

A Midwinter 'Nature Study' pattern plate, designed by Sir Terence Conran, transfer-printed.

c1955   9.5in (24.5cm) diam

$40-60   **FFM**

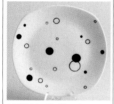

A Midwinter Fashion shape 'Pierrot' pattern plate, designed by Jessie Tait, transfer-printed.

c1955   6.25in (16cm) diam

$40-60   **FFM**

A Midwinter Fashion shape 'Plant Life' trio set, by Terence Conran, transfer-printed.

This is the later version of the original 1954 design.

c1960   6in (15cm) diam

$50-80   **FFM**

A Midwinter Fashion shape 'Primavera' pattern plate, designed by Jessie Tait, hand-painted, extremely rare, minor crack.

c1954   12.5in (32cm) diam

$30-50   **FFM**

A Midwinter Fashion shape 'Plant Life' pattern plate, designed by Sir Terence Conran, transfer-printed.

c1956   7.75in (19.5cm) diam

$30-50   **FFM**

A hand-painted Midwinter Fashion shape 'Primavera' pattern TV set plate, designed by Jessie Tait, originally with tea cup.

c1955   8.5in (22cm) diam

$20-30   FFM

A Midwinter Fashion shape 'Quite Contrary' pattern plate, designed by Jessie Tait, transfer-printed.

c1959   6in (15.5cm) diam

$10-12   FFM

A hand-painted Midwinter Stylecraft shape 'Red Domino' pattern plate, designed by Jessie Tait.

c1953   8.5in (21.5cm) diam

$20-30   FFM

A Midwinter Fashion shape 'Saladware' pattern tea plate, designed by Sir Terence Conran, with printed and enameled decoration.

c1955   6in (15.5cm) diam

$30-40   FFM

A Midwinter Fashion shape 'Riviera' pattern plate, designed by Sir Hugh Casson, with printed and enameled decoration.

The 1950s saw a huge boom in foreign vacations as flying by air became affordable for many more people. Seen as very fashionable and even glamorous, people were able to travel to Europe and beyond for comparatively short periods. Patterns like Hugh Casson's 'Riviera' and 'Cannes' designs represented an evocative memory of past vacations.

c1954   8.5in (22cm) diam

$30-40   FFM

A Midwinter Fashion shape 'Savanna' pattern plate, designed by Jessie Tait, with hand-painted yellow detail and printed and enameled decoration.

c1956   9.5in (24.5cm) diam

$30-40   FFM

A Midwinter Stylecraft shape 'Shalimar' pattern plate, designed by Jessie Tait, with printed and enameled decoration.

c1953   9.5in (24.5cm) diam

$30-40   FFM

A Midwinter Fine shape 'Sienna' pattern milk jug and sugar bowl, designed by Jessie Tait, transfer-printed.

c1962   2.25in (5.5cm) high

$10-15   FFM

A Midwinter Stylecraft shape 'Silver Bamboo' pattern teapot, designed by Jessie Tait, hand-painted, damage to inside of lid.

c1953   5in (13cm) high

$30-40   FFM

A Midwinter Fashion shape 'Stardust' export pattern meat plate, designed by Jessie Tait, hand-painted speckled glaze, chipped rim.

This pattern was made for export to Canada.

c1958   13.75in (35cm) diam

$20-30   FFM

A Midwinter Stonehenge shape 'Wild Oats' pattern milk jug, designed by Eve Midwinter, transfer-printed.

c1974   4in (10cm) high

$10-12   FFM

A Midwinter Fashion shape 'Zambesi' pattern trio set, designed by Jessie Tait, hand-painted.

c1956   Plate 6in (15.5cm) high

$30-50   FFM

A Moorcroft MacIntyre Florian ware vase, with blue flowers against a white ground.

4in (10cm)

$1,800-2,200 **GorL**

A Moorcroft MacIntyre Florian ware slender baluster vase, with dark blue poppies against a pale blue ground, small area of restoration on rim.

9.75in (25cm)

$800-1,200 **GorL**

A pair of Moorcroft MacIntyre 'Yellow Iris' pattern vases, with frilled rims, slender stems and bulbous bases, tiny foot rim chips on one vase.

12.25in (31cm)

$3,000-4,000 **GorL**

A Moorcroft Florian ware baluster vase, in an unusual reverse painted style with yellow poppies and blue flowers.

7in (18cm) high

$3,000-4,000 **GorL**

A Moorcroft MacIntyre green and gold Florian ware two-handled vase, cover missing.

7in (18cm)

$1,000-1,500 **GorL**

A Moorcroft MacIntyre Florian ware two-handled inverted baluster vase, with sprays of spring flowers on a cream ground, restored rim.

8.75in (22cm)

$1,000-1,500 **GorL**

A Moorcroft Art Deco peacock feather design pitcher, in orange and browns.

9.5in (24cm)

$800-1,000 **GorL**

A Moorcroft columbine bowl, hand-decorated flowers to well, deep green ground, with paper label, flaw to rim.

5in (12.5cm) diam

$150-200 **FRE**

A Moorcroft orchid cabinet vase, with hand-decorated flowers on a deep cobalt ground, paper label.

A Moorcroft ovoid vase, with clematis on a blue ground.

A Moorcroft 'Tudor Rose' pattern vase, of bellied form decorated in pinks and blues against a rare turquoise ground, registered no. 431157, crack to rim.

5.25in (13.5cm)

4in (10cm) high

8in (20cm) high

$300-400   **GorL**

$300-400   **FRE**

$2,200-2,800   **GorL**

An unusual Moorcroft vase, of irregular tapered oval form with ribbed body in blues and greens, possibly an experimental piece.

A Moorcroft baluster vase, with wisteria within palmette-shape leaves against a dark blue background.

Two Moorcroft hibiscus cabinet vases, one with a cobalt ground, the other green.

8.75in (22cm)

7in (18cm)

Tallest 4.25in (11cm) high

$80-120   **GorL**

$1,000-1,500   **GorL**

$180-220   **FRE**

A Moorcroft magnolia ashtray and leaf/berry dish, each with hand decoration to well against a cobalt glaze.

Three Moorcroft cabinet vases, two hibiscus, one with a blue ground, the other green, and clematis on a cobalt ground.

Ashtray 6in (15cm) diam

Tallest 4in (10cm) high

$150-200   **FRE**

$220-280   **FRE**

A Moorcroft ovoid vase, with hibiscus on a yellow green ground.

A Moorcroft vase, painted with cornflowers against a white ground, blue script signature.

A Moorcroft pomegranate cabinet vase, hand-decorated in soft tones, cobalt interior.

7.25in (18.5cm)

9in (23cm)

3.25in (8cm) high

$220-280   **GorL**

$3,500-4,500   **GorL**

$350-400   **FRE**

A B C D E F G H I J K L M N O P Q R S T U V W XYZ

CERAMICS

POOLE

- In 1873 Jesse Carter (1830-1927) bought James Walker's tile company, in Poole, Dorset. The pottery became known as Carters in 1901. Owen Carter died in 1919 and two years later the Carter pottery became Carter, Stabler and Adams. Charles Carter, Owen's brother continued the business with Harold Stabler and John Adams, a potter from Stoke.

- A subsidiary was formed in 1921 to make domestic artistic ceramics. Carter's son Owen developed the production of art pottery with different glazes. Wares were hand-thrown and hand-decorated, often with stylized floral motifs.

- The Thirties saw a boom at the pottery, with some of the most memorable Poole designs being produced. Truda Carter, Charles Carter's wife, and John Adams produced a succession of outstanding patterns that have become classics.

- The Forties saw a slump in production as a result of wartime recession, but by the Fifties the pottery was at the forefront of contemporary design. In 1962 the factory became Poole Pottery Ltd and the following years saw an abundance of abstract patterns in orange, yellows and browns that corresponded with the fashions of the Sixties and Seventies. Today the pottery is still active and Poole Pottery has become highly collectable.

A Carter, Stabler & Adams Poole two-handled vase, painted with wild birds and stylized foliage in polychrome, impressed mark.

c1925   7in (18cm) high

$350-450   **GorL**

A Carter, Stabler and Adams Poole Pottery footed fruit bowl, incised "464", blue hand-painted "OT & H" in foot rim, small chip to foot rim, and with stained crazing.

8in (20.5cm) diam

$150-200   **AS&S**

A Carter, Stabler & Adams square honey pot and cover, impressed mark and "TK" signature.

5in (12.5cm) wide

$100-150   **AS&S**

A large 1920s Carter, Stabler and Adams Poole Pottery jug.

8.5in (21.5cm) high

$200-250   **OACC**

A Poole Pottery 'Blue-bird' pattern jug, designed by Truda Carter, painted in vivid colours with two blue-birds in flight amid flowers and trellises, between formal bands, impressed "Carter Stabler & Adams Ltd" mark, "316/PN".

4.5in (11cm) high

$250-300   **DN**

A Poole Pottery vase, painted by Ruth Paveley to a Truda Carter design, of compressed globular shape with a broad frieze of stylized flowers and foliage, impressed "Carter Stabler Adams" and "Poole England" numbered "338/ZX".

8.25in (21cm) high

$250-300   **DN**

A Poole Pottery shallow bowl, decorated with a geometric band.

8in (20.5cm) diam

$100-150   **GorB**

A Poole Pottery compressed round bowl, painted by Rita Curtis to a design by Truda Carter, the rounded sides showing a broad band of large stylized blooms interspersed with foliage impressed "Carter Stabler Adams Ltd. Poole England" with painter's mark and "0564/OT".

9in (23cm)

$400-500   **DN**

A Poole Pottery water jug, impressed "Poole England".

7.75in (20cm) high

$80-120   **AS&S**

A Poole Pottery vase, painted with a stylized array of foliage in polychrome.

4.5in (11.5cm) high

$100-150   **GorL**

A Poole vase, decorated with birds and flowers.

6in (15cm)

$250-300   **GorL**

A 1930s-60s Poole Pottery four egg cup set on stand, "seagull" and turquoise glaze decoration, unnamed designer.

Stand 6in (15.5cm) wide

$30-40   **FFM**

A Poole Pottery cylindrical vase, painted in colored glazes in shades of iron-red, brown and ocher with a stylized interwoven leaf band, incised mark for Carol Cutler.

A Poole Pottery 'Aegean' circular wall plate, designed and decorated by Carolyn Wills, showing a landscape at sunset with tall trees in the foreground in muted colors with an autumnal colored sky, impressed "Poole England" and signed "C.Wills".

13in (32.5cm) diam

$400-500   **DN**

A set of four 1980s Poole Pottery dishes.

$10-15 (set)   **AS&S**

Tallest 10.5in (26.5cm) high

$100-150   **DN**

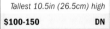

A 1970s Poole Pottery bowl.

6in (15cm) diam

$30-40   **AS&S**

A CLOSER LOOK AT A POOLE PLATE

Robert Jefferson, a designer at Poole, introduced the Delphis 'studio ware' range in 1958.

Brightly colored decoration and individual styling are characteristic of the Delphis pattern.

The Delphis range tends to have a finer texture than that of the Aegean range, which was made to complement Delphis.

A 1970s Poole Pottery fruit bowl, chipped and repaired, rim losses.

8in (20.5cm) diam

$15-20   **AS&S**

An impressive Poole Pottery 'Delphis' circular wall plate, painted with a large owl perched on a branch against a moonlit sky and having brightly colored geometric plumage, "Poole England" and Dolphin mark and painter's mark which resembles that of Carolyn Bartlett.

16.25in (41cm) diam

$700-1,000   **DN**

CERAMICS

ROOKWOOD

■ Maria Longworth Nichols (1849-1932) first developed an interest in art pottery while painting china blanks as a hobby with other Cincinnati ladies. In 1880 she founded the Rookwood Pottery, which produced some of the first underglaze slip decorated ware in America. William Watts Tyler, a friend of Mrs Nichols, was brought in to manage the pottery in 1883 and he set about organizing the structure of the company. Ten years after starting Rookwood, Mrs Nichols moved abroad and Tyler was left in change.

■ Under Tyler's care, production of existing lines was standardized and new ideas, often risky ones, were encouraged. The risks paid off and Rookwood won a number of international prizes including the 1893 World Columbian Exposition in Chicago and the gold medal at the Paris Exposition of 1900.

■ The pottery closed in 1961, but production was continued until 1965 by the Mississippi Clock Company which purchased the rights and molds. These are currently owned by a Michigan-based dentist who produces a limited amount each year.

A Rookwood Standard Glaze dark squat vessel, by Anna Marie Bookprinter, decorated with cherry blossoms under a partially tiger's-eye overglaze, flame mark, dated.

As the name suggests, the Standard Glaze line was the main range and was produced for 16 years from 1884. Pieces typically have underglaze decoration with floral designs and a hard clear brown overglaze.

1886   5in (12.5cm) diam

$600-700   **CR**

A Rookwood Standard Glaze light basket, by Sallie Toohey, painted with amber pansies, flame mark, hairline to handle, dated.

1889 6.75in (17cm) wide

$220-280   **CR**

A Rookwood Standard Glaze light organically-shaped platter, by Edward Abel, beautifully painted with strawberry plants on a light green ground, flame mark, uncrazed, dated.

1892   11in (28cm)

$800-900   **CR**

A Rookwood Standard Glaze humidor, by Bruce Horsfal, painted with orange nicotina blossoms, flame mark, hairline to inside of lid, dated.

1893 6.25in (16cm) high

$550-650   **CR**

A Rookwood Standard Glaze ovoid vase, by Lenore Asbury, painted with narcissus, flame mark, a few scratches, dated.

1894 7in (18cm) high

$550-650   **CR**

A Rookwood Standard Glaze commemorative mug, by Mary Nourse, "Commercial Club of Cincinnati, 1894", and painted with orange carnations, flame mark "/MN", silver band around handle is missing.

5in (12.5cm) high

$250-350   **CR**

A Rookwood Standard Glaze vase, by Edith Felton, painted with crocuses, flame mark "/162D/" artists cipher, dated.

1899 5.5in (14cm) high

$600-700   **CR**

A Rookwood Standard Glaze stoppered jug, by E.T. Hurley, with brown berries on the vase and embossed sterling stopper, flame mark, abrasion around base, dated.

1900 7.75in (19.5cm) high

$600-700   **CR**

A Rookwood Standard Glaze baluster vase, by Lenore Asbury, decorated with oak leaves and acorns, "flame mark /l/849/L.A./X", seconded mark, dated.

1901 9.75in (24.5cm) high

$550-650   **CR**

A Rookwood Standard Glaze bulbous vessel, by Marianne Mitchell, decorated with golden blossoms, flame mark, dated.

1903   6in (15.5cm) high

$450-550   **CR**

A pair of Rookwood Production candlesticks, covered in turquoise matte glaze, flame mark "/XVIV/822D", dated.

1919   6in (15.5cm) high

$180-220   **CR**

A tall Rookwood Production vase, designed by Louise Abel, embossed with a Classical scene of maidens and a flute player under a matte green glaze, flame mark, dated.

1922   11in (28cm) high

$550-650   **CR**

A Rookwood Standard Glaze vase, by Caroline Steinle, decorated with yellow tulips against a black, green and orange shaded ground, flame mark "/V/950D/C.S.", dated.

1905   8.25in (21cm) high

$750-850   **CR**

A small Rookwood Production vase, with bulbous form and three feet covered in a smooth green semi-matte glaze, flame mark "XIX/2093", datedf.

1919   3in (7.5cm) high

$220-280   **CR**

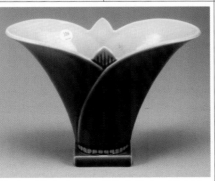

A Rookwood Production vase, with faceted body and flaring rim covered in a blue semi-matte glaze, flame mark, dated.

1924   5.5in (14cm) high

$120-180   **CR**

A Rookwood Standard Glaze vase, by Caroline Steinle, painted with amber columbines on a black-to-brown ground, flame mark "/VII/904D/CS", dated.

1907   8in (20.5cm) high

$650-750   **CR**

A Rookwood Production bulbous vase, with band of rooks, flame mark "/XIX/2174", dated.

1919   5.25in (13.5cm) high

$400-500   **CR**

A Rookwood Production footed dish, in an amber to green glaze, flame mark "/V/S1781C", small tight line to interior rim, most likely in making, dated.

1905   7in (18cm) high

$250-350   **CR**

A tall Rookwood Production vase, embossed with band of floral swags in white against a chocolate brown ground, flame mark "/XXII/2489", dated.

1922   11.75in (30cm) high

$450-550   **CR**

A Rookwood Production vase, with faceted body covered in a blue semi-matte glaze, flame mark, dated.

1924   5.5in (14cm) high

$250-350   **CR**

A Rookwood Production vase, with embossed leaves under a mottled pink and green matte glaze, flame mark "XXIV/2095", dated.

1924   5in (12.5cm) high

$250-300   **CR**

A Rookwood Production ovoid vase, embossed with stems of stylized flowers, flame mark "/XXVIII/2431", stilt-pull chip, glaze fleck to rim, dated.

1928   9.25in (23.5cm) high

$400-500   **CR**

A Rookwood Production ovoid vase, with triangular-shaped trees under a waxy blue glaze, flame mark, seconded mark for grinding chips, dated.

1928   7in (18cm) high

$200-250   **CR**

A Rookwood Production ovoid vase, neck embossed with a stylized pattern under a green and pink butterfat matte glaze, flame mark "/XXVIV/2318".

1929   9.25in (23.5cm)

$200-250   **CR**

A Rookwood Production bullet-shaped vase, covered in a blue glaze, flame mark "/XXXIV/2426", dated.

1934   7.5in (19cm) high

$250-350   **CR**

A tall Rookwood Production vase, covered in a fine robin's-egg blue glaze, and embossed with wisteria, flame mark "/XLVIII/6871", dated.

1948   14in (35.5cm) high

$300-350   **CR**

A Rookwood modeled matte pink bud vase, by Sallie Toohey, with stylized flower on a pink ground, flame mark "/V/969E/ST", glaze miss visible, dated.

1905   4in (10cm) high

$400-500   **CR**

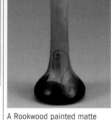

A Rookwood painted matte bud vase, by C.S. Todd, with stylized floral design, flame mark "/XX/2309/C.S.T./X".

1920   7in (18cm) high

$550-650   **CR**

A Rookwood incised matte tapering vase, by C.S. Todd, with berries, flame mark "/XVIII/1655E/C.S.T", long crack from rim, dated.

1918   7.75in (19.5cm) high

$300-400   **CR**

A Rookwood wax matte bulbous vase, by Katherine Jones, decorated with stylized wild roses in pink and yellow on turquoise ground, flame mark "/935D/XXV/KJ", dated.

1925   8in (20cm) high

$900-1,000   **CR**

A large Rookwood matte squeezebag vase, by Elizabeth Barrett, artist's cipher and flame mark, dated.

1927   16.5in (42cm) high

$2,500-3,000   **FRE**

A Rookwood Vellum glaze landscape vase, by Frederick Daniel Henry, of tapering ovoid form painted with pink flowers and pale green stems on a blue shading to ivory ground, impressed and incised date, artist and shape marks.

1907   10.5in (26.5cm) high

$1,800-2,.200   **SI**

CERMICS

A Rookwood Vellum glaze peacock vase, by Sara Sax, of waisted cylindrical form, decorated with a band of peacocks at the base on a teal green/blue ground, impressed and incised date marks.

1911   *7in (18cm) high*

$5,000-6,000   **SI**

A Rookwood Vellum glaze landscape vase, by Sarah Elizabeth Coyne, of tapering cylindrical form painted with a landscape at sunrise, impressed and incised date, artist and shape marks.

1920   *8.5in (21.5cm) high*

$2,200-2,800   **SI**

A Rookwood carved matte ovoid vase, by Sara Sax, painted with a band of parakeets on branches with fruit, flame mark "/XIII/892C/V/" artist's cipher.

1913   *9in (23cm) high*

$1,500-2,000   **CR**

A CLOSER LOOK AT A ROOKWOOD VASE

This vase in larger than normal, making it rare.

The pink tones in the sky are unusual and make this piece more interesting.

After floral decoration, landscapes are the most common form of decoration on Vellum wares.

Kataro Shirayamadani is one of Rookwood's most sought after artists.

A large Rookwood scenic Vellum vase, by Kataro Shirayamadani, with serene landscape scenes in soft green and pink hues, signed flame mark for 1912.

Kataro Shirayamadani (1857-1947) and Maria Nichols first met at the 13th Cincinnati Industrial Exposition in 1886, where he was representing the Japanese government's trade interest. Rookwood's designs and glazes are clearly influenced by Japan and a year later Shirayamadani joined the pottery, bringing with him a very high quality of painting, design skills and a knowledge of Japanese iconography. He worked at the pottery until his death.

15in (38cm)

$4,500-5,000   **FRE**

A Rookwood carved matte bulbous vase, by C.S Todd, decorated with stylized flowers in red and amber on a matte green ground, flame mark "/XV/973/C.S.T."

1915   *4.5in (11.5cm) high*

$1,000-1,500   **CR**

A rare Rookwood carved matte two-handled factory lamp base, by William Hentschel, the "lid" carved with a floral pattern in green and blue on a dripping ocher ground, flame mark "/XV/638/WEH".

1915   *8in (20cm) wide*

$850-950   **CR**

A Rookwood incised Vellum ovoid vase, by Margaret McDonald, decorated with morning glories in pink, white, yellow and green against a shaded blue and pink ground, flame mark "/XVII/904D/V/ 454/" artists cipher.

1917   *9in (23cm) high*

$1,200-1,500   **CR**

A Rookwood carved matte vase, by William Hentschel, flame mark "/XIII/ 1659D/ WEH/X", seconded mark for mottling of background color.

1913   *9in (23cm) high*

$800-900   **CR**

A Rookwood carved matte vase, by Charles S. Todd, decorated around the shoulder with an abstract pattern in red, yellow and green against a cobalt matte ground, flame mark "/XVI/1927/C.S.T.", tight line to rim, several to base.

1916   *5.25in (13.5cm) wide*

$550-650   **CR**

A Rookwood jewel porcelain vase, by Arthur P. Conant, with panels of branches and blossoms, flame mark "/XVIII/1930/" artist's cipher, opposing cracks from rim.

1918   6.5in (16.5cm) high

$350-450   **CR**

A large Rookwood porcelain vase, by Arthur P. Conant, of bulbous form with painted floral and bird motifs in the Chinese manner, artist's cipher, flame mark, paper labels.

1920   15.5in (39.5cm) high

$4,000-5,000   **FRE**

A Rookwood jewel porcelain baluster vase, by Harriet Wilcox, painted with bachelor's buttons against a Sung plum ground, flame mark "/XXV/2721/HEW", restoration to shallow chip or nick at base.

1925   6.25in (16cm) high

$1,600-2,000   **CR**

A Rookwood porcelain bulbous vase, covered in a mottled sang de boeuf glaze, flame mark/50th Anniversary mark.

1930   4.5in (11.5cm)

$600-700   **CR**

An unusual Rookwood bisque vessel, painted with mice, stamped "Rookwood/1884".

1884   10in (25.5cm) wide

$1,500-2,000   **CR**

A Rookwood bulbous porcelain vase, with waterlilies in relief on a pale blue ground, flame mark "/XLIII/6833".

1943   6.5in (16.5cm)

$600-700   **CR**

A Rookwood jewel porcelain vase, by Jens Jensen, decorated abstract forms of fish and fowl in black on a mottled ocher ground, flame mark "XLVIII/30E/artists cipher", small crack from rim.

Jens Jensen was born in Denmark in 1898, he studied at Ryslinge and the Askov Academy in Jutland, and came to America in 1927. By 1928 he had settled in Cincinnati and was working as a decorator at Rookwood where he remained until 1948. He died in 1978.

1948   9in (23cm) high

$600-700   **CR**

An unusual early Rookwood four-sided plate, by Matt Daly, with white lotus, flame mark.

1886   10in (25.5cm) diam

$500-600   **CR**

An early Rookwood vase, with applied pottery flowers, leaves and buds, two leaves on one flower show signs of repair, signed "Rookwood 1883".

23.5in (59.5cm) high

$2,000-2,500   **JDJ**

A Rookwood cameo pitcher, artist unknown, flame mark "/1327W", a few deep crazing lines, water stains.

1887   7in (18cm) high

$220-280   **CR**

A Rookwood iris glaze bulbous bottle, by Rose Fescheimer, decorated with mistletoe, flame mark "/III/861/RF/X", seconded mark for firing flaw around rim and heavy crazing over decoration.

1903   *6.25in (16cm) high*

$550-650   **CR**

A Rookwood iris glaze ovoid vase, by Sara Sax, decorated with yellow nasturtiums on a white ground, flame mark/VII/artists cipher/941D/W", restoration to rim, dated.

1907   *7.75in (20cm) high*

$650-750   **CR**

A Rookwood trivet, decorated in cuenca with an abstracted flower under a green and brown mottled matte glaze, flame mark "/XV", several small nicks, dated.

1915   *5.5in (14cm) wide*

$280-320   **CR**

A Rookwood Coramandel bulbous vase, covered in a tan to rust mottled glaze, flame mark "/XXXII/6315".

1932   *6.25in (16cm) high*

$350-450   **CR**

A Rookwood flaring vase, with embossed figures, all covered in a turquoise glaze, flame mark "/XXXIV/6536".

1934   *9in (23cm) high*

$350-450   **CR**

A Rookwood bulbous vase, by C.S.Todd, covered in an olive green glaze with design at rim, flame mark "/XX/966/C.S.T."

1920   *4in (10cm) wide*

$600-700   **CR**

A Rookwood flambé cabinet vase, flame mark "/XXXII/6307/F"

1932   *3in (7.5cm) high*

$350-450   **CR**

A Rookwood trivet, embossed with bird on a branch in yellow on an ivory ground, flame mark, dated.

1929   *5.5in (14cm)*

$400-500   **CR**

A rare Rookwood elephant paperweight, covered in a fine tiger's-eye glaze, flame mark "/XXXVI/6488", several small chips to underside of base, dated.

1936   *3.75in (9.5cm) wide*

$500-600   **CR**

ROSEVILLE

- The Roseville Pottery started making utilitarian stoneware in Roseville, Ohio, in 1890. By 1900, the pottery had relocated to Zanesville and, in line with public demand began producing art pottery under the 'Rozane' label. This art ware was hand painted in the Victorian style and was clearly influenced by Rookwood's Standard Glaze line.

- In 1904, the English potter Frederick Rhead joined the company, followed by Frank Farrell in 1915, and under their direction, Roseville began producing a number of original art pottery ranges such as 'Della Robbia', 'Fudji', 'Woodland' and 'Crystallis'.

- Farrell continued working for Roseville until 1953 and designed 96 different lines in total, including 'Dahlrose', 'Jonquil', 'Wisteria' and 'Pine Cone'.

- Mid-period production pieces are noted for their high quality glazes and production standard and for popular ranges such as 'Sunflower' and 'Futura'.

- 1953 saw the last new design leave Roseville. A year later, the company's assets were sold several times, eventually becoming the the property of New England Ceramics of Connecticut.

A Roseville brown Artcraft pedestal, unmarked, small chip to base, two small glaze flakes to top, and short tight line.

17in (43cm) high

$550-650 CR

A Roseville blue Bleeding Heart basket, 360-10", raised mark.

$400-500 CR

A large and unusual Roseville brown Bushberry basket, 372-12", raised mark, large repair to chips at base, two reglued cracks to handle, two small chips to handle.

$150-200 CR

A Roseville green Bushberry basket, 371-10", raised mark, small chip to rim, and repaired lines and nicks to handle.

$150-200 CR

A large Roseville Carnelian II ewer, covered in a mottled pink glaze with purple drips from rim, remnants of paper label, repairs to handle.

15in (38cm) high

$700-800 CR

A Roseville brown Bushberry basket, 370-8", raised mark, a couple of very minor nicks at base.

$180-220 CR

A Roseville red Carnelian II bulbous vase, unmarked, a couple of grinding chips.

7in (18cm) high

$450-550 CR

A Roseville brown Cherry Blossom spherical vase, unmarked, minor nick to one blossom.

8.5in (21.5cm) high

$750-850 CR

A Roseville pink Cremona four-sided vase, with blue blossoms, unmarked, small chips at base and one at rim.

10in (25.5cm) high

$200-250 CR

A Roseville Egypto bulbous two-handled vessel, unmarked, fleck at base, burst bubbles throughout.

5.5in (14cm) high

$350-450 CR

A Roseville Crocus bulbous vase, restoration to glaze chips at base, fleck to rim.
9.75in (25cm) high

$350-450   CR

A Roseville Dahlrose jardinière and pedestal set, unmarked, several small chips and lines.
24.75in (63cm) high

$550-650   CR

A Roseville Dahlrose oval center bowl, unmarked, reglued flat chip to rim.
10.25in (26cm) wide

$150-200   CR

A Roseville blue Falline bulbous two-handled vase, unmarked, two minor bruises and a small repaired chip, all to one handle.
7.5in (19cm) high

$900-1,000   CR

A tall Roseville green Foxglove vase, 55-16", raised mark, several flat chips to flowers and base.

$400-500   CR

A Roseville pink Foxglove basket, 373-8", raised mark, minute nick to one flower.

$200-250   CR

A Roseville blue Fuchsia vase, 903-12", impressed mark, with strong mold and color.

$550-650   CR

A Roseville green Fuchsia bulbous vase, unmarked, burst bubble to one handle.
8.25in (21cm) high

$220-280   CR

A Roseville blue Fuchsia vase, with strong mold, unmarked.
9.25in (23.5cm) high

$450-550   CR

A Roseville Imperial II vessel, and decorated with a yellow band around the rim, remnant of foil label, some flecks and abrasions to body.
7in (17.5cm) high

$350-450   CR

A Roseville Futura spherical vase, with stepped neck, unmarked, base entirely repaired and several scratches to body.
10in (25.5cm) high

$300-400   CR

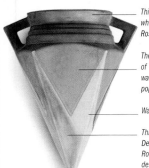

This piece is molded, which is typical of Roseville.

The Futura range was one of the first production wares made and is very popular with collectors.

Wall pockets are scarce.

This design shows Art Deco influence and Roseville's maturing designs.

A Roseville Futura wallpocket, with stylized leaf-like design in purple, yellow, green and blue, a couple of small chips to tip.

8.5in (21.5cm) high

$350-450   **CR**

A Roseville Futura four-sided vase, chips to rim, bruise and writing to base.

12in (30.5cm) high

$550-650   **CR**

A large Roseville Jonquil bulbous vase, with crisp mold, unmarked, restored chip at rim, a couple of very minor nicks at base.

12.25in (31cm) high

$550-650   **CR**

A large Roseville yellow Laurel flaring vase, unmarked.

10.25in (26cm) high

$550-650   **CR**

A Roseville Matt Green wallpocket, impressed with geometric pattern, unmarked.

10.25in (26cm) high

$300-400   **CR**

A Roseville green Montacello flaring vase, unmarked, bruise and small colored-in chip to rim.

11in (28cm) high

$600-700   **CR**

A Roseville Mostique corseted vase, with yellow spade-shaped leaves, unmarked, restored chip at base.

10.25in (26cm) high

$220-280   **CR**

A Roseville Mostique large jardiniere, with yellow and red Glasgow roses, marked "593", hairline from rim and some glaze flakes.

12in (30.5cm) high

$550-650   **CR**

A Roseville brown Panel flat vase, decorated with nudes, RV ink mark, two shallow scratches near base.

8.5in (21.5cm)

$200-250   **CR**

A tall Roseville green Pine Cone ewer, 416-18", raised mark, restored chip to spout, and minor firing flaw to base.

500-600   **CR**

A large Roseville Pauleo classically shaped vase, covered in a fine variegated red glaze, unmarked, several scratches to body and factory drill hole.

20.75in (52.5cm) high

$1,500-2,000 CR

A Roseville brown Pine Cone planter, 124, impressed mark.

5in (12.5cm) high

$220-280 CR

A Roseville brown Pine Cone hanging basket, with soft mold, unmarked, bruise and nick to hanging holes.

7.5in (12.5cm) high

$220-280 CR

A Roseville brown Pine Cone pitcher, 1321, marked, with restoration to rim.

8in (20cm) high

$350-450 CR

A Roseville blue Pine Cone bowl, unmarked, minutest bruise to body, two shallow scratches near base, flea bite to one handle.

11.5in (29.5cm) wide

$300-400 CR

A Roseville blue Pine Cone wave-shaped basket, 472-6", with strong mold, raised mark, some peppering to rim and short firing line to interior.

$450-550 CR.

A Roseville blue Pine Cone flaring vase, 936-10", marked, with basket handle.

$500-600 CR

A Roseville green Pine Cone basket, 338-10", impressed mark.

$350-450 CR

A Roseville brown Pine Cone vase, 907-7", with flaring rim and good mold, impressed mark, fleck at base.

$350-450 CR

A Roseville blue Pine Cone vase, 712-12", with squat base, raised mark, very strong mold.

$850-950 CR

A Roseville blue Pine Cone triple bud vase, unmarked.

8.5in (21.5cm) high

$500-600 CR

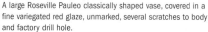

A Roseville green Pine Cone jardinière, with foil label, minor line under one handle and short firing line to base.

11in (28cm)

$400-500   **CR**

A Roseville green Pine Cone hanging basket, marked "U.S.A.", nick to hanging hole, tight line through body.

8in (20cm) wide

$450-550   **CR**

A Roseville brown Pine Cone flaring vase, 747-10", impressed mark, very minor restoration to one handle near base.

$280-320   **CR**

A Roseville brown Pine Cone planter, 633-5", raised mark, missing underplate, very tight short line to interior rim.

6.5in (16.5cm) wide

$150-200   **CR**

A Roseville Rosecraft Vintage bowl, RV ink mark, with crisp mold.

7.5in (19cm) wide

$280-320   **CR**

Two Roseville brown Rosecraft Vintage jardinières, RV ink marks, small chip and two bruises to base of one, a couple minor flecks to both.

Largest 6.25in (16cm) high

$400-500   **CR**

A Roseville Sunflower bulbous vase, with strong mold and good color, unmarked, tight bruise to rim.

9.5in (24cm) high

$1,700-2,000   **CR**

A Roseville Rosecraft Vintage squat vessel, RV ink mark.

4.5in (11.5cm) wide

$250-300   **CR**

A Roseville Vista bulbous vase, with buttressed handles, unmarked, repaired rim chip.

9.75in (24.5cm) high

$500-600   **CR**

A B C D E F G H I J K L M N O P Q R S T U V W XYZ

A Roseville Vista footed vase, unmarked.

10in (25.5cm) high

$750-850 CR

A large Roseville Vista jardiniere, long line and minor burst to rim.

10.75in (27.5cm) high

$350-450 CR

A Roseville pink Waterlily hanging basket, complete with hanging chains, marked "81".

5.5in (14cm) high

$200-250 CR

A Roseville brown Wisteria jardiniere and pedestal, unmarked.

28in (71in) high

$2,000-3,000 CR

A CLOSER LOOK AT A ROSEVILLE VASE

- This range was introduced around 1920.

- This molded vessel has embossed decoration.

- The colors were then added by hand.

- Despite being mass-produced, this is still a striking piece.

A Roseville Vista floor vase/umbrella stand, unmarked, a couple of very minor flecks.

20in (51cm) high

$2,000-2,500 CR

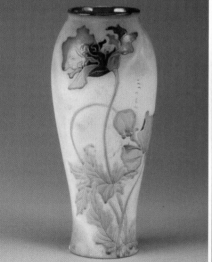

A large Roseville Rozane Woodland bulbous vase, decorated with glossy brown poppies and leaves on an ivory bisque base, marked "Rozane Ware Woodland", incised "ED" and "ET" written along base.

"Rozane", taken from Roseville and Zanesville, the two sites of the Roseville factory, was Roseville's art pottery range, emulating the success of Rookwood.

16.25in (41.5cm) high

$1,500-2,000 CR

A Roseville Vista hanging basket, unmarked.

6.5in (16.5cm) high

$300-400 CR

A Roseville brown Wincraft four-sided vase, 274-7", with panels of blowing wind, raised mark.

The Wincraft line was introduced in 1948. It was covered in a high gloss and came in a number of colors including chartreuse, blue and yellow.

$150-200 CR

A Roseville brown Wisteria tapering vase, unmarked.

10.5in (26.5cm) high

$750-850 CR

A Roseville brown Wisteria ovoid vase, unmarked, short line inside rim.

6in (15.5cm) high

$450-550 CR

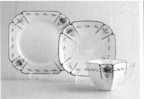

A Shelley 'Floral' trio, no. 11564.

Largest plate 5.5in (14cm) diam

$120-180 SCG

A Shelley 'Iris' trio, no. 2160.

1927-29 Largest plate 6in (15.5cm) diam

$150-200 SCG

A Shelley 'Garden' trio, no. 11607.

1927-29 Largest plate 5.5in (14cm) diam

$120-180 SCG

A Shelley 'Garland of Flowers' trio, no. 11504.

1927-29 Largest plate 6in (15.5cm) diam

$100-150 SCG

A Shelley 'Blue Iris' trio, no. 11561.

1927-29 Largest plate 6in (15.5cm) diam

$120-180 SCG

A Shelley 'Sunrise and Tall Trees' trio, no. 11670.

1927-29 Largest plate 6.25in (16cm) diam

$100-150 SCG

A Shelley 'Urn' trio, no. 11565.

1927-29 Largest plate 6.25in (16cm) diam

$180-220 SCG

A Shelley green 'Vogue Shape' trio, no. 114740.

1931 Largest plate 6.25in (16cm) diam

$320-380 SCG

A Shelley orange 'Vogue Shape' trio.

1931 Largest plate 6.25in (16cm) diam

$320-380 SCG

A Shelley 'Sun Ray Vogue Shape' coffee pot and six cups, no. 11742.

c1931 *Jug 7in (18cm) high*

$1,800-2,200 SCG

A Shelley Intarsio ware character teapot and cover, modelled as Austin Chamberlain wearing a green jacket, printed marks, some damage.

7.5in (19cm) long

$220-280 WW

CERANICS

STAFFORDSHIRE

■ From the early 17th century Staffordshire has been pre-eminent in the English ceramics industry. The area has abundant supplies of clay, salt and lead for glazing, and coal, used to fire the kilns. Staffordshire potteries were made up of five towns, Stoke-on-Trent, Burslem, Hanley, Longton and Tunstall. Other areas involved were Fenton, Lane Delph, Longport, Shelton, Cobridge and Newcastle-under-Tyne.

■ By the 19th century there were over 1,000 firms in production in the Staffordshire region. The expansion of the canal system in the beginning of the 19th century and the proximity of the port at Liverpool meant that English ceramics spread far and wide. By the late 19th century the railway system aided the ceramics trade even further and as a result Staffordshire had become the pottery center of the world. The factories produced figures, dinner services and various domestic wares in earthenware and stoneware.

■ Today Staffordshire is still at the forefront of the British ceramic industry, and is the largest clayware producer in the world.

A pair of mid-19thC Staffordshire models of King Charles spaniels, sitting up and decorated with red patches, moulded '4' marks, one with base cracks.

7.5in (19cm) high

$150-200 (pair)   **WW**

Two similar mid-19thC models of poodles with pups, with extruded clay clipped coats, on blue gilt-line bases, sparsely colored and gilt.

5.75in (14.5cm) high

$250-300 (both)   **DN**

A pair of mid-19thC models of spaniels, facing left and right, seated on their haunches, painted with iron-red patches, gilt collars and black chains.

8.75in (22cm) high

$500-600   **DN**

A pair of mid-19thC models of spaniels, facing left and right, seated on their haunches, iron-red patches and gilt collars, some slight enamel flaking.

7.5in (19cm) high

$300-400   **DN**

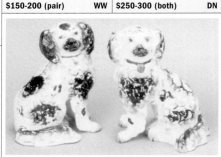

A pair of mid-19thC models of spaniels facing left and right, seated on their haunches, painted with black patches and gilt collars separate front legs, enamel flaking.

6.75in (17cm) high

$400-500   **DN**

A mid-19thC group of two spaniels, each seated on its haunches, one on a barrel, painted with iron-red patches and with gilt collars, on a gilt line and flecked base.

8.25in (21cm) high

$300-350   **DN**

A pair of mid-19thC spaniel and pup groups, modelled facing left and right, the spaniels painted with iron-red patches, the pups with black patches, on blue gilt-line bases, one with small chip to the base.

6.25in (16cm) high

$600-700 (pair)   **DN**

A pair of Staffordshire spaniels, with green and luster decoration.

This pair is desirable for two reasons, firstly, their front legs are separate from their bodies which is a sign of quality and the use of green and luster paint is unusual.

c1880   *7in (15cm) high*

$200-250 (pair)   **OACC**

Three 19thC Staffordshire seated spaniels, comprising a pair of spaniels holding flower baskets and King Charles spaniel, imperfections.

Tallest 4.75in (12cm)

$180-220 SI

A pair of Staffordshire seated spaniels, pink noses, gilt decoration.

13in (33cm) high

$200-250 OACC

A pair of mid-19thC recumbant hound penholders, painted with black patches and gilt collars, on blue gilt-line bases, one head glued.

6in (15cm) long

$450-550 DN

A pair of late 19thC recumbant greyhound penholders, painted in iron-red with gilt collars, on blue gilt-line bases, one has small chips to nose and ears.

6in (15.5cm) wide

$250-300 DN

A pair of greyhound models, seated on their haunches facing left and right, painted in iron-red with gilt collars, on blue gilt-line bases, both worn.

c1860   6in (15.5cm) high

$300-400 DN

A pair of Victorian earthenware models of greyhounds, holding dead game.

7.5in (19cm) high

$250-300 GorL

A pair of Victorian Staffordshire models of recumbant sheep.

3.5in (9cm) high

$150-200 GorL

A Staffordshire model of a ram, standing four square on a gilt-lined base, its shaggy coat of grated porcelain.

4.5in (11cm) high

$250-300 Chef

A mid-19thC Staffordshire model of a ram, standing on a green gilt lined base.

4in (10cm) wide

$450-550 WW

A late 18thC Staffordshire figure of a seated deer, with bocage back and mound base.

5.5ins (14cm)

$400-500 GorL

A late 18thC Staffordshire group of a cow and calf, with bocage back and scroll mound base.

4.5ins (11.5cm)

$600-700 GorL

Two similar 20thC William Kent Ltd models of cats, seated on cushion bases, painted with iron-red patches and seated on green and pink cushion bases, some enamel flakes, chips to ears.

7.25in (18.5cm) high

$400-500 DN

A Crown Staffordshire pintail duck, from a limited edition of 250, modelled by Peter Scott, with plinth and certificate, small hairline crack to base.

$400-500 PSA

A late 18thC Walton Staffordshire group of a lady and gentleman musician, "Rural Past Time" on square base, drum stick replaced, minor fretting.

7.75in (19.5cm)

$400-500 GorL

A Walton bocage group of a boy fighting off two girls, a hat full of grapes at his feet, modeled standing before flowering bocage, on a scroll-molded base, painted with colored enamels, some damage and losses.

c1820   7.75in (20cm) high

$400-500 DN

A Walton 'Tenderness' group, typically modeled with a shepherd and companion before bocage, on a scroll-molded titled base, the reverse with Walton banner mark, repaired.

c1820   8.25in (21cm) high

$800-1,000 DN

An early 19thC Staffordshire bust of Elijah, with floral bocage back on square base.

$400-500 GorL

An Obadiah Sherratt-type 'Tithe Pig' group, the vicar and his parishioners standing before a leafy tree, on a scroll-molded base, painted with colored enamels, top section of tree lacking.

c1825   6.25in (16cm) high

$800-1,000 DN

A 19thC Staffordshire flat-back model, of a hunter on horseback.

10in (25.5cm) high

$250-300 WW

A 19thC Staffordshire flat-back model, of a lady and gentlemen on a boat with a spaniel at their feet.

8.5in (21.5cm) high

$250-300 WW

Two small 19thC Staffordshire groups, one of a woman and child standing on a rocky base, the other of two figures in a boat, the first with a crack to the reverse.

7in (18cm) high

$150-200 WW

A mid-20thC Stangl medium Cockatoo, #3580, original sticker and price tag.

9in (23cm) high

$150-200 CR

Two mid-20thC Stangl White Wing Crossbills, #3754D, marked, drill-hole with break to underside.

9in (23cm) high

$300-400 CR

A mid-20thC Stangl Shoveler Duck, #3455, marked.

12in (30.5cm) high

$1,200-1,800 CR

A mid 20thC Stangl Scissor-tailed Flycatcher, #3757.

11in (28cm) high

$1,200-1,800 CR

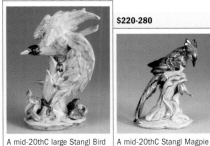

Two mid-20thC Stangl Hummingbirds, #3599, marked.

10.5in (26.5cm) high

$220-280 CR

A mid-20thC Stangl penguin, #3274, marked.

6in (15.5cm) high

$750-850 CR

A mid-20thC large Stangl Bird of Paradise, #3625, marked.

13.5in (34.5cm) high

$3,000-4,000 CR

A mid-20thC Stangl Magpie Jay, #3758, marked.

10.75in (27.5cm) high

$1,700-2,000 CR

Two mid-20thC Stangl Western Tanagers, #3750, marked.

8in (20cm) high

$500-600 CR

A mid-20thC Stangl Rooster, #3445, and Hen, #3446.

Tallest 9in (23cm) high

$500-600 CR

Two mid-20thC Stangl White-Headed Pigeons, #3518D, marked.

12.5in (31.5cm) wide

$900-1,000 CR

A mid-20thC Stangl Key West Quail Dove, #3454, marked.

9in (23cm) high

$700-800 CR

A 1.5 gallon stoneware jug, by N.White & Co., Birmingham, New York, decorated with a cobalt blue peony.

11.5in (29cm) high

$450-500 RAA

A two gallon stoneware jug, "Geddes N.Y.", with large blue flower and leaf decoration, finish burn on back side, flaw on top rim from making, glaze drip to right of flower.

$160-260 TWC

A two gallon stoneware jug, "N.A. White & Son, Utica N.Y.", with cobalt bird on branch design, fried areas on high spots of cobalt, glaze drips at handle, glaze burn on back.

$800-1,200 TWC

A one gallon stoneware jug, "Whites, Utica", with cobalt Christmas tree design, some staining, some frying on design.

$100-200 TWC

A one gallon stoneware jug, "Geddes N.Y.", with blue leaf decoration, large brown stain to right of design, smaller stain to left of design.

$80-125 TWC

A CLOSER LOOK AT A STONEWARE JUG

This example is clearly marked with the factory name, a known maker.

The design is attractive, depicting a fantail bird, leaf and mount.

The handpainted decoration is exceptional, with a more detailed design than is usually found on stoneware items.

Even though this piece is damaged, the other features make this a highly desirable example.

A two gallon stoneware jug, "W.H. Farar & Co. Geddes N.Y.", with elaborate bird and flower on mound decoration, tight hairline to right of bird, thumb-size chip at bottom edge on right side, crisp cobalt design, overall finish appears dull.

$8,000-10,000 TWC

A four gallon stoneware jug, "New York Stoneware Co.", with elaborate blue scrolling flower decoration, minor rim chips, somewhat dull finish.

$200-300 TWC

A two gallon stoneware jug, "C.E. Pharis & Geddes N.Y.", with cobalt feather decoration, minor staining and minor frying of blue decoration.

$80-125 TWC

An ovoid stoneware jug, by Julius Norton of Pennington, Vermont.

c1845 *11in (28cm) high*

$650-750 RAA

A four gallon stoneware jug, "New York Stoneware Co.", with elaborate blue scrolling flower decoration, minor rim chips, somewhat dull finish.

$200-300 TWC

A three gallon ovoid crock, "White's Utica", with cobalt blue "3" design, some rim chips, overall dull finish and some staining, hairline along bottom.

$80-125 TWC

A three gallon stoneware crock, "N.A White & Son Utica N.Y.", with elaborate cobalt blue floral decoration, chips to underside of right handle, two short hairlines on backside of rim.

$250-450 TWC

A four gallon stoneware crock, "S.S. Taft & Company Keene N.H.", with cobalt bird on branch, professional restoration on rim, minor stain spots.

$400-600 TWC

A four gallon stoneware crock, "N.A. White & Son, Utica N.Y.", with elaborate paddle tail bird on flowering branch in cobalt blue, cobalt on tail incomplete, yet original, minor rim chip above right handle, minor flaking.

$600-900 TWC

A half-gallon stoneware crock, with cobalt blue flower and incised pin wheel decoration, two short hairlines at lip, maker unknown.

$80-125 TWC

A one gallon stoneware crock, "White's Utica", with two handles and scrolling flower decoration in cobalt blue, overhanging lip rim.

$80-125 TWC

A "White's Utica, N.Y." two gallon stoneware crock, with cobalt blue leaf design, some staining and unprofessional blister repair below handle and on rim, mistake on inscription.

$160-260 TWC

Four two-gallon cobalt-decorated stoneware crocks, by Ottman Bros, (1872-1892) and New York Stoneware Co. (1851-1885), Ft. Edward, New York, and J. E. Norton prior 1859, Bennington, Vermont, each decorated with a bird or floral device.

All 9.5in (24cm) high

$400-600 SI

FIND OUT MORE...

Don & Carol Raycraft, 'American Stoneware', Wallace-Homestead Book Co., 1995.

A two gallon stoneware crock, cobalt design features winged "V", cylindrical body, dark finish, maker unknown.

$80-125 TWC

A salt glaze stoneware pitcher, with relief decoration, including men and women and a child in a wicker basket, maker unknown but possibly White's Utica, cobalt blue highlights.

9in (23cm) high

$160-260 TWC

A stoneware inkwell, hockey puck form, two quill holes and inkwell, from New York State.

c1830   4in (10cm) diam

$40-60 RAA

CERAMICS

VAN BRIGGLE

- Artus Van Briggle was born in Ohio in 1869. He studied at the Art School in Cincinnati and then joined the Cincinnati-based Rookwood Pottery.
- Rookwood were impressed with his skills and sent him to study in France where he met his future wife, Anne Gregory.
- The pair returned to Cincinnati in 1896 and Artus set about developing the dead matte glaze that was to become his trademark at the Rookwood Pottery.
- In 1901 ill-health forced Artus to move to Colorado Springs, Colorado, where he set up his own pottery, The Van Briggle Pottery Co.
- The Van Briggles married in 1902 and worked together until Artus' death in 1904 when Anne took over the running of the company. The company is still in existence today.

A Van Briggle bulbous vase, embossed with poppy pods under a sheer, incised "AA/Van Briggle/Colo. Spgs./694", T-line from rim.

1908-11   7in (17.5cm) high

$400-500   CR

A Van Briggle bulbous vase, embossed with stylized trefoils under a Persian Rose matte glaze, incised "AA VAN BRIGGLE/Colo.Spgs./727".

1908-11   5in (12.5cm) high

$500-600   CR

An early Van Briggle squat vessel, embossed with pine cones on a robin's-egg blue ground, incised mark/1913, several tight cracks from rim.

1913   10.25in (26cm) high

$500-600   CR

A 1920s-30s Van Briggle bulbous vase, embossed with leaves under a turquoise and blue matte glaze, incised AA/49?".

7in (18cm) high

$350-450   CR

An exceptional Van Briggle shouldered vessel, embossed with spade-shaped leaves, and covered in an unusual dripping matte blue glaze, mark obscured by glaze.

9.25in (23.5cm) high

$850-950   CR

A late Van Briggle flaring vase, with squat base, embossed with crocus and covered in a matte turquoise glaze, incised "AA/Van Briggle/Colo. Spgs./2/AO".

5.5in (14cm) high

$120-180   CR

A late Van Briggle 'Lorelei' vase, covered in a turquoise matte glaze, in script "Van Briggle/Colo. Spgs".

The Art Nouveau influenced "Lorelei" vase is Van Briggle's most famous design and is still in production today. Those produced during Van Briggle's lifetime are the most sought after as they show a subtlety and quality of glazing lacking in later pieces.

11in (28cm) high

$280-320   CR

A late Van Briggle figural centerbowl and flower frog, the bowl with a half-naked maiden peering in, and the frog with a turtle, both covered in a shaded turquoise glaze, both marked.

15in (38cm) diam

$280-320   CR

A Van Briggle vase, with Native American busts, covered in a Persian Rose glaze, incised "VAN BRIGGLE/COLO.SPGS", grinding chips and flat chip to footring.

11.25in (28.5cm) high

$400-500   CR

A pair of Van Briggle bookends, of owls standing on books, covered in a Persian Rose glaze, one incised "AA".

5in (12.5cm)

$220-280   CR

A pair of 1930s Wade Heath vases, with inserts.

5.25in (13cm) high

$220-280   **RH**

Two Wade Natwest pig money boxes, 'School Girl' and 'Baby'.

$20-30   **PSA**

A Wade Hat Box series, including 'Lady', 'Jock coat', 'Jock no coat', 'Tramp', 'Trusty', 'Peg' and 'Scamp'.

$120-180   **PSA**

Six Wade Minikins figures.

$60-100   **PSA**

A Wade Wynken figure, first version, minute chips.

$70-100   **PSA**

A Wade 'Kissing Rabbits' posy bowl, slight damage.

$30-50   **PSA**

A Wade Blynken figure, first version, minute chips.

$70-100   **PSA**

A Wade Blynken figure, second version, minute chips.

$100-150   **PSA**

Three Wade ABC cats.

$270-330   **PSA**

Three Wade farm animals: 'Cow', 'Goat' and 'Dog'.

$20-30   **PSA**

A Wade 'Faust Lang Panther on Rock', with green base and unusual colorway.

8in (20cm) high

$1,000-1,500   **PSA**

Six Wade Lilliput Lane Cottages, including 'Victoria Cottage', 'Woodman's Retreat', 'Old Mother Hubbard's', 'Anne Hathaway's Cottage' and 'Sadler's Inn'.

$180-220   **PSA**

Keith Murray

A Wedgwood Keith Murray moonstone-colored fluted shallow bowl, signature mark.

10.25in (26cm)

$200-280 | **GorL**

A Wedgwood Keith Murray moonstone-colored pedestal fruit bowl, with fluted body, crack, Etruria and monogram mask.

10in (25.5cm)

$80-120 | **GorL**

A Wedgwood Keith Murray moonstone-colored pedestal fruit bowl, with fluted body, monogram mark.

10.25in (26cm)

$320-380 | **GorL**

A Wedgwood matt green dinner plate, with fluted border, a matt green two-handle soup bowl and stand, both Keith Murray designs.

Dinner plate 10.25in (26cm)

$120-180 | **GorL**

A Wedgwood Keith Murray ribbed ovoid vase, in a dark green signature mask, small crack to foot rim.

10in (25.5cm)

$400-600 | **GorL**

A Wedgwood Keith Murray ribbed cylindrical green glaze pot, and a similar ashtray, monogram marks.

$180-220 | **GorL**

A Wedgwood Keith Murray moonstone-colored salt or small bowl, on tapered fluted conical pedestal and a miniature mug with fluted body, both with monogram marks, small rim chip.

Bowl 3in (7.5cm) high

$120-180 | **GorL**

A Wedgwood Keith Murray rectangular inkstand, with pen depression and well with liner but no cover, signature mark.

10.5in (26cm)

$270-330 | **GorL**

A pair of Wedgwood Keith Murray green tankards, signature marks.

5in (12.5cm)

$180-220 | **GorL**

A pair of Wedgwood Keith Murray moonstone-colored dwarf candlesticks, signature marks, one restored.

3in (7.5cm)

$180-220 | **GorL**

Two Wedgwood Keith Murray green circular ashtrays, with fluted bodies, one with monogram, one with signature.

4.5in (11.5cm)

$180-220 | **GorL**

A Wedgwood Keith Murray moonstone-colored mug, with blue printed badge for the Royal Highland Regiment of Canada, monogram mark and three plain mugs, all with signature marks.

4.75in (12cm)

$270-330 | **GorL**

A Wedgwood Keith Murray bowl and cover, with silvered lustre knop and fluted decoration.

3.5in (9cm)

$180-220 | **GorL**

Two Wedgwood Keith Murray moonstone-colored circular ashtrays, both with signature marks, both chipped.

4.5in (11.5cm)

$120-180 | **GorL**

A small Wedgwood Keith Murray moonstone-colored cream jug, with a broken silver luster handle and ribbed body, signature and moonstone marks.

3in (7.5cm)

$120-180　　　　　　　　　**GorL**

A Wedgwood Keith Murray moonstone-colored fluted tapered cylindrical vase, monogram Etruria mark.

11.5in (29cm)

$600-1,000　　　**GorL**

A Wedgwood Keith Murray moonstone-colored fluted tapered cylindrical vase, signature and moonstone marks, two large cracks and area of glaze damage.

11.5in (29cm)

$120-180　　　**GorL**

A Wedgwood Keith Murray fluted ovoid vase, in a rare turquoise color, monogram and Etruria marks.

6in (15cm)

$500-700　　　**GorL**

A Keith Murray ribbed globular vase, with beige glaze.

$320-380　　　**GorL**

A Wedgwood Keith Murray moonstone-colored semi-circular fluted wall pocket, signature mark.

8.5in (21.5cm)

$180-220　　　**GorL**

A Wedgwood Keith Murray green semi-circular fluted wall pocket, signature mark.

8.5in (21.5cm)

$270-330　　　**GorL**

A Wedgwood Keith Murray fruit bowl, with lightly fluted rim in an unusual blue grey color, signature mark, small internal chip.

9.5in (24cm)

$270-330　　　　　　　　　**GorL**

KEITH MURRAY (1892-1981)

- Keith Murray was a New Zealand born architect and glass and ceramic designer, who became a pioneer of Art Deco styling.
- He designed glass for Stevens & Williams and, from 1933, ceramics for Wedgwood. His designs are typically modern, with bold, simple and streamlined forms, often with fluted or ribbed designs.
- Colors are muted, including duck-egg blue, straw, light green, ivory white and pale grey. Glazes are matt, semi-matt and celadon-satin.
- All his pieces are marked and highly desirable today. His vases in particular are highly sought after.

A Wedgwood Keith Murray matt green pedestal bowl, with banded decoration.

$400-600　　　　　　　　　**GorL**

A Wedgwood matt straw coffee set with ribbed bodies comprising coffee pot, cream jug, sugar bowl and six cups and saucers (sugar bowl cracked, one side chipped).

$600-1,000 GorL

A Wedgwood moonstone two-handle sugar bowl and cover with fluted body, Etruria and Moonstone marks.

7.5in (19cm) across the handles

$200-280 GorL

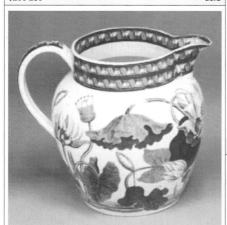

A Wedgwood 'Water Lily' pattern jug, of tall Dutch shape with strap handle, printed in blue with the composite botanical pattern and with the usual cut-reed stringing adapted for use as a border around the neck, inside the rim and down the handle, impressed mark, cracked, glaze rubbing to spout.

1811-20 *6.5in (16.6cm) high*

$270-330 DN

A Wedgwood matt straw square ashtray (each corner chipped on the underside).

7.25in (18.5cm)

$100-150 GorL

A set of six Wedgwood matt green side plates with fluted borders.

7in (18cm)

$300-400 GorL

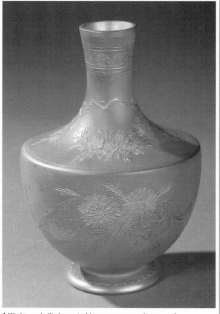

A Wedgwood gilt-decorated jasperware vase, impressed "Wedgwood", decorated with floral sprays.

19thC *6in (15cm) high*

$250-350 SI

A Wedgwood basalt plaque, made to commemorate Winston Churchill's centenary.

1974 *6.25in (16cm) wide*

$70-100 H&G

A Wedgwood 'Garden Pattern' plate, designed by Eric Ravilious.

c1939 *9.25in (23.5cm) diam*

$150-200 REN

A Wedgwood 'Queensware' Veilleuse and fittings, painted in the Dutch style in shades of iron-red, blue and green with oriental flowering shrubs, birds and insects, impressed marks, date code, repaired.

c1884   *11in (28cm) high*

$150-200   **DN**

A Wedgwood dragon luster vase, variegated blue background with a dragon encircling the vase, inside of vase shades from bluish-purple to green and the inside rim is decorated with three panels of Oriental village scenes, alternating between the panels are gold stylized flowers, some minor wear to the gold floral trim on the inside of the vase.

8.5in (21.5cm) high

$800-1,200   **JDJ**

A Wedgwood 'Heartsease' pattern plate, produced for the Orient Shipping Line, designed by Edward Bawden.

c1952   *6in (15cm) diam*

$100-150   **REN**

A Wedgwood plate, produced for the Orient Shipping Line, designed by Robert Gooden.

c1960   *8.5in (22cm) diam*

$40-60   **REN**

A Wedgwood sporting souvenir black basalt Jasperware mug, designed by Professor Richard Guyatt.

c1969   *4.25in (11cm) high*

$300-500   **REN**

A Wedgwood Anniversary mug, designed by Professor Richard Guyatt.

1984   *4.25in (11cm) high*

$180-220   **REN**

A Wedgwood lemonade jug, with four matching beakers, produced for Liberty's of London, designed by Professor Richard Guyatt.

1953   *7.5in (19cm) high*

$1,800-2,200 (set)   **REN**

A Wedgwood bone china limited edition plate, from a series depicting historic British castles and country houses, here "Warwick Castle", designed by David Gentleman, with original box and certificate.

c1980 10.75in (27.5cm) diam

$80-120   **REN**

A Wedgwood bone china limited edition "Ashdown House" plate, designed by David Gentleman, from a series depicting historic British castles and country houses, with original box and certificate.

c1980 10.75in (27.5cm) diam

$80-120   **REN**

A pair of Wedgwood bone china vases, pattern number Z3620.

3.75in (9.5cm) diam

$300-400   **WW**

A Wedgwood Fairyland Dana series luster bowl, designed by Daisy Makeig Jones, of octagonal form, printed and painted in gilt and colored enamels to the exterior in the 'Castle on a Road' pattern and to the interior with 'Fairy in a Cage' pattern, with an all-over luster wash, printed and painted marks Z4968.

10.75in (27cm) diam

$3,000-4,000   **L&T**

CERAMICS

WELLER

- The Weller Pottery was established by Samuel Weller in Fultonham, Ohio, in 1872. In 1888, he moved the pottery to Zanesville and like his local rival Roseville, began producing utilitarian wares. However, by 1895 he had begun to produce art pottery in the style of Rookwood. The Louwelsa range is a copy of Rookwood's Standard Glaze and the Eocean, the Iris range.

- World War I forced Weller to concentrate on easily and cheaply made production wares, but the invention of a number of new glazes such as "Burnt Wood" and "Graystone" do make these wares more interesting.

- The inter-war years saw changes to the owners of Weller Pottery, Harry Weller, Samuel's nephew, took over the running of the pottery when Samuel died in 1925. Harry died in 1932 and the company was taken over by Samuel's two sons-in-law.

- World War II forced changes in the company and although the Weller Pottery was still producing, it was much smaller. By 1948 it had closed for good.

A Weller Dickensware jug, by AH, incised with a monk, and painted with chains of flowers, impressed "Dickensware Weller/incised AH".

6in (15.5cm) high

$350-450   **CR**

A Weller Eocean jardinière, embossed with thistles, marked Eocean in script, one inch area of glaze scaling to interior, and small burst bubble to rim.

10.5in (26.5cm) wide

$250-350   **CR**

A rare Weller blue Louwelsa factory boudoir lamp, painted with clover blossoms, stamped "Louwelsa Weller".

6.5in (16.5cm) high

$550-650   **CR**

A Weller LaSa vase, with tropical landscape in nacreous gold and blue glazes, marked, cracked.

6.5in (16.5cm) high

$180-220   **CR**

A Weller faceted vase, covered in a smooth matte green glaze, unmarked.

8.5in (21.5cm) high

$350-450   **CR**

A monumental Weller Hudson light floor vase, painted with cattleya orchids, stamped "WELLER/CTX-TRX", some small glaze chips around rim and smaller flakes at base.

36.5in (92.5cm)

$7,500-8,500   **CR**

A CLOSER LOOK AT A WELLER VASE

Production pieces are typically molded.

The large size of this vase makes it unusual and valuable.

Sicard ware is usually hand-painted.

A rare Weller Sicard floor vase, decorated with lilies under a green, gold, and purple iridescent glaze, signed "Weller Sicard", small glaze scaling inside rim and at base.

In 1902, Weller employed Jacques Sicard to recreate the recently developed iridescent metallic glaze called 'Reflets Metalliques'. As only a third of the pieces fired were saleable and had to be hand finished, they were expensive and not popular with buyers. Sicard left Weller in 1907 and returned home to France and production ceased.

26.25in (66.5cm) high

$15,000-20,000   **CR**

A Weller Sicard twisted vase, decorated with flowing lines, unmarked, some damage and repairs.

5in (12.5cm) high

$450-550   **CR**

A Weller Sicard tapering vase, decorated with flowers under a gold, green, purple and red iridescent glaze, signed "Sicard Weller", fleck near base.

5.25in (13.5cm) high

$550-650   **CR**

A CLOSER LOOK AT A WEMYSS PIG

Pigs are a popular Wemyss design. In Bohemia, the birthplace of Karel Nekola, the Wemyss painter, pigs are symbols of good luck.

Wemyss ware is renowned for its distinctive style and high quality paintwork.

Bold floral decoration such as the flowering clover on this pig is typical, and usually botanically accurate.

A Wemyss pottery pig, seated on its haunches, painted with pink roses, impressed "WEMYSS" and with ocher script mark "MYS", one ear and a foot restored.

Wemyss ware was produced at the Fife Pottery in Kirkcaldy, Scotland, from the mid 1800s. Wares include jug-and-basin sets, large pig doorstops, inkstands, tablewares and candlesticks, all hand-painted with brightly colored fruit, flowers, cats and birds in the distinctive Wemyss style. In 1930, the Bovey Tracey pottery took over the manufacture of Wemyss ware until 1942.

A Wemyss Lady Eva vase, painted with thistles.

6.25in (16cm) long

$1,200-1,800 **DN**

6.5in (16.5cm) high

$400-500 **GorL**

A large Wemyss pottery pig, painted with pink flowering clover, marked "Wemyss, Made in England", fine crack on forehead and tiny glaze chips to tips of ears.

16.5in (42cm) long

$3,000-4,000 **GorL**

A Wemyss pottery pig, painted with three-leaf clover, marked "Wemyss" in yellow, one ear chipped.

6.25in (16cm)

$600-700 **GorL**

A small Wemyss honey pot, painted by Nekola, with bees and hive.

c1890 *2.75in (7cm) high*

$350-450 **RdeR**

A small Wemyss early morning preserve pot, painted with plums, minor restoration to chips on lid.

c1890 *2.75in (7cm) high*

$200-300 **RdeR**

A Wemyss commemorative mug, with motto "Nae Sic Queen Was Ever Seen" minor restoration to original handle.

This piece was part of a series of Wemyss ware produced to commemorate Queen Victoria's diamond jubilee in 1897.

1897 *5.75in (14.5cm) high*

$650-750 **RdeR**

A Wemyss fern pot, painted with sweet peas, minor restoration to rim.

c1890 *3.5in (8.5cm) high*

$200-300 **RdeR**

A Hadley's Worcester baluster vase, painted with roses.

3.75in (2.5cm)

$150-200 GorL

A pair of Worcester small jugs, printed with floral sprays on an ivory ground, gilt loop handles, puce-printed mark, shape number "1094".

c1891 *4.75in (12cm)*

$220-280 BonS

A Royal Worcester blush vase, painted with roses, no.991.

3in (7.5cm)

$100-150 GorL

A mid-19thC Kerr & Binns Worcester two-handled vase, painted with butterflies above foliage, raised on a fluted socle base and square foot, printed mark.

7.25in (18.5cm) high

$300-400 WW

A Royal Worcester blush globular vase, painted with a bird on gilt branches.

2.75in (7cm)

$220-280 GorL

A Grainger Worcester reticulated teapot and cover, pierced with scrolling foliage, within gilt band borders, printed marks.

c1880

$500-700 DN

A Royal Worcester baluster vase, painted with blackberries, no.285.

4.25in (10.5cm)

$270-330 GorL

A Royal Worcester candle-snuffer, in the form of a nun.

1949

$50-80 DN

A Royal Worcester floral-painted miniature tyg, a similar basket and a trinket dish.

$180-220 GorL

A Royal Worcester 'The French Cook' candle-snuffer.

2.75in (7cm)

$180-220 GorL

A set of eight Royal Worcester fish plates, retailed by Tiffany & Co., each painted with a fish and marine plants on a basket weave-molded ground, with purple-printed mark.

c1865 *9.5in (24cm) diam*

$500-700 SI

A pair of Royal Worcester gilt blush figures of musicians, boy's pipe broken.

1803 *6in (15cm)*

$500-700 GorL

A pair of American Art and Clay Company female busts, both covered in a bright blue glossy glaze, stamped mark.

7in (17.5cm) high

$220-280 **CR**

An American Art and Clay Company bust of a woman, well-modeled in a bright blue glossy glaze, stamped mark, small hairline to base.

8.5in (21.5cm) high

$150-200 **CR**

Two Batchelder tiles, each depicting a peacock with grape clusters and vines in relief on a teal matt ground, impressed "Batchelder/Los Angeles", minor flecks to back edges.

8.75in (22.5cm) high

$1,600-2,000 **CR**

A book flask for whiskey, flint enamel glaze, made by the Bennington Company, Vermont.

c1845 *5.5in (13.5cm) high*

$500-600 **RAA**

A Bennington Company pitcher.

$100-150 **BCAC**

An early Arequipa gourd-shaped vase, marked "Arequipa/California/1912" in blue.

1912 *6in (15cm) high*

$500-600 **FRE**

A tall and unusual Arequipa baluster vase, Salon period, incised "GC/Arequipa/" illegible markings.

c1916 *13.5in (34cm) high*

$3,000-4,000 **CR**

A Benevolent and Protective Order of Elks flask, hairline crack in neck.

The clock on one side signifies it's always the right time for a drink.

$45-55 **BAC**

A Brouwer squat vessel, covered in a mottled green, brown and umber glaze, wishbone mark, small hole and bruise to body.

4.75in (12cm) wide

$350-450 **CR**

A Brouwer flame-painted bulbous vase, in shades of umber and brown, wishbone mark.

4.5in (11.5cm) wide

$450-550 **CR**

A Californian Art Tile framed tile, with a Viking ship on waves in matte polychrome glaze, some wear to color on surface, stamped "California Art Tile Co./Richmond, Calif."

6in (15.5cm)

$280-320 **CR**

A rare Denver Denaura column-shaped vase, with flaring rim and base, covered in a shaded semi-matte green glaze, stamped 'Denaura" and numbered.

10.25in (26cm) high

$550-650 **CR**

A Chicago Crucible bulbous vase, embossed with leaves and covered in a mustard over blue-green semi-matte glaze, stamped "CHICAGO CRUCIBLE", restoration to hairlines from rim and to small chip at base.

6in (15cm) high

$600-700 **CR**

A Clifton corseted Crystal Patina vase, etched mark.

6in (15.5cm) high

$250-350 **CR**

A pair of Cowan elephant bookends, covered in a lustered blue and green mottled glaze, stamped "Cowan", and "flower", restoration around feet of one, a few shallow scratches to both.

7.5in (19cm) high

$550-650 **CR**

A pair of Cowan "Sunbonnet Girls" bookends, covered in a green crystalline glaze, stamped "Cowan", and "flower", restoration to necks on both.

7.25in (18.5cm) high

$250-350 **CR**

A large Dedham crackleware plate, in the 'Rabbit' pattern, ink and impressed marks, small pea-size abraded area to center.

12.5in (31.5cm) high

$220-280 **CR**

A large Dedham crackleware plate, in the 'Elephant' pattern, ink and impressed marks, very dark, firing glaze bubbles around rim, ink and impressed marks.

12.5in (31.5cm) diam

$1,500-2,000 **CR**

A Grueby tile, with monk in wax-resist decoration in matte yellow, unmarked.

6in (15cm) wide

$250-350 **CR**

A small Grueby vessel, covered in a blue-gray frothy glaze, marked.

2in (5cm) high

$700-800 **CR**

A Hampshire cabinet vase, stamped "Hampshire/183".

4.25in (11cm) high

$350-450 **CR**

A Hampshire bulbous vase, embossed with stylized flowers under a fine leathery teal blue and green matte glaze, stamped "Hampshire Pottery/123", a couple of tight lines to base from firing.

7.25in (18.5cm) high

$800-900 **CR**

A Hampshire oil lamp, complete with glass chimney and shade painted with red roses, Miller fittings, stamped "Hampshire".

19in (48.5cm) high

$800-900 **CR**

A Hampshire midnight blue bottle-shaped vase, marked.

6.5in (16.5cm) high

$400-500 CR

A Jugtown small ovoid vase, covered in a Chinese red and blue glaze, stamped mark.

4in (10cm) high

$500-600 CR

A Jugtown bulbous lamp base, covered in a flowing white semi-matte glaze over a dark body, circular stamp.

9.5in (24cm) high

$300-400 CR

A signed Swastika Keramos art pottery vase, with bright gold background with iridescent flower and leaf.

8in (20.5cm) high

$350-450 JDJ

A Mountainside Pottery bust of a woman, covered in an ivory glaze, etched mark, minute nick to base.

8.5in (21.5cm) high

$150-200 CR

A Niloak Mission Ware cylindrical vase, in brown and terracotta scroddled clay, stamped "Niloak".

10in (25.5cm) high

$450-550 CR

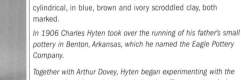

Two Niloak Mission Ware vases, one corseted and one cylindrical, in blue, brown and ivory scroddled clay, both marked.

In 1906 Charles Hyten took over the running of his father's small pottery in Benton, Arkansas, which he named the Eagle Pottery Company.

Together with Arthur Dovey, Hyten began experimenting with the process of swirling color through the clay. These unglazed pieces were named "Niloak", taken from the local kaolin clay spelt backwards. Later the wares became known as Mission Ware and in 1911 the company changed its name to the Niloak Pottery Company.

These colorful wares proved popular, but the combination of debts and the Depression forced them to produce cheaper glazed wares in the late 1920s.

A fire badly damaged the pottery in 1945 and by 1947 it had closed.

Tallest 11in (28cm) high

$500-600 CR

An early Newcomb College high-glaze cylindrical vase, by Lillian Ann Guedry, decorated with stylized band in mustard and black on a tan ground, marked "NC/D24/X/dot in diamond symbol/JM/L.A.G.", cracks and chips.

1901   11in (28cm) high

$1,000-1,500 CR

Two Niloak Mission Ware classically shaped vases, in blue, ivory and brown scroddled clay, both marked, chip to each, one has a scratch.

9.5in (24cm) high

$220-280 CR

A Norweta bulbous vase, embossed with broad leaves and covered in a frothy blue-green mate glaze, impressed Norweta, several hairlines from rim.

Two Niloak pieces, comprising a vase and a low bowl in marbled blue and gray clay, impressed mark.

4in (10cm) diam

$180-220 CR

A pair of Niloak tall candlesticks, of blue and gray marbled clay, impressed mark.

8in (20cm) high

$350-450 CR

6in (15cm) high

$550-650 CR

A George Ohr small cup pitcher, with pinched rim, covered in a rare amber volcanic glaze, stamped "G.E. OHR/BILOXI", restored chip to rim and minor nick.

4.75in (12cm)

$1,700-2,000 CR

A George Ohr squat vessel, covered in a speckled brown and green glaze, stamped "GEO E. OHR/BILOXI, MISS", repair to rim chip.

5.5in (14cm) wide

$1,200-1,500 CR

A George Ohr gourd-shaped vase, with closed-in rim, covered in a gunmetal glaze, script signature, small bruise to base.

3.75in (9.5cm) wide

$1,500-2,000 CR

A George Ohr squat vessel, covered in a gunmetal brown glaze, stamped "GEO E. OHR/BILOXI, MISS.", repair to rim chip and a few small nicks to shoulder.

4.25in (11cm) high

$900-1,000 CR

A George Ohr bulbous cabinet vase, with "ripped," scalloped rim, covered in a black gunmetal glaze with green and yellow interior, stamped "G.E. OHR/BILOXI", nicks to points.

2.75in (7cm) wide

$1,500-2,000 CR

A Ben Owen bulbous shouldered vessel, covered in a white semi-matte glaze, circular stamp, firing line at base does not go through.

6.75in (17cm) high

$120-180 CR

A pair of Ott & Brewer decorative plates, hand-painted with a dendrobium orchid, the other with parrot tulips, both with scalloped gilded edge, both bear red Belleek mark, a few minor nicks to edge of square plate.

8.5in (21.5cm) wide

$450-550 CR

Two Pewabic cabinet vases, covered in amber lustered glazes, both stamped, one with "PP".

3.25in (8cm) high

$450-550 CR

A Ben Owen salt-glazed jug, with incised ribs, covered in a buff glaze, circular stamp mark.

11in (28cm) high

$180-220 CR

An Owens Utopian ovoid vase, by Mae Timberlake, painted with a cat, a couple of very minor flecks to body.

10.5in (26.5cm) high

$120-180 CR

A Ridgway pitcher, relief-molded to resemble bamboo.

c1835

$60-80   **BAC**

A Roblin barrel-shaped cabinet vase, covered in a fine speckled blue glaze, impressed "ROBLIN".

2.25in (5.5cm) high

$500-600   **CR**

A pair of Roycroft/Buffalo Pottery salt and pepper shakers, stamped pottery mark and orb and cross decoration, base chip and bruise to top of salt, glaze fleck to top of pepper shaker.

3in (7.5cm) high

$250-350   **CR**

A Saturday Evening Girls flaring bowl, covered in a lavender semi-matte glaze.

1922   *8in (20cm) diam*

$90-100   **CR**

A Saturday Evening Girls cup, decorated with a band of rabbits at rim, all on a blue-gray ground, marked "S.E.G."

4in (10cm) high

$1,200-1,500   **CR**

A tall Shearwater bulbous vase, embossed with geometric bands and covered in a mottled charcoal and green matte glaze, circular Shearwater stamp.

8.75in (22.5cm) high

$1,500-2,000   **CR**

A Teco bulbous vase, with lobed rim covered in a medium matte green and charcoal glaze, stamped mark, small chip to foot ring, bruise to rim and base.

5in (12.5cm) high

$400-500   **CR**

A Teco baluster vase, covered in a lemon yellow matte glaze, stamped "TECO", restoration to several hairlines.

11in (28cm) high

$300-400   **CR**

A W.J. Walley squat flower frog vase, in brown and green matte glaze, stamped "WJW", a couple of very minor nicks.

5in (12.5cm) diam

$550-650   **CR**

A rare Willets woven porcelain basket, with two "branch" handles, and applied flowers, stamped "Willets/Belleek", a few chips to leaves and petals.

The Willet brothers purchased the Excelsior Pottery Company in Trenton, New Jersey, in 1879 and changed the name to Willets.

The pottery produced a number of different wares including American "Belleek". This line was developed by William Bromley Sr. and Walter Scott Lenox, who had trained at Ott & Brewer. Lenox went on to become head of decorating at Willets.

The pottery went into receivership in 1909 and then became the New Jersey Pottery Company.

9in (23cm) wide

$1,200-1,500   **CR**

A Willets Belleek shell-shaped vase, with "coral" handle, with light gilding and pink glaze on an ivory ground, red Willets stamp.

8.25in (21cm) high

$2,000-2,500   **CR**

A Wheatley tile, impressed with stylized flower and petal medallion in rose, yellow and blue glazes, unmarked.

6in (15cm) wide

$250-350 **CR**

A Willets Belleek urn, with silver overlay, on a pink to green ground, with reticulated handles, brown ink stamp.

8.5in (23cm) high

$1,000-1,500 **CR**

A Willets Belleek ewer, with silver overlay on a green ground, china-painted with wild roses, brown ink stamp, tight line to body.

9in (23cm) high

$450-550 **CR**

A Willets Belleek three-piece porcelain tea set, all with silver overlay, consisting of a teapot, a creamer and a sugar bowl, brown ink stamps, some damage.

Teapot 8.25in (21cm) high

$250-350 **CR**

A 1930s Crown Devon luster vase.

7.5in (18.5cm) high

$400-500 **RH**

A 1930s Crown Devon wall charger.

12in (30.5cm) diam

$850-950 **RH**

A 1930s Crown Devon "Matilda" fairy castle vase.

8in (20.5cm) high

$900-1,000 **RH**

A 1930s Crown Devon "Malta" jade fairy castle vase.

6.25in (15.5cm) high

$750-850 **RH**

A 1930s Crown Devon geometric jug.

3.5in (8.5cm) high

$150-200 **RH**

Two 1930s Crown Devon green glazed dogs.

$30-40 **AS&S**

An unusual mid-19thC Alcock bone china relief-molded milk jug, modeled with witches in a wood fanning a cauldron, the reverse with figures in a tent beneath trees, molded mark, a crack across the top of the handle.

5.5in (14cm) high

$150-200   **WW**

A Mabel Lucy Atwell elf-shaped milk jug, modeled standing and saluting, painted in green with rosy red cheeks, printed facsimile signatures, factory marks and RD No 724421, part of "Boo-Boo" nursery tea set.

Mabel Lucy Atwell (1897-1964) was born in London, where she attended art school and classes. In her early career she sold sketches to magazines but by 1900 she had started to illustrate books. These include "Mother Goose", "Alice in Wonderland" and "Peter Pan and Wendy", at the personal request of author J. M. Barrie.

Atwell went on to design other ephemera as well as figurines, wall plaques and china and sets of her china were used in the Royal Nursery.

c1926   *6in (15cm) high*

$120-180   **BonS**

A Mabel Lucy Atwell mushroom form teapot and cover, printed in black with a house, an elf and a mouse at one door and painted in green and orange, restored cover, some overpainting to pot, interior discolored, part of "Boo-Boo" nursery tea set, printed facsimile signatures, factory marks and RD No 72442.

c1926   *5in (12.5cm) high*

$220-280   **BonS**

A Mabel Lucy Atwell mushroom form sucrière, painted with red spots and green grass at the base, part of "Boo-Boo" nursery tea set, printed facsimile signatures, factory marks and RD No 724421.

c1926   *4in (10cm) high*

$70-100   **BonS**

A Mabel Lucy Atwell canted square cake plate, with foliate molded handles, printed with an illustrated verse, "To work in the garden is ever such fun, With fairies to help you to get the job done", printed marks, RD number 721562.

9.5in (24cm) diam

$70-80   **BonS**

A Mabel Lucy Atwell nursery bowl, printed with an illustrated verse "Fairies, fairies everywhere, Dancing in the sun, Flying here and flying there Yet — I can't catch one", printed marks, RD number 721562.

7.75in (20cm) diam

$70-90   **BonS**

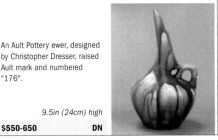

An Ault Pottery ewer, designed by Christopher Dresser, raised Ault mark and numbered "176".

9.5in (24cm) high

$550-650   **DN**

An Ault Pottery vase, the shape designed by Christopher Dresser and probably decorated by Clarissa Ault, the vessel of conical shape tapering to a slender neck, and simply painted in naturalistic colours with a kingfisher carrying a fish in its beak, and flanked by pink flowers and leaves, impressed facsimile designer's signature, restored patch on base.

Christopher Dresser (1834-1904) was born in Scotland in 1834. He trained and later lectured on botany at the Government School of Design in London and went on to produce a number of illustrated plates and three books on the same subject, including an article entitled "Botany as Adapted to the Art and Art Manufacture".

While studying, Dresser came into contact with the works of Owen Jones and he later contributed to Jones' 'Grammar of Ornament', which was published in 1856. He published his first book on design in 1862 called 'The Art of Decorative Design'.

Dresser spent four months in Japan in 1876 and was stimulated by Japanese design.

He designed for a number of well-known manufacturers and in a wide range of media including metalware, textiles, ceramics, glass and furniture.

8.25in (21cm) high

$300-350 | **DN**

A pair of Berlin double sweetmeat dishes, surmounted by putti.

5.5in (14cm) wide

$450-550 | **GorL**

A Beswick Figures 'The Mad Hatter's Tea Party' tableau, limited edition number 533 of 1998, no. LC001.

$120-180 | **PSA**

A Booth's silicon china miniature teapot, decorated in the first period Worcester style with exotic bird reserves on a blue scale ground.

$180-220 | **Chef**

A Beswick Birds 'Penguin Family', nos. "MN800/801/802/803", some damage.

$45-55 | **PSA**

A Beswick gold back stamp Beatrix Potter figure, 'Peter Rabbit'.

4.5in (11.5cm) high

$150-200 | **OACC**

A Beswick 'Circus' pattern toast rack.

6in (15cm) wide

$35-45 | **GorL**

A large Brannam pottery oviform vase, by James Dewdney, signed "C.H. Brannam Barum" and "JD", dated.

1904 16.25in (41cm) high

$250-300 | **DN**

A 1930s Burleigh ware parrot vase, with liner.

7.5in (19cm) high

$1,000-1,500 | **RH**

A 1930s 22-piece Burleigh ware zenith-shape 'Vine' pattern tea set.

6in (15cm) high

$750-850 | **RH**

A Burmantofts earthenware stove, of Moorish design, glazed in red, the cylindrical body with shell carrying handles, pierced with all over flowerheads and a "mihrab" opening for the fire, the domed cover similarly decorated with flue aperture, the whole raised on molded base with arcaded bracket feet, impressed marks.

34.25in (87cm) high

$1,000-1,500   **L&T**

A late 1960s Carol Daw Pottery small pot.

$100-150   **V**

A Denby 'Burlington' pattern vase, hand-painted, unnamed designer.

c1959 11.25in (28.5cm) high

$40-50   **FFM**

A Cauldon goblet, the semi-oval bowl boldly printed with floral sprays and entwined gilt handles, printed mark.

7in (18cm) high

$500-600   **LC**

A Cauldon goblet, the semi-oval bowl boldly printed with floral sprays and entwined gilt handles, printed mark.

7in (18cm) high

$550-650   **LC**

A Davenport caneware baluster water jug, with independent decoration attributed to Robert Allen, painted with a figure before a bathing machine, coastal shipping in the distance and to one side indistinctly inscribed "Trifle Lowestoft", above an engine-turned basketweave lower section and blue enamel rims and borders, impressed mark, extensive wear, some stains and restoration.

For an almost identical scene on a Lowestoft flask see "Sheena Smith", Lowestoft Porcelain in the Castle Museum Norwich Vol. 2 , pl. 21a. Robert Allen (1745-1831), seems to have become established as an independent decorator in Lowestoft following the closure of that factory c1800.

c1810   *5.5in (14cm) high*

$65-75   **DN**

A Denby 'Arabesque' pattern coffee pot, hand-painted, designed by Gill Pemberton.

1964-70s 12.25in (31cm) high

$25-35   **FFM**

A Copeland earthenware jug, with frieze of classical figures against a green ground, and a matching beaker.

Jug 5.5in (14cm) high

$100-150   **GorL**

A pair of early 19thC plates, possibly Davenport or Ridgway.

8.25in (21cm) diam

$25-35 (pair)   **Chef**

An 18thC Derby figure of a lady, amidst floral bocage and a sheep at her side.

5.75in (14.5cm)

$180-220   **GorL**

An 18thC Derby figure of a shepherd girl, in a pink dress on a pierced gilded rococo base with floral encrusted bocage back.

6in (15cm) high

$100-150   **GorL**

An early 20thC Dresden circular floral encrusted box and cover, with bird decoration.

5in (12.5cm) diam

$70-100   **GorL**

One of a series of Fornasetti opera plates, featuring José from Carmen, by George Bizet.

1838-1875 10in (26cm) diam

$200-250   **FM**

A Fornasetti ceramic paperweight, with crossed keys motif.

3.5in (9cm) wide

$150-200   **FM**

A Fornasetti 'crème de cocu' ashtray.

6in (15cm) diam

$120-180   **FM**

A Fornasetti ceramic biscuit barrel.

9.5in (24cm) high

$800-1,200   **FM**

A Fornasetti ceramic pot.

1958

$100-150   **FM**

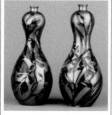

A pair of T. Forrester & Sons double gourd vases, floral painted in blue against a gilded ground, necks restored.

12in (30.5cm) high

$400-500   **GorL**

A Goebel wall pocket, modeled in the form of a horse and rider, decorated in shades of brown, black and orange, heightened with gilt.

5in (12.5cm) high

$80-120   **PSA**

A Goebel decorative ornament, modeled as two budgies on a perch, one decorated in green and the other in blue.

$60-80   **PSA**

A Goebel figure of a lady.

$50-70   **PSA**

A 1960s Isle of Wight Pottery pencil pot, hand-painted, designed by Jo Lester.

4.75in (12cm) high

$8-12   **FFM**

A 1960s Isle of Wight Pottery jug, hand-painted, designed by Jo Lester.

3.5in (8.5cm) high

$10-15   **FFM**

A Robert Jacob porcelain coffee set.

Coffee pot 9.5in (24cm) high

$80-120 CA

Three Liliput Lane Figures, comprising a Land of Legend figure, "Mr. Bronzer", "Ranol" and "The Swamp Bird", with box.

$25-35 PSA

A Liliput Lane "Under the Hedge" figure, "Deck the Halls", limited edition.

$25-35 PSA

A 1960s Stig Lindberg high-fired earthenware bowl, transfer-decorated with geometric leaf design pattern.

6.35in (16cm) diam

$55-65 MHT

A Linthorpe pottery bowl, of compressed form on spreading circular foot painted in naturalistic colours with branches of pink blossom against a ground shading from yellow to gray, impressed "Linthorpe", printed "FB" monogram and numbered "466", having a metal neck rim.

10.75in (27cm) diam

$250-350 DN

A Maling earthenware two-handled vase, painted in luster enamels.

6in (15cm) high

$100-150 GorL

A Linthorpe Pottery jardinière, of compressed globular shape with wavy rim and dimpled sides and applied with six double loop handles, molded with florets, the red clay streaked with a milky greenish amber glaze, only number "179" visible on base.

5.25in (13cm) high

$300-400 DN

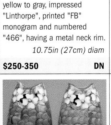
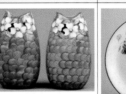

A pair of Maling earthenware vases, relief-molded and painted with flowers and leaves.

8in (20.5cm) high

$200-250 GorL

An Alfred Meakin "Gay Nineties" plate, transfer-printed.

c1960 *22.5cm diam*

$12-15 FFM

A Martin Brothers stoneware "double-face" jug, modeled on one side with the face of a man whistling, the other side shows a man with a grimacing visage, signed on base "Martin Bros., London & Southhall" and dated "5-1910", repaired on spout.

5.25in (13cm) high

$2,500-3,000 DN

A 19thC Meissen sweetmeat basket, two-handled, pierced and painted with flower sprays, painted mark, incised numeral.

10.25in (26cm) long

$120-180 GorL

A early 20thC Meissen chaffinch No.798, restored tip of wing.

4in (10cm) high

$100-150 GorL

A pair of late 19thC Meissen blue and white 'onion' pattern sweetmeat dishes, flanked by reclining figures in period costume, No.2872 and 2875, chips to fingers and toes.

6.75in (17cm) wide

$1,300-1,500 | **GorL**

A Mettlach plaque, with castle scene and boats, numbered 2195.

7.5in (19cm) diam

$450-550 | **JDJ**

A Mettlach plaque, with castle scene and boats, numbered 2196.

7.5in (19cm) diam

$500-600 | **JDJ**

A Minton flower-encrusted teapot.

c1835   1.75in (4.5cm) high

$600-700 | **Gro**

A Minton pottery Japanoiserie garden seat, of barrel-shaped form, molded in relief and painted in colours with sprays of chrysanthemum and with a large turquoise ribbon, impressed marks, date code, some small cracks through the footrim, minor wear.

c1881   17.5in (44.6cm) high

$800-1,000 | **DN**

A large Minton jardinière, of shaped ovoid form, decorated with shaped panels of flowering poppies and painted in colors, molded mark "Mintons England", incised no "3434".

13in (33cm) diam

$500-600 | **L&T**

A Minton baluster vase, designed by Christopher Dresser, applied with ring 'handles', painted in gilt and colored enamels with floral motifs in a faux cloisonné style on a turquoise ground, impressed marks.

9.5in (24cm) high

$1,300-1,500 | **L&T**

A Minton framed tile, printed and painted in colored enamels with the figures of Ferdinard and Ariel, in a floral landscape, impressed and incised marks verso.

7.75in (20cm) wide

$400-500 | **L&T**

Three Moore Bros. figural table center pieces, each modeled as a putto playing a musical instrument, seated beside a blackberry encrusted bowl, chips and losses.

c1880   6.25in (16cm) high

$350-450 | **DN**

A New Hall porcelain bowl, oriental decoration on the outside with small painted decoration on the inside base of the bowl, some wear to the decoration on the inside of the bowl.

6in (15cm) diam

$180-220 | **JDJ**

A Nippon four-handled vase, paneled decoration of two birds on a branch with dogwood blossoms, blue and white handled decoration of grapes and leaves, signed on base, handpainted "Nippon".

12.5in (31.5cm) high

$2,000-3,000 | **JDJ**

An Omega Workshops tin-glazed pottery plate, painted in the center with a red spiral and on the everted rim with four further spirals, alternating with green banding, against a milky off-white ground, impressed on the underside with an Omega symbol in a square.

9.75in (24.5cm) diam

$900-1,000 **DN**

A Pendelfin rabbit, 'Peeps'.
c1970 *4in (10cm) long*

$40-50 **PC**

A Pendelfin rabbit, 'Rocky'.
c1970 *4in (10cm) high*

$30-40 **PC**

A Pendelfin rabbit, 'Bongo'.
c1970 *3in (7.5cm) high*

$45-55 **PC**

A Pendelfin rabbit, 'Margo'.
c1970 *3in (7.3cm) high*

$150-200 **PC**

A Pendelfin rabbit, 'Squeezy'.
c1970 *3in (7.5cm) high*

$150-200 **PC**

A Pinder Bourne plaque, hand-painted with a bulldog lying in woodland, edged with gilt, slight crazing.
6.5in (16.5cm) high

$200-250 **PSA**

A 20thC Potschappel figure of a grape harvester, with bare feet, grape basket, printed marks.
5.5in (14cm) high

$40-50 **Chef**

Two Plichta models of seated cats, with thistle decoration.
Largest 5.5in (13.5cm)

$280-320 **GorL**

A Pratt "Belle Vue Pegwell Bay" paste pot.

$100-150 **GorB**

A Pratt "Belle Vue Pegwell Bay" pot.
5.25in (13.5cm) diam

$120-180 **PSA**

A Pratt pot, decorated with a scene of "The Room in which Shakespeare was born".
4.25in (10.5cm) diam

$80-100 **PSA**

A Pratt pot, decorated with a scene of Osbourne House, restored.
4.5in (11cm) diam

$70-100 **PSA**

A Pratt pot lid, decorated with a scene of "The Times".

$70-100 **PSA**

A Pratt pot lid, signed Mayer, decorated with a scene of bears on a rock.
3.75in (9.5cm) diam

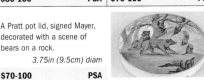

$70-100 **PSA**

A B **C** D E F G H I J K L M N O P Q R S T U V W XYZ

A Porquire-Beau Quimper oval platter, decorated with a mother and baby and a geometric border, marked "Briec".
c1880   15.75in (39.5cm) high

$1,000-1,400   **FLA**

A rare Henriot Quimper demilune vase, decorated with a Breton and Bretonne on one side, flowers on the other side and with a border of flowers and cross hatching, marked "HR".
c1905

$1,500-1,700   **FLA**

An Henriot Quimper scalloped plate, decorated with a finely painted Breton couple in muted colors, with a wide green décor border.
     10in (25.5cm) diam

$650-750   **FLA**

A pair of Henriot Quimper urn-shaped vases, marked.
c1922   15in (37.5cm) high

$2,000-2,500   **FLA**

An Odetta vase, decorated with a man smoking a pipe, signed "Fouillex HB Quimper".
c1925   10in (25.5cm) high

$800-1,200   **FLA**

A Rorstrand Sweden 'Picknick' pattern tureen with lid, printed and hand-painted, designed by Marianne Westmann.
c1954   8.5in (22cm) high

$60-80   **FFM**

Three Rorstrand cups and saucers.
c1965

$55-65   **MHT**

A Rorstrand Sweden 'Picknick' pattern serving dish, printed and hand-painted, designed by Marianne Westmann.
c1954   14.25in (36cm) wide

$55-65   **FFM**

A Gunnar Nylund for Rorstrand porcelain pitcher, engraved "R" and crown mark, "G. N." initials.
     13.5in (34.5cm) high

$400-500   **FRE**

Two Royal Bayreuth devil and card pitchers.

Large: $500-600, small: $200-300   **BAC**

A Royal Bayreuth apple jug.

$200-250   **BAC**

A Royal Bayreuth lobster jug.

$100-150   **BAC**

A Royal Bayreuth elk jug.

$250-300   **BAC**

A Royal Dux porcelain centerpiece, maiden kneeling beside foliated pond, applied pad mark, chipped.

10in (25.5cm) high

$400-500   **GorL**

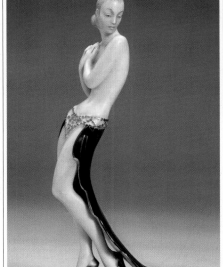

A Royal Dux porcelain figure, modeled as a partially nude woman with cobalt blue skirt, applied triangle mark.

The Royal Dux porcelain factory was founded in Duchov, also known as Dux, in Bohemia in 1860. It produced wares in terracotta, faience and majolica in the style of Copenhagen, Worcester and Sèvres, and in 1878 won a silver medal at the Paris exhibition.

At the turn of the century, Royal Dux started using porcelain and its Art Nouveau designs attracted international customers and also won a number of gold medals at exhibitions in Milan, Liberec and St Louis, Missouri. The factory also produced some good Art Deco figures during the 1930s.

The factory was taken over by the Nazis in 1938 and used to produce propaganda material. It was later nationalized by the Communists.

The company is still producing porcelain figurines today.

11in (28cm) high

$450-550   **FRE**

A Royal Dux camel and rider group, with a boy holding carpet bags below, on a natural base, No.1725.

19.5in (49.5cm)

$2,800-,3200   **GorL**

A set of six late 19thC Sarreguemines pig jugs, the pink-tinged snouts forming the spout, the tails the handles.

8.75in (22cm) high

$300-400   **Chef**

A Royal Dux Art Nouveau mirror, with bevelled plate, No.1097.

23.5in (59.5cm)

$1,000-1,500   **GorL**

A Sevres wall sconce.

c1890

$1,000-1,500   **ACM**

A Sèvres card tray, with pink border decorated in center with roses, cherries and strawberries surrounded by a gold enamel wreath, topped in the border with a Royal Crest, ormolu stand.

12in (30.5cm) long

$1,000-1,500   **JDJ**

An American blue and white spongeware pitcher.

$300-400　　　**BCAC**

An American tri-colored pitcher, sponge-decorated.

$200-300　　　**BCAC**

A Royal Stone China covered vase, by Ralph Stevenson & Williams, of tapered hexagonal shape with dog handles, the domed cover with seated dog finial, decorated with a typical Japan pattern, red-printed royal arms mark with maker's initials, some enamel flaking on body, cover holed and chipped.

c1825　　*16in (40.5cm) high*

$200-300　　　**DN**

A 1980s Janice Tchalenko Vessel bowl, for Next.

Artist potter Janice Tchalenko who originally worked for Dartington Pottery, collaborated with James Kent to produce these studio pottery inspired vessels for Next in the 1980s.

4.75in (12cm) high

$100-150　　　**MHT**

A 1980s Janice Tchalenko Vessel vase, for Next.

8.75in (22cm) high

$100-150　　　**MHT**

A 1950s pitted glazed earthenware bowl by Vallauris, France, stamped "Vallauris".

8in (20.5cm) wide

$150-200　　　**MHT**

A Reginald Fairfax Wells "Soon" vase.

c1919-51 7.25in (18.5cm) high

$550-650　　　**ADE**

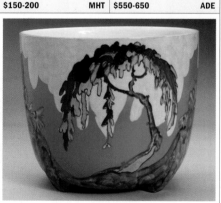

A Wilkinson Memory Lane jardinière, with abstracted trees and landscape, in the style of Clarice Cliff.

8.5in (21.5cm) diam

$220-280　　　**FRE**

A Willow model of John Knox's house, colored version with inscription "model of the house in Edinburgh where John Knox, the Scottish reformer, died, 24th Nov. 1572".

$70-100　　　**DN**

A Withernsea rabbit jug.

8in (20cm) high

$45-55　　　**OACC**

A 1930s Zsolnay Pecs ceramic model of two deer.

6.25in (16cm) wide

$200-300　　　**OACC**

A late 19thC German china fairing "Daily News Sir?", in the form of a painted figure of a newsboy standing in front of a match container with strike surface to the back, impressed shield mark and number "3198".

28in (11cm) high

$400-500　　　**DN**

A fairing, "Two Different Views".
c1900   3.5in (9cm) high
$80-120   **OACC**

A fairing, untitled.
c1900   4in (10.5cm) high
$70-100   **OACC**

A fairing, untitled, crack to base.
c1900   4in (10cm) high
$60-80   **OACC**

A fairing, "Paddling His Own Canoe".
c1900   4in (10cm) high
$100-150   **OACC**

A fairing, "The Power of Love".
c1900   3in (8cm) high
$100-150   **OACC**

A mid-19thC porcelaineous pastille burner and separate stand, modelled as a turreted house.
$600-700   **DN**

A mid 19thC porcelaineous pastille burner and separate stand, modeled as a cottage, stand damaged and repaired.
4.25in (11cm) high
$100-150   **DN**

A mid-19thC porcelain pastille burner and separate stand, modeled as a gothic church, with tower.
5.5in (14cm) high
$600-700   **DN**

A pair of mid-19thC porcelain models of cottages, with moss-encrusted gables and with two large flowers in the garden.

4.25in (11cm) wide

$400-500 **DN**

A 19thC English biscuit porcelain group, of three children at play on an oval base, tiny chips.

5.75in (14.5cm) high

$300-400 **WW**

A pair of Continental porcelain figures, of a lady and gentleman in period costume with sheep at their sides.

10.5in (26.5cm) high

$250-350 **GorL**

A pair of 20thC German porcelain figures, one seated with a dog and the other with a cat.

5.25in (13.5cm) high

$550-650 **GorL**

A mid-19th-century English biscuit porcelain model of a girl, with her dog sitting up and wearing a bonnet, all on a molded base.

5.75in (14.5cm) high

$120-180 **WW**

A 19thC porcelain-handled desk seal, with pastoral landscape and gold-colored base, set with a cornelian engraved with a coronet and "G&R".

$1,300-1,500 **GorL**

A pair of 20thC German porcelain figures, of lady and gentleman in period costumes with lambs at their feet.

7in (18cm) high

$200-250 **GorL**

An American Boy Scout mug.

c1910-1920

$200-250 **BAC**

A pair of 19thC American chalkware decorated dogs.

$1,000-1,500 **BCAC**

A pair of late 19thC Austrian Secessionist green-glazed vases.

9.75in (25cm) high

$120-180 **AS&S**

A creamware mug, scroll handle, black printed hunting scene within silver resist luster border.

c1820 *3.75in (9.5cm) diam*

$100-150 **OACC**

A small Continental ceramic figure, probably Austrian, in the manner of Preiss, modeled as a naked female child sucking her finger and sitting on a large book with green and golden binding, incised only with number "6227" on base.

3.25in (8.5cm) high

$350-450 **DN**

A 19thC faience tulip vase, with five tapering necks, painted in the Rouen-style with flowers and leaves, marked "JJ-V, 25-3".

7.25in (18.5cm) high

$85-95 **WW**

A late 19thC faience plate, painted with two crests and sprigs of flowers within a gilded wavy rim, painted mark "RD" and "1756".

9.25in (23.5cm) diam

$60-70 **Chef**

A Victorian bone china centerpiece, two semi-nude children supporting floral encrusted vase, on oval base, chips and cracks.

9in (23cm) high

$600-700 **GorL**

A luster tea set, comprising teapot, sugar bowl, creamer, eight cups and ten saucers.

c1820 *Saucer 5.5in (14cm) diam*

$500-550 **OACC**

A B **C** D E F G H I J K L M N O P Q R S T U V W XYZ

An early 20thC pink luster mustache cup, with view of The Pier, Hastings.

3.5in (9cm) diam

$65-75 **OACC**

A late 19thC Staffordshire pastille burner.

5in (13cm) high

$150-250 **OACC**

A late 19thC majolica candlestick, modeled as a cherub holding bulrushes.

9.5in (24cm) high

$200-250 **GorL**

A late 19thC American spongewear pitcher.

8.25in (21cm) high

$300-400 **BCAC**

A Danish pottery money box, in the form of a seated King Charles spaniel, the coin slot in the back of the mottled ocher and brown animal.

5.25in (13.5cm) high

$45-55 **Chef**

A late 19thC American blue and white stoneware pitcher.

$200-250 **BCAC**

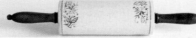

A stoneware rolling pin, decorated with blue flowers.

$250-350 **BCAC**

A 1970s stoneware studio vase, unsigned.

$250-350   **V**

An American art pottery jardinière, with embossed leaves covered in a frothy green matte glaze, unmarked, shallow spider line to bottom, and a grinding chip to one foot.

11.5in (29.5cm) wide

$500-600   **CR**

A Victorian bone china cat ornament, at play within a bonnet encrusted with foliage, impressed date mark for 1878, handle cracked.

1878   *7in (18cm) high*

$200-300   **GorL**

Two Rococo-style vases, applied with colorful flowers on a blue ground, some restoration.

c1830   *8.75in (22.5cm) high*

$60-80   **WW**

A 20thC scallop-shaped dish.

9in (23cm) high

$15-20   **WW**

A framed pot lid, depicting New St Thomas's Hospital.

$60-70   **GorL**

A turtle and shell mustard pot, unmarked, chip to base.

$120-180   **BCAC**

A mid-19thC floral encrusted vase, the two-handled baluster shape heavily applied with various flowers on a deep blue ground.

10.75in (27.5cm) high

$60-70   **Chef**

COMICS

COMICS

- Condition is vital as comics are often damaged and worn when read. Early comics were also not 'made to last', being printed on inexpensive paper. The paper darkens with age and its color affects the value. Look for doodles and scrawlings by previous owners, detached (or missing) covers, tears and lost pages or areas. Restoration is possible and is considered necessary on some of the rarer comics found.

- Major superheroes, such as Superman and Spider-Man, are likely to be interesting to collectors. Popular interest in some superheroes is reawakening due to the 2002 release of the 'Spider-Man' film, soon to be followed by many more, including 'The Incredible Hulk'. Widely popular characters are always likely to be more desirable.

- The first issue of any comic is likely to be the most valuable, but prices will drop considerably for any later issues.

- As well as collecting by 'age', publisher, superhero or character, the work of individual comic book artists is often collected. Some artists are better known than others, such as Bob Kane (Batman), Jerome Siegel & Joe Shuster (Superman), Carl Banks (Donald Duck), Steve Ditko (early Spider-Man) and Harvey Kurtzman (early M.A.D.).

- Many comics are moralistic or patriotic in their themes and stories and are intended as a form of proaganda to educate the young. Themes such as America battling 'evil forces' like Nazi Germany is a good example.

- Comics are usually divided into three eras:

  Golden Age: 1938-c1955. Began with the first Superman story in 'Action Comics' No.1 in Spring 1938. New characters appeared regularly as the market boomed, such as Batman in 'Detective Comics' No.27 in May 1939. Wonder Woman, the Green Lantern, and the Flash were also popular characters introduced at this time.

  Silver Age: c1956-c1969. Saw the rebirth of many superheroes after a lull in the 1950s. This period saw the arrival of Spider-Man, the Incredible Hulk. Comic collecting also began in earnest during this period.

  Bronze Age: c1970-c1979 and beyond. More modern classics, some targeted at serious readers, and a continuation of surviving popular characters. Comic collecting is now a well-established activity.

'Action Comics' #100 by DC Comics, fine condition, off-white pages.

1946

$220-280   HC

'America's Greatest Comics' #1, by Fawcett Comics, very good condition, cream to off-white pages.

1941

$500-700   HC

'Animal Comics' #6, by Dell Comics, near mint condition, cream to off-white pages.

1944

$220-280   HC

'The Avengers' #3 by Marvel Comics.

This is the first Sub-Mariner crossover issue.

1964

$50-80   HC

'The Avengers' #4, by Marvel Comics, very fine condition, off-white pages, top edge of cover trimmed.

This is the first Silver Age appearance of Captain America, with Jack Kirby cover artwork.

1964

$500-700   HC

'The Avengers' #9, by Marvel Comics, off-white pages.

1964

$120-180   HC

'Batman' #130, by DC Comics, water stain on the bottom of the first few pages.

1960

$15-25   HC

'Batman' #18, by DC Comics, with Hitler, Tojo and Mussolini cover.

1943

$180-220 HC

'Batman' #23, DC Comics, off-white pages, with Joker cover, very fine condition.

'Batman' #25, DC Comics, very fine condition, white pages.

This is the only Golden Age Joker/Penguin team-up, the first team-up between two major villains.

1944

$1,500-2,000 HC

1944

$1,000-1,500 HC

'Batman' #3, DC Comics, fine condition, off-white to white pages.

This is the first appearance of the Puppet Master and the first Catwoman in costume.

1940

$1,200-1,800 HC

'Captain America Comics' #13, Timely Comics, cream to off-white pages, classic cover, very fine condition.

'Captain America Comics' #19, by Timely Comics, cream to off-white pages, with Human Torch story, good condition.

1942

$1,800-2,200 HC

1942

$300-400 HC

'Batman' #67, by DC Comics, fine condition, off-white to white.

'Black Cat' #25, by Harvey Comics, very fine condition.

1951

$180-220 HC

1950

$100-150 HC

'Captain America Comics' #62, by Timely Comics, off-white pages, very good condition.

1947

$200-300 HC

Captain America Comics #4, by Timely Comics, cream to off-white pages, Alex Schomburg cover, Simon and Kirby artwork, fine condition.

1941

$800-1,000 HC

A
B
C
D
E
F
G
H
I
J
K
L
M
N
O
P
Q
R
S
T
U
V
W
XYZ

Walt Disney's Comics and Stories #1 Rare Star Copy, by Dell, off-white pages.

Note the black star printed at the spine, to the left of "Walt".

1940

$1,200-1,800   HC

'Dandy Comics' #1, by EC Comics, off-white pages, very good condition.

1947

$120-180   HC

'Daredevil Comics' #1, by Lev Gleason's Comic House, off-white pages, with Hitler cover, near mint condition.

1941

$7,000-9,000   HC

'Detective Comics' #53, by DC Comics, with double cover and off-white to white pages, very fine condition.

1941

$550-650   HC

'Detective Comics' #66, by DC Comics, off-white to white pages, origin and first appearance of Two-Face, near mint condition.

1942

$1,000-1,500   HC

'Green Lantern' #8, by DC Comics, very good condition.

1961

$40-60   HC

'The Incredible Hulk' #2, by Marvel Comics, white pages, Jack Kirby and Steve Ditko artwork, fine condition.

1962

$450-550   HC

'Dick Tracy Monthly' #1, by Dell Comics, first issue, inside cover edges are tan, fine condition.

1948

$120-180   HC

'Flash Comics' #21, by DC Comics, off-white pages, staples cleaned, with classic Hawkman cover, very fine condition.

1941

$550-650   HC

'The Incredible Hulk' #1, by Marvel Comics, off-white to white pages, fine condition.

This premiere issue features the origin and first appearance of the Hulk by Jack Kirby. It is one of the most sought after of all the Marvel Silver Age keys, and one of the toughest to find in any condition.

1962

$2,200-2,800   HC

COMICS

'The Incredible Hulk' #6, by Marvel Comics, off-white to white pages, all Steve Ditko artwork in this issue, very good condition.

1963

$250-300 HC

'Mad' #1, by EC Comics, cream to off-white pages, very fine condition.

1952

$1,800-2,200 HC

Mad #18, by EC Comics, good condition, centrefold and next page detached from top staple, water stains.

1954

$30-40 HC

'Marvel Mystery Comics' #55, by Timely Comics, off-white to white pages, cover and centerfold detached, Schomburg cover, good condition.

1944

$120-180 HC

'Marvel Super-Heroes' #1, by Marvel Comics, fine condition.

1966

$20-25 HC

'Silver Surfer' issues #1, #4, #5 and #14, by Marvel Comics.

1968

$350-450 HC

'The Amazing Spider-Man' #1, by Marvel Comics, Winnipeg pedigree, white pages, very fine condition.

1963

$10,000-15,000 HC

'The Amazing Spider-Man' #17, Marvel, good condition, water damage.

1964

$55-65 HC

'The Amazing Spider-Man' #13, Marvel, very good condition.

1964

$80-120 HC

'The Amazing Spider-Man' #2, Marvel, white pages, very fine condition.

This is the first appearance of the Vulture and the Terrible Tinkerer, with a Steve Ditko cover and artwork.

1963

$1,500-2,000 HC

A papier-mâché plate, commemorating the coronation of Queen Victoria.

1838   *8in (20.5cm) diam*

$60-100   **OACC**

A rare Prince Albert memorial earthenware plate, printed in brown with a profile portrait within a paneled border depicting the achievements of his reign, rim chipped, restored, printed with "published by J.T. Close".

c1862   *11in (28cm) diam*

$300-400   **HamG**

An octagonal earthenware "Balance of Payments" plate, made for Queen Victoria's Golden Jubilee.

This plate was made to commemorate the Golden Jubilee of Queen Victoria and illustrates the Commonwealth by means of a map of the world on two globes in the bottom center of the plate. The plate also cites the figures in 1885 (although this plate was produced in 1887) for the population (303,347,924) and total area of the British Empire (9,101,699 miles). It also shows the total value of imports (£390,18,569) and exports (£295,967,583). These plates were produced in large numbers but it is rare to find one in mint condition today.

1887   *9.5in (27cm) high*

$180-220   **H&G**

An octagonal Golden Jubilee earthenware plate, printed in black with Victoria's portrait, chips to rim.

9.75in (24.5cm) diam

$70-100   **HamG**

A Doulton earthenware beaker, made to commemorate Queen Victoria's Golden Jubilee.

1887   *3.75in (9.5cm) high*

$180-220   **H&G**

A Coalport Diamond Jubilee plate, printed in blue with the standing figure of Victoria within a border naming dominions of the British Empire, rim cracks, green printed mark.

10.5in (26.5cm) wide

$80-120   **HamG**

A Doulton bone china plate, made to commemorate Queen Victoria's Diamond Jubilee.

1897   9in (22.5cm) high

$200-250   **H&G**

A Royal Worcester bone china plate, made to commemorate Queen Victoria's Golden Jubilee.

1887   10.5in (27cm) diam

$180-220   **H&G**

An Aynsley bone china mug, made to commemorate Queen Victoria's Diamond Jubilee.

1897   3in (7.5cm) high

$200-250   **H&G**

A Doulton earthenware mug, made to commemorate Queen Victoria's Diamond Jubilee.

1897   3.25in (8.5cm) high

$150-200   **H&G**

An earthenware beaker, made for Queen Victoria's Diamond Jubilee and presented by Sir Henry Doulton.

1897   3.75in (9.5cm) high

$200-300   **H&G**

A Copeland earthenware mug, made to commemorate Queen Victoria's Diamond Jubilee.

1897   3in (8cm) high

$180-220   **H&G**

A Doulton three-handled vase, made to commemorate Queen Victoria's Diamond Jubilee.

1897   6.5in (16.5cm) high

$400-600   **H&G**

A Copeland earthenware jug, made to commemorate Queen Victoria's Diamond Jubilee.

1897   6.25in (16cm) high

$320-380   **H&G**

A Doulton earthenware silver rim jug, made to commemorate the coronation of Edward VII.

1902 *7.5in (19cm) high*

$400-450 **H&G**

A Radford bone china mug, made to commemorate the coronation of Edward VII.

1902 *3in (7.5cm) high*

$80-120 **H&G**

A Crown Staffordshire bone china jug, for Thomas Goode, made to commemorate the coronation of Edward VII, from a limited edition of 500.

Thomas Goode Ltd, founded in 1827, is a well known retailer of ceramics and holder of the Royal Warrant, located in Mayfair, London.

1902

$700-1,000 **H&G**

A Bros bone china mug, made to commemorate the coronation of Edward VII.

Most of these mugs are dated 26th June, the planned date for the coronation. Before this date, Edward was struck down with appendicitis and the coronation was delayed until August 9th. Those items that display both dates or the August postponement will usually command a premium.

1902 *3.25in (8.5cm) high*

$150-200 **H&G**

A pair of Wedgwood plates, made to commemorate the coronation of Edward VII.

1902 *10.25in (26cm) diam*

$400-600 **H&G**

An Royal Doulton earthenware mug, made to commemorate the coronation of George V.

1911 *3.25in (8.5cm) high*

$80-120 **H&G**

An earthenware pub advertising jug, with "Ask for Worthington in a Bottle" printed on the side, made to commemorate the coronation of George V.

1911 *4.75in (12cm) high*

$150-200 **H&G**

COMMEMORATIVE WARE

An Aynsley bone china mug, made for the coronation of King George V.

1911   2.75in (7.5cm) high

$80-120   **H&G**

A Royal Doulton bone china plate, made to commemorate the coronation of George V.

      10.25in (26cm) diam

$150-200   **H&G**

An earthenware vase, made to commemorate the Allies during World War I.

1914-16   8.25in (21cm) high

$150-200   **H&G**

An Aynsley bone china beaker, made to commemorate the Silver Jubilee of George V.

1935   4in (10cm) high

$80-120   **H&G**

A Wedgwood creamware beaker, made to commemorate the Silver Jubilee of George V.

1935   4.5in (11.5cm) high

$100-150   **H&G**

A Mason's earthenware jug, made to commemorate the Silver Jubilee of George V.

1935   6.75in (19.5cm) high

$350-400   **H&G**

A Radfords Crown China loving cup, to commemorate the coronation of Edward VIII.

1936-37   3.25in (8cm) diam

$70-100   **OACC**

A Crown Ducal earthenware mug, designed by Charlotte Rhead, made for the proposed coronation of Edward VIII.

1936-37   4.75in (12cm) high

$200-250   **H&G**

A Royal Doulton bone china beaker, with a green ground, made to commemorate the proposed coronation of Edward VIII.

1936-1937   3.75in (9.5cm) h

$300-500   **H&G**

A Coalport cobalt-blue bone china plate, made to commemorate the coronation of George VI.

1937   9.5in (24cm) diam

$200-300   **H&G**

A Wedgwood earthenware mug, designed by Eric Ravilious, made to commemorate the proposed coronation of Edward VIII.

Eric Ravilious (1903-1942) was a well-known and influential designer and book illustrator, often using wood block designs. He was lost at war whilst acting as an official war artist during World War II.

1936   4in (10cm) high

$800-1,200   **H&G**

A Royal Doulton bone china mug, with G-handle, made to commemorate the coronation of George VI.

1937   3.25in (8.5cm) high

$220-280   **H&G**

A Hammersly bone china mug, made to commemorate the coronation of George VI.

1937   3in (8cm) high

$80-120   **H&G**

A Pountney & Company Ltd earthenware mug, made to commemorate the coronation of George VI.

1937   4.25in (11cm) high

$80-120   **H&G**

A Fieldings Crown Devon earthenware musical "super jug", made to commemorate the coronation of George VI.

1937   11.75in (30cm) high

$2,500-3,000   **H&G**

A small Paragon china plate, made to commemorate the coronation of George VI, printed and over-enameled with "The Royal Coat of Arms" within an inscribed border, printed marks.

1937   8.75in (22cm) diam

$60-100   **HamG**

An English transfer-printed mug, made to commemorate the coronation of King George VI.

1937   3.5in (9cm) high

$30-50   **PC**

A Wedgwood green band earthenware mug, designed by Eric Ravilious, made to commemorate the coronation of George VI.

1937   *4in (10cm) high*

$800-1,200   **H&G**

A Wedgwood blue band earthenware mug, designed by Eric Ravilious, made to commemorate the coronation of King George VI.

1937   *4in (10cm) high*

$600-1,000   **H&G**

A Royal Doulton loving cup, made to commemorate the 80th birthday of Queen Elizabeth the Queen Mother.

1980   *3.75in (9.5cm) diam*

$30-50   **OACC**

A Spode bone china mug, made to commemorate the 80th birthday of H.M. Queen Elizabeth the Queen Mother.

1980   *3.5in (9cm) high*

$50-80   **H&G**

A Caverswall bone china loving cup, made to commemorate the 80th birthday of H.M. Queen Elizabeth the Queen Mother and the 50th birthday of Princess Margaret, from a limited edition of 100.

1980   *3.5in (9cm) high*

$100-150   **H&G**

A Spode for Mulberry Hall bone china plate, made to commemorate the 80th birthday of H.M. Queen Elizabeth the Queen Mother, from a limited edition of 1,000.

1980   *10.5in (27cm) diam*

$80-120   **H&G**

A Royal Crown Derby bone china loving cup, made to commemorate the 90th birthday of H.M. Queen Elizabeth the Queen Mother, from a limited edition of 500.

1990   *3in (7.5cm) high*

$320-380   **H&G**

A Coalport bone china plate, made to commemorate the 90th birthday of H.M. Queen Elizabeth the Queen Mother, from a limited edition of 5,000.

1990   *10.5in (27cm) diam*

$100-150   **H&G**

A Caverswall bone china plate, made to commemorate the 90th birthday of H.M. Queen Elizabeth the Queen Mother, from a limited edition of 250.

1990   *10.75in (27.5cm) diam*

$100-150   **H&G**

A Bradmere House bone china mug, made to commemorate the 99th birthday of H.M. Queen Elizabeth the Queen Mother, from a limited edition of 99.

1999   *3.5in (9cm) high*

$40-60   **H&G**

A Caverswall bone china lionhead beaker, made to commemorate the 100th birthday of H.M. Queen Elizabeth the Queen Mother, from a limited edition of 500.

2000   *4.25in (11cm) high*

$50-80   **H&G**

A Chown bone china mug, made to commemorate the 101st birthday of H.M. Queen Elizabeth the Queen Mother, from a limited edition of 70.

2001   *3.75in (9.5cm) high*

$80-120   **H&G**

A Caverswall bone china lionhead beaker, made to commemorate the life *in memoriam* of H.M. Queen Elizabeth the Queen Mother, from a limited edition of 2002.

2002   *4.25in (11cm) high*

$40-60   **H&G**

A Salisbury bone china mug, made to commemorate the coronation of Queen Elizabeth II.

1953   *3in (7.5cm) diam*

$20-30   **OACC**

A china mug, made to commemorate the coronation of Queen Elizabeth II, illegible mark, ink stains inside.

1953   *3.25in (8cm) diam*

$15-25   **OACC**

A Royal Doulton bone china beaker, made to commemorate the coronation of Queen Elizabeth II.

1953   *4in (10cm) high*

$50-80   **H&G**

An English transfer-printed mug, made to commemorate the Silver Jubilee of Queen Elizabeth II.

1977   *3.25in (8.5cm) high*

$10-15   **PC**

An Aynsley mug, made to commemorate the Silver Jubilee of Queen Elizabeth II, with a list of the kings and queens of England on the reverse.

1977   *3.25in (8.5cm) diam*

$40-60   **OACC**

A Wedgwood print band earthenware mug, designed by Eric Ravilious, made to commemorate the coronation of Queen Elizabeth II.

Ravilious was dead by this time, but Wedgwood resurrected his 1936-37 design for the coronation. This piece is worth less as it was produced after the designer had died.

1953   *4in (10cm) high*

$270-330   **H&G**

An earthenware "Ajax" mug, made to commemorate the Silver Jubilee of Queen Elizabeth II.

1977   3.25in (8.5cm) high

$30-50   **H&G**

An Ovaltine pottery earthenware mug, for Woman's Own magazine to commemorate the Silver Jubilee of Queen Elizabeth II.

These mugs were sent to women who had had a baby in Silver Jubilee week.

1977   4.5in (11.5cm) high

$30-50   **H&G**

A large Wedgwood earthenware mug, made to commemorate the Silver Jubilee of Queen Elizabeth II.

1977   4.5in (11.5cm) high

$30-50   **H&G**

A Sunderland China for the Royal Collection bone china lionhead beaker, made to commemorate the Golden Jubilee of H.M. Queen Elizabeth II, from a limited edition of 2,500.

2002   4.75in (12cm) high

$60-100   **H&G**

A Royal Doulton earthenware loving cup, made to commemorate the Queen's Silver Jubilee, from a limited edition of 250.

1977   10in (26cm) high

$1,200-1,800   **H&G**

A large Wedgwood earthenware mug, made to commemorate the investiture of Prince Charles.

1969   4.75in (12cm) high

$40-60   **H&G**

A Royal Worcester mug, made to commemorate the marriage of Prince Charles and Lady Diana Spencer.

1981   3.25in (8cm) diam

$30-40   **OACC**

A Rye Pottery hand-painted half-pint tankard, made to commemorate the Golden Jubilee of H.M. Queen Elizabeth II.

2002   3.75in (9.5cm) high

$30-50   **H&G**

A Denby mug, made to commemorate the marriage of Prince Charles and Lady Diana Spencer.

1981　　　　　　*3.5in (9cm) diam*

$20-30　　　　　　**OACC**

An Elizabethan Bone China royal commemorative mug, the marriage of Prince Charles and Lady Diana Spencer.

1981

$20-30　　　　　　**OACC**

A Spode bone china mug, made to commemorate the wedding of Prince Charles to Lady Diana Spencer.

1981　　　　　　*3.5in (9cm) high*

$50-80　　　　　　**H&G**

A Kiln Cottage Pottery earthenware teapot, made to commemorate the wedding of Prince Charles to Lady Diana Spencer.

1981　　　　　　*6.75in (17.5cm) high*

$200-250　　　　　　**H&G**

A Kevin Francis 'Charles and Diana' Spitting Image mug, from a limited edition of 350.

$80-120　　　　　　**PSA**

A bone china mug, by Chown, to commemorate the divorce of the Prince and Princess of Wales, limited edition of 150.

1996　　　　　　*4in (10.5cm) high*

$80-120　　　　　　**H&G**

An Aynsley footed bowl, made to commemorate the marriage of Princess Anne and Captain Mark Phillips.

1973　　　　　　*5.5in (14cm) diam*

$30-40　　　　　　**OACC**

A B C D E F G H I J K L M N O P Q R S T U V W X Y Z

COMMEMORATIVE WARE

A Buffalo Pottery blue-on-white George Washington pitcher, Stuarts' portrait of Washington and Mt. Vernon, some staining at rim, retains much of its original gilded lip decoration.

c1910 7.5in (19cm) diam

£300-400 TWC

A Caverswall bone china lion head beaker, made to commemorate the birth of Prince William.

This mug was a limited edition of 1,000.

1982 4.5in (11.5cm) high

$70-100 H&G

A Coalport bone china mug, made to commemorate the bestowing of the title 'Princess Royal' on H.R.H. Princess Anne, from a limited edition of 2,000.

1987 3in (7.5cm)

$60-100 H&G

A royal commemorative mug, celebrating the birth of Prince William. Made for the National Trust by Cardigan Pottery.

Following the Princess of Wales' death, commemorative wares related to her children are now a growing collecting area.

1982 3in (8cm) diam

$30-40 OACC

An Aynsley small bone china loving cup, made to commemorate the birth of Prince Henry.

1984 2.25in (6cm) high

$70-100 H&G

A bone china mug, made to commemorate Buckingham Palace.

1996 2.75in (7cm) high

$30-40 H&G

A Chown bone china loving cup, made to commemorate the life *in memoriam* of H.R.H. Princess Margaret, from a limited edition of 70.

2002 2.75in (7cm) high

$70-100 H&G

A bone china mug, to commemorate in memoriam, H.R.H. Princess Margaret.

Only a very small number of these mugs were commissioned.

2002 3.5in (9cm) high

$40-60 H&G

DOG COLLARS

- ▦ Rare dog collars dating from the 15th century to the 18th century are usually made from iron and bear spikes as they were designed to protect the vulnerable throats of hunting dogs from attacks by wolves and boars, as much as to restrain them.
- ▦ German and Austrian collars are more richly made than British ones. They are usually made from ornately engraved and embossed precious metals and lined with fabrics and were as much a display of the wealth and status of the owner as utilitarian items.
- ▦ 19th century dog collars are generally less ornate than earlier examples and are made from silver or brass with rolled edges to prevent chafing. They commonly bear engraved names or wording used for identification.
- ▦ Collars often bear the popular decorative motifs of the period they were made in, which helps when dating them.
- ▦ Dog collars are often misidentified as slave or prison collars, which are much scarcer.
- ▦ There is a comprehensive collection of historic dog collars at Leeds Castle, Kent, England.

A plated chain link dog collar, with rectangular panel and initials M.R.

$150-200   **LFA**

A plated chain link dog collar, with rectangular panel inscribed 'J Usher, Keynsham'.

$150-200   **LFA**

A mid 19th century plated and leather bound dog collar, with plaque inscribed 'Won by Dick at Birmingham, in a sweepstakes, 12 rats each, dogs of all weight, Nov. 10'.

1852   *3.75in (9.5cm) diam*

$800-1,200   **LFA**

A brass dog collar, with a panel inscribed 'John Jones,' and bearing the date 1847, flanked by chain link panels.

$1,000-1,500   **LFA**

A plated chain link dog collar, with rectangular panel with initials M.R.

$150-200   **LFA**

A 19th century brass plain dog collar, with padlock.

5.5in (13.5cm) diam

$200-300   **LFA**

A brass dog collar, with padlock and inscribed 'W. Smith, Rushenden,' within a scroll band.

4.5in (11cm) diam

$400-500   **LFA**

A 19th century plated dog collar, with leather mounts, inscribed 'J. F. Fell, Kilburn Wells'.

5in (13cm) diam

$350-400   **LFA**

An unusual 19th century white metal cat collar, inscribed 'Tiny Tim'.

3in (8cm) diam

$400-600   **LFA**

EPHEMERA

EPHEMERA

- Ephemera is the collective term for many different types of printed or handwritten objects, usually on paper or card, that were made for specific, often short term, purposes and discarded thereafter. This includes Valentine and Christmas cards, postcards, trade cards, catalogs, invitations, calendars and all forms of paper advertising and packaging.

- Condition of ephemera is very important. As they are primarily made from paper or card, damage can easily occur over the years. This includes tears, creases, crumples and folds, missing portions and tatty edges. All of these factors will affect the value of a piece detrimentally. Some level of discoloration is to be expected, but fading and stains are to be considered seriously.

- Storing of ephemera is important to protect the often delicate paper or card. This is best done in acid free card, paper or high quality plastic folders. Keep ephemera away from strong light, both natural and artificial as this will fade and discolor pieces and can make them more brittle. Damp conditions are unsuitable.

- Always handle ephemera with clean hands and keep ink and other substances that may stain them away from it. Never trace or write on ephemera, or stick "Post-It" notes or other adhesives on pieces as this can stain and discolor them.

An English Valentine, with embossed lace paper, with a hand-painted silk center of flowers and hand-colored circle.

c1855   6.75in (17cm) high

$80-120   **PC**

An English Valentine, with embossed lace paper and background of silk netting, silk and linen flowers and leaves and hand-painted flowers, maker unknown.

1850-1860

$70-100   **PC**

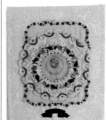

A gold and white English Valentine, with embossed lace paper, silk background and gold die-cuts with hand-colored die-cut flowers.

c1855   10in (25.5cm) high

$270-330   **QUAD**

An English Valentine, on unusual lace paper with background of silk-mesh and hand-painted flowers, dated, slight fading.

1851

$120-180   **PC**

An English Valentine, with embossed lace paper, with cut-out on silk background, the main body of work in a heart-shaped frame.

c1855   6.75in (17cm) high

$100-150   **QUAD**

An English Valentine, with embossed lace paper, with hand-painted die-cut detail, by Wood.

c1855   6.75in (17cm) high

$100-150   **PC**

An English Valentine, made with rare embossed lace paper, unusually decorated underneath silk gauze, hand-painted with flowers, fruit, shells, leaves and feathers, with gilt-edged flags showing "Constancy will Triumph", and "Love is my Shareland", by Dobbs Bailey & Company.

c1855

$350-400   **PC**

An English Valentine, with superb embossed lace paper of the finest quality, with hand-colored die-cut flowers and leaves, by Kershaw & Sons.

6.75in (17cm) high

$100-150   **PC**

An English Valentine, with embossed lace paper and original hand coloring, made by Dobbs & Company.

c1855   5.25in (13.5cm) h

$70-100   **PC**

VALENTINE CARDS

An unusual English Valentine, with embossed lace paper, silk background and hand-colored die-cut flowers, silk leaves and glass stones, maker unknown.

c1855 6.75in (17cm) high

$270-330 PC

A pair of Valentine poetry booklets, written by English Valentine writers, in mint condition.

c1840-50 7in (17.5cm) high

£200-300 (each) QUAD

A German Biedermeier friendship Valentine card, with gold leaf die-cuts and original hand-coloring, made in Dresden, Germany.

c1820 3.25in (8.5cm) w

$650-750 QUAD

A German Biedermeier friendship Valentine card, with gold leaf die-cuts and original hand-coloring, made in Dresden, Germany.

c1820 3.25in (8.5cm) w

$500-800 QUAD

- The first references to tokens given on Valentine's Day can be dated to the 15th and 16th centuries, in Samuel Pepys' famous 'Diary' (although these were mainly trinkets) and in documents describing the giving of religious 'devotional' tokens at various events throughout the year. These were intricately cut from paper and it is perhaps from here that the exquisitely cut paper cards of the 19th century date.

- Most handmade Valentine's tokens made during this period show high levels of craftsmanship. In America, German immigrants introduced 'fraktur' (paper designs using German imagery and lettering) and 'scherenschnitte' (paper cutting).

- Paper making methods soon began to improve and by 1834, techniques for creating designs in impressed open work 'lace' paper had been developed which remained popular until the 1860s. Cards of this period were beautiful, often finished by hand with gilt, painted and cut decoration using different silks, lace, ribbons and card as materials.

- As the Industrial Revolution spread in Europe and the USA, people spent less time making cards. Chromolithographic images also took over from the intricate lace-like cards, with colored Victorian 'die-cut' scraps and heavy layers becoming popular.

An English Valentine, with embossed lace paper and a cut-out of a lady with a gauze and silk overskirt, original hand-coloring and an unusual blue border, maker unknown.

c1855 6.75in (17cm) high

$100-150 QUAD

An early English Valentine, printed and with original hand-coloring, published by A. Park, Leonard Street, London.

c1840 10in (25.5cm) high

$180-220 PC

An early wood-cut comic Valentine card, depicting a cricketer with original hand-coloring.

c1840 7in (18cm) high

$70-100 QUAD

A comic Valentine, with inscription "All the way from Manchester and got no work to do".

c1840 7in (18cm) high

$50-80 PC

An English Valentine, with embossed lace paper, showing glove motif, with silvered die-cut leaves.

Gloves have been given as a token of love since the late 16th century.

c1855 6.75in (17cm) wide

$180-220 PC

A very rare early English chromolithographic Valentine, printed in color by F. Scherick, Edinburgh, published by B.F. Lloyd & Co., Edinburgh, drawn by Adolf Schrodler.

c1850 10in (25.5cm) high

$350-400 PC

FIND OUT MORE...

Robert Brenner, 'Valentine Treasury: A Century of Valentine Cards', published by Schiffer Publishing, 2000.

Katherine Kreider, 'One Hundred Years of Valentines', published by Schiffer Publishing, 1999.

An unusual English Valentine, showing a galleon in sail.

c1840 10in (25.5cm) h

$320-380 PC

EPHEMERA

CHRISTMAS CARDS

- Although handwritten messages of best wishes have been sent at Christmas time to family and friends for many centuries, it was not until 1843 that the Christmas card was first used.

- Sir Henry Cole, the first director of London's Victoria & Albert Museum, wanted to save time sending best wishes to his family, friends and acquaintances. Rather than use festively decorated headed paper for personalized messages, he commissioned John Calcott Horsley, a member of the Royal Academy, to design and produce a lithographed card, of which 1,000 copies were produced, the spare copies being sold in a shop.

- Sending messages this way soon caught on and was aided by the introduction of the 'Penny Post' in 1840, allowing letters to be sent anywhere for one penny. 1844 saw another card being produced, by W.C.T. Dobson, symbolizing the 'Spirit of Christmas'.

- By the 1850s, improved color lithographic printing processes allowed colored cards to be produced inexpensively. The 1880s saw millions of cards sold as the fashion took hold and the industry grew, with cards being sold in tobacconists, toy and other shops.

- Cards produced during the 1860s to 1890 are the most commonly found and present great variety to the collector. Cards can have delicate cut edges or designs, embossed patterns and the addition of materials such as silk.

A Christmas card, by Ernest Nister, printed in Bavaria.

c1890   4.5in (11.5cm) high

$15-18   **PC**

A Christmas card, depicting Pierrot seated on snowball, by Raphael Tuck & Sons.

c1890   4.75in (12cm)

$15-18   **PC**

An English chromolithographic Christmas card, by Raphael Tuck & Sons.

c1890   5.25in (13.5cm) high

$10-15   **PC**

A Christmas card, with three babies, published by Hagelbrag, Berlin.

c1890   5in (13cm) high

$15-18   **PC**

A fine chromolithographic Christmas card, by Shidesheimer & Company.

c1890   6in (15cm) high

$15-18   **QUAD**

A De la Rue Christmas card, showing a woman with a candle, looking at the moon.

De La Rue, founded by Thomas de La Rue in London, England in 1821 are also very well known for printing British stamps from 1855 and various banknotes from 1860 as well as for making the famous 'Onoto' range of fountain pens. As one would expect from a company that printed money and stamps, the quality of lithography, and printing in general, is very high with sophisticated and very well colored pieces.

c1895   2.75in (7cm) high

$10-15   **QUAD**

An unusual moveable Christmas card, showing girls with pigs.

c1890   4.25in (11cm) high

$20-30   **QUAD**

A die-cut English Christmas card, dated.

1892   5in (12.5cm) high

$15-18   **QUAD**

Two early English moveable Christmas cards, by Goodall.

c1870   4.75in (12cm) high

$50-80 each   **PC**

An unusual pull-out Christmas card of a dog.

c1890   4in (10cm) high

$15-25   **QUAD**

An unusual die-cut English Christmas card, depicting a robin, by Ernest Nister.

c1895   4.75in (12cm) h

$15-25   **PC**

An unusual early chromolithographic Christmas card, in four parts.

c1870   4in (10cm) high

$40-60   **PC**

An unusual German die-cut card, printed in England, dated.

1891   4.25in (11cm) high

$20-30   **PC**

An unusual die-cut Christmas card, depicting a policeman.

c1890   4.25in (11cm) high

$12-18   **QUAD**

LITHOGRAPHY & CHROMOLITHOGRAPHY

■ Lithography (from the Greek 'lithos' for 'stone') was developed in Germany by Aloys Senefelder in 1798 and spread to other parts of Europe and the USA over the following 20 years. A design is drawn on the surface of a highly polished stone using a grease 'lithographic' crayon. Where the crayon adheres to the stone, the ink also adheres so that when the stone is pressed onto paper, the design is transferred in ink.

■ Chromolithography uses many colors rather than a single color. For every color used a new stone is drawn up. Providing the paper remains at the same 'register' or positioning, each stone with a different color is successively pressed down, resulting in a multi-colored image.

■ It was developed during the 1840s and popularized during the 1860s. The most successful American chromolithographer was Louis Prang, who produced scenes of Civil War battles as well as reproductions of art works.

■ The development of chromolithography allowed the production of many intricately designed and colored cards.

■ Cards from the 1870s onwards tend to lose the simplicity of color that is found in earlier cards and are very heavily colored with great detail.

An unusual set of four embossed chromolithographic cards, with various fruits, each with the image of a child inset, made for any occasion with no wording.

c1880   5in (12.5cm) high

$50-80   **PC**

A set of three award winning cards, for "Exposition Palais d'Industrie", Champs Elysées, Paris, by Raphael Tuck & Sons.

1882

$50-80   **PC**

An unusual die-cut card, in the form of a tambourine with cat.

c1895

$12-18   **QUAD**

A moveable card, in the form of a posy of flowers, the flowers lift up to show the greeting inside.

c1865

$180-220   **QUAD**

An unusual chromolithographic Lifeboat card, sold in aid of the National Lifeboat Institute for the Christmas season.

c1895   6.75in (17cm) w

$50-80   **QUAD**

A rare moveable card, from Germany, die-cut with cherubs in a tree and two lovers on a park bench.

Moving parts can be damaged in themselves, but also cause wear to the surrounding area. Condition is imperative, with damaged and worn cards being worth much less.

c1870

$320-380   **QUAD**

An unusual German moveable card, in the form of a table, made for the English market.

c1870

$350-400   **QUAD**

An unusual moveable peep-show appearance card.

These cards are particularly prone to damage due to their delicate nature. Although they fold flat, protruding elements and folds can easily be damaged. Collectors should look for examples in the best condition with strong, vibrant colors and intact details. Damage will reduce value.

c1865

$220-280   **QUAD**

TRADE CARDS

- Trade cards were used to advertise the services or products of tradesmen and manufacturers. The earliest cards date from the early 17th century and were used in London, but these are extremely rare.
- The woodcut or letterpress method was used to print very early trade cards until copperplate engraving was introduced in the 18th century. Printing during this period was still monochrome.
- Cards often contained complicated graphic designs, in ornate script with detailed lettering, or in block letters with simple designs. Illustrations and motifs of the products or services offered were also incorporated. If the maker held a Royal Warrant this would also be proudly displayed. Names would usually take a prominent position.
- Custom-made cards were printed specifically for individual tradesmen but cards with standardized designs and blank spaces for a tradesman's stamp were also available and are often known as 'stock cards'.
- The spread of color lithography in 1870 led to a boom in advertising. Companies began manufacturing their own cards for products and there was a decline in trade cards for individual tradesmen. Late Victorian advertising cards are more readily available and affordable than earlier trade cards.

A trade card, for Robert Vincent, scale maker, "At the Hand and Scales on London Bridge the Second Door from the Bear Tavern".

Robert Vincent, the scale maker worked from 1751 until 1793, based mainly around the Southwark area of London. The address listed on this card is his earliest known location.

c1751   6.25in (16cm) high

$2,200-2,800   **PJC**

A trade card for Thomas Ripley & Co., scientific instrument makers.

Thomas Ripley is listed as working as a maker of scientific and optical instruments from 1765-1790.

c1760

$2,500-3,000   **PJC**

A trade card, for John Grant, son of the late Mrs. Ann Pitman, a brushmaker, the shop was on London Bridge.

The shops on London Bridge were demolished in the 1750s.

c1750   7in (18cm) high

$1,800-2,200   **PJC**

A trade card, for Maydwell & Windles of London, cut glass works.

1751-1778 11.25in (28.5cm) h

$3,000-4,000   **PJC**

A trade card, for Jacques Songy, instrument maker, made with a plate dating from c1690, overprinted with new wording and dated in 1732.

$1,200-1,800 QUAD

A trade card, for Henry Hastings, night-watchman.

c1745   9.75in (25cm) high

$1,800-2,200   PJC

A trade card, for Richard Hand, "The oldest original Chelsea bun maker", by William Hogarth, dated.

1718   8.75in (22cm) high

$1,800-2,200   QUAD

A trade card, for Thomas Norris, gold chain and swivel maker, trimmed.

c1720   6.25in (16cm) high

$800-1,200   PJC

A trade card, for Harrison, Norwich, saddler and harness maker.

1800-1810   3.5in (9cm) high

$180-220   QUAD

A trade card for Blair & Company, makers of guns and pistols, printed in blue.

c1790   4.5in (11.5cm) h

$400-600   QUAD

A trade card, for Le Blond & Company, engravers, copper platers, lithographic printers, letter press and account book maintainers, London.

c1860   4.5in (11.5cm) wide

$180-220   QUAD

A CLOSER LOOK AT A TRADE CARD

This extremely fine quality trade card was printed with a lithographic stone by R. Martin of 124 High Holborn, London, during the 1830s and is arguably one of the finest cards found. It is not in the usual format of a trade card with the name being hidden within the design and it almost has the appearance of a print rather than an advertising card.

A trade card for J. Southby, artist in fireworks, Vauxhall Gardens, main theater.

c1820   4.5in (11.5cm)

$500-800   QUAD

A trade card for a C.L. Wulcko, manufacturer of tobacco and snuff, Covent Garden.

c1820   3.5in (9cm) wide

$180-220   QUAD

The detail is of extremely high quality, showing an attention to fine detail, with a range of shades and good handling of perspective. The small 'stone plaque' in the center reads 'A SPECIMEN OF INK LITHOGRAPHY FROM R.MARTIN 124 HIGH HOLBORN' revealing that this was a trade card produced by the tradesman himself to display the skill and quality of his work to potential clients.

A trade card, for Thomas Pritchard, a chimney sweep and night-watchman.

c1760

$1,000-1,500   PJC

A trade card, for J. F. Salter, hat maker.

c1790   6in (15cm) high

$1,200-1,800   PJC

Many of the objects depicted have been chosen, not only for their ability to show the virtuosity and skill of the lithographer, but also as they were indicative of popular fashions of the time such as the 'Grand Tour', Palladian and Classical architecture, anatomy and Egypt.

An early lithographic trade card, designed, drawn on stone and printed at the Robert Martin Lithographic Establishment, dated.

1830

$1,800-2,200   PJC

FUNERAL EPHEMERA

- The Victorian period saw the peak of funeral ephemera. The Victorian preoccupation with death, mourning and remembrance is illustrated by their jewelry which includes mourning rings and lockets, often containing the hair of dead relatives. This national sentiment increased further after the death of Queen Victoria's husband, Prince Albert, in 1861.

- Funerals of high profile figures were often public affairs and the Victorian predilection for organization and formal approach to grieving dictated the production of tickets and programs in many instances.

- However, the printing of invitations is not unusual and had been in existence in the 18th century. Invitations were not usually issued publicly, so few were made. As with trade cards, standard designs were offered with blank spaces upon which the specific details could be handwritten or printed.

- Despite this morbid subject matter, this type of ephemera is sought after, with collectors looking for invitations, programs and announcements associated with renowned historical figures and items with fine artwork and printing.

A ticket to the funeral of prime minister Mr. William Pitt, the Younger.
1806   *10.25in (26cm) wide*

$1,000-1,500   **QUAD**

A ticket to the funeral of Sir Joshua Reynolds, by Bartolozzi, dated.
1792   *8.75in (22cm) wide*

$1,800-2,200   **QUAD**

A funeral ticket, for a Mr. Richard Mackleston, dated.
1732   *8.5in (21.5cm) high*

$1,800-2,200   **QUAD**

A blank funeral ticket, also an advertisement for C. Jennings undertakers.
c1740   *9.5in (24cm) wide*

$1,200-1,800   **QUAD**

A ticket to the funeral of Queen Victoria, at St. Paul's Cathedral, with inscription "Admit the Bearer to Service of Solemn Supplication".
1901   *3in (7.5cm) high*

$70-100   **QUAD**

A memorial card, in memory of HRH Prince Albert, embossed by Windsor, on an original black velvet background.
1861-1862 10in (25cm) high

$300-500   **QUAD**

A Queen Victoria memorial card, detailing her death on 22th January 1901 at Osborne House, the Isle of Wight.
1901   *5in (13cm) high*

$20-30   **QUAD**

An advertisement for patent iron coffins, with inscription "Safety for the Dead!".
Metal coffins were made in order to prevent grave robbers. There is an example of this coffin in St Bride's Church, London.
1800-1820 10in (25.5cm) h

$300-500   **PJC**

A page of certificates of proof of burials.
The act for "compelling the burying of corpses in Woollen" was passed in 1679 to help the wool market. All corpses had to be buried in woolen garments.
c1700-1775

$800-1,200 each   **PJC**

A ticket for the coronation of William IV and Queen Adelaide, at Westminster Abbey.

Despite the importance of the event and the richly ornate decoration on comparable tickets to coronations, this ticket is extremely plain. The reason for this was that William was shocked by the expense and extravagance of his brother's coronation and vowed not to be so lavish with his.

1831

$180-220　　　　　**PJC**

A chromolithographic ticket to the Guildhall for International Municipal Entertainment, by F.J. Fitch, printed with the names of the Lord Mayor and Aldermen of London.

The removable coupon that should have been retained at the Guildhall is intact.

1875　　7.25in (18.5cm) high

$250-300　　　　　**PJC**

A ticket to the Guildhall, for a dinner given by the Lord Mayor, with steel engraving.

1788　　9.5in (24cm) high

$300-500　　　　　**PJC**

An invitation to The Corporation of London, for the inauguration of the Metropolitan Cattle Market, (today Caledonian Market), HRH Prince Albert in attendance.

1855　　11.5in (29.5cm) high

$250-300　　　　　**PJC**

A chromolithographic ticket for a banquet, given by the Lord Mayor, by Blades, East & Blades.

1878　　7.25in (18.5cm) high

$200-250　　　　　**PJC**

A ticket to the Guildhall City of London, in honor of the coronation of Queen Victoria, embossed by Dobbs.

1837　　7.5in (19cm) high

$300-500　　　　　**QUAD**

A ticket for a reception by the City of London, for his Imperial Majesty Alexander II, Emperor of all Russias.

1874　　7in (18cm) high

$300-500　　　　　**PJC**

A ticket for the reception of HRH Prince of Wales, to celebrate his return home from India, printed by S.W. Rowsell & Son.

1876　　8.5in (21.5cm) high

$200-250　　　　　**PJC**

A ticket for the "Visit of the National Corporation of London to Epping Forest", with photographs.

An actual photograph is attached to the ticket because there was no way of reproducing photographs until the 1890s.

1875　　8.25in (21cm) high

$180-220　　　　　**PJC**

A benefit ticket, with all the proceeds going to Mr Grimaldi the clown, held at Sadler's Wells, North London.

1813　　3in (7.5cm) high

$400-600　　　　　**PJC**

A Christmas calendar, die-cut in one piece, printed in Germany and made for the Davidson brothers, New York, dated.

1909   13.25in (34cm) high

$80-120   **QUAD**

A broadside advertisement, for the New Vauxhall Gardens, printed by W. Mason.

1826   20in (51cm) high

$1,800-2,200   **PJC**

A broadside detailing Mr. Green's 109th Ascent with his balloon, dated 1832, printed by T. Wilson, Whitehaven.

It is unusual to find such a high quality of printing outside London during this period. Memorabilia relating to ballooning is extremely popular amongst a band of devoted collectors and can fetch very high prices. Ballooning was very popular in the late 18th century when, as well as being followed and developed seriously by its early proponents, it almost became a 'sport' for aristocratic adventurers. It was also popular through the 19th century, with pieces from the 18th and early 19th centuries tending to be the most popular and, due to their scarcity, fetching high prices when offered. Mr Charles Green (1785-1870) the aeronaut, ascended in his balloon for the 109th time on 29th August 1832 at Whitehaven. His balloon was 100 feet in circumference and was made of alternate panels of crimson and gold silk cloth.

An advertisement for a cricket match, Northampton Arms, Islington, dated Tuesday October 6th.

1846   15.75in (40cm) high

$2,000-3,000   **PJC**

An advertisement for the grand opening of the Argyll Rooms, (what is today the Trocodero), lithograph by Day & Sons, proprietor R.R. Bignell.

1850   16.25in (41cm) high

$1,000-1,500   **PJC**

1832   19.75in (50cm) high

$1,800-2,200   **QUAD**

An unusual advertisement for a cricket match, in two-color printing.

It is rare to find two-color printing at this date.

1854   15in (38cm) high

$1,800-2,200   **PJC**

An unusual advert for Rimmel's perfumed Valentines, showing the range of Valentines and prices, dated.

Rimmel are still making cosmetics today.

1871

$40-60   **PC**

An advertising leaflet, for the Lumiere Cinematograph's first screening before a paying audience, it opened on Regent Street Polytechnik on 20th February.

1896   4.75in (12cm) high

$3,500-4,500   **PJC**

An advertisement for British cinema in Piccadilly Circus.

This was Britain's first attempt at establishing a permanent cinema, after a few weeks it was destroyed by a fire.

1896   8.5in (21.5cm) high

$1,800-2,200   **PJC**

An English fan-shaped calendar, made with coated paper, dated.

1874   *4.5in (10.5cm) high*

$80-120   **QUAD**

Four of a set of twelve German calendar cards, with superb chromolithographic printing, published by Sackett, Wilhelms and Betzig, New York, dated.

1884   *7in (18cm) high*

$300-400 (set)   **PC**

A German calendar, for the "Calendria Antikamnia" Chemical company, USA, depicting macabre skeleton figures, designed in 1899 for the calendar of 1900, made for English, French and German distribution.

1899-1900 10in (25.5cm) high

$400-600   **QUAD**

A skip note, made to look like a bank note and designed to dupe those who could not read into thinking that they were real, with inscriptions "Bank of Folly" and "Fool".

1847   *5in (12.5cm) high*

$180-220   **QUAD**

A skip note, made to look like a bank note and in protest against hanging, by George Cruikshank.

The penalty for producing counterfeit bank notes was death by hanging. Cruikshank campaigned against hanging and was horrified that people, including women, could be hung for passing a false banknote. He designed these skip notes in ironic protest.

1819   *5in (13cm) high*

$320-380   **PJC**

A hairdressing skip note, with inscriptions "promise to cut any lady or gentleman's hair superior to any man in England or forfeit on demand the sum of ten thousand pounds" and "Bank Of Elegance", by C.B. Macalpine.

1823   *5in (12.5cm) high*

$180-220   **QUAD**

POLICE NOTICE.
TO THE OCCUPIER.

On the mornings of Friday, 31st August, Saturday 8th, and Sunday, 30th September, 1888, Women were murdered in or near Whitechapel, supposed by some one residing in the immediate neighbourhood. Should you know of any person to whom suspicion is attached, you are earnestly requested to communicate at once with the nearest Police Station.

A rare leaflet, issued by the police requesting information regarding Jack the Ripper, dated 30th September.

1888   *8.75in (22cm) high*

$300-500   **PJC**

A penny dreadful leaflet, describing the arrest of Dr. Crippen and girlfriend Le Neve aboard the S.S. Montrose, for the brutal murder of his wife.

c1910   *10in (25.5cm) high*

$300-500   **PJC**

THE LONDON MURDER MYSTERY.
Mutilated Body found in a Cellar
Arrest of Crippen & Le Neve On board S.S. Montrose
THE NAUGHTY DOCTOR
The Crippen Diary.

A broadside detailing the murder of Maria Marten. The murderer, William Corder, was later apprehended in Ealing.

The woodblock engraving and hand-coloring make this particular piece very rare.

1828   *18.5in (47cm) high*

$1,800-2,200   **PJC**

A set of three coupons, with the head of George IV, from Atlas newspaper, embossed by Dobbs.

These were the first ever free offers in a publication.

1821   *5in (12.5cm) high*

$300-500   **QUAD**

FIFTIES & SIXTIES

FIFTIES AND SIXTIES

- Collectors should look for pieces that have a strong 'retro' feeling that sums up the period. This can be represented in terms of form or in the decorative motifs used.
- Many new forms were introduced during the period, some with an exaggerated streamlined and 'modern' feel that was inherited from the 1930s. Man-made materials such as vinyl and Dralon were very popular.
- The 1950s also saw the emergence of 'Popular' music, the birth of the teenager as a social and economic force and a move away from the austerity of the post-war years. Color, frivolous motifs and a return to a preoccupation with glamor are some of the hallmarks of the period.
- Popular motifs of the 1950s include diamonds, spades, clubs and hearts from playing cards and 'glamorous' scantily clad ladies posing. Cats were also popular subjects and there are many thousands of ceramic cats available on the market, mostly with elegantly elongated forms.
- Items connected to household names, such as 'I Love Lucy' and stars, musicians and celebrities, are also desirable and often cross collecting fields making them desirable to different collectors.
- Due to the 'throw away' nature of modern society, once styles changed, pieces in then 'old-fashioned' styles were thrown away, meaning selective pieces can be scarce. 'Retro' styles are still currently fashionable and decorating your interiors in a 1950s style is still largely affordable and easy, as well as possibly being a good investment!
- As many items were produced in great numbers, condition is vital to make a piece desirable. Sets should be complete and individual items undamaged as damage will seriously affect value.

A Ridgways 'Homemaker' series plate, transfer-printed, designed by Enid Seeney.

The 'Homemaker' series of tableware is perhaps one of the most recognisable objects from the 1950s. Sold in vast numbers through 'Woolworths', they gave any home an inexpensive, but very fashionable, table setting. As so many were made, they are commonly found now, but are now worth much more than they sold for during the period, if in excellent condition. Both the simple forms and the highly characteristic motifs used sum up the essence of 1950s styling.

c1957 (made to early 1970s)   25.5cm diam

$15-25   FFM

A Ridgways 'Homemaker' series side-plate, transfer-printed, designed by Enid Seeney.

1957-1970s   7in(18cm) diam

$15-18   FFM

A Ridgways 'Homemaker' series trio, transfer-printed, designed by Enid Seeney.

This range was only available with black cups with white interiors.

1957-1970s   7in (18cm) diam

$30-40   FFM

A Ridgways 'Homemaker' series cereal bowl, transfer-printed, designed by Enid Seeney.

1957-1970s 6in (16cm) diam

$15-25   FFM

A Ridgways 'Parisienne' pattern plate, transfer-printed.

c1957   9.75in (25cm) diam

$15-25   FFM

A Ridgways 'Barbeque' pattern meat plate, print and enamel, unnamed designer.

1958   11in (28cm) diam

$20-30   FFM

Four 1950s playing card glasses.

Playing card symbols were highly popular motifs during the 1950s.

4.5in (11.5cm) high

$50-80   MA

A 1950s pin-up girl glass, decorated on both sides with transfers.

4.25in (11cm) high

$20-30   CVS

A stainless steel Danish teapot.
c1965   *5in (13cm) high*

$50-80   **MHT**

A Robert Welch five-piece cruet set, by Old Hall, stamped "Old Hall".
c1965   *7.75in (20cm) wide*

$50-80   **MHT**

Two Robert Welch toast racks, for Old Hall.

Robert Welch first became interested in stainless steel while visiting Scandinavia during the 1950s.

Largest 9.5in (24cm) wide

$30-50   **MHT**

Six Alveston coffee spoons, by Robert Welch (RCA), for Oldhall, in original box, each stamped.
c1963   *4.5in (11.5cm) high*

$70-100   **MHT**

A set of Venus salt and pepper shakers.
c1950   *4in (10cm) high*

$80-120   **SM**

A set of six 1930s Australian pale blue Bakelite kitchen canisters.

A full set of these canisters in blue is extremely rare, although separate pieces are found. Blue is a very sought after color for Bakelite.

Largest 9.5in (24cm) high

$220-280   **MA**

A 1960s serviette holder and salt and pepper set, with reindeer motif.

$8-12   **MA**

A 1950s Prince Pineapple string holder, some damage.

$120-180   **DAC**

An electrical mixer, by Excelsior.
1955

$120-180   **TK**

A Dutch boy laundry sprinkler.

$220-280   **DAC**

A 1950s picnic set, with four settings.
19in (48.5cm) wide

$70-100   **MA**

A 1960s picnic set, with plastic flower motif carrier.

16in (40.5cm) wide

$50-80   **MA**

LADY HEAD VASES

■ 'Lady Head Vases' are rapidly becoming a sought after collectable. The earliest examples from the 1940s are often marked 'Glamour Girl', from which the vases of the 1950s, 1960s and early 1970s derive. However, these early examples are not as stylish or sought after as those from the 1950s. They were made to display flowers and some examples have decorative features such as jewelry and hands with painted nails resting against the faces. The most desirable vases are those modeled on personalities of the period such as Marilyn Monroe, Jackie Kennedy and Lucille Ball. Some are hard to recognise, so refer to a book for guidance.

■ Many 'Lady Head Vases' were made in Japan and the U.S.A. with manufacturers names including 'Napco' or 'Napcoware' (National Potteries Company), Enesco, Relpo, Ruebens and Betty Lou Nichols. In many instances however, the styling of the vase is more important than the maker, so a mark does not necessarily make a vase more valuable.

A 1950s Lady Head Vase.

$100-150   **DAC**

A 1950s Lady Head Vase, marked "INARCO" (registered symbol) on base.

$120-180   **DAC**

A 1950s Lady Head Vase.

$120-180   **DAC**

A 1950s Lady Head Vase.

$30-50   **PC**

A CLOSER LOOK AT A LADY HEAD VASE

This example has delicately rouged cheeks and a good hairstyle. Collectors look for features such as well-modeled and well-painted hair and good quality painting, especially on the 'made-up' face. Also look for applied eyelashes.

The way the head is modeled is also important, with many having an attractive tilt to the head.

Condition is very important. Clean interiors attract a premium, as do examples with no chips to the rim or base and paint that has not crazed or flaked. Colors should be bright and not faded.

The applied flowers that stand out from the body of the vase are another feature that makes this example desirable. They are easily damaged, but the flowers on this example are not. The earrings and 'pearl' necklace are also original and intact.

A 1950s Lady Head Vase.

$120-180   **PC**

A 1940s plaster wall mask.

11in (28cm) high

$70-100   **MA**

A 1940s plaster reproduction face wall mask.

10in (25.5cm) high

$50-80   **MA**

Two 1950s ceramic cat vases and matching fan vase, made in Western Germany.

The fan vase is not as commonly found as the cats.

Fan $40-60, cats $30-50 each MA

A 1950s Pilkingtons ceramic free-form bowl, designed by Mitzi Cunliffe.

10.5in (26.5cm) diam

A 1960s ceramic Siamese cat.
11.5in (29cm) high

$20-30 MA

A 1960s ceramic Siamese cat.
14.5in (36.5cm) high

$40-60 MA

$180-220 REN

A 1950s alabaster vase, with musical theme design.
9.75in (25cm) high

$150-200 V

A Robert Welch candlestick, made from vitreous cast iron at Chipping Campden.
c1964 5.75in (14.5cm) high

$50-80 MHT

A 1950s 'bridge' cigarette lighter and ashtray, made in China.
3.5in (9cm) high

$40-60 MA

A Poul Henningsen PH5 hanging lamp, produced by Louis Poulsen, Denmark, designed 1958, tiered, enameled metal shade with red and blue interior.
c1958 19in (48cm) diam

$500-700 FRE

A Gae Aulenti Pipistrello lamp, designed in 1967, produced by Martinelli-Luce in Italy, with black enameled metal base, telescoping stainless steel shaft and white methacrylate shade, labeled.

36in (91.5cm) high

$1,500-2,000 FRE

A B C D E F G H I J K L M N O P Q R S T U V W XYZ

A 1960s bronze and Baccarat crystal chandelier, with nickeled bronze dome over an illuminated interior with stepped rows of 80 crystal teardrop pendants, stamped "BACCARAT Bronze".

16in (40.5cm) diam

$3,000-4,000   **FRE**

A 1950s Lightolier table lamp, with plastic shade, enameled metal shaft and base.

19in (48cm) high

$400-600   **FRE**

A 1950s table lamp, with plastic shade.

39in (99cm) high

$80-120   **MA**

A rare Fornasetti 'magic' mirror.

c1950 11.75in (30cm) diam

$2,000-2,500   **FM**

A psychedelic pop mirror triptych, two panels with bubble border framing mirror plate, a third panel with 'Saturn Ring'.

Largest 36in (91.5cm) high

$500-700   **FRE**

A pair of Dralon-upholstered and wire constructed dressing table chairs.

31.5in (80cm) high

$60-100   **CA**

A 1950s artist's easel table, by Dennis & Robin Portslade SX D&R products.

This table is rare. The legs are detachable and can be clipped to the base and whole hung from the wall to resemble an artists easel with 'brushes'. This also acts as a useful 'space-saving' device, which was another popular theme during this period.

19.75in (50cm) high

$100-150   **MA**

A 1940s Hoover.

$30-50   **MA**

A Photoplay magazine, featuring Elvis Presley on the cover, November edition.

1962 11.5in (29cm) high

$30-40   **CVS**

A Picture Goer magazine, featuring Sal Mineo on the cover, March edition.

1960 11.75in (30cm) high

$8-12   **CVS**

A Picture Goer magazine, featuring Valerie Alan, March edition.

1957 11.75in (30cm) high

$8-12   **CVS**

A Tit Bits magazine, featuring Zsa Zsa Gabor, January edition.

1954 12.5in (31.5cm) high

$5-8   **CVS**

An 'I Love Lucy' comic no. 18, published by Dell.

1958

$15-25   **HC**

A 1950s 45rmp record case.

The 1950s saw both the explosion of the pop music movement and the emergence of the 'teenager'. For the first time, young people had music aimed specifically at them that was different to other popular music. With freedom growing, teenagers were able to work in their spare time to earn money with which they bought 'singles'. These inexpensively produced, brightly colored bags were produced to store collections, but as they were heavily used and not made to last, many have not survived.

9.5in (24cm) high

$20-30 MA

A 1950s 45rmp case, with a jiving couple.

$30-40 MA

A 1960s 45rmp record case.

7.5in (19cm) high

$20-30 MA

A Bush transistor radio.

1959

$50-80 MA

A radiogram musical cigarette box.

9in (23cm) wide

$40-60 MA

A 1950s pin-up girl lighter.

$10-15 CVS

A 1950s pin-up girl lighter, with box.

$70-100 CVS

An English toffee tin.

c1960 4.25in (11cm) diam

$15-25 DH

A 1950s battery-powered Moon Rocket toy.

The 1960s saw a growing fascination with outer space, which reached its high point with the first man landing on the moon in 1969.

9.5in (24cm) wide

$300-400 DH

A 1960s tin money box, with outer space scene.

4.5in (11.5cm) high

$15-25 DH

A 1950s 'Elvis is King' badge.

1in (2.5cm) diam

$15-25 CVS

A 1950s 'I Love Lucy' badge.

1.75in (4.5cm) diam

$20-30 CVS

A Warner Brothers animation art cel from "Another Froggy Evening", featuring Michigan J. Frog, fourth cel in series, limited edition 673/750, signed by Chuck Jones, with Warner Brothers, Certificate of Authenticity, framed.

1995   *21in (53.5cm) high*

$1,000-1,500   **SI**

A Warner Brothers animation art cel from "Another Froggy Evening", featuring Michigan J. Frog, CJ02-070-006, with Certificate of Authenticity 24238, signed "Chuck Jones 1995 Warner Brothers", framed.

1995   *18in (45.5cm) wide*

$3,000-4,000   **SI**

A Warner Brothers animation art cel, featuring Bugs Bunny as a knight, signed by Chuck Jones, framed.

1980   *19in (48.5cm) wide*

$3,000-4,000   **SI**

A Warner Brothers animation art cel no. 200696, depicting Bugs Bunny, Marvin Martian and a dog hanging from the moon, limited edition 377/500, signed by Chuck Jones, framed.

1998   *21.25in (54cm) high*

$1,500-2,000   **SI**

A Turner Entertainment Company animation art cel no. CJ75-257-007 from "How The Grinch Stole Christmas!", featuring the Grinch carving the "Christmas Beast", with Certificate of Authenticity 17955, signed by Chuck Jones, framed.

1966   *21in (53.5cm) wide*

$3,000-4,000   **SI**

A Turner Entertainment Company animation art cel no. CJ75-332-013 from "How The Grinch Stole Christmas", featuring the Grinch holding onto Max's foot, with Certificate of Authenticity 21412, signed by Chuck Jones, framed.

1966   *21in (53.5cm) wide*

$3,000-4,000   **SI**

A Turner Entertainment Company animation art cel no. CJ75-329-010 from "How The Grinch Stole Christmas", featuring the Grinch discovered stripping decorations, with Certificate of Authenticity 29598, signed by Chuck Jones, framed.

1966   *21in (53.5cm)*

$3,000-4,000   **SI**

An MGM animation art cel no. CJ75-093-018 from "How The Grinch Stole Christmas", featuring the Grinch on a sled with Max, with Certificate of Authenticity 05593, signed by Chuck Jones, framed.

1966   *21in (53.5cm)*

£3,000-4,000   **SI**

An MGM animation art cel no. CJ75-153-011 from "How The Grinch Stole Christmas", featuring the Grinch holding Max, with Certificate of Authenticity 16903, signed by Chuck Jones, framed.

18in (45.5cm) wide

$3,000-4,000   **SI**

Two Lone Ranger animation cels, depicting Indian chiefs, one showing the head of "Chief Running Water", pegbar punched on the bottom edge, the other a colour model sheet showing chiefs "Devil Spirits" and "Running Water", extensively annotated, also pegbar punched on the bottom edge, each framed and glazed.

Both 11in (28cm) wide

$180-220   **DN**

Two Lone Ranger animation cels, depicting the character "Sheriff Twogun", pegbar punched on the bottom edges, each framed and glazed.

Largest 13in (33cm) wide

$180-220   **DN**

Two Lone Ranger animation cels depicting the character "Town Tamer Jake", pegbar punched on the left hand side, each framed and glazed.

13in (33cm) wide

$180-220 **DN**

Two Lone Ranger animation cels, depicting the characters "Farmer Fred" and outlaw "McLeod", the first pegbar punched on the right hand side, the other pegbar punched on the bottom edge, each framed and glazed.

Largest 13in (33cm) wide

$180-220 **DN**

Two Lone Ranger animation cels, depicting the characters "Wallace Volunteer" and "Honest Abe", pegbar punched on the left hand sides, each framed and glazed.

Largest 13in (33cm) wide

$180-220 **DN**

Two Lone Ranger animation cels, one depicting a hunter wearing a pith helmet and holding a shotgun, the other a blond-haired man with knife and rifle, pegbar punched on the left hand sides, each framed and glazed.

13in (33cm) wide

$180-220 **DN**

Two Lone Ranger animation cels, one depicting three outlaws with guns drawn, pegbar punched on the top edge, the other showing "Clarence Undertaker (called Terrible Tiny Tom)", pegbar punched on the bottom edge, each framed and glazed.

12in (30cm) wide

$180-220 **DN**

Two Lone Ranger animation drawings, one in color depicting a young girl in three poses, pegbar punched on the bottom edge, the other a black and white sketch titled "Sheriff" and numbered LR511, pegbar punched on the bottom edge, each framed and glazed.

13in (33cm) wide

$180-220 **DN**

Two Lone Ranger black and white animator's models, one depicting "Soldier Sam (hero of Gettysburgh), two-stripe soldier", numbered LR516/130 and S1, the other showing "Colonel Wakefield, congressional medal, Victor at the Battle of Charlestown", annotated "clean-up as this" and numbered LR9/139 and G1, each cut to shape and pegbar punched on the lower edges, each framed and glazed.

13in (33cm) wide

$180-220 **DN**

Three Lone Ranger black and white animator's model drawings of bandits, variously inscribed "Cecil, Bandit One, one tough hombre", "Bandit Two, trace as this clean-up", numbered LR1, and "Girlie Jackson, Bandit Three", pegbar punched on the lower edges, each framed and glazed.

13in (33cm) wide

$320-380   **DN**

A Peanuts animation cel, depicting Charlie Brown, shown reading a letter with simple color landscape background, framed and glazed.

10.25in (26cm) high

$100-150   **DN**

A Peanuts animation cel, depicting Lucy, shown wearing a yellow dress and seated on a sketched chair, framed and glazed.

8.75in (22cm) square

$100-150   **DN**

A Peanuts animation cel, depicting Schroeder, shown looking anxious and wearing an orange shirt, pegbar punched on the bottom edge and annotated "Reg to BG", framed and glazed.

10in (25.5cm) wide

$100-150   **DN**

A Warner Brothers animation art cel no. CJS 27 - 156024 for "Pullet Surprise", featuring Foghorn Leghorn, with Certificate of Authenticity 32464, signed by director Darrell Van Citters, framed.

1996   *20in (51cm) wide*

$1,000-1,500   **SI**

An animation art cel featuring Sylvester, framed.

21in (53.5cm) wide

$8,000-12,000   **SI**

A Warner Brothers animation art cel, featuring Tweety in a sailor's hat, framed.

21in (53.5cm) wide

$3,000-5,000   **SI**

A pair of Yellow Submarine animation cels, featuring Paul, one where he is falling (only the top half of his body visible), the other of him landing, gouache on celluloid on an orange and black background

c1968   *Overall 12in (30cm) high*

$1,000-1,500   **CO**

Two animation cels from the Beatles "Yellow Submarine", depicting clowns, each with a half-side view and a rear view, both peg bar punched near the bottom edge, one titled "The Clown", the other untitled, separately framed and glazed.

1968   *Largest 13in (33cm) wide*

$1,500-2,000   **DN**

PROPS AND MEMORABILIA

- Authenticity and provenance are vitally important, so always buy from a reputable dealer or auction house. If the item is a prop, ensure that it comes with a good provenance or a letter of authenticity guaranteeing it is what it claims to be. Try to find out how the item was obtained.

- Look for props that can be clearly seen in the film, preferably having been used in key scenes or if they represent an important facet of an actor's or an actress' character. Costumes are often very popular and can command high prices.

- Unless there are personal reasons for collecting a particular film, collectors should buy props and memorabilia that come from films that captured the public imagination or are classed as popular or period classics. "Star Wars", "James Bond" and "Titanic" are good examples. Props from unpopular, largely unsuccessful films or films that pass out of public interest will command lesser values and be less likely to retain a value.

- Large, bulky or cumbersome props that are difficult to display and store, or parts of props, generally command lesser prices for these reasons.

- Condition is also important, with some props being treated badly during or after the film. Do not be surprised if the prop is not of high quality production. Unless they had a specific function, many were made only to appear visually correct on screen, often seen only from a distance.

A 1:4 scale Sulaco cargo area floor tile from "Aliens", metal effect plastic mounted on card with the film's logo die-cut into it.

1986   *Overall 12in (30cm) wide*

$180-220   **CO**

A painted latex Alien claw from "Aliens", of a complete alien costume worn in the film.

1986

$400-600   **CO**

A prop diamond from "Batman & Robin", clear cast special effects diamond used by the character Mr Freeze (Arnold Schwarzenegger) and kept in his backpack, mounted over a custom-made background featuring digital stills from the film together with descriptive text, in a perspex display case.

1997   *11in (28cm) wide*

$400-600   **CO**

Two prosthetic model pig facial parts from "Babe – Pig In The City", comprising the end of the snout and a mouth palate, box framed with a small version of the film poster.

This piece is accompanied by a Certificate of Authenticity explaining the items' origins.

1998   *18in (46cm) high*

$300-500   **CO**

Four prop Smylex products from "Batman", comprising three boxes and an aerosol can used as set dressings in the Joker's Smylex commercial, together with a color image of the scene where the Joker (Jack Nicholson) can be seen with similar items, and a Certificate of Authenticity.

$600-1,000   **CO**

A brown cocktail dress from "Batman & Robin", as worn by Poison Ivy/Dr. Pamela Isley (Uma Thurman), unlabeled, together with a matching clutch purse, labeled "Saks New York" inside, with a one paper label reading "paisley drk brn. sample purse only do not use!" and another numbered "232", with two Certificates of Authenticity, the first from Warner Bros. Studios, the second from the original purchaser of the costume.

1997

$1,000-1,500   **CO**

An Army camouflage hat and pants from "Black Hawk Down", as worn by Specialist Danny Grimes (Ewan McGregor), hat inscribed on the interior in black marker pen "Gordon, Delta Master Sgt." and additionally inscribed "EMcG", together with a pair of pants also inscribed "Gordon" and a black cast-rubber stunt rifle.

Nikolaj Coster-Waldau who played Delta Master Sergeant Gary Gordon and Ewan McGregor swapped costumes as this one fitted McGregor better and McGregor then gave the costume to the vendor.

2001

$600-1,000 **CO**

A stunt rifle from "Black Hawk Down", believed to have been used by Sgt. Matt Eversmann (Josh Hartnett), mounted with a signed color still of Hartnett in character on a custom-made background with digital stills and descriptive text, in a perspex display case.

475in (1205cm) wide

$400-600 **CO**

A teaser and illegal release warning poster for "James Bond – The Living Daylights".

During the last few weeks of production, unedited footage was stolen and circulated, masquerading as the new film. This poster advises the public that illegal copies are available, but that the authorised version opens in British cinemas on 30th June.

1987 *30in (76cm) high*

$150-200 **CO**

A central console from "James Bond – Tomorrow Never Dies", forming part of Bond baddie Elliot Carver's (Jonathan Pryce) black stealth boat, the silver-painted console with one of the original screens fitted and features wiring, switches and lights, inscribed on the interior in black marker pen "Ops Room Ceiling Command Console", obtained from the Bond stage at Pinewood Studios, where the boat was built.

1997

$320-380 **CO**

A rubber stunt machine gun from "James Bond – Tomorrow Never Dies", as used by Colonel Wai-Lin (Michelle Yeoh), sold together with an index card signed by Yeoh in blue marker pen.

1997 *17in (43cm) wide*

$500-700 **CO**

A prop satellite wing from "James Bond – Tomorrow Never Dies", forming part of Elliot Carver's 'Carver Media Group News' satellite, made of white-painted wood with applied blue mirrored tiles and red lettering, some scratches and minor marks.

Bond is clearly seen battling past and around two of these wings in fight scenes in the film, which was set in a high tech building actually located in Hamburg. Props from memorable scenes such as this have added value, particularly if they are clearly visible in the film.

1997 *55in (140cm) wide*

$800-1,200 **CO**

Three prop casino chips and a check from "James Bond - The World Is Not Enough", in denominations of $25, $100 and $1000, together with a Casino D'Or Noir client check made payable to Electra King, both mounted with digital stills featuring similar chips and checks together with descriptive text, the whole in a perspex clip frame.

1999 *16.5cm (42cm) high*

$270-330 **CO**

A Zukovsky caviar jar and box label from "James Bond – The World Is Not Enough", comprising a glass jar, one of many visible in Zukovsky's caviar factory scenes and box label, both featuring the profile of Zukovsky (Robbie Coltrane), mounted in a display including digital stills featuring Coltrane with the jars in the background together with descriptive text, in a perspex case.

1999 *11in (28cm) high*

$100-150 **CO**

A $25 casino chip from "James Bond – The World Is Not Enough", mounted on a custom-made display with digital stills featuring similar chips and descriptive text, in perspex clip frame.

1999 *8.5in (22cm) high*

$100-150 **CO**

A prop axe head from "Braveheart", a special effects axe-head painted to resemble steel and used in the production of the film, mounted over a custom-made background featuring digital stills and descriptive text, in a perspex display case.

1995   *11in (28cm)*

$300-400   **CO**

A prop dagger with knuckle duster handle from "Cutthroat Island", painted to resemble steel with a brass handle, the latter doubling as a knuckleduster in the shape of a skull, mounted on a custom-made background featuring digital images from the film and descriptive text, in a perspex display case.

1995   *11in (28cm) wide*

$100-150   **CO**

A prop New York Post newspaper front page from "15 Minutes", with the headline "Double Homicide – Eddie's On It!" and an image of Detective Eddie Fleming (Robert DeNiro), mounted with a descriptive plaque, framed and glazed, accompanied by a letter of authenticity from New Line Cinema.

2001   *21in (53cm) high*

$120-180   **CO**

A rubber stunt weapon from "Braveheart", a wide-bladed, falchion-like weapon, painted to resemble steel, used in battle sequences in the film, mounted on a custom-made background with descriptive text, in a perspex display case.

     40in (102cm) wide

$180-220   **CO**

A prop New York State police badge from "Drowning Mona", as worn by Wyatt Rash (Danny DeVito), Chief of the town of Verplanck, matted with a signed color photo of DeVito in character, and two on set polaroid images from the film's production, box framed and glazed.

     22in (56cm) high

$400-600   **CO**

A large prop parchment document from "Elizabeth", an illuminated document on parchment-style paper with stylized script beginning "Omnibus Christi Fidelibus...", Elizabeth I's coat of arms, a large gold-colored seal and the royal insignia.

1998   *27in (68cm)*

$180-220   **CO**

A montage of images from "Enter the Dragon", signed by John Saxon (Roper), mounted with "Enter the Dragon"-style graphics, framed and glazed.

     30in (76cm) wide

$180-220   **CO**

A large flail-like weapon from "Gladiator", the large spiked rubber ball painted to resemble iron, attached to a wooden handle by a length of plaited leather, used in arena fight scenes in the film.

2000   *54in (137cm) long*

$180-220   **CO**

A full Scottish warrior costume from "Braveheart", comprising a large tartan kilt which wraps over to form a shawl, brown cotton padded breast plate, brown heavy woolen tunic, two belts (one plastic), leg wraps, a pair of knee high brown suede boots and a black long-haired wig, as worn by an extra in the film, also includes a wooden shield with handles on the back and written instructions and a diagram on how wear the costume.

1995

$700-1,000   **CO**

A Paper Street Soap wrapper from "Fight Club", as featured in the soap factory scene, mounted with a letter of authenticity from 20th Century Fox, framed and glazed, together with a letter of authenticity from Pinewood Studios.

1999   *14in (36cm) high*

$100-150   **CO**

A prop Barbarian sword and scabbard from "Gladiator", resin painted to resemble steel with wooden handle ornately carved with the figure of a head accompanied by a leather scabbard with brass detail, used in the Germania battle scenes in the film, mounted on a custom-made display, in a perspex case.

2000 *40in (102cm) wide*

$270-330 **CO**

A special effects Barbarian sword and holder from "Gladiator", used in early scenes in the film, mounted on a background featuring an image of General Maximus Decimus Meridus (Russell Crowe) and digital stills with descriptive text, in a perspex display case.

2000 *39in (99cm) wide*

$320-380 **CO**

A prop Roman sword from "Gladiator", a Gladius-style wood and steel sword, the blade painted to resemble steel with blood on the tip, together with its accompanying scabbard used in Arena scenes in the film, both mounted on a custom-made background with descriptive text, in a perspex display case.

2000 *40in (102cm)*

$500-600 **CO**

A oversized Harry Potter promotional postcard, signed by author J.K. Rowling in black marker pen, together with a copy of a letter from Rowling's PA to the charity this item was originally donated to.

10in (25cm) high

$600-1,000 **CO**

A prop wand box from "Harry Potter and the Philosopher's Stone", used as set dressing in Ollivander's Wand Shop where Harry purchases his wand prior to entering Hogwarts School, with green faux lizard skin top with brass-look studded loop on one end, a gold and black label reading "Ollivander's Makers of Fine Wands since 382BC. This is to certify that the wand box is a genuine Ollivander's article".

These props were given as gifts at the UK premier of the film and can be seen in their hundreds when Harry is choosing his wand in Ollivander's shop in one of the early parts of the film.

2001 *14in (36cm)*

$800-1,000 **CO**

A Red Army Bell Bolas prop from "Planet of the Apes", consisting of a strap made of three plaited leather strips, individually connected to foam bell shapes, conicals at one end, matted with an image of a member of the Red Army, and a die cut card of the film title/logo, box framed.

27in (68cm) high

$500-700 **OD**

A large fighting net from "Gladiator", with black rubber crab/spider-like creatures attached, used in arena fight sequences.

2000

$180-220 **CO**

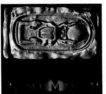

A gold colored ingot from "The Mummy", with the impression of a scarab beetle used in production, mounted in a perspex display case.

11in (28cm)

$70-100 **CO**

A prop Sankara stone from "Indiana Jones and The Temple of Doom", solid resin with chiseled, incised markings, with a color image from the film.

This item was previously sold at Christie's in London.

1989 *6in (15cm) high*

$6,000-10,000 **CO**

Two solid rubber prop hand guns from "Resident Evil", one marked "Smith & Wesson TZS6614 Mod 596", the other "Springfield Armory G422", mounted with an image of Alice/Janus Prospero, box framed and glazed.

27in (68cm) high

$1,800-2,200 **CO**

An original painted foam and leather axe from "Robin Hood: Prince of Thieves", mounted on a custom-made background with descriptive text, in a perspex case.

1991   *40in (102cm)*

$180-220   **CO**

A special effects severed limb from "Saving Private Ryan", a realistic, mud-splattered silicone cast human arm and hand with hand-punched hair detail, used in the Normandy landing scenes, mounted on a custom made background, in a perspex display case.

1991   *40in (102cm)*

$300-500   **CO**

A small prop crystal from "Superman", used in the Fortress of Solitude, mounted over a custom made background featuring digital stills with descriptive text, in a perspex display case.

1978   *11in (28cm) high*

$600-1,000   **CO**

A 19thC-style lady's day dress from "Sleepy Hollow", comprising a bodice of black sheer fabric embroidered with gold floral detail trimmed with lace over a gold full skirt, with bustle.

1999

$270-330   **CO**

A current flow filter from "Star Wars: Episode I - The Phantom Menace", used in the Pit Droid scenes, juggled by the animated character Jar Jar Binks in Watto's shop, mounted over a custom-made background featuring digital stills and descriptive text, in a perspex display case.

1999   *11in (28cm)*

$320-380   **CO**

A prop Daily Planet newspaper from "Superman III", with the headline "Superman Scandal", featuring a photograph of Superman (Christopher Reeves), framed and glazed.

5in (63cm)

$300-400   **CO**

A montage of digital images from "Terminator 2: Judgment Day", signed by Edward Furlong (John Connor), in silver ink, mounted with a descriptive plaque, framed and glazed.

1991   *29in (74cm)*

$300-400   **CO**

An 1:8 scale model ship's whistle from "Titanic", mounted with an image of the film's stars Leonardo DiCaprio and Kate Winslett and a descriptive plaque, box framed and glazed.

1997   *19in (48cm)*

$500-700   **CO**

A replica White Star Line prop dinner fork from "Titanic", used as set dressing, mounted with an image from the dining scene, box framed.

1997   *13in (33cm) high*

$180-220   **CO**

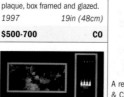

A replica White Star Line Moët & Chandon champagne bottle from "Titanic", labelled "White Star Moët & Chandon Eperney".

1997   *12in (30cm) high*

$270-330   **CO**

A part of the replica ship's hull and a section of bench from "Titanic", both mounted on a custom-made background featuring digital stills from the film together with descriptive text, in a perspex display case.

For certain scenes in the film, director James Cameron built a scale model of the Titanic at Rosarito Beach in Mexico. After filming had finished and the crew had left, the area was littered with left over parts and 'props'. This piece was collected from the beach at this point.

1997   *11in (28cm)*

$100-150   **CO**

A pair of 1930/40s Mickey and Minnie toothbrush holders, marked "copyright Walt Disney".

4in (10cm) high

$350-450 **RH**

A rare French cast aluminum Mickey Mouse penny bank, by Depeche Company.

6in (15cm) high

$250-350 **TK**

A ceramic Mickey Mouse figure, together with two smaller figure, by Severn China.

c1970 *3.25in (8cm) high*

$60-80 **WHP**

A Walt Disney's Mickey Mouse "Maestro Michel Mouse" figure.

1993

$150-250 **MSC**

A 1930s Walt Disney's Pinocchio figure, made by Knickerbocker.

$800-1,000 **FRA**

A Walt Disney's Pinocchio "I'll Never Lie Again ..." figure.

2000

$200-300 **MSC**

A pair of 1950s Walt Disney's Snow White and the Seven Dwarfs ceramic toothbrush holders, by Walt Disney Designs.

Snow White 6in (15cm) high

$250-350 **WHP**

A Walt Disney's Sneezy from Snow White and the Seven Dwarfs felt toy.

$200-300 **FRA**

A Walt Disney's Snow White and the Seven Dwarfs "Soup's On" group.

2000

$1,500-2,000 **MSC**

A Walt Disney's The Lion King "Pals Forever" figure.

1995

$120-180 **MSC**

A B C D E F G H I J K L M N O P Q R S T U V W XYZ

A Walt Disney's Toy Story Buzz Lightyear "To Infinity and Beyond" figure.
1998

$120-180 MSC

A Walt Disney's Peter Pan Tinkerbell "A Firefly! A Pixie! Amazing!" figure.
1993

$450-550 MSC

A Walt Disney's 101 Dalmations Cruella De Vil "Anita Daahling!" figure.
1995

$300-400 MSC

An original Disney Studios "Mickey Mouse" printing slate, with two original gift box samples featuring six images of Mickey in different poses.
29in (73.5cm) long

$750-850 TK

Barks, Carl, "The Fine Art of Walt Disney's Donald Duck", published by Rainbow Publishing, Inc., hardcover edition featuring glossy prints and fold-outs of the work of "the good Duck artist", autographed by the author, limited edition 0096/1875.
1981

$1,000-1,500 HC

A boxed set of Mazda Disneylights, manufactured by the British Thomson-Houston Co, consisting of 12 bell-shaped Christmas tree lights, each printed with Disney characters including Mickey Mouse, Dumbo, the Seven Dwarfs, and Bambi, complete in original colour printed box.

$70-90 DN

A typed letter signed by Walt Disney, a personal letterhead, boldly signed "Walt Disney", dated December 29, 1964, written to John Hurt of the Curtis Publishing Company, with a letter of authenticity.
1964

$2,800-3,200 HC

A 1970s Mickey Mouse Disneyland promotional badge.
3.5cm (9cm) diam

$20-30 CVS

A Wadeheath six piece nursery tea set, transfer-printed by Walt Disney Designs.
Teapot 3.25in (8cm) high

$18-22 WHP

Left: A Walt Disney Blow-Up Thumper figure, by Royal Albert.
1961-1965

$250-350 PSA

Right: A Walt Disney Blow-Up Bambi, by Royal Albert.
1961-1965

$150-250 PSA

AMBERINA

- During the 1880s, the American decorative glass industry moved away from cut and pressed glass and began experimenting with more sophisticated art glass techniques.
- Amberina was primarily used for tableware and decorative pieces, such as vases.
- The distinctive coloring is produced by using heat sensitive glass, containing colloidal gold, which is reheated before letting it cool, resulting in the deep ruby red color. The color shades from dark ruby at the top to light amber at the base on the best pieces with a whole range of delicate tones between them.
- The technique for making Amberina was patented by Joseph Locke in 1883, and was made at the factory he worked at – the New England Glass Company in Cambridge, Massachusetts.
- In 1888, the company moved to Toledo, Ohio, where it became known as the 'Libbey Glass Co.' It is still in existence today, producing tableware, having departed from art glass during the 1940s.
- Cased 'plated' Amberina was patented by Locke in 1886 and was largely produced in the USA by the New England Glass Co. who licensed Sowerby, based in England, to produce it. It is differentiated from standard Amberina by having a second, opaque layer of glass inside the piece which is colored creamy white. It is rare and desirable to collectors and fetches high prices at auction.
- 'Reverse Amberina' occurs where the glass is heated at the base, resulting in red at the base and amber at the top.
- Two other variations in Amberina are 'I.T.P.', for 'inverted thumbprint' where the surface is covered with many inverted impressions that look like thumb prints and 'D.Q.' for 'diamond quilted' where a repeated pattern of diamond designs covers the piece.

An Amberina inverted thumbprint water pitcher, with applied amber reeded handle, slight chip to rim.

8in (20.5cm) high

$60-80　　　　**JDJ**

An Amberina water pitcher, with square top spout, inverted thumbprint design and applied amber reeded handle.

7in (18cm) high

$300-400　　　　**JDJ**

An Amberina milk pitcher, with inverted thumbprint tricorn-shaped spout, applied handle.

5.5in (14cm) high

$120-180　　　　**JDJ**

An Amberina water pitcher, the swirl pattern with applied amber handle, ground pontil.

7in (18cm) high

$350-450　　　　**JDJ**

An Amberina bulbous water pitcher, with vertical ribbing, applied amber reeded handle and ground pontil.

7.5in (19cm) high

$180-220　　　　**JDJ**

Two Amberina pitchers, a petticoat-shaped creamer with inverted thumbprint design, square top spout and ground pontil and a square-topped milk pitcher with inverted thumb print design, and minor roughage to top, the creamer with minor scratches to exterior

Largest 5.5in (14cm) high

$600-700　　　　**JDJ**

An Amberina milk pitcher, melon ribbed shape with herringbone design, applied amber handle and ruffled top, handle appears to have been ground.

8in (20.5cm) high

$180-220　　　　**JDJ**

A decorated Amberina creamer, with enameled floral decoration and applied reeded amber handle.

5in (12.5cm) high

$280-320　　　　**JDJ**

An Amberina inverted thumbprint pitcher, with triangular spout, applied amber handle and enamel decoration

8.5in (21.5cm) high

$50-80 | **JDJ**

An Amberina tankard pitcher, with fuchsia shading to amber and applied Amberina handle.

9.5in (24cm) high

$1,700-2,000 | **JDJ**

A large Amberina inverted thumbprint pitcher, with reeded handle and ground pontil.

10 .25in (26cm) high

$180-220 | **JDJ**

An Amberina pitcher, diamond quilted with a ruffled top and applied amber handle, ground pontil.

9.5in (24cm) high

$280-320 | **JDJ**

An Amberina pitcher, with vertical ribbing and applied amber handle and foot.

8.25in (21cm) high

$450-550 | **JDJ**

An Amberina inverted thumbprint decanter, with ruffled top, ground pontil, applied crystal-reeded handle and a clear lapidary stopper

9in (23cm) high

$150-250 | **JDJ**

An Amberina footed ewer, the swirled glass with applied amber handle and pedestal foot with an amber stopper, one minor flake to the stopper.

12in (30.5cm) high

$600-700 | **JDJ**

An Amberina decanter, the inverted thumbprint design with fuchsia shading to amber with ground pontil, matching hollow blown stopper.

12in (30.5cm) high overall

$1,000-1,500 | **JDJ**

Two Amberina cruets, one bulbous-shaped with inverted thumbprint design, clear stopper and applied clear reeded handle, the second petticoat-shaped with amber lapidary stopper and applied amber handle, some interior staining to one.

Tallest 9.5in (24cm) high

$350-450 | **JDJ**

A plated Amberina cruet, with fuchsia shading to cranberry, vertical ribs and applied amber handle with lapidary stopper, creamy white lining, handle cracked and stopper has roughage at base.
Plated Amberina is very rare.

5.25in (13cm) high

$2,000-3,000 | **JDJ**

An Amberina syrup jug, with original silver-plated fittings, lid is marked "1954".

5.5in (14cm) high

$2,500-3,000 | **JDJ**

Two Amberina cruets, with applied amber handles and amber lapidary stoppers, ground pontils.

5.5in (14cm) high

$550-650 **JDJ**

An Amberina celery vase, with fuchsia color shading to amber with a square-scalloped top, ground pontil and diamond quilted design, some scratches to side.

6in (15cm) high

$200-400 **JDJ**

An Amberina celery vase, with fuchsia color shading to amber with a square scalloped top, ground pontil and inverted thumbprint design.

6.5in (16.5cm) high

$180-220 **JDJ**

An Amberina celery vase, with vertical ribbing and scalloped top.

5.5in (14cm) high

$150-250 **JDJ**

An Amberina celery vase, with inverted thumbprint decoration and a tightly crimped ruffled top,

7in (18cm) high

$150-250 **JDJ**

An Amberina spooner, with swirl pattern, ground pontil, and fuchsia to amber coloring.

4.25in (11cm) high

$300-400 **JDJ**

A plated Amberina spooner, with fuchsia shading to amber and vertical stripes and creamy white lining.

4.25in (11cm) high

$4,000-5,000 **JDJ**

An Amberina vase, with four pinched-in sides and applied rigaree around the neck, with tricorn-shaped top, has scratch on side.

6.25in (16cm) high

$180-220 **JDJ**

An Amberina egg-shaped vase, with diamond quilted pattern, tricorn-shaped top and applied reeded feet, ground pontil.

5.5in (14cm) high

$600-800 **JDJ**

An Amberina square vase, with vertical ribs, applied amber edge around the top and rough pontil.

8.5in (21.5cm) high

$180-220 **JDJ**

An Amberina swirl vase, with enamel floral decoration of pink and white blossoms with gold branches and leaves, ground pontil.

9in (23cm) high

$300-400 **JDJ**

A B C D E F G H I J K L M N O P Q R S T U V W XYZ

An Amberina stalk vase, with blown-out molded decoration of a stalk and cattails, by Joseph Locke.

Joseph Locke (1846-1936) was born in Worcester, England where he gained experience working for many British glass factories. In 1882 he emigrated to the USA to work for the New England Glass Company in Massachusetts. Here, in addition to Amberina, he developed Pomona and a type of Peachblow glass.

4.5in (11.5cm) high

$4,000-5,000 JDJ

Two Amberina lily vases, the first vertically ribbed with fuchsia coloring shading to amber with an applied amber foot, the second with fuchsia coloring shading to amber with applied amber foot and ruffled top.

Tallest 8.25in (23cm) high

$500-600 JDJ

A Libbey Amberina ruffled vase, the polished pontil with acid-etched Libbey insignia and signed "Amberina".

6in (15cm) high

$450-550 JDJ

A decorated Amberina swirl vase, with enamel decoration of flowers and a bird, applied amberina ruffled top and applied amber foot .

9.5in (24cm) high

$900-1,000 JDJ

A Libbey Amberina tall vase, fuchsia coloring shading to amber, vertically ribbed vase with applied amber foot, signed on base with Libbey acid etched insignia, interior staining.

14in (35.5cm) high

$1,700-2,000 JDJ

A Libbey Amberina trumpet vase, with vertical ribbing and fuchsia shading to amber, hollow ball stem, signed on base with acid-etched "Libbey" insignia.

11in (28cm) high

$2,500-3,000 JDJ

An Amberina lily vase, the metal holder comprised of cattails and signed "TUFTS".

6.25in (16cm) high

$250-350 JDJ

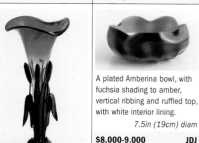

A plated Amberina bowl, with fuchsia shading to amber, vertical ribbing and ruffled top, with white interior lining.

7.5in (19cm) diam

$8,000-9,000 JDJ

An Amberina bowl, diamond quilted pattern with fuchsia color shading to amber with ground pontil and ruffled top.

7.5in (19cm) diam

$850-950 JDJ

An Amberina bowl, ruffled top, ground pontil.

9in (23cm) diam

$120-180 JDJ

An Amberina finger bowl, ruffled top with fuchsia coloring.

5.25in (13.5cm) diam

$80-120   **JDJ**

Four Amberina bowls, two ruffled top finger bowls with ground pontils, a tricorn-shaped bowl with ground pontil, and a small shallow Amberina bowl.

Largest 5.25in (13.5cm) diam

$350-450   **JDJ**

A Sandwich Amberina fuchsia toothpick holder, with diamond lattice pattern and tricorn top.

c1890   2.25in (5.5cm) high

$440-500   **RAA**

A six-sided reverse Amberina toothpick holder.

2.5in (6.5cm) high

$100-150   **JDJ**

An Amberina bucket, with two ears.

5.5in (14cm) high

$150-200   **JDJ**

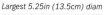

A square daisy and button Amberina bowl, deep fuchsia shading to amber, various rim chips.

9in (23cm) square

$220-280   **JDJ**

A set of four Amberina tumblers, with ground pontils.

4in (10cm) high

$200-300   **JDJ**

One of a set of four Amberina lemonades, with fuchsia coloring shading to amber with applied amber reeded handles, slight vertical ribbing.

3.5in (9cm) high

$220-280   **JDJ**

One of a set of four Amberina cordials, in lily form with fuchsia shading to amber.

4.5in (11.5cm) high

$2,200-2,800   **JDJ**

An Amberina cheese dish, with applied clear lapidary knob and matching under plate.

8in (20cm) diam

$180-220   **JDJ**

An Amberina celery vase, with original silver-plated holder, the glass with scalloped top and vertical ribbing.

9in (23cm) high

$1,500-2,000   **JDJ**

DAUM

- In 1878, Jean Daum (1825-1885) bought a glass factory at Nancy, France. After his death, it was run by his sons, Antonin and Auguste and was known as 'Daum Freres'. After being inspired by the work of Emile Gallé at the Paris Exhibition in 1889, they started to produce art glass.

- Under influence of Antonin Daum, the factory produced work in the Nancy style of Art Nouveau, using wheel carving, engraving, etching and enameling. In 1893, the first acid-etched cameo glass was shown at the Chicago World's Fair. Technically sophisticated, 'vitrification' was developed which resulted in a cloudy, mottled effect through reheating enamel particles.

- Decoration was typically organic, incorporating flowers, foliate designs, fish and leaves, and a common shape is the 'Berluze' vase with its elongated neck.

- 'Pate de verre' was produced from 1906-1914 with figures and small vases in the shape of insects and birds. In 1909 Auguste's son Paul took over and after World War I, seeing the decline of the Art Nouveau style, he introduced transparent vases. These were typically made with embedded bubbles or silver or gilt decoration. Some were decorated with lines and dots or trailing vines and berries over colored, opaque glass.

- Pioneering the Art Deco styling in glass, low relief vases with stylized flowers were produced, some with gilded details. As the 1920s progressed, forms became simpler with more stylized and formal designs and textured surfaces.

- The designer Maurice Marinot was a strong influence during the 1920s, leading to production in single colors with slightly rough surfaces combined with polished surfaces and bold 'deco' style acid-etched patterns.

- After World War II, the factory produced clear, uncolored glass. Designed by Michel Daum, pieces were organic and spiky in form.

- In 1962, the name of the factory changed to 'Cristallerie Daum' and production centered on juxtaposing areas of smooth, polished glass with deep-cut, abstract, rough and textured patterning.

- The factory is still in existence today, producing colored glass and high quality clear lead crystal.

A Daum vase, with applied enameled red glass berries, cameo leaves and vines, signed in cameo "Daum Nancy".

21.75in (55cm) high

$18,000-20,000　　**JDJ**

A rare enameled and gilt Daum bumble bee vase, decorated with leaves and flowers surrounded by twenty bees, signed on the bottom "Daum Nancy".

8.75in (22cm) high

$9,000-10,000　　**JDJ**

A Daum summer scene vase, with green trees and foliage against an orange background, possibly cut down from a taller vase, two burst bubbles in the background, one ground, possibly during manufacturing, signed "Daum Nancy".

7in (18cm) high

$550-650　　**JDJ**

A Daum day lily vase, the diamond-shape waisted vase with acid-cut day lilies and stems on all sides, each enameled in rich orange and yellow tones, signed in cameo "Daum Nancy".

4.5in (11.5cm) high

$2,000-2,500　　**JDJ**

An early Daum cameo vase, red acid-etched background with deeply cut purple cameo flowers, etched into the base "Daum Nancy".

5in (12.5cm) high

$900-1,000　　**JDJ**

A Daum cameo and enamel sugar bowl, rim fitted with silver collar, probably added to cover possible damage.

7in (18cm) long

$700-800　　**JDJ**

An unusual Daum cameo and enameled lamp, very good to excellent condition, signed "Daum Nancy".

Shade 6in (15cm) diam

$4,500-5,000　　**JDJ**

A Daum cameo lamp, the base is impressed "MADE in FRANCE".

Shade 8.5in (21.5cm) diam

$4,000-6,000　　**JDJ**

A Daum Nancy cameo bowl, decorated with leaves and berries on mottled glass, signed in decoration "Daum Nancy".

6.25in (16cm) diam

$1,000-1,500 — **JDJ**

A Daum cranberry cameo tumbler, signed on the bottom "CRISTAL Nancy FRANCE", one small chip at the base.

3.5in (9cm) high

$500-600 — **JDJ**

A signed Daum mini tumbler, with acid-cut gilt leaves and stems on a green ground and gilt trim to lip.

2in (5cm) high

$450-550 — **JDJ**

A Daum cameo enameled and gilt salt.

2in (5cm) diam

$1,100-2,100 — **JDJ**

A miniature Daum tumbler, acid-cut and enameled violets, signed in cameo "Daum Nancy FRANCE".

2in (5cm) high

$1,100-2,100 — **JDJ**

A signed Daum miniature tumbler.

2in (5cm) high

$1,100-2,100 — **JDJ**

A signed Daum Nancy toothpick holder, some very minor wear to gilt.

2in (5cm) high

$180-240 — **JDJ**

A Daum cameo bucket salt, with acid-cut and enameled bellflowers, stems and leaves on a yellow and purple ground, signed "DAUM NANCY FRANCE".

1.75in (4.5cm) diam

$1,300-2,300 — **JDJ**

A signed Daum cameo and enameled salt, with cameo and enameled sailing ships on a yellow and orange ground, one tiny chip to the rim.

2in (5cm) diam

$1,500-2,000 — **JDJ**

FIND OUT MORE...

Clothilde Bacri, Noel Daum, Claude Petry, 'Daum: Masters of French Decorative Glass', published by Rizzoli, 1993.

Musee des Beaux Arts, 3 Place Stanislas, 54000 Nancy, France. A collection of over 600 pieces partly built from donations from the Daum factory.

A rare miniature Daum vase, signed "Daum Nancy" on the base.

2.5in (6.5cm) high

$2,500-3,500 — **JDJ**

An early miniature Daum pitcher, signed on the bottom "Daum Nancy".

3.25in (8.5cm) high

$400-500 — **JDJ**

A miniature Daum long neck vase, with acid-cut and enameled Dutch winter scene, signed on the base "Daum Nancy".

3in (7.5cm) high

$800-1,200 — **JDJ**

EMILE GALLÉ

- The origins of the Gallé factory date back to a mirror glass workshop founded by Charles Gallé in the 1840s, in Nancy, France. After studying glass making, his son Emile (1846-1904)established a workshop there and began to design glass.

- Emile initially produced transparent glass with colored enameled or engraved designs.

- Soon, he became interested in natural motifs and, influenced by the colored glass of Rousseau at the Paris Exhibition of 1878, he began experimenting with colored glass.

- In 1884, he publicly displayed glass with opaque and translucent enamels and by the late 1880s had mastered cameo glass techniques. Pieces included up to seven layers which were cut back by acid and then by carving. Some had enameled or gilt decoration and had added decoration in the form of insects.

- A major influence in the developing Art Nouveau movement, Gallé's work was shown at the Paris Exhibition in 1889. In 1894, he built his first factory at Nancy and produced three ranges. These were one off, often experimental, pieces; high priced limited editions and more standard pieces. Gallé personally oversaw all designs produced.

- He won the 'grand prix' at the Paris Exhibition of 1900. After his death in 1904, his widow Madame Gallé ran the factory. All production between 1904 and 1914, when the factory closed for the war, is marked with a star.

- The factory reopened in 1919, but production was limited to less sophisticated two or three layer pieces, mainly vases and lamps in cameo glass. Pale colors and animal motifs dominated the 1920s, including elephants, seagulls, otters, polar bears and penguins. The factory is still in production, making particulary high quality limited edition pieces. However, it is important that collectors beware reproductions.

A large Gallé enameled green glass vase, the tapering cylindrical vessel painted with lady slipper blossoms and ferns, with molded and engraved signature.

c1900   *17.5in (44cm) high*

$1,800-2,300   **SI**

A Gallé enameled vase, cylindrical and in smoky amber, decorated with enameled thistles and cross of Lorraine on the back, signed on the bottom "E. Galle Nancy", base restored.

10in (25.5cm) high

$120-180   **JDJ**

A Gallé cameo vase, peach-colored cameo decoration of chrysanthemums on a frosted white background. signed on the side in cameo "GALLE".

13.5in (34.5cm) high

$2,000-2,500   **JDJ**

A Gallé enameled glass tall vase, the cushion base with long cylindrical vessel painted with thistles and the cross of Lorraine, enameled on base "E.Galle".

c1900   *17.5in (44.5cm) high*

$2,500-3,000   **SI**

A Gallé cameo stick vase, decorated with green and purple columbine blossoms and leaves, signed in decoration "GALLE".

11in (28cm) high

$1,000-1,500   **JDJ**

A Gallé cameo glass banjo vase, with purple acid-cut flowers, leaves and buds on a yellow-green background, signed in cameo "GALLE".

6.75in (17cm) high

$2,200-2,800   **JDJ**

A Gallé enameled glass vase, onion-shaped with slender cylindrical neck, with pale smoky tone acid-etched with leaves and enameled in naturalistic colors with stems and flowerheads, centers applied in relief as bosses, finely painted on base "Cristallerie d'Emilie Galle a Nancy" and "Modele et decor depose".

7.75in (19.5cm) high

$1,000-1,500   **DN**

A large Gallé scenic cameo vase, with amethyst, green and blue trees and mountains, signed within the decoration "GALLE".

14in (10cm) high

$6,500-7,500   **JDJ**

A Gallé scenic cameo vase, with brown and green acid-cut trees, shrubs, and a boat on a pond, with background color shading from blue to green.

13in (33cm) high

$3,500-4,000   **JDJ**

A Gallé cameo scenic vase, with overall panoramic scene of a lake, trees and a boat, on a frosted yellow and grey background, signed "Gallé" in script on the side.

12.75in (32.5cm) high

$3,000-4,000   **JDJ**

A Gallé cameo fern vase, decorated with ferns on a frosted ground shading from amber to green, signed "GALLE" in cameo.

7in (18cm) high

$750-850   **JDJ**

A small Gallé cameo vase, decorated with hanging trumpet lilies and buds with leaves and branches on a raisin-colored ground.

6.5in (16.5cm) high

$800-900   **JDJ**

A Gallé cameo vase, decorated with lavender bellflowers, stems and leaves on a frosted ground, signed in cameo "Gallé" with a star.

8.25in (21cm) high

$900-1,000   **JDJ**

A signed Gallé scenic cameo vase, with trees, pond and bridge in shades of brown on a rich orange background.

15.5in (39.5cm) high

$3,000-4,000   **JDJ**

A Gallé cameo vase, amethyst over frosted glass with amethyst flower blossoms, leaves and stems on a frosted ground, signed in decoration, possible bruise to lip of vase.

6.5in (16.5cm) high

$800-1,200   **JDJ**

A large Gallé cameo glass vase, with deep purple tiger lilies over opalescent yellow.

18in (45.5cm) high

$2,250-2,750   **JDJ**

A Gallé iris vase, with amethyst irises on frosted amber glass, signed "Gallé" within the decoration, ground top, two minor flakes to the base.

11.5in (29cm) high

$3,000-4,000   **JDJ**

A Gallé cameo glass vase, with purple floral stems, on a frosted gray glass shaded pink, signed in cameo "Gallé".

c1900

$630-730   **SI**

A Gallé enameled vase, in translucent brown with applied enameling of flowers, leaves and branches, signed on base "E. GALLE DEPOSE".

5.5in (14cm) high

$1,000-1,500   **JDJ**

A Gallé cameo vase, with amethyst over pastel blue cameo decoration of flowers and leaves, signed on side "GALLE".

3.75in (9.5cm) high

$650-750   **JDJ**

FIND OUT MORE...

Tim Newark, 'Art of Emile Gallé', published by Books Sales, 1989.

Francois-Therese Charpentier, 'Gallé', published by Harry N. Abrams, April 1988.

Musee de l'Ecole de Nancy, 36-38 Rue du Sergent Blandan, 5400 Nancy, France.

The Corning Museum of Glass, One Museum Way, Corning, New York 14830, U.S.A.

A small Gallé cameo vase, in green over blue over frosted pink glass with blue blossom and green branches and leaves, signed on side "GALLE"

6in (15cm) high

$1,500-2,000 JDJ

A small Gallé cameo vase, burnt orange glass over oyster white, fire-polished cameo decoration of leaves, signed in the decoration.

4.75in (12cm) high

$600-700 JDJ

A small Gallé cameo vase, with peach-colored cameo decoration of lily pads and blossoms, signed within the decoration.

3.75in (9.5cm) high

$650-750 JDJ

A rare Gallé fire-polished cameo decanter, with green cameo leaves, vines and berries, highlighted with gilt, silver collar on the neck with grapes engraved, signed on the bottom "EMILE GALLE".

10in (25.5cm) high

$2,250-3,250 JDJ

A rare early Gallé carved decanter, in smoky amber color, carved with a roaring lion and a stylized fleur-de-lis, four flat knobs applied on either side, signed on the bottom "GALLE DEPOSE" with an engraved flower, small bruise to the ground pontil, near signature, minor staining to the inside of the decanter.

9.5in (24cm) high

$1,000-1,500 JDJ

A Gallé enameled smoky glass bottle and stopper, of flattened teardrop shape with applied ribbons of glass and painted en grisaille with a hunting scene and embellished with floral sprays in colored enamels, finely signed on the base "E. Gallé Nancy depose".

8.5in (21.5cm) high

$700-800 DN

An early Gallé tumbler, signed on the underside "E. GALLE NANCY", an unusual signature.

4.5in (11.5cm) high

$350-400 JDJ

A miniature fire-polished Gallé tumbler, with red fire-polished leaves, vines and berries, signed.

2in (5cm) high

$675-775 JDJ

A signed Gallé chandelier, red acid-cut flowers, leaves and foliage on a shaded green and cream background, signed in cameo "GALLE", supported by three cast brass chains with decorative Art Nouveau motif.

Shade 12in (5cm) diam

$3,750-4,250 JDJ

A Gallé cameo glass bowl, cameo leaves and vine on a frosted background, signed "GALLE" in the design, bowl appears to have been ground on the lip as well as the base.

4in (10cm) long

$350-400 JDJ

A Gallé cameo glass tazza, with acid-etched flowering orchids on grey glass overlaid with yellow and ruby glass, raised on a turned foot, cameo signature, crack to foot.

8in (20cm) diam

$800-1,200 L&T

GLASS

RENÉ LALIQUE

- René Lalique (1860-1945) was born near Reims, France. Lalique began his career designing popularly acclaimed jewelry. A pioneer of the Art Nouveau movement, his clients included stars such as the actress Sarah Bernhardt.

- In the 1890s he began to experiment with glass, both for jewelry and for small vessels, using the lost wax technique. In 1905 he opened a shop in Paris and began to make glass perfume bottles.

- By 1911, he had ceased making jewelry to concentrate on glass, establishing three factories by the 1920s.

- Using molded glass, his pieces could be clear, frosted or opalescent. Opalescent glass is particularly desirable amongst collectors. Translucent milky glass was one of Lalique's specialities. Some pieces were stained with color.

- Most of his designs were modernistic and clean. Repetition of an animal or plant motif or abstract design that covers the entire surface in a sophisticated pattern is common.

- Marks are important and help with dating. Marks for Lalique can be both etched and molded. Before his death in 1945, marks used an 'R' before Lalique's name. This could appear with or without the word 'France' and was sometimes in script and sometimes in capitals. After 1945 the mark is simply 'Lalique, France' with no 'R'.

- Due to the popularity of Lalique's work, there are fakes. Crude production often identifies them, so familiarize yourself with authentic Lalique by viewing and handling as many pieces as possible. Other signs are wrong colors, thick rims and examples that are lighter in weight than genuine Lalique.

A Lalique 'Actina' pattern opalescent shallow bowl, signed "R.Lalique, France".

10in (25.5cm) diam

$750-850   **GorL**

A Lalique 'Vaguest No.1' pattern clear glass bowl, signed "Lalique, France".

9.5in (24cm) diam

$320-380   **GorL**

A Lalique opalescent bowl, designed by Cremieu, molded mark "R. LALIQUE FRANCE" with inscribed "No. 400", small scratches to the well and two bruises to the lip, one appears to have been ground.

1928   *12in (30.5cm) diam*

$1,000-1,500   **JDJ**

A Lalique 'Ondines' pattern opalescent bowl, molded on the exterior with a group of six mermaids swimming amid bubbles, signed "R. Lalique France" and numbered "380".

8.25in (21cm) diam

$1,000-1,500   **DN**

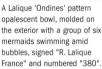

A mid-20thC Lalique opalescent bowl, molded in a spiral with serrated edged leaf motifs, molded "R. Lalique France" mark.

8in (20.5cm) diam

$300-400   **BonS**

A mid-20thC Lalique bowl, tapered towards the foot and cut with a design of thistle heads divided by thorned canes, engraved script "Lalique France" mark.

10.25in (26cm) diam

$400-500   **BonS**

A small Lalique clear glass bowl.

$120-180 GorL

A Lalique dish, with green petal and cut decoration, signed "Lalique, France".

12in (30.5cm) diam

$700-800 GorL

A Lalique 'Poisson' clear glass dish, signed "Lalique, France".

14in (35.5cm) diam

$750-850 GorL

A R. Lalique 'Fauvettes' pattern clear glass ashtray.

7in (18cm) diam

$120-180 GorL

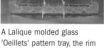

A Lalique molded glass 'Oeillets' pattern tray, the rim molded with stylized blossoms, stamped "R. LALIQUE/FRANCE".

1936   15.75in (40cm) wide

$700-800 SI

A Lalique ashtray, decorated with a galleon, signed "Lalique".

7ins (18cm) diam

$100-150 GorL

A Lalique clear glass ashtray, decorated with impressed frosted flowerheads.

7in (18cm) diam

$120-180 GorL

An octagonal Lalique bowl, with petaled rim, signed "Lalique, France".

8.5in (21.5cm) diam

$180-220 GorL

A frosted Lalique fan-molded ovoid bowl, signed "Lalique, France".

8.5in (21.5cm) diam

$225-275 GorL

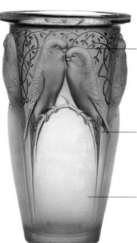

Opalescent glass was produced by adding phosphates, fluorides and aluminium oxide. This was followed by carefully controlled amounts of pigment to give very subtle hints of color.

As in this example, colors are typically delicate, becoming part of the design.

Animals are a typical form of imagery used by Lalique. As well as birds, he used fish, reptiles and insects.

A mid-20thC cylindrical Lalique vase, molded with long leaves and berries towards the rim, stained in blue, molded "R. Lalique France" mark to side of vase.

7in (17.5cm) high

$750-850 BonS

A Lalique 'Rampillon' pattern frosted and clear glass vase, engraved "R. LALIQUE".

5.25in (13cm) high

$375-475 GorL

A Lalique 'Ceylan' pattern frosted and opalescent vase, of tapering cylindrical form with broad rim, molded with a frieze of budgerigars, blue staining, wheel etched marks.

9.75in (25cm) high

$5,000-6,000 L&T

A square Lalique 'Roses' pattern bowl, signed "Lalique, France".

9.5 in (24cm) wide

$420-480   **GorL**

A Lalique 'Bagatelle' pattern frosted glass vase, the sides with birds in foliate compartments, inscribed with "Lalique, France".

6.75in (15.5cm) high

$375-475   **SI**

An R. Lalique opalescent vase, all-over fish decoration with waves, signed on underneath side "R. Lalique".

5.5in (14cm) high

$2,000-3,000   **JDJ**

An R. Lalique 'Ronces' pattern opalescent vase, with molded thorny vines, engraved "R. Lalique France"

9.25in (23.5cm) high

$2,700-3,200   **FRE**

An R. Lalique Archer vase, frosted amber glass with a blown-out molded decoration of ten archers and ten birds, signed in block letters on the underside as well as in script.

10.5in (26.5cm) high

$13,000-14,000   **JDJ**

A green colored R. Lalique vase, with molded design of leaves, signed on base "R. Lalique FRANCE H984".

6.5in (16.5cm) high

$3,000-4,000   **JDJ**

A Lalique crystal vase, of urn-form with molded and frosted sparrows, engraved "Lalique France".

4.75in (12cm) high

$270-330   **FRE**

An R. Lalique 'Ornis' pattern opalescent vase, signed on the underneath side "R. Lalique, FRANCE", repair to foot.

7.5in (19cm) high

$225-275   **JDJ**

An R. Lalique frosted glass 'Thais' figure, signed "R. LALIQUE"

8.5in (21.5cm) high

$9,000-10,000   **JDJ**

A Lalique frosted glass 'Chrysis' figure, signed on base "LALIQUE FRANCE".

6.25in (16cm) long

$1,500-2,000   **JDJ**

A Lalique opalescent atomizer, with ten molded nudes, signed on base "R. LALIQUE FRANCE 2654".

9in (23cm) high

$600-700   **JDJ**

An R. Lalique 'Grape' pattern decanter set, with six matching tumblers and tray, all signed in block letters "R LALIQUE", slight damage to tray and tumblers.

Decanter 10.5in (26.5cm) high

$1,000-1,500   **JDJ**

A Lalique 'Eventail' pattern molded glass ice cream cup.

1928   *3in (7.5cm) diam*

$90-120   **SI**

SCANDINAVIAN

- Scandinavian glass designs are typically very 'modern', often with strong angular elements and clear lines. Pieces were aimed at being aesthetically pleasing but also affordable and were produced in large amounts. As such, they are still affordable today as this area has only begun to be appreciated by collectors.
- Production centred around mold blown glass which can be machine made or free-blown into a mold by a blower. It was highly popular during the 1960s and 1970s when glass was improving due to increased competition between factories.
- The striking clarity of Swedish glass is highly sought after, so beware of scratched or scuffed examples.
- Collectors should look for pieces that were designed by famous designers working at well-known factories.
- The Riihimaki Glassworks, based in Finland and founded 1910, is considered a key factory. Examples of glass production are often known as 'Lasi' after the factory's full title, 'Riihimäen Lasi Oy', meaning 'Riihimäen Glass Company'.
- During the 1940s and 1950s a team of skilled designers including Nanny Still and Helena Tynell joined forces. Their collective improved methods in glass blowing ensured the company took a leading role in post-war glass production.
- In 1976, glass making went fully automatic and blown glass was discontinued. After a small series of sales to different companies and a merger, the factory was closed in 1990.
- Iittala was another key factory. It was based in Finland and founded in 1881, initially making household glass. The early 1930s saw competitions bringing in new modernist designers.
- From 1945, Iittala's production was confined to container glass, with Tapio Wirkkala joining in 1946 as Chief Designer. Timo Sarpaneva joined in 1950s and, with a team of innovative designers, Iittala became Finland's largest art glass maker and merged with Nuutajarvi glassworks in 1987.

A Nanny Still vase, for Riihimaën Lasi Oy.
7.75in (20cm) high
$70-90 MHT

A Nanny Still vase, for Riihimaën Lasi Oy.
11.75in (30cm) high
$145-165 MHT

Three Nanny Still vases, for Riihimaën Lasi Oy.
1970s 11in (28cm) high
$100-120 each MHT

NANNY STILL

- Born 1926 in Finland, Nanny Still worked for Riihimaki from 1949-1976 and is considered one of their chief designers, working in ceramics, enamels, jewelery, glass and other materials.
- Her earliest designs exploited the plastic nature of glass, but during the 1950s they became more geometric with strong colors. In 1954 she won the 'diplome d'honneur' at the Milan Triennale.
- She had great success in 1963 with her 'Flinari' decanters which were decorated with a diagonal grid-like relief pattern. From then her designs became more textural, starting with these 'Fantasma' and 'Kehra' vases of the late 1960s and 1970s.
- Elongated bottle shaped vases designed by her are commonly found and are affordable.

A Nanny Still cased vase, for Riihimaën Lasi Oy, pattern no. 1436 and acid stamp "Riihimaën Lasi Oy" with polar bear on base.
7.75in (19.5cm) high
$70-90 MHT

Two Nanny Still still-mold blown vases, for Riihimaën Lasi Oy.
8.25in (21cm) each high
$60-70 each MHT

A Nanny Still cased vase, for Riihimaën Lasi Oy, pattern no. 1339 and acid stamp "Riihimaën Lasi Oy" with polar bear on base.

7.75in (21.5cm) high

$70-90 MHT

Two Nanny Still 'Tiimalasi' vases, for Riihimaën Lasi Oy.

1970s *7in (18cm) high*

$80-100 each MHT

A Nanny Still cased vase, for Riihimaën Lasi Oy, pattern no. 1436 and acid stamp "Riihimaën Lasi Oy" with polar bear on base.

6in (15cm) high

$70-90 MHT

Three Tamara Aladin vases, for Riihimaën Lasi Oy.

c1976 *9.75in (25cm) high*

$60-70 each MHT

TAMARA ALADIN

- Tamara Aladin was born 1932 in Finland and joined Rihiimaki in 1959. She is considered one of their chief designers.

- Her designs are typical of the period, with bright, jewel-like and strong colors and simple, clean designs, often using geometrical features.

- Her work is typified by these vases where the vertical line is cut with undulating sections, either with rippling ribs or stronger, horizontal flanges.

Two Tamara Aladin large undulating vases, for Riihimaën Lasi Oy.

1960s *11in (28cm) high*

$80-100 each MHT

A Tamara Aladin large undulating vase, for Riihimaën Lasi Oy.

1960s *11in (28cm) high*

$80-100 MHT

A Tamara Aladin undulating vase, for Riihimaën Lasi Oy.

1960s *9.75in (25cm) high*

$80-100 MHT

A Tamara Aladin undulating vase, for Riihimaën Lasi Oy.

1960s *7.75in (20cm) high*

$65-85 MHT

A Tamara Aladin 'Tuulikki' vase, for Riihimaën Lasi Oy.

c1976 *7.75in (20cm) high*

$60-70 MHT

Two Tamara Aladin vases, for Riihimaën Lasi Oy.

c1970s *7.75in (20cm) high*

$60-70 each MHT

A Vicke Lindstrand vase, for Kosta, randomly decorated with pale blue, red and amethyst threads, signed "Kosta LH 1089".

6.75in (17.5cm)

$450-500 MHT

A Vicke Lindstrand dish, for Kosta, internally decorated, signed "Kosta LH 1386".

6.25in (16cm) wide

$180-220 MHT

A Vicke Lindstrand vase, for Kosta, Sweden, internally decorated, signed "_KOSTA LH 1260".

c1960 6.25in (16cm) high

$380-420   **MHT**

Two Vicke Lindstrand "Dark Magic" vases, for Kosta, signed to base "Kosta LH 1605".

5in (12.5cm)

$400-450 each   **MHT**

A colored Vicke Lindstrand vase, for Kosta, with trapped air bubble from the 'Mambo' range, signed "Kosta LH 1889".

9in (23cm) high

$250-300   **MHT**

A small ovoid Vicke Lindstrand 'Moonshine' bowl, for Kosta, signed "Kosta LH 1316/90".

3in (7.5cm) high

$80-130   **MHT**

VICKE LINDSTRAND

■ Born in 1904, Lindstrand began working for Kosta in 1950 as Chief Designer after twelve years at Orrefors. He held the position until 1973 and died in 1983 after a successful and varied career.

■ Many of his designs use trees as inspiration or as motifs. He also worked as a book illustrator and this experience helped him with his decorative abilities in glass.

■ He captured contemporary feelings during the 1950s with natural, bud shaped forms. He is well known for his use of color and organic forms. His inventive use of asymmetrical figural or abstract designs also make him noteworthy.

A Tapio Wirkkala 'Pinus' vase, for Iittala, signed "TW" on base.

8.75in (22.5cm) high

$120-180   **MHT**

TAPIO WIRKKALA

■ Born in 1915 in Finland, Wirkkala studied sculpture at Helsinki from 1933-36.

■ He was inspired by the Finnish and Laplandish countryside and the patterns of nature, such as those found in wood and bark.

■ He worked for Iittala from 1946-1985 and Venini from 1959-1985.

■ He won the first prize at the Iittala glass competition in 1946 after which he took the position of Chief Designer. This was followed by gold medals at Faenza all during the 1960s. After a successful career, he died in 1985.

A Tapio Wirkkala 'Cog' vase, for Iittala, acid etched and polished, signed "Tapio Wirkkala 3552".

6.5in (16.5cm) high

$400-450   **MHT**

A Tapio Wirkkala kanto (tree stump) vase, for Iittala, signed "_3241 Tapio Wirkkala".

4.5in (11.5cm) high

$150-200   **MHT**

Two Tapio Wirkkala 'Ultima Thule' tankards, for Iittala, still-mold blown, designed by Wirkkala for Finnair's transatlantic flights.

1968   4.75 in (12cm) high

$80-100   **MHT**

A Helena Tynell vase, for Riihimaën Lasi Oy.

c1970s 7.75in (21.5cm) high

$80-110   **MHT**

GLASS

HELENA TYNELL

- Tynell started designing for Riihimaën Lasi Oy in 1946 and became known for her household glass designs.
- Forms are organic, often with undulations and wavy optical designs.
- During the late 1960s, her work became more geometric and surfaces became more textured.

A Helena Tynell 'Pala' vase, for Riihimaën Lasi Oy.

c1969-76   4.5in (11.5cm) high

$60-70   **MHT**

A Helena Tynell 'Sun' juice carafe, for Riihimaën Lasi Oy.

'Sun' bottles were available in four different sizes.

c1964-74   9in (23cm) high

$100-150   **MHT**

A reproduction of a 1930s Alvar Aalto 'Savoy' vase, for Iittala.

The Finnish designer Alvar Aalto (1898-1976) is better known for his architectural, interior and furniture designs. As well as glass, he also worked in lighting and textiles.

1990s   4in (10cm) high

$70-90   **MHT**

A Swedish dark green Elis Bergh 'Ribbed Optic' vase.

c1948   7.75in (20cm) high

$100-140   **MHT**

An Otto Brauer white cased "Gul" vase, for Kastrap / Holmegaard.
1960s

$100-140   **MHT**

A selection of Otto Brauer "Gul" vases, for Kastrap/Holmegaard.
1960s

$120-180 each   **MHT**

A Kiejl Engman vase, for Kosta, with abstract landscape on white ground, signed "Kosta Boda 48638 K Engman".
            9.5in (24cm) high

$100-150   **MHT**

A Boda Sun Catcher, by Eric Hogland, with impressed abstract animals, signed "H866/F".
            11.75in (30cm) wide

$100-150   **MHT**

A Paul Kedelv still-mould blown vase, for Reijmyre.
c1965   8.25in (21cm) high

$70-80   **MHT**

A Holmegaard ice bucket, by Per Lutken, signed "Holmegaard 8715".
            6in (15cm)

$60-70   **MHT**

A Strombergshyttan Free Form vase, by Gunnar Nylund, signed to base "Strombergshyttan G. Nylund".

c1955   54.25in (11cm) high

$100-140   **MHT**

A late 1950s Aimo Okkolin Free Form vase, for Riihimaën Lasi Oy, with air-bubbled decoration around the base, signed "AIMO OKKOLIN Riihimaën LASI OY" on base.

9.25in (23.5cm) high

$100-150   **MHT**

A Bengt Orup vase, for Johansfors, graduated color, signed to base "J Fors Orup".

16.6in (42cm)

$170-210   **MHT**

A Bengt Orup olive green tail glass, for Johansfors, signed "Johansfors Orup".

16.5in (42cm) high

$170-210   **MHT**

An Orrefors 'Selena' dish, by Sven Palmqvist, signed "Orrefors Pu 3092/31".

6in (15.5cm) wide

$70-90   **MHT**

An Orrefors vase, by Sven Palmqvist.

6.75in (17.5cm) high

$100-140   **MHT**

One of a set of four Timo Sarpaneva 'Klinka' whiskey glasses, for littala, boxed.

3.5in (8.5cm) high

$80-100 (set)   **MHT**

Three Timo Sarpaneva 'Festivo' candlestick holders, signed "TS" to base.

Largest 8.5in (21.6cm) high

$120-180 set   **MHT**

A Boda vase, with abstract celestial motifs, signed "Boda Artist B Vallien 48330".

5.75in (14.5cm) high

$80-110   **MHT**

A Kosta vase, decorated internally with amethyst swirls, signed "_KOSTA LH 1405".

c1960   6.25in (16cm) high

$200-270   **MHT**

FIND OUT MORE...

Jennifer Opie, 'Scandinavian Ceramics & Glass in the Twentieth Century, Victoria & Albert Museum, 1989.

A Finnish ruby red carafe and a turn-mold blown tumbler, for Nuutajatui Notsjo.

1962-63   7.5in (19cm)

$100-140   **MHT**

A Mona-Morales-Schildt vase, for Kosta, signed "Kosta".

4.5in (11.5cm) high

$70-90   **MHT**

STEUBEN GLASS

- Founded in 1903 by Thomas G. Hawkes and Frederick Carder in Steuben County, New York. The Steuben Glassworks initially supplied blanks to Hawkes' factory. Later, Carder began experimenting with art glass after his experience with John Northwood at the English company Stephens & Williams.

- In 1904, Carder patented an iridescent glass which he called 'Aurene' (from 'aurum', the Latin word for gold) which resembled Tiffany's 'favrile' range, prompting Tiffany to sue due to its success. Proving he had developed Aurene independently, the range was produced from 1905 in blue, brown, green and red including plain and patterned pieces and pieces with combined colors.

- In 1918, the company was bought by The Corning Glass Works and took this factory as part of its name. The range was expanded enormously in color and form over the next 30 years and other ranges such as 'Calcite' (translucent ivory glass) and 'verre de soie' (clear glass with a gentle colored iridescence) were introduced.

- 'Cluthra' was made during the 1920s and used large particles of powdered enamel on clear glass which incorporated bubbles. Etched, engraved and carved cameo glass was also produced at this time.

- In 1932, Carder was replaced as Director by John Mackay who stayed until Arthur Amory Houghton took control. In 1933 the company was renamed 'Steuben Glass Incorporated'. The company is still in production today.

A signed Steuben gold Aurene vase, scratch to one side and a slight roughness at the base.

8in (20.5cm) high

$1,000-1,500 | **JDJ**

A Steuben blue Aurene vase, of classical form, etched "STEUBEN", scratch to lip.

8in (20.5cm) high

$900-1,000 | **FRE**

A Steuben blue Aurene vase, ribbed design and flared lip, iridescence inside and out, signed on the bottom "Steuben", several minor scratches to the exterior.

5in high

$1,000-1,500 | **JDJ**

A Steuben blue Aurene vase, with applied foot, signed on base "Steuben".

10in (25.5cm) high

$1,500-2,000 | **JDJ**

A Steuben gold Aurene on Calcite trumpet-shaped vase.

6in (15cm) high

$400-500 | **JDJ**

A Steuben gold Aurene on Calcite glass compote, unsigned.

c1920 *7.25in (18cm) high*

$400-500 | **SI**

A Steuben gold Aurene on Calcite footed bowl, gold aurene, unsigned.

7in (18cm) diam

$400-500 | **JDJ**

A Steuben blue Aurene on Calcite bowl, minor surface scratches to the interior of the bowl.

8in (20.5cm) diam

$650-750 | **JDJ**

A Steuben blue Aurene on Calcite centerpiece bowl, slightly flared rim, several minor scratches.

14in (10cm) diam

$1,200-1,800 | **JDJ**

A Steuben blue Cluthra vase, printed "fleur-de-lis" mark.
c1920

$900-1,000   **SI**

A Steuben plum jade glass bowl, with acid-cut back decoration of flowers and scrolls, ground pontil.
8in (20.5cm) diam

$5,000-6,000   **JDJ**

A Steuben grotesque fan vase, ruby shading to clear crystal with applied foot, signed on base with fleur-de-lis mark.
11.25in (28.5cm) high

$500-600   **JDJ**

A Steuben pink Cluthra vase, urn-shaped with all over bubbles, ground pontil.
6.5in (16.5cm) high

$1,400-1,600   **JDJ**

A large Steuben amethyst low bowl with frog, ground pontil with fleur-de-lis signature, several scratches to the bowl.
12in (5cm) (30.5cm) diam

$400-500   **JDJ**

A Steuben grotesque vase, amethyst shading to clear footed vase, signed with fleur-de-lis mark.
11.25in (28.5cm) high

$500-600   **JDJ**

A threaded Steuben clear glass vase, with controlled bubbles and applied pink threading, unsigned.
8in (20.5cm) high

$300-400   **JDJ**

A Steuben rosaline glass vase, of baluster form with printed "fleur-de-lis" mark, drilled.
c1910   *8in (20.5cm) high*

$220-280   **SI**

A Steuben ruby and clear glass vase, the ribbed fan-form vessel on a knopped stem and circular foot, faintly inscribed "STEUBEN".
c1910   *8.25in (21cm) high*

$280-320   **SI**

A Steuben jade green urn-shaped vase, with two applied opalescent "M" handles, unsigned.
10in (25.5cm) high

$2,300-2,500   **JDJ**

A Steuben jade green three-prong vase, set on an alabaster foot, unsigned.
10.5in (26.5cm) high

$1,800-2,200   **JDJ**

A B C D E F G H I J K L M N O P Q R S T U V W XYZ

A Steuben green fan vase, engraved with a ship, signed on the base "STEUBEN".

8.5in (21.5cm) high

$200-300 | **JDJ**

A Steuben alabaster and black glass vase, shape 7457, the ovoid vessel with flaring rim of alabaster glass and applied with three black glass feet, unsigned.

c1920 | *8in (20.5cm) high*

$700-800 | **SI**

A Steuben blue jade shade vase, vertical ribbed with fluted top, unsigned.

5.5in (14cm) high

$4,000-5,000 | **JDJ**

A Steuben Bristol yellow bowl, with wide brim, ground pontil, unsigned, scratches to underneath side.

13.5in (34cm) diam

$180-220 | **JDJ**

A Steuben celeste blue and amber glass candlestick, with lily pad foot and tulip candle holder.

12in (30.5cm) high

$1,500-2,000 | **JDJ**

A Steuben green jade stick vase, applied alabaster foot, unsigned, roughness to the top of the vase.

10in (25.5cm) high

$250-350 | **JDJ**

A pair of Steuben blown amber candlesticks, with hollow stem and a turquoise rim to the base and top, signed on the underside with the fleur-de-lis mark.

10in (25.5cm) high

$800-1,000 | **JDJ**

Three Steuben candlesticks, with pink threading applied over iridescent frosted glass.

Largest 7in (18cm) high

$800-900 | **JDJ**

LATER & CLEAR STEUBEN GLASS

- In 1932, Houghton employed the renowned industrial designer Walter Dorwin Teague as design consultant, whose influence saw the phasing out of colored glass. In the same year, Corning developed a new lead crystal glass of incredible purity, which became known as '10M'.

- By 1935, the newly reinvigorated company was effectively relaunched with a new image, based around this new clear crystal.

- After the war, design became less geometrical and more organic and fluid. Continuing a tradition, many famed designers, such as Jacob Epstein (1880-1959) and Graham Sutherland (1903-1980) worked on a variety of prestigious themed ranges. The 1970s saw simple stylized animal figurines becoming popular and a leaning towards simpler, plainer styles.

- The employment of renowned designers has continued. Simplicity and strength of design has ensured that pieces from this factory have remained highly collectable.

A Steuben crystal compote, with broad flaring rim on a quadrilobate base, engraved signature.

7in (17.5cm) high

$500-600 | **FRE**

A mid-20thC Steuben glass vase, of trumpet form applied with two curved disks, signed "Steuben".

6.5in (16.5cm) diam

$120-180 SI

A Steuben glass vase, the flaring vessel on a twisted stem and thick circular foot, signed "Steuben".

10.5in (26.5cm) high

$400-500 SI

A mid-20thC Steuben glass bowl, the deep vessel on a six-petaled scroll foot, signed "Steuben".

6.5in (16.5cm) diam

$180-220 SI

Two Steuben crystal pieces, comprising a flaring vase on knopped stem and a bowl with swirled base, both with engraved signature.

Vase 9in (22.5cm) high

$350-450 FRE

Two mid-20thC Steuben glass bowls, each shallow vessel on four scroll feet, signed "Steuben".

Largest 10.25in (26cm) diam

$500-600 SI

A set of six Steuben crystal cocktail glasses, each with conical cup and base encasing a single air droplet, signed "S".

4in (10cm) high

$500-600 FRE

A Steuben compote, green threading applied over clear crystal with controlled bubbles, very good to excellent condition.

7in (18cm) diam

$180-220 JDJ

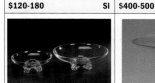

A set of eighteen 20thC signed Steuben glasses, comprising twelve tall wines and six short wines, each with conical bowl on knopped stem enclosing an air bubble, on a circular foot.

Tallest 7in (18cm) high

$1,000-1,500 set SI

A pair of mid-20thC Steuben glass candlesticks, each cylindrical candle holder with three curved loop supports, signed "Steuben".

4.5in (11cm) high

$400-500 SI

A pair of 20thC signed Steuben glass candlesticks, of tapering cylindrical form enclosing a teardrop air bubble, with a ring-turned neck.

4.5in (11.5cm) high

$450-550 SI

A Steuben crystal apple, with engraved signature.

4in (10cm) high

$280-320 FRE

A Steuben glass mushroom, modeled as a toadstool with polka dots, signed "Steuben".

8.25in (21cm) high

$1,700-2,000 SI

FIND OUT MORE...

James M. Houston, 'Fire into Ice: Adventures in Glass Making', Tundra Books, 1998.

Rockwell Museum, Cedar Street at Denison Parkway, Corning, New York 14830, USA. www.stny.1run.com. Contains the best collection of Steuben Glass produced before 1933, comprising over 2,500 pieces.

A Steuben glass elephant, modeled with trunk raised, signed "Steuben".

7.25in (18.5cm) high

$300-400 SI

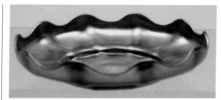

A Tiffany gold iridescent dish, with blue highlights and a scalloped edge, signed on base "L.C.T. FAVRILE".

5in (12.5cm) diam

$375-475 JDJ

A signed Tiffany gold iridescent bowl, with ruffled and fluted top edge with a ribbed outside design, signed on the bottom "L.C.T FAVRILE", a few very minor scratches to the interior of the bowl.

7in (18cm) diam

$500-600 JDJ

A Tiffany gold iridescent shallow bowl, with pulled out feet, signed "L.C.T. M 9142".

5.5in (14cm) diam

$675-775 JDJ

A Tiffany green and gold iridescent bowl, with a gold and beige exterior, applied iridescent foot, signed on foot "L.C. TIFFANY FAVRILE".

7.5in (19cm) diam

$900-1,000 JDJ

A Tiffany gold iridescent stretched glass compote, with applied pedestal and foot, signed on base "L.C.T.".

8in (20.5cm) diam

$900-1,000 JDJ

A signed footed Tiffany bowl, with creamy yellow rolled rim, clear opalescent bowl and cupped foot with swirled panels of opalescence, signed on the bottom "LC Tiffany FAVRILE 1839", some very minor scratches to the inside of the bowl.

10in (25.5cm) diam

$2,700-3,200 JDJ

TIFFANY

- The son of an American jeweler, Louis Comfort Tiffany (1848-1933) traveled widely and was inspired by the different decorative styles he encountered.

- He founded 'Tiffany Glass & Decorating Co.' in 1892 and became chairman of his father's jewelers, Tiffany & Co, in 1902. 'The Tiffany Glass Company' was set up in 1885 and he became further interested in glass as a medium after seeing the work of Emile Gallé at the Paris Exhibition in 1889.

- In 1902, the 'Stourbridge Glass Company', run by his employee A. Douglas Nash, was renamed 'Tiffany Furnaces'.

- Tiffany began to produce lamps in 1890, the shades coming to be made from many pieces of his patented glass, 'Favrile'. Favrile, originally called 'Fabrile' means 'made by a craftsman or from his craft' and was patented in 1894. The glass was treated with metal oxides and exposed to acidic fumes to give it its particular appearance.

- The iridescence and luster of many Tiffany pieces was produced by spraying surfaces with metallic salts. This style was inspired by excavated Roman glass and became very popular.

- Tiffany produced many different types of glass, including 'Cypriote' which was produced from 1896-1927 and has a lustrous but rough surface, 'Lava' glass with lustrous drips running down the surface and 'Agate' glass, opalescent colored glass. He also produced glass that included sections of millefiori to represent flowers.

- In 1924, Tiffany dissolved the glass company and it was bought by A.D. Nash. Although Tiffany would not allow his name to be used, many of his styles continued to be produced. The A. Douglas Nash Corporation finished production in 1931.

A Tiffany gold iridescent footed bowl, with ruffled top and applied foot, signed on base "L.C.T.".

6in (15cm) diam

$750-850 JDJ

A Tiffany pastel gold iridescent compote, with oyster-white iridescent exterior finish, signed on base "L.C. TIFFANY FAVRILE V234".

8.25in (21cm) diam

$800-900 JDJ

A Tiffany Favrile glass dish, of bulbous form, with flared rim, etched "L.C.T."

3.75in (9.5cm) diam

$500-600 FRE

A Tiffany pastel pink finger bowl and underplate, both signed "LCT FAVRILE".

Underplate 7in (18cm) diam

$1,000-1,500 JDJ

Two Tiffany Favrile glass salts, one circular with ruffled rim, signed "L. C. T.", the other roughly octagonal on four feet, signed "L. C. T.", chips to feet.

First 2.5in (6.5cm) diam

$300-400 FRE

A Tiffany gold intaglio-cut finger bowl and underplate, with green, blue and purple iridescence, both bowl and underplate intaglio-cut with grapevines, grapes and leaves, signed "LCT" on the bottom of the underplate.

Underplate 5.75in (14.5cm) diam

$1,000-1,500 JDJ

A Tiffany gold iridescent floriform vase, with a stretched ruffled top and an applied foot, signed on base "L.C.T. 4872B", some interior staining.

11in (28cm) high

$3,000-3,500 JDJ

A Tiffany Favrile glass compote, with circular pedestal, bulbous body and wide ruffled rim, signed "1529-5633 K L C Tiffany - Favrile".

4.25in (10.5cm) high

$1,000-1,200 FRE

A Tiffany gold iridescent floriform vase, with green and blue highlights and ruffled top, signed on base "L.C.T. W5977".

5in (12.5cm) high

$800-900 JDJ

A Tiffany gold iridescent floriform vase, with ruffled top, signed on base "L.C.T. W1737".

4.75in (13cm) high

$900-1,000 JDJ

A Tiffany iridescent vase, with gold and green finish, vertical ribs and pinched in sides, button pontil, signed "L.C.T. U970".

4.75in (12cm) high

$2,250-3,250 JDJ

A Tiffany gold iridescent ribbed vase, with uneven ribs from top to base, marked on the bottom "7314C".

3.5in (9cm) high

$800-1,200 JDJ

A Tiffany gold iridescent floriform vase, of melon ribbed design with slightly domed foot, marked on the bottom "48788", some staining to the interior.

6in (15cm) high

$800-1,200 JDJ

A Tiffany iridescent vase, with brown, gold and beige striped decoration and gold collar, signed on base "TIFFANY FAVRILE B-522", ground pontil.

11.25in (28.5cm) high

$4,200-4,800 JDJ

A Tiffany ididescent vase, blue-gray background with silvery blue pulled leaves and vines, signed on the base "LCT F698", base drilled and patched.

21in (53.5cm) high

$10,000-12,000 JDJ

A CLOSER LOOK AT A TIFFANY VASE

This example is made from Agate glass, which was produced from the mid-1890s and is highly desirable. Sometimes known as 'laminated glass', the stunning effect was produced by mixing carefully chosen, often contrasting, colors together in a pot with heat reactive glass that changed color after being cooled and reheated.

Pieces were finished for display or sale by cutting and polishing the glass to show the sophisticated striations in the glass.

This piece bears the original paper label and is signed on the base " L.C. Tiffany INC FAVRILE EXHIBITION piece in 5545M".

A Tiffany agate exhibition piece, green, brown and beige with all over faceting, original Tiffany paper label, very minor chips to the side, two small holes in the center of two of the cane panels, done in the making.

This piece was made to exhibition quality and would have been used to demonstrate and represent Tiffany's glassmaking skills.

4.5in (11.5cm) high

$12,000-14,000 JDJ

A Tiffany Favrile glass loving cup, classic form with three applied handles, etched "L. C. Tiffany - Favrile 2684 D".

7.25in (18.5cm) high

$1,800-2,200 FRE

A Tiffany blue iridescent covered compote, with purple highlights, signed on base "L.C. Tiffany inC FAVRILE 5679M", also cover is signed "L.C. Tiffany INC FAVRILE 5679M".

9.5in (24cm) high

$2,000-3,000 JDJ

A Tiffany gold iridescent candle lamp, of ruffled stretched shade with gold and purple iridescence, the swirled base signed on the base "LCT" and supporting the original candle holder.

15in (38cm) high

$3,000-4,000 JDJ

A Tiffany Favrile glass lamp, with twisted vasiform base, cylindrical pulled glass electrified bobeche and ruffled stretch glass shade, base and shade signed "L. C. T. Favrile".

14in 35.5cm) high

$1,800-2,200 FRE

A Tiffany turquoise iridescent vase, dark blue bands on a light blue ground, button pontil, signed on underneath of base "L.C. TIFFANY FAVRILE PANAMA PACIFIC EXHIBITION 9439".

7.25in (18.5cm) high

$3,500-4,500 JDJ

A Tiffany gold iridescent stick vase, in a brass and green and gold enameled metal holder, signed on base "LOUIS C TIFFANY FURNACES INC 152", some interior staining.

16.5in (42cm) high overall

$1,200-1,800 JDJ

WHITEFRIARS & GEOFFREY BAXTER

- A glassworks was founded in Whitefriars, London, in the 17th century. In 1834 it was acquired by James Powell and became known as 'Powell & Sons' until 1962 when its name reverted to 'Whitefriars Glassworks'.

- During the 19th century designs included pieces by renowned designer William Morris. The 20th century saw a move towards more Art Deco designs and coloured and textured glass.

- In 1954 the talented Geoffrey Baxter was employed and during the 1960s designed ranges that injected a new impetus into Whitefriars. Today they are highly sought after. His designs varied between those that were unusually shaped, had textured finishes or resembled the pure and brilliant colors found in Scandinavian glass of the time.

- Textured finishes were fashionable during the 1960s and Baxter initially used nature as his inspiration.

- Mold-blown pieces such as those with bark-like textured exteriors were produced from 1967. Other popular textured pieces were made using carpet nails hammered into the wooden molds so that the nail heads left an impression.

- Baxter was also influenced by man-made subjects, as can be seen in the innovative and asymmetric 'Drunken Bricklayer' vase.

- As molds were slightly burnt by the hot glass each time they were used, look for pieces that were produced early in the mold's life and show a fine and varied level of texture.

- Despite being highly popular during the 1960s and 1970s, the difficult economic climate meant that Whitefriars began to decline, until its eventual closure in 1980.

A large ruby Geoffrey Baxter for Whitefriars vase, with bulbous pinched form.

10.5in (27cm) high

$90-120   MHT

A pair of Geoffrey Baxter for Whitefriars ruby bud vases,.

c1960s   7.85in (20cm) high

$30-40 each   MHT

A Geoffrey Baxter Kingfisher blue bud vase.

c1960s   8.5in (21.5cm) h

$40-50   MHT

A Geoffrey Baxter for Whitefriars textured 'Nailhead' vase, pattern no. "9683".

c1967   6.75in (17cm) high

$45-55   MHT

Above left: A Whitefriars "drunken bricklayer" glass vase, designed by Geoffrey Baxter, of rectangular section formed as three blocks with the central portion dislodged and in "pewter" toned glass.

13in (33cm) high

$1,500-2,000   DN

A Geoffrey Baxter amethyst soda glass vase, for Whitefriars.

1962-64   4in (10cm) high

$70-100   MHT

Two Geoffrey Baxter small shadow green soda glass vases, in shadow green, for Whitefriars, pattern no.9548.

4in (10cm) high

$50-70 pair   MHT

Above right: Whitefriars "ribbon-trailed" glass lamp base, designed by Barnaby Powell, the body of pale green tone and decorated with a horizontal spiralling band.

8.25in (21cm) high

$270-320   DN

A Geoffrey Baxter willow cased bowl, for Whitefriars, pattern no "9660".

c1965   11.5in (29.5cm) wide

$90-120   MHT

A Geoffrey Baxter four-sided cased dish, for Whitefriars.

1960s/1970s 5.25in (13.5cm) h

$40-50   MHT

A Geoffrey Baxter ruby dish, with splayed rim, for Whitefriars.

1960s/1970s 6.25in (16cm) h

$40-50   MHT

GLASS

LOETZ

- Founded by Johann B. Eisner von Einstein at Kostermuhle in Austria in 1836, the factory was bought by Susanna Gerstner, the widow of glassmaker Johann Loetz and renamed 'Loetz-Witwe', in 1851.

- Gerstner's grandson Max Ritter von Spaun took over in 1879. Assisted by Eduard Prochaska, a glass technician, they produced new designs in iridescent art glass and in Art Nouveau-styles.

- Inspired by Tiffany's 'Favrile' range they used stronger, unusual and sophisticated color combinations, incorporating reds, cobalt blues and golds. Due to this range, the period around the turn of the century were highly successful years for Loetz.

- Forms were inspired by Tiffany's pieces, but Loetz also produced other new forms with applied ribs, metal mounts and numerous handles. Papillon with its 'oil spot' design and 'Phaomen' with pulled trails over iridescent glass, were popular ranges.

- Many well-known designers were employed during this period, including the Secessionist architect Leopold Bauer and Koloman Moser, who designed simple but strong forms.

- After 1905, production moved away from Art Nouveau styles with forms becoming more regular and colors brighter. Silver became the dominant metallic color in use, and a 'cracked ice' design was introduced.

- In 1906, Josef Hoffman joined and the factory was reinvigorated, with new designs using stylized leaf and geometric patterns and acid-etched cameo techniques.

- After 1914, the factory produced pieces for Weiner Werkstatte, including those by designers such as Arnold Nechansky, Michael Powolny and Dagobert Peche.

- The 1930s saw a serious fire at the factory and the 1939 Wall Street Crash. Although it was declared bankrupt in 1939, the factory carried on until 1948 when it finally closed.

A Loetz 'Candia Papillon' nautilus shell, designed 1898, unsigned.

7.5in (19cm) long

$600-700   **FRE**

A Loetz decorated and silver overlay vase, with light blue iridescent pattern, topped with silver overlay in a flowing Art Nouveau pattern.

5.25in (13.5cm) high

$3,500-4500   **JDJ**

A Loetz 'Phaomen' vase, of classical form, etched signature "Loetz Austria".

5.25in (13.5cm) high

$1,500-2,000   **FRE**

A Loetz 'Papillon' glass vase, possibly designed by Michael Powolny, lobed form with ruffled rim on three ball feet, "CZECHOSLOVAKIA" in oval stamped mark, minor scratches in interior.

c1920   *5in (12.5cm) high*

$820-880   **FRE**

A Loetz iridescent 'King Tut' vase, gold body swirled with blue lines.

4in (10cm) high

$850-950   **JDJ**

A Loetz 'Octopus' vase, brown glass with air-trapped scrolls highlighted with applied enameling, pink interior.

10in (25.5cm) high

$2,500-3,500   **JDJ**

A Loetz oil spot and silver overlaid vase, brown and blue oil spot design with silver overlaid snap dragons on the front.

8.75in (22cm) high

$650-750   **JDJ**

A Loetz iridescent glass vase, of conical shape with random splashes of silvery blue luster, further decorated with a sinuous floral appliqué, cracked on neck and with added collar.

4.5in (11.5cm) high

$150-200   **DN**

A small Loetz iridescent glass vase, of tapering form with slightly flared neck, the slightly dimpled and frosted body with soft iridescent sheen and applied with three golden scrolling vertical bands in relief.

4.75in (12cm) high

$250-350   **DN**

A Loetz iridescent bottle, with light blue iridescent free-form threading, tiny chip to edge of base.

7in (18cm) high

$120-180 JDJ

A rare Loetz glass bowl, peach-colored shading to raspberry at the base, entirely threaded with fluted rim.

10in (25.5cm) diam

$650-750 JDJ

A Loetz glass footed bowl, with ruffled edge and three curved feet, in clear glass with iridescent oil spot decoration, unsigned, falsely inscribed "Tiffany".

c1900 *8.5in (21.5cm) wide*

$250-350 SI

A Loetz floriform vase, shades from green base to red top with blue-green iridescence.

13.5in (34.5cm) high

$200-300 JDJ

An unusual iridescent green Loetz vase, with green snake wrapped around the body, several tiny fleabites to the lip.

9in (23cm) high

$120-180 JDJ

An unusual glass 'creature' pouring vessel, attributed to Loetz and a design by Richard Techner.

7in (18cm) high

$320-380 DN

A red Loetz vase, with pinched body, ribbed shoulder and bulbous mouth with irregular silver iridescence.

5.5in (14cm) high

$180-220 JDJ

BARBER'S BOTTLES

- Barber's bottles were popular from the late 19th century onwards. They primarily take a familiar form with a bulbous base and a tall, slim neck terminating in a spout. Early bottles are lighter in weight than later examples.
- Many bottles are highly decorative, usually being decorated with painted designs or being made from brightly colored glass.
- They contained hair tonic, bay rum, shampoo, cologne and other necessary lotions for the barber to use. Colors corresponded to contents so the barber knew which bottle to pick. Bottles for generic lotions were often branded, sometimes with labels under the glass, or with painted lettering.
- Many barbers mixed their own tonics and cologne until around 1906, when the food and drug act made it illegal to fill unlabelled bottles with alcohol based products and the production and use of these bottles declined rapidly.
- Collectors should look for decorated bottles, or bottles bearing labels, which are the most desirable. Plain and early bottles are usually inexpensive.

A cranberry barber's bottle, with enamel floral decoration and damaged metal stopper.

$100-150 JDJ

A cranberry opalescent barber's bottle with china stopper.

$80-120 JDJ

A cranberry barber's bottle with opalescent hobnails.

$120-180 JDJ

A cobalt blue Mary Gregory type barber's bottle with metal stopper.

$100-150 JDJ

A Victorian green barber's bottle with enamel decoration.

$100-150 JDJ

A Victorian cut glass barber's bottles with metal stopper.

$70-100 JDJ

A Victorian cut glass barber's bottles with metal stopper.

$80-120 JDJ

A Victorian cut glass barber's bottles with metal stopper.

$60-90 JDJ

An amethyst barber's bottle with enameled decoration, with a china stopper, and a blue barber's bottle with enamel decoration, lacking stopper.

$150-250 JDJ

Two green barber's bottles (one shown) with white enamel decoration and metal stoppers.

$150-200 JDJ

An amethyst barber's bottle, with gold and yellow enameled floral decoration, missing stopper.

$150-250 JDJ

An amethyst barber's bottle, with gold and yellow enameled floral decoration, with metal stopper.

$200-300 JDJ

A cobalt blue barber's bottle with white enamel and gold decoration, with metal stopper.

$200-300 JDJ

An amethyst opalescent barber's bottle, with metal stopper.

$200-250 JDJ

One of a set of four molded cranberry barber's bottles, with metal stopper.

Tallest 9.5in (24cm) high

$300-500 (set) JDJ

One of a set of four bay rum decorated barber's bottles, with china stopper, paint worn

Tallest 10.5in (26.5cm) high

$200-400 (set) JDJ

A pair of white cut to cranberry overlay barber's bottles, cut in a raised diamond pattern.

$400-600 JDJ

VERLYS

- In 1920, the American Holophane Company set up a subsidiary at L'Andelys near Rouen in France which initially produced car headlamps. The name 'Verlys' is derived from the French words for the glassworks – 'Verrerie d'Andelys'.
- By the mid 1920s, the factory had moved into art glass with internal decoration and a smooth exterior. After 1933, production focused on fine quality press molded glass. Pieces bear molded signatures reading 'Verlys France' or 'Verlys Made In France'.
- Designs were strongly inspired by the styles of Lalique and it is easy to confuse Verlys with Lalique at first glance.
- Frosted, opalescent, clear and colored items were all produced. Patterns were also in the manner of Lalique, and of the 1930s in general, with sophisticated patterns using geometrical designs, birds, fish and plants. Collectors prefer the opalescent and frosted pieces, with smoky gray, blue and pink being less popular.
- In 1935, a Verlys factory was established at a glass factory in Newark, Ohio. Although molds were supplied to the American factory from France, not all designs were shared.
- The period just before the Second World War saw a slow decline in production of this glass, and during the war the factory made industrial and commercial products. Production finally ceased around 1952.
- From 1955 until 1957 some of the Verlys molds were leased to the Heisey glass factory, in Newark, Ohio, who produced a limited range of original designs. In 1966, the Fenton Art Glass Company, Virginia, acquired the molds and produced some pieces, but these were not marked with the Verlys mark.

A Verlys molded and frosted glass charger, molded on the surface with three orchid blossoms, inscribed "Verlys".

c1940   14in (35.5cm) diam

$90-120   SI

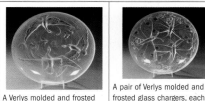

A Verlys molded and frosted glass charger, molded on the underside with three ducks and fish, marked "Verlys".

c1935   13.5in (34cm) high

$90-120   SI

A pair of Verlys molded and frosted glass chargers, each molded on the underside with three butterflies and flowers, inscribed "Verlys".

c1940 13.5in (34.5cm) diam

$180-250   SI

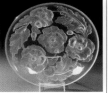

A pair of Verlys chargers, each molded on the underside with hibiscus blossoms, inscribed "Verlys".

c1940 13.5in (34.5cm) diam

$180-230   SI

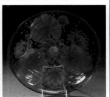

A Verlys molded turquoise glass charger, molded on the interior and underside with water lilies, inscribed "Verlys".

c1940   13.25in (35cm) diam

$150-200   SI

A Verlys Art Deco blue glass centerpiece bowl, circular on short foot, molded with radiating ribs, , molded "Verlys France".

c1935   16in (41cm) diam

$60-100   SI

A Verlys molded and frosted topaz glass centrepiece bowl, and matching vase, the vase with conforming decoration, vase molded "Verlys France".

c1935   15in (38cm) diam

$120-180   SI

A Verlys molded topaz glass center bowl, the underside molded with six tassels or grasses, inscribed "Verlys".

c1940   11.75in (30cm) diam

$60-80   SI

A Verlys molded and frosted glass vase, the ovoid vessel molded with dogwood, inscribed "Verlys".

c1940   7.5in (19cm) high

$70-100   SI

A Verlys molded opalescent glass vase, molded with stylized berries on vines, inscribed "Verlys".

c1940   6.5in (16.5cm)

$70-100   SI

A Verlys chrome-mounted molded topaz glass vase, the trumpet-form vessel on a circular stepped metal foot molded with latticework and an acid-textured ground, molded "Verlys France".

c1935   6.75in (17cm) high

$150-200   SI

A Verlys molded and frosted topaz glass wine cooler, of stepped tapering form on a ten-sided base with triple scroll handles, molded with stylized foliage on a textured ground, molded "Verlys France".

c1935   9.5in (24cm) high

$200-250   SI

A Verlys molded glass four seasons vase, molded with two frosted figures of women depicting summer and fall, inscribed "Verlys" and signed "Carl Scmitz/1940".

c1940   8.5in (20.5cm) high

$150-200   SI

A Verlys molded and frosted glass powder box, the cover molded with three butterflies, mounted with a glass and metal handle, molded "Verlys".

c1935   6.5in (16.5cm) diam

$100-150   SI

A Verlys molded amber glass powder box, the cover molded with a chrysanthemum, molded "Verlys France".

c1935   4.75in (12cm) diam

$120-180   SI

CRANBERRY GLASS

■ As its name suggests, cranberry glass has a characteristic ruby pink color. This comes from the addition of copper oxide or gold chloride to the glass mix. Although it was produced by the ancient Romans, it became most fashionable in Victorian England, where the center of production was at Stourbridge. In America it was widely produced, primarily at the Boston & Sandwich Glass Co. (1826-1888) in Sandwich, Massachusetts.

A cranberry glass two-handled vase, slight damage.

6in (15cm) diam

$90-120   **OACC**

Two opalescent cranberry glass vases, comprising a triple tree trunk vase with a clear fluted base and a light amber green glass vase with cranberry opalescence at the heavily fluted rim, clear glass rigaree spirals down the body.

Largest 10in (25.5cm) high

$225-275   **JDJ**

A religious cranberry glass bowl, with white enamel decoration "IHS" (In His Service).

2.75in (7cm) diam

$60-100   **OACC**

An American freeblown cranberry glass apothecary's shop trade sign, wooden base.

Apothecary's shops had two of these signs: one red and one blue. If the blue sign was in the window visitors knew there was disease in the town. A red sign meant it was safe to visit.

c1840   *15in (38cm) high*

$1,500-2,000   **RAA**

A Victorian cranberry glass sweet basket.

4.5in (11cm) diam

$120-180   **OACC**

A cranberry glass tankard, engraved "To Madame Fontana as souvenir from Mr Voisin, 1840".

c1840   *5.5in (14cm) high*

$200-300   **OACC**

A Victorian cranberry glass jug, gilded and hand-painted.

c1870   *4in (10cm) high*

$120-180   **OACC**

A pair of cranberry glass tumblers.

4in (10cm) high

$70-100   **OACC**

A cranberry glass wine glass.

5in (12.5cm) high

$20-40   **OACC**

GLASS

CARNIVAL GLASS

Carnival glass is an inexpensive decorative glass characterized by its bright colors and iridescence. It is most commonly found in orange (marigold), through to green and blue. Red is very rare and is the most valuable. Often known as the 'poor man's Tiffany', the iridescence was produced by spraying the molded glass with metallic salts suspended in oil. It was popular in England from the late 19th century and in America from around 1900. It was produced in vast quantities and was even given away as prizes at fairs, hence its name.

A Carnival glass marigold dish.

$20-30   OACC

A Carnival glass bowl, with rose and dragon decoration, peacock color.

8in (20.5cm) diam

$15-25   AS&S

A Carnival glass punch bowl.

12.25in (31cm) diam

$100-150   OACC

A Carnival glass bowl.

7.5in (19cm) diam

$15-25   OACC

A Carnival glass boat-shaped dish.

7in (18cm) long

$40-50   OACC

Pressed glass

A late 19thC molded glass dish.

c1900   7.75in (20cm) diam

$20-30   OACC

A pressed glass chamber stick, bearing the motto 'Good Night'.

c1900   5.25in (13cm) diam

$50-70   OACC

A pressed glass tazza.

7.75in (20cm) diam

$12-18   OACC

Two small 19thC green pressed glass plates, decorated with flowers and foliage.

Largest 10.5in (26.5cm) diam

$40-50 pair   WW

PICKLE CASTORS

■ Pickle castors were used in wealthy homes in the late 19th century to serve pickles at the table. Look for sets that include the original tongs as well as those by well-known manufacturers. As well as being colored, some glass inners have enameled or painted decoration. They are currently becoming highly collectable.

A Mount Washington Amberina pickle castor, with hobnail Amberina insert and silver-plated holder, signed "James W Tufts".

12in (30.5cm) high

$2,000-3,000   JDJ

A late 19thC cranberry pickle castor, the panel sprig insert set in a Cincinnatus quadruple-plate frame.

10.5in (26.5cm) high

$600-700   JDJ

A late 19thC blue enameled pickle castor, the inverted thumbprint insert decorated with enameled flowers and beads with gold trim and outlines, in Derby quadruple-plate frame without tongs.

10.5in (26.5cm) high

$680-720   JDJ

A Depression glass candlewick desk mirror.

$100-150   PR

A late 19thC ruby glass pickle castor, set in a Pairpoint quadruple-plate frame with tongs,

10.25in (26cm) high

$550-650   JDJ

A late 19thC pigeon-blood pickle castor, the inverted thumbprint insert set in an unmarked silver-plated frame with tongs.

9.5in (24cm) high

$550-650   JDJ

An amber coin-spot pickle castor, in frame with tongs.

10.5in (26.5cm) high

$400-500   JDJ

A late 19thC double pickle castor, set in a double Forbes quadruple-plate frame

10.5in (26.5cm) high

$350-450   JDJ

DEPRESSION GLASS

Depression glass was produced in the USA during the economically poor times of the 1920s and 1930s. Machine-made pressed glass is typified by heavily molded kitchen or tableware and was produced in a range of pale colors. Blue is the most desirable color, followed by pink and green. Manufacturers include Anchor Hocking, Federal and Hazel Atlas. The glass was made in huge quantities, often being given away as a promotional gift.

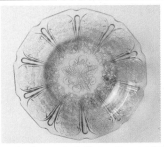

A flat Depression glass soup bowl, with cherry blossom pattern.

$50-100   PR

A flat Depression glass soup plate, with iris pattern.

$120-180   PR

A Depression glass iced tea tumbler, with 'Sharon' pattern.

$40-60   **PR**

A Depression glass gravy boat and platter, with 'Florentine' pattern.

$80-110   **PR**

A Depression glass floral lamp.

$200-300   **PR**

MOUNT WASHINGTON

■ The Mount Washington Glassworks was founded in 1837, in Boston, MA. From around 1880 until the early 20th century, it was known for its satin finished art glass. It often had enameled decoration and silver mounts. It also patented 'Burmese' glass in 1885, the color of which faded from yellow to pink at the top.

A Mount Washington blown-out box, with blown-out cabbage head and leaves.

8in (20.5cm) diam

$1,300-1,500   **JDJ**

A Mount Washington Crown Milano cookie jar, with Persian enamel decoration of flowers and leaves, unsigned, original signed "Pairpoint" hardware, minor paint loss.

7.5in (19cm) high

$520-580   **JDJ**

A Mount Washington satin glass biscuit jar, drape-molded pink with enameled decoration of amethyst leaves and white and blue blossoms, original metal hardware.

9in (23cm) high

$480-520   **JDJ**

A Mount Washington temple jar, with blue draping flowers, green leaves and vines all highlighted with gold enamel, lip of jar beaded and decorated in gold.

8in (20.5cm) high

$650-750   **JDJ**

A Mount Washington cased bride's bowl, signed "Pairpoint" silver-plated stand, base inscribed in German and dated, the base with some wear to silver plating.

1888   *11.5in (29cm) high*

$460-500   **JDJ**

A Mount Washington Burmese syrup jug, decorated with blue and white flower blossoms, applied Burmese handle and original silver-plated hardware.

6in (15cm) high

$5,000-6,000   **JDJ**

A pair of Mount Washington Burmese salt and pepper shakers, vertically ribbed with original silver-plated tops and fancy silver-plated holder.

6in (15cm) high

$800-900   **JDJ**

A mold-blown Wave Crest hinged box, decorated with blue forget-me-nots and a Dutch windmill scene, highlighted with gold enamel scrolls.

6.5in (16.5cm) wide

$400-500   JDJ

A green mold-blown Wave Crest box, with enamel pink flowers and leaves on the lid and gold scroll highlights, areas of green missing on top corner, lining is missing.

7in (18cm) square

$300-400   JDJ

A signed Wave Crest shell pattern box, with blue and white flowers on a pink ground, signed on the bottom "Wave Crest", some wear to painted flowers on top.

4in (10cm) diam

$350-450   JDJ

A Wave Crest covered jar with hinged lid, decorated with fern bows in green, tan and blue, and small red forget-me-not type flowers, very slight wear to the finish.

7.5in (19cm) high

$450-550   JDJ

A Wave Crest Helmschmidt swirl cracker jar, with pink floral decoration, original metal hardware, retains original Wave Crest label.

10in (25.5cm) high

$350-450   JDJ

A pair of hand-decorated Wave Crest ewers, with brass collars at top and bottom and white metal ewer top, handle and base, tail of one handle slightly bent and corroded.

15.5in (39.5cm) high

$250-350   JDJ

A signed Wave Crest sweetmeat dish and perfume bottle, signed on the bottom "Wave Crest", the bottle signed on the bottom "Wave Crest", missing collar and cap.

Dish 5.5in (14cm) diam

$280-320   JDJ

Two C.F. Monroe pieces, comprising a signed "Wave Crest" planter, decorated with pink and yellow flowers and a brass collar and a signed "NAKARA" and a brown Nakara box decorated with blue flowers.

Largest 5.5in (14cm) long

$300-400   JDJ

An unusual signed Kew Blas stick vase, with wide flat bottom and gold iridescent damascene design.

5.5in (14cm) high

$1,000-1,500   JDJ

A hand-decorated Burmese creamer, applied handle and ruffled rim.

2.5in (6.5cm) high

$300-400   JDJ

Three Burmese items, comprising a Mount Washington finger bowl with ruffled top and two tumblers.

Bowl 6in (15cm) diam

$350-450   JDJ

A rare Burgun and Scheverer & Co. two-handled bowl, with cameo and enamel decoration of various animals including griffins, salamanders and dragons, base with enamel black and white collar, signed on base "MEISENTHAL BS & CO".

5.75in (14.5cm) diam

$3,000-4,000   JDJ

A B C D E F G H I J K L M N O P Q R S T U V W XYZ

Two Burmese lily vases, one Mount Washington, the other, attributed to Webb, ribbed with applied foot.

6in (15cm) high

$500-600 | **JDJ**

A small Burmese vase, ruffled lip with applied rigaree at the neck, with faint hobnail type design.

3in (7.5cm) high

$350-450 | **JDJ**

A Burmese glass fairy lamp, base marked "S. CLARKE FAIRY PYRAMID", shade has flake to the inside at the bottom rim as well as edge roughness.

3.75in (9.5cm) high

$50-80 | **JDJ**

A tall Clutha green glass vase, by James Couper & Sons, designed by George Walton, the body of tapering cylindrical form, with a broad rim and trailing opaque inclusions.

15.75in (40cm) high

$4,000-4,500 | **L&T**

A Clutha green glass vase, by James Couper & Sons, the ovoid body with knopped and tapering neck and everted rim, the body having aventurine and trailing opaque inclusions.

9in (23cm) high

$400-500 | **L&T**

A signed D'Argental cameo vase, in shades of purple and depicting a tropical island scene with palm trees, water and mountains.

11.5in (29cm) high

$2,000-3,000 | **JDJ**

A Degue cameo glass vase, orange ground with brown leaves extending upward half way from the base, four groupings of four flowers each extend up from the leaves, three rub marks between two of the flower groupings.

14in (35.5cm) diam

$800-1,200 | **JDJ**

An A. Delatte enameled glass vase, signed "A. DELATTE NANCY".

4.5in (11.5cm) high

$500-600 | **JDJ**

A rare signed De Vez cameo bowl, round base extending to square top, with sailing ships and islands viewed through an arbor draped with floral garlands, the brown cameo ships, flowers and arbor set against a cream-colored background.

3.75in (9.5cm) high

$700-1,000 | **JDJ**

A De Vez acid-cut cameo vase, decorated with a landscape with a castle overlooking a lake, signed in cameo "DE VEZ".

8in (20.5cm) high

$1,200-1,800 | **JDJ**

A Durand gold and blue iridescent vase, bulbous body extending to a long slender neck, signed on the base "Durand" in block letters.

6.25in (16cm) high

$450-550 | **JDJ**

A Dorflinger presentation piece, engraved "DORFLINGER GLASS STUDY GROUP 1972-1982", signed on base "R V S #5 OF 26".

1972-1982   75in (24.5cm) high

$120-180   JDJ

A Durand 'King Tut' decorated bowl, unsigned, the rim appears "out of round", crack on the pontil at the base of the bowl.

10.5in (26.5cm) diam

$700-800   JDJ

An Etling opalescent bowl.

Edmond Etling & Cie, active in France in the 1920s and 30s, produced molded opalescent glass comparable in standards of design to Sabino, the figures of draped female nudes are especially collectable.

1920-30   9in (23cm) diam

$450-500   OACC

An Etling molded opalescent glass vase, molded with stylized blossoms, molded "ETLING".

As can be seen, Etling was influenced by René Lalique.

c1930   7in (18cm) high

$300-500   SI

A Findlay onyx spooner, with good color retention, several chips and roughness to the lip.

4.25in (11cm) high

$300-400   JDJ

A rare raspberry Findlay onyx spooner.

4in (10cm) high

$1,000-1,500   JDJ

A signed Handel 'Teroma' vase, decorated with a mountainous landscape in shades of greens, blues and lavender, signed on the base "Handel 4221".

10in (25.5cm) high

$1,800-2,200   JDJ

An enameled Handel vase, with flared, fluted rim and decorated in brown enamel depicting trees, shrubs and grass with simplistic birds in the sky, signed in the polished pontil "Handel".

7in (18cm) high

$400-500   JDJ

A Higgins striped glass bowl, in beige, white and gray, with gold striped accents, marked.

9.5in (24cm) diam

$120-180   CR

A six-sided Kelva box, signed, bottom liner is missing, collar appears to be reattached.

3.5in (9cm) diam

$350-400   JDJ

A Kelva box, signed on the bottom "KELVA", top liner missing, top collar re-glued, hinge has some wear.

3.5in (9cm) diam

$220-280   JDJ

A large Val St. Lambert cameo glass vase, in clear glass overlaid with mottled green, russet, brown and yellow and cut with vines and pendant blossoms, signed in cameo.

c1900   20in (50.5cm) high

$4,000-5,000   SI

A Legras enameled acid-etched glass landscape cylindrical vase, painted and acid-etched with a landscape of boats on a lake, signed "Legras".

c1910   6.75in (17cm) high

$450-550   SI

A Legras bulbous stick vase, with cameo decoration of green leaves and vines over frosted glass, signed within the decoration.

14.75in (37.5cm) high

$1,000-1,500   JDJ

A Legras scenic cameo vase, decorated with a village and trees, signed on the side of the vase.

3.75in (9.5cm) high

$850-950   JDJ

A Legras winter scene vase, square-shaped with enameled decoration of trees surrounded by snow, signed.

5in (12.5cm) wide

$550-650   JDJ

A Libbey Brilliant Period 'Wedgemere' pattern tray, signed "Libbey".

c1900

$4,500-5,500   PTA

A Libbey vase, flaring ruffle top with vertical ribbing, signed on base.

6.5in (16.5cm) diam

$500-600   JDJ

A large Kathleen Mulcahy blown glass globe, of onion form with orange and yellow variegated stripes, small opening, engraved "Kathleen Mulcahy".

22in (56cm) high

$800-900   FRE

A Muller cameo vase, blue opalescent body with burgundy cameo flowers, leaves and stems, signed on the bottom "MULLER CROISMARE".

10in (25.5cm) high

$1,000-1,500   JDJ

A Pairpoint bubble glass and silver-plated lumiere, the glass globe with internal air bubble design fitted into a lighted base cast with acanthus, guilloche and bellflowers, base impressed "PAIRPOINT/E3013" and with a "P" in a diamond.

c1910   7.25in (18.5cm) high

$800-900   SI

A Pairpoint vase, ruby cut to clear on a diamond stem and square base, chips to each corner of the base and a fishscale to one of the cut ribs.

13.25in (33.5cm) high

$1,000-1,500   JDJ

A pair of matching Pairpoint green glass candlesticks, engraved in the vintage pattern.

6in (15cm) high

$1,000-1,200   JDJ

A Quezal compote, with blue-green iridescent bowl supported by an amber iridescent stem, signed on the base "QUEZAL".

6.25in (16cm) high

$800-1,000   **JDJ**

A 20thC Sabino molded green glass vase, molded with leaves and berries, inscribed "Sabino France".

4in (10cm) high

$280-320   **SI**

A 1930s Czechoslovakian Curt Schlevogt malachite glass vase, with entwined female nudes and tree branches on a faceted base.

5in (12.5cm) high

$350-400   **FRE**

A large Schneider vase, signed "Schneider" with an etched outline of a vase next to the signature.

6in (15cm) high

$1,800-2,200   **JDJ**

A Schneider yellow bowl, with brown tortoiseshell design on the upper third, signed "Schneider" at the base.

4.5in (11.5cm) diam

$220-280   **JDJ**

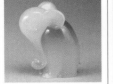

A blue and white glass elephant, attributed to Seguso, etched "Seguso Murano", unmarked.

6in (15cm) high

$120-180   **CR**

A Smith Bros. temple jar, melon-ribbed with chrysanthemum decoration on a pastel green background with gold beads around the top, signed with a rampant lion mark, repair to top of the vase.

8.5in (21.5cm) high

$100-150   **JDJ**

A Smith Bros. biscuit jar, white blossoms highlighted with gold on a blue background, unsigned, original hardware, wear to silver plating.

10.5in (26.5cm) high

$600-700   **JDJ**

A Stevens and Williams red cameo glass vase, ovoid with white dogwood branch and bleeding heart decoration.

c1890   *7in (18cm) high*

$1,500-2,000   **SI**

A pair of St. Louis crystal glass candlesticks, with a teardrop bubble in the center of the candlestick, signed on base with acid etched insignia, interior bubble has "in the making" staining.

8.75in (22cm) high

$250-350   **JDJ**

A Thomas Webb jardinière, triple-cased rainbow glass.

1900-1930   *10in (25cm) high*

$2,000-3,000   **PTA**

A pâte-de-verre boat-shaped pin tray, mottled yellow glass set with a bumble bee at one end, the bee striped with various shades of brown and the wings in green, signed "WALTER".

4in (10cm) long

$1,400-1,600   **JDJ**

A Murano presentation goblet, with floral design, accented in gold, unmarked, some losses to gold.

10in (25.5cm) high

$150-200   **CR**

An early 20thC Vaseline glass bonbon dish, in Walker & Hall silver-plated stand.

6.75in (17cm) diam

$120-160 **AS&S**

A late 19thC French art glass vase, with a flared neck.

6n (15cm) high

$50-80 **AS&S**

A late 19thC French hand-blown vase, with bubble decoration.

6in (15cm) high

$90-120 **AS&S**

A French art glass vase, with twisted decoration.

6in (15cm) high

$70-100 **AS&S**

An enamel-decorated art glass vase, probably French, green shading to clear iridescent glass, painted with yellow and white irises, inscribed in enamel "F.H. 493/3 H146".

c1900 *8in (20.5cm) high*

$350-400 **SI**

A pair of cameo and enamel winter scene vases, with trees and snow, signed on the bottom sometime after manufacture with "Daum Nancy".

8.5in (21.5cm) high

$1,000-1,500 **JDJ**

An American pink blown-glass vase, the globular vessel with ruffled rim painted with white enameled flowers on a thorny branch, inscribed in enamel "794/5".

c1880 *5.5in (14cm) high*

$200-300 **SI**

A gold iridescent Austrian art glass vase, with clear free-form lines.

28.5in (72.5cm) high

$1,400-2,000 **JDJ**

An unusual Bohemian agate glass vase, similar to lithyalin, the exterior cut through to the tan base glass forming lotus buds and blossoms, small grinding to the corner of the vase on a lotus leaf, probably done in the making.

4.5in (11.5cm) high

$400-500 **JDJ**

A silver overlaid bottle vase, of thin Loetz-type green glass with elaborate repoussé silver overlay, unsigned.

13in (33cm) high

$550-650 **JDJ**

A Moser-type cobalt blue vase, with gold decoration and three color panels with figures.

12.75in (30.5cm) high

$220-280 **JDJ**

A Moser-type vase, with applied enamel salamander, crystal rigaree and enameled floral decoration, the top ground down on the points.

10.5in (26.5cm) high

$450-550 JDJ

A cased glass vase, attributed to Webb, shaded yellow glass with gold enamel decoration of blossoms, leaves and branches, signed with a propeller mark.

7.5in (19cm) high

$180-220 JDJ

A late 19thC art glass vase, yellow cased in white with gold leaves and branches and four jewelled bugs, the collar with Egyptian type lettering.

6in (15cm) high

$550-650 JDJ

A French art glass vase, with mottled green and blue metallic decoration, pinched rim.

4in (10cm) high

$80-120 AS&S

A late 19thC French Art Nouveau glass vase, applied with green glass mouldings and with a wide flat rim.

5in (12.5cm) high

$120-180 AS&S

An Art glass vase, blue shading to clear inverted thumbprint decoration.

6.5in (16.5cm) high

$350-450 JDJ

A yellow satin glass vase, ovoid-shape with white lining.

8in (20.5cm) high

$70-100 JDJ

A raspberry satin glass vase, ovoid-shape with creamy white lining, acid finish.

5in (12.5cm) high

$140-180 JDJ

A 1920s hand-blown blue Art glass vase, with wave decoration to waist.

7.75in (20cm) high

$80-120 AS&S

An English green glass vase, with applied teardrop decoration.

8in (20.5cm) high

$250-300 AS&S

A grey glass vase, with abstract flower motifs.

c1960   11.75in (30cm) high

$70-100 MHT

Two Italian Art glass vases, one of cylindrical form with bands of orange, green and blue, unmarked, together with a vase of bulbous form with alternating yellow and white stripes, small fracture to foot.

Tallest 11.5in (30cm) high

$450-550 FRE

A Loetz-type iridescent diamond quilted pattern bowl, with metal cover.

6.5in (16.5cm) diam

$60-100 JDJ

A Loetz-type gold iridescent bowl, with purple highlights.

6in (15cm) diam

$180-220 JDJ

A pink diamond quilted satin glass jar, the silver-plated lid with floral decoration and beaded lip, roughness to the lip.

6in (15cm) diam

$75-85 JDJ

A Loetz-type green iridescent triangular bowl, with rolled rim, decorated inside and out with enameled flowers, the stems highlighted in gold.

8in (20.5cm) diam

$220-280 JDJ

An Art Deco opalescent green glass bowl, circular with molded "V" geometric panels between three supporting legs.

5.25in (13.5cm) high

$130-180 FRE

A 1960s Murano glass dish, unsigned.

17in (43cm) high

$180-230 V

A 1960s art glass bowl.

9in (22cm) diam

$30-50 AS&S

An art glass center bowl, with a pierced rim.

11in (28cm) diam

$25-35 AS&S

An Italian 'Canedece' glass bowl, with polychrome swirled design, unmarked, fleck to one edge.

9.5in (24cm) diam

$250-300 CR

An art glass dresser box, iridescent blue with applied enameled decoration of pink and white flowers.

4.75in (12cm) diam

$250-300 JDJ

A late 19thC box, decorated with a young boy and girl with kitten on a blue background.

5.5in (14cm) diam

$200-300 JDJ

A late 19thC cupid box, decorated with two cherubs gardening, on a blue background, on a brass three-legged foot.

4in (10cm) high

$250-350 JDJ

A hinged art glass dresser box, with enameled pansies and green leaves on a beige background, original metal hardware.

8in (20.5cm) diam

$200-250 JDJ

A satin glass water pitcher, coin spot decoration with red color shading to white, ruffled top and an applied frosted reeded handle.

8.5in (21.5cm) high

$350-450 JDJ

A blue coin spot syrup jug, with applied handle, original nickel-plated brass top, dated.

1882 6.5in (16.5cm) high

$450-500 RAA

A rare and early blown glass footed bottle, with separately blown and applied disk base, twisted lobe column, inverted tear drop-shape body

An old note stuck in bottle reads "Extremely Rare Lace Workers Bottle, Listed in McKerin's Book on Glass, value $65 or more".

9in (23cm) diam

$200-300   **TWC**

A hand-decorated opal glass cream and sugar set, each with plated metal collar with attached handles, some minor wear to plating.

$120-180   **JDJ**

A pair of Bohemian amber-flashed candlesticks, engraved with grapes, leaves and strawberry.

13.5in (34.5cm) high

$400-500   **JDJ**

A 'Midwestern' pattern globular bottle, aqua-colored with ribs swirling to the right.

9in (23cm) high

$220-280   **JDJ**

A 1960s blue brandy glass, with internal jeweling.

10in (25.5cm) high

$8-12   **AS&S**

A late 19thC cheese dish, light amber glass with all-over enameled flowers, slight roughness to the edge of the underplate as well as two small chips.

8.75in (22cm) diam

$120-180   **JDJ**

A free-blown 'end-of-day' glass punch ladle, with white powder sulphide lining.

c1890   *14.5in (37cm) long*

$200-250   **RAA**

An amethyst free-blown flip glass, broken pontil, used for making a syllabub drink.

c1840   *8in (20.5cm) high*

$260-300   **RAA**

A large Murano lamp, by Cenedese.

c1960   *18.5 in (47cm) high*

$400-450   **MHT**

A late 19thC glass castor set.

$300-400   **BAC**

A milk glass rabbit, bearing mark "pat 1886".

$225-275   **BCAC**

A set of twelve serving compotes, attributed to Dorflinger, with glass inserts and gold enamel decoration, two missing inserts.

7in (18cm) high

$650-750 (set)   **JDJ**

A commemorative consolidated glass boudoir lamp, commemorating the fraternal order of Elks, in the form of an elk's head with a clock between its horns, a couple of chips.

13in (33cm) high

$300-400   **JDJ**

A pair of Italian glass figures, a lady and gentleman each holding a bundle of wheat, in pale blue, clear and gold-flecked glass.

c1940

$200-300   **SI**

JEWELRY

CHRISTIAN DIOR

- Christian Dior started making costume jewelry at the end of World War II as part of his extravagant New Look.
- Early designs were made to look deliberately 'fake' and showy, using unconventional stones such as aurora borealis and petal-shaped glass.
- Soon, Dior started using these 'new' stones in conventional 18thC designs and the company's trademark costume jewelry look was born.
- Early designs are couture pieces, made by craftsmen to complement a particular outfit for one client. Later pieces were made in greater numbers – but not mass-produced – for the company's boutiques.
- Dior's designs were produced by Kramer in the US until 1955 and by Mitchell Maer in England from 1950-52. Then in 1955, the German firm Henkle & Grosse was given an exclusive licence to produce Dior's designs.
- Collectors look for pre-1970 evening necklaces and earrings, although there is a growing market for more affordable pieces from the 1970s.

A mid-late 1950s Christian Dior rhinestone and paste unicorn pin, by Mitchell Maer.

$80-120   **RG**

A mid-late 1950s Christian Dior clear paste and faux pearl flower pin, by Mitchell Maer, signed Christian Dior.

$120-180   **RG**

A Christian Dior necklace and earrings, set with iridescent glass and aurora borealis stone, signed by Christian Dior.

c1958

$400-500   **RG**

A mid-late 1950s Christian Dior necklace and earrings set with clear paste stones and green marble effect cabochons, by Mitchell Maer.

$400-600   **RG**

A Christian Dior pin, set with royal blue and aurora borealis stones, signed and dated 1958.

$120-180   **RG**

A Christian Dior necklace and earrings, set with faux rubies and diamonds.

1959 Earrings 1.5in (4cm) long

$400-600   **Rox**

A 1960s Christian Dior necklace, bracelet and earrings, by Kramer.

Earrings 1in (3cm) long

$200-300   **Rox**

A Christian Dior pearl and diamanté pin.

1963   *4in (9cm) long*

$220-280   **Rox**

A Christian Dior abstract apple pin, set with red, blue and clear rhinestones and faux pearls, signed "Christian Dior", made in Germany.

1962

$300-500   **RG**

A 1960s Christian Dior heart-shaped pin, set with clear stones with pink or white inclusions and pastel yellow, blue and green stones, signed Christian Dior.

$180-220   **RG**

A Christian Dior necklace, earrings and pin, set with faux emerald and lapis stones, signed "CD Germany".

1966

$300-500   **RG**

A rare Christian Dior circus seal pin.

1966   *3in (8cm) long*

$220-280   **Rox**

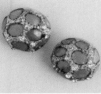

A pair of Christian Dior earrings.

1967   *1in (3cm) diam*

$100-150   **Rox**

A 1970s Christian Dior pin.

3in (7cm) long

$60-100   **TR**

A Christian Dior necklace and earrings, set with emerald green and clear paste, signed Christian Dior.

1967

$300-500   **RG**

A Christian Dior Indian influence necklace, set with faux pearl and faux lapis beads, signed and dated.

From the the estate of the singer and actress, Vivienne Blaine.

1970

$350-400   **RG**

A pair of 1930s Miriam Haskell pink and diamanté drop earrings, unmarked.

2.25in (6cm) long

$120-180   **Rox**

A 1940s Miriam Haskell pearl and diamanté pin and earrings.

Earrings 1in (3cm) long

$300-500   **Rox**

A 1940s Miriam Haskell pearl, diamanté and gold flower pin.

3.25in (8cm)

$270-330   **Rox**

MIRIAM HASKELL

- Miriam Haskell's jewelry is always handmade using glass beads and simulated seed and baroque pearls threaded onto brass wire and secured to filigree backings. Another common feature are rose montée – clear paste stones set closely together.

- She only started signing her jewelry in the late 1940s, but earlier unsigned pieces can be identified by the quality of the workmanship and materials.

- Haskell opened her boutique at the McAlpin Hotel in New York in 1925 and sold the company in the early 1950s. The company continues to produce reproductions of classic designs from the 1940s and 50s today.

- Collectors of vintage pieces should learn to tell reproductions from originals. An inspection of the metal can help. The metal used in vintage pieces – known as 'antique Russian gold' – has a warm matt finish. Modern pieces look yellower in comparison.

- Buyers should also inspect the faux pearls closely. Poor storage often chips the surface irreparably and perfume, soap and creams will also erode the finish.

A Miriam Haskell pin, with matching earrings.

Pin 2.5in (6cm) high

$200-300   **Rox**

A 1940s Miriam Haskell pearl and diamanté necklace.

Drop 2in (5cm) long

$400-500   **Rox**

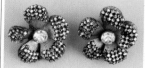

A pair of 1940s Miriam Haskell gold and diamanté flower earrings.

1.5in (4cm) long

$180-220   **Rox**

A pair of 1940s Miriam Haskell pearl and diamanté flower earrings.

1.5in (4cm) long

$180-220   **Rox**

A 1940s Miriam Haskell "cherry" design pearl and diamanté pin and earrings.

Earrings 2in (5cm) long

$400-500   **Rox**

A 1940s Miriam Haskell necklace, bracelet and earrings, with faux pearl and brass spacers and beads.

$300-500   **RG**

A 1940s Miriam Haskell faux pearl and brass necklace.

$200-250   **RG**

A 1940s Miriam Haskell pink flower pin.

2.5in (6.5cm) long

$300-400   **Rox**

A 1940s Miriam Haskell red and clear glass bead pin.

2in (5cm) long

$220-280   **Rox**

A pair of 1940s Miriam Haskell earrings, with large pink stones.

1.25in (3.5cm) long

$180-220   **Rox**

A 1940s Miriam Haskell bird of paradise stick pin, set with blue, green and pink beads.

$60-100   **RG**

A 1940s Miriam Haskell necklace.

$270-330   **Rox**

A 1940s Miriam Haskell pink and pearl bead bracelet.

Clasp 1.5in (3.5cm) long

$180-220   **Rox**

A 1940s Miriam Haskell multi-colored bead bracelet and earrings.
Earrings 2.25in (6cm)

$400-600   **Rox**

A pair of 1940s Miriam Haskell yellow flower earrings.
1.25in (3.5cm) long

$180-220   **Rox**

A pair of 1940s Miriam Haskell earrings.
1in (2.5cm) long

$120-180   **Rox**

A 1940s Miriam Haskell gold, blue and green pin.
3in (7.5cm) long

$150-200   **Rox**

A 1940s Miriam Haskell white bead pin.
3in (7.5cm) long

$180-220   **Rox**

A 1940s Miriam Haskell amber and gold necklace.
Drop center 2in (5cm) long

$300-400   **Rox**

A 1940s Miriam Haskell amber and gold necklace.
Drop center 2in (5cm) long

$300-400   **Rox**

A 1940s Miriam Haskell amber and pearl bead pin and earrings.
Earrings 1in (3cm) long

$270-330   **Rox**

A 1950s Miriam Haskell blue and white bead necklace and earrings.
Earrings 1.75in (4.5cm) long

$300-400   **Rox**

A 1950s Miriam Haskell stick pin, with baroque pearls and filigree stampings.
2.75in (7cm) long

$100-150   **CRIS**

A 1960s Miriam Haskell pearl pin and earrings.
3.5in (9cm) long

$220-280   **Rox**

A 1960s Miriam Haskell pink and white necklace.
15.75in (40cm) long

$180-220   **Rox**

A 1960s Miriam Haskell tutti-frutti necklace.
16in (41cm) long

$220-280   **Rox**

A 1960s Miriam Haskell necklace, with brass chains and faux pearls.

$220-280   **RG**

An early Joseff of Hollywood pin, set with faux emeralds and diamonds.

c1930   *2.5in (6cm) high*

$220-280   **Rox**

A pair of Russian gold and amethyst glass butterfly earrings, by Joseff of Hollywood.

c1940

$100-150   **PC**

A pair of Russian gold and diamanté star earrings, by Joseff of Hollywood.

c1940

$60-100   **PC**

A 1940s star pin, by Joseff of Hollywood.

4.5in (11cm) wide

$300-500   **CRIS**

A pair of 1940s Art Deco-style red cabochon earrings, by Joseff of Hollywood.

2.5in (6cm) long

$80-120   **CRIS**

A monarch butterfly pin, by Joseff of Hollywood.

3.5in (9cm) wide

$320-380   **CRIS**

A 1940s bee chatelaine pin, by Joseff of Hollywood.

Large bee 2.25in (5.5cm)

$320-380   **CRIS**

A 1940s horse chatelaine pin, by Joseff of Hollywood.

Shortest chain 7in (18cm) long

$180-220   **CRIS**

A 1940s French bull dog pin, by Joseff of Hollywood.

1.5in (3.5cm) diam

$60-100   **CRIS**

A pair of 1940s French bull dog earrings, by Joseff of Hollywood.

2.75in (7cm) long

$80-120   **CRIS**

Three 1940s fish pins, by Joseff of Hollywood.

1.5in (4cm) wide

$30-40 each   **CRIS**

A pair of 1940s owl earrings, by Joseff of Hollywood.

2.25in (5.5cm) high

$180-220   **CRIS**

A set of Kenneth J. Lane earrings and pin.

Pin 5in (2cm) long

$800-1,000 set   **TR**

A rare 1950s/60s Kenneth J. Lane pin.

5in (13cm) long

$400-600   **Rox**

A 1950s Kenneth J. Lane necklace.

$50-70 TR

A Kenneth J. Lane bracelet.

1in (2.5cm) wide

$150-180 TR

A Kenneth J. Lane necklace.

Longest drop 7.75in (20cm)

$800-1,000 TR

A Kenneth J. Lane bracelet and earrings.

Earrings 1in (3cm) long

$400-500 TR

A Kenneth J. Lane bracelet.

3.25in (8.5cm) wide

$300-400 TR

A Kenneth J. Lane bracelet.

3.25in (8.5cm) wide

$300-400 TR

A pair of Kenneth J. Lane earrings.

1in (3cm) long

$120-180 TR

A pair of Kenneth J. Lane earrings.

1.5in (4cm) long

$50-80 TR

A pair of Kenneth J. Lane earrings.

1.5in (4cm) long

$40-50 TR

A pair of Kenneth J. Lane earrings.

1in (3cm) long

$30-40 TR

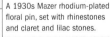

A 1930s Mazer rhodium-plated floral pin, set with rhinestones and claret and lilac stones.

$200-300 RG

A late 1930s Mazer rhodium-plated pin, set with rhinestones.

$180-220 RG

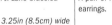

A late 1940s Joseph Mazer rhodium-plated necklace and earrings, set with rhinestones.

$220-280 RG

A 1940s Mazer sterling silver and gold-plated bow pin, marked "Mazer Sterling".

$220-280 RG

A 1940s Mazer sterling silver and gold-plated retro pin and earrings, set with faux emeralds and rhinestones.

$320-380 RG

A 1960s Joseph Mazer necklace, bracelet and earrings, set with faux turquoise, pearls and rhinestones, marked "Jomaz".

Joseph Mazer started out with his brother Lincoln in the 1930s, they split in 1947 and Joseph carried on as Joseph Mazer and Jomaz. Early pieces are marked Mazer or Mazer Brothers.

$300-500 RG

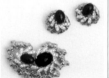

A pair of 1960s Jomaz gold-plated clip earrings, set with cranberry cabochons and rhinestones.

$150-200 RG

A 1960s Jomaz gold-plated pin and earrings, set with faux emeralds and lapis cabochons.

$150-200 RG

A 1960s Jomaz gold-plated double-flower pin, with faux coral-colored glass and yellow rhinestones, signed "Jomaz".

$50-80 RG

A late 1960s Jomaz necklace, pin and earrings, set with red, blue and green cabochons and rhinestones.

$200-300 RG

A 1960s Jomaz leaf pin, with faux turquoise and lapis stones.

$80-120 RG

A Jomaz jester pin.

3.25in (8.5cm) high

$180-220 Rox

A 1960s Jomaz gold-plated pin and earrings, set with faux turquoise pearls and rhinestones.

$100-150 RG

A rare early Réja flower pin.

Réja jewelry was only produced in 1940s-50s, and this short production period makes pieces hard to find.

3.25in (8.5cm) long

$500-600 Rox

A 1940s Réja sterling silver blackamore pin and earrings.
Pin 2.25in (6cm) long

$500-800 Rox

A Réja sterling silver and gold-plated bracelet, pin and earrings, set with clear rhinestones and opaque pink cabochons, signed and dated "Réja Sterling".
1947

$270-330 RG

A 1940s Réja sterling silver pin, set with rhinestones, faux sapphires and pearls, signed "Réja Sterling".

$200-300 RG

A 1940s Réja sterling silver and gold-plated turtle pin, set with green and clear rhinestones, signed "Réja Sterling".

$180-220 RG

A 1940s Réja sterling silver and gold-plated stork pin, with faux emeralds, rhinestones.

$120-180 RG

A 1940s Réja sterling silver and gold-plated leaping stag pin, set with rhinestones and a large faux aquamarine, signed "Réja Sterling".

$180-220 RG

A 1940s Réja sterling silver and gold-plated bird pin and earrings, set with rhinestones and faux citrines.

$270-330 RG

SANDOR

- Sandor was founded in New York, USA c.1938 by Sandor Goldberger and made jewelry until 1972.
- Very little is known about the company, but it is believed to have been the first to use enamel to decorate costume jewelry.
- Pieces rarely come on to the market and are therefore highly collectable.
- When buying any enameled costume jewelry, do check the condition. Enamel can chip and peel and while small areas can be retouched, large areas of damage significantly reduce the value of a piece.

A 1930s Sandor enamel and diamanté pin.
4.25in (10.5cm) long

$700-1,000 TR

A 1930s Sandor pin, with yellow flowers and a green pot.

3in (7.5cm) long

$700-1,000 TR

A 1930s Sandor pin, with blue and pink flowers.

3.5in (9cm) long

$700-1,000 TR

A 1930s Sandor ribbon and flowers pin.

3.5in (9cm) long

$400-600 TR

A 1930s Sandor yellow flower bouquet pin.

3.25in (8cm) long

$400-500 TR

A 1930s Sandor flower pin, with purple petals.

4in (10cm) long

$800-1,200 TR

A 1950s Schiaparelli necklace and earrings, with Bakelite cabochons and aurora borealis crystals.

Earrings 1.25in (3cm) long

$300-400 CRIS

A 1930s Sandor pin.

3.5in (9cm) long

$1,000-1,300 TR

A 1940s Schiaparelli gold and pearl bracelet.

3in (7.5cm) wide

$120-180 TR

A 1950s Schiaparelli bracelet, with light sapphire and aurora borealis beads and leaf motif.

6.25in (16cm) long

$300-400 CRIS

ELSA SCHIAPARELLI

- Elsa Schiaparelli (1890-1973) was an Italian-born fashion designer who worked in Paris and America.
- She is famous for introducing brightly colored fabrics to the austere world of Post War Parisian Haute Couture – especially the shocking pink which has come to bear her name.
- From the late 1930s, Jean Schlumberger designed a limited number of unsigned pieces for Schiaparelli. These are highly sought after today.
- Signed pieces from the 1940s and 50s are coveted for their stunning use of unusual stones.
- Schiaparelli's avant garde style embraced Surrealism and Dada and her artist friends, including Salvador Dali and Jean Cocteau, designed pieces for her.
- In the 1950s Schiaparelli moved to America where she designed jewelry using aurora borealis and frosted glass beads. These pieces are more common than her earlier designs and popular with collectors.

A 1950s Schiaparelli bracelet, pin and earrings, gilt metal and green stones, signed "Schiaparelli".

$400-500   **RG**

A 1950s Schiaparelli bracelet and earrings, with iridescent blue and aurora borealis stones, signed "Schiaparelli".

$320-380   **RG**

A 1950s Schiaparelli bracelet, pin and earrings, set with aurora borealis stones and faux pearls, signed "Schiaparelli".

$320-380   **RG**

TRIFARI

- Trifari was founded in New York by Gustavo Trifari and Leo Krussman in 1918. The firm was known as Trifari and Krussman until 1925 when Carl Fishel joined and its name was changed to KTF.
- Its early success can be attributed to its successful imitation of the Art Deco jewelry being produced at the time by firms such as Cartier and Van Cleef and Arpels.
- In the 1940s its 'jelly-belly' animal jewelry – which featured large Lucite stones – was the perfect antidote to wartime shortages. Jelly bellies are still popular with collectors today, although later examples are less valuable.
- In the 1950s Trifari developed Trifanium, an ultra-shiny, non-tarnishing metal alloy. Complete Trifanium parures, set with richly colored stones, are highly collectable.
- The firm's success was sealed in 1952 when America's First Lady, Mamie Eisenhower, commissioned a faux pearl and rhinestone parure for the presidential inauguration ceremony. She repeated her request in 1956.
- Trifari won a landmark legal case in 1954 when it gained a ruling that costume jewelry is a work of art and therefore copyrightable. The aim was to prevent competitors stealing its designs. Jewelry made after 1954 bears a copyright mark.

A 1930s Trifari white metal and enamel birds on a branch pin.
2.25in (6cm) long

$300-500   **Rox**

A 1930s Trifari enamel and white metal pea pod pin.
2.5in (6.5cm) long

$220-280   **Rox**

A Trifari enamel and white metal sailor pin.
2.25in (6cm) long

$320-380   **Rox**

A very rare 1930s Trifari elephant's head pin.
2in (5.5cm) long

$300-400   **Rox**

A rare 1930s Trifari enamel, diamanté and faux topaz pin.

$400-600   **Rox**

A 1930s Trifari enamel pin.
4in (10cm) long

$400-600   **Rox**

A 1930s Trifari bug pin.
1.5in (4cm) long

$150-250   **Rox**

A 1930s Trifari enamel pansy pin.
2.75in (7cm) long

$220-280   **Rox**

A very rare 1930s Trifari lantern pin.
2.75in (7cm) long

$600-800   **Rox**

A 1930s Trifari bunch of flowers pin.
4.75in (12cm) long

$1,500-2,000   **Rox**

A 1930s Trifari pin.
4in (10cm) long

$400-500   **Rox**

A 1930s Trifari diamanté pin.
3in (8cm) long

$300-350   **Rox**

A 1930s Trifari "fruit salad" pin
and earrings.
Earring 1in (2.5cm) diam

$300-350   **Rox**

A Trifari "jewels of India" pin.
2in (5cm) high

$350-450   **Rox**

A 1930s Trifari white metal
bunch of flowers pin.
3.75in (9.5cm) long

$220-280   **Rox**

A 1930s Trifari bunch of
grapes pin.

$220-280   **Rox**

A 1930s Trifari duet pin.
3.25in (8.5cm) diam

$400-500   **Rox**

A very rare 1930s Trifari bug pin.

3in (7.5cm) long

$800-1,000   Rox

A 1930s Trifari turtle pin.

2.25in (6cm) long

$270-330   Rox

A 1930s Trifari fish pin.

2.25in (6cm) long

$250-350   Rox

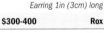

A 1940s Trifari smooth metal necklace, bracelet and earrings, one stone missing.

$300-500   Rox

A 1940s Trifari pin and earrings.

Earring 1in (3cm) long

$300-400   Rox

A CLOSER LOOK AT A TRIFARI PIN AND EARRINGS

This pin and earrings were designed by Alfred Philippe, a French-born jeweler who had worked for Van Cleef and Arpels and Cartier.

He joined Trifari in 1930, following the Wall Street Crash the previous year, and worked for them for 40 years. His use of multicolored stones led to Trifari being known as the 'Rhinestone Kings'.

The stones are caliber-cut, which means they were cut to fit the shape of the design. This is a sign of high quality and is rarely seen in costume jewelry.

The stones are in an 'invisible setting'. This technique was developed by Van Cleef and Arpels in the 1930s, and is used here 10 years later.

The clear rhinestones offset the brightly colored stones.

A 1940s Trifari flowers pin and earrings.

Earring 1.25in (3.5cm) diam

$800-1,000   Rox

A 1940s Trifari pin and earrings.

Earring 1.25in (3.5cm) long

$750-850   Rox

A 1940s Trifari pin and earrings.

Earring 0.75in (2cm) diam

$300-500   Rox

A 1940s Trifari American flag pin.

2.25in (6cm) long

$200-300   Rox

A 1940s Trifari American eagle pin.

1.75in (4.5cm) long

$200-300   Rox

A 1940s Trifari American eagle pin.

2in (5cm) long

$100-150   TR

A Trifari 'Jelly Belly' chick in egg pin.

2in (5cm) long

$1,000-1,200   **TR**

A Trifari 'Jelly Belly' fly pin.

2in (5cm) long

$800-1,000   **TR**

A Trifari 'Jelly Belly' crab pin.

3in (7.5cm) long

$800-1,000   **TR**

Three Trifari duck pins and a duck emerging from egg pin.

Largest 1.45in (2.5cm)

$300-500   **Rox**

A 1940s Trifari sterling silver and gold-plated bird of paradise pin, designed by Alfred Philippe.

$320-380   **RG**

A 1940s Trifari sterling silver and gold-plated bird on a branch pin.

$180-220   **RG**

A very rare 1940s Trifari swan pin.

2.75in (7cm) wide

$700-1,000   **Rox**

A 1940s Trifari bug pin.

2.25in (6cm) long

$300-350   **Rox**

A 1940s Trifari leaf and bug pin.

2.75in (7cm) long

$200-300   **Rox**

A 1940s Trifari bug pin.

1.75in (4.5cm) long

$200-250   **Rox**

A 1940s Trifari Alfred Philippe sterling silver butterfly pin, with red and blue cabochons.

2.5in (6cm) long

$120-180   **CRIS**

A 1940s gold-plated Trifari pin, with blue and green stones.

$120-180   **RG**

A 1940s Trifari rose pin.

$180-220   **Rox**

A rare Trifari crab pin.

3.25in (8.5cm) wide

$1,800-2,200   **Rox**

A 1950s gold-plated Trifari snake pin and earrings, with simulated ruby and emeralds.

$180-220   **RG**

A 1950s gold-plated Trifari pin, set with red, blue, green and clear stones.

$80-120   **RG**

A 1950s Trifari "jewels of India" necklace and earrings.

Earring 1in (3cm) long

$300-350   **Rox**

A Trifari crown pin, set with pearls.

2.25in (5.5cm) long

$200-300   **TR**

A early 1950s Trifari blue and gold stylized fruit pin.

2in (5cm) long

$100-150   **CRIS**

A 1950s Trifari peapod pin, with faux pearls mounted in cold enamel on gilt metal.

2.75in (7cm) long

$120-180   **CRIS**

A 1950s Trifari emerald and crystal rhinestone fruit pin.

2.5in (6cm) long

$70-100   **CRIS**

A 1950s Trifari shell pin, decorated with cold enamel.

3.25in (8cm) long

$120-180   **CRIS**

A 1950s sea motif Trifari pin and earrings, set with cabochon imitation rose-pink and white moonstones.

Pin 3.5in (8.5cm) long

$180-220   **CRIS**

A 1950s Trifari owl pin, set with faux coral cabochons and pavé-set crystals.

3.75in (5.5cm) long

$70-100   **CRIS**

A 1950s Trifari toadstool pin, decorated with faux angel skin coral.

1.5in (4cm) long

$70-100 | **CRIS**

A 1950s Trifari balloon pin, with satin finish.

2.25in (5.5cm) long

$40-60 | **CRIS**

A 1950s Trifari enamel bee pin.

1.5in (3.5cm)

$30-50 | **CRIS**

A 1950s Trifari small cat pin, with a Bakelite turquoise belly and glass eyes.

1.75in (4.5cm) long

$40-60 | **CRIS**

A 1950s Trifari seahorse pin, with Bakelite turquoise cabochons.

1.75in (4.5cm) long

$30-50 | **CRIS**

A 1960s Trifari watch ring, face under diamanté panel.

Head 2in (5cm) long

$200-250 | **Rox**

A 1950s Art Christmas tree pin, set with multi-colored crystal rhinestones.

2.5in (6cm) high

$40-60 | **CRIS**

A Cadora Christmas tree pin, with cherubs set with pearls.

2.75in (7cm) high

$80-100 | **Rox**

A Cristobal-designed Christmas tree pin, using 1950s Swarovski crystals, with peridot and emerald green glass.

3.25in (8cm) high

A 1950s Art Christmas tree pin, in enamel with multi-colored crystal rhinestones, with copyright mark.

2.5in (6cm) high

$40-60 | **CRIS**

$30-40 | **CRIS**

A Cristobal-designed Christmas tree pin, set with ruby-red and emerald-green stones.

2.75in (7cm) high

$30-40   **CRIS**

A Cristobal Christmas tree pin, set with emerald, ruby-red and green glass stones.

4in (10cm) high

$70-100   **CRIS**

A 1980s Eisenberg Ice Christmas tree pin, with multi-colored crystal rhinestones on gold-plated casting, with copyright mark.

2in (5cm) high

$15-25   **CRIS**

A 1980s Eisenberg Ice Christmas tree pin, with emerald-green navette, with ruby-red and clear crystal rhinestones.

2.25in (5.5cm)

$30-40   **CRIS**

A 1950s Hollycraft Christmas tree pin, with multi-colored crystal rhinestones.

2.25in (5.5cm) long

$40-60   **CRIS**

A Mylu Christmas tree pin, set with pink and green stones.

2.75in (7cm) long

$320-380   **Rox**

A 1960s English Sphinx Christmas tree pin, with green enamel leaf with ruby-red crystal rhinestones.

2.25in (5.5cm) long

$30-50   **CRIS**

A 1960s English Sphinx Christmas tree pin, with green enamel and diamanté.

2.75in (7cm) high

$30-50   **CRIS**

A Trifari Christmas tree pin.

2in (5.5cm) long

$60-80   **Rox**

A 1950s Trifari Christmas pin.

This is one of three designs that Trifari made.

2in (5cm) high

$70-100   **CRIS**

A Trifari partridge in a pear tree pin.

2in (5cm) long

$60-80   **Rox**

A 1980s French 'bijoux stern' Christmas tree pin, with green enamel and crystal rhinestones.

2.5in (5cm) long

$40-60   **CRIS**

A 1980s French 'bijoux stern' Christmas tree pin, with multi-colored crystal rhinestones.

2.75in (7cm) high

$30-50   **CRIS**

An Emporio Armani bead necklace, from the Spring/Summer 1997 collection, with original box, storage bag and certificate of authenticity.

$50-80   **PC**

A 1950s American Art turtle pin, set with Bakelite cabochons, coral moonstones and faux lapis stones.

2.25in (5.5cm) long

$40-60   **CRIS**

A 1950s Marcel Boucher rose pin and earring set, the carved ebony rose on rhodium-plated pavé rhinestones.

Pin 4.25in (10.5cm) long

$180-220   **CRIS**

A 1930s Marcel Boucher rhodium-plated and pearlized enamel sweet pea pin, signed "Sterling" and with Marcel Boucher logo.

$400-500   **RG**

A 1950s Marcel Boucher pin, gold-plated, rhinestones and faux sapphires, signed "Boucher".

$100-150   **RG**

A late 1990s Butler and Wilson pin.

$8-12   **PC**

A 1950s Hattie Carnegie Bakelite pin.

3in (5.5cm) wide

$180-220   **CRIS**

A 1950s-60s Hattie Carnegie seahorse pin and earrings.

4.35in (11cm) long

$300-350   **Rox**

A 1960s Hattie Carnegie necklace and earrings.

Earrings 1in (3cm) long

$100-150   **Rox**

A pair of 1980s Chanel gilt earrings.

$70-100   **RG**

A 1940s Coroduette jelly belly pin, by Corocraft, studded with crystals.

Coroduette pins are comprised of two pieces that may be taken apart to be worn individually.

A rare 1950s-60s Hattie Carnegie merman pin.

4.25in (11cm) long

$350-450 | **Rox**

A 1950s-60s Hattie Carnegie lionhead pin.

4in (10.5cm) long

$300-350 | **Rox**

1.75in (4.5cm) long

$500-600 | **CRIS**

A Corocraft fish pin in sterling silver, enamel and Lucite/Perspex, signed "Corocraft Sterling America".

Designed by Adelpho Katz. During World War II designers used less metal and more plastic.

1942-45

$320-380 | **RG**

A Corocraft sterling silver and gold-plated starfish baby pin, signed "Corocraft Sterling".

1942-45

$220-280 | **RG**

A 1940s Corocraft sterling silver and gold-plated rose pin.

$320-380 | **RG**

One of a pair of 1940s De Rosa sterling silver and gold-plated fur clips, set with red and clear rhinestones.

The De Rosa company was owned by Ralph de Rosa and its head designer was his wife Elvera de Rosa.

A 1940s Corocraft sterling silver and gold-plated rose pin.

$320-380 | **RG**

$320-380 (pair) | **RG**

A 1940s De Rosa sterling silver gilt and blue enamel bracelet, set with rhinestones.

$220-280 | **RG**

A 1940s De Rosa sterling silver pin, with rhinestones and faux sapphires.

$100-150 RG

A 1930s Eisenberg pearl and diamanté pin.

3in (7.5cm) long

$600-800 TR

A pair of Eisenberg earrings.

2in (5cm) long

$550-650 TR

A 1930s Fahrner pin.

2.25in (6cm) long

$3,000-4,000 TR

A 1960s Stanley Hagler poinsette flower pin, with murano glass leaves and petals, and a wired filigree base.

4in (10cm) wide

$220-280 CRIS

A 1960s Stanley Hagler Murano glass fruit pin.

2.56in (6cm) long

$50-80 CRIS

A 1990s Histoire de Verre pin, with poured glass in metal frames.

3.5in (8.5cm) long

$220-280 CRIS

A 1940s Hobé sterling bow pin, set with faux peridot, rose quartz, jonquil and amethyst.

4in (10cm) long

$200-300 CRIS

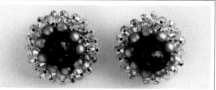

A pair of Hobé earrings, set with blue and clear crystals.

1in (3cm) long

$30-40 TR

A 1940s Hobé sterling heart pin, with a faux amethyst stone.

2.5in (6.5cm) long

$320-380 CRIS

A pair of mid-1990s Christian Lacroix gold and imitation pearl clip earrings.

$50-80   PC

A 1930s Robert pin.

3in (7.5cm) long

$700-1,000   TR

A 1940s Nettie Rosenstein crab fur clip, gold-plated silver and enamel, signed "Nettie Rosenstein" and "Sterling".

$120-180   RG

A rare 1940s Nettie Rosenstein sterling silver, gold-plated and enamel butterfly fur clip, signed. *Nettie Rosenstein was a couturier who made jewelry, and pieces by her are quite rare.*

$300-500   RG

A 1940s Vogue gold-plated sterling silver blackamoor pin and earrings.

$320-380   RG

A 1940s Warner mechanical day and night flower pin, with the petals which open and close.

2.5in (6cm)

$60-100   CRIS

A 1950s costume jewelry pin, unmarked.

$30-40   PC

A mid-1980s costume jewelry pin, from Miss Selfridge.

1983

$5-8   PC

A 1950s costume jewelry pin, unmarked.

$50-80 PC

A 1930s basket of flowers pin, set with channel-cut ruby and pavé crystals, unsigned.

5in (7.5cm) long

$200-300 CRIS

A 1930s American rhodium-plated silver pin, with prong-set fruit salad stones, unsigned.

2in (5cm) long

$300-500 CRIS

A 1930s French pin, rhodium-plated silver with prong-set fruit salad stones, unsigned.

1.75in (4.5cm) long

$300-500 CRIS

An early hand-beaded pin, with matching earrings, unsigned.

Pin 6in (15.5cm) high

$300-500 Rox

A 1940s American panda duet pin, set with a pearl belly, black enamel and diamanté, unsigned.

1.5in (4cm) long

$180-220 CRIS

A pair of 1940s American sterling silver and gold-plated wing pins.

$180-220 RG

A 1940s American sterling silver and gold-plated 'jelly-belly' penguin pin, set with rhinestones and Lucite.

$80-120 RG

An American sterling silver and gold-plated blackamoor clip, the black glass face set with clear rhinestones.

$80-120 RG

A French Art Deco chrome-plated shield dress clip.

$80-120 RG

A 1940s American pin, sterling silver and gold-plated, with colored faux pearls.

$120-180 RG

A 1930s enamel lobster pin, claws on springs.

1930s   *3.25in (8cm) long*

$60-80   **TR**

An enamel and diamanté lobster pin.

4.25in (11cm) long

$80-120   **TR**

A 1940s American blackamoor pin, with black enamel head and gold-plated turban.

1.75in (4.5cm) long

$300-500   **CRIS**

A 1930s clear Lucite "Scotty dog" pin.

3in (8cm) long

$320-380   **Rox**

A 1930s black Lucite "Scotty dog" pin.

3in (7.5cm) long

$180-220   **Rox**

An extremely rare 1930s-1940s apple juice Bakelite figural pin.

$2,000-3,000   **Rox**

A 1930s Lucite parrot pin.

3.5in (9cm) long

$100-150   **TR**

A "Scotty dogs" pin.

$300-350   **Rox**

A CLOSER LOOK AT A BAKELITE FISH CUFF

In the 1930s, when the use of plastics was seen as the material of the future and craftsmen used it to great effect – treating it with far more respect than we do plastic today. This witty fish design is typical of the creativity put into Bakelite jewelry.

Each fish has been hand-carved from the plastic to give a three-dimensional effect.

The fish have been hand-painted to give the illusion of movement as they 'swim' around the wrist.

This pale orange Bakelite is known as 'apple juice'.

An 1940s apple juice Bakelite fish cuff.

2.5in (7cm) wide

$1,500-2,000   **Rox**

A B C D E F G H I J K L M N O P Q R S T U V W XYZ

A Victorian 18ct gold, turquoise and pearl pin and matching screw-on drop earrings, in original box.
c1870

$800-1,200 SSp

A Victorian tortoiseshell, gold and silver pique demi-parure, comprising a pin and a matching pair of drop earrings.
c1870

$500-800 SSp

A Victorian three-piece demi-parure, comprising matching gold earrings and pin, set with cabouchon garnets.

$1,800-2,200 GS

A gold bracelet, set with diamonds and emeralds.

$5,000-7,000 GS

A Georgian 18ct gold foil link and barrel bracelet.

$1,000-1,500 SSp

A Victorian 15ct gold and platinum horseshoe bracelet.
1870

$500-800 SSp

A diamond and platinum rectangular pin, by Mappin & Webb, London.

$800-1,200 GS

A white gold and diamond rose pin, set with a sapphire.

$4,000-6,000 GS

A gold and diamond pin, of a leaping stag with ruby stones.

$1,000-1,500 GS

A blue enameled silver butterfly pin.

$50-80 SSp

A circular micromosaic gold pin, with beetle design.

Micromosaics are currently enjoying a revival in popularity.

$400-600 GS

A late Victorian silver lizard pin, marked "Sterling".
c1880

$200-250 RG

A Victorian silver pin.

2in (5cm) long

$30-50 PC

An Art Nouveau enameled silver pansy pin.
c1890

$100-150 SSp

A diamond-set portrait of a woman, on ivory.

$1,200-1,800 GS

A 1920s Italian cameo pin, made for the tourist market.

2in (5cm) long

$30-50 PC

A Victorian silver "Bella" name pin.

$40-60 SSp

A Victorian silver "Bertha" name pin.

$40-60 SSp

A Victorian silver "Clara" name pin.

$40-60 SSp

A Victorian silver "Ethel" name pin.

$40-60 SSp

A Victorian silver "Lilian" name pin.

$40-60 SSp

A Victorian silver and blue enamel "Mother" name pin.

$40-60 SSp

A horn pin.

2in (5cm) long

$15-20 OACC

A cameo, with a scene of a mother with children and cherubs.

$500-800 GS

A cameo, with a woman's head.

$700-1,000   **GS**

A cameo, with woman's head in two colors.

$500-800   **GS**

An elaborate Georgian seed pearl necklace.
c1800

$1,000-1,500   **SSp**

A Victorian yellow amber bead necklace.

32.25in (82cm) long

$150-200   **SSp**

A row of cultured pearls, with an 18ct white gold, diamond and sapphire clasp.

24in (61cm) long

$800-1,200   **SSp**

A row of cultured pearls, with a 18ct white gold and diamond chip ball clasp.

1960s   *12in (30.5cm) long*

$800-1,200   **SSp**

A Victorian silver, diamond and star sapphire pendant.
c1870

$800-1,200   **SSp**

An Edwardian platinum, diamond and citrine pendant.

$300-500   **SSp**

A small diamond pin, of a flying pheasant.

$1,200-1,800　　　　　　　　　　**GS**

An important Georgian 18ct gold rosecut diamond ring, set with three diamonds on either side.

$2,000-3,000　　**SSp**

A stylish ring, probably Italian, with alternating ribbed and plain curved bands enclosing a garnet-topped doublet, stamped "750" and an indistinct mark.

$70-100　　**DN**

An 18ct white gold ring, with an exeptionally large white South Sea pearl in the center, surrounded by diamonds.

South Sea pearls are cultured pearls from Australia or the Philippines. They usually grow up to 0.75in (1.5cm).

$3,000-4,000　　**SSp**

FIND OUT MORE...

'Understanding Jewellery', by David Bennett & Daniela Mascetti, published by Antique Collectors' Club, 2000.

'Jewels and Jewellery', by Clare Phillips, published by V&A Publications, 2000.

'Earrings' by Daniela Macetti & Amanda Triossi, published by Thames and Hudson, 1999.

A set of three 18ct gold press studs, with Greek Key decoration and set with seed pearls.

c1870/1880

$200-300　　**Wim**

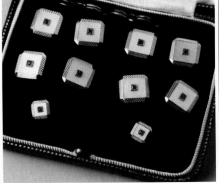

An Art Deco dress set, set with square cut rubies, in fitted case.
c1930

$1,200-1,800　　**Wim**

A late 19thC baby's gilt whistle, with coral teether, bells missing, maker TH.

With all its bells this would be worth $320-380.

$180-220　　**PC**

A pair of Victorian 9ct gold and enamel cuff links.
c1870

$300-500 SSp

A pair of 9ct gold oval cuff links, in a fitted case.
c1885

$270-330 Wim

A pair of 18ct gold and enamel oval cuff links, in a fitted case.
c1900

$800-1,200 Wim

A pair of 15ct gold "coffee-bean" cuff links, in a fitted case.
c1900

$270-330 Wim

A pair of 9ct gold "bowling" cuff links and pin, in a fitted case.
c1900

$300-500 Wim

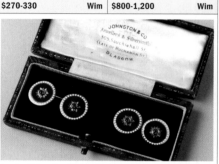

A pair of Edwardian 18ct gold and enamel bar cuff links, set with sapphires, in a fitted case.
c1905

$1,000-1,500 Wim

A pair of Edwardian 18ct gold and enamel bar cuff links, set with sapphires, in a fitted case.
c1905

$1,000-1,500 Wim

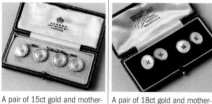

A pair of 15ct gold and mother-of-pearl cuff links, with enamel decoration and set with seed pearls, in a fitted case.
c1915

$500-800 Wim

A pair of 18ct gold and mother-of-pearl cuff links, decorated with enamel and gold "button threads", in a fitted case.
c1915

$700-1,000 Wim

A pair of 18ct gold and guilloche enamel cuff links, in a fitted case.
c1915

$1,200-1,800 Wim

A pair of green bakelite Eloware cuff links, manufactured by Birkby's of Liversedge, England.
1920s   *face 0.75in (2cm) long*

$30-50 MHC

A pair of enamel double-sided cuff links.

1920-30s

$100-150 CVS

A pair of French black and white enamel double-sided cuff links.

1920-30s

$80-120 CVS

A pair of green and blue double-sided cuff links.

1920-30s

$100-150 CVS

A pair of 18ct gold and lapis lazuli square cuff links, in a fitted case.

c1930

$1,000-1,500 Wim

A pair of 1950s black and Bakelite oversized dice cuff links.

$80-120 CVS

A pair of 1950s leather and metal gun-in-holster cuff links.

1.5in (4cm) wide

$70-100 CVS

A 1950s bowling motif tie bar and cuff links set.

2.5in (6.5cm) wide

$30-50 CVS

A pair of sterling silver Volkswagen cuff links and tie pin.

$100-150 Koz

A pair of silver Georg Jensen cuff links, marked "Georg Jensen", "925 S Denmark" and "114".

1961

$200-300 SSp

A pair of 1960s silver Georg Jensen cuff links, decorated with a horseshoe, marked "Georg Jensen", "925 S Denmark" and "123".

$300-400 SSp

A pair of 1960s 18ct gold Kutchinsky "D" cuff links.

$500-800 SSp

A pair of 18ct gold, onyx and citrine cuff links.

1970

$180-220 SSp

A pair of 1980s silver gilt, lapis lazuli and pearl bar cuff links, by Mappin & Webb.

$120-180 SSp

KITCHENALIA

DOORSTOPS

- Doorstops are often confused with cast-iron bookends. Doorstops are generally heavier and larger – usually 6-14in (15-35.5cm) high – and have a horizontal wedge for placing under the door.
- Used from the 19thC to keep doors open to aid ventilation, most doorstops were produced between the late 19thC and the 1940s. Animals, people and garden plants and flowers are all very popular subjects.
- In the late 1930s and 1940s, companies reduced the amount of iron used in manufacturing doorstops to cut costs, with the result that items from this period tend to weigh less than older versions.
- Condition is important. Badly damaged paint, rust and repainting reduces value considerably.
- Important makers include Hubley (founded 1894), Bradley & Hubbard (founded 1854), The Albany Foundry Company (1897-1932) and Littco Products (established 1916).
- Modern reproductions are commonly found. These usually have rough and sandy-feeling surfaces and, if cast in two pieces, the joins will not fit snugly. If the paint is bright, it may be repainted or a reproduction. Examine the molding and material closely as the details will also not be as fine.

A Bradley & Hubbard corgi doorstop, with turned head and well detailed fur molding.

9in (23cm) high

$350-450   **BERT**

A large Bradley & Hubbard turkey doorstop.

12.5in (31.7cm) high

$3,500-4,500   **BERT**

A Hubley tiger lilies doorstop.

10.5in (26.6cm)

$400-500   **BERT**

A Hubley Cape Cod doorstop, with trees and flowers surrounding a white cottage, in near mint condition.

5.5in (13.5cm) high

$450-550   **BERT**

A Hubley Lil' Red Riding Hood doorstop.

This is one of the more popular nursery rhyme doorstops.

9.5in (24cm) high

$700-1,000   **BERT**

A CLOSER LOOK AT A DOORSTOP

Humorous, 'characterful' subject matter with comical facial expressions and designs that echo cartoons of the time.

Signed 'Fish' - this piece was designed by the popular and well-known English cartoonist 'Mr Fish'.

Made by Hubley, one of the foremost names in quality collectable doorstops. Stylish Art Deco design with bold and bright colors.

Surface wear is very light and the original colors are retained.

A Hubley bathing beauties doorstop, signed by Fish, featuring two bathers sharing a parasol.

10.75in (27cm) high

$3,500-4,500   **BERT**

A Hubley pheasant doorstop, designed by Fred Everett, with fine painted details overall.

7.25in (18cm)

$400-500   **BERT**

A Hubley parlor maid doorstop, signed by Fish, depicting a parlor maid in colorful outfit holding a serving tray.

9.25in (23.5cm) high

$3,500-4,500   **BERT**

A Hubley messenger boy doorstop, designed by Fish, showing a boy holding flowers in his arms, a scarce example.

10in (25cm) high

$1,500-2,000   **BERT**

A small Hubley footmen doorstop, signed by Fish.

9in (23cm) high

$1,500-2,000   **BERT**

A wine seller doorstop, heavy cast iron depiction of man holding bunches of wine bottles in hands.

9.5in (24cm) high

$2,000-3,000   **BERT**

LEARN MORE ABOUT...

'Doorstops' by Jeanne Bertoia, published by Collector Books, Kentucky 1985.

A rare clown doorstop, brightly painted and well cast, of a highly whimsical subject. This doorstop, by an unknown manufacturer, is very hard to find and is desirable amongst collectors.

10in (25.5cm)

A scarce Taylor Cook koala doorstop, one in the series of Cook designs, painted in bright orange and yellow, black body with orange log base.

7.5in (19cm) high

$1,000-1,500   **BERT**

A white caddie doorstop, depicting a young golfing caddie carrying a golf bag.

8in (20.3cm)

$1,000-1,500   **BERT**

A rare clown doorstop, brightly painted and well cast, of a highly whimsical subject. This doorstop, by an unknown manufacturer, is very hard to find and is desirable amongst collectors.

10in (25.5cm)

$2,000-3,000   **BERT**

A 1950s 'Elsie the Cow' cookie jar, marked "Pottery Guild".

12in (30.5cm) high

$400-450   **Rox**

A 1950s 'Sheriff Pig' cookie jar, marked "RRP Co, Roseville, Ohio".

12in (30.5cm) high

$125-150   **Rox**

A 1950s 'calf head' cookie jar, marked "Made in California - Poppytrail Pottery by Metlox".

11in (28cm) high

$400-450   **Rox**

A 1950s 'Cinderella' cookie jar, marked "J. C. Napco 1957 K2292".

10in (25.5cm) high

$350-425   **Rox**

A 1950s 'Pinocchio' cookie jar, with paper label marked "Poppytrail".

11.5in (29cm) high

$450-500   **Rox**

A 1950s Humpty Dumpty cookie jar, marked "W29 Brush USA".

12in (30.5cm) high

$350-425   **Rox**

A 1950s clown cookie jar, marked "Maurice of California, USA, JA10".

13in (33cm) high

$250-300   **Rox**

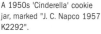

A 1950s 'the cow jumped over the moon' cookie jar, marked "J2USA made by Doranne of California".

13.5in (34.5cm) high

$350-300   **Rox**

A 1950s 'Woodpecker on acorn' cookie jar, with paper label.

11.5in (29cm) high

$850-950   **Rox**

A "The Nightmare Before Christmas" Jack Skellington cookie jar, by Treasure Craft.

1993   *16in (40.5cm) high*

$175-250   **MSC**

A 1950s 'Cinderella's Pumpkin Coach' cookie jar, marked "W32 Brush USA".

10in (25.5cm) high

$350-375   **Rox**

A metal hen on nest-form chocolate mold, used condition.

11in (28cm) high

$200-250   **TWC**

A metal Easter Bunny riding rooster-form chocolate mold, used condition.

5in (12.5cm) high

$85-100   **TWC**

A classic metal seated Easter Bunny-form chocolate mold, used condition.

10in (25.5cm) high

$45-80   **TWC**

Two matching metal chocolate molds, standing rabbits with baskets on back, used condition.

11in (28cm) high

$75-100   **TWC**

A metal Easter egg in basket-form chocolate mold, relief decoration with Easter Bunny, used condition.

6in (15cm) high

$45-80   **TWC**

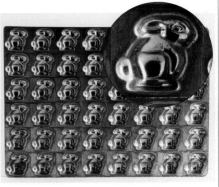

A metal tray-form chocolate mold, produces 48 separate candies, all with hopping bunny theme, used condition.

13in (33cm) long

$55-80   **TWC**

A metal Santa-form chocolate mold, Santa with sack of toys, used condition.

9.5in (24cm) high

$135-175   **TWC**

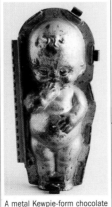

A metal Kewpie-form chocolate mold, used condition.

11.5in (29cm) high

$105-150   **TWC**

A metal tray-form chocolate mold, produces 24 separate candies, all with a circus theme including elephant, bear, monkey, performer on horseback, lion and clown, used condition.

10.5in (26.5cm) long

$45-80   **TWC**

Three metal chocolate molds, two kitten-form, one pug-form.

Tallest 7.25in (18.5cm) high

$55-85   **TWC**

An early knife box.

$300-350   BCAC

A tiger maple eating plate.

Both sides of this plate would have been used during a meal, one side for savory food, the other for sweet. Wooden plates were never washed as it would cause them to warp. Instead, they were scrubbed clean.

c1720   8in (20.5cm) diam

$900-1,500   RAA

A maple burl wood bowl, extremely deep shape.

c1740

$3,500-4,000   RAA

A rare burl two-handled mixing bowl, with elaborate graining.

18.25in (46.5cm) long

$1,200-1,500   TWC

A skewer set, in hand-forged iron, all original.

c1740

$800-1,200   RAA

A mid-18thC cast bronze posnet, with maker's name "Washbrough" cast at handle.

15.75in (40cm) long

$650-750   SI

A tilting tea kettle, with cast-iron body, hand-forged iron tilter and handle.

c1780   15in (38cm) wide

$850-950   RAA

A shell-shaped maple cream skimmer, with original surface.

c1750   7in (17.5cm) wide

$350-395   RAA

A boat mill, used to grind herbs and spices.

c1760   13in (33cm) long

$1,100-1,250   RAA

An extremely rare tin nurser, for mothers' milk, with raw tin pewter nipple.

c1770   4in (10cm) high

$570-650   RAA

A potato masher, made from turned maple.

c1810   9.75in (24.5cm) long

$40-45   RAA

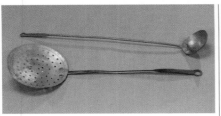

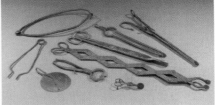

An 18th/19thC brass and iron skimmer, and a brass and iron ladle, the bowl of the skimmer engraved with concentric circles.

Longest 25.5in (64.5cm)

$300-350 SI

An 18th/19thC group of iron fireplace and kitchen items, including coal tongs, sugar cutters, pipe tongs, ice tongs, tongs, scissor-form tongs and a skimmer.

$700-800 SI

A bass wood lollipop butter stamp, with pattern on both sides.

Lollipop butter stamps are not common and stamps like this one, with a carved design on both sides, are even rarer, adding to its value.

c1810 *9.5in (24cm) long*

$1,000-1,300 RAA

A pierced tin foot-warmer, in wooden frame and decorated with multiple heart designs, with original tray and bail handle, good finish, worn on frame.

c1820

$100-200 TWC

An early 19thC New England brass-hinged warming pan, with turned wooden handle, the cover of pan decorated with punch work.

45in (114cm) long

$200-300 SI

A very rare piggin-handled cream churn, with original dasher, lid and hickory bands, signed by maker Fearing of Hingham, Massachusetts.

This miniature churn would have been used to make whipped batters for dishes such as syllabub and marshmallows.

c1820

$2,900-3,500 RAA

A folding iron candle-lantern, with six arched ribs ending in baluster-shaped feet, enclosing a single candle-cup.

17in (43cm) high

$1,000-1,500 SI

A 19thC painted leather fire bucket, with brass-studded rim and two handles cast with masks.

15in (38cm) high

$450-550 DN

A cast-iron trivet, made to commemorate the Independent Order of Odd Fellows, cast in one piece.

c1830 *9in (23cm) long*

$180-220 RAA

A dustpan, with original combed and grained paint.

c1830   *12in (30.5cm) high*

$550-650   **RAA**

A raw tin hatchet cookie cutter.

c1830   *9.5in (24cm) long*

$180-220   **RAA**

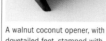

A walnut coconut opener, with dovetailed feet, stamped with the stars of Zoar, Ohio.

c1830   *5in (12.5cm) long*

$175-195   **RAA**

A heart-shaped hickory butter stamp, with star pattern and leaves.

c1830   *4in (10cm) long*

$400-450   **RAA**

A pine butter stamp, with cow design.

This pattern is uncommon, making this butter stamp more valuable than other examples.

c1830   *4.5in (11.5cm) diam*

$700-800   **RAA**

A maple butter stamp, with peace eagle design.

c1830   *4.5in (11.5cm) diam*

$450-500   **RAA**

A very rare apple parer, in cherry, walnut and hand-forged iron, dated and signed JHS.

1836   *9.5in (24cm) long*

$1,300-1,500   **RAA**

A group of 19thC wooden kitchen items, including a burl bowl, scoop, ratchet, whisk broom, long-handled ladle, apple corer, long-handled beechwood peel, candle drier and octagonally shaped cutting board.

$600-900   **SI**

A 19thC crimping machine, with heating bars.

12.5in (31.5cm) high

$500-700   **BS**

Two burlwood mortars, each of tapering cylindrical form, one with molded foot.

7.75in (20cm) high

$500-700   **SI**

A 19thC lemon squeezer.

11in (28cm) wide

$200-300   **BS**

A set of 19thC wood and iron kitchenware, including a paint-decorated oval tin tray, an iron roasting device, an oval bowl, a cutlery box, and an oval-handled Shaker box from Sabbath Day Lake, Maine.

$300-400   **SI**

Three 18th/19thC wrought iron trivets.

16in (40.5cm) long

$400-500   **SI**

A cast-iron cake board, with rare pattern depicting a beehive on a table, by Albany and Troy New York foundry.

c1850   6.5in (16.5cm) long

$450-500   **RAA**

A complete patented walnut spice set.

c1850 lg box 7.5in (19cm) diam

$300-350   **RAA**

A Peaseware maple sugar bowl, with original finish.

This was made by a family of wood turners from Painesville, Ohio.

c1850   5in (12.5cm) high

$570-650   **RAA**

A naughty Nelly or lewd lady bootjack.

c1860   10in (25.5cm) long

$180-220   **RAA**

A 19thC brass pastry crimper and cutter.

5.5in (14cm) long

$70-100   **BS**

A raw tin song bird cookie cutter.

c1880   5in (12.5cm) long

$35-40   **RAA**

A 19thC cast-iron fish scaling grip and scraper, US patented.

1889   16in (40.5cm) long

$320-380   **BS**

A mid-to late 19thC wooden pantry box, with swing handle and metal trim, maker unknown, old finish worn on top.

9in (23cm) diam

$80-120   **TWC**

A 19thC Hudson & Co USA 'Little Star' cast-iron mechanical apple peeler, relacquered and replaced cutting blade, patented.

1885

$180-220   **BS**

A set of eight fancy tin cookie cutters, one grip missing.
Largest 4.5in (11.5cm) wide

$50-80 BS

An American three-piece crimping iron.
c1880 *5.75in (14.5cm) long*

$120-180 BS

A 1920s iron stand, heated by methylated spirits.
9.25in (23.5cm)

$30-50 BS

An early 19thC blacksmith-made box iron.
6.5in (16.5cm) wide

$200-250 BS

A nutmeg grater.
c1900 *5.25in (13cm) long*

$50-80 BS

A nutmeg grater.
c1900 *5.25in (13cm) long*

$50-80 BS

An unusual nutmeg grater, US patented.
c1880 *7.25in (18.5cm) long*

$400-600 BS

A cast iron potato sheer, US patented.
c1900 *10.5in (26.5cm) high*

$300-400 BS

A set of 15 tin pastry cutters.
c1900 Case 6.75in (17cm) wide

$70-100 BS

A pair of steel glove drying frames.
c1900 *11.5in (29cm)*

$70-100 BS

A 19thC Goodell Co USA cast-iron mechanical apple peeler, patented.
1898 *10.5in (26.5cm) long*

$320-380 BS

A can opener, US patent date 1922.
8.5in (21.5cm) long

$120-180 BS

A tin flour dredger.
c1900 *5.25in (13.5cm) high*

$70-100 BS

A Singer sewing machine, with fresh decoration in excellent condition.

Despite their often decorative finishes, with many ornate gilt and colored transfers, Singer sewing machines do not fetch high prices as they were made in enormous quantities. Only examples in the very best condition will be of interest to collectors but compared to other machines the prices will be low.

$60-100 TK

A very rare French sewing machine, by Thabourin.
c1880

$500-800 TK

An extremely rare French Peugeot No. 0 sewing machine, no shuttle.
c1883

$1,200-1,800 TK

An original metal sign for Pfaff vintage sewing machine, signed "E. Doepler".

c1920 21.75in (55.5cm) high

$180-220 TK

An original Gritzner sewing machine metal sign.

c1920   29.5in (75cm) high

$120-180 TK

An extremely rare French sewing machine, "Paris-Louvre", similar to "Todd Champion", circular shuttle, missing its winder.
c1890

$800-1,000 TK

A 19thC sewing machine, with scroll-molded cast-iron base and frame japanned with gilt foliate decoration, the work table bearing the serial number "63431".

11.25in (28.5cm) long overall

$60-100 DN

A CLOSER LOOK AT A SEWING MACHINE

The Maine-based company Shaw & Clark made sewing machines between 1857 and 1866. Amongst a range of chain-stitch and running-stitch models, they made the 'Monitor' from 1860-1864. In 1867, the company moved to Cicopee, Mass., adopting the name 'Cicopee Sewing Machine Company' but closed one year later. This example dates from just before the relocation occurred. It is in good condition but shows some wear to the paint and ornate transfers. If its condition were better, the value would be higher. Despite this, it was produced by a short-lived company and so is more valuable than most machines.

A decorative American chain-stitch sewing machine, by Shaw and Clark, in very good condition.
c1865

$700-1,000 TK

Two 19thC oblong necessaires, one in an ivory case, the other in a gilt metal case.

Largest 5.5in (14cm) long

$600-1,000 DN

A mid-18thC gilt scissors case, engraved with rococo scrolls, flowers and cartouches, and a pair of scissors.

4.25in (11cm) long

$500-800 DN

MECHANICAL MUSIC

MECHANICAL MUSIC

- Mechanical music devices take a number of forms; a musical box with a revolving cylinder, the disk musical box, the phonograph and the gramophone. The majority were produced during the second half of the 19th century and were driven by winding springs which drove gears to operate the mechanism.
- Musical boxes using cylinders with embedded protruding pins striking metal teeth of different lengths on a 'comb' to produce sounds were popular from the Great Exhibition of 1851 until the 1880s. The center of production was Switzerland, and desirable names include B.A. Bremond, Paillard and Nicole Freres.
- Disk musical boxes, often known as 'Symphonions' after the most popular manufacturer, reached the height of their popularity around the 1890s, which lasted until the first few decades of the 20th century.
- Look closely for damage to the mechanism or the 'comb' used to produce sounds. Missing or broken teeth and seized mechanisms can be expensive to repair. Take care not to damage the springs and gears by overwinding or winding a seized mechanism.
- The gramophone, the precursor to the last century's record player, which could play specially recorded disks, was developed by Emile Berliner in 1887, with the format becoming popularized around the turn of the century on both sides of the Atlantic.
- Gramophones use a needle and 'soundbox' to pick up sound from the grooves on the disk and a horn, which can be built in or applied, to amplify the sound. As well as the desirable and decorative table mounted horn gramophones, there are many portable gramophones which are usually more affordable.

A Victor Three gramophone, with original oak horn and in full working order.

$3,000-4,000　　**ACM**

An unmarked brass horn gramophone, with oak case and Fidelio reproducer.

$300-400　　**TK**

A gramophone, wooden body with inlaid decoration to front, reproducer marked 'Polyphon Concert', original horn, minor repairs.

c1910

$600-1,000　　**TK**

A portable gramophone, with original horn soundbox, in working order.

$270-330　　**TK**

A Mikiphone clockwork pocket gramophone, nickled case, needs some restoration.

This was the smallest commercial gramophone ever produced and all the parts fold up compactly into a portable instrument the size of a large, thick pocket watch.

4.5in (11.5cm) diam

$500-700　　**TK**

A novelty Excelda portable gramophone, in the shape of a Kodak 'Autographic' camera, case repaired, working well.

$180-220　　**TK**

A Swiss Thorens 'Excelda' portable gramophone in the form of a folding camera.

c1930

$320-380　　**OACC**

A small German Symphonion disk musical box, playing 6.25in disks, with original seaside scene in lid.

c1890

$1,000-1,500　　**AMM**

A German Symphonion disk music box, playing 10 5/8in disks, with walnut cabinet, 84 teeth in double comb, with 12 disks, complete but needs small regulation.

$700-1,000　　**TK**

A Symphonion Style 28 hand-cranked musical box, plays 5.75in disks, with 40 teeth comb, one broken, black finished case with decals on top, with 19 disks.

$400-600　　**TK**

A late 19thC mahogany-cased disk musical box, the comb mechanism marked with a windmill trademark and serial number 48274, the lid with inset reverse-painted glass panel named "Alice Butcher", with a collection of 30 disks by Kalliope.

11.25in (28.5cm) wide

$500-700　　**DN**

A Swiss bells and drum in sight cabinet musical box, playing six airs on 52 teeth with four bells and drum with nine hammers, Stop/Play levers to side recesses, bird's-eye maple veneered two-door cabinet with ebonized band and box-strung inlaid panel fronts, ogee-molded base with block feet.

c1880   *20in (53cm) wide*

$2,200-2,800   **BAR**

A Swiss musical box, with brass cylinder for 12 tunes and 62 notes, in wooden case with inlaid top, original tune-sheet, zither attachment, one tooth missing, not working.

c1880

$700-1,000   **TK**

A National musical box, made in Switzerland, with six tunes, lever wind, painted wood box with ebonized edges, with original tune sheet.

c1900   *13in (33cm) wide*

$2,000-2,500   **AMM**

A French clockwork singing bird snuff box, in composition case with snuff compartment and animated singing bird with moving beak, tail and wings, with a repoussé scene of putti releasing a caged bird on the lid.

c1880   *4in (10cm) wide*

$3,000-4,000   **AMM**

441

A mechanical singing bird cage, brass cage, mechanism with small bellows, operated slide whistle created a warbling sound, not working but complete.

$400-600   **TK**

A continental silver singing bird music box, with repoussé decoration, box has fine detailing with griffins, faces, birds and scrolls, hallmarked on the bottom "E B" in an oval and "925".

4in (10cm) long

$4,000-6,000   **JDJ**

A Crystal radio set by Regent.

c1920

$50-80   **OACC**

An American 'Colonial Globe' radio.

c1930

$1,500-2,000   **TK**

A Pillow Speaker Radio model no. 413-S, by the Dahlberg Company, Minneapolis.

c1955

$220-280   **TK**

An Ultra R906 Coronation twin deluxe receiver, with hinged back panel and twin sliding doors concealing speaker aperture and controls.

$100-150   **DN**

FIND OUT MORE...

Arthur W.J.G. Ord-Hume, 'The Musical Box, A Guide for Collectors', published by Schiffer Publishing, 1995.

Benet Bergonzi, 'Old Gramophones & Other Talking Machines', published by Shire Books, 1995.

- During the 19th century, there were no chemists and doctors may have been located far from certain houses, so medical chests containing medicines and drugs were common in the homes of families who could afford them.
- They take many forms, from the very simple to the very large and sophisticated, complete with accessories such as balances and pestles and mortars. The more sophisticated and larger chests will fetch higher prices than smaller, simpler ones.
- Some have concealed compartments behind panels at the rear of the chest to hold poisons and dangerous drugs. These are sometimes only opened by operating a small lever or bar located in a unusual place, such as inside a drawer.
- When buying chests, check that the bottles match and are not replaced, as this can devalue a chest. Medical bottles of all sizes are in themselves highly collectable. They are often very decorative, particularly leech jars.
- When considering post mortem sets or surgeon's instruments, there are three factors to consider. Firstly, the maker – a set will be more valuable if it is made by a noted maker. Secondly, the set should be as complete as possible as missing pieces will devalue a set considerably, although some collectors will buy an incomplete set with a view to completing it over time. Thirdly, condition is important. Damage and rust will affect the value.

Four 19thC apothecary jars with paper labels, all with original stoppers, all in good condition, some loss to labels.

8.5in (22cm) high

$80-120　　　　**TWC**

Three 19thC apothecary bottles, with original stoppers, paper labels, varying condition, from poor to good.

9in (23cm) high

$60-80　　　　**TWC**

Three 19th/20thC apothecary jars, original stoppers, good condition.

Tallest 9.5in (24cm) high

$50-70　　　　**TWC**

Three ceramic medicine jars, with applied printed labels.

Largest 9.5in (24cm) high

$200-250　　　　**BA**

A large apothecary bottle, with original stopper, good condition.

13in (33cm) high

$60-80　　　　**TWC**

A 19th/20thC apothecary bottle, polished bottom with 'poison' type stopper.

9in (23cm) high

$50-70　　　　**TWC**

A 19thC mahogany apothecary's box, the doors holding six glass stoppered bottles each and opening to reveal five pull-out drawers containing an assortment of glass vessels under a recess holding five further bottles.

14in (35.5cm) high

$2,000-2,400　　　　**BA**

A 19thC mahogany apothecary's box, the top lifting up to reveal eight glass stoppered bottles, over a pull-out drawer with five compartments containing an assortment of glass vessels and a glass pestle and mortar.

12in (30.5cm) wide

$800-1,200　　　　**BA**

A 19thC mahogany apothecary's box, with nine compartments holding glass stoppered bottles, six with printed labels reading "Dandelion Pills, C. H. Booth, Chemist, Kings Road, Chelsea SW" and pull-out drawer to base.

6in (15.5cm) wide

$650-700　　　　**BA**

A late 19thC apothecary set, possibly American, in a leather trunk.

c1890-1910

$350-450　　　　**BAC**

A large 19thC French marine surgeon's instrument set, with two layers in padded, fitted wooden case with printed paper label.

Case 22.75in (58cm) wide

$8,000-12,000　　　　**BA**

A 19thC cased surgeon's set, with stainless steel blades and black stained wooden handles, case with ivory label marked "Evans & Wormull, 31 Stamford Street, Blackfriars, London".

Case 18in (46cm) wide

$1,200-1,800 | **BA**

A cased postmortem set, with stainless steel blades and black stained wooden handles, blades marked "J. Gray & Son, Sheffield".

Box 9.5in (24cm) wide

$800-1,200 | **BA**

A 19thC lacquered brass and glass cupping set, in velvet-lined, fitted mahogany case, including a glass medicine bottle with printed label "Godfrey".

$1,000-1,400 | **BA**

An "Improved Patent Magneto-Electric" machine, in fitted mahogany case with printed paper label.

A great many 'amazing' benefits were promised from regular treatment with minor electric shocks during the 19th century. These included more rapid recovery from illnesses, prevention of hair loss and all manner of physiological ailments. The machine would be wound using the handle to generate a charge and electrodes applied to deliver the shock to the right area.

Box 8.75in (22.5cm)

$200-250 | **BA**

A pessary mould.

c1900 | *6.75in (17cm)*

$70-90 | **BS**

A steel folding corn razor, with original case.

c1900 | *5in (12.5cm)*

$40-60 | **BS**

A 19thC gum lancet, with tortoiseshell cover.

6.75in (17cm) long

$70-100 | **BS**

An early 19thC steel cranium rasp.

7.5in (19cm)

$200-250 | **BS**

A late 18thC "Heys" steel cranium saw, with ebony grip.

6.75in (17cm)

$180-220 | **BS**

FIND OUT MORE...

Keith Wilbur, 'Antique Medical Instruments', published by Schiffer Publishing, 1998.

A CLOSER LOOK AT A TOOTHKEY

A 19thC steel toothkey, with horn grip, marked "Charriere, Paris".

Toothkeys, used to extract teeth, were first mentioned in records in 1742. They are also known as 'clef de Garegeot', 'Fothergill key', 'English key' and 'French key'. The first examples had a straight shaft and were made from iron. Handles were initially plain and shaped like a turnkey, but were made later on from horn, ivory and other material over time, sometimes incorporating instruments, such as this example which contains screwdrivers, to adjust the grip or claw.

7in (17.5cm) long

$100-150 | **BS**

A selection of 1920s-30s glass eyes.

Glass eyes were used as false eyes by people who had lost an eye. They were stored in large quantities as every patient had a differently shaped eye and the colour had to be matched as closely as possible to the other eye. Today, they are sought after by collectors, with large collections in original cabinets fetching very high prices at auction.

$35-45 (each) | **BS**

A Buffalo Art Craft Shop three-sided chamberstick, with stylized flowers in green, red and black, some dents, stamp marked.

4.5in (11cm) high

$550-650   **CRA**

A Keswick School of Industrial Arts copper tray, of rectangular form, repoussé decorated with a band of fruiting Arbatus, stamped mark, together with a Keswick School of Industrial Arts brass bowl, of ovoid form with repoussé decoration, stamped marks, also a small Celtic design copper tray.

Largest 20.5in (52cm) wide

$400-500   **L&T**

A CLOSER LOOK AT A CANDLESTICK

This candlestick was designed by Christopher Dresser (1834-1904) and is indicative of his work with its clean lines and simple design.

Ornamentation is minimal, and the style of the piece is very modern. Dresser is credited with being the first 'modern' industrial designer.

The angled position and design of the handle is typical of his designs.

The pared down 'Moroccan' or Middle Eastern feel of the piece is also indicative of Dresser, who was skilled at combining the best elements of designs from other cultures with an understanding for mass production and machines.

A Kardofan brass chamber candlestick, designed by Christopher Dresser, for Richard Perry, Son & Co., the dished drip tray above cylindrical neck on a domed base with curved cylindrical mahogany handle, bears factory mark.

56.25in (143cm) high

$650-750   **L&T**

An oval twin-handle brass tray, the rim and handles decorated in Celtic inspired repoussé.

29.5in (75cm) wide

$450-550   **L&T**

Two Heintz silver-on-bronze verdigris pieces, some wear, stamped mark and patent.

Ashtray 8in (20cm) diam

$300-400   **CRA**

A large Stickley Brothers hammered copper coal scuttle, with two riveted handles, a few minor dents, lip slightly bent, stamped "406" on base.

Gustav Stickley (1857-1942) was a prominent and renowned furniture maker in the American Arts & Crafts style. He founded 'The Craftsman Workshops' under the name 'Gustav Stickley Company' in 1898, mostly making oak furniture. In 1916, his brothers took over and renamed the company 'L & JG Stickley'. The family ended its association with the company in 1974, but it still retains the Stickley name.

14.5in (37cm) wide

$1,000-1,500   **CRA**

A Dirk Van Erp hammered copper bowl, with scalloped rim.

7.5in (19cm) diam

$600-700   **CRA**

An Arts and Crafts silver overlaid copper desk set, comprising a calendar frame, a pen tray, a rolling blotter and four blotter corners, each with geometric overlay.

c1900 Pen tray 9in (23cm) high

$200-300   **SI**

A large Stickley Brothers hammered copper bulbous vessel, with rolled rim, stamped "83".

16in (40.5cm)

$1,000-1,500   **CRA**

A pair of Tudric pewter candlesticks, designed by Archibald Knox, each with broad drip trays and tapered supports with three flared brackets on a broad circular base cast with entwined tendrils, stamped mark "0221".

5.75in (14.5cm) high

$1,500-2,000   **L&T**

TUDRIC WARE

■ Tudric is the trade name for decorative and table ware made by William Haseler of Birmingham and marketed by Liberty & Co. of London from 1903.

■ It is made from a form of pewter with a high proportion of silver, and accompanied Haseler's solid silver range which was called 'Cymric'.

■ Decoration is typically Art Nouveau, and uses many interlaced Celtic motifs as well as stylized leaves and flowers. Pieces also often have enameled decoration.

■ The designer Archibald Knox (1864-1933), an exponent of the Celtic interpretation of the Art Nouveau movement, designed many pieces.

A pair of Tudric pewter candlesticks, the scrolled drip trays above molded tapering columns on circular spreading bases cast with leaves and set with turquoise enamel roundels, stamped marks "023".

5.5in (14cm) high

$1,200-1,800   **L&T**

A Liberty's Tudric two-handled comport, pierced and embossed with shamrocks, impressed numeral "0287".

11in (28cm) wide

$150-200   **GorL**

A Tudric pewter cake tray, designed by Archibald Knox, cast with stylized fruiting branches and centerd by a Moorcroft panel, painted in the 'pomegranate' pattern, stamped mark "0357", and a similar twin-handled bowl the body pierced and cast with stylized bands, stamped marks "0350".

Tray 12in (30.5cm) wide

Tray $1,500-2,000, Bowl $600-700   **L&T**

A Liberty's Tudric sugar bowl, with single handle, cast with stylized organic forms, stamped "BOM 0231".

4.5in (11.5cm)

$80-120   **GorL**

A Liberty & Co. Tudric pewter timepiece, from a design by David Veasey, of square section with a spreading base and top surmounted by a squared dome with cross-banding, the sides and back hinged door panel embellished with branches of stylized honesty, the front copper dial embossed with Roman numerals and with pewter hands, stamped "Tudric" and numbered "0159".

The original design for this timepiece was an elaborate silver tea-caddy. For that design and a Liberty version of a pewter caddy see 'The Designs of Archibald Knox for Liberty & Co.' by Adrian J. Tilbrook, Ornament Press, 1976, p.58 figs. 29 & 30.

6.5in (16.5cm) high

$2,500-3,500   **DN**

Two Scottish School brass jardinières, the first decorated with polychrome enamel hearts and panels of stylized dragonfly, the second with broad rim over flaring sides, decorated with Celtic galleons and roundels of swimming fish.

L $1,000-1,500, R $300-400   **L&T**

A Scottish School brass and enamel inlaid stationery rack, with shaped back above divided interior, inlaid with a roundel of a downcast maiden in coloured enamels.

11.5in (29cm) wide

$1,200-1,800   **L&T**

From left to right:
A Scottish School brass wall mirror, the rectangular frame repoussé decorated with entwined Celtic mythical beasts, bears inscription "Wool Prize, Gargunnoch Show, the gift of F.H. McLeod & Sons, 1927".

15.5in (39.5cm) high

$450-550   **L&T**

A Scottish school brass wall mirror, of rectangular outline, the rectangular mirror enclosed within repoussé decorated frame depicting stylized roses on a hammered ground, bears inscription "Wool Prize: Killearn Show 1921, The Gift of F.H. McLeod & Sons".

14in (36cm) high

$450-550   **L&T**

A Scottish school brass picture frame, possibly by Agnes Bankier Harvey, of rectangular outline, repousse decorated with a band of flowering stems.

13.5in (34.5cm) high

$600-700   **L&T**

A German pewter easel mirror, attributed to Kayser, of arched shape embellished at the top with rose blooms and thorny branches, the sides extending to form feet and further embellished with roses, having a brass wire hinged support.

$750-850   **DN**

A WMF style pewter dressing mirror, cast with classical maiden and foliage.

14in (35.5cm) high

$300-400   **GorL**

A WMF pewter soda-syphon coaster, of openwork cylindrical shape embellished with geometric plant form motifs, and sinuous twin handles, maker's marks on base.

2.75in (20cm) high

$300-400   **DN**

An Art Nouveau copper gimbal lamp and tray, the tray is with flowing silver designs, which extends up to form the frame, tray monogrammed "RL" and signed on back "SHREVE & CO. sterling & other metals"

10in (25.5cm) long

$1,500-2,000   **JDJ**

An Art Nouveau WMFB silver calling card tray, with a maiden standing in the middle, her flowing gown drapes to the ground and flows out to form the tray on either side of her.

13.75in (35cm) wide

$750-850   **JDJ**

Three Art Nouveau patinated metal table articles, comprising a candlestick of tapering square shape with green slag glass panels held by stylized foliage, on a similar square base, a tall bud-shaped candleholder on a circular base, and a mother-of-pearl and brass inkstand, the first stamped "Apollo Studios".

Candlestick 14in (35.5cm) high

$400-500   **SI**

An Austrian Art Nouveau rosewood and inlaid desk set, comprising a letter rack, the domed lid enclosing a divided interior, the sides with brass tendril straps, the whole with whiplash foliate inlay, also an inkwell, with two glass wells and inlaid lids on an inlaid twin-handled tray with pen rests, a blotter of rectangular form with inlaid panel, and a pair of table candlesticks.

11.5in (29cm) high

$1,500-2,000   **L&T**

An Art Nouveau copper jardinière, probably English, cylindrical form riveted with three stylized cast handles and paw feet, stamped "Emantee" underneath.

c1900   *12.75in (32.5cm) high*

$300-400   **FRE**

A collection of Chase Art Deco chromeware, comprising a pair of bubble candlesticks, a mint and nut dish with banded middle, designed by Ruth and William Gerth, a mustard jar with frosted glass liner, all with stamped archer mark, together with a Revere chrome creamer, sugar and tray set, stamped mark.

Dish 8.5in (21.5cm) wide

$80-120   **FRE**

A Chase Diplomat coffee service, designed by Walter Von Nessen, including coffee pot, sugar and creamer, copper with black plastic handles and knobs, stamped archer mark, , chip to handle of pot.

c1932

$150-200   **FRE**

A Chase copper pretzelman, designed by Lurelle Guild, cutout silhouette design with brass rod and tray, stamped mark.

16in (40.5cm) high

$150-200   **FRE**

A Chase chrome Art Deco breakfast set, designed by Ruth and William Gerth, with semi-spherical creamer and lidded sugar with black Bakelite handles, on a tray with concentric circle design, stamped archer marks.

The Chase Brass & Copper Company was founded in Waterbury, Connecticut in 1876. The bulk of production was for industrial uses, until the 1930s when they released a range of homeware. Primarily in chrome, but available in other finishes, its clean lines and Art Deco styling made it immensely popular. Renowned period designers such as Walter von Nessen, Russell Wright, Ruth and William Gerth and the in-house designer Harry Laylon were employed to work on the range. The war effort in the 1940s meant that production of the range ceased and after the war, the company chose not to revive the range. Produced for a short period, Chase domestic metalware is now highly collectible.

$100-150   **FRE**

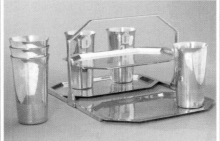

A Chase chrome Art Deco metalwork triple collapsible tray, designed by Harry Laylon, with scribed concentric design and six iced drink tumblers with scribed lines, stamped archer marks.

Tray 7in (17.5cm) high

$150-200   **FRE**

A Chase Connoisseur Art Deco cigarette box, designed by Ruth and William Gerth, in a satin nickel finish with scribed geometric designs, wood lining, chip to lining.

6.75in (17cm) wide

$100-150   **FRE**

A Chase Diana Art Deco chrome console set, designed by Harry Laylon including a flower bowl with ribbed white plastic base and sawtooth rim, and a pair of matching candlesticks, stamped and molded archer mark.

Bowl 10in (25.5cm) diam

$100-150   **FRE**

Three Chase Art Deco boxes, a divided candy dish with black metal base, glass insert and nickel lid with black metal finial, designed by Ruth and William Gerth, a one-tray box in chrome with shell finial designed by Harry Laylon and a dolphin box with brown Bakelite base and brass lid designed by Helen Bishop Dennis, tiny chip to base, stamped archer marks.

Largest 7in (17.5cm) diam

$60-80   **FRE**

A Chase copper Art Deco bud vase, designed by Ruth and William Gerth, together with a copper napkin holder with orange Bakelite handle, designed by Harry Laylon, stamped archer mark.

First 9in (23cm) high

$60-80   **FRE**

A B C D E F G H I J K L M N O P Q R S T U V W XYZ

An Art Deco chrome appetizer stand, in the shape of a swan with red Bakelite head and body pierced to hold toothpicks, on a dished base.

7in (17.5cm) high

$100-150   **FRE**

A Max Le Verrier Art Deco pelican lamp, bronze figure on a marble base, unwired, signed "FRANCE LE VERRIER".

c1930 7.25in (18.5cm) high

$250-300   **FRE**

A pair of European pewter domed base candlesticks.

c1680-1720 7in (18cm) high

$1,500-2,000   **JDJ**

Two hog scraper pushup candle holders.

6.5in (16.5cm) high

$200-250   **TWC**

An Art Deco pewter caddy.

6in (15cm) high

$30-50   **OACC**

A Machine Age chrome coffee service, designed by Michael W. McArdle for Sunbeam, including a pitcher, creamer, sugar and tray, executed in chrome with black Bakelite handles and line inlay.

1934 Pitcher 9.5in (24cm) high

$150-200   **FRE**

A pair of mid 19thC brass beehive-type push-up candle holders.

Many candlesticks have scratches from where solidified wax has been cleaned off over the years. Beware of sticks in pristine condition and in bright yellow coloured brass, as these are likely to be modern reproductions.

10in (25.5cm) high

$40-60   **TWC**

A 19thC hog scraper candlestick, with side ejector.

7in (18cm) high

$70-100   **OACC**

A silver-plated Mappin & Webb Art Deco three-piece tea service, monogrammed initials, stamped "MAPPIN & WEBB PARIS FAB. ANGLAISE".

5.5in (14cm) high

$100-150   **FRE**

A pair of 19thC small brass push-up candlesticks.

11in (28cm) high

$200-250   **JDJ**

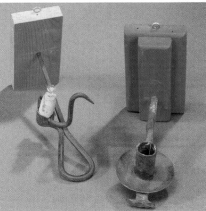

Two 18thC/19thC American wrought iron candle holders, with jamb spikes.

$250-300   **SI**

A 1950s table lamp, with chrome stem with Lucite leaves and large spherical bulbs

38in (96.5cm) high

$250-300   **FRE**

A pair of Victorian brass candlesticks.

8.25in (21cm) high

$150-200   **OACC**

A set of three early copper measuring jugs, comprising a half gill, one gill, and one-and-a-half gills.

Largest 4.5in (11cm) high

$250-350   **OACC**

A set of six graduated English pewter lidless bellied measures, from a quarter gill to a quart, some dents and imperfections.

$450-550   **JDJ**

A Mexican silver and copper Modernist pitcher, the spherical body with applied silver band, simple strap handle and stylized silver ice guard to spout, unmarked.

8.25in (21cm)high

$150-200   **FRE**

A vintage cream can.

11.5in (29cm) high

$40-60   **OACC**

A brass hot water can.

1880s   11.5in (29cm) high

$50-80   **OACC**

A brass hot water can.

1880s   14.25in (36cm) high

$70-100   **OACC**

A 19thC American pierced tin hanging candle lantern.

14in (35.5cm) high

$120-180   **SI**

A Norwegian enameled metalware bowl.

$50-80   **V**

Top: A large 19thC Martingale horse decoration, comprising cast and pattern brasses, surmounted by various small boss-like studs, including heart, cross, crescent and shield patterns, leather work in generally good condition.

38.5in (98cm) long

$120-180   **HamG**

Middle: A large 19thC Martingale horse decoration, comprising all cast brasses including a plough, chained bear and a brass of North Eastern Railway, surmounted by a small brass with maker's name "J. Watson, Maker, Pickering", leather work in generally good condition with some perishing.

16.25in (41cm) long

$80-120   **HamG**

Bottom: A group of four Martingale horse decorations, comprising three small and one large, all of 19thC period, including anchor pattern and bell, the large Martingale consisting of cast barrels denoting brewery transport, all in generally good condition with some perishing.

Longest 37in (94cm) long

$150-200   **HamG**

A set of three 20thC steel fire irons, with gilt metal baluster handles.

$700-800   **DN**

An early 20thC cast bronze figure of a Boy Scout, on square base, staff missing.

7.75in (19.5cm) high

$150-200   **GorL**

PISTOLS

- Pocket pistols, used by journeymen to protect themselves, are the most affordable form of pistol. Duelling pistols are more expensive, with cased pairs fetching the highest prices.
- Makers' names are important as those by good makers are of higher quality. Look for pistols made by Manton and Mortimer.
- Reproductions are found, usually originating from Spain. These low quality pieces are easy to spot when compared to an authentic weapon or firearm.
- Pay close attention to firearm licensing laws, with details available from your local police station. Sometimes a licence is needed simply to own a piece.
- Handle the metal parts as little as possible. Natural acids on fingers cause small red spots known as 'finger rust' to appear. To avoid this and spots caused by air pollution, apply a thin protective layer of beeswax.

An early 18thC flintlock holster pistol, signed "John Harman" on the lock and "Harman, London" on the breech of the three-staged swamped barrel.

John Harman was made a freeman of the Gunmakers Company on 15th April 1714. Appointed gunsmith to HRH Frederick Prince of Wales in 1729.

c1725   16in (40.5cm) long

$2,500-3,000   **L&T**

An English Sea Service standard issue pistol, dated.

1800

$2,000-3,000   **CS**

A percussion dueling pistol, the octagon barrel with gold inlaid legend "Canon A. Rubens D'Acier", with side loading breech and foliate engraving.

14.25in (36cm) long

$1,000-1,500   **SI**

A mid-18thC flintlock Caucasian holster pistol, in the English tradition, the lock signed "CjC Burrij", the stock split at the pistol grip.

19in (48.5cm) long

$1,000-1,500   **L&T**

A percussion pistol, .68 calibre, Pedro Eibar, with snaphaunce lock.

$1,000-1,500   **SI**

A mid-18thC side-by-side double-barreled flintlock box lock tap-action carriage pistol, by Bond of London.

9.5in (24cm) long

$3,000-4,000   **L&T**

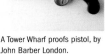

A Tower Wharf proofs pistol, by John Barber London.

$700-1,000   **CS**

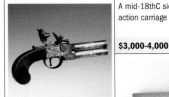

A flintlock box lock tap-action under-over turn-off barrel pocket pistol, signed "G Wallace" within a trophy of arms, the barrels numbered "3" and "4".

8in (20.5cm) long

$700-800   **L&T**

An 18thC brass under-over flintlock overcoat pistol, by Ketland & Co., Birmingham.

$800-1,200   **CS**

A mid-19thC percussion six-barreled revolving pepper-box pistol, with engraved round action lock, Birmingham proof marks, finely checkered butts, engraved steel butt plate trigger guard and butt strap.

8.5in (21.5cm) long

$550-650   **L&T**

A copper powder flask, body with medallion of two dogs and hunter, common top stamped "Dixon & Sons Patent", twin hanging rings, retains much original finish overall, minor dents, one screw missing from top.

7.5in (19cm) long

$250-350　　　**W&W**

A copper powder flask, stamped "Sykes", common brass tip, fixed nozzle, retains some original finish overall.

3.75in (9.5cm) long

$250-350　　　**W&W**

A Continental brass-mounted powder horn, hinged charger, graduated nozzle, shaped retaining spring, brass border and four hanging rings, some age wear overall.

c1800　　　6in (15cm) long

$200-300　　　**W&W**

A late 18thC brass-mounted cowhorn powder flask, probably for Rifle Volunteers, common brass tip with sprung lever and adjustable nozzle, brass hanging band with suspension loop, concave brass base with suspension loop, original leather charger cover.

11in (28cm) long

$550-650　　　**W&W**

A Y-shaped Enfield rifle combination tool, comprising nipple key, oil bottle, turnscrew and pricker, stamped "T & CG", worm missing.

4.5in (11cm) long

$120-180　　　**W&W**

A late 17thC engraved flattened cow horn powder flask, engraved with a hunter, dogs, and animal in forest, reverse engraved with circles, branded "WL", later mounts.

9in (23cm)

$850-950　　　**W&W**

A T-shaped Enfield rifle combination tool, comprising nipple key, spring cramp, oil bottle, pricker, two turnscrews, ball spike, ball worm missing.

5.25in (13.5cm) long

$150-200　　　**W&W**

A nickel silver percussion cap dispenser, blued spring, cover plate stamped "M-Sykes".

2.75in (7cm) wide

$200-300　　　**W&W**

An "Air Raid Defences - NSDAP" steel helmet, without chinstrap, engraved "RL2 - 39/11".

$250-300　　　**TK**

An 1867-pattern Prussian pickelhaube, as worn during the Franco-Prussian war.

$800-1,000　　　**CS**

OIL LAMPS

OIL LAMPS

- ◼ Early oil lamps were fuelled by 'whale oil', which was highly flammable blend of alcohol and distilled turpentine. It was dangerous to use and expensive. By the late 1850s, kerosene had been introduced as a safer and more economical option.

- ◼ In 1878, Edison developed electric light which began to threaten oil lamp manufacturers. Partly to provide designs that fitted in with increasingly lavish rooms and later to compete with the revolution of electricity, late 19th century lamps became more decorative and attractive. Many glass manufacturers produced examples in a rainbow of colors and varied forms.

- ◼ Electricity eventually took over and the oil lamp industry died, but lamps were used up until the 1940s in rural areas without electricity supply and are still used by Amish communities today.

- ◼ Burners are also collected, partly to restore lamps that had been electrified and partly to gather parts for incomplete burners. Thousands of patents were taken out to protect new designs, so the variety of types is enormous.

- ◼ Condition is important. Lamps were functional objects that were the centre of many rooms. Chips, cracks and wear will affect value and desirability considerably. Replaced parts and electrification will also affect value, especially if the piece has been drilled to fit electrical parts.

- ◼ Reproductions are common, so use a good reference book to familiarise yourself with common styles and forms. Also look at levele of wear, particularly on the base of the lamp.

A pressed green satin glass mini lamp, square base with round shade, very good condition.

8in (20.5cm) high

$300-500 JDJ

A miniature red satin 'Gone with the Wind' or parlor lamp.

c1890 8.5in (22cm) high

$400-600 RAA

An amber pressed satin glass mini lamp, amber exterior and white cased interior, small chip to inside top rim of shade.

9in (23cm) high

$300-500 JDJ

A hand-painted 'Gone with the Wind' lamp, globes hand-painted with yellow and white flowers, flowers are highlighted with heavy white enamel, chip to fitter rim on top globe, lamp electrified, otherwise very good condition.

19in (48.5cm) high

$150-200 JDJ

A very large 'Gone with the Wind' lamp, with green shading to yellow background and hand-painted chrysanthemums, foot of lamp impressed with lion's faces at the feet and smiling cherub faces in between, lamp electrified, top globe appears to be a replacement painted to match and has a nine inch crack extending from the top opening, downward.

33in (84cm) high

$400-600 JDJ

A Pairpoint painted lamp, painted with rust and green background and white and purple flowers, two flakes to top rim of shade, otherwise good condition.

11in (28cm) high

$300-500 | **JDJ**

A decorated milk glass mini lamp, the shaded yellow background with red flowers, several chips to top of shade, roughness to bottom of shade, otherwise good condition.

8in (20.5cm) high

$120-180 | **JDJ**

A hand-painted kerosene lamp with shade, light blue background with pink flowers and green leaves, original burner replaced with electric burner, metal foot has been painted gold, otherwise good condition.

15in (38cm) high overall

$250-300 | **JDJ**

A blue swirl mini lamp base and shade, shade with several flakes to the fitter rim, two small flakes to the top rim, base in good condition, spider replaced.

7.75in (19.5cm) high

$600-700 | **JDJ**

A honey-colored reverse swirl mini lamp, two tiny fleabites to bottom fitter rim.

8.25in (21cm) high

$1,200-1,800 | **JDJ**

A blue diamond quilted and 'mother-of-pearl' mini lamp, on eight petal-shaped frosted feet, shade has ruffled lip.

10.5in (26.5cm) high

$700-1,000 | **JDJ**

An Amberina mini-lamp, melon-ribbed body with five applied amber glass feet extending in a feather-type design on the lamp base, burner marked "PAT FEBY 27 1877".

8in (20cm) high

$3,500-4,000 | **JDJ**

A cranberry beaded swirl miniature lamp.

c1890 *8.5in (22cm) high*

$500-800 | **RAA**

A mid-20thC pink satin glass diamond quilted and 'mother-of-pearl' mini lamp, with shade, shade cut down, bruise to shoulder of base.

10.25in (26cm) high

$250-300 | **JDJ**

A cranberry mini lamp, tiny fleabites to fitter rim as well as top rim, otherwise good condition.

8.75in (22cm) high

$300-500 | **JDJ**

A Thomas Webb & Son oil lamp and shade, double wick burner, bronze feet stamped "JD" and "71", signed "THOMAS WEBB & SONS", good condition.

20in (51cm) high

$2,200-2,800 | **JDJ**

A Hinks No. 2 oil lamp, wth cranberry glass shade.

Hinks is considered to be the 'Rolls-Royce' of the oil lamp.

c1860 *28in (71cm) high*

$300-400 | **OACC**

A Victorian oil lamp, with green glass shade.

29.5in (75cm) high

$300-500   **OACC**

A cranberry glass oil lamp.

c1860   *18.5in (57cm) high*

$400-600   **OACC**

A cut overlay fluid lamp, several minor chips to marble base, otherwise good condition.

10in (25.5cm)

$300-400   **JDJ**

A EPNS oil lamp, with "Messenger" burner.

24.75in (63cm) high

$250-300   **OACC**

A cut overlay fluid lamp, small burst air bubble on the edge of one quatrefoil, otherwise good condition, lamp electrified, but not drilled.

14.25in (36 cm) high

$1,800-2,200   **JDJ**

A pair of Sandwich Glass Factory camphene lamps, blown glass, made in three parts, waterfall bases, engraved with grapes, vines and berries, original burners.

c1835   *14in (35.5cm) high*

$2,500-3,000   **RAA**

A cut overlay lamp, floral cutting on font is trimmed with gold, wear to gold trim on font, several open air bubbles on both font and stem, electrified but not drilled.

16.5in (42cm) high

$600-1,000   **JDJ**

A Sandwich Glass Factory whale oil lamp, with patterned glass.

c1830   *9.5in (24cm) high*

$600-1,000   **RAA**

A Victorian room heater, with ruby glass shade.

17.75in (45cm) high

$400-600   **OACC**

A pink melon ribbed hall light, with a white opalescent top to pink at the bottom, in brass pull-down frame, slight bend to filigree top collar, otherwise good condition.

10in (25.5cm) high

$180-220   **JDJ**

A rare hand-blown crystal lace maker's whale oil lamp, with applied handle, together with original lace maker's lens and wooden stool, lamp and lens are good condition, stool appears to have been top coated at some point.

Lens 11in (28cm) high

$1,800-2,200   **JDJ**

OPTICAL

- Popular in the 19th century, opera glasses can be found in huge variety. The most desirable have ornately decorated tubes, with painted enamel patterns or scenes, guilloche enamel and inset metals. Ivory is a common material, which is well carved in the best examples. Opera glasses with plain cases will not be as desirable or valuable. Most are contained in soft-sided cases or small bags.

- Splits to ivory coverings or loss or damage to enameling will reduce value. These items were made to be used which often led to them being damaged.

- Makers' names will add value. Look out for Lemaire, who used a small bee as his motif and Chevalier of Paris. Both were well-known French optical instrument makers. Opera glasses can be signed around the eyepiece lens or on the bridge between the tubes.

A pair of opera glasses, gilded brass enamel, mother-of-pearl eye pieces, by Chevalier, Paris.
c1880   *4.25in (10.5cm) wide*

$300-500   **OACC**

A pair of opera glasses, gilt enamel and mother-of-pearl.

3.5in (9cm) wide

$270-330   **OACC**

A pair of French enameled opera glasses, in a suede bag with silver gilt base.

$180-220   **L&T**

A pair of opera glasses, mother-of-pearl, with case.

3.75in (9.5cm) wide

$40-60   **OACC**

A pair of Victorian mother-of-pearl and gilt brass opera glasses, in original leather bag.
c1870   *4.25in (10.5cm) wide*

$100-150   **MB**

A pair of late 19thC brass and tortoiseshell pique covered opera glasses.

4.75in (11cm) wide

$350-450   **DN**

A pair of opera glasses, engraved brass.

4.25in (10.5cm) wide

$70-100   **OACC**

A pair of opera glasses, ivory and gilded brass with tortoiseshell eye pieces, by Jumelle Duchesse, Paris.
c1890   *4in (10cm) wide*

$180-220   **OACC**

A velvet opera bag, designed with three compartments to hold opera glasses, make-up and a purse, by Chevalier, Paris.

4.75in (12cm) wide

$100-150   **OACC**

SPECTACLES

- Since their development in the 15th century, spectacles have always been viewed as lending the wearer an air of intelligence. 18th century gentlemen and aristocrats would often purchase spectacles to vainly create a certain studious and intellectual air about themselves.

- Early spectacles did not have arms and are sometimes wrongly called 'pince nez'. Some early models, such as 'Nuremburg types' are now less common and can command high prices. Other armless types, dating from the 19th century when the style regained popularity, are more affordable.

- Arms, which were developed in the 18th century, initially had loops at the ends which pressed against the temples to hold them in place. The loops could also be used to attach cords.

- These types can also be known as 'wig spectacles' as they were secured by poking the arms into a wig. They often had shorter arms for this purpose. Initially lens shape was round, with octagonal and square shapes being used in the late 18th and 19th centuries.

- Having been produced in quantity for many centuries, spectacles offer collectors a wide and varied collecting area. Look for notable makers, such as Benjamin Martin, McAllister and Sageant.

A pair of silver-framed spectacles, with green lenses, made by M Boster.

1740s

$300-400   VE

A pair of solid gold-framed spectacles, made by the son of the founder of McAllister, Philadelphia.

1820s

$400-600   VE

A pair of steel-framed spectacles, dating from the American Revolution, dug up near Old Fort, Niagara, NY.

c1770

$200-300   VE

A maple haircomb and a pair of spectacles, dating from the Revolutionary War, found at Fort Campbell, Cherry Valley.

$200-300   RAA

A pair of double horseshoe silver-framed spectacles, made by McAllister, Philadelphia.

c1800

$1,000-1,500   VE

A pair of solid silver double-D spectacles, with original sun lenses, made by McAllister, Philadelphia.

Benjamin Franklin was a customer of McAllister.

c1800

$2,000-2,500   VE

A pair of French double-D spectacles, with K-bridge tortoiseshell frames with original sun lenses, sterling silver arms and a trim pin hinger.

1730s

$2,000-3,000   VE

A pair of tortoiseshell-framed 'Martin's Margin' spectacles.

c1840

$1,000-1,500   VE

Two pairs of marksmen's spectacles.

The lenses of marksmen's spectacles were designed to correct defective eyesight. Both the colour of the lenses and the depth of the translucent border were believed to help the long-and short-sighted.

c1860

$100-150 each   VE

Two pairs of English tortoiseshell-framed wig spectacles.

left c1750, right c1850

L $650-750, R $350-450 VE

Three pairs of spectacles, by unknown makers.

1840-60

$100-150 each   VE

Three pairs of pince nez with coloured lenses.

1840-60

$100-150 each   VE

FIND OUT MORE...

Nancy N Schiffer, 'Eyeglass Retrospective: Where Fashion meets Science', published by Schiffer Publishing, 1999.

A Chinese blue and white porcelain vase, Wanli, of lobed oval form, overall with floral and foliate decoration, Ming Dynasty.

7in (17.75cm) high

$1,500-2,000   **SI**

A pair of Chinese export porcelain sauceboats, , of silver shape with barbed rims and loop handles, painted with a bird above a peony and pine tree, on an oval foot decorated with lambrequins, some restoration, Qianlong period.

9.5in (24.5cm) wide

$400-450   **BonS**

A large Chinese export porcelain meat dish, painted in blue with pagodas in landscape within a cracked ice border, the rim painted with foliate scrolls, cell diaper panels and peony flowers, Qianlong period.

19.75in (50.5cm) wide

$600-700   **BonS**

A Chinese export deep meat plate, with an extensive river landscape within a cell diaper border, the rim decorated with foliate scroll lambrequins. Qianlong period, chip to rim.

14.75in (37.5cm) wide

$120-180   **BonS**

A Chinese export porcelain oval meat plate, decorated in blue with a river landscape within a cell diaper border, gilding worn, together with another similar plate, Qianlong period.

17.25in (44cm) wide

$500-600   **BonS**

A 19thC Chinese export platter, painted in underglaze blue with a koro in a flower garden, within Fitzhugh-style borders.

The Fitzhugh pattern, which contains peony blossoms, the auspicious objects and pomegranates, was a popular Chinese export pattern. It is unknown where the design originated, but it is thought that it is named after the family that originally commissioned it.

10.5in (26.5cm) wide

$100-150   **HamG**

A 19thC Chinese blue and white square-section vase, each face decorated with watery landscapes.

14.25in (36cm) high

$2,300-2,800   **WW**

A miniature Chinese blue and white vase, decorated with repeating figures, bearing Kang Hsi marks.

10.5in (26.5cm) wide (?)

$120-180   **HamG**

An early 20thC Chinese blue and white vase.

16.5in (42cm) high

$400-450   **OG**

A pair of Chinese bowls, painted with bands of chrysanthemums and scrolling tendrils, within foliate borders, bearing Kang Hsi marks, small abrasion to one rim, one bowl damaged.

5.25in (13cm) wide

$150-200   **HamG**

A Chinese blue and white hotplate, octagonal and painted with a traditional riverscape in underglaze blue.

9.25in (23.5cm) high

$150-200   **GorL**

A Chinese blue and white vase, with scepter handles and landscape decoration.

8in (20.5cm) high

$120-180   **GorL**

A Chinese export porcelain tureen and cover, of canted rectangular section, between foliate S-scroll handles, the cover with lotus blossom strap handle, the tureen painted with pagodas in extensive landscapes, the cover with foliate lambrequin design within diaper borders.

14.5in (37cm) wide

$1,200-1,800 | **BonS**

FAMILLE ROSE

- The famille rose (pink family) palette was developed from famille verte (green family), which in turn was based on Wucai or five-colored decoration.

- The name refers to a palette of enamel colors used in overglazed decoration and is typified by the use of mainly pink or purple. The pink colour was invented by Andreas Casssius of Leyden in the mid-17th century and is derived from gold chloride. It was introduced into China by a Jesuit priest in around 1720, where it was perfected.

- This new color palette was of a very high quality and proved very popular in Europe where is was exported in huge quantities in the 18th, 19th and 20th centuries. As demand increased, quality was often sacrificed and as a result later pieces are not as collectible.

A Chinese famille rose plate, decorated with a cockerel and a bird amongst flowers on blue and green backed scrolls, all on a ruby ground with chrysanthemum flower heads, Yongzheng period, crack.

8.5in (22cm) diam

$500-550 | **DN**

A pair of Chinese famille rose baluster vases, decorated with panels of flowers, figures, dragons and phoenix on a blue floral ground, six character Qianlong marks in iron red.

c1900   16in (40.5cm) high

$600-700 (pair) | **DN**

A Canton famille rose part dinner service, comprising a well and tree platter, a tureen, a covered vegetable dish, two sweatmeat dishes, five dinner plates, five dessert plates, four small side plates, one lobed saucer, two small sweatmeat dishes, two soup bowls, five plates, three cups, two square vegetable dish covers, an oval mazarin and an oval platter.

c1840   Platter 16.5in (42cm) long

$4,500-5,000 | **SI**

A 19thC Chinese famille rose porcelain vase, of ovoid form, cylindrical neck, the shoulders applied with peach tree branches in high relief on a black ground, Qing Dynasty.

22.5in (57cm) high

$1,200-1,800 | **SI**

A 19thC Chinese famille rose porcelain vase, of baluster form, with alternating cartouches enclosing figural and floral decoration, domed cover.

26in (66cm) high

$600-700 | **SI**

A 19thC Chinese famille rose hu-shaped vase, with iron red side handles, each face painted with figures in various pursuits, unmarked.

10.75in (27cm) high

$750-850 | **WW**

A 19thC famille rose baluster vase, decorated with phoenix perched amongst flowering peony and magnolia issuing from pierced rockwork, and pierced wood cover.

3.75in (35cm) high

$500-600 | **DN**

A late 19thC Chinese export porcelain rose mandarin covered vegetable dish.

9.5in (24cm) long

$500-600 SI

A late 19thC Chinese rose mandarin gravy boat.

$300-400 SI

A late 19thC Chinese export porcelain rose mandarin platter.

18.5in (47cm) long

$1,500-2,000 SI

A late 19thC Chinese small rose mandarin teapot.

4.5in (11.5cm) high

$300-400 SI

Four late 19thC Chinese export porcelain rose medallion plates.

9.75in (24cm) diam

$150-200 SI

A 20thC Chinese export rose medallion porcelain umbrella stand.

24in (61.3cm) high

$1,000-1,500 SI

An early 19thC Canton dish, painted with a figure scene within a fret-pierced border.

$600-700 HamG

A large 19thC Chinese jar, decorated in underglaze blue in Transitional-style with figures, rocks and plantains.

15.5in (39cm) high

$1,500-2,000 DN

A China trade porcelain plate, painted to the center with a bird-of-prey on an anchor, the rope forming the initials "J.H.", within an unusual blue enamel banded and gilt foliate scroll-decorated border.

The naval theme probably related to a London merchant who either traded or controlled ships to Canton.

c1800   *7.75in (19.5cm) diam*

$80-120 HamG

A Jiaqing coffee can, painted in famille verte enamel colours with a crest, probably for Radcliff or Walcott, between two five clawed dragons amidst scrolled clouds, against a café au lait ground.

c1815   *2.5in (6.5cm) high*

$150-200 HamG

A pair of Chinese porcelain baluster vases, with domed covers painted with prunus blossom against a dark blue ground.

11in (28cm) high

$300-400 GorL

A pair of Chinese green lead-glazed censers, raised on five legs issuing from dragon masks, paw feet, in Han-style, with wood covers and stands.

3.25in (8.5cm) high

$300-350 DN

Two Chinese wine cups, with green interiors, the exteriors decorated with dogs of Fo and dragons and a phoenix, with ormolu mounts.

2.5in (6.5cm) high

$50-80 DN

A pair of Chinese porcelain bowls and covers, decorated with lotus, with later gilt metal mounts and set up as censer and cover with vine knops and pierced border, some damage.

6.75in (17.5cm) high

$500-600   **DN**

A Japanese Satsuma earthenware vase, decorated with panels of warriors and domestic scenes with brocade panels, in polychrome enamels and gilding.

12in (30.5cm) high

$1,800-2,200   **GorL**

A 19thC Satsuma vase, cylindrical and painted with flowers in bright enamels.

10.5cm (26cm) high

$100-150   **GorL**

A Kutani earthenware bowl, the interior decorated with a square reserve depicting immortals surrounded by floral and bird reserves on a iron red ground with gilt scrolling foliage, the exterior with floral, figural and landscape reserves and a leaftip border, Meiji period.

8.75in (22.5cm) diam

$180-220   **SI**

A Japanese Satsuma earthenware bowl, with satsuma mon, figural and dragon decoration, signed, Meiji period.

12in (30.5cm) diam

$900-1,000   **SI**

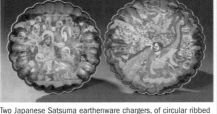

Two Japanese Satsuma earthenware chargers, of circular ribbed form, with scalloped rim, with dragon and figural decoration, Meiji period.

12.5in (32cm) diam

$900-1,000   **SI**

A Japanese Satsuma earthenware teapot, of flattened circular form, with a gilt dragon form handle and spout, floral decoration, Meiji period.

6in (15cm) diam

$300-350   **SI**

A late 19thC Satsuma ovoid vase, relief-molded with male figures against an iron red and gilt ground, inscribed Hododa.

9.5in (24cm) high

$150-200   **GorL**

A late 19thC Japanese earthenware bottle vase, decorated with flowering branches of prunus and chrysanthemum within decorative border, with pierced and carved wood stand.

7.5in (19cm) high

$450-500   **DN**

A Satsuma pottery vase, of paneled baluster form, painted and gilded with immortals resting on clouds on a dotted ground, the shoulder decorated with fan and star-shaped motifs, seal mark to base, late Meiji period.

9.5in (24.5cm) high

$300-350   **BonS**

A Satsuma pottery vase, of baluster form, the shoulder and neck applied with pierced demi "mon" handles, decorated with Samurai warriors, birds amid peonies verso, probably late Meiji.

15.5in (39cm) high

$500-600   **BonS**

A Satsuma figure of bearded man, carrying a fan and bucket on back, clothed in a loose-fitting robe, brocaded with roundels.

12.5in (31.5cm) high

$300-350 GorL

A Japanese Kutani deep-footed bowl, decorated inside with a bird and clouds within iron red borders, the exterior with a continuous band of ducks and water plants, leaf band to the foot.

7.5in (19cm) diam

$300-350 DN

A Chinese agate snuff bottle, of pebble form, carved to depict a tree.

$300-400 SI

A 19thC Chinese agate snuff bottle, of flattened rectangular form with rounded shoulders, carved in high relief to depict a crane under a pine tree.

$500-600 SI

A Japanese earthenware U-shaped bowl, decorated with a band of fruiting branches.

4.75in (12cm) diam

$80-100 DN

A Japanese Raku-type bowl, the slightly conical body covered in a crackled glaze trailed in green and with stylized characters, seal mark.

5.25in (13.5cm) diam

$80-100 DN

A pair of Oriental slender baluster earthenware vases, each decorated with panels of figures on a brocade ground, both damaged.

6in (15cm) high

$80-100 DN

A Japanese Imari pail, with high-arched handle and decorated in underglaze blue with brocade panels over crashing waves.

15.5in (39.5cm) high

$1,200-1,800 DN

SNUFF BOTTLES

- Snuff is made from ground tobacco, often mixed with herbs or spices to improve its aroma. Tobacco originated in the Americas but had reached major European ports by the early 1600s. It was considered a more genteel way of consuming tobacco than smoking and reached the height of its vogue in Europe in the late 17th century.

- It is unclear how snuff and tobacco were first introduced to China, but it is possible that it came via Japan from Portuguese and Spanish traders. The first recorded mention is of a gift from the Jesuit missionary Father Enrico Ricci to the Qing Dynasty emperor in the late 17thC.

- As with Europe, smoking was unpopular with authorities in China and was banned during the Ming dynasty and into the Qing dynasty. As a result, with further influence from the West, snuff became the acceptable way of taking tobacco.

- As snuff became more popular, so the production of snuff bottles became more artistic and diverse. This was particularly so during the reign of emperor Chien Lung (1736-1796) under whose patronage the imperial workshops reached their peak. As well as practical vessels, these increasingly elaborate bottles became popular as gifts to dignitaries or court officials.

Two early 20thC Chinese snuff bottles, comprising one in agate of flattened ovoid form, carved to depict a bird perched on a rockery, the stone with russet and chocolate inclusions and one in celadon jade of flattened ovoid form, carved to depict a pagoda amongst flowering trees.

$200-300 SI

A fine Chinese shadow agate snuff bottle, of flattened rectangular form with rounded shoulders, carved to depict a large raptor standing on one talon and a smaller bird flying above, the stone of gray tone with café-au-lait and chocolate inclusions.

$700-800 SI

A 19thC Chinese moss agate snuff bottle, of flattened rectangular form, the stone a light gray tone suffused with moss-like green.

$300-400 SI

A 19thC Chinese shadow agate snuff bottle, Qing dynasty, of flattened rectangular form with rounded shoulders, carved through the brown skin to depict a cat, butterfly and flying magpie, the reverse a cicada, carved lion mask ring handles on the shoulders.

$600-700 SI

A Chinese cinnabar snuff bottle, of flattened ovoid form, carved to depict a dragon chasing the flaming pearl of wisdom.

$180-220 SI

A Chinese enameled glass snuff bottle, Qianlong mark, of flattened rectangular form, with a bird and floral decoration.

$750-850 SI

A Chinese copper enamel European-subject snuff bottle, Qianlong mark, of flattened ovoid form, painted to depict a European lady in an orchard, enclosed within a medallion with blue foliate border, surrounded by a floral and foliate motif.

$1,500-2,000 SI

A Chinese blue glass overlay snowfleck snuff bottle, of flattened form, carved to depict scholars and attendants.

$300-400 SI

A 19thC Chinese inside-painted glass snuff bottle, Qing dynasty, of flattened ovoid form, painted on one side to depict a mountainous landscape, the reverse a praying mantis stalking two crickets on rockery, signed 'Yan Yutian', inscribed with red seal of Yutian.

$1,000-1,500 SI

A Chinese three-color overlay on snowflake glass snuff bottle, of flattened rectangular form, carved in green, blue and pink overlay to depict fish, fans, chimes and lotus.

$600-700 SI

A Chinese ivory snuff bottle, of flattened ovoid form, carved in low relief to depict a man on horse back and boy, the reverse with calligraphy.

This is a commemorative snuff bottle, produced for one of the snuff bottle conventions.

$200-300 SI

A Chinese gray jade bottle, of pebble form.

$250-300 SI

A 19thC Chinese jade snuff bottle, of double-gourd form, carved in high relief through the darker skin to depict on one side opposing dragons; the other, fruiting gourd vine.

$200-300 SI

A 19thC Chinese celadon jade snuff bottle, of flattened rectangular form, carved to depict a frog overlooking fruiting gourds with vine and tendrils, the stone of celadon tone with apple green inclusions.

$1,000-1,500 SI

A 19thC Chinese celadon jade snuff bottle, carved to depict a goldfish, with carved details.

$200-300 SI

An unusual Chinese porcelain snuff bottle, modeled as a chilli pepper, with spinach jade stopper and overall red glaze. *c1800*

$1,300-1,800 SI

A 19thC Chinese rock crystal snuff bottle, Qing dynasty, of flattened rectangular form, undecorated body with bevelled corners.

$600-700 SI

A 19thC Chinese rock crystal coin snuff bottle, Qing dynasty, of flattened circular form, carved with a Spanish coin portrait design and inscription, the reverse with clock dial with Roman numerals.

$800-900 SI

A CLOSER LOOK AT A SNUFF BOTTLE

The technique of inside-painting was invented specifically for snuff bottles and is unique to China.

Legend has is that inside painting began after a court official scratched the inside of his glass bottle when he scraped out the snuff with a sharpened bamboo stick.

Artists used matchstick-sized bamboo sticks with a hooked end to paint the inside of the bottles.

A 20thC Chinese inside-painted rock crystal snuff bottle, of flattened ovoid form, painted to depict a river landscape amongst mountains, signed Wang.

$300-400 SI

Two Tibetan stone inlaid silver snuff bottles, one of rectangular form with turquoise and coral inlay and one of flattened ovoid form inlaid with stones on a filigree ground.

$180-220 SI

BRUSHPOTS

■ Japanese or Chinese brushpots were made as containers for artists' or calligraphers' brushes. The first ones were made in the 16th century and were usually made from bamboo, porcelain or jade, and decorated with calligraphy or Oriental scenes. They are usually cylindrical in form. The use of polished hardwood was introduced from the 17th century. Today Oriental calligraphy is considered to be an elegant art form and brushpots have become highly sought after.

A white biscuit brushpot, intricately carved in low relief with figures in a landscape, mark of Chen Guozhi (1820-1860).

Chen Guozhi was a famous ceramic artist during the Qing Dynasty (1644-1911). He produced ceramic pieces that imitated the appearance of wood, bamboo and ivory.

5.75in (14.5cm) high

$750-850 **DN**

Two pale brown-glazed brushpots, one carved with two horses playing on a riverbank; the other a brown-glazed brush pot with prunus.

c1900   5in (12.56cm) high

$450-550 (pair) **DN**

A brown-glazed brushpot, carved in low relief with mountainscapes, mark of Zhang Maiyi.

5.25in (13.5cm) high

$500-600 **DN**

A pale-green glazed brushpot, carved in high relief with a Shou Lao and a boy beside a deer and five bats, mark of Tang Huxing.

6in (15.5cm) high

$800-900 **DN**

A tall green-glazed brushpot, by Li Yuchen, carved in high relief with cranes and deer under pine trees, wood stand.

11in (27.9cm) high

$1,200-1,800 **DN**

A green-glazed brushpot, carved with the eight horses of Mu Wang, mark of Li Yucheng.

6in (15cm) high

$1,200-1,800 **DN**

Two green-glazed brushpots, one carved in low relief with a landscape, the base with four character Guangxu mark, the other green-glazed and carved with cockerels.

c1900   5in (13cm) high

$450-550 (pair) **DN**

A pale yellow-glazed brushpot, by Li Yucheng, carved with monkeys playing in a landscape.

5.75in (14.5cm) high

$1,200-1,800 **DN**

A white biscuit brushpot, of lozenge section, carved in low relief with fishermen in a riverscape; and three further white biscuit brushpots, two carved with figures and one with rabbits.

6.75in (17.5cm) high

$300-350 **DN**

A Chinese light celadon jade brush washer, of cylindrical form, carved to depict a flowering prunus tree and calligraphy, late Qing/early Republic period,

4.7in (12cm) high

$450-550 **SI**

Three Yixing brushpots, each carved in imitation of a tree trunk, one with a 16-character inscription at the base.

Largest 5.75in (14.5cm) high

$300-350 **DN**

A fine Japanese gilt bronze figure of a fisherman, incised with gilt roundels fixed to a gilt brass inlaid rosewood stand, signed "Miyao", Meiji period.

13in (33cm) high

$6,500-7,500 **GorL**

A Chinese ivory cylindrical vase and cover, deeply carved with flowers and foliage, the cover with a knop carved as a farmer with an oxen, the knop damaged.

c1900 *8.75in (22cm) high*

$300-400 **WW**

A Japanese gilt bronze figure of a carpenter, fixed to a gilt brass inlaid rosewood stand, signed "Maiyau", Meiji period.

8in (20.5cm) high

$2,000-3,000 **GorL**

A mid-19thC Chinese ivory cricket cage, in the form of a gourd finely pierced with flowering branches on a pierced cell ground.

3.25in (8.5cm) high

$500-600 **DN**

A Japanese bronze round plaque, modeled in high relief with a lion's head, signed.

14.5in (37cm) diam

$1,000-1,500 **DN**

A Chinese rock crystal figure of Pudai, the corpulent figure reclining on a cushion.

$150-200 **DN**

A Chinese white jade carving of a Ruji Scepter, Qing dynasty.

6.7in (17.2cm) long

$400-500 **SI**

A pair of yellow-glazed seals, each square column topped by a seated lion; and another yellow-glazed seal surmounted by an eagle perching on a pine tree.

Largest 4.25in (10.5cm) high

$600-700 **DN**

A Japanese iron and gilt tsuba, pierced and cast with five ducks in flight within a gilt diaper border, and a plain iron tsuba cast with three cranes.

3in (7.5cm) diam

$1,000-1,500 **DN**

A pair of 19thC Japanese iron tsuba, finely cast and pierced with scaly dragons, signed "Hiotsuyanagi Tomoyoshe at the age of 68".

3.5in (8.5cm) diam

$1,000-1,500 **DN**

A Japanese iron tsuba, probably 18thC finely pierced with stylized tendrils and droplets in gold.

3in (7.5cm) diam

$500-600 **DN**

A fine Japanese katana, with single-edged blade, the tang signed "Tsunemitsu", the grip covered with ray-skin, gilt copper tsuba and mounts with black lacquer scabbard with lacquer stand.

Blade 28in (71cm) long

$3,500-4,000 **L&T**

A 19thC Japanese red lacquer zushi, the doors with chased gilt metal mounts, the interior in gilt with the four armed Kannon seated on a pedestal.

9.75in (25cm) high

$700-800 **DN**

A Japanese black lacquer cabinet, of rectangular outline, with two doors opening to an interior with three small drawers, painted with feather decoration.

10in (25.4cm) wide

$180-220 **SI**

A 20thC Japanese carved ivory concentric ball on stand, having naturalistic decorated shell containing approximately. ten pierced balls.

2in (5cm) high

$180-220 **GorB**

A carved ivory mystery ball, exterior carved with dragons and vines, the five interior balls pierced with holes around the exterior, ivory stand carved with an oriental gentleman holding a pillar on top of his head, which supports the ball, very minor loss to fins.

8.25in (21cm) high

$180-220 **JDJ**

Three views of a 19thC Japanese lacquer suzuribako and cover, the black ground decorated with a figure gazing at a rural landscape, the interior with figures pulling barges in a river landscape.

9in (23cm) high

$3,000-4,000 **DN**

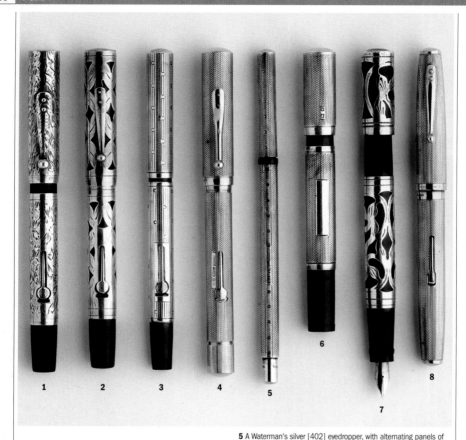

1 A 1920s Waterman's 452 'Hand Engraved Vine', marked "Sterling", with 2 nib, excellent, a lovely writer, engraved, replaced cap crown, recently overhauled.

$400-500   **CO**

2 A 1920s Waterman's 452 'Basketweave', marked 'Sterling', with 'Sterling' Clip Cap and 2 nib, lightly engraved name and initials, cap crown lip damaged.

$250-300   **CO**

3 A Waterman's silver overlaid 52, 'line and dot' overlaid lever-filler with Waterman's 2 medium nib, a rare pattern, slight oxidation on hard rubber, London hallmarks.
1933

$300-400   **CO**

4 A Waterman's 9ct gold 52, engine-turned overlaid lever-filler with 9ct gold clip and Waterman's 2 medium flexible nib, presentation inscription otherwise excellent/near mint, recently overhauled, London hallmark.
1939

$600-700   **CO**

5 A Waterman's silver [402] eyedropper, with alternating panels of barley and line-and-dot decoration, and Ideal 2 nib, quite rare, three dings in cap, 6mm split in barrel by section, London hallmarks.
1916

$200-300   **CO**

6 A Waterman's silver-overlaid 42, 'barleycorn' pattern overlaid black hard rubber retractable safety pen, with Waterman's 2 nib, in red Waterman's presentation box with papers, excellent/near inked mint, London hallmarks.
1920

$500-600   **CO**

7 A 1920s Waterman's 442V 'Filigree' safety, marked 'Sterling', with 2 nib, model number rubbed, two initials lightly scratched into the plate.

$250-350   **CO**

8 A Waterman's 9ct gold overlaid pen, 'barley' pattern engine-turned S.J. Rose overlaid lever-filler, with Waterman's 2 nib, excellent, London Coronation year hallmarks.
1953

$500-600   **CO**

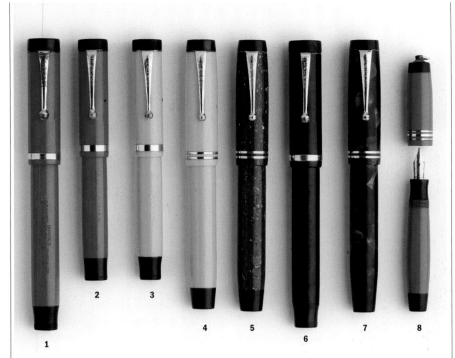

1 An American Parker Lucky Curve Duofold Senior, red Permanite, Canadian Duofold nib, very good but some brassing, clip screw chewed.

c1927

$150-200　　　　　　　　　　　　　　　　**CO**

2 An American Parker Lucky Curve Duofold Junior, red Permanite, broad Duofold nib, ball on clip brassed, two scratches.

c1927

$60-80　　　　　　　　　　　　　　　　**CO**

3 An American Parker Lucky Curve Duofold Junior, mandarin Permanite, Duofold nib, excellent, slight color difference.

Yellow is one of the rarer colors for Duofolds. Collectors should examine the cap lip for cracks, which show up as grey hairlines.

c1927

$250-300　　　　　　　　　　　　　　　　**CO**

4 An American Parker Duofold Senior, mandarin Permanite, Duofold nib, very good, band of color difference beneath threads, light brassing.

1930s Duofolds can be told apart from 1920s versions by the streamlined shape of the ends. Compare those on this pen to No.1.

c1930

$600-700　　　　　　　　　　　　　　　　**CO**

5 A Canadian Parker Duofold Senior, lapis Permanite, Canadian Duofold nib, near mint.

c1929

$750-850　　　　　　　　　　　　　　　　**CO**

6 An American Parker Lucky Curve Senior, black Permanite button-filler with early Parker Lucky Curve medium nib, very good.

c1927

$200-300　　　　　　　　　　　　　　　　**CO**

7 A Canadian Parker Duofold Senior, burgundy and black marble Permanite button-filler, nib split, otherwise excellent/near mint.

c1931

$250-350　　　　　　　　　　　　　　　　**CO**

8 A Canadian Parker Vest Pocket Duofold Pen and Pencil, red Permanite button-filler with Parker Duofold pen nib, and matching rotary pencil, rare, especially in red, light brassing on cap bands.

Although red is one of the most common colors for other Duofolds, Vest Pocket Duofolds are rare in this color.

c1932

$450-550 (set)　　　　　　　　　　　　　　**CO**

1   2   3   4   5   6   7   8

1 A Wahl Eversharp Oversize 'Deco Band' pen and pencil, black hard rubber lever-filler with Greek Key decoration and Gold Seal Manifold nib, with matching rotary pencil, minor brassing on pen, pencil near mint.

c1929

$450-550   **CO**

2 A Wahl Eversharp Oversize Gold Seal 'Deco Band', jade green plastic, with Gold Seal Manifold Post nib and roller clip, some discoloration.

c1929

$300-400   **CO**

3 A Wahl Eversharp Gold Seal Personal Point, coral Pyrolin, roller clip, and Gold Seal M Signature nib, excellent.

c1929

$500-600   **CO**

4 A Wahl Eversharp Gold Seal Personal Point, black and pearl Pyrolin, roller clip, Gold Seal B Flexible nib, a difficult color to find.

c1929

$250-350   **CO**

5 A mid-1920s Sheaffer Lifetime Senior, black lever-filler, with two bands and Lifetime 'number' nib, very good.

$100-150   **CO**

6 A Sheaffer's Lifetime Extended Balance Senior, pearl and black Radite, Lifetime nib, good, barrel pinched lightly in two places.

This plastic is often "browned" on the barrel due to sulphur on the ink sac. This is irreversible.

c1930

$120-180   **CO**

7 A Conklin Nozac, red, silver and black herringbone celluloid faceted Nozac-filler with Cushion Point medium nib, very good.

This is the most desirable color Nozac

c1932

$750-850   **CO**

8 A Carter's lever-filler, 'Pearl White' Pearltex, replaced 14K Warranted nib, together with a framed "Carter's, You Set the Pace" advert illustrating this pen, pen a rare color in excellent condition.

c1931

$300-400   **CO**

1 A 1920s American Waterman's 42, chased black hard rubber, with 2 nib, excellent.

This style of pen is known as a 'safety'. Twisting the bottom of the pen retracts the nib into the barrel. Safety pens were popular during the 1920s.

$50-60 **CO**

2 A Canadian Waterman's Patrician pen and pencil, black hard rubber, Canadian Patrician medium nib, propeling pencil, lacks globe, light brassing and oxidation, clear imprints.

Black hard rubber Patricians are rare.

c1929

$350-450 (set) **CO**

3 A 1930s Canadian Waterman's 94, steel-quartz celluloid lever-filler with chrome trim and Waterman's medium nib, replaced, otherwise excellent.

$85-95 **CO**

4 A 1930s Candian Waterman's 32?, red-flecked brown-black woodgrain celluloid, with Waterman's fine 2 nib, near mint, clip ball slightly brassed.

$120-180 **CO**

5 A Canadian Waterman's 94 ripple, blue ripple hard rubber lever-filler, with 9ct gold cap band and Ideal 4 fine nib, replaced lever, otherwise excellent.

Blue is one of the rarer ripple colors, the more common is the red/orange and black ripple which is worth less in a similar size.

1929

$300-400 **CO**

6 A rare Canadian Waterman's 94 ripple, olive ripple hard rubber, with 9ct gold cap band and Ideal 4 generous-medium nib, very good.

1928

$300-400 **CO**

7 A 1930s Canadian Waterman's Ink-Vue Deluxe, 'emerald ray' celluloid, keyhole 7 Canadian nib, fair to good.

This pen has a semi-transparent barrel allowing the user to see the ink supply.

$250-350 **CO**

8 A Canadian Waterman's 92, 'brown lizard' celluloid lever-filler, with slightly later English Waterman's 2 fine nib, very good, slight brassing on clip.

c1935

$250-350 **CO**

1 A De La Rue 9ct gold Onoto, barley design engine-turned fully-covered full-length plunger-filler with Onoto 3 nib, Onoto brown leather box, engraved "M. Y. Mary Rose 18-7-31" otherwise excellent / near mint, London hallmarks.

1919

$600-700 CO

2 A rare De La Rue silver-overlaid Onoto, 'snail' overlaid cap and barrel marked "Sterling" with De la Rue nib, very good.

'Snail' refers to the ornate curling pattern on the overlay that resembles a snail's shell.

1915-20

$1,000-1,500 CO

3 A 1940s-50s De La Rue Onoto Magna 1703-35, chased black lever-filler with plain Onoto 7 medium nib, light marks on post.

Magna lever-fillers are rarer than the piston-filling mechanism that is usually found on Onoto pens.

$250-350 CO

4 A 1930s-40s De La Rue 'The De La Rue Pen', un-numbered opaline pearl and black marble celluloid lever-filler, with bandless cap and unusual Onoto 14ct 5 nib, rare, hairlines in cap lip.

The cap on this pen is very prone to cracks due to the relative fragility of the plastic.

$120-180 CO

5 A Burnham 'The Burnham', lapis blue and turquoise flecked caesin lever-filler, with Burnham 14ct gold fine nib, excellent.

c1927

$70-100 CO

6 A mid-1930s Ford's 'Large' Patent Pen, black hard rubber, phenomenally broad Ford 428 Mill 'spade' nib, with original instructions, inked mint.

$250-350 CO

7 A 1930s Dickinson 'The Croxley' Pen, lilac pearl marble lever-filler with juicy broad Dickinson nib, mear mint.

$50-80 CO

8 A scarce 1930s-40s Kingswood pen, rose herringbone celluloid button-filler, with correct Warranted nib, , an attractive color in excellent condition.

$70-100 CO

1 A Conway Stewart Duro, mottled red hard rubber, Conway Stewart nib with matching section and feed, near mint, noting minor brassing on clip and lever.

c1927

$500-600 CO

2 A 1920s Conway Stewart No. 200M, mottled red hard rubber, bandless cap, later Conway nib, excellent.

$120-180 CO

3 A rare Conway Stewart 1206, black celluloid lever-filler with two hallmarked 18ct gold bands and Duro nib, light posting wear, otherwise excellent.

1941

$70-100 CO

4 A Conway Stewart No. 266, blue pearl and black-veined marble celluloid button filler, with Conway Stewart medium nib, excellent, ball brassed, quite rare.

c1935

$180-220 CO

5 A 1950s Conway Stewart 60, blue and black-lined celluloid lever-filler, with firm fine Duro nib, excellent.

$150-200 CO

6 An extremely rare Conway Stewart 60, grey herringbone celluloid lever-filler, with broad cap band and 60 Duro nib, excellent/near mint.

The attractive grey herringbone Conway Stewart is far scarcer than well-publicized rarities such as the No.22 'Floral'. It was first brought to collectors' attention by Andreas Lambrou with the publication of "Fountain Pens of the World' in 1995, when the model 58 he illustrated was thought to be the only example. However, Conway Stewart also used the grey herringbone celluloid for their model 60 (essentially the same pen, but with different trim) and recent discussion among senior collectors has now identified a total of four or five known examples in these two versions. None has yet surfaced in any other size or model.

c1951

$1,000-1,500 CO

7 A 1950s Conway Stewart 60, 'cracked ice', silver pearl veined black celluloid, lever filler with Duro firm nib, excellent.

$250-350 CO

8 A Conway Stewart 22 'Floral', 'floral' celluloid laminated lever-filler with 5 nib, and box, very good, light darkening on barrel.

c1955

$400-500 CO

1 A 1920s Montblanc 2, octagonal black hard rubber safety pen, with Montblanc 2 nib, excellent, some wear to milled cap top.

$300-400   CO

2 A 1930s Danish Montblanc Masterpiece 25, coral push-knob filler, replaced Danish nib, good color, engraved name on barrel.

$300-400   CO

3 A late 1930s/early 1940s Montblanc Meisterstück 136, black celluloid and hard rubber piston-filler, with long ink window, unusual white cap star set within a metal ring, and metal 4810 nib, lacks tip, burn mark in threads.

The format of the cap star makes this an unusual pen.

$250-350   CO

4 A 1940s Danish Montblanc 244, green marbled celluloid piston-filler, with 4 nib, very good, one cap band slightly loose.

$150-200   CO

5 A 1950s Montblanc Meisterstück 144G, light silver-green striated celluloid piston-filler, with two color 4810 nib, even discoloration.

$450-550   CO

6 A late 1950s Montblanc 254, black plastic piston-filler, with 'wing' nib, and original box and instructions, excellent/near mint.

$250-350   CO

7 A 1940s Pelikan 100, with grey and black striated celluloid sleeve, and Pelikan 14 K nib, fair, needs restoration.

$250-300   CO

8 A rare Pelikan 101N Weißgold, white rolled gold overlaid piston filler, with Pelikan .585 fine nib, cap top slightly brighter, otherwise excellent.
1938-39

$1,000-1,500   CO

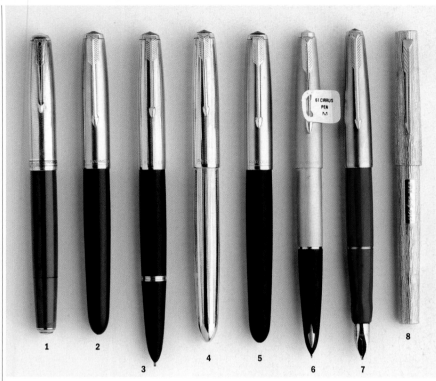

1 A Parker 51 'First Year' Blue Diamond Vacumatic, dove grey, with "Parker Made in USA" imprint around the blind cap, aluminum jewels, lined sterling silver cap and broad italic nib, good/very good.

Earlier Parker 51s from the 1940s used the 'vacumatic' system filling developed by Parker. To fill the pen, unscrew a small cap at the end of the barrel and press the small plastic or metal plunger.

1941

$450-550   **CO**

2 A 1950s English Parker 51 Insignia, teal blue aerometric-filler, with lustraloy cap and medium nib, a nice pen.

The 'aerometric' filler was used from the 1950s onwards and replaced the 'vacumatic' filling system on Parker 51s. To fill the pen, unscrew the barrel and squeeze the part of the metal cylinder that contains the latex ink sack.

$50-80   **CO**

3 A 1950s American Parker 51 Insignia, Midnight Blue aerometric-filler, with rolled gold cap and broad italic nib, juicy nib, pen worn.

$100-150   **CO**

4 A 1950s English Parker 51 Signet, with rolled gold cap and barrel and medium nib, a couple of small dings on barrel, light tool marks under clip.

$180-220   **CO**

5 A 1950s English Parker 51 Insignia, black aerometric-filler, with lustraloy cap and medium nib, excellent.

$70-100   **CO**

6 A 1970s Parker 61 Cirrus, finely-lined rolled gold 'cloud series' cartridge/convertor pen, with medium nib, tag and box, near mint, light scratch on barrel.

The delicately lined matt finish on this pen is very susceptible to wear. The 'Cirrus' is part of a series of pens with finishes that represented different cloud forms.

$100-150   **CO**

7 A Parker VP, red clean-filler, with transparent filler section, steel cap and broad oblique 75 'dial' nib, excellent.

This is a rare color for a VP.

c1962

$120-180   **CO**

8 A Parker 'Royal Wedding' Pen, No 0491/1000, rolled gold bark-effect 'Royal Oak' 105, with medium nib, box, instructions, certificate and brown card outer, mint.

This pen was produced by Parker to celebrate the wedding of Prince Charles and Lady Diana Spencer.

1981

$700-1,000   **CO**

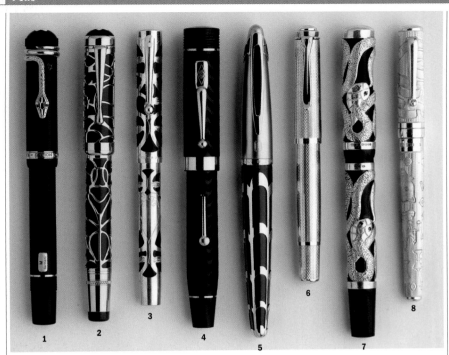

1 2 3 4 5 6 7 8

A Montblanc Agatha Christie No. 0116/4810, black Montblanc resin piston-filler, with vermeil snake clip marked "925", inlaid sapphire eyes and medium two-color Agatha Christie 18k nib, with box, reply card, personal service card, card box and outer sleeve, mint.

The edition size of 4810 refers to the height of Mont Blanc in meters.

1993

$1,200-1,800   CO

A Montblanc Prince Regent No 4352/4810, gold-plated filigree-overlaid blue Montblanc resin piston-filler, with crown motif on cap and Prince Regent 18k medium nib, box, leaflet and card outer, mint.

1995

$1,500-2,000   CO

A mid-1990s Sheaffer Nostalgia 800, silver filigree cartridge/convertor pen, with import hallmark, two-color Sheaffer medium nib, box and packaging dated 1997, mint.

$400-500   CO

A Conway Stewart Churchill 'The Writing Equipment Society 20th Anniversary' No 089/200, chased black hard rubber lever-filling pen, with Conway Stewart broad nib, box and packaging, mint.

2000

$200-300   CO

A Waterman Edson Signé Boucheron No 0622/3741, with 18ct gold filigree overlay by Boucheron on a blue Edson pen, with Waterman medium nib, with box.

1996

$1,000-1,500   CO

A Pelikan Souveran M850, green and black striped piston-filler, with vermeil cap marked "925", and two-color 18k gold broad nib, mint and boxed.

c2000

$300-350   CO

A Henry Charles Simpole Snake pen No 250/250, hard-rubber button-filler with silver filigree overlay of two snakes each set with emerald eyes, mint and boxed.

This pen was inspired by the legendary Waterman and Parker snake pens of the 1900s-1910s.

2001

$600-800   CO

An Anthony Elson "Worshipful Company of Goldsmiths" pen, silver Montegrappa-style cartridge/convertor pen, with an engraved design showing the leopard's head, demi-maiden and motto "justitia virtutum regina" of the Worshipful Company of Goldsmiths with 18ct gold nib, mint, London millennium hallmark.

2000

$350-400   CO

A 1920s Wahl-Eversharp fountain pen desk set, onyx base decorated with a spelter dog (probably an English Setter), with two "Wahl-Eversharp Fountain Pen Desk Set" stickers, green/bronze marble celluloid tulip and matching Gold Seal desk pen with Wahl-Eversharp Signature nib, dog fatigued and lacks a paw.

$250-300   **GorL**

A 1930s Dunhill Namiki maki-e lacquer bridge pencil, signed by Kosai and bearing the Namiki kanji, depicting three playing cards in takamaki-e on a roiro-nuri background.

3in (8cm) high

$300-400   **PC**

An olive green blown three-mold diamond-pattern glass inkwell, made by Keene, New Hampshire.

c1830 2.25in (5.5cm) diam

$600-700   **RAA**

A 1930s Dunhill Namiki urushi-e and maki-e lacquer deskbase, signed by Kosan and depicting a bird eating cherries from a basket, executed in takamaki-e and urushi-e on a roiro-nuri background.

Produced under the shortlived partnership of Namiki Manufacturing of Japan and Alfred Dunhill Ltd of London, this rare and unusual deskbase shows two types of lacquerwork, the more usual maki-e where the pigment is sprinkled onto the lacquer before it hardens and the scarcer urishi-e where lacquer and pigment are applied with a brush.

6in (15cm) wide

$450-550   **PC**

An 1890s F. Soennecken Soennecken's Tintenfasser No. 276, shaped wooden base with grooved pen rest on three sides, ornate metal corner mounts, and ornate circular brass lift-up inkwell cover marked "SOENNECKEN'S PATENT" over a pale blue glass liner with graduated base, two chips to liner.

6in (15cm) wide

$150-250   **GorL**

A 1930s marbled cast phenolic pen desk base, with hard rubber tulip.

4in (10cm) high

$50-60   **JBC**

A European pewter writing set, probably Dutch, comprising three holders with long drawer on bottom, removable sander, covered ink box and open round box, possibly later.

11in (28cm) wide

$200-300   **JDJ**

A Tiffany Studios 'Zodiac' pattern eight-piece desk set, comprising a pair of bookends, hexagonal inkwell, rolling blotter, calendar frame, pen tray and a pair of blotter ends.

1899-1928 19.5in (49.5cm) l

$2,000-2,500   **SI**

A Tiffany Studios 'Zodiac' pattern seven-piece desk set, comprising two blotter ends, pin tray, inkwell, stamp box, covered pad holder and paper clip, signed on bottom "TIFFANY STUDIOS NEW YORK", some wear to finish.

$1,800-2,200   **JDJ**

A Bradley & Hubbard seven-piece desk set, cast bronze with pattern of draped garlands, ribbons and shield center, comprising letter rack, calendar, flat blotter and four blotter corners, signed "BRADLEY & HUBBARD".

$200-300   **JDJ**

An American gilt-bronze seven-piece desk set, probably by Bradley & Hubbard, including inkwell, stamp box, pen tray, letter opener, calendar, envelope rack and blotter corners, each with pierced foliate design against mother-of-pearl, unmarked, hinge broken on stamp box, stand missing from calendar.

c1920

$450-550   **FRE**

PENS & WRITING EQUIPMENT

A George III oval silver inkstand, with gadrooned and pierced borders on four ball-and-claw feet, with a cut glass well and a pounce pot, by John Weldring or James Wiburd, London hallmarks.

1771   *7in (18cm) high*

$450-500   **DN**

A silver inkwell, by J.C.E. Dington, London.

1845

$1,500-2,000   **GS**

A silver inkstand, with two glass inkwells, by Charles and George Fox, London.

1848   *7in (18.5cm) wide*

$1,000-1,500   **JBS**

A Viennese bronze and crystal inkstand.

c1870   *5in (13cm) wide*

$320-380   **SS**

An unusual Victorian olive wood plough inkstand.

c1870   *7.75 (20cm) wide*

$300-400   **MB**

A brass lobster inkwell.

1860   *13in (33cm) long*

$600-1,000   **SS**

A Victorian papier-mâché rectangular inkstand, with two square-section cut glass wells, painted with landscapes, within gilt scroll borders.

           10.5in (26.5cm) wide

$120-180   **LFA**

A French cut glass and silver inkwell, with miniature portrait of a lady in 19thC dress set in lid, by Tiffany and Co, Paris.

c1890   *5.5in (14.5cm) high*

$1,200-1,800   **JBS**

A mid-to late 19thC pottery phrenology head pen stand, the regions of the brain inscribed in gilding, on a scroll-moulded base, chip to tip of nose, light wear to gilding.

Phrenology was invented in the late 18th century by a Viennese doctor. It explained how the brain was the source for all human intellectual capacity and character traits, and that each part of the brain represented a different trait. According to this science the shape of the head reveals the character and intellect of a person. Hence, by measuring the shape of the head, practitioners could tell what type of a person they were. Unsurprisingly, phrenology had been dismissed as a 'quack science' by the mid-19th century. Collectors should beware of the great many modern reproductions on the market.

$350-400   **DN**

A CLOSER LOOK AT AN INKWELL

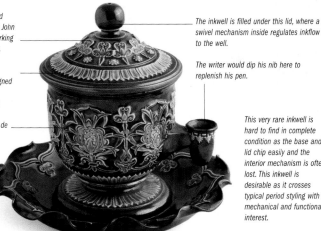

Very strong high Victorian styling and decoration with the entire design by John Huskinson, an in-house designer working in the 1880s at the Doulton factory.

Each piece is hand decorated and signed by the artist. This piece is signed 'ES' for Eliza Simmance, a famous woman artist in the Doulton factory.

The 'Isobath' was made for Thomas de la Rue who are better known for producing bank notes and also the 'Onoto' range of fountain pens.

Crimped edge acts as a pen rest, allowing pen to be laid down.

The inkwell is filled under this lid, where a swivel mechanism inside regulates inkflow to the well.

The writer would dip his nib here to replenish his pen.

This very rare inkwell is hard to find in complete condition as the base and lid chip easily and the interior mechanism is often lost. This inkwell is desirable as it crosses typical period styling with a mechanical and functional interest.

A rare Royal Doulton Lambeth 'isobath' inkwell.
c1888

6.5in (16.5cm) high

$600-1,000   **MHC**

A late 19thC cast-iron inkwell, with sphinx to front and vertically-mounted thermometer to rear, with rose-glass inkwell, the whole mounted on a base with acanthus leaf motifs.

9in (23cm) high

$120-180   **MHC**

A silver inkstand, with two inkwells, London hallmarks.
1903

$1,000-1,500   **GS**

An Edwardian single inkstand, on a silver base, with London hallmarks and dated.
1911

$600-1,000   **GS**

A silver inkstand, of shaped outline, with two square glass and silver-mounted inkwells and inscribed with a presentation inscription, by Horace Woodward & Co Ltd, London hallmarks.
1906

10.75in (27.5cm) wide

$400-500   **DN**

A cut glass and silver inkwell, with desk calendar, by Mappin & Webb, Birmingham hallmarks.

1909   *3.5in wide*

$1,000-1,500   **Tag**

A silver double inkstand, with Birmingham hallmarks and dated.
1912

$800-1,200   **GS**

An oblong silver inkstand, with reed-and-ribbon border, a central oval sand box and two pen recesses, on ball-and-claw feet and with silver-mounted inkwells, by Horace Woodward & Co Ltd, London hallmarks.

1913   *10.25in (26cm) wide*

$350-400   **DN**

A cut glass inkwell, with silver watch set into the cap, Birmingham hallmark.

1917   *3.5in (9cm) high*

$2,500-3,000   **Tag**

A 1920s carved wooden inkwell and pen rest, the head of a terrier forming the lid of the inkwell.

7.25in wide

$600-1,000   **Tag**

FIND OUT MORE...

'Inkstands and Inkwells', by Ted & Betty Rivera, Crown Publishing, June 1973, ASIN: 0517504197.

'The Collector's Guide to Inkwells', by Veldon Badders, Collector Books, October 1997, ISBN: 1574320203.

Scrytion Museum, Spoorlaan 434a, 5038 CH Tilburg, The Netherlands. A museum housing over 1,200 inkwells and inkstands, amongst other exhibits relating to the evolution of script.

A silver inkstand, of concave oblong outline, by Asprey & Co Ltd, Birmingham hallmarks.

1935   *7.75in (19.5cm) wide*

$270-330   **DN**

A silver desk inkwell, of oblong shape with waisted and faceted well, with Birmingham hallmarks and dated.

$400-600   **GS**

A Continental Art Deco marble two-piece desk set, including a double inkwell and pen tray of heavily veined gray marble, with matching letter rack, one inkwell missing glass liner.

c1935

$150-200   **FRE**

BAKELITE

- Not all early plastics are 'Bakelite'. Real Bakelite can be identified by rubbing it for two minutes with your finger. If the item is Bakelite this will produce a strong carbolic smell.

- Tagged as 'the material of 1,000 uses', Bakelite was developed by the Belgian Dr Leo Baekeland in 1907. Bakelite is considered the first important truly synthetic plastic after the discovery of celluloid in the 19thC.

- The adaptability of Bakelite and related plastics allowed for cost-effective mass production of products, hence some pieces are common.

- Bakelite and early plastics were produced in a multitude of colors. It is commonly found in shades of brown and black, but also blue, red and green which are scarcer and more collectable. These colored pieces broke away from the dull monotony of wood, ceramics and metal, ushering in a new age of style and were connected with new fashions such as Art Deco and Industrial styling.

- Many plastic objects were aimed at the domestic market, most notably the radio but also kitchenalia. Plastic also had office and even industrial uses, such as with switches and insulators.

- Fabulously colored Bakelite jewelry is extremely collectable and can fetch high prices. Look for bright colors and deep-cut designs made from a single piece of plastic.

- Although it provided cheer during the Depression and World War II, the post war invention of cheaper injection molded plastics saw the end of the golden age of plastics.

A brown Bakelite cigarette box for Teofani cigarettes.

1920s   *6.25in (15.5cm) wide*

$40-60   **MHC**

A selection of English celluloid simulated tortoiseshell dressing table items.

1920s

$5-8 each   **JBC**

Two Bakelite Thermos flasks with chrome plated metal handles.

1920s   *10.25in (26cm) high*

$40-60 each   **JBC**

A tabletop crumb sweeper in green and black Bakelite.

1920s   *6in (15cm) wide*

$30-50   **JBC**

A De La Rue Enduraware multi-colored Bakelite inkwell.

1920s   *2.5in (6.5cm) diam at base*

$20-30   **JBC**

A brown mottled Bakelite lidded circular pot.

1920s   *5in (12.5cm) diam*

$15-25   **JBC**

A brown mottled Bakelite vase on a pewter base.

1920s   *7.5in (19cm) high*

$50-80   **JBC**

A maroon mottled Bakelite box by Stadium.

1920s   *3.5in (9cm) square*

$20-30   **JBC**

A tortoiseshell celluloid jewelry box in the form of a grand piano.

The legs and lid prop are extremely delicate and are often found damaged.

1920s   5in (13cm) long

$60-100   **JBC**

A brown mottled Bakelite Kodak Hawkette No.2 folding camera.

This camera was given away as a free gift with selected products such as Cadbury's chocolates and was designed by E.K. Cole.

1927   7in (18cm) high

$40-60   **MHC**

A French brown mottled Bakelite mantle clock, by Blangy.

The distinctive Art Deco styling of this clock makes it highly desirable.

1930s   5.25in (13cm) high

$180-225   **MHC**

A Plastalite desk lamp, designed by Wells Coates and manufactured by E.K. Cole Ltd.

E.K.Cole Ltd is better known as manufacturer of the famous round 'EKCO' Bakelite radios.

1930s   14.5in (37cm) high

$320-380   **MHC**

A Dunlop promotional ashtray, by Roanoid Ltd.

These came in a variety of colors but cracks affect the value considerably. The three black cigarette rests fold inward into the ball over the ashtray to complete the sphere.

c1930   5in (12cm) diam

$180-225   **MHC**

A brown mottled Bakelite toast rack.

1930s   5.5in (14cm) wide

$15-25   **MHC**

A blue Bakelite wall mirror.

These popular mirrors were made in a variety of colors, brown was the most common.

1930s   9in (23cm) wide

$30-50   **MHC**

A marbled Bandalastaware plate, cup and saucer.

Bandalastaware was used extensively in 1930s picnic sets. Manufactured by Brookes & Adams, it was made from urea formaldehyde under the tradename 'Beatl'. In 1929 a shop called the Beatl shop opened in London's Regent Street.

1930s   Saucer 5in (13cm) diam

$30-50   **MHC**

A orange catalin cruet set.

1930s   2.5in (6cm) high

$40-60   **MHC**

Three novelty animal-shaped cast-phenolic napkin rings.

These were made in a variety of animal shapes and bright colors, some being mounted on small wheels.

1930s   Hen 3in (7.5cm) high

$20-30   **MHC**

Four novelty animal-shaped cast-phenolic napkin rings.

1930s   squirrel 3in (7cm) h

$20-30   **JBC**

A blue urea formaldehyde lemon squeezer.

1930s   5.25in (13.5cm) diam

$30-50   **JBC**

An Art Deco cream and brown swirl urea formaldehyde Hurricane cigarette box, made by Nutt Products Ltd.

c.1930   *8.75 in (22cm) wide*

$70-100   **JBC**

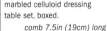

A 1930s pale blue and copper marbled celluloid dressing table set, boxed.

comb 7.5in (19cm) long

$60-100   **JBC**

Two urea formaldehyde and Bakelite Thermos ice buckets.

1930s   8.75in (22cm) wide

$60-100 (each)   **JBC**

A multi-colored urea formaldehyde six-person tea service.

1940s   plate 6in (15cm) diam

$60-100   **JBC**

A Parker brown Bakelite "Baccy Flap" tobacco holder.

1930s   3.5in (9cm diam)

$20-30   **JBC**

A brown Bakelite lidded pot with ribbed feet, marked 'Seaforth'.

1930s   4in (9.5cm) diam

$15-25   **JBC**

A green and white mottled urea formaldehyde jelly mold.

1930s   2.75in (7cm) diam

$5-8   **JBC**

An Art Deco carved blue acrylic horse pin.

1930s   4.25in (10.5cm) long

$30-50   **JBC**

A rare pale green urea formaldehyde chandelier.

1930s   21in (53cm) wide

$120-180   **JBC**

A Lingalonga Ware muffin dish, in orange marbled urea formaldehyde.

1930s   6in (15cm) diam

$70-100   **JBC**

A marbled Bandalasta tea cup and biscuit tray.

1930s cup 3.25in (8cm) diam

$40-60   **JBC**

A pale green and white marbled urea formaldehyde Thermos flask from a picnic set.

1930s   8.25in (21cm) high

$30-50   **JBC**

A set of four egg cups, in marbled urea formaldehyde.

1930s   1.75in (4.5cm) diam

$30-50   **JBC**

A salt and pepper set, in blue and white marbled urea formaldehyde.

1930s   2.75in (7cm) high

$40-60   **JBC**

A brown Bakelite and cream urea formaldehyde bird cigarette dispenser.

1930s   *7.5in (19cm) long*

$70-100   **JBC**

A carved phenolic chess set, boxed, by Grays of Cambridge, one pawn missing.

1930s   *pawns 1.5in (4cm) high*

$70-100   **JBC**

A brown mottled Bakelite 'Eloware' desk stand and double inkwell manufactured by Birkby's of Liversedge, England.

This piece is very rare as it is usually found as a cigarette box rather than as a desk stand with two internal inkwells mounted on a pen rest. The lid design is typical of the Art Deco styling of the period.

c1936   *9in (23cm) wide*

$180-225   **MHC**

A green Carvacraft stamp sponge holder.

These holders were often used as ashtrays and burns inside the well reduce the value considerably.

1940s   *3in (8cm) wide*

$80-120   **MHC**

A rare green acrylic and black Bakelite ink stand.

1940s   *6.5in (16.5cm) wide*

$180-225   **MHC**

A Kodak Bullet camera, black Bakelite with box.

1940s   *4.75in (12cm) wide*

$10-15   **JBC**

A brown mottled Bakelite desk telephone directory.

1940s   *8in (20cm) high*

$15-25   **MHC**

A maroon mottled Bakelite torch.

1940s   *4.75in (12cm) long*

$15-25   **JBC**

A pink urea formaldehyde floral flask, marked 'The British Vacuum Flask Co Ltd.'

1940s   *10.5in (27cm) high*

$40-50   **JBC**

An red and yellow urea formaldehyde egg cup.

1940s   *1.75in (4.5cm) diam*

$5-8   **JBC**

A set of four mottled Bakelite napkin rings.

1940s   *1.75in (4.5cm) diam*

$15-25 for set   **JBC**

A brown mottled Bakelite fruit bowl on a Celtic Plate plated base, English registration number for 1945.

8in (20.5cm) diam

$180-225   **MHC**

An amber Carvacraft double pen holder.

c1948   *6.5in (16.5cm) wide*

$80-120   **MHC**

A CLOSER LOOK AT BAKELITE

This ink stand features period Art Deco styling with stepped sides. Collectors should look for design features that exemplify the styles of a period.

The form is 'streamlined' following the popular designs of the period.

The color of the plastic is bright and colorful, breaking away from the dull browns and blacks of the preceding years.

The item is well made and bears the maker's stamp depicting a hammer on the underside – for Dickinson Products.

This item is in amber, one of the three colors used for Carvacraft. Green is the rarest. The third color used was yellow.

This item is typical of collectable plastics in that it was manufactured for use in the home and office.

An amber Carvacraft double ink stand.

Carvacraft objects were manufactured by the English company Dickinson in the late 1940s from a cast phenolic resin. The range included blotters, calendars and notepad holders. Collectors need to look for cracks, chips, inkstains and burns which reduce the value considerably.

c1948   *10.5in (27cm) wide*

$120-180   **MHC**

A yellow Carvacraft memo holder.

c1948   *5.75in (14.5cm) wide*

$70-100   **MHC**

A white urea formaldehyde 'Rototherm' desk thermometer.

Made in England, the styling is typical of the popular Industrial design of the period.

late 1940s   *6.75in (9cm) high*

$30-50   **MHC**

A Carvacraft amber blotter, with the rare original box.

c.1948   *6in (15cm) wide*

$70-100   **JBC**

An amber Carvacraft notepad holder, paper knife and stamp sponge holder.

The paper knife is a rare item.

c1948   *8in (20.5cm) long*

$180-225 (set)   **JBC**

A green marbled Halex dressing table set (part shown).

1950s   *Tray 10.75in (27.5cm) wide*

$15-25 (part set)   **MHC**

Two polythene duck-shaped clothes brushes and holders.

1950s   *11.25in (28.5cm) high*

Grey $15-25 Blue $20-30   **JBC**

A lacquered wooden tray with cast phenolic handles, by Belvane Ltd of Andover, England.

1950s   *14.5in (37cm) l*

$40-60   **JBC**

A Park Green 'The Peter Piper' pepperpot, in red urea formaldehyde.

1950s   *3.75in (9.5cm) high*

$30-50   **JBC**

A blue and cream celluloid child's dressing table set, boxed.

1950s   *comb 4.5in (11.5cm) long*

$30-50   **JBC**

Two urea formaldehyde electric clocks, marked 'Smiths English Clocks Ltd.'

1950s   *5in (12.5cm) high*

$15-25 each   **JBC**

POSTERS

- Condition is vital when considering posters. Collectors should look for tears, water stains (although these can often be removed), fading and missing areas that extend into the design as these will have a detrimental effect on value. However, as posters were made to be used, made from easily damaged paper and often folded for storage (particularly before 1970), it is difficult to find a poster in mint condition. Creases and multiple folds, whilst affecting value, should be taken into mind when working out a price but can be corrected.

- Good restorers can be found who can correct many problems, so collectors should always ask about restoration. Many posters are backed onto linen to make them more robust and easier to display. This work should always be completed by a specialist, who will probably give the poster a 'full service' at this point.

- Posters from the country of a movie's original release are usually the most desirable. Posters were produced for each country the movie was released in, and although these are still collected, collectors should be aware of differences – for example Belgian posters tend to be smaller, are in an unusual language but often have visually stunning artwork, whilst Australian posters, whilst in English and being more impactful due to their larger size, tend to have artwork of a lesser quality.

- The artwork and artist of any poster will count towards value. Although you should always choose an image that you like, some artists and images will be very desirable and prices may be high.

- Collectors should look for posters for movies that captured the public's imagination, are considered cult movies or classics, and are thus still popular. Posters for unknown or unpopular movies will not be as desirable.

- One sheet movies posters are the most popular amongst collectors and are sized at 27in x 41in. British quads are also popular at 30in x 40in.

- The romance of travel has always appealed, and railway posters have commanded a premium for some time. Look for attractive scenes of the landscape or destination. Posters for the main British domestic railways, GWR, LMS, LNER and SR, are desirable and fetch high prices. Collectors are now looking for the later British Rail posters.

- Fakes and forgeries are comparatively rare and can usually be readily identified. Reproductions are common however: these are often photographic images of a design printed on poster paper. Seeing originals will enable you to spot these easily, so visit an auction or a reputable dealer. Do not confuse 're-issue' posters for reproductions as these were made when the movie was re-released.

"1941", US one sheet poster, matted, with an autograph of John Belushi (Captain Wild Bill Kelso), in blue ink, mounted, framed and glazed.

1979   *48in (122cm) high*

$500-700   **CO**

"An American Werewolf in London", one-sheet video and DVD release promotional poster signed by director John Landis and Griffin Dune (Jack Goodman) in black marker pen, framed and glazed.

42in (100cm)

$270-330   **CO**

"Barbarella", US 'B' style one sheet poster, linen-backed.

1968   *41in (104cm) high*

$1,000-1,500   **ATM**

"Blade Runner", US one sheet poster, second printing, linen-backed.

1982   *41in (104cm) high*

$300-400   **ATM**

"The Blues Brothers", US one sheet poster.

1980   *41in (104cm) high*

$200-300   **ATM**

"James Bond - Dr. No", US one sheet poster, linen-backed.

This US version is scarce. 2002 also marks the 40th anniversary of the release of this movie.

1962   *41in (104cm) high*

$2,000-2,500   **ATM**

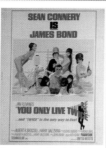

"James Bond - You Only Live Twice", US 'C' style one sheet poster, artwork by Robert McGinnis, linen-backed.

1967   *40in (101cm) high*

$1,200-1,500   ATM

"James Bond - Moonraker", US one sheet poster, linen-backed.

1979   *41in (104cm) high*

$200-300   ATM

"James Bond – From Russia with Love", US one sheet 'B' style poster, linen-backed.

1964   *40in (101cm) high*

$3,500-5,500   ATM

"James Bond - Tomorrow Never Dies", UK quad poster.

This version was withdrawn from circulation as 'Tommorrow' is mis-spelt in the credits.

1997   *40in (101cm) wide*

$80-120   ATM

"Breakfast At Tiffany's", US 40x60 poster, linen-backed, framed and glazed.

With its stylish and iconic image of Audrey Hepburn with her cigarette holder, this classic poster has enormous appeal to poster collectors, film fans and many others.

1961   *60in (152.5cm) high*

$15,000-23,000   ATM

"James Bond – Die Another Day", advance US one sheet poster.

2002   *41in (104cm) high*

$50-80   ATM

"Triple-O-Seven", UK one sheet triple bill promotional poster, advertising "Three James Bond Adventures In One Action Packed Programme" Octopussy, "For Your Eyes Only", "Thunderball", together with a double bill poster for "The Spy Who Loved Me" and "Moonraker".

$300-400   CO

"Bullitt", US one sheet poster, linen-backed.
1969   41in (104cm) high
$800-1,200   **ATM**

"Bunny Lake Is Missing", Spanish one sheet poster.
1965   39in (99cm) high
$120-180   **CO**

"Cat on a Hot Tin Roof", US 'B' style half sheet poster, paper-backed, framed and glazed.
1958   28in (71cm) wide
$600-1,000   **ATM**

"Charade", US one sheet poster, paper-backed, framed and glazed.
1963   41in (104cm) wide
$500-800   **ATM**

"Chinatown", German language A1 poster, artwork by Amsel, framed and glazed.
1974   33in (84cm) high
$500-800   **ATM**

"Get Carter", international one sheet poster, lined-backed.
1971   41in (104cm) high
$400-600   **ATM**

"The Godfather: Part II", US one sheet poster.
1974   41in (104cm) high
$180-220   **ATM**

FIND OUT MORE...

The International Vintage Poster Dealer Association.
www.ivpda.com

R. Allen, 'Vintage Hollywood Posters' (Volumes I & II), published by Bruce Hershenson, 1998.

"The Godfather", UK one sheet poster.
1972   41in (104cm) high
$600-1,000   **ATM**

"The Graduate", US one sheet poster, first year release 'B' Style Academy Award poster, linen-backed.
1967   41in (104cm) high
$300-500   **ATM**

"Halloween", one sheet promotional poster, signed by Jamie Lee Curtis, in black ink, framed and glazed.
1978   37in (94cm)
$320-380   **CO**

"A Hard Day's Night", US one sheet poster, linen-backed.

1964   41in (104cm) high

$800-1,300 ATM

"Jaws", US one sheet poster, linen-backed.

1975   41in (104cm) high

$500-700 ATM

"The Magnificent Seven", US one sheet poster.

1969   41in (104cm) high

$320-380 CO

"Manhattan", US one sheet 'B' bridge style poster.

1979   41in (104cm) high

$400-600 ATM

"Magnum Force", UK quad poster, designed by Bill Gold.

1973   40in (101cm) wide

$500-800 ATM

"Colpo Grosso" (Ocean's Eleven), Italian due foglio (two sheet) poster.

1960   55in (140cm) high

$400-600 CO

"Mary Poppins", Italian locandina (insert) poster.

1964   28in (71cm) high

$120-180 CO

"The Party", US one sheet poster, paper-backed, framed and glazed.

The artwork for this poster is by Jack Davis, who is better known as the artist for M.A.D. comics.

1968   41in (104cm) high

$300-450 ATM

"Psycho", Italian language photobusta, linen-backed, framed and glazed.

1960

$500-700 ATM

"Raiders of the Lost Ark", UK quad poster.

1981   40in (102cm) wide

$150-200 CO

"Raging Bull", advance US one sheet poster, photography by Kunio Hagio.

1980   41in (104cm) high

$300-500 ATM

"Raging Bull", US one sheet poster.

1980   41in (104cm) high

$250-350 CO

"Raiders of the Lost Ark", US one sheet poster.

1981   *41in (104cm) high*

$150-200   **CO**

"Return to Oz", design for promotional posters, highlighted in paint and pen, by artist Michael Ploog, mounted, framed and glazed.

1985   *27in (68cm)*

$600-1,000   **CO**

"Return to Oz", design for promotional posters, comprising overlaid printed images, highlighted in paint and pen, by artist Michael Ploog, mounted, framed and glazed.

1985   *27in (68cm)*

$500-700   **CO**

"Blanche Neige et les Sept Nains (Disney's Snow White and the Seven Dwarfs)", Belgian language one sheet poster, paper-backed, framed and glazed.

1937   *34in (86.5cm) high*

$2,500-3,000   **ATM**

"Shaft", US one sheet poster, linen-backed.

1971   *41in (104cm) high*

$400-600   **ATM**

"Walt Disney's Sleeping Beauty", US window card.

1959   *22in (56cm) high*

$300-500   **ATM**

"The Sound of Music", US roadshow-style one sheet poster, linen-backed.

1965   *41in (104cm) wide*

$1,000-1,500   **ATM**

"The Sting", US one sheet poster.

1973   *41in (104cm) high*

$300-500   **ATM**

"Spider-Man", advance US one sheet double-sided poster.

This poster is extremely rare, it was re-called by Sony after the September 11th tragedy as it features the World Trade Center reflected in Spider-Man's eyes, making it a collector's item overnight.

2002   *40in (101cm) high*

$300-500   **ATM**

"Star Wars V: The Empire Strikes Back", 'Gone with the Wind'-style US one sheet poster, linen-backed.

1980   *41in (104cm) high*

$500-700   **ATM**

"Star Wars Episode I - The Phantom Menace", US 'B' style one sheet poster.

With artwork still remaining in the style of previous Star Wars movie posters, despite being produced over 20 years later, this poster fits seamlessly into a Star Wars poster collection.

1999   *41in (104cm) high*

$300-500   **ATM**

"The Terminator", UK quad poster.

1984   *40in (102cm)*

$300-400   **CO**

"The Thomas Crown Affair", UK quad poster, linen-backed.

1968   *40in (101cm) wide*

$300-500   **ATM**

"Thunderbirds Are Go", UK quad poster, framed, glazed.

1966   *41.5in (105cm)*

$700-1,000   **CO**

Lobby cards

- Known as 'lobby cards' in the U.S. and 'front of house cards' in the U.K., these cards were made for advertising forthcoming movies and placed in the foyer or entrance of cinemas.
- Lobby cards were usually produced in sets of eight (but sets of four and ten can also be found) with a title card accompanied by seven stills (single snapshots of scenes) from the movie. They are nearly always produced in color and numbered.
- At 11in x 14in, lobby cards are larger than British front of house cards which are often only black and white stills from scenes in the movie.
- Although it is most often preferable to have a complete set, single cards showing key scenes, lead characters or a visually appealing scene from the movie are highly desirable. Value relates directly to the image depicted and its connection to the movie.
- Pioneering and seminal genre movies, such as science fiction or horror movies, are highly popular amongst collectors, as are title cards.
- These cards can provide a way for collectors to collect contemporary visual imagery related to a movie at a more affordable price than posters.

"2001 – A Space Odyssey", UK quad poster, re-release of the 1968 movie.

2001   *40in (101cm) wide*

$80-120   **ATM**

"Titanic", US one sheet poster, signed by cast members including Kate Winslett (Rose De Witt Bukater), Leonardo DiCaprio (Jack Dawson), Billy Zane (Caledon 'Cal' Hockley) and Bill Paxton (Brock Lovett), framed and glazed.

1997   *42in (107cm) high*

$1,000-1,500   **CO**

"Black Christmas", set of eight UK front of house cards.

1974   *10in (25cm) wide*

$30-50   **CO**

"James Bond – Goldfinger", U.S. lobby card no. 1.

1964   *14in (35.5cm) wide*

$100-150   **ATM**

"James Bond – The Man with the Golden Gun", US lobby card no. 1.

1974   *14in (35.5cm) wide*

$70-100   **ATM**

"James Bond - Octopussy", lobby card no. 8, mounted.

1983   *14in (35.5cm) wide*

$50-80   **ATM**

"Casablanca", Mexican lobby card, 1960s re-release of the 1946 movie, mounted, central image replaced.

17in (43cm) wide

$200-250   **ATM**

"Casablanca", Mexican lobby card, 1960s re-release of the 1946 movie, mounted, central image replaced.

17in (43m) wide

$200-250   **ATM**

"To Catch a Thief", US lobby card, mounted.

1955   *14in (35.5cm) wide*

$200-250   **ATM**

"Charade", lobby card no. 3, mounted.

14in (35.5cm) wide

$220-280   **ATM**

"The Hill", set of eight US lobby cards.

1965   *11in (28cm) wide*

$50-80   **CO**

"Let's Make Love", US lobby card no. 2, mounted.

1960   *14in (35.5cm) wide*

$180-220   **ATM**

"Marnie", US lobby card no. 4, mounted.

1964   *14in (35.5cm) wide*

$100-150   **ATM**

"Mary Poppins", set of twelve UK front of house stills.

1964   *10in (25cm) wide*

$150-200   **CO**

"The Nightmare Before Christmas", set of eight US lobby cards.

1993   *14in (35cm) wide*

$150-200   **CO**

"The Seven Year Itch", US lobby card no. 2, mounted.

1955   *14in (35.5cm) wide*

$320-380   **ATM**

POSTERS

"The Terminator", set of eight US lobby cards.

1984   11in (28cm) wide

$50-80   **CO**

"Vertigo", lobby card no. 3, mounted.

1958   14in (35.5cm) wide

$180-225   **ATM**

A KLM Airlines three-color lithograph poster, depicting a single engine Focker airplane, signed, dated and framed.

1924   33in (84cm) high

$400-600   **TK**

A Beheer der Luchtvaart lithograph poster of the Belgian cargo airline, impressive illustration of several biplanes, background with "Hermes" and his winged helmet, signed "T.Michielsson", framed.

1925   39.25in (99.5cm) long

$2,000-2,500   **TK**

A Transaerienne, Paris lithograph poster, showing a dirigible balloon over the roofs of Paris, very colorful design, signed "Gatier", framed, some damage at edges.

This poster advertises airship flights above Paris and suburbs.

1915   46.75in (119cm) long

$1,800-2,200   **TK**

An early Imperial Airways lithograph poster, for the Baghdad-Basra air route, with illustration of a tri-motor biplane flying over the pyramids of Giza, signed "H. Cuther", framed and dated.

1927   38.5in (98cm) long

$2,200-2,800   **TK**

A Geneva Intercontinental Airport Switzerland poster.

39in (99.5cm) high

$350-450   **DO**

A Koninklijke Luchtvaart lithograph poster, for the Dutch Airline airfreight company, showing the 'Flying Dutchman' with a pilot who explains the progress of aviation, framed.

1930   41in (104cm) high

$1,800-2,200   **TK**

A Hamburg-Amerika Linie five-color lithograph poster of the airship 127 Graf Zeppelin, showing the air route from Hamburg, Germany to Rio de Janeiro, South America in three days, framed.

Due to their brief life as a reliable mode of mass transport, posters showing airships in this way are scarce. This example shows a very long distance route which seems incredible to us now.

1931

$2,200-2,800 TK

A Deutsche Luftfahrt-Werbewoche 1932 five-color lithograph poster, with two-seater aircraft, glider and hot-air balloon, framed.

1932   29in (48.5cm) long

$800-1,200 TK

A Soc. An. Aero Espresso Italiana lithograph poster, with an illustration of a single engine sea plane over the Aegean Sea, with the air routes, dated and signed "Keverta".

1932   39.25in (99.5cm) long

$1,200-1,800 TK

A British South American Airways 'A l'Amérique du sud' poster.

40in (101cm) high

$400-600 DO

A Lufthansa, Air France lithograph poster, showing the flight route Europe-South America, with an illustration of a Junker aircraft which goes around the world, with the German national emblem, showing all stopovers, framed.

1935   26.25in (66.5cm) long

$1,500-2,000 TK

An American Overseas Airlines double Royal poster, designed by Jan Lewitt and George Him.

c1946   40in (101.5cm) high

$1,800-2,200 REN

An Air France three-color lithograph poster, depicting an airplane flying over the jungle in Africa, signed "Guena", printed in France, framed and dated.

1946   39.25in (99.5cm) long

$1,200-1,800 TK

A British European Airways 'Meet the Spring - fly BEA' lithograph poster, with expressionistic depiction of an elegant lady on the runway signed, framed.

1948   41.25in (105cm) long

$700-1,000 TK

A Frederiksberg poster.

Frederiksberg is a popular beach in Denmark.

1938

$400-600   **DO**

A North Eastern Railways 'The Yorkshire Coast' quad royal poster, from the "Alice in Holidayland" advertising campaign, designed by Frank Mason.

c1910   *50in (127cm) wide*

$10,000-15,000   **REN**

A London & North Eastern Railways double royal woodcut-style 'Batchworth Heath' poster, unnamed artist.

c1924   *40in (101.5cm) high*

$1,800-2,200   **REN**

A London & North Eastern Railways double royal woodcut-style 'Batchworth Heath' poster, unnamed artist.

c1924   *40in (101.5cm) high*

$1,800-2,200   **REN**

A Southern Railways 'Canterbury' quad royal poster, designed by Leslie Carr.

c1928   *50in (127cm) wide*

$2,000-3,000   **REN**

A Great Western Railways 'Stratford Upon Avon' quad royal poster, from the series "This England of Ours", designed by Michael Reilly.

c1930   *50in (127cm) wide*

$5,000-7,000   **REN**

A Shell 'Mousehole, Penzance' poster from the "To Visit Britain's Landmarks" series, originally displayed on Shell lorries, designed by A. Stuart-Hill.

c1932   *45in (114.5cm) wide*

$6,000-10,000   **REN**

A London & North Eastern Railways 'Clyde Coast' quad royal poster, designed by Frank Mason.

1931   *50in (127cm) wide*

$3,000-4,000   **REN**

A Shell 'Folly Houses, Darley Abbey' poster from the "To Visit Britain's Landmarks" series, originally displayed on Shell lorries, designed by Rowland Suddaby.

c1935   *45in (114.5cm)*

$2,000-3,000   **REN**

A Shell Conchofile 'Explorers Prefer Shell' poster, designed by Edward McKnight Kauffer.

McKnight Kauffer is a celebrated poster artist. Born in Montana, he studied in Paris and San Francisco. After coming to London in 1914, he was commissioned by Frank Pick at London Transport to design posters. From there his popularity and commissions mushroomed. His work has been the subject of many retrospectives, including at the Museum of Modern Art, New York, and at the Victoria & Albert Museum, London.

1934   *45in (114.5cm) wide*

$6,000-10,000   **REN**

A London Transport 'Cut Travelling Time' double royal poster, designed by Tom Eckersley of Eckersley Studio.

c1968   *40in (101.5cm) high*

$800-1,200   **REN**

A London Transport 'Extension of the Piccadilly Line to Heathrow Airport' double royal poster, designed by Tom Eckersley, the foremost exponent of this "Swiss typographical" style.

1971   *40in (101.5cm) high*

$2,500-3,000   **REN**

Miscellaneous

A Bal du Moulin Rouge 'Femmes, Femmes, Femmes' poster.

24in (60.5cm) high

$120-180   **DO**

A Monis Cognac Fine Champagne poster.

17in (43cm) high

$220-280   **DO**

A Huntley & Palmers 'Dainty Afternoon Tea Biscuits' poster.

14.5in (36.5cm) wide

$60-100   **DO**

A Gibbs Cold Cream Soap poster.

14in (35.5cm) wide

$35-45   **DO**

A du Maurier 'The Most Widely Smoked Filter Cigarette in the World' poster.

30in (76cm) high

$180-225   **DO**

A Dunlop 'Fit Dunlop Tubes for Longer Life' poster.

30in (76cm) high

$320-380   **DO**

A Pneu Hutchinson 'Plus Solid que l'Acier' poster.

21.5in (55cm) high

$270-330 DO

A South African Oranges 'The Only Empire Summer Orange' poster.

20in (51cm) high

$270-330 DO

A Kodavox 'Pour Votre Magniphone, Produit Kodak' poster.

23.5in (60cm) high

$120-180 DO

A Daily Express 'A Help Your Neighbour...' poster.

23in (58cm) high

$80-120 DO

A Ministry of Food 'The Effects of Over-cooking and Keeping Hot' double crown poster, designed by Jan Lewitt and George Him.

c1941 *30in (76cm) high*

$800-1,200 REN

A Ministry of Food 'The Vegetabull' double crown poster, designed by Jan Lewitt and George Him.

c1941 *30in (76cm) high*

$800-1,200 REN

A Post Office Savings Bank 'War Production' quad crown poster, designed by Auben Cooper.

c1944 *40in (101.5cm) long*

$1,800-2,250 REN

A General Post Office 'Helps the Export Drive' quad crown poster, designed by Tom Eckersley of the Eckersley Studio.

1948 *40in (101.5cm) wide*

$2,000-3,000 REN

A 'Dick Whittington' David Allen & Sons poster.

27in (69cm) high

$350-450 DO

'A La Francaise Diamant' poster.

23.5in (60cm) high

$200-300 DO

An 'Exposition Internationale Mai-Novembre, Ministre du Commerce et de l'industrie' poster.

1937 *12in (35.5cm) high*

$220-280 DO

PRINTS

- Although not traditionally considered as 'collectibles', modern prints are an accessible way of building a collection of works by usually unaffordable modern masters.

- There are three types of collectable prints: prints where production has been controlled by the artist; prints where the artist has full control but uses somebody else to assist; and finally prints where the artist has granted somebody else permission to make prints from an image. They are not poster prints where the image has been photomechanically reproduced on poster paper.

- Value is determined on the popularity of artist, the subject and visual appeal of the image, edition size and condition. The convention of numbering was introduced c1915. Look carefully at signatures, as some were 'in the block' meaning that the signature is part of the print (sometimes in reverse) and not signed by hand.

- Condition is vital, with scuffs and tears that affect the image reducing value. Although mint condition is best, it can be difficult to find older prints in such a condition. Crinkles, folds and even tears can be restored professionally.

- Prints should be handled with clean hands and should not be rolled for storage, but laid flat in acid free tissue paper. When framed, use acid free board and make sure the glass is not in contact with the print. Keep the image out of strong light, which can bleach the colors.

Peter Blake, (born 1932) 'Girl in a Poppy Field', screenprint, signed, from an edition of 125. 1974

$800-1,000   **WO**

Georges Braque, (1882-1963), 'Si Je Mourais La Bas', original color wood engraving, signed in pencil and numbered X/X, edition of ten, and extra special edition of parchment.

18.25in (46.5cm) wide

$5,000-6,000   **WO**

Georges Braque, 'Le Tir a l'Arc', original color lithograph, signed in pencil and numbered 16 from the edition of 20 on Japanese nacre paper.

This piece was inspired by 'Le Zen dans l'art chevalevesque du tir a l'arc' by T.D. Suzuki and E. Cahiers (1917-1952), published by Louis Broder, Paris.

1960

$3,500-4,000   **WO**

Georges Braque, 'Le Tir a l'Arc', original color lithograph, from the edition of 20 on Japanese nacre paper, signed lower right in pencil and numbered "16/20".

Birds as shown here were a favourite motif for Braque. He also used them when painting a gallery ceiling in the Louvre in Paris.

1960   *6in (15cm)*

$3,000-4,000   **WO**

Georges Braque, 'Le Tir a l'Arc', original lithograph, signed in pencil, numbered 16 from an edition of 20.

1960

$2,500-3,000   **WO**

Max Ernst, (1891-1976) 'Oiseau Bleu', original etching with aquatint, signed in pencil and inscribed 'essai'.

16.25in (41.5cm)

$5,000-6,000   **WO**

Elizabeth Frink, (1930-1993), 'Nude', an original lithograph in two colors, signed in pencil from an edition of 85 plus 5 artist's proofs, printed by the Royal Academy.

25.5in (65cm) wide

$2,500-3,000   **WO**

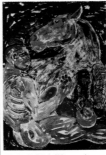

Elizabeth Frink, 'Man and Horse', original screenprint, signed in pencil, edition of 70.

1990   *27in (69cm) wide*

$4,000-4,500   **WO**

Elisabeth Frink, 'Viszla II', original etching and aquatint, signed in pencil, edition of 50.

36in (91.5cm)

$4,000-4,500   **WO**

Sir Terry Frost, (born 1915), 'Camberwell Green', original etching with aquatint and woodcut collage, signed, from an edition of 250.

19.75in (50cm) wide

$400-500   **WO**

Sir Terry Frost RA, 'Trewellard Sun', original linocut with hand-coloring, signed in pencil and numbered from the edition of 70 on Zerkall paper, published by the Paragon Press.

25.25in (64cm) wide

$650-750   **WO**

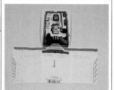

Sir Terry Frost RA, 'Green and Black Q'.

1997

$1,000-1,500   **WO**

Patrick Heron, (born 1920), 'Blue with Lime, Umber, Dull Red and Orange in Violet', original screenprint, signed in pencil from an edition of 50.

1978   *7in (18cm)*

$3,000-4,000   **WO**

David Hockney, (born 1937), 'The Old Guitarist', hardground and aquatint, signed in pencil.

1977   *13.5in (34.5cm)*

$5,500-6,500   **WO**

David Hockney, 'What is this Picasso?', original etching in colors, signed in pencil, edition of 200.

1979   *20.75in (53cm) wide*

$5,500-6,000   **WO**

David Hockney, 'Red Square and the Forbidden City', original lithograph, signed in pencil, edition of 1000.

1982   *21.75in (55cm) wide*

$1,000-1,500   **WO**

Howard Hodgkin, (born 1932), 'David's Pool', original etching with hand-coloring, signed with initials in pencil, numbered from an edition of 100.

1979   *24.5in (62cm) wide*

$10,000-12,000   **WO**

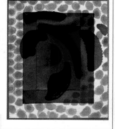

Howard Hodgkin, 'Snow', original carborundum etching with hand-coloring, signed in pencil, edition of 80.

1995   *14in (36cm) wide*

$3,000-3,500   **WO**

John Hoyland, (born 1934), 'Space Born', original screenprint with woodblock. *1993*

$1,000-1,500   **WO**

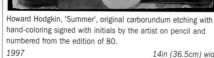

Howard Hodgkin, 'Summer', original carborundum etching with hand-coloring signed with initials by the artist on pencil and numbered from the edition of 80.

1997   *14in (36.5cm) wide*

$3,000-3,500   **WO**

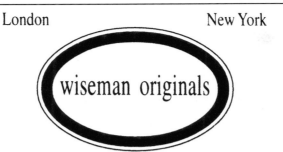
A
B
C
D
E
F
G
H
I
J
K
L
M
N
O
P
Q
R
S
T
U
V
W
XYZ

John Hoyland, 'Sanur Seal', original screenprint, signed in pencil, edition of 75.

1994   *26.75in (68cm) wide*

$700-1,000   **WO**

Henri Matisse, (1869-1954) 'Visages', original lithograph, edition of 250.

1946   *10in (25.5cm) wide*

$700-1,000   **WO**

Henri Matisse, 'Tête de Femme', original lithograph, signed in pencil, edition of 300.

1948

$5,500-6,000   **WO**

Henry Moore, (1898-1986), 'Reclining Nude I', original etching, inscribed 'Bon a Tirer HM', a unique proof in black aside from the edition of 50.

1978   *7.75in (20cm) wide*

$1,000-1,500   **WO**

A CLOSER LOOK AT A HENRY MOORE PRINT

The 'Mother and Child' is a typical and favorite theme for Moore, whose primitive forms are inspired by natural and landscape forms.

The 'Bon a Tirer' inscription means the artist approves the appearnce of the print and the subsequent edition is compared to this visually.

Henry Moore, (1898-1986), 'Mother and Child XXVIII', original etching with aquatint.

This print was inscribed 'Bon a tirer HM' in pencil on the lower right before being printed on Arches paper in an edition of 80.

1983   *10.75in (27.5cm) wide*

$4,500-5,000   **WO**

Henry Moore, 'Three forms in orange and yellow', original lithograph.

1967   *11.5in (29cm) wide*

$3,500-4,000   **WO**

Pablo Picasso, (1881-1973), 'Six Contes Fantasques', original drypoint.

1953

$1,500-2,000   **WO**

Pablo Picasso, 'Buste de Femme au Corsage Blanc', original lithograph, from an edition of 50, 17th December 1957.

19.75in (50cm) wide

$45,000-50,000   **WO**

Pablo Picasso, 'Minotaure Caressant Une Femme', etching from an edition of 250, plate 84 from 'La Suite Vollard'.

Named after the influential art dealer Ambroise Vollard, who launched many artists' careers and hosted Picasso's first exhibition in 1901, the Vollard Suite depicts the conflicts between Picasso's love affair with Marie-Therese Walter and his artistic drive. Dating from between 1930 and 1937, it is made up of 100 etchings and is considered an important part of Picasso's work.

1933   *14.5in (37cm) wide*

$25,000-30,000   **WO**

ROCK & POP

- The general rule when collecting Rock & Pop memorabilia is 'the bigger the name, the bigger the price ticket'. As more people are interested in collecting a star's memorabilia, they will drive the prices up.

- A key rule to consider is provenance. Always buy from a reputable dealer or auction house and check that the item is what it purports to be. This may require the vendor showing adequate research, an unbroken history of the item's owners from the star, or a letter of provenance.

- Clothing is a popular area, with many stars defining the fashions of the period, such as The Beatles. 'Hallmark' clothing in a style that the star is known for, will usually be more popular, as will those used at key events and on album covers.

- Guitars are ever-popular, and cross value ranges. There are three types – those owned and played by a star at a major event, those owned and played by a star, and those simply signed but not owned by a star. Values will be the highest for those in the first two categories, and considerably lower for the third.

- Signatures form one of the widest areas of collecting. Again, collectors should ensure that they are not forgeries or signatures by supporting staff. Ephemera connected to events is also popular, with those related to key events in an artist's career fetching higher prices.

Jerry Garcia's Hawaiian-style shirt, in faded blue and purple, worn by Jerry.

$2,200-2,800   **G**

Jerry Garcia's Hawaiian-style shirt, in green, blue and white, worn by Jerry.

$2,200-2,800   **G**

Jerry Garcia's Hawaiian-style shirt, in blue and white, worn by Jerry.

$2,200-2,800   **G**

Jerry Garcia's black T-shirt, pictured wearing it while relaxing at the beach in Kona, Hawaii in 1992.

$2,200-2,800   **G**

Ten Grateful Dead backstage passes, for different concerts between March 6 and June 24 1994.

$2,200-2,800   **G**

Ten Grateful Dead backstage passes, for different concerts between July 24 and December 18 1994.

$2,200-2,800   **G**

Jerry Garcia's Pacific Bell calling card, issued to 'J. Garcia'.

$300-500   **G**

A set list handwritten by Jerry Garcia, for concerts of the Jerry Garcia Band in the 1980s; the list is written in pencil.

$1,500-2,000   **G**

A signed cheque from the Grateful Dead's account, dated "10-4-1966" and signed by original band members Phil Lesh and Bill Kreutzman.

$600-1,000   **G**

A Grateful Dead concert poster, featuring the Grateful Dead and the New Riders of the Purple Sage, fair condition with some fading, partially mounted.

This poster advertises the last concert that Ron McKernan, better known as "Pig Pen", played with the Grateful Dead. He was the original front man and a founding member.

22in (56cm) high

$1,500-2,000   **G**

Ace Frehley's platform boots, worn during the Kiss Farewell Tour 2000-2001, custom-made six inch silver lamé-covered leather platform "space" boots which were worn onstage by Ace throughout the Farewell Tour.

$1,500-2,000   G

Peter Criss' platform boots, worn during the Kiss Farewell Tour 2000-2001, custom-made six inch silver and black snakeskin leather platform boots which were worn onstage by Peter throughout the Farewell Tour.

$1,500-2,000   G

Paul Stanley's platform boots, worn during the Kiss Farewell Tour 2000-2001, custom-made seven inch black and silver leather platform boots with rhinestone and studded "vein" designs which were worn onstage by Paul throughout the Farewell Tour.

$1,500-2,000   G

Gene Simmons' platform boots, worn during the Kiss Farewell Tour 2000-2001, worn onstage by Gene throughout the Farewell Tour.

$1,500-2,000   G

Vinnie Vincent's red shirt, Vinnie can be seen wearing this shirt on the back cover of his rare 1988 "Vinnie Vincent Invasion" compilation album and in worldwide media photographs in the same year.

$3,500-4,500   G

Vinnie Vincent's Indian jacket, Vinnie can be seen wearing this jacket on the cover of 1984 Guitar World magazine.

$6,000-10,000   G

Handwritten lyrics for "Lick It Up", by Vinnie Vincent, this song appeared on the 1983 album of the same name.

$2,200-2,800   G

Vinnie Vincent's belt, decorated with Japanese symbols, he was given this belt by Gene Simmons for Christmas 1982 and can be seen wearing it on the cover of the 1983 Kiss album "Lick It Up" and in successive press and publicity photos.

$20,000-30,000   G

Handwritten lyrics for "A Million to One", by Vinnie Vincent, this album appears on the 1983 Kiss album "Lick It Up".

$1,000-1,500   G

An original employment contract between Vinnie Vincent and The KISS Company, dated July 18, 1984.

$2,200-2,800   G

An official Kiss/Sterling Marlin car banner, displayed at the NASCAR race at the Homestead-Miami Speedway on November 11, 2001 and featuring the band wearing the Kiss Farewell Tour "four faces" design above the No. 40 Sterling Marlin car with the classic Kiss logo.

96in (244cm) high

$3,000-4,000   G

A set of Beatles' signatures, John, Paul and Ringo in green ballpoint pen on a clipped piece of paper, matted with a black and white photograph of the 'Fab Four.'

16in (40cm) high

$2,200-2,800 **CO**

"A Hard Day's Night", US half sheet poster signed by Paul, George and Ringo.

1964 *22in (56cm) high*

$2,200-2,800 **G**

A Beatles 'Sgt Pepper's Lonely Hearts Club Band' picture disc, on Parlophone Records (PHO 7027 Stereo), together with a promotional sampler, shrink-wrapped CD titled Paul McCartney's 'Standing Stone Celebration'.

$40-60 **CO**

A rare Beatles 'butchers' album cover for "Yesterday and Today", together with an original letter with post-marked envelope from Capitol Records, describing the recall of the cover, minor discoloration.

This original cover features the four Beatles dressed in butcher's overalls and surrounded by lumps of meat and dismembered dolls and was apparently a protest against the way Capitol Records had "butchered" their catalog in the USA. Early copies shocked D.J.s, reviewers and store owners and the album was recalled, the cover being replaced with an innocuous picture of John, Ringo and George standing around a trunk with Paul sitting inside.

$1,800-2,200 **DRA**

"Help!", a set of eight original UK front of house stills.

1965 *10in (25cm) wide*

$350-400 **CO**

A printer's block for the Beatles movie "Help!", hand-crafted blocks photo-engraved on metal in reverse and used to produce the pressbook advertisements.

3in (7.5cm) wide

$150-200 **G**

Seven pieces of 1960s Beatles memorabilia, including two Beatles ads for dolls and posters.

$270-330 **DRA**

A Beatles mechandising talcum powder tin, by Margo of Mayfair (U.K.), printed with images of the band and their autographs.

c1964 *7in (17.5cm) high*

$180-220 **CO**

Five pieces of Beatles memorabilia, including a rare Yellow Submarine pop-out decoration book, and four Beatles buttons with mirror backs.

1968

$500-700 **DRA**

Six pieces of Beatles memorabilia, including a Beatles metal tray, four souvenir buttons, gold-colored commemorative coin.

1964

$500-700 **DRA**

A 1960s George Harrison figure.

$60-80 **Fra**

A souvenir menu from the Summer Festival at the International Hotel, Las Vegas, signed Elvis Presley in black ballpoint pen, on the front cover.

11in (28cm)

$700-1,000   **CO**

A Summer Festival at the Las Vegas Hilton souvenir concert menu, signed by Elvis Presley, in black ballpoint pen on the front.

15in (38cm) high

$1,000-1,500   **CO**

A souvenir concert photo album, signed by Elvis Presley in blue ballpoint pen on the front cover.

14in (36cm) high

$500-700   **CO**

A Christmas card signed by Elvis Presley, the one-sided printed card signed and dedicated "To Mary from Elvis Presley" in blue ballpoint pen, with an image of Elvis and "Seasons Greetings Elvis and the Colonel 1966" on the front.

8.5in (16 cm) high

$600-1,000   **CO**

A Japanese Elvis Presley Panel Delux double album boxed set, on RCA RP-9201-2, both records unplayed.

This exotic album package has become the most coveted Elvis boxed set ever made.

c1970   *16in (40.5cm)*

$1,200-1,800   **G**

A 1964 Country and Western Gibson acoustic guitar, purportedly owned by Elvis Presley, together with case and accompanied by a letter of authenticity.

$12,000-18,000   **CO**

A typed letter from Elvis to Colonel Parker, dated March 23, 1971 and signed by Elvis in blue ink, includes Certificate of Authenticity.

$6,000-10,000   **G**

Elvis Presley's black leather briefcase, covered with various tour stickers from Elvis's shows and other music groups, including International Kenpo Karate Association sticker, slightly worn, includes an Elvis Presley Museum Certificate of Authenticity.

$10,000-15,000   **G**

A Graceland Security badge, marked "Cauley 5".

$800-1,200   **G**

Elvis Presley's Smith and Wesson Pistol, with 'TCB', and a lightening bolt on the black pearl handle.

On December 19, 1970, a captain of a Trans World Air flight was told that a V.I.P. on board was carrying a gun. At this point Elvis Presley was escorted into the cockpit where he explained that he had just met President Nixon, and showed the captain a letter stating that he was an agent for the D.E.A., allowing him to carry a concealed weapon. The captain agreed to let Elvis carry the gun on board. After landing, the captain gave Elvis a behind-the-scenes tour and helped Elvis out with the captain of his next flight. Elvis was so impressed with this man that he insisted he accept his Smith & Wesson pistol as a gift. Presley's fascination with guns is well-documented and forms a popular area of interest to collectors.

T.C.B. stood for 'Taking Care of Business' and was a favored motto used by Elvis Presley.

$40,000-60,000   **G**

A Carlo Robelli acoustic guitar, signed by Cat Stevens in black marker "Peace Train/Holy Roller, Yusuf Islam", sold with a photo of him posed with the guitar after signing.

$1,000-1,500 G

A red Fender Squier Telecaster guitar, signed by the Rolling Stones, signed on the body by Mick Jagger, Keith Richards, and Ron Wood and on the pickguard by Charlie Watts, Bill Wyman, and Mick Taylor.

Guitars signed by all six members of The Rolling Stones are very rare. With a five-page handwritten letter of provenance from the collector who obtained five of the autographs, detailing where and when each member signed it.

$5,000-7,000 G

A black E-ROS 12 string acoustic guitar, signed by the Rolling Stones in silver marker pen by Mick Jagger, Charlie Watts, Keith Richards and Bill Wyman and on the scratchplate in gold marker pen by Mick Taylor.

$1,200-1,800 CO

A white Fender Squier Telecaster guitar, signed by The Who, signed boldly on the body by bassist John Entwistle and on the pickguard by Pete Townsend and Roger Daltrey.

$1,500-2,000 G

An autographed Cher CD cover, issued as a promotional item.

$75-100 MSC

A 1973 Beach Boys In Concert signed album sleeve, on Reprise Records, signed byBrian Wilson, Carl Wilson, Dennis Wilson, Al Jardine and Mike Love, each in black marker pen.

12in (31cm) wide

$270-330 CO

A signed contract between The Doors and the Kaleidoscope club, Los Angeles, dated 30th March, 1967 and signed by Robbie Krieger of the Doors.

$3,000-5,000 G

A handwritten poem "Explosion" by Jim Morrison, unsigned, 'instant of creation (fertilization), not an instant seperate from breakfast, it all flows down & out, flowing, ...'.

12in (31cm)

$14,000-15,000 CO

Elton John's red stage platform shoes, owned and worn by Elton John.

$6,000-10,000 G

A Cher poster, signed "To Mark all my love Cher".

$75-100 MSC

A handmade brown suede vest worn by Jimi Hendrix, possibly made by Omar's of the Village, NYC, and given to Hendrix by Steve Paul, a club owner and manager, subsequently signed inside by James "Booty" Neil, Noel Redding and Eugene McFadden, in silver pen, accompanied by a letter from the vendor explaining the vest's history.

c1968

$1,800-2,200 CO

A miniature Colt 45 pistol charm, removed from Sid Vicious' jacket and given to the late Helen Wheels, attached to a note signed and dedicated by Vicious: "CBGB For Helen SID" with his bloody thumb print, together with a Helen Wheels and the Skeleton Crew concert flyer, one of her business cards and a letter of provenance from the vendor.

7in (18cm) wide

$1,200-1,800 CO

ROCK & POP

ACK

A giclee print of Aerosmith, performing at Madison Square Garden, by Roberto Rabanne.

A giclee is a faithful reproduction of a fine art archival print using state-of-the-art printing technology.

19in (48cm) wide

$1,500-1,800 G

A giclee print of James Brown, performing at John Harms Theater, N.J., 2000, by Roberto Rabanne.

19in (48cm) high

$1,500-2,000 G

A giclee print of L.L. Cool J., by Roberto Rabanne.

19in (48cm) high

$1,500-2,000 G

A giclee print of Ray Charles, performing at the Great American Music Hall, 1976, by Roberto Rabanne.

19in (48cm) high

$800-1,200 G

A giclee print of Sheryl Crow and Keith Richards, performing at Central Park, NYC, 2000, by Roberto Rabanne.

19in (48cm) high

$1,500-2,000 G

A giclee print of Miles Davis, performing at Montreaux Switzerland, late 1980s, by Roberto Rabanne.

19in (48cm) high

$1,500-1,800 G

A giclee print of Bob Dylan, performing at U.C. Berkley Greek Theater in the 1970s, by Roberto Rabanne.

19in (48cm) high

$1,500-2,000 G

A giclee print of Bob Dylan and Eric Clapton, performing at the Crossroads Benefit at Madison Square Garden, 2001, by Roberto Rabanne.

19in (48cm) wide

$1,500-2,000 G

A giclee print of Dizzy Gillespie, backstage at the Great American Music Hall, 1975, by Roberto Rabanne.

19in (48cm) high

$1,500-2,000 G

A giclee print of Dizzy Gillespie and Carmen Miranda, by Roberto Rabanne.

19in (48cm) high

$1,500-2,000 G

A giclee print of Debbie Harry, performing at Berkley, 1977, by Roberto Rabanne.

19in (48cm) high

$1,200-1,800 G

A giclee print of Hole, Los Angeles, mid 1990s, by Roberto Rabanne.

19in (48cm) wide

$1,500-2,000   G

A giclee print of John Lee Hooker, performing at Keystone, Berkley, 1975, by Roberto Rabanne.

19in (48cm) wide

$1,200-1,800   G

A giclee print of Mick Jagger, by Roberto Rabanne.

19in (48cm) high

$1,500-2,000   G

A giclee print of Dr. John, at Keystone, Berkley, 1975, by Roberto Rabanne.

19in (48cm) high

$1,500-2,000   G

A giclee print of Grace Jones, performing in San Francisco, 1973, by Roberto Rabanne.

19in (48cm) high

$1,500-2,000   G

A giclee print of Janis Joplin, performing in San Francisco, 1967, by Roberto Rabanne.

19in (48cm) high

$2,200-2,500   G

A giclee print of B.B. King, performing at the Apollo Theater, NYC, 1993, by Roberto Rabanne.

19in (48cm) high

$1,500-2,000   G

A giclee print of Lenny Kravitz, performing in NYC, late 1990s, by Roberto Rabanne.

19in (48cm) high

$1,500-2,000   G

A giclee print of Madonna, by Roberto Rabanne.

19in (48cm) high

$2,200-2,500   G

A giclee print of Madonna, by Roberto Rabanne.

19in (48cm) high

$2,200-2,500   **G**

A C-print of Bob Marley, by Roberto Rabanne.

60in (152.5cm) wide

$2,500-3,000   **G**

A giclee print of Bob Marley, performing at the Boarding House, San Francisco, by Roberto Rabanne.

20in (51cm) high

$1,400-1,600   **G**

A giclee print of Slick Rick, NYC, early 1990s, by Roberto Rabanne.

19in (48cm) high

$1,200-1,800   **G**

A giclee print of the Sex Pistols, performing at the Winterland, San Francisco, by Roberto Rabanne.

This was the last perfomance by the group.

19in (48cm) wide

$1,500-2,000   **G**

A giclee print of Rod Stewart, in Frankfurt, Germany, 1989, by Roberto Rabanne.

19in (48cm) high

$1,200-1,800   **G**

A giclee print of Bruce Springsteen, performing at the Amnesty International Benefit, Paris, 1989, by Roberto Rabanne.

19in (48cm) high

$1,500-2,000   **G**

A giclee print of Bruce Springsteen and Patti, Amnesty International Benefit in Paris, 1989, by Roberto Rabanne.

19in (48cm) high

$1,500-2,000   **G**

A giclee print of Tricky, NYC, 1999, by Roberto Rabanne.

19in (48cm) high

$1,200-1,800   **G**

A giclee print of Stevie Wonder, by Roberto Rabanne.

19in (48cm) high

$1,500-2,000   **G**

An English clear cut-glass double-ended scent bottle, with silver stoppers.

$200-300   **Trio**

An English ruby glass double-ended scent bottle, with silver-gilt stoppers.

$250-350   **Trio**

A Victorian ruby glass scent bottle.

$250-350   **Trio**

A Sandwich Glass Factory paneled paperweight perfume bottle, smokey canary color.

c1840   *7.5in (17.5cm) high*

$1,000-1,500   **RAA**

A pair of early 20thC Baccarat crystal scent bottles, each of geometric form with lobed stopper and acid-stamped signature.

3.75in (35.5cm) high

$120-180   **FRE**

A clear cut-glass scent bottle, with silver top.

1897

$200-250   **Trio**

A clear cut-glass scent bottle, with silver top.

1919

$120-180   **Trio**

A set of three Art Deco cut glass sunburst perfume bottles.

c1935   *Tallest 12.5cm (5in) high*

$70-100   **OACC**

A 1930s Czechoslovakian carved glass atomizer.

4.5in (11.5cm) high

$200-300   **LB**

A Steuben gold Aurene perfume bottle, unsigned.

6in (15cm) high

$750-850   **JDJ**

A Venetian latticino glass scent bottle.

The name 'latticino' refers to the milk-colored thread-like design incorporated into the glass. It was a technique typically used by Venetian glass manufacturers.

$200-300   **Trio**

An Art Nouveau silver overlaid iridescent blue glass perfume bottle, overlaid with scrolling foliage, the stopper of clear glass with silver overlay, marked "Sterling", monogrammed "JRB".

c1900   *6.5in (16.5cm) high*

$550-650   **SI**

A Daum-covered perfume bottle, with purple ground and acid-cut thistles, stems and leaves, and enamel and gilt decoration, signed, some minor wear to gilt.

3in (7.5cm) high

$1,200-1,800   **JDJ**

A Daum 'Nancy' cameo scent bottle, green over clear glass, acid-etched with gold highlighting, signed on base in gold script "Daum Nancy", some wear to the gold enameling.

6.25in (16cm) long

$700-800   **JDJ**

An English cameo scent bottle, white over yellow glass with a wheel-cut decoration of branches and leaves with a silver top.

2.5in (6.5cm) high

$550-650   **JDJ**

A Galle cameo perfume bottle, purple flowers and leaves against a white background, signed "GALLE" in one of the cameo leaves.

3.5in (9cm) high

$700-800   **JDJ**

A Lalique atomizer, opalescent glass with ten molded nudes, brass metal hardware, signed on base "R. LALIQUE FRANCE J6 2687".

9in (23cm) high

$1,000-1,500   **JDJ**

A Webb Burmese scent bottle, pink shading to yellow glass with enamel decoration of leaves, berries and branches, original silver top.

4.75in (11cm) high

$1,000-1,500   **JDJ**

A French blue opaline scent bottle.

$200-300   **Trio**

A clear glass scent bottle, painted with flowers, with pinchbeck stopper.

$200-300   **Trio**

A clear glass scent bottle, decorated with filigree set with pearls and a garnet, with pinchbeck stopper.

$200-300   **Trio**

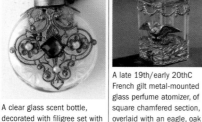

A late 19th/early 20thC French gilt metal-mounted glass perfume atomizer, of square chamfered section, overlaid with an eagle, oak branches and laurel garlands.

7in (18cm) high

$300-400   **SI**

Two scent bottles, one heart-shaped, the outer sleeve decorated with putto, C-scrolls and roses, London 1898, William Comyns, the other drop-shaped with screw-off cap, the body with stippled ground, floral and bird decoration, Birmingham, 1884.

Largest 4in (10cm) high

$700-1,000   **L&T**

A 1960s Avon black cat perfume bottle.

4.5in (11.5cm) long

$40-50   **LB**

A small porcelain scent bottle.

$100-150 **Trio**

A Caron "Les Pois de Senteur de Chez Moi" perfume bottle.

1927 *4.5in (11.5cm) high*

$150-200 **LB**

A Christian Dior "Miss Dior" perfume bottle, with box.

c1947 *5.5in (14cm) high*

$200-300 **LB**

A 1920s Richard Hudnut "Dubarry" perfume bottle, compact and lipstick.

Perfume 2.75in (7cm) high

$200-300 **LB**

A Guerlain "Parure" glass perfume bottle.

1974 *6.75in (17cm) high*

$100-150 **LB**

A Gabilla "La Rose de Gabilla" perfume bottle, by Baccarat, in box.

c1912 *3in (7.5cm) high*

$450-550 **LB**

A 1950s Guerlain "Shalimar" perfume bottle, by Baccarat.

6in (15cm) high

$150-200 **LB**

A Charles Kaziun paperweight perfume bottle, decorated with a spider lily on a white ground, signed with gold "K" on base and stopper.

3.25in (8.5cm) high

$1,000-1,500 **JDJ**

A 1950s Max Factor perfume bottle.

6in (15cm) high

$55-65 **LB**

A 1960s/70s Nina Ricci "L'Air Du Temps" perfume bottle, by Lalique.

4in (10cm) high

$200-300 **LB**

A 1930s "Saturday Night Lotion" bottle.

5in (12.5cm) high

$45-55 **LB**

A
B
C
D
E
F
G
H
I
J
K
L
M
N
O
P
Q
R
S
T
U
V
W
XYZ

SCIENCE & TECHNOLOGY

- Instruments from the 18th century can be found but these will most often command high prices. Earlier instruments from the 1600s and 1500s are generally unavailable to private collectors, unless common or of basic construction.

- The majority of science and technology instruments available to collectors today date from the 19th century, which was a period of prolific production and many new inventions and ingenious innovations. Many are stored in fitted wooden boxes, often made from mahogany.

- The quality of production in the 19th century was high; bodies are usually finely made in brass with precise optical components.

- Instruments fall into a number of categories which include those for navigation, surveying, scientific purposes, optical instruments and functional mechanical and technical instruments, such as the telephone and typewriter.

- Look for good workmanship when examining a piece. Pieces should be well-engineered and 'fit' and function together. If an instrument came with a range of accessories, they should be as complete as possible as this helps increase value and desirability.

- Collectors favor pieces in good condition or bearing a maker's mark. If a piece was made by a renowned maker this can increase its value considerably.

- Makers' addresses can help identify a period of manufacture. From 1767, street numbers replaced signs and makers often moved. Specialist reference works allot dates ranges to specific addresses.

- Beware of cleaning brass instruments, abrasive cleaners can remove the surface of lacquer on brass.

A black lacquered brass three drawer pocket telescope, with leather-covered tube, signed "Parascope W. Watson & Son Ltd, 313 High Holborn, London".
Extended 16.75in (42.5cm) long

$70-100 BA

A 19thC four drawer lacquered brass and mahogany telescope, marked "Thos. Harris & Son, Opticians to the Royal Family, Oppos. the British Museum London".
Extended 43.5in (110.5cm) long

$300-400 BA

A six drawer lacquered brass pocket telescope, with black ribbed grip and screw-in mount, in velvet-lined fitted mahogany case, signed "Edwd Davis, 65 Bold St, Liverpool".
Extended 5in (12.5cm) long

$650-750 BA

A five drawer brass telescope, with tripod and fitted mahogany case, signed "Ramsden, London".
Extended 40.5in (103cm) long

$700-900 BA

A Victorian tortoiseshell and brass two drawer spy glass.
Extended 5.5in (14cm) long

$200-300 BA

A pair of military regulation field glasses.
4.5in (11.5cm) wide

$25-35 OACC

A pair of racing binoculars, marked "Le Jockey Club, Paris".
4.75in (12cm) wide

$100-150 OACC

A pair of Leitz Fernglass 08 field glasses, marked, with leather case.
c1916

$120-180 TK

A pair of early 20thC Baker binoculars.

$70-90 OACC

An early Zeiss monocular field glass, marked "Carl Zeiss, Jena", with old Zeiss company logo, with maker's case.
c1896

$300-350 TK

A pair of Carl Zeiss 6 x 30 binoculars, No. 2021729, in hard black plastic case, well worn.

$40-50 W&W

A late 19thC mahogany and black painted tin magic lantern.

The magic lantern has existed since the 17thC and used a light source behind a glass plate with an image painted or printed onto it. A magnifying lens at the front of the lantern projected an enlarged image onto a surface for viewing.
24in (61cm) long

$650-750 BA

A Skioptikon magic lantern, with original electrical lighting mechanism.

c1920   18.5in (47cm) wide

$100-150   **TK**

An Ernst Plank magic lantern, with original box and 13 glass slides, no burner, reflector loose.

c1910

$150-200   **TK**

An 1860s Pestalozzi handheld stereo viewer, with stereocards.

Stereographic images have two seemingly identical images of the same scene beside each other on a card or on a glass plate. They are taken using a special camera with two lenses mounted side by side which capture the same scene but from a slightly different viewpoint. When viewed through a stereographic viewer, the eyes are tricked into merging the images to create an almost 'three-dimensional' image.

Established as a principle by Sir Charles Wheatstone in 1832, stereography reached the height of popularity during the third quarter of the 19th century. Popularity declined after the 1860s, but it was still popular around 1900 when cards mounted with photographic images were being mass produced.

These cards typically show tourist scenes of popular venues such as the Alps, Rome, the Holy Land and Chicago. Rarer subjects include historical events or scenes.

A large mahogany and japanned tinplate magic lantern, with tilt facility and brass knob adjustments for front bellows and rear light, with early electric fitting.

                          23in (58.5cm) long

$100-150   **DN**

A wooden Graphoscope viewer.

The Graphoscope was used for viewing photographs easily and comfortably. The image would be placed on the rest behind the magnifying lens which was angled to allow viewing.

                          5.5in (14cm) high

$120-180   **TK**

                          3in (33cm) long

$80-120   **MHC**

MICROSCOPES

- There are two different types of microscope, the simple with one lens and the compound with more than one, usually mounted apart in a tube. Tubes can be made from card, brass or wood. The invention of the microscope in 1608 is credited to Sacharias Janssen, a spectacle maker in the Netherlands.

- Earlier microscopes are usually very valuable and fetch high prices when offered. 19th century microscopes are more readily available. They are typically made from brass and are often contained in wooden boxes that also contain accessories.

- Makers' names are very important and can give an indication of date. Unmarked versions, unless in a rare type or from an early period, will generally not be as desirable. Some names, such as George Adams and Benjamin Martin attract great attention and high prices. Others have lent their names to types of design, such as the 'Cuff' type and the 'Culpeper' type with its three distinctive curving legs and centrally placed tube. Twentieth century microscopes with blackened metal stands by makers such as Leitz are usually less valuable and desirable.

- Accessories are also important, with those having a complete or near complete set of accessories being more valuable than those without.

A large lacquered brass monocular microscope, in brass bound mahogany case.

$1,000-1,700   **BA**

A lacquered brass binocular microscope, with fitted mahogany case containing different objectives, eyepieces and other accessories, signed "R. & J. Beck, 31 Cornhill, London".

Closed 15.25in (39cm) high

$1,800-2,200   **BA**

A lacquered brass compound drum microscope, in a fitted wooden box, unmarked.

                          10in (25.5cm) high

$600-700   **BA**

A lacquered brass microscope, in fitted wooden case, marked "Gardner & Co., 21 Buchanan Street, Glasgow".

The opticians and mathematical instrument makers Gardner & Co are recorded as being at 21 Buchanan St, Glasgow from 1839-1859, and then at 53 Buchanan Street from 1860-1882. They were active and working between 1837 and 1883. With this microscope, the stand and tube are separate and are screwed together after removing them from the case, which also contains an array of eyepieces, objectives and accessories.

Case 11.5in (29cm) high

$1,900-2,700   **BA**

A lacquered brass microscope, in fitted mahogany case, marked "Watson & Son, 313 High Holborn, London".

Watson & Son are recorded as being active and working at 313A High Holborn, London between 1869 and 1872.

16in (40.5cm) high

$700-1,000   **BA**

A painted and lacquered brass microscope, in fitted wooden case, marked " Henry Crouch, London, 4085".

11in (28cm) high

$300-400   **BA**

A brass microscope, by Bausch & Lomb, in locking walnut case, includes instruction manual, cover glasses, slides and extra lens.

Case 14in (35.5cm) high

$180-220   **TWC**

A lacquered brass pocket microscope, with fitted mahogany box and ivory slides.

This microscope is taken to pieces and the stand folded away to fit into the mahogany box, which also has fitted areas to hold accessories.

10.5in (26.5cm) high

$750-850   **BA**

An early brass microscope, by Carl Zeiss, No. 11890, with three lenses, one later and two different oculars, in original mahogany box, with key.

$650-750   **TK**

A black microscope, by Ernst Leitz, No. 367.690.

Ernst Leitz are a famous optical manufacturer based in Wetzlar, Germany. They also developed and manufactured the famous 'Leica' cameras.

$180-220   **TK**

A lacquered brass microscope, by R. & J. Beck, No. 8.212.

c1860   15.25in (39cm) high

$1,200-1,800   **TK**

A brass mounted bullseye, on ball-jointed arm.

A bullseye lens was used for focusing light to allow use of a microscope. These lenses have a flat and a bulbous side, the latter giving them their characteristic name.

1.75in (4.5cm) diam

$100-150   **BA**

A lacquered brass transit theodolite, in fitted wooden case, signed "T. Cooke & Sons, York, England No. 5115", the case with printed label dated December 1932.

11in (28cm) wide

$700-1,000   **BA**

A brass theodolite, signed "Fraget A Paris".

11in (28cm) high

$700-1,000   **BA**

A black lacquered brass Starke & Kammerer theodolite, No. 8.705.

c1890   *11.75in (30cm) high*

$700-800   **TK**

A brass French cross staff, by Radiguet, Paris, silver nonius scale.

c1860   *6.25in (16cm) high*

$100-150   **TK**

A lacquered brass octagonal cross staff, the top set with a compass, in a wooden box.

5in (12.5cm) long

$200-250   **BA**

Two early French brass cross staffs, with original boxes.

c1860

$150-200   **TK**

A lacquered brass "Director No. 5 Mark I" level, in fitted wooden case, marked "E. R. Watts & Son, 1916, No. 3397".

14.75in (37.5cm) long

$450-550   **BA**

A lacquered brass Abney level, marked "F.B. & Son Ltd 2904".

5.75in (14.5cm) long

$100-150   **BA**

A lacquered brass dial, in fitted wooden case, signed "Pyefinch, London".

$2,000-2,500   **BA**

A lacquered brass miners dial, on wooden base, signed "John King, Bristol".

Dial 5.5in (14cm) diam

$650-750   **BA**

A lacquered brass protractor, in fitted mahogany case, signed "Troughton & Simms, London".

Case 13in (33cm) wide

$350-450   **BA**

A pocket sextant, with leather case, marked "Liddon & Co. London B818 1916".

The pocket sextant was invented by Edward Troughton around 1800 and was one of the most useful surveying instruments available, particularly for trigonometric purposes. The tiny scales are read with a magnifier.

2.5in (6.5cm) diam

$300-400   **BA**

A lacquered brass octant, signed "H.C. Coles, London", with later conservation varnish, complete.

$400-500   **TK**

A lacquered brass octant, in fitted mahogany case, case marked "J. Sewill, Chronometer Manufacturer, 30 Cornhill, Royal Exchange".

9.5in (24cm) long

$700-1,000   **BA**

A black lacquered brass sextant on stand, marked "Bottomley, 11 Billiter Street, London".

20in (51cm) high

$2,000-3,000   **BA**

A lacquered brass flying boat sextant, with fitted wooden box and printed paper label "for Henry Hughes & Son Ltd, London", dated 10/6/44.

1944   *8in (20.5cm) wide*

$450-550   **BA**

A wood and brass octant, with ivory label "Browning maker, Boston".

Octants were used to measure angles in navigation from c1750 to c1900. As the name suggests, they take the form of an eighth of a full circle.

Its invention is credited to John Hadley, who modified and adapted another navigational instrument, the back staff, into the octant in the early 1730s.

The earliest frames, dating from before 1800, were made of mahogany, but octants are usually found in ebony in styles identical to this example.

Browning, based in Boston MA, is a known maker and his name is found on a small inset ivory plaque on the cross bar.

13in (33cm) high

$650-750   **BA**

A marine chronometer, in fitted, gimbaled case, marked "Kelvin, White & Hutton, 11 Billiter Street, London", case marked "Kelvin, White & Hutton 5464" and with paper label "J. Sewill Ltd, makers to the Royal Navy, 36 Exchange Street, East Liverpool, L2 3PT, Date: May 1982".

Marine chronometers are mounted on a series of moving mounts, known as 'gimbals'. Accurate chronometers were essential for discerning longitude to enable correct navigation at sea and a competition was held in the early 18thC to devise the most accurate timepiece. John Harrison, a talented British clockmaker, developed the first reliable marine chronometer that was not affected by the movement of the sea or the varying temperature – it was tested successfully in 1736.

Dial 4.75in (12cm) diam

$2,000-2,500   **BA**

A brass compass, signed "Dent & Co Ltd" and "No. 3039 Patt 20".

12in (30.5cm) high

$1,500-2,000   **BA**

A near pair of brass and copper ship lanterns, marked "Port" and "Starboard".

12in (30.5cm) high

$150-200   **BA**

A lacquered brass ship's log, with painted enamel dial, marked "T. Walker's Patent Harpoon Ship Log A1, London".

19.25in (49cm) long

$650-750   **BA**

A ships flare gun, with brass and wood grip and painted metal barrel, marked "SFRA".

19.5in (49.5cm) long

$350-450   **BA**

An American 'The Fox' typewriter.

c1902

$600-700 TK

A Hammond No. 12 typewriter, with wooden case and ten part documentation, three type sleeves in original boxes and three box ribbons.

c1893

$450-550 TK

A very rare Imperial Visible typewriter, with sloping type bar by Triumph Visible Co., Kenosha, Wisconsin.

This typewriter is the forerunner of the rare Burnett model, but even scarcer. Only three examples are known worldwide, and this one bears the low serial number of 304, adding to its desirability.

c1907

$10,000-12,000 TK

A Mignon Model 2 typewriter.

c1905

$600-700 TK

A Royal Bar-Lock typewriter, with original wooden hood.

c1902

$400-500 TK

A CLOSER LOOK AT A VIROTYP MACHINE

The circular plate had a series of letters printed on it. Below this was a series of letter stamps and under that, rollers to hold the paper.

The knob was turned to point at a letter the printing key pressed and letter stamped onto the paper.

A French 'Virotyp' index machine, in good working condition.

The Virotyp, invented by the Frenchman H. Viry in 1914, was a comparatively small machine primarily made for use during the First World War.

It had a strap and series of hooks that meant it could be cradled between both hands and operated without needing a hard surface to rest it on.

Combined with its small size and lightness of weight, it became popular for people who had to type whilst on the move. A further strap allowed it to be attached to a forearm enabling it to be used even on horseback!

c1914

$550-650 TK

An American Odell 'Type Writer' index typewriter, wooden case replaced.

This model was one of Chicago-based Odell Type Writer Co's most popular machines and used a sliding linear index fixed at a 90 degree angle to the paper. A patent was issued in 1889 and versions with upper and lower case as well as upper case only (as with this example) were sold. The user would select the letter with the slide and rock the slide to print the letter.

c1890

$1,000-1,500 TK

A rare Urania-Piccola portable typewriter, with scarce German Gothic type, the successor of Perkeo.

c1925

$250-350 TK

FIND OUT MORE...

Scryption Museum, Spoorlaan 434a, 5053 CH Tilburg, The Netherlands. www.tref.nl, This 'museum of writing' contains an incredible and diverse collection of typewriters.

Michael Adler, 'The Writing Machine – A History of the Typewriter', published by George, Allen & Unwin, 1973.

A rare Swedish table telephone, by L. M. Ericsson, for 10 lines.
c1905

$1,500-2,000 **TK**

A French table telephone, with wooden case, and coil, minimal damage on edge of case.

c1910

$300-400 **TK**

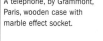

A telephone, by Grammont, Paris, wooden case with marble effect socket.

c1900

$1,000-1,500 **TK**

L. M. ERICSSON

- L.M. Ericsson, known for their mobile telephones today, were founded in Stockholm in 1876 by Lars Magnus Ericsson as a telephone repair company.
- They began to manufacture their own telephones in 1878 and began selling in America in the 1890s. By 1905, when a factory was set up in Buffalo, New York, a sales office had been in existence for three years.
- Their candlestick telephones are sought after by collectors, as is the highly decorative skeleton model, which is also sometimes known as the 'Eiffel Tower' telephone. It shows many of the internal workings as decorative features.
- Condition is important, as the black finish is prone to wear and scratches. The gilt transfers on the legs can also be scratched and show signs of wear. Damage such as this will affect value.

An L. M. Ericsson telephone.
c1910 13in (33cm) high

$120-180 **OACC**

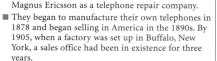

An L.M. Ericsson skeleton telephone.
c1900

$1,200-1,800 **TK**

A rare Swiss wall telephone, by G. Hasler, Bern, with original receiver, fixed microphone.
c1925

$550-650 **TK**

A white painted candlestick telephone.

$200-250 **BA**

A wall telephone, by L.M. Ericsson, Stockholm, with turnable microphone protectors for use during a thunderstorm, no receiver.
c1900

$3,000-3,500 **TK**

An early 20thC Western Electric oak wall telephone.

19in (48.5cm) high

$150-200　　　**TWC**

A pocket barometer, with silvered dial, marked "W. H. Blackler Bulawayo".

2.75in (7cm) diam

$150-250　　　**BA**

A brass pocket barometer, with silvered dial, signed "P. H. Steward, 457 West Strand, 406 Strand & 7 Greenchurch Street, London 3520".

2in (5cm) diam

$100-150　　　**BA**

A brass holosteric pocket barometer, signed "H A Reens, Opticien Rotterdam".

2in (5cm) diam

$100-150　　　**BA**

A cased barograph, with pull-out drawer.

12in (30.5cm) wide

$700-1,000　　　**BA**

A German barometer, by G.Müller, Braunschweig.

c1900

$150-200　　　**TK**

A marine barograph.

12in (30.5cm) wide

$700-900　　　**BA**

A compass, in carved wooden case, with printed paper dial and carved wooden meridian ring, signed "Thomas Heath".

1720-33　　　*Case 6in (15cm) wide*

$800-1,200　　　**BA**

A Sestral clock and barometer, mounted on a wooden board, signed "The Seaway Co."

13.5in (34.5cm) wide

$350-450　　　**BA**

A pocket compass, in fitted wooden case, with printed paper dial and yellow paper label "Hudson, Optician, Greenwich".

2in (5cm) wide

$80-120　　　**BA**

A compass, in carved wooden case, with engraved brass dial, marked "I. Coggs, Fleet Street, London".

Case 6in (15cm) wide

$1,000-1,700   BA

A brass equinoctial dial, in a fitted case, marked "KOHN Onmukb".

4.5in (11.5cm) diam

$1,500-2,000   BA

A pocket compass, with silvered dial and wooden case.

3in (7.5cm) wide

$70-100   BA

A brass compass, in fitted wooden case, signed "J. Wardale & Co., London No. 7906 1918".

3.25in (8cm) wide

$70-100   BA

A pocket compass, with printed paper dial and brass case.

3.5in (9cm) wide

$150-200   BA

A silvered brass pocket sundial, signed "Lynch, Dublin".

3.5in (9cm) wide

$700-1,000   BA

A "Willis World Time Clock", in seven-sided wooden case, with printed dial, lacks hands.

13in (33cm) diam

$800-1,200   BA

A CLOSER LOOK AT AN ORRERY

The oil lamp on the main body of the instrument represents the sun, with the globe at the end of the arm being the Earth, mounted at the correct angle. The small sphere held near it on another arm is the moon.

By turning the handle, the whole revolves including the Earth and the moon and the Earth's orbit around the sun associated with the moon's placement can be seen.

A German painted metal orrery, with hand-cranked mechanism, the globe marked "ZEMÉKOULE VYDAU J. FELKLASYN ROZTOKYAPRAHY".

Through use of winding, gears and revolving spheres, orreries illustrate the movement of planets and solar system. They are found in various degrees of sophistication with one or numerous planets. They are a good example of demonstration instruments and are popular with collectors of globes.

20in (51cm) wide

$2,500-3,000   **BA**

A 17thC Continental set of bronze weights, the hinged case with punchwork decoration and hallmarks fitted with eight stacking weights.

3.5in (9cm) wide

$1,200-1,800   **SI**

A minimum-maximum thermometer, cased.

8.5in (21.5cm) wide

$120-180   **BA**

A set of 18thC monetary beam scales.

7.25in (18.5cm) wide

$500-600   **OACC**

A minimum-maximum thermometer, cased.

8.5in (21.5cm) wide

$120-180   **BA**

A Curta Type 1 calculator, input imperfect, with original metal box. *c1948*

$500-600   **TK**

An ivory and brass hydrometer, in fitted mahogany case, marked "Buss, 48 Hatton Garden, London".

Hydrometers were used by brewers and excise officers to measure the gravity of liquids, from which the alcohol content could be discerned. A common maker of hydrometers is 'Sikes', whose highly accurate patent was introduced in 1817. The small disc weights are often missing from sets, so collectors should examine boxes closely.

Case 8in (20.5cm) wide

$100-150   **BA**

A lacquered brass pantograph, in fitted wooden case, signed "Allen, London".

A pantograph was used for copying and enlarging or reducing the size of maps and diagrams.

15.25in (39cm) wide

$350-450   **BA**

A mahogany and brass Cuthbert electricty generating machine, with large glass disc rotating between to sets of leather pads.

19in (48.5cm) high

$700-900   **BA**

SILVER

A George III caddy spoon, by Duncan Urquhart and Napthali Hart, with wriggle-engraved round bowl and bright-cut engraved handle with monogram, London hallmarks.

1799 3in (7.5cm) long

$180-220 DN

Two George III shell bowl caddy spoons, one by S. Godbehere & Co., with an old 'English' pattern handle and London hallmarks, the other with a short handle, London hallmarks rubbed.

1801 & 1809 3.5in (9cm) long

$250-300 DN

CADDY SPOONS

- Caddy spoons were used for transferring tea from a tea caddy to a teapot.
- They are often fancifully shaped and highly decorative and were made from the 1770s until the decline in use of tea caddies in the late 19th century.
- They are made from a single sheet of silver which is stamped into the form, and stamped with the design and pattern, so they are often fragile. Collectors should look for repaired bends, which reduce value if serious, and splits.
- Handles are often made from bone, ivory or mother-of-pearl. Popular motifs include shells, jockey's caps, hands and an eagle's wing.

A Victorian caddy spoon, by Hilliard and Thomason, the lobed bowl embossed with shells and leaves, the handle in the form of a lily, London hallmarks.

1852 3.5in (9cm) long

$650-750 DN

A Liberty & Co silver caddy spoon, the oval-shaped bowl decorated with a panel resembling basket weave, the handle with scrollwork and a further panel of basket weave, marked "L&Co" for Birmingham.

1924 3.3in (8.5cm)

$400-500 DN

A silver spoon, by Sibyl Dunlop, the almost heart-shaped bowl with the handle terminating in a pointed oval, with overall planached surface, marked "SD" and stamped "S. Dunlop", with London hallmarks.

1969 6in (15cm) long

$250-300 DN

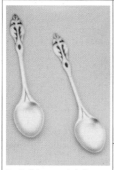

A set of six enameled silver coffee spoons, by W. H. Haseler, each with a oval bowl and a slender handle with foliate terminal, the detail heightened with coloured enamels, each marked with "W.H.H.", Birmingham hallmarks, fitted case.

1906 4.5in (11.5cm) each

$700-800 (set) DN

A silver gravy ladle, by Georg Jensen, the curved handle terminating in a stylized blossom.

1933-44 8in (20.5cm) long

$450-550 SI

A silver sauce ladle, by Georg Jensen, with deep elliptical bowl, the handle with central slender beaded knop and bud finial, stamped with maker's marks, Copenhagen date mark and London import marks.

1927 5.5in (14cm) long

$350-450 DN

Two pairs of 20thC silver serving pieces, comprising a serving fork and spoon cast with rosebud decoration on handles and terminals, and a serving fork and spoon cast and pierced with scrolls and shells.

$300-350 SI

50 pieces of 19thC coin silver and plated flatware, including 30 engraved "Oregon" bearing maker's mark of Salisbury, 212 Broadway, New York, NY, together with flatware similarly designed by E.W. Moir, and coin silver serving spoons bearing the maker's mark of Griffen.

The ship "Oregon" sunk in Boston Harbor in 1863. The engraved flatware was salvaged and used by the family of Phillip White of Boston as their family silver. All pieces bear the White family monograms.

$450-550 SI

A 156-piece silver flatware service, by Georg Jensen, 'Acanthus' pattern, comprising 18 dinner forks, luncheon forks, salad forks, dinner knives, coffee spoons, dessert spoons and table serving spoons, twelve teaspoons and bouillon spoons, one cake server, three cold meat forks, a pie server and salad spoon.

$7,500-8,500 SI

A George V silver circular tray, by Mappin & Webb, Sheffield, the centre engraved with C-scrolls, flowers and foliage, the rim chased with conforming decoration and the scalloped rim applied with foliage.

1913   *14in (35.5cm) diam*

$650-750 SI

A silver circular tray, by Frank M. Whiting Co., North Attleboro, MA, chased with floral and foliate swags, applied with a fruit and leaf rim.

12.25in (31cm) diam

$150-200 SI

A silver circular platter, by Tiffany & Co., moulded with a laurel chain border and a central reserve within a radiating petal surround, monogrammed "HAF".

1907-38   *15in (38cm) diam*

$1,200-1,500 SI

A silver two-handled oval dish, by Tiffany & Co., with cut-out shaped handles, bright cut with triangular panels of bellflowers, monogrammed "MMC".

1907-38 9.25in (23.5cm) wide

$450-550 SI

A silver-plated salver, by G. Forbes, New York, NY, of oblong form with gadrooned edge with the initials "M.O." at the center, on paw feet.

c1810   *10in (25.5cm) long*

$350-450 SI

One of a pair of Austro-Hungarian Art Nouveau silver trays, possibly used as wine coasters, each with a wavy everted rim embossed with lilies-of-the-valley with sinuous foliage, marked with Diana head standard mark and maker's mark "FR".

4.5in (16.5cm) diam

$150-200 (pair) DN

A silver and enamel small dish, by Omar Ramsden, with planached surface and a notched rim, centered with a pierced rose motif revealing a red enameled panel beneath, marked "OR" with London hallmarks for 19.. and signed "Omar Ramsden Me Fecit".

4.25in (10.5cm)

$800-900 DN

A Taxco Mexican silver and copper bird dish, modeled as a stylized bird with silver wings, brass beak and inlaid silver and malachite eye, stamped "METALES [_____] HANDWROUGHT LOS CASTILLO TAXCO".

12in (30.5cm) high

$280-320 FRE

A silver centerpiece dish, by Tiffany & Co., the circular bowl with everted wide rim applied with leaf tip edge, rosettes and scallop shells, engraved with scrolling foliage and monogrammed "MFG".

1907-38 13.5in (34.5cm) diam

$1,500-2,500 SI

A silver bowl, designed by Harald Nielsen for Georg Jensen, of half-spherical form with hammered texture and simple ring base, date mark for 1933-44, "HN" initials, "580A" and other markings.

4.75in (12cm) diam

$1,000-1,500 FRE

A late 19thC/early 20thC German silver vase, of tapering lobed ovoid form, applied with two lions' mask and ring handles and with leaf tip borders.

7in (18cm) high

$450-550 SI

A silver vase, by Tiffany & Co, waisted vessel chased in high relief with flowers.

7in (17.7cm)

$1,400-1,800 SI

A George III silver creamer, of baluster form, engraved with bands of foliage, ovolus and serpentine lines and a vacant shield-form cartouche, London hallmarks.

1799   4.25in (10.5cm) high

$400-500 SI

A late 19thC Continental silver small ewer, of pear form, chased with Biblical scenes, the hinged cover surmounted by a phoenix with chicks.

9in (23cm) high

$650-750 SI

A Danish-style silver coffee pot, probably American, lobed body with hammered texture and floral bulb to lid, applied spout and carved ivory handle on three "webbed" feet, stamped "STERLING".

c1930   7.5in (19cm) high

$900-1,000 FRE

A modern English silver creamer, modeled as a cow wearing a garland of flowers and with a bumble bee on her back.

6in (15cm) long

$850-950 SI

A contemporary Italian silver five-piece tea service, by Miniati, Florence, comprising teapot, coffee pot, creamer, sugar and two-handled tray, each of angular pentagonal section with hinged cover and angular handle mounted with square lapis lazuli tiles.

20in (51cm) wide

$4,500-5,500 SI

A Continental silver and glass liqueur set, comprising two bottles and eight glasses on a stand.

c1900   9.5in (24cm) wide

$350-450 JBS

A Victorian pepper pot, by Hukin & Heath, naturalistically modeled as a toadstool, the domed cover unscrewing from the shaped stem, London hallmarks.

1889   2in (5cm) diam

$600-700 DN

A pair of cased silver beakers, by Elfin, of cylindrical form, with inset discs inscribed "ELFIN".

c1850   2.75in (7cm) diam

$250-300 DN

A salt cellar in the form of a canoe, by Saunders and Shepherd, the canoe Birmingham 1904, the spoon London 1903.

3.25in (8.5cm)

$250-350 DN

A Japanese silver-mounted and enameled ostrich egg cup, the egg painted brown and enamelled in gilt and red with insects and plants, the mixed metal base in the form of a flower stem on a mound applied with a cricket and cover.

Ostrich egg cups were made from a cleaned-out shell that was mounted onto a silver or gold stem and foot which is usually highly and intricately decorated. Although this example is certainly 19th century due to its form and country of manufacture, they were popular during the 16th and 17th centuries, having originated in Europe as an exotic curiosity during the 15th century.

7.5in (19cm) high

$650-750   **SI**

Two pairs of contemporary American silver salt and pepper shakers, by Pampaloni, of asymmetric pyramidal form.

Largest 4.25in (10.5cm) high

$1,000-1,500   **SI**

A pair of silver wine glass coasters, by Georg Jensen, of circular shape with beaded rims and embossed in the center with buds and foliage, stamped "GI", "925" and numbered "41", with London import marks.

1930   3.3in (8.5cm)

$180-220   **DN**

A pair of Victorian bath-shaped silver spoon stands, by Edward Smith, each engine-turned with a cartouche, one lacking a small section of border, Birmingham hallmarks.

1864   4in (11.5cm) long

$450-550   **DN**

A pair of silver shaped rectangular menu stands, by Samuel Jacob, cast, pierced and chased with winged putti amid foliate scrolls, London hallmarks.

1899   2.75in (7cm) wide

$250-350   **DN**

A set of six George III wine labels, 'Port' and 'Madeira', London 1805 by John Rich; 'Brandy', 1800 by Mary Hyde and John Reily; 'Sherry', 1803 by Phipps and Robinson; and two 'Sherry', 1794 by Phipps and Robinson, 1820 by George Knight.

$300-400   **DN**

A late 19thC Derby crumb scoop, the handle painted in the Imari palette with stylized flowers, the electroplated scoop engraved with scrolling foliage.

12.5in (31.5cm) long

$60-80   **Chef**

A pair of silver sugar tongs, by George Jensen, marked "925".

1910

$250-350   **SSp**

A silver toast rack, by H.G. Murphy, marked for the Falcon works, "HGM" and London hallmarks.

1934   3.5in (9cm) high

$1,800-2,200   **DN**

A silver box, by John Linnit, with lid depicting scene from 'The Pickwick Papers'.

$1,500-2,000   **GS**

A late 19th/early 20thC Continental silver box, rectangular with hinged cover, repoussé with floral baskets, floral sprays, foliage and scrolls and with a vacant cartouche, lined with purple velvet, partial hallmark and marked "925".

5in (12.5 cm) wide

$400-450 **SI**

A 20thC Continental silver-mounted glass box, of casket form, mounted with ribbon-tied bellflower garlands, ovolo and beaded edges, the domed cover engraved with laurel branches, ribbons and flowerheads.

5in (12.5 cm) long

$450-550 **SI**

A Dutch silver cabinet-shaped tea caddy, embossed with figured and foliate scrolls, the cover with an animal finial, date letter.

1912 *5.5in (14cm) high*

$550-650 **DN**

A silver repoussé tea caddy, by S. Kirk & Son, Baltimore, the ovoid vessel and cylindrical cover chased with flowers and foliage on a stippled ground, the base monogrammed "GPG".

1868-1896 *3.5in (9cm) high*

$750-850 **SI**

Two silver vinaigrettes, by John and Joseph Wilmore, both with cast border, engine-turned panels and pierced grill, Birmingham hallmarks.

1827 and 1836 *1.5in (3.5cm) wide*

$550-650 **L&T**

A silver embossed pot, with foliate and floral decoration, Birmingham hallmarks.

1890 *2in (5cm) diam*

$120-180 **PSA**

A Dutch silver trinket box, the top with pastoral scene with pierced mother-of-pearl behind.

2.25in (5.5cm) wide

$100-140 **PSA**

A single sovereign holder, by Mordan and Storr, Birmingham.

$200-300 **GS**

A silver double sovereign holder, engraved with initials "W.W.", Birmingham.

1912

$200-300 **GS**

A silver compact, by Georg Jensen.

c1925

$900-1,000 **PC**

A silver vesta, engraved with initials "E.H.", Birmingham.

$60-80 **GS**

A silver hip flask, with pull off lid, Edinburgh hallmarks.

1924 *6in (15cm) high*

$1,000-1,500 **Tag**

A plain silver playing card case, Birmingham hallmarks.

1909

$180-220 **L&T**

A silver stamp box, by A. & J. Zimmerman, in the form of a serpentine side table, with a hinged lid, one dummy drawer on square legs, Birmingham hallmarks.

1910 *2.25in (6cm) wide*

$400-450 **DN**

A silver vesta/match case, by William Hornby, in the form of a dog kennel with a hinged roof and a nephrite bulldog at the door, a chip to one ear and leg, London hallmarks.

1907   *2.25in (5.75cm)*

$1,300-1,500   **DN**

A silver and enamel five-piece toilet set, the grey enamel backs mounted with Art Deco influenced mounts, Birmingham hallmarks, some damage.

1936

$60-80   **LFA**

A late 19thC/early 20thC American enameled silver traveling set, comprising of hand mirror, hair brush, clothes brush, comb, two canisters, two bottles, jar, pill box, button hook, two fingernail files, fingernail scissors and fingernail buffer, all in a fitted case.

Dressing sets need to be complete to fetch the highest prices. Damage to the enameling will affect value. These were functional pieces and were used frequently, so were easily damaged. Where possible, bottles should have original stoppers. Many such sets were contained in fitted boxes with a myriad of accessories, as well as being loose and displayed on a dressing table. Incomplete sets still have a value as collectors may buy incomplete sets to 'make up' complete sets.

$500-600   **SI**

A 20thC enameled silver and engraved glass dresser set, decorated with blue, pink, yellow and green birds, ribbons and flowers on a green engine-turned ground, with an engraved glass pin.

Mirror 13.5in (34cm) long

$2,800-3,200   **SI**

A five-piece silver dressing table set, Birmingham hallmarks.

1924 Brush 11in (28cm) long

$180-220   **OACC**

A silver-backed clothes brush, by William Hutton & Sons, embossed with the profile of a girl wearing a cap, flanked by stems of lilies, from a design by Kate Harris, maker's mark for London.

1902   *7in (18.5cm)*

$80-120   **DN**

A silver pin cushion, by Levi and Salaman, in the form of the coronation throne, Birmingham hallmarks.

1901   *2.75in (7cm) high*

$180-220   **DN**

A silver pin cushion, by Levi and Salaman, in the form of an ostrich, standing on a round composition base, Birmingham hallmarks.

1911   *2.5in (6.5cm) high*

$600-700   **DN**

A Dutch silver shoe-shaped basket, embossed with pastoral scenes, lacking the swing handle, date letter for 1902.

6in (15cm) long

$400-500   **DN**

A George IV 'King's Husk' pattern silver-gilt grape scissors, engraved with a crest, London hallmarks.

1822

$600-700   **DN**

An 18thC silver scissors case, the rounded oval top with simple acanthus engraving and "Eliz Mills Bristol", plain lower section, ball end finial, unmarked.

4in (10cm) long

$800-1,000   **L&T**

A Victorian silver pocket knife, with integral scissors, corkscrew, hook, knife and more, engraved monogram, London hallmarks.

1870   *3in (7.5cm) wide*

$600-700   **Tag**

A Victorian miniature watering can, by Henry Wilkinson & Co, engraved with initials, handle to the lid detached, Sheffield hallmarks.

1888   *1.75in (4.5cm) high*

$300-400   **DN**

A silver rattle, Birmingham hallmarks.

1915   *4.75in (12cm) long*

$300-400   **OACC**

An early 20thC silver-plated and horn trophy, on ball feet, inscribed 'HOGMANAY/ 1914'.

6in (15cm) high

$250-350   **SI**

A silver rattle, by Crisford & Norris, compressed round form, pierced with a pig, suspended from a plastic teether, Birmingham hallmarks.

1920   *2in (5.5 cm) diam*

$100-150   **DN**

An Edwardian silver-mounted horse's hoof, by George Neal & George Neal, London, the interior fitted with an inkwell, the cover inscribed 'In memory of Brigand / died February 26th 1918 / a favourite and the last Hunter of W.H.P. Jenkins, Frenchay Park, Bristol.'

Desk accessories made from horses' hooves were popular Victorian and Edwardian items and were often finely made by noted silversmiths. Intensely personal, they were made from the hooves of favorite horses, or local horses who achieved success with their rider. They are often engraved with an inscription and dated, commemorating the horse's life or the event.

1918   *6.5in (16.5cm) long*

$1,000-1,500   **SI**

An early 20thC silver Torah breast plate, chased with foliate scrolls, mounted with a crown with bird finial, flanked by lions and columns hung with bells, centering a small door enclosing a model of the Torah within a bird and foliate pierced surround, inscribed in Hebrew and dated "5711".

13.5in (34.5cm) high

$1,400-2,000   **SI**

A silver and green marble postal scale, with ivory scale, Birmingham hallmarks.

1922   *3.75in (9.5cm) high*

$300-400   **Tag**

A cast silver model of a pig, maker S.C., retailed by A. Barrett & Sons, inscribed "Ye Ancient Lucky Pig" on the back ridge, London hallmarks.

1902

$550-650   **L&T**

CLAY PIPES

- Clay pipes are the most common and inexpensive type of pipe found due to the huge volume made.
- Made from kaolin (china clay), they were produced in vast quantities from the 17thC to the 19thC.
- The shape of clay pipes has changed over the centuries – either due to fashion or to the falling price of tobacco. The earliest pipes from the 17thC are very small. After c1700, pipe bowls became larger and stems longer. The 1800s saw bowls becoming shorter and fatter, allowing for more decoration. Stems became shorter.
- Collectors should look for clay pipes bearing arms or crests, maker's names, initials or trademarks. 'Churchwardens' – pipes with elongated stems up to 24in (60cm) long – are very desirable. There is little interest in clay pipes produced after 1900.

A leather clay pipe wallet, dated 1761, and an 18thC facsimile packet from Willsons Snuff Shop, 27 St John Street, West Smithfield, also labelled Wills, Bristol.

$500-700   **BAR**

A collection of five 19thC European black clay character pipe bowls.

$60-100   **BAR**

A collection of five French polychrome clay pipes: two with character bowls, three with flower motifs.

Longest 8in (20cm) long

$300-400   **BAR**

A collection of five 19thC French clay pipes and bowls, representing hands, feet and a leg.

Longest 6in (15cm) long

$180-220   **BAR**

A pair of 19thC large clay pipes, one carved in full relief as a Christ-like character, the other bas relief molded with a football game.

8in (20cm) long

$100-150   **BAR**

A collection of four 19thC European clay pipes, of various animals including an unusual full relief fish pipe.

Longest 6in (14cm) long

$150-200   **BAR**

A collection of four 19thC French red clay pipes, named Negresse, Le Tzar, Un Maroc and another of a lady's head.

$270-330   **BAR**

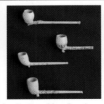

A collection of four French polychrome clay pipes, three with a floral motif and one with a French Navy anchor.

2in (5cm) long

$150-200   **BAR**

A collection of four 19thC European clay pipes, one with large bowl with Crystal Palace motif and amber mouthpiece, one double-bowl pipe, one in full relief of an owl, the other as Atlas holding up the world.

Longest 8in (20cm) long

$100-150   **BAR**

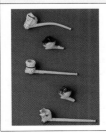

A collection of five 19thC French polychrome clay pipes, representing a horse, cat, monkey, dog and bull.

Longest 6in (15cm) long

$500-700   **BAR**

A collection of six English clay pipe bowls, in full relief, of Disraeli, Edward VII, George V and others.

$150-200   **BAR**

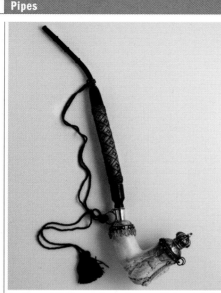

A well-carved 19thC meerschaum pipe, carved in bas relief with the head of Prince Albert flanked by pair of angels, the silver colored metal mounts and cover with a Royal Crown surrounded by medallions and turquoise stones.

Albert, Queen Victoria's beloved Prince Consort, died in 1861.

21.5in (55cm) long

$1,200-1,800   **BAR**

A collection of four 19thC meerschaum cheroot holders, one full relief carved a boy (some damage), one carved as a bearded head, one full relief carved as two stallions, and a suave gentleman with monocle and top hat (damage to hat brim).

$70-100   **BAR**

An unusual 19thC meerschaum cigar holder on stand, carved with two Saxon figures, silver-colored metal mount and lion claw feet to base, Wills Collection label No. M92.

7in (18cm) high

$5,000-7,000   **BAR**

A 19thC meerschaum pipe, finely carved as a young lady's head, with coiffured hair and a flower-and-ribbon bedecked bonnet perched above her forehead, silver colored mount and amber stem.

Bowl 3in (8cm) high

$350-400   **BAR**

A collection of three 19thC meerschaum pipe bowls, one full relief carved as a bearded man with Wills Collection label No. M225, one two-tone colored plain bowl, the top off white, the rest biscuit, the last with engraved floral motif and silver-colored metal mount.

Max 4.75in (12cm) long

$40-60   **BAR**

MEERSCHAUM PIPES

- The name 'meerschaum' is taken from the German words for 'sea scum' alluding to the color of sea foam. It is made from a form of magnesium silicate found in rock veins.
- Meerschaum was first used by the Hungarians in the 18thC after they discovered that it sweetened tobacco, was largely resistant to heat and was easily carved to great decorative effect.
- As meerschaum pipes are smoked, they turn from a pale creamy beige color to a much stronger yellowy amber color.
- Many fantastic and intricate shapes were produced and the most unusual and deeply carved, or those with precious metal parts, are highly sought after and fetch high prices. Bowls decorated with or in the form of an old man's face are relatively common.

A 19thC meerschaum pipe, finely full relief carved as a cuffed hand holding an egg, with silver-colored metal band on two-piece amber stem.

9.5in (24cm) long

$400-500   **BAR**

A good 19thC meerschaum bird claw pipe, the claw holding a pipe bowl, with an amber stem.

7in (18cm) long

$100-150   **BAR**

A hand-carved meerschaum pipe, in the form of a Turk's head, with an amber stem.

c1900   *6in (15cm) long*

$5-8   **TWC**

A 19thC Persian Nargileh, decorative pink flash glass bowl, decorative brass stand, fitments and flexible stem.

$100-150 **BAR**

A Qajar period decorative Persian Nargileh water pipe, colored enamel, matching base.

$2,200-2,800 **BAR**

A 19thC Persian Nargileh, inlaid bi-metal ovoid body, scroll tripod base.

$600-1,000 **BAR**

A 20thC leather and metal water pipe, probably Middle Eastern.

$70-100 **BAR**

WATER PIPES

- Water pipes were used in Asia, Africa and Persia (the Middle East). It is believed they spread from Africa into Arab countries, India and China, from the 17th century onwards. Styles became more elaborate according to fashion and as they grew in popularity.
- They are also known as 'nargileh' pipes, an Indian word meaning 'coconut', which echoes the shape, and also the original material, of the water container.
- The container holds water through which the smoke is passed, which cools and cleanses the smoke.
- Smaller ornate and handheld water pipes are generally Chinese in origin. Larger, floor or table mounted water pipes are usually Middle Eastern or Indian in origin. To use them, smokers reclined on cushions or a low divan, or sat cross-legged on the floor.

A 19thC Persian water pipe, inlaid with various metals in a geometric design, on a circular base with feet.

$70-100 **BAR**

A 19thC Persian Nargileh, the bowl formed from a gourd, decorative brass finish.

$600-1,000 **BAR**

A 19thC Turkish water pipe, with plain glass bowl.

$60-100 **BAR**

A 19thC decorative Turkish water pipe, European cut glass ovoid bowl, metal arrow-decorated mount.

$120-180 **BAR**

A 19thC decorative glass water pipe, frosted and white enamel, embossed brass top.

$100-150 **BAR**

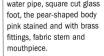

A 19thC Bohemian decorative water pipe, square cut glass foot, the pear-shaped body pink stained and with brass fittings, fabric stem and mouthpiece.

$120-180 **BAR**

An unusual 18thC root wood pipe in the Kalamasch style, inlaid with green and red cut glass and brass, with decorative silver-colored metal mounts and horn stem.

2in (30cm) long

$400-600 **BAR**

An unusually painted early 19thC long bowl porcelain pipe, handpainted with figures in military uniforms, with wood and horn stem and brass mounts.

Bowl 4in (10cm) long

$300-500 **BAR**

An early 19thC Prattware puzzle pipe, with pot bellied bowl, three outer rings and looped coils to center, restored and missing a small section.

8.5in (21.5cm) long

$600-1,000 **BAR**

An Austro Hungarian pipe, with finely relief carved portrait of Napoleon, the plain bowl with silver-colored metal hallmarked mounts and lid.

c1830 *6in (15cm) long*

$600-1,000 **BAR**

A 19thC Japanese wood opium pipe holder, of an elongated man with a well-carved bamboo pouch in full relief of a man hanging by a cord, a carved wood bowl and a copper and brass long decorative pipe, possibly Burmese.

$200-250 **BAR**

A 19thC Chinese porcelain famille rose dry opium pipe with porcelain bowl.

21.25in (54cm) long

$2,200-2,800 **BAR**

An unusual painted 19thC porcelain pipe, formed as a rabbit in full dress, the lid being its head, with wood and horn stem.

Bowl 6in (15cm) long

$350-400 **BAR**

A 19thC Chinese embroidered pipe holder, with tassel and two porcelain balls, containing a white metal and black wood pipe, a 19thC silver-colored metal miniature Chinese water opium pipe, and a Persian water pipe bowl, silver-colored metal on brass.

Pipeholder 14.5in (37cm) long

$1,000-1,500 **BAR**

A 19thC German porcelain pipe, with mountain goat scene, white metal lid, wood and horn stem.

14.5in (37cm) long

A polychrome porcelain pipe bowl, with a man in a green hat in bas relief.

4.75in (12cm) high

A porcelain pipe bowl, painted with a running deer.

4in (10cm) high

$100-150 **BAR**

A scarce 19thC carved amber pipe, the bowl formed as a tower with bear in full relief, plain silver ferrule and amber stem, slight damage.

6.25in (16cm) long

$250-300 **BAR**

A large English pottery Codgers pipe, with transfer print entitled 'The Pig Race' to bowl, black and white glaze, damaged stem.

c1860 *12in (30cm) long*

A brown glazed Codgers clay pipe with a football game in bas relief.

c1860 *9in (23cm) long*

$200-250 **BAR**

FIND OUT MORE...

Pipe Museum, 1 Bis Rue Cambetta, Saint-Claude, France.

Pitt-Rivers Museum, Parks Road, Oxford, England.

The Victoria & Albert Museum, Cromwell Road, London, England.

A large 19thC English decorative clear glass pipe, with tulip-shaped bowl and knopped stem.

19in (48cm) long

$100-150   **BAR**

A 19thC Bristol blue glass pipe.

25.5in (65cm) long

$320-380   **BAR**

A 19thC molded blue glass pipe, cut glass pipe and blue twist glass cheroot holder.

Max 6.25in (16cm) long

$300-400   **BAR**

A Matsikolumbwe zoomorphic black clay pipe, bowl shaped as an antelope, and two Botswan engraved stone pipe bowls.

Pipe 5.5in (14cm) long

$350-400   **BAR**

FIND OUT MORE...

'The Pipe Book' by Alfred Dunhill, published by Arthur Barker Ltd, London, 1969. Out of print, but an excellent book.

'The Intriguing Design of Tobacco Pipes' by Benedict Goes, published by Uniepers b.v., Leiden, 1993.

A Wedgwood blue jasper pipe bowl, applied with a cherub scalding an insect with a torch, another with a flower garland, upper case mark.

2.5in (6.5cm) long

$450-600   **BAR**

A Wedgwood blue jasper pipe bowl, applied with anthemion leaves, four paterae to bowl edge, impressed STAITE S PATENT and WEDGWOOD.

2.75in (7cm) long

$270-330   **BAR**

Two 19thC German porcelain pipes, one bowl with a transfer print of a horse, abalone inlaid wood, horn and woven stem, the other with two-piece bowl handpainted with blue cornflowers, wood and horn stem; plus a white porcelain bowl, naively painted with a lady.

Max 13in (33cm) long

$60-100   **BAR**

A collection of three 19thC pipes: a silver-colored metal studded Hungarian pipe, part of stem missing; a wood pipe, full relief carved as a man's head, with horn mouthpiece; and a meerschaum pipe, in full relief as a head held by a hand, bone stem.

Max 15in (38cm) long

$70-100   **BAR**

A German porcelain pipe, with bas relief of a sailor boy on a dock, the silver lid marked London 1881, with light wood and horn stem.

4.25in (11cm) long

$120-180   **BAR**

A 19thC memento mori porcelain pipe of a skull, a pottery pipe in full relief of man with large nose, metal hat as lid, and a large 19thC Negro head pottery pipe.

Max 4in (10cm) long

$320-380   **BAR**

A 19thC African Mahsikulumbwe pipe, the black pottery bowl in the form of an antelope, the stem of wood and ivory inlaid with abalone.

21.25in (54cm) long

$600-1,000   **BAR**

A B C D E F G H I J K L M N O P Q R S T U V W XYZ

DUNHILL LIGHTERS

- Alfred Dunhill opened his first shop in 1907 in Duke St., London and retailed lighters from the 1920s. These lighters are amongst the most desirable and collectible today, with many fetching the highest prices.

- Their popular proprietary lighters were developed by Willey Greenwood and Frederick Wise. They patented a new design in 1919 that placed the flint horizontally and allowed the lighter to be triggered with one hand. Dunhill built a prototype using a mustard can that directly led to their new lighter, the 'Unique', which was released in 1922-1923.

- The Unique came in many different sizes and designs, including the tiny 'bijou' and novelty designs including a desk ruler lighter.

- Precious metal lighters are very desirable as are those with 'maki-e' lacquered decoration. The most desirable and valuable versions include extra or concealed features such as a lady's compact or, more commonly, a watch.

- Some wear is expected as these lighters were used, with entirely mint examples being extremely scarce. Dents, splits and missing or non-original replaced parts will devalue a piece. Prices have risen steeply in recently years for top quality pieces in fine condition.

A late 1940s French Dunhill Salaam manual petrol pocket lighter, with lacquer-over-aluminium decoration.

Thanks to the aluminum case, this lighter is very light in weight. The Salaam was introduced in 1946.

2.25in (5.5cm) high

$200-250   **RBL**

A Swiss Dunhill Unique Sport manual petrol pocket lighter, brass and leather with lift-arm.

Early Unique lighters have a single wheel for the user to trigger the lighter, after 1932 they consistently have two – a wheel for the user to turn which is below the wheel that strikes.

1926   *2.25in (5.5cm) high*

$250-300   **RBL**

A 1940s English Dunhill Unique manual petrol table lighter, silver-plated and shagreen decoration with lift-arm.

3.75in (9.5cm) high

$450-500   **RBL**

A Swiss Dunhill Unique manual petrol pocket lighter, silver with lift arm and engine-turned decoration.

c1926   *2.25in (5.5cm) high*

$650-750   **RBL**

A 1940s French silver Dunhill Handy manual petrol pocket lighter.

Earlier versions of this model were called the Savory.

2in (5cm) high

$200-250   **RBL**

A 1940s Dunhill Squareboy manual petrol pocket lighter, silver-plated with engine-turned decoration.

The Squareboy was introduced by Dunhill in 1937.

1.5in (4cm) high

$100-150   **RBL**

A CLOSER LOOK AT A DUNHILL LIGHTER

Parts can often be replaced. Check for consistent markings such as a serial number.

The integral watch first appeared as a special commission for a wealthy South American in 1926 and went into production in 1927.

The body is made from solid silver, gold versions are also known. Larger table sizes, some with eight day inset watches were also made.

The Sports' model with raised flame guard was introduced in 1926. It protected the flame from wind when used outside.

A Swiss Dunhill Unique Sports manual petrol pocket watch lighter, silver with lift-arm.

1927   *2.25in (5.5cm) high*

$3,000-4,000   **RBL**

FIND OUT MORE...

The Dunhill Museum, 48 Jermyn Street, London, SW1Y 6DL, England. www.dunhill.com

A late 1920s Swiss Dunhill Unique Club manual desk lighter, silver-plated, with single wheel.

5.5in (14cm) high

$300-400 | **RBL**

A 1930s French Parker manual petrol pocket lighter, silver-plated with ribbed decoration and lift-arm.

Parker was a sub-brand of Dunhill, founded in 1923.

2in (5cm) high

$100-150 | **RBL**

A 1930s German Everest manual petrol pocket lighter, silver with engine-turned decoration.

These lighters were imported into the UK marked with other manufacturers' names.

1.75in (4.5cm) high

$150-200 | **RBL**

A 1940s French Dupont Jeroboam manual petrol table lighter, silver-plated with engine-turned decoration, lift-arm and pipe wand.

3.75in (9.5cm) high

$700-900 | **RBL**

OTHER LIGHTERS

- Cigarette lighters began to be developed as the cigarette grew in popularity at the beginning of the 20th century. The field of lighter collecting has developed in the past five to ten years and is now supported globally. As the field has widened, more collectors and further research has led to a growing interest and higher prices.

- Collectors should look for innovative design, precious materials and notable names such as Dunhill, Ronson, Zippo, Thorens and Colibri as well as those by well-known jewelers such as Van Cleef & Arpels and Cartier.

- Although modern and generally similar in form and materials, Zippo lighters (founded 1933) are hotly collected, with a multitude of patterns and decoration available to the collector at comparatively inexpensive prices.

- Most collectable lighters used fluid or 'petrol' with gas being introduced and superseding fluid in the 1950s. There are three main categories – smaller pocket lighters, larger table or desk lighters and finally lighters that are part of something, such as a ladys' compact. Novelty shapes such as airplanes and figures are popular.

- Trench Art lighters are commonly found. They were made by civilians and soldiers during the World Wars from materials they found, such as bullet shells and coins. They are generally of comparatively low value but due to the variety on offer make a superb collection.

- Lighters are devalued by bad wear to plating, damage to lacquered decoration, missing or non-original replaced parts.

A Swiss Thorens manual petrol pocket lighter, chrome-plated Christmas edition given to German soldiers.

Thorens (founded in 1883) were based in Sainte-Croix, Switzerland and were well known for their production of fine quality musical boxes. Production of lighters began during the First World War and continued until c1964.

1944 | *2in (5cm) high*

$100-150 | **RBL**

A 1960s chrome-plated advertising Zippo manual petrol pocket lighter.

2.25in (5.5cm) high

$45-55 | **RBL**

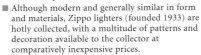

A late 1940s Polish Duplex or Tandem manual petrol pocket lighter, aluminum with two gas tanks.

2in (5cm) high

$100-150 | **RBL**

An early 1930s Austrian Princess advertising semi-automatic petrol pocket lighter, chrome-plated with removable fuel tank.

2.25in (5.5cm) high

$35-45 | **RBL**

A 1930s Swiss Pall Mall manual petrol pocket lighter, gold-plated and simulated snake skin, the flint wheel with horizontal striking surface.

2.25in (5.5cm) high

$200-250 | **RBL**

A no-name 1940s simple manual petrol pocket lighter, chrome-plated the lift-arm with cigar-cutter.

2in (5cm) high

$250-300 RBL

A 1940s French no-name manual petrol pocket lighter, with celluloid wrap and lift-arm.

1.75in (4.5cm) high

$35-45 RBL

A 1940s German no-name manual petrol pocket lighter, with mother-of-pearl wrap and lift-arm, marked "Foreign".

1.75in (4.5cm) high

$70-90 RBL

A 1930s American Pollak ladies' manual petrol pocket lighter, chrome-plated with lift-arm, rouge and compact.

2in (5cm) high

$450-550 RBL

A late 1940s Ronson Banker automatic petrol pocket lighter, 14ct gold with engine-turned decoration.

2.25in (5.5cm) high

$350-450 RBL

A 1930s American Ronson Standard automatic petrol pocket lighter, with wind shield, leather wrap and monogram shield.

2in (5cm) high

$200-250 RBL

A 1940s French Atomy manual petrol pocket lighter, aluminium with interesting fuel and flint access system.

2in (5cm) high

$100-150 RBL

A 1940s German Myflan Strato semi-automatic petrol pocket lighter, nickel-plated.

2.75in (7cm) high

$70-90 RBL

A 1930s ladies' semi-automatic petrol pocket lighter, chrome-plated, unknown maker, probably German.

1.75in (4.5cm) wide

$70-90 RBL

A WWII hand-made Trench manual petrol pocket lighter, the body formed from two penny.

2in (5cm) high

$100-150 RBL

An artisan's netsuke miniature tinder pistol, in the form of a walnut, decorated with silver and copper on brass with florettes on a hammered surface.

The flint produces a spark which ignites charred silk floss in the base, creating a flame.

c1880　　　　　　*1.75in (4.5cm) high*

$2,200-2,800 RBL

A WWII Trench miniature manual petrol pocket lighter, with engraved initials.

1.5in (4cm) high

$35-45 RBL

An early 1960s Zippo Coca-Cola advertising manual petrol pocket lighter, with lanyard, mint and boxed.

2.25in (5.5cm) high

$450-550 RBL

A French Sarhon "spinner" manual petrol pocket lighter, with clockwork mechanism and niello-style and engraved decoration.

c1880 *2in (5cm) high*

$350-450 RBL

A French Cito bijoux manual petrol pocket lighter, probably 1920s, silver, with special mechanism.

2.75in (7cm) high

$200-300 RBL

An Austrian TCW Pretty manual petrol pocket lighter, chrome-plated in fitted leather case.

c1920 *2.25in (5.5cm) high*

$100-150 RBL

A Carlton Ware 'Rouge Royale' table lighter.

8.5in (22cm) long

$70-100 OACC

Six late 1950s to mid-1990s loss-proof Zippo manual petrol pocket lighters, all mint and boxed.

'Loss Proof' Zippo lighters have small loops or 'lanyards' that can be attached to objects or a belt to prevent loss.

2.25in (5.5cm) high

$700-900 RBL

A 1930s American Ronson automatic petrol table lighter.

The standard model, without feet, is worth about $5.

4.25in (7cm) high

$250-350 RBL

A Dorset Light Industries petrol table lighter, Bakelite with electronic ignition, special Coronation edition.

1953 *4.5in (11.5cm) high*

$120-180 RBL

A 1930s Thorens bar fuel dispenser, nickle-plated.

5.75in (14.5cm) high

$120-180 RBL

An American Ronson Beauticase combination cigarette case and automatic petrol lighter, chrome-plated with lacquer decoration.

c1930 *4.5in (11.5cm) high*

$200-300 RBL

An early 1920s Austrian Juwel silver semi-automatic petrol ring lighter.

These ring pocket lighters were also made in brass, which is more common.

Face 0.75in (2cm) high

$1,000-1,500 RBL

FIND OUT MORE...

Stefano Bisconcini, 'Lighters', Edizioni San Gottardo, 1984.

A.M.W. van Weert, 'The Legend of the Lighter', published by Abbeville Press, 1995.

Ira Pilossof & Stuart Schneider, 'Handbook of Lighters', published by Schiffer Publishing, 1999.

National Lighter Museum, 107 South 2nd Street, Guthrie, OK 73044.

A
B
C
D
E
F
G
H
I
J
K
L
M
N
O
P
Q
R
S
T
U
V
W
XYZ

A Scottish ivory and silver-mounted table snuffbox.

c1770   3.25in (8cm) long

$500-800   **MB**

A George III tortoiseshell and silver snuffbox.

c1780   13.25in (8.5cm) wide

$300-500   **MB**

A yo-yo snuffbox, in partridge wood.

c1790   *3.5in (9cm) diam*

$100-150   **MB**

SNUFFBOXES

- Snuff-taking became popular at the French court during the late 1500s, spreading and becoming generally fashionable by the late 1600s, but did not spread to Britain until the early 1700s. Snuffboxes tend to be hinged, rather than having lift-off lids.

- Snuff was originally made by grating tightly rolled blocks of tobacco leaves with a snuff rasp or grater. Use of rasps ended by the mid 1700s with the proliferation of ready-ground snuff.

- The Scots continued taking snuff into the late 19th century, long after the habit had become less fashionable elsewhere in Europe.

- Enamelled copper snuffboxes were mass-produced in Staffordshire and Birmingham, England, during the late 18th and early 19th centuries. These snuffboxes are highly decorative, with brightly colored, transfer-printed scenes.

- Thanks to new mechanical die-stamping and rolled silver sheet techniques, silver snuffboxes from the early to mid-19th century could be mass-produced to meet demand. Such Victorian examples are more flamboyantly engraved and decorated than simpler and plainer 18th century boxes.

- Silver boxes by the maker Nathaniel Mills are highly sought after and will usually command a premium over similar boxes by other makers.

- Silver boxes with lids showing cast scenes such as battle scenes or castles are particularly desirable. Cast pieces are heavier than die-stamped examples, which use a thinner grade of silver sheet.

- Collectors should look carefully for damage to hinges and splits or dents which will affect value. Beware of lids that do not fit tightly and of worn engraved decoration that lacks precision.

A late 18thC French tortoiseshell snuffbox, the hinged cover inset a miniature painting of a young couple in landscape under glass and with gold banding and initials to tablet "JP to JR".

3.5in (8.5cm) long

$300-400   **BAR**

A late 18thC octagonal snuffbox, in silver-mounted mother-of-pearl, engraved with flower borders and dotted lines.

3.25in (6cm) wide

$180-220   **BAR**

A late 18thC English oval enamel snuffbox, the cover polychrome-painted with a stag hunt, the front with a bear and back with stag on a white ground.

2.25in (6cm) wide

$400-600   **BAR**

A brass one dial puzzle snuffbox.

c1880   2.75in (7cm) long

$150-200   **MB**

A papier-mâché circular snuffbox, the cover painted with a view titled "Lindau am Bodensee" in red inside and incised indistinctly "...1833, Brunsvig".

1833   3.5in (9cm) diam

$600-1,000   **BAR**

A mid-19thC Austro Hungarian tortoiseshell snuffbox, with silver mounts and massed flowers thumbpiece, 13 lothige, maker's mark "F.V.".

3in (7.5cm) diam

$350-400   **BAR**

A Victorian silver snuffbox, of serpentine outline, engraved acanthus scrolls and presentation inscription, Birmingham hallmarks for Nathaniel Mills.

1846 3in (7.5cm) wide

$400-500 **L&T**

A mid-19thC circular papier-mâché snuffbox, the cover printed and painted, showing an itinerant violinist with daughter, cracking.

3.25in (8.5cm) diam

$220-280 **BAR**

An English, black papier-mâché rectangular snuffbox, the hinged cover with a printed and painted scene of three card players.

3.5in (8.5cm) wide

$220-280 **BAR**

A 19thC Bavarian wood snuffbox, carved as a hound's head, with glass eyes and open mouth displaying its bone teeth, painted tongue, and hinged fox mask cover.

4.25in (11cm) long

$700-1,000 **BonS**

A tortoiseshell banjo snuffbox, inlaid with mother-of-pearl with ivory pegs.

c1870 4in (10cm) long

$300-400 **RdeR**

A late 17thC Netherlandish ivory snuff rasp, carved as a figure of a man with full wig wearing long robes with arms together, worn features, cracked, lacking iron rasp.

The Redfern Collection, no.32.

7in (18cm) long

$2,200-2,800 **BAR**

A 19thC Scottish rootwood snuff mull, of asymmetric form, the hinged split lid also with applied root.

8.5in (22cm) long

$1,500-2,000 **L&T**

A 19thC Scottish burr-boxwood snuff mull, of carved asymmetric form, the corresponding lid with chased brass hinge.

2.75in (7cm) long

$350-400 **L&T**

An 18thC French ivory snuff rasp, well-carved with a classical maiden in diaphanous robes holding a tablet and resting on a pillar, with fruit and leaves above and shell terminal, chipped to one side, lacking iron rasp.

From the Redfern Collection, no.28.

7.25in (18.5cm) long

$2,500-3,000 **BAR**

An 18thC French ivory snuff rasp, carved with a woman representing Summer with sickle and cornucopia between scrolls, a crowned coat of arms and shell above, with iron rasp.

7.5in (19.5cm) long

$3,000-4,000 **BAR**

A B C D E F G H I J K L M N O P Q R S T U V W XYZ

A silver Mappin & Webb cigarette box, on four plain feet, cedar-lined with engine-turned decoration, in original Garrards cardboard box, Birmingham or London hallmarks.

1947

$150-200   **BAR**

A Victorian silver cigar box, with two compartments with lift-up lids, two cigar cutters and a lighter, London hallmark.

1893   *10.25in (26cm) wide*

$3,000-4,000   **Tag**

An enameled cigarette case, painted with the head of a black horse.

3.25in (8.5cm) high

$800-1,200   **Tag**

A Victorian lacquer cigar box.

5in (13cm) long

$65-75   **OACC**

An early 20thC pietra dura and ebonised wood matchbox with striker, probably Florentine.

2in (5cm) wide

$45-55   **MHC**

A decorated Handel tobacco jar, with a hunting dog on point in a field, the reverse with lightly painted Bavarian pipe, the silver-plated lid with pipe mounted on top, plated top shows pitting and loss of plating, some wear.

7in (18cm) high

$800-1,200   **JDJ**

A late 19thC walnut table top smoker's companion, with central two-handled jar with domed cover, apertures for ten pipes with match holder, striker and ashtray on a circular base.

9.5in (24cm) high

$200-300   **Clv**

An Australian WWII commemorative ashtray.

6.25in (16cm) wide

$100-150   **OACC**

A 1930s clown ashtray, unmarked.

$500-600   **BAC**

A novelty dog ashtray.

3.5in (8.5cm) high

$40-60   **RH**

A tobacco cutter, NY State, butternut board, cutting blade has whirling decorative center, used to cut tobacco plugs for smoking / chewing.

c1830   *19in (48.5cm) long*

$1,000-1,500   **RAA**

A kitsch clockwork cigarette dispenser, with devil's feet and angel finial, Italian with Swiss mechanism.

13.5in (34cm) high

$350-450   **V**

SPACE MEMORABILIA

- Space memorabilia has become increasingly popular over the past 10 years. A realization of the historical importance of these items twinned with increased visibility and availability at auctions has led to growing interest and thus rapidly rising values.

- Space memorabilia can be divided into categories: items carried to the moon; items carried in space; items used by astronauts in training; items used in training but not flown; space agency documents; astronauts' autographs; and commemorative items.

- Although lunar and space used items, such as clothing, fetch high prices, the vast majority of items are affordable. Collections of non-unique items such as autographs, small pieces of craft, training items, associated documents and commemorative pieces can be bought comparatively inexpensively.

- Condition is important, but as much was stored (often improperly) by ex-employees, wear is common. Many items are unique, so rarity takes precedence over condition.

- Russian pieces are more common than American pieces as Russian cosmonauts were allowed to take pieces home after flights, whilst American astronauts were only allowed limited 'souvenirs'. Collectors are usually unfamiliar with Russian programmes and language so it can be difficult to tell how a piece relates to a mission. American memorabilia is therefore more valuable, particularly as the Americans landed on the moon.

An extremely rare flown two-piece white Beta cloth flight suit, worn by Command Module pilot Dick Gordon, onboard the Command Module "Yankee Clipper", with correct NASA and Apollo XII tags and badges.

This important suit was worn by Gordon onboard the orbiting Command Module for over 10 days whilst in earth and lunar orbits. The seams contain moon dust that was picked up from contact with Gordon's crew members (Charles Conrad and Alan Bean) after their mission on the moon's surface. Provenance: Ex Dick Gordon Collection.

$100,000-150,000   **AGI**

A tan cloth communications flight cap, by David Clark Co., worn by Robert Overmyer, with openings for a pair of earphones and an open-ended pocket with three snaps across the top, together with a white cloth cap designed to be worn under a hard flight helmet.

$180-220   **AGI**

A blue flight coverall, worn by Dick Gordon during the Gemini Program training, with "R. F. Gordon / M.S.C. N.A.S.A." nametag and NASA meatball patch on the chest.

$5,000-6,000   **AGI**

A flown component threaded screw, recovered from the Liberty Bell 7 from a depth of 16,043 feet on July 20, 1999.

'The Kansas Cosmosphere', sponsors of the recovery and restoration of the capsule from the sea, encased certain parts that could not be reinstalled due to corrosion, in Lucite blocks and sold them as fundraisers to help offset costs of restoration and exhibition of the spacecraft.

$400-500   **AGI**

A flown piece of shuttle tile, encased in clear Lucite block, with descriptive sheet enclosed.

$400-500   **AGI**

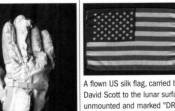

A training/prototype white Beta cloth right-handed glove, for Gordon Cooper, with red wrist ring, battery pack and light on one finger, interior ID label "Glove, Space Suit; NASA designation GC-4C-10; Mfg. David Clark Company, Inc.; P/N A-1715D Serial No. 410-A; Size Cooper August 1965."

$1,800-2,200   **AGI**

A flown US silk flag, carried by David Scott to the lunar surface, unmounted and marked "DRS Aug 71" in blue ink in the lower right hand corner.

6in (15cm) wide

$4,000-4,500   **AGI**

A flown Russian silk flag, carried by STS-105 crew member Vladimir Dezhurov to the International Space Station.

6in (15cm) wide

$400-500   **AGI**

A presentation plaque, given to George R. Faenza upon his retirement from McDonnell Douglas at KSC in 1996, reading "This piece of Orbiter Columbia (OV-102) Thermal Protection System (TPS) tile has successfully flown all twenty Columbia missions, including the first STS-1 on 12 April 1981. The tile was removed after the LMS STS-78 mission, launched 20 June 1996", together with a piece of "Multilayer Insulation (MLI)" that was successfully flown on four Spacelab Module missions, including the Spacelab-MIR rendezvous docking mission (STS-71, the 100th United States Manned Space Flight".

$400-500 AGI

Two Challenger Shuttle tiles.
6in (15cm) wide

$300-400 AGI

A flown parachute line cutter, from the Space Shuttle.

This was flown as part of the Shuttle's solid rocket booster assembly. When the boosters are jettisoned from the shuttle, at T+2 minutes and 7 seconds, they drop from an altitude of about 30 miles into the Atlantic for recovery. Their descent is controlled by a series of parachutes. This device is part of the system. At specified time delays, the cutters use an explosive charge applied to a metal guillotine blade to sever the main chute's reefing lines, allowing the chutes to inflate to their second reefed and then full open positions. A "Clarkson" photo certificate of authenticity for this unit is included.

$70-100 AGI

SKIN FROM APOLLO 11 SPACECRAFT "COLUMBIA"

A piece of flown gold foil, mounted on a green "Slezak" certificate of authenticity that reads: "This is to certify that the attached material was part of the outer reflective skin of the Apollo spacecraft CM-107, that carried astronauts Armstrong, Aldrin and Collins on their historic flight to the moon, 16-21 July 1969".

$300-400 AGI

A flown Soyuz mission clock, No. 653b/1081 from the main control panel, in wooden carry case and with instruction manual indicating the unit was flown, but not which flight.

$600-700 AGI

A flown titanium film canister, with Federal Scientific-Research and Industrial Center "Priroda" certificate of authenticity and with a colour back-up film "Kodak-Rallfilm-120-EPR", numbered "6".

The film was used for interior photo shoots aboard the space crafts during the mutual experimental "Apollo-Soyuz" flight as part of the "EPAS" program. The shoot was carried out using a Hasselblad camera by the crew of the space craft "Soyuz-19" with cosmonauts A. Leonov and V. Kubasov between July 15 and 21 1975.

$200-300 AGI

REMOVE BEFORE FLIGHT

A red "Remove Before Flight" tag.

This tag is used to ensure that key connectors are not pulled prior to launch and as a safety check to ensure that those that should be disconnected prior to launch are pulled.

$30-40 AGI

A flown mission summary card, signed by Rominger, Ashby, Parazynski, Phillips, Hadfield, Guidoni and Lonchakov and annotated by Lonchakov "Flown on STS-100 to ISS".

$250-300 AGI

Two similar food cubes, each wrapped in rice paper, and designed to have been eaten by the astronauts without having to be unwrapped.

$180-220 AGI

A flown miniature lunar rover license plate, carried by David Scott aboard the first manned lunar rover vehicle during the entire exploration of the Hadley-Apennine from July 30 to August 2, 1971.

$15,000-20,000 AGI

A NASA publicity photo of Neil Armstrong, wearing his white spacesuit, uninscribed.

10in (25.5cm) high

$800-1,000   **AGI**

Four NASA publicity photos of Fred Haise, wearing his white spacesuit, each signed by Haise.

10in (5.5cm) high

$80-100 (set)   **AGI**

A NASA publicity photograph of Vladimir N. Dezhurov, wearing his orange NASA spacesuit, signed.

10in (25.5cm) high

$40-50   **AGI**

An NASA publicity photo of James McDivitt and Ed White, signed by both.

10in (25.5cm) high

$70-80   **AGI**

A NASA publicity photo of John Young, wearing his Gemini spacesuit as taken during training, signed.

Informal signed photos such as this are scarce today.

10in (25.5cm) high

$600-700   **AGI**

A publicity photo, signed by Shepard, Krikalev and Gidzenko, plus back-up crew Bowersox, Dezhurov and Tyurin.

10in (25.5cm) high

$450-550   **AGI**

A set of 15 NASA publicity photos and lithographs.

$180-220   **AGI**

A NASA publicity lithograph, signed by Neil Armstrong and Buzz Aldrin, trimmed.

3.5in (9cm) high

$550-650   **AGI**

A McDonnell Douglas photo, taken in space and signed by James Lovell and Buzz Aldrin, together with a NASA montage lithograph inscribed and signed by Buzz.

$250-350   **AGI**

A colour lithograph of the International Space Station, signed by Shepard, Gidzenko and Krikalev.

$80-100   **AGI**

A NASA lithograph of the first seven Mercury astronauts, signed by Scott Carpenter, Gordon Cooper, John Glenn, Virgil Grissom, Wally Schirra, Deke Slayton and Alan Shepard.

10in (25.5cm) wide

$6,000-7,000   **AGI**

A WonderWorks replica Apollo capsule, used as back-up model to that used in the movie "Apollo 13", with highly detailed interior.

$15,000-20,000 AGI

A full-scale WonderWorks Mercury capsule replica, used in the movies "Rocket's Red Glare" (2000) and "Race to Space" (2002), with highly detailed interior.

$10,000-15,000 AGI

Worden, Alfred M., "Hello Earth – Greetings from Endeavor", first edition signed on the front page by the author.

Al Worden was the pilot during the 67 hours his fellow astronauts Scott and Irwin were on the Moon. He was in complete solitude, floating in space. The overwhelming experience of being completely alone in the universe gave him a profound feeling of rejuvenation. That experience changed his life.

1974

$100-150 AGI

A Robbins silver commemorative medallion, no. 91.

This mission patch commemorates the third Space Shuttle flight supporting the assembly of the ISS. The flights' primary tasks are to outfit the ISS, extend its lifetime and to conduct a spacewalk to install external components in preparation for docking of the Russian Service Module "Zvezda" and the arrival of the first ISS crew. The Space Shuttle is depicted on the medallion in an orbit configuration prior to docking with the ISS. Only 114 silver medallions were produced for this mission, of which 24 were flown and 90 were not. This medallion was not flown. A Weinberger certificate of authenticity is included.

2in (5cm) wide

$300-400 AGI

Space Shuttle Mission 51-L

Press Kit   January 1986

A Challenger STS-51L press kit, dated January 1986, detailing general information, mission statements, timetables and diagrams of the ill-fated Space Shuttle, together with a biography and training history of teacher astronaut Christa McAuliffe and others and a certificate of authenticity.

$250-300 AGI

Mission Cards
STS-81 SHUTTLE/MIR DOCKING 5   **81**

Eight unopened sets of Mission Space trading cards, comprising STS-81 to -87, and STS-94.

3.25in 98.5cm) high

$100-150 AGI

A Wonderworks replica Saturn V launch vehicle rocket, configured for the Apollo 11 launch and includes the engines, piping, Apollo capsule, escape tower, graphics and paint.

144in (366cm) high

$20,000-25,000 AGI

A silver "Snoopy" lapel pin, wearing a space helmet and space suit, together with a photo of Fred Haise presenting the pin to Ossie Reid, with original issue plastic box.

1in (2.25cm) high

$400-500 AGI

An Apollo 16 earth orbit chart, displaying the proposed earth orbit, revolution 2.

41.5in (105.5cm) high

$100-150 AGI

A John Glenn Orbit Globe, showing the three orbits made by MA-6.

8in (20cm) high

$100-150 AGI

A presentation brass ashtray, with 12 raised images around the edges, a cloisonné inset in the center with the inscription "For your contribution to the First Manned Lunar Landing, 1969, NASA-MSC".

5.75in (14.5cm) diam

$180-220 AGI

BASEBALL CARDS

■ Baseball card collecting finds its origins in the 19th century with tobacco companies producing trading cards, depicting athletes and celebrity entertainers, with an aim of selling more cigarettes. They had plain reverses and the personalities were often identified by second names only.

■ In 1933, the Goudey Gum Company copied the idea and began to use cards with the hope of selling more gum. They featured famous baseball players such as Babe Ruth and Lou Gehrig and were aimed primarily at children.

■ By 1951, many other companies had adopted cards, such as Bowman Gum and Topps Chewing Gum. In 1956, Topps acquired Bowman and became the largest sports card maker in the world.

■ It was primarily children who collected and swapped these cards during the 1950s and 1960s, but by the 1970s, adults began collecting too. This caused a leap in values, as scarce and desirable cards were traded by people with disposable incomes.

■ 'Centering' on a baseball card is a vital aspect to collecting. The printed image should be surrounded by as even amounts of white space as possible – these cards will be most desirable. Backs can also differ, for example as with the Ty Cobb card shown here.

■ Condition will affect value, with creases, abrasions, folds and other wear and tear affecting value detrimentally.

■ Counterfeit cards, although illegal, are often seen. These are usually printed on thicker or thinner card than authentic cards and the image is often blurred.

■ Errors and low print runs will often create a valuable card if the market for the player exists. An example is the legendary 1909-1911 Honus Wagner card, of which only a few hundred examples exist. Many theories exist for this; from demands for large sums of money from the tobacco company by Wagner, or the fact that Wagner disliked smoking and refused to be associated with it.

A Williams Caramel E103 Ty Cobb card, key card to the set, a few light creases.

1910

$1,000-1,500 HA

A T-206 Ty Cobb, red portrait version, even corner wear and creasing, 'Piedmont' back.

1909-11

$300-400 HA

A T-206 Ty Cobb card, red portrait version is well centered with some light surface wear, 'Polar Bear' back.

1909-11

$500-600 HA

A Play Ball Joe DiMaggio #26 card, in near original condition, four sharp corners and remains well centered, back equally clean.

1939

$1,400-1,600 HA

A T-206 Christy Mathewson card, portrait variation, retains strong color with three fairly sharp corners and one slightly dinged corner, 'Piedmont' back has a stain at bottom left, top edge also has small area of wear.

1909-11

$220-280 HA

A Dan Dee Mickey Mantle card, vertical crease on right side.

1954

$350-450 HA

A T-206 Bill O'Hara card, rare St. Louis variation, some creasing while retaining strong color, 'Polar Bear' back.

1909-11

$520-580 HA

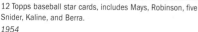

12 Topps baseball star cards, includes Mays, Robinson, five Snider, Kaline, and Berra.

1954

$300-400 HA

A set of 52 Topps Red Backs baseball cards, including Spahn, Hodges, Berra, and Rizzuto, set also includes four unopened wax packs and four single cards.

1951

$700-800   HA

A set of Topps baseball cards, missing 25, 31 (Spahn), 40, 80, 139, 157, 155 (Mathews), 164 (Clemente), 189 (Rizzuto), 195, and 198 (Berra).

1955

$1,000-1,500   HA

A lot of 1957 and 1958 Topps baseball star cards, includes 22 1957 Topps such as Berra, Aaron, Snider, three Dodgers Sluggers, two Campanella, and two Reese, and five 1958 Topps with Aaron, yellow letters, two Mays, B. Robinson, and Snider.

1957/1958

$350-450   HA

A set of Topps baseball cards, missing 97, 100, 175, 270, 271, 290, 293, 300, 302, 307, 309, 312, 323, 328, 335, 327, 339, 343, 352, 368, 407 for completion.

1957

$1,800-2,200   HA

A set of 48 Bowman baseball cards, in very good to excellent condition.

1948

$1,500-2,000   HA

A partial Topps baseball card set, missing 69 cards for completion, balance of set has mixture of cards in good condition.

1958

$600-700   HA

A complete set of 494 Topps baseball cards.

1958

$1,600-2,000   HA

A set of Topps baseball cards, strong set with numerous high grade stars, missing cards 310, 350, 356, and 455 for completion.

1969

$1,500-2,000   HA

A partial set of 208 Bowman baseball cards, majority in excellent to mint condition.

1950

$1,800-2,200   HA

A partial set of 242 Bowman baseball cards, majority in very good condition, includes letter of authenticity from James Spence PSA/DNA regarding Williams autographed card.

1951

$2,000-2,500   HA

FIND OUT MORE...

Thomas Owens, 'Collecting Baseball Cards: 21st Century Edition', published by Millbrook Pr Trade, 2001.

Robert F. Lemke & Dwight Chapman, '2002 Standard Edition of Baseball Cards, 11th Edition', published by Krause Publications, 2001.

A complete set of Fleer Ted Williams baseball cards, with the exception of rare card #68.

1959

$850-950   HA

Eight T-206 Hall of Fame members portrait cards, including Beckley, Marquard, Collins, Chesbro, Waddell, Huggins, Walsh, and Griffith, all but one have 'Piedmont' backs.

1909-11

$550-650   HA

A complete set of Fleer baseball cards, superb example complete except for checklist card, mostly new mint cards.

1963

$3,000-3,500   HA

A rare Ron Davis Houston Astros home jersey, flannel shirt with #22 on back and original Astrodome patch on sleeve, includes letter of authenticity.
1968

$1,200-1,800   **HA**

A rare Bob Cerv Kansas City Athletics home jersey, flannel shirt with #33 on back, elephant patch on sleeve, light wear, includes letter of authenticity.
1959

$1,800-2,200   **HA**

BASEBALL UNIFORMS

▪ Before the early 1970s, baseball uniforms were made from flannel. They were not collected at this period. By around 1973, every major league team had switched from flannel to polyester.

▪ When polyester became fashionable in the 1970s these sleeker, more modern uniforms attracted more attention, and collecting began.

▪ By the early 1980s, polyester uniforms had become standard and more widely collected. Collectors soon began to appreciate the heritage in the older flannel uniforms.

▪ Uniform collectors should beware, as many samples for uniforms made for big league teams were sold at events and games, often leading to people considering these uniforms as being 'game worn'. Furthermore, the manufacturer 'Scoreboard', made replicas of players' shirts which were then signed by the players, under licence. Even though they were termed 'game jerseys', they are not to be confused with game worn jerseys.

▪ Over the past 15 years, the major league teams have often sold their entire stocks of uniforms to retailers and dealers, so it is now much easier to obtain an authenticated game-worn uniform, if you are prepared to pay the asking price. In 2001, Major League baseball announced a deal whereby they would market and sell team uniforms, adding further weight to authenticity.

A Bob Chipman Boston Braves home uniform, flannel jersey, Indian head patch on sleeve, original #17 remains on back, Horace Partridge tag in collar, with pair of matching pants, includes letter of authenticity.
1950

$2,000-3,000   **HA**

A rare Gabby Street St. Louis Browns home jersey, flannel button-down pullover-style jersey, with #31 on back, Rawlings tag and size tag remains in collar with some wear to piping on neck and a small hole repair on front, shows light to moderate general wear retaining original patch on sleeve, faint signature of Ray Coleman on tail added later, scarce one year style from popular manager of defunct team, includes letter of authenticity.
1938

$3,000-4,000   **HA**

A Gene Hermanski Brooklyn Dodgers home jersey, flannel shirt with #22 on reverse, retains collar tag, name chain-stitched on tail, includes letter of authenticity.
1950

$2,200-2,800   **HA**

A Larry Stahl New York Mets home jersey, worn in 1967, with numbers on front and back, logo patch on sleeve, includes letter of authenticity.
1967

$3,000-4,000   **HA**

A Ron Northey St. Louis Cardinals home uniform, flannel shirt with #5 on back, matching pants.
1948

$1,500-2,000   **HA**

A 1950s Brooklyn Dodgers souvenir T-shirt, child's size shirt with color player graphic.

$120-180   **HA**

A Jackie Brandt Philadelphia Phillies home jersey, flannel shirt retaining original embroidered team name on front and #20 on reverse, name and year tag chain-stitched in collar, includes letter of authenticity.
1967

$2,200-2,800   **HA**

A
B
C
D
E
F
G
H
I
J
K
L
M
N
O
P
Q
R
S
T
U
V
W
XYZ

A rare Seattle Pilots home jersey, flannel shirt, missing MLB 100th Anniversary patch on sleeve, includes letter of authenticity.
1969

$3,500-4,000 HA

A Richie Hebner Pittsburgh Pirates home jersey, vest-style flannel shirt with original lettering and #20 on front and back, includes letter of authenticity.
1970

$850-950 HA

A significant Chicago White Sox mascot uniform, worn by E.J. Silvers, retains original "Mascot Brand, Chicago" tag in collar, "SOX" breast patch on the front and applique U.S. flag affixed to sleeve, matching hat, includes letter of authenticity.
c1917

$5,500-6,500 HA

A California Angels professional model hat, blue hat with red bill and lowercase "a" on front with halo, retains original Pro KM label and stamping inside headband, shows minimal usage wear, includes letter of authenticity.
1971

$40-50 HA

A rare Houston Colt 45s professional model hat, retains original tag and cap stamp on interior headband, "W" written under bill, letter of authenticity.
1962-64

$450-550 HA

A 1950s Brooklyn Dodgers hat, royal blue with embroidered white "B" on front, retains rectangular "Tim McAuliffe Inc., by Leslie" tag on interior leather band.

$450-550 HA

A Montreal Expos professional model hat, unused, retains original cap label and stamping on interior headband, includes letter of authenticity.
1970s

$50-60 HA

A Baltimore Orioles professional model hat, retains Wilson tag on interior band and signed under brim by player, includes letter of authenticity.
1960-70s

$200-250 HA

A rare Seattle Pilots professional model hat, issued to Fred Talbot or Jack Aker, original tag on interior headband, "23" written under bill, letter of authenticity.
1969

$550-650 HA

A Boston Braves professional model hat, original "B" on front, interior headband retains Wilson label, with letter of authenticity.
c1950

$220-280 HA

A rare Spalding Ambidextrous fielder's glove, with red label on backstrap and original webbing between fingers intact, interior shows moderate usage wear.
c1900

$3,500-4,500 HA

A set of vintage baseball catcher's equipment, including a Peerless Bill Dickey model glove.
1890-1930

$500-600 HA

A Ted Williams store model baseball glove, with autograph inside, retaining majority of its original silvering, large adult size, owner's name on back strap.
12in (30.5cm) wide

$80-120 HA

FIND OUT MORE...

Marc Okkonen, 'Baseball Uniforms of the 20th Century – the Official Major League Baseball Guide', published by Sterling Publishing Co., 1993.

Mark Stang & Linda Harkness, 'Baseball By The Numbers, A Guide to the Uniform Numbers of Major League Teams', published by Scarecrow Press, 1997.

A Chub Feeney NL size 9 ball, boxed, box missing panel at top.

$25-35 HA

A D & M Youth League baseball, near white condition with black markings, with Lucky Dog Logo on panel above sweet spot, red and white box complete.

$80-120 HA

A Mickey Cochrane and Bill Dickey autographed baseball, signed in black ink on side panel by the two premier catchers of their era, includes letter of authenticity.

$600-700 HA

A large sized 19thC Lemon Peel ball, constructed crudely of heavy leather and large lacing, weight about the same as a regular baseball, classic four panel style.

3in (7.54cm) diam

$350-450 HA

A Brooklyn Dodgers team autographed baseball, rare early team ball one year removed from the NL Championship, official NL ball, signed by 25 players including a rare manager W. Robinson, Wheat, Myers, Grimes, and Taylor, includes letter of authenticity.

1921

$500-600 HA

Two 19thC baseballs, a regular-sized brown leather ball with very tight small stitches, and a typical lemon peel-size ball which appears to be hand-stitched.

$100-150 HA

A Barry Bonds single signed ball, blue ink sweetspot signature on a Selig ball features the Bonds Hologram and a PSA/DNA letter.

$100-150 HA

A 1930s Babe Ruth Home Run Special baseball, clean ball with crisp original stampings on sweet spot, opposite sweet spot has very faded Babe Ruth 'clubhouse' signature, box features image of Ruth on one side and ball on opposite end, missing portion of top.

$1,000-1,500 HA

A 1940s Hall of Fame induction autographed baseball, signed by 22 players including Ruth, Speaker, Mack, Grove and Ott, includes letter of authenticity.

$3,500-4,500 HA

A Charles O. Finley orange baseball, unused.

$60-80 HA

A Ty Cobb signed ball, in original cellophane.

1928

$900-1,000 HA

Four views of a Babe Ruth and Lou Gehrig autographed Spalding Official NL baseball, off-white ball signed in blue ink by Babe Ruth and Lou Gehrig.

1927

$25,000-28,000 HA

A Pittsburgh Pirates team autographed baseball, signed by 22 players including Clemente, Stragell, Mazeroski, and Virdon, includes letter of authenticity.

$550-650 HA

A mini Spalding baseball, marked "National Association Professional BB Leagues" with the Reach logo above the sweet spot and Spalding logo below.

$70-100 HA

A Joe Torre professional Adirondack model 302 baseball bat, with "94A" stamped on knob end with #15 written in black, shows good usage wear with crack at handle and heavy pine tar, includes letter of authenticity.

1961-67   *35in (89cm) long*

$550-650   HA

A Bill Salkeld game-used L. Slugger 125 baseball bat, autographed by members of the 1948 Braves NL Championship team, with Salkeld's autograph stamped on barrel, knob has some chipping otherwise bat is fairly clean, signed on barrel by eight team members including Spahn, Sain, Dark, and Stanky, includes letter of authenticity. for bat and autographs.

1948   *35in (89cm) long*

$250-350   HA

A folk art display baseball bat, two-toned sectional bat-style display shows light overall wear with wood graining and surface.

1940s   *32in (81cm) high*

$55-65   HA

A Dizzy Dean autographed "Yale" baseball bat, made by The Moneco Co. New Haven, CT, signed on barrel "Dizzy Dean", very clean with original blond finish, includes letter of authenticity .

                                            29in (73.5cm) long

$120-180   HA

A Giants Model No. G100 baseball bat, with script team name of Giants stamped at center of bat, "Special" stamped on barrel end, with slight fissure on handle and small area of deadwood at back of barrel.

1915-20   *35in (89cm) long*

$350-450   HA

A vintage Washington Senators signed H.G. Spalding & Bros. No. 36 baseball bat, bearing the signatures of 21 1924 World Championship team members and President Calvin Coolidge, all signatures in bold ink and entirely legible, noteable signatures include Walter Johnson, Bucky Harris, Sam Rice, Roger Peckinpaugh and Calvin Coolidge.

1924

$12,000-17,000   SI

A Babe Ruth signed and game-used baseball bat, Louisville Slugger model 125JFS Special Jimmie Foxx, with foil-stamped markings and handle crack and period black tape, includes letter of authenticity regarding signature and notarized letter of provenance regarding bat from the vendor's son detailing the history.

The black tape, according to family history, was placed on the bat by Ruth before he presented it to Morton Gillman who was the 16-year-old batboy for the Gems. After the game Gillman and Fred Silliman, the boy who caught the home-run ball, had Babe autograph their respective treasures, the photo captures this moment. The bat markings are clearly visible in the photo adding a "fingerprint" to the authentication of the piece. The bat was used for many years after by Gillman's son so the signature has faded. This historical object was obtained at an exhibition game played in Hartford, CT at Bulkeley Stadium, the teams were the Savitt Gems, a semi-pro team owned by Connecticut jeweler Bill Savitt, and a traveling exhibition team for which Ruth was playing. During the course of the game, as retold by former Hartford Times sports reporter Harold Ogden, Babe Ruth hit several home runs, one of which cracked the offered bat.

c1943   *Bat 34in (86cm) long*

$3,500-4,500   HA

BASEBALL BATS

There are four types of bat that are collected:

1. Game-used bats, with or without cracks caused by use. These will show wear and tear caused by use in a game. Larger cracks devalue a bat. These bats are made to the players specifications and carry his signature, name or the team's name branded onto it. Always buy these from a reputable source as game-type wear can easily be added.

2. Bats made to a player's specifications, but that were not used during the game. These were often made for promotional purposes and are often used for autographing.

3. Store bats that are bought in sports' stores. They may not be made to a player's specifications but may carry his name as an endorsement. Pre 1950s examples are popular, but they are not to be confused with the first two types of bat. They usually bear numbers and letters relating to the named player's initials and the model number. Knobs also bear inch markings.

4. Commemorative bats are produced from time to time to celebrate an event such as the entry of a player into the Hall of Fame. Collectors often get these signed by the associated player, which increases their value.

A Willie Mays professional Adirondack model 302 bat, with "M63" stamped on knob end, crack on handle and good usage wear and ball marks, stampings clearly legible with some wear to inking on player name stamp, includes letter of authenticity and letter of provenance.

1961-67   *35in (89cm) long*

$2,500-3,500   **HA**

A Frank Robinson coaches L. Slugger model 125 bat, with autograph stamped on barrel end with "Mc 44" above name, bat shows good usage wear with some abrasions to brown surface, uncracked, includes letter of authenticity.

1977-79   *34in (86.5cm) long*

$250-350   **HA**

A Spalding "Wagon Tongue" model bat, with strong logo stampings at center, including "Model #000", paint on end of barrel remains approximately 70% intact.

1890-1910   *33in (84cm) long*

$550-650   **HA**

A Richie Allen professional L. Slugger 125 model baseball bat, with P89 stamping on knob end, shows good usage wear with ball marks and crack to handle, includes letter of authenticity.

$1,200-1,800   **HA**

An Ed Mathews professional L. Slugger model 125 baseball bat, with "S2" stamped on knob end along with "41" written in black, with heavy cracking to handle, includes a vintage Mathews single signed ball on Giles NL ball personalized to bat recipient, letter of authenticity, and letter of provenance.

1965-68   *35in (89cm) long*

$2,000-3,000   **HA**

A Muesel professional Spalding model #200 bat, double diamond stamped with "MUESEL" on barrel end, retains original finish and patina with some period nail repair around name stamping, also side written "School--11-30", includes letter of opinion regarding bat and player specifications from David Bushing.

There were two Meusel brothers in the Major Leagues; Bob and Irish. The dimensions of this bat match those known to Bob Meusel and not the two known Irish Meusel bats. Based on this the bat is attributed to New York Yankee Bob Meusel.

1926-30   *35in (89cm) long*

$500-600   **HA**

A Wally Schang professional L. Slugger 125 model baseball bat, with player autograph stamping on barrel end, pronounced thickness to barrel and handle crack, desirable Yankee player bat includes letter of authenticity.

1922-25   *34.25in (87cm) long*

$450-550   **HA**

A Jimmie Foxx mini bat, with strong gold-colored signature, wear to H. & B. logo in the center that may have been as issued.

16in (40.5cm) long

$50-70   **HA**

A Babe Ruth photograph by Paul Thompson, with Thompson stamp on back along with handwritten note, "The opposing pitcher commences to get nervous - "Babe" enroute to the plate - Batter Up", crisp overall contrast and clarity with virtually no wear.

1920s   8.5in (21.5cm) high

$6,500-7,500   HA

A Babe Ruth and Lou Gehrig photograph, with strong clarity and contrast with excellent detail, rare image of affection between the two players that often had differences on and off of the field, matted and framed with some light abrasions on back.

1927-30   9in (23cm) high

$2,000-3,000   HA

A Babe Ruth portrait photograph, by Paul Thompson, with image of Ruth smiling in front of dugout, stamped on back by Thompson with period titling notations.

1920s   8.5in (21.5cm) long

$1,800-2,200   HA

A Babe Ruth photo, of Ruth playing the bagpipes in front of a couple in Scottish Highland dress.

1938   9in (23cm) long

$20-30   HA

A Lefty O'Doul autographed photograph, image of O'Doul batting signed in black fountain pen, "To Vinnie My old pal, Best Always From Frank "Lefty" O'Doul", includes letter of authenticity.

8.5in (21.5cm) high

$350-450   HA

A Ty Cobb portrait photograph, close-up image of Cobb in typical scowl dated "June 28, 1921" on back, with some chipping to edges.

1921   10in (25.5cm) long

$420-480   HA

A Ty Cobb autographed photograph, image of Ty Cobb sliding by Charles Conlon signed in green ink, "To Vince From Ty 3/23/55", and has "T.R. Cobb 48 Spencer Ln. Menlo Park, CA" on reverse, one of only a handful of signed copies of this famous image are known to exist, includes letter of authenticity and letter of provenance.

1930-40s

$6,000-7,000   HA

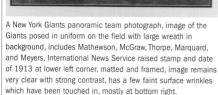

A New York Giants panoramic team photograph, image of the Giants posed in uniform on the field with large wreath in background, includes Mathewson, McGraw, Thorpe, Marquard, and Meyers, International News Service raised stamp and date of 1913 at lower left corner, matted and framed, image remains very clear with strong contrast, has a few faint surface wrinkles which have been touched in, mostly at bottom right.

1913   28in (71cm) long

$3,500-4,500   HA

A rare October 12, 1927 Bustin Babes and Larrupin Lous barnstorming team photograph, image of the famed barnstorming duo of Babe Ruth and Lou Gehrig in uniform taken in Brooklyn's Dexter Park where they played the Bushwicks, with some minor border chipping at bottom left corner and top right corner, not visible in frame, matted and framed.

1927   10in (25.5cm) long

$3,500-4,500   HA

A 1912 Boston Red Sox photo postcard, image of the World Champion Red Sox posed in uniform on the field, players identified include Speaker, Wood, Hooper, Stahl, and Lewis, unused on back.

1912

$550-650   HA

A World Series panoramic photograph, image taken at Game Seven of the Series on October 10, 1924 and clinched the title for the Senators, exceptional clarity exhibited with numerous dignitaries visible including President Coolidge, framed, marked "Schutz Studios, Washington" at lower right.

1924   46in (117cm) long

$5,000-6,000   HA

BASEBALL PENNANTS

- The first pennants appeared at stadiums around 1900, with pennants featuring teams and city names appearing around 1905-1910. It was not until 1914 that the first commemorative pennant, for the World Champion Boston Braves, appeared.
- There is little information about baseball pennants from before 1970, making them very hard to research. Some pennants dating from before 1940 had a maker's tag, but these are not usually found between 1940 and 1970.
- Early pennants were often available for many successive years and were made from scrap felt. The same design may appear on different colored materials which would have been available at different locations.
- In the 1970s, new materials meant pennants became thinner and more rigid with the addition of synthetics. 'Trench Manufacturers' and 'Wincraft' have dominated their manufacture since then. Pennants commemorating events, such as the World Series and retirements, are the easiest to find.
- Colorful, pre 1970 pennants are the most popular with collectors, but these are hard to find and date accurately. Examples with holes (where they were pinned to walls), fading from display and missing tips or tassels will be worth less than examples in better condition.

A 1950s green Brooklyn Bushwicks pennant, with full game scene graphics on left side.

24in (61cm) long

$150-200 HA

A Cincinnati Reds Pennant, full pennant features a batter at left on red felt, Cincinnati Redlegs on right.

30in (76cm) long

$35-45 HA

A red Brooklyn Dodgers pennant, with crossed bat and ball graphics.

c1944 *23in (58.5cm) long*

$180-220 HA

A full-size purple Brooklyn Dodgers pennant, with color-tinted lettering having two player graphics at left and right.

1940-1960

$250-350 HA

A 1940s blue New York Giants pennant, with crisp white lettering and game scene graphics.

$55-65 HA

A blue New York Mets pennant, features the Mr Met Family, some soiling.

29in (73.5cm) long

$50-80 HA

A rare Pittsburgh Pirates pennant, early blue and orange pennant, with applied team name lettering and skull and crossbones logo, retains original Kaufmann's Sporting Goods Department tag on back and original tassels, exhibits very little overall wear with fresh original color.

c1910 *39in (99cm) long*

$1,800-2,200 HA

A 1950s full-size navy blue Philadelphia Phillies pennant, unusual color, missing one tassle set and has loose tip.

$70-100 HA

An oversized red Boston Red Sox pennant, very clean with only three typical pinholes.

1910-15 *34in (86.5cm) long*

$1,500-2,000 HA

A 1940s-50s full-size white Washington Senators pennant, fairly clean with very light toning.

$120-180 HA

A full-size red Joe DiMaggio "Yankee Clipper" pennant, has some wear to tip.

c1950

$450-550 HA

A University of Virginia baseball hat and pennant, early small bill cap with orange "V" on front, Spalding silver stamping on interior silk liner, and wool pennant with applied lettering.

1900-1910 *30in (76cm) long*

$650-750 HA

An All-Star Game Houston Astrodome pennant, red, white, and blue with yellow trim featuring the Astrodome on the right side.

1968 *29in (73.5cm) long*

$45-55 HA

A rare full-size 1969 New York Yankees Old Timers Day pennant, with four inset photos of Yankee greats Ruth, Gehrig, DiMaggio, and Mantle along with Yankee stadium graphic, front has some fading, otherwise remains in fairly clean condition.

1969

$180-220 HA

A large St Louis Cardinals team photo pin, probably sold at the World Series against the Red Sox, retains original easel back.
1967   *6in (15cm) diam*

$40-50   **HA**

A 1949 Brooklyn Dodgers World Series press pin.
1949

$280-320   **HA**

A Philadelphia Phillies Pm10 pin, National League Champs.
1950

$10-20   **HA**

A 1946 Boston Red Sox World's Champions pin, red and white pin.
                1.5in (4cm) diam

$50-60   **HA**

A rare 1944 Detroit Tigers Phantom World Series press pin, red, white and blue enameled pin with inset tiger head.
1944

$450-550   **HA**

A Jackie Robinson Rookie of the Year pin, featuring a young Jackie Robinson after his groundbreaking season.
1947   *1.75in (4.5cm) diam*

$220-280   **HA**

A Little Pinkies the Ball Player pinback, unusual character holding a ring bat, very reminiscent of a young Yellow Kid.
1896   *1in (25.5cm) diam*

$40-50   **HA**

A 1943 New York Yankees World Series sterling silver press pin, with ball and bat decor.

$600-700   **HA**

An Orlando Cepeda Pm10 pin.
        1.75in (4.5cm) diam

$30-40   **HA**

A Don Newcombe Pm10 pin, with ribbon.
        1.75in (4.5cm) diam

$20-30   **HA**

A GoGo Chicago White Sox "Beat The Dodgers" pin.
1959   *3in (7.5cm) diam*

$20-30   **HA**

A Philadelphia Whiz Kids Pm10 pin, National League Champs.
1950

$30-40   **HA**

A Philadelphia Athletics souvenir pottery plate, has some age toning and two small rim chips along with a light hairline crack.
1911

$600-700   **HA**

A rare New York Giants souvenir plate, with two light hairline fissures on left side.
1889   *8.5in (21.5cm) diam*

$900-1,000   **HA**

A Staffordshire "alphabet" plate, titled "Base Ball Pitcher", with some age toning and a rim chip.
1860s   *8in (20.5cm) diam*

$180-220   **HA**

A rare baseball decorated porcelain tobacco jar, marked "M&Z Austria" on base, tiny interior rim flake under inside base rim.
1890-1900 *6in (15cm) high*

$1,700-2,000   **HA**

An early Staffordshire china children's mug, color-transfer decorated scene titled "Trap Bat & Ball" with three children playing a baseball-style game.

1860s   3in (7.5cm) high

$300-400   HA

A rare "Roogie's Bump" Brooklyn Dodgers movie poster, full color lithograph, has typical fold lines with some small tears at two center joints, framed.

1954   9in (23cm) high

$120-180   HA

A 1940s Wheaties baseball advertising poster, with large illustration of batter superimposed over several game action scenes.

21in (54cm) high

$250-350   HA

A 1960s Los Angeles Dodgers Cooper Tires advertising poster, with five Dodger players endorsing Cooper Tires, has some wear to far left edge at bottom.

22in (56cm) high

$50-60   HA

A Sport Magazine with Ted Williams cover, dated September, vivid cover with light foxing, interior clean but 1in piece missing from one page.

1951

$10-20   HA

A Baseball Stars Magazine with Ted Williams cover, has coupon clipped from back cover.

1954

$10-15   HA

A Life Magazine wtih Brooklyn Dodger Jackie Robinson cover.

Despite its age and the famous player on the front cover, the value is comparatively low. Time had a huge distribution because it was a general news magazine, rather than a specialist title, meaning a great many copies could have survived.

1950

$25-35   HA

A Philadelphia Phillies vs Chicago Cubs program, interior scored in pencil, some light general wear including a few border chips on cover.

1905

$220-280   HA

A rare Montreal Royals program, with Jackie Robinson cover, 18 pages, issued for game played between Montreal and Louisville featuring a centerfold team photo of Montreal with Robinson, a few pencil notations.

1946

$150-250   HA

A rare 1882 Philadelphia vs Chicago scorecard, clean fold-out card with handsome lithographic cover picturing Recreation Park and inset game scene, printed line-ups inside include Anson, Willamson, and Ferguson.

$720-780   HA

A Spalding's Base Ball Guide, contains great photos and reference material.

1910

$70-100   HA

A pair of original baseball charcoal illustrations of New York Giant and Brooklyn Dodger players each drawing matted and framed and signed by artist Vincent Bova.

c1916   26in (66cm) high

$720-780   HA

A color lithographic baseball silk, modeled after Nap Lajoie batting, dated and marked "Bernhard Ulmann & Co., N" at bottom left, very clean with vibrant color and very minor toning in a few areas and possibly slightly short on left edge, laid down on board for stability.

c1906   22in (56cm) high

$1,500-2,000   HA

A Babe Ruth painting, oil on board, and is titled at bottom "Babe Ruth 1932" and signed by artist "Chas. D. Wiliam 1942", with original uncleaned and unrestored surface, remains in original gilt frame.

c1942   *17in (43cm) high*

$320-380   **HA**

A rare green base Washington Senators blackfaced boy nodder, a tiny flake touch up under hat bill and two minute touch-ins on top of hat, small chip on hand with bat and some wear to team name on base.

1962-64

$750-850   **HA**

A green base Philadelphia Phillies boy nodder, a couple of small paint flecks and no hairlines.

$60-80   **HA**

A gold base Detroit Tigers mascot nodder, some overall wear including a few chips.
1967-69

$30-40   **HA**

A "Darktown Battery" baseball mechanical bank, with original paint and patina mainly intact, players parts all original including rare intact bat, interior base spring replaced and period replaced coin trap, manufactured by J.E. Stevens Co.
1888

$2,500-3,500   **HA**

A 1930s Bat-A-Ball baseball coin-operated game, in working order and retaining painted metal sign on top.

$1,200-1,800   **HA**

A pair of bronze Arts and Crafts style baseball-decorated bookends, stamped "Bronze" with foundry number on back.
1910-15   *6in (15cm) high*

$600-800   **HA**

A rare baseball figural napkin ring, by Pairpoint, New York featuring 19thC style player with bat and pillow glove atop textured base.
1890s

$1,500-2,000   **HA**

A 1940s Exacta Time Co. Babe Ruth wristwatch, with metal band and featuring color image of Ruth on face, in original ball-shaped plastic case with Ruth signature on exterior.

$900-1,000   **HA**

A rare Philadelphia Phillies white leather tobacco premium, featuring photos of the 1915 NL Champion Phillies.
1915   *39in (99cm) long*

$2,500-3,500   **HA**

A 1930s wooden-cased Play Ball baseball coin-operated game, on original cast metal stand, featuring painted backboard and ping-pong style balls, game in working order.

$600-700   **HA**

A vintage baseball announcer's microphone, used by "Rosie" Rosewall to call games for the Pittsburgh Pirates at Forbes Field, marked "Hudinco" on front of microphone.

16in (40.5cm) high

$1,800-2,200   **HA**

A B-18 baseball tobacco blanket pillowcase, featuring 22 B-18 baseball blankets including Cobb, Maranville, Wheat, and Covaleski surrounding a large U.S flag.
1914   *30in (76cm) long*

$250-350   **HA**

AMERICAN FOOTBALL

- American football developed in the United States from a hybrid of Association Football and rugby. The first professional football game took place in Latrobe, Pennsylvania in 1895.

- Over the next ten years, more professional teams were founded, including the Duquesnes of Pittsburgh, Pennsylvania, the Olympics of McKeesport, Pennsylvania and the Bulldogs of Canton, Ohio.

- For the first three decades of the 20th century, American Football did not become popular and attracted only minimal public interest, failing to capture the popular imagination.

- The American Professional Football Association, changed its name in 1922 to the National Football League (NFL).

- It was Harold 'Red' Grange's exciting play for the Chicago Bears after 1925 that began to draw crowds and thus the game became increasingly popular.

- The globally renowned 'Super Bowl' saw its origins in 1967 when the champions of the American Football League (AFL) and the National Football League met at the AFL-NFL Championship Game. In this game, the Green Bay Packers beat the Kansas City Chiefs 35-10 at the Los Angeles Coliseum. Shortly afterwards, the game was renamed the 'Super Bowl' after a child's toy.

- Memorabilia from American Football runs a close second to baseball. The earliest pieces usually date from around 1900. As with baseball and other high profile sports, attention focuses on important players and major events. The main collecting areas are autographs, photographs, kit and historical items that show the development of the sport.

- Football trading cards have been printed since the 1890s, but it was not until Goudey released the first football card in 1933 in gum packets that it really took hold. Although not as expensive or as widely collected as baseball cards, some cards attract extremely high values.

A green base Toes Up nodder, several hairlines and wear to the NFL decal.

$120-180   **HA**

A burgundy base Washington Redskins nodder, head clean, body and base have some small chips.

$70-100   **HA**

A blue base Los Angeles Rams nodder, appears as new with some slight touch-ups on edge of base, head has no chips or cracks.

$30-50   **HA**

A purple base Minnesota Vikings nodder, displays as near mint but has a tight hairline on the reverse of the head.

$75-85   **HA**

A gold base Washington Redskins nodder, decorative shelf piece with damage to back of head and a few other hairlines.

$55-65   **HA**

A gold base Washington Redskins nodder, yellow helmet nodder has a few small chips and a couple of hairlines.

$120-180   **HA**

A 1930s painted bisque football figurine, marked "Japan" under foot, with nicely detailed helmet and ball.

1930s   *5in (13cm) high*

$400-500   **HA**

A collection of 28 National Chicle football cards, includes two Strong #7, Battles #10, and Feathers #23.

1935

$1,500-2,000   **HA**

A collection of 64 large Bowman football cards, includes two Gifford, two P. Brown, Graham, two Tittle, two Baugh, and a Van Brocklin.

1952

$1,700-2,000   HA

A collection of 25 Joe Namath football cards, including two 1966 Topps #96, one 1967 Topps #98, one 1968 Topps #65, two 1968 Topps Stand-ups #17, four 1969 Topps, including one autographed, #100, one 1970 Topps #150, three 1971 Topps #250, four 1972 Topps #100, one 1971 Topps Game #3, two 1973 Topps #400, three 1970 Topps Super Glossy #29, and 1972 Fabric Card #26, includes letter of authenticity from James Spence PSA/DNA regarding Namath autographed card.

1966-1973

$220-280   HA

A "Football - A Collision at the Ropes" engraving, Frederic Remington, depicting a game between two teams wearing union suits and stocking caps, blank backed, framed in reverse-painted glass matting and molded edge frame.

c1890   22in (56cm) long

$350-450   HA

A football team cabinet photograph, mounted image of team in full union suits including one African American player with dated ball in front row, gilt stamping on mount from Notman Photo Co. in Boston, some wear to corners of mount.

1892   16in (40.5cm) long

$450-550   HA

An early football photo button, depicting a player in a lace-up uniform with reeded football pants, clear image surrounded by green and yellow floral-patterned border.

8in (20.5cm)

$140-180   HA

A rare 1930s "Red" Grange large format photographic display piece, of Grange in uniform throwing a ball, name painted in white at bottom of image, has a few minor tears at base and small edge stain on right side, period pencil notation on back, "A.G. Spalding Bros." along with address.

22in (56cm) long

$2,800-3,200   HA

A late 20thC decorative football tinted glass panel, with football player etching in center surrounded by frosted glass and intaglio decor.

37in (94cm) long

$70-100   HA

An early "The Foot Ball Game" board game, by Parker Bros., featuring attractive Yale vs Princeton color lithograph illustration, includes color lithograph playing board and box bottom, missing box top and bottom aprons, spinner, and ball.

1900

$1,800-2,200   HA

An Arts and Crafts-style football themed ink blotter with game scene which was intended to be Harvard and Yale with period notation taken from Teddy Roosevelt, dated, small tack hole at the top.

1909

$40-50   HA

A "Big Time Football Game" by Richard Veazey, New Orleans, color lithograph cover with three football scenes, interior has color lithograph board and wooden die and chalk, lid aprons have some minor wear and lid top has light water stain, color remains very strong.

1934

$450-550   HA

A decorative wooden block football puzzle, featuring color lithograph label on lid of young football player, puzzle blocks form several different puzzles.

c1900

$450-550 HA

A Munsing football union suit cardboard advertising sign, die-cut sign depicting players running with melon-style ball, with repaired tear to neck.

c1900 13in (33cm) high

$600-700 HA

A D. & M. football cardboard advertising sign, crisp unused color easel-back sign depicting football player kicking D. & M. model J5V football, with minimal overall wear and original color.

1920s 19in (48.5cm) long

$600-700 HA

A pair of Wilson football die-cut cardboard advertising signs, colorful easel-back signs picturing game scenes in each with Wilson equipment, with minor general wear.

1930-40s 20in (51cm) high

$1,000-1,500 HA

An Army vs Navy football program, played at Soldier Field in Chicago, 144 pages, features full page pictures of captains, colorful cover has wear and pictures President Coolidge in the top left corner.

1926

$150-200 HA

Warner, Glenn "Pop", "Football for Coaches and Players", double autographed "Yours Truly Glenn S. Warner" on interior cover page and again, "Yours Truly Glenn Warner 'Pop'" under his photo on title page, some typical light wear, includes letter of authenticity.

$220-280 HA

Zuppke, Robert, "Football Technique and Tactics", by famous University of Illinois coach Robert Zuppke, signed on interior title page under his photo, some typical age wear, includes letter of authenticity.

1924

$200-300 HA

Two vintage football related pennants, includes 1944 Philadelphia Eagles pennant with players' names and Eagle graphic and 1940s Chicago Cardinals pennant.

$500-600 HA

A rare Spalding Army and Navy model football, includes box with Spalding end label containing uninflated Spalding ball.

1915-25

$500-600 HA

An assortment of 1960s-70s felt sports pennants, 1960s New York Jets, Washington Redskins, California Angels and Washington Senators and 1970s Washington Redskins, Green Bay Packers, Baltimore Orioles and 1970 Baltimore Orioles "World Champions", some with tabs, some with pin holes, most creased.

$50-60 SI

A large Goldsmith leather football helmet, with slightly elongated ear pads stamped with Goldsmith logo on back, missing chin strap.

1915-25

$300-400 HA

A rare pair of Winchester Sporting Goods football shoulder pads, adult size pads with leather trim.

$1,500-2,000 HA

A Reach leather football helmet, with unusual pointed style front, stamped Reach on front and logo on top, missing chin strap and has some typical age/usage wear.

1915-25

$250-350 HA

A Philadelphia Eagles team autographed Sonnett model AFB football, includes letter of authenticity.

1963

$800-900 HA

A C. Hunter putter, the head stamped.

$1,500-2,000 | **L&T**

A T. Morris putter, the head stamped.

$2,200-2,800 | **L&T**

A T. Morris Juvenile putter, head stamped.

$1,500-2,000 | **L&T**

A Schnectady putter, with patent "March 24 1903".

$250-300 | **L&T**

A Slazenger 'Emperor' gooseneck putter, the face insert with brass plate and five screws.

$1,000-1,500 | **L&T**

A putter, the shaft stamped "R.R. Wilson, St. Andrews", patent "1000".

$1,800-2,000 | **L&T**

A Roller golf club, the back of the head stamped "M.N.7", the shaft stamped "Moodie".

$1,000-1,500 | **L&T**

A Mills brassie spoon, with patent "142038".

$400-500 | **L&T**

An R. Simpson short spoon, with three additional lead weights to sole, indistinctly stamped.

$1,500-2,000 | **L&T**

A presentation golf club, with silver blade and fittings and leather wrapped shaft, engraved "Putting Competition", London hallmarks.

1895   *36in (91.5cm) long*

$2,000-3,000 | **Tag**

An Osmond's patent "The Automaton Caddie", the canvas pencil bag and conforming ball and tee pouch with brass mounted wood frame and leather strap handles.

$1,200-1,800 | **L&T**

Two "Special Argus" Bramble rubber core balls, both unused with added owners' early identification numbers.

$350-450 | **MM**

A framed copper plaque, relief-decorated with a scene of Charles I on Leith Links receiving news of the Irish Rebellion, with floral outer border and ebonized frame.

9.75in (25cm) wide

$300-400 L&T

A half-plate glass negative, depicting an unidentified golfing scene as two golfers on a links course, one playing a fairway shot, a caddie looking on.

c1870   8.5in (21.5cm) wide

$1,000-1,500 L&T

A half-plate glass negative, believed to depict members of the Bruntsfield links Golfing Society, Edinburgh.

c1890   8.5in (21.5cm)

$550-650 L&T

A half-plate glass negative, depicting a studio portrait of the renowned Musselburgh caddie John Carey (known as Fiery), standing against a white cloth and holding a bag of clubs under his left arm, inscribed to the upper border, "Photo of 'Fiery' for J.F. McClymont, Sandwick Pl.48, 24/8/98".

c1898   8.25in (21cm) high

$1,800-2,200 L&T

A half-plate glass negative, depicting an unidentified golf scene, one golfer holing out at the 11th and ladies looking on.

c1900   8.5in (21.5cm) wide

$600-700 L&T

A half-plate glass negative, depicting a double portrait of Harry Vardon and James Braid at Murrayfield Golf Club, Edinburgh.

$2,200-2,800 MM

A half plate glass negative of Harry Vardon and James Braid in competition, Vardon teeing off, the border inscribed "Murrayfield".

8.5in (21.5cm)

$1,200-1,500 L&T

A Staffordshire baluster tobacco jar and cover, decorated with a cartoon golfing scene and golfing trophies, the reverse with a humorous eight line verse.

5in (12.5cm) diam

$280-320 BG

A Royal Doulton biscuit barrel, with swing handle, the circular white metal lid surmounted by a mesh gutty ball, the circular tapering body with a scene of golfers with mountains behind.

6in (15cm) high

$1,200-1,800 L&T

A Lenox pottery tyg, hand-painted by W. Clayton with a wraparound scene of a lady golfer putting, watched by her caddy with the clubhouse in the background.

7in (18cm) high

$15,000-20,000 L&T

A glass tankard, with hinged pewter lid and hand-enameled decoration of a lady golfer at the top of her swing.

7.5in (20cm) high

$600-700 L&T

A figural golf trophy, with multi-sport decor and three-handle footed cup, the lid with figural golfer hitting a ball, the base painted metal with an engraved silver plate band featuring various sports scenes, trophy winners engraved on side from 1929-1935, replaced golf club.

22in (55.5cm) high

$400-500 HA

An impressive golfing medal, with a thistle and oak leaves emblem and crossed long nosed club behind, enclosed in a wired ribbon band above a pennant, bears the motto "never up, never in", for Edinburgh Burgess Golfing Society, instituted 1735, the center with crossed clubs and three balls amidst thistles, the back engraved "won by Mr John Cruickshank with 52 strokes", Edinburgh, makers mark "J. B", cased.

c1873   *3in (8cm) high*

$4,500-5,500 L&T

A golfing prize medal, cast to the obverse with a scene of a golfer in the follow-through, with traces of gilding, made by Walker & Hall and inscribed "XVIth Golf Club", and another, the obverse cast with a scene of golfers and caddies, one figure in the foreground at the top of his swing, the obverse with a vacant scroll and a figure emblematic of victory, made by J. & F. Anderson, Birmingham, cased.

c1905   *3in (7.5cm) diam*

$400-500 L&T

An Honorary Life Membership Gold Card, presented to Robert Tyre Jones Jnr. by the Board of Directors, Detroit Golf Club for distinguished service, William G. Burton Secretary, William A. Sells President, Sept 22 1941.

c1941

$10,000-12,000 L&T

A silver and niello cigarette case, decorated in silhouette with a golfer at the top of his swing, with caddy on a fairway, possibly Japanese, stamped "950" and three characters mark to the interior.

c1930   *3.25in (8.5cm) wide*

$300-400 L&T

An early Open Championship Memorabilia Victorian snuffbox, by George Unite, with shaped sides, cast scroll thumb piece, gilt interior, the oval cartouche to the cover engraved in various Victorian scripts "A gift to W. (Willie) Park on his achievement on winning the championship at the Prestwick Golf Club, presented by his friends and colleagues as a testimony of their esteem, 1867", Birmingham.

4in (10cm) wide

$7,500-8,500 BG

A white metal cigarette case, chased and engraved, with a wraparound scene of a golfer teeing off, with attendant caddy, the gilt interior with clip, reverse engraved with cursive initials "INS", stamped "Sterling-B9".

3in (8cm) wide

$150-200 L&T

A glass humidor, with white metal lid depicting a Victorian golfer at the top of his swing.

6.75in (17cm) high

$400-500 L&T

A glass decanter and two matching glasses, overlaid with sterling silver bands depicting golfers.

Tallest 12.25in (31cm)

$750-850 L&T

A pair of silver-plated "golfing" candle sticks, with three golf clubs forming the stem and a golf ball in the middle.

7in (18cm) high

$800-1,000 Tag

A Scottish silver and enamel Trushot "golfing" shoe horn, in the shape of a golf club.

7in (17.75cm) long

$1,200-1,500 Tag

A propelling pencil, in the form of a golf club.

$100-150 LFA

A pair of bronze bookends, depicting a golf player and golf caddy, the golfer in plus fours, his diminutive caddy in similar attire, on marble bases.

Tallest 9.5in (24cm) high

$600-700 L&T

A painted plaster Dunlop advertising figure, depicting the familiar golf ball headed man, in golfing attire and carrying a bag of clubs on a naturalistic shaped square base, inscribed twice "We Play Dunlop".

16in (40.5cm) high

$450-550 L&T

A Golf Calendar by Edward Penfield, with twelve calendar months to ten pages, published by R.H. Russell.

c1900

$5,500-6,000 L&T

A brass golf inkwell, with crossed clubs in front of a ball.

c1900

$300-400 PC

A small silver-mounted pottery vesta holder, modelled as a gutty ball, marked "Chester 1894"

$280-320 L&T

FIND OUT MORE...

The British Golf Museum, Bruce Embankment, St Andrews, Fife, Scotland. www.britishgolfmuseum.co.uk

The Heritage of Golf, West Links Road, Gullane Golf Club, East Lothian, Scotland. The private collection of Archie Baird, a long time avid collector.

James River Country Club Museum, 1500 Country Club Road, Newport News, Virginia, 23606, USA. www.ouimet.org. Founded in 1932 by Archer M. Huntington a keen golf collector who never actually played, this claims to be the first golf museum in the world.

Ouimet Museum, The Golf House, 190 Park Road, Weston, Massachusetts, USA. Frances Ouimet rose from being a caddie to make golfing history, winning against champions Harry Vardon and Ted Ray in 1913. He went on to win the US Amateur twice. His life is now celebrated in this museum and also by a caddie scholarship fund.

An Edward Vom Hofe "The Van Vleck Tarpon Trolling Hook", hook stamped to shank "Van Vleck" and "E. Vom Hofe N.Y.", together with original linked chain and wire trace and in maker's paper packaging printed with hook and Vom Hofe address details.

$100-150 MM

A fine Wadham's "The X-Ray" celluloid live May fly box, transparent celluloid with corrugated and highly perforated side and pivoted circular lid, the top with solid rim forming a trap to keep live insects inside and twin locking catches, lid stamped "Dreadnought Casting Reel Co. Ltd., Newport, I.W.".

1920s   3in (7.5cm) diam

$1,000-1,500 MM

A 1930s Hardy "The Fisherman's" rustless steel gauge, the combined hook/gut gauge stamped "Chesterman, Sheffield, England" and Hardy Bros. Ltd. and details, the steel plates with finely engineered tapering slot for measuring gut size and line thickness, stamped with salmon hook gauge and inch scale to one side and with fine scale in one thousands of an inch to the other.

4in (10cm) long

$400-600 MM

A scarce Allcock's "The Otter" wading net, with iron knuckle joint, brass tube ferrule to either end, oval bentwood frame, brass belt clip and whole cane handle, brass butt cap stamped with maker's bordered oval logo.

c1915

$300-350 MM

A Hardy The No. 2 "Alma" rustless swivel, the larger of the two sizes made at the request of Mr H. White-Wickham to lift a deadweight of 750lbs, made from "Sildur" non-corrosive metal and nickel silver, together with the smaller No. 1 size "Alma" Swivel, both stamped "Hardy's England".

c1935

$120-180 MM

A spool of 1930s Hardy "Atlas" flax line, the black-painted softwood spool with black-on-white circular trade label "Hardy's 'Atlas' Square Plaited Flax Line No. 4, 100yd", with line and in a Hardy card box.

3in (7.5cm) diam

$100-150 MM

An unusual combination priest and knife, the tapering alloy priest with weighted head and integrally cast ridge, threaded to screw onto handle section, this with knife that fits into hollow priest head, together with an unnamed alloy priest of tapering form with brass head and a Hardy the "Driflydresser", this lacking felt and amadou pads.

First 8in (20.5cm) long

$300-350 MM

A leather bound reedwork creel, probably American, sides and lid woven into traditional corrugated patterning, with hole in lid for putting in the trout, leather bound rims with attractive strap work decoration, lacks carry strap.

15in (38cm) wide

$450-550 MM

An Allcock's No.34 trade catalog, large 8vo.

1937

$100-150 MM

A DAM catalog No.25, with illustrations in both color and black and white.

c1954

$120-180 MM

A C. Farlow & Co. Ltd. fishing tackle catalog, 75th edition.

c1916

$220-280 MM

A Wadham's catalog, spine detached, cover rubbed, tears.

1920

$250-300　　　　MM

A 1930s anonymous fishing tackle catalog, 90 pages featuring Allcock's tackle and entitled "Illustrated Price List of High-Class Fishing Rods and Tackle".

$200-250　　　　MM

Buller, Fred, "Pike", first edition, Macdonald, 4to, photos, dust wrapper.

1971

$300-400　　　　MM

A Hardy Angler's Guide, 39th edition.

1912

$550-650　　　　MM

Martin J.W. (The Trent Otter), "My Fishing Days and Fishing Ways", first edition, W. Brendon & Son Limited, photos, green cloth with gilt spine, signed copy.

1906

$650-750　　　　MM

Wheat, Peter, "The Fighting Barbel", first edition, Ernest Ben Limited, illustrations, photos, dust wrapper, signed.

1967

$270-330　　　　MM

A pair of perch by J. Cooper & Sons, mounted in a setting of reeds and grasses against a turquoise background in a gilt-lined bow front case with gold on black plaquette reading "Perch. Caught by S.F. Maybrick, Warminster, July 14th 1934" and with J. Cooper & Sons label to case interior, restorations.

Case 27.75in (70.5cm) wide

$1,000-1,500　　　　MM

A fine perch by F.W. Anstiss, the fish mounted in a setting of reeds and grasses against a blue background in a rare gilt-lined wrap-around case with gilt inscription "Perch 21/2lbs. Caught by Mr H. Webb in the Avon. March 21st 1918" and with F.W. Anstiss label to case interior.

Case 18.5in (47cm) wide

$3,000-4,000　　　　MM

A fine pike attributed to W.F. Homer, mounted in a setting of reeds and grasses against a typical reed painted green background in a gilt-lined bow front case with gilt inscription "The Fenton & District Angling Society. Pike 10lbs. Caught by Mr J. Wilkes. Jany. 1928.

Case 38.75in (98.5cm) wide

$1,500-2,000　　　　MM

A fine carved pike by Brian Mills, the half-block fish with scale and fin ray detail and stained wood backboard to match the pike's distinctive markings, mounted against a stained weed backboard and set within a frame, inscribed "Pike. 15 lbs. Hand carved by" and signed "B.W. Mills".

42.5in (108cm) wide

$400-600 **MM**

A fine and very rare Jack pike in a picture frame case attributed to J. Cooper & Sons, the fish mounted to graduated green background with ivorine label "4lbs 8oz. Length 24ins. Caught by John P. Ashcroft. 30.8.53".

Backboard 30in (76cm) wide

$6,000-10,000 **MM**

An exceptionally fine Fochabers Studio carved wooden salmon, the half block fish naturalistically painted and with characteristic finely carved fin detail, mounted to oak backboard with the lure that caught the fish and painted with details "44lbs. Killed by Barbara Williams in the Wye, Aramstone, 17th April 1930, on a 2" wood minnow. Length 48" Girth 261/2", with a facsimile of the fishing register recording details of the capture and an article appearing in the "Field" June 1930.

Backboard 56in (142cm) wide

$10,000-15,000 **MM**

A carved and painted wooden rainbow trout by Brian Mills, mounted to painted wooden backboard within frame, signed, dated Sept. '82.

17in (43cm) wide

$200-300 **MM**

R.A. Johnson "Common Carp", 20thC, signed, oil on board.

24in (61cm)

$500-700 **MM**

R.A. Johnson "Mirror Carp", 20thC, signed, oil on board.

24in (61cm) wide

$500-700 **MM**

Esther Blaikie Mackinnon, 'The Young Fisherman', signed, oil on canvas.

$3,500-4,500 **L&T**

John Russell, British 1820-1893, "A Day's Catch", oil on canvas.

36in (91.5cm) wide

$1,500-2,000 **MM**

English School, 20thC, "Loch Katrina", still life of salmon, trout and fishing tackle in a highland landscape, oil on board.

12.25in (31cm) wide

$500-700 **MM**

A mid-19thC Dutch tile, a blue-on-white glazed earthenware tile, depicting two anglers.

$100-150 **MM**

A Royal Doulton Isaac Walton ware series plate, the central reserve with two 17thC gentlemen anglers, within tree-decorated rim and with verse, signed "Noke" printed factory mark.

1901-38

10.75in (27.5cm) diam

$120-180 **MM**

A Staffordshire porcelain cabinet plate, with molded celadon border, the central reserve hand-painted with Gregory "Bug-eyed Stoker" lure and inscribed "Gregory (Maker) Birmingham, England c1885", signed "L. Woodhouse", in original box.

c1885 9.25in (23.5cm) diam

$150-200 **MM**

A Beswick porcelain model of a trout, impressed and printed factory marks and impressed "1032 Trout".

6.5in (12.5cm) high

$150-200 **MM**

BASKETBALL

- As with many high profile sports, basketball memorabilia is widely collected. Pieces include kit, the basketballs themselves and players' autographs.

- Like baseball, basketball has trading cards to collect although these are not as widely traded nor as highly regarded as baseball cards which have a much wider audience.

- Collectors should look for items connected to important players and key games and moments, although the value is likely to rise with the importance of the player or moment.

A Billy Cunningham Philadelphia 76ers rookie uniform, red jersey with original #32 and "PHILA" on front and back, Pearson tag and "42 65 32" applied chain-stitched tag remain inside tail, shorts are blue satin with Pearson tag inside on quilted hip pads along with size/year/number chain-stitched tag, includes letter of provenance.

Cunningham's uniforms are seldom found from any era let alone his rookie season.

1965-66

$6,000-7,000   HA

A Charles Barkely Philadelphia 76ers road uniform, complete red mesh jersey and shorts retaining all original numbers and lettering, champion tag, size tag, year tag, and 76ers tags, all remain in both jersey and shorts, faded Barkely autographed "4" on front and on shorts in black, both jersey and shorts show great usage wear, includes letter of authenticity from Global David Bushing/Dan Knoll.

1990

$1,500-2,500   HA

A Hal Greer Philadelphia 76ers road jersey, blue knit jersey with original #15 and team name on front, "Greer" and #15 on back, retains Spanjian tag on tail, very clean with light usage wear, includes letter of provenance and letter of authenticity.

1972-73

$4,000-5,000   HA

This vest was worn during Wilt 'The Stilt' Chamberlain's last season as a 76'er when he scored his 25,000th point, explaining its high value.

Chamberlain is considered one of best players in the world, and is one of only two players to score more than 30,000 points in his career.

A rare Wilt Chamberlain Philadelphia 76ers home jersey, white jersey with original "PHILA" and #13 on front, #13 on back retaining Wilson tag on tail, shows excellent usage wear with only a few light perspiration stains.

1967-68

$25,000-30,000   HA

A rare Wilt Chamberlain Philadelphia 76ers warm-up jacket, Wilson tag in collar with chain-stitched "13" on applied felt tag alongside, unrestored with some light staining, includes letter of provenance.

1967-68

$8,000-10,000   HA

A 1980s Isiah Thomas Detroit Pistons warm-up jacket, with original Pistons breast patch and #11 on tail, Wilson tag, size 42, remains in collar, shows appropriate usage wear, includes letter of authenticity.

$500-600   HA

A rare Wilt Chamberlain Philadelphia 76ers road jersey, #13 on back retaining Wilson tag on tail, no damage or staining, includes letter of provenance.

1967-68

$22,000-28,000 HA

A 1950s Syracuse Nats warm up jacket, with #5 on sleeve, attributed to Paul Seymour 1956-57, Joe Charles Co. and Coane tags remain in collar with size 44, includes letter of provenance.

$5,000-6,000 HA

Two 1960s Philadelphia 76ers warm-up shirts, each blue with zipper front and embroidered Sixers logo on breast, retain Wilson tags in collars with size 42 on each, players are unclear, includes letter of authenticity.

$850-950 HA

A Philadelphia 76ers warm-up suit, rare fleece zipper front jacket with #5 on sleeve attributed to Paul Neumann, retaining black Wilson tag in collar, and a pair of matching fleece pants with #10 who was John Kerr with Wilson tag in waist, includes letter of authenticity from Global David Bushing/Dan Knoll/Mike Baker.

1963-64

$1,500-2,000 HA

A lace-up basketball, light brown, with good form, labeled "interscholastic approved #404".

$60-80 HA

A Maurice Podoloff NBA basketball, Wilson stampings and name remain strong, autographed on side "1963 Johnny Kerr".

1949-63

$850-950 HA

A Robert S. Carlson ABA basketball, rare red, white, and blue stylish ball with bold Rawlings stampings and commemorative autograph, stamped on panel "Denver Rockets 73", shows minimal usage wear with some light toning.

c1973

$1,200-1,500 HA

A 1970s New York Knicks blue and orange logo bag.

$10-20 HA

A selection of items relating to Wilt Chamberlain's 100th point game on March 2, 1962, including March 2, 1962 "The Wigwam" program signed "Wilt Chamberlain", ticket stub, modern signed photo of Chamberlain.

1962

$18,000-22,000 HA

A 1970s Hal Greer die-cut stand up figure, particle board stand up of Hal Greer in full Sixers uniform having wooden back brace, once displayed at the stadium in Philadelphia.

58in (147.5cm) high

$220-280 HA

An unusual 1930-40s folk art-painted vanity, with basketball-themed oil painting on top featuring world map with various notations and symbols, includes large ball with "Duke R.E.D. Victory & Pyramid", some chips to door frame.

32in (81.5cm) wide

$15-20 HA

A Henry Armstrong autographed photo, full body pose of this boxing Hall of Fame member who held three World Championships at the same time, personalized in black ink, signature is strong.

10in (25.5cm) long

$150-200 HA

A Jack Dempsey signed photo, personalized in bold black ink, classic full body shot.

10in (25.5cm) long

$150-200 HA

A Benny Leonard autographed photograph, classic bust shot of this boxing great, autographed in bold black ink, personalized.

1947   10in (25.5cm) long

$700-1,000 HA

An autographed color press photograph of Cassius Clay, standing over Sony Liston, signed in felt-tip pen "Muhammed Ali aka Cassius Clay", mounted with engraved plaque, which reads "Phantom Punch", framed and glazed.

21.5in (54.5cm) high

$220-280 MM

An autographed color press action photograph of Muhammad Ali and Frazier, signed by both in silver pen, mounted with engraved plaque "The Thriller in Manila", framed and glazed.

21.5in (54.5cm) high

$270-330 MM

An autographed color press photograph of Muhammed Ali, standing over a floored Ken Norton signed by both fighters in blue felt-tip ink, engraved plaque "The Rumble in the Jungle", matching frame.

21.5in (54.5cm) high

$270-330 MM

An autographed color press photograph, signed in gold felt-tip pen by Ali, Joe Frazier, Ken Norton, George Foreman and Larry Holmes, plaque "Champions Forever", in matching frame.

$400-600 MM

An autographed display, comprising scorecard detailing each fight including World Heavyweight Championship bout between Rocky Marciano v Don Cockell, 15 rounds; black and white magazine action photograph mounted with brass plate engraved with fight details which Rocky won by T.K.O. in 9th round.

1955   21.5in (54.5cm) high

$700-1,000 MM

A signed boxing glove, mounted on mahogany based display case with engraved brass name plate "Ali, Foreman, Frazier, Norton, Lennox Lewis, Holmes, Tyson, Holyfield and Riddick Bowe".

16.5in (42cm) wide

$1,000-1,500 MM

A Joe Louis funeral service program, dated April 12, 1981.

$60-100 SI

A Joe Louis World's Heavyweight Champion pinback button, featuring Joe in classic white training tanktop.

1.25in (3cm) diam

$60-100 HA

SPORTING COLLECTIBLES

A full-size replica Grand Prix racing helmet, signed on visor in silver marker pen by Michael Schumacher, World Champion, with Ferrari, Marlboro and Asprey sponsors' logos.

$3,000-4,000 MM

A large signed color photograph of Ayrton Senna, on the winners' podium, signed in black felt-tip pen, mounted, framed and glazed.

16in (40.5cm) long

$800-1,200 MM

A signed limited edition print of Ayrton Senna, fighting off Nigel Mansel's challenge in the closing laps of the Monaco Grand Prix on 31st May 1992 where he clinched victory driving Marlboro McLaren, the border signed in pencil by Ayrton Senna and artist Alan Fearnley, No. 14/850.

$3,000-5,000 MM

Three Winter Olympic Programs in Oslo 1952, covering ice hockey, skiing and Nordic events on 5th, 6th and 11th day of the Games held during the month of February.

$70-100 MM

Four pieces of Olympic ephemera, including two tickets for 1936 Games in Berlin; 1974 Munich Games Athletic Ticket; and program for the Closing Ceremony in Helsinki 1952.

$150-200 MM

A rare late Victorian/early Edwardian table billiards game, with one original red and one white ball, plus a set of later snooker balls.

19in (48.5cm) long overall

$220-280 MM

Mannock, J.P, 'Billiards Expounded – to all Degrees of Amateur Players', two early first editions, red cloth and gilt boards, some wear and dust staining.

c1920

$70-100 MM

A scarce signed sepia photograph of national champion H.W. Payne, on his racing cycle, signed in ink "Yours sincerely H.W. Payne 1899".

$60-100 MM

A D&M hockey puck, embossed with the Lucky Dog logo, this practice puck shows use but logo remains strong.

$100-150 HA

An interesting silver-plated and enamel Albion Auto Racers winged motif, mounted on silver hallmarked plate, with three matching silver hallmarked name plates, each decorated with rose motifs including enamel red rose.

$60-100 MM

A brass sculpture of single rower, mounted on black marble base in the shape of a rowing boat, with brass plaque engraved "M.C.R.C. – Singles - 1922", possibly of U.S. origin.

$270-300 MM

A good R. Wylie Hill & Co, Glasgow boxed table tennis set, including accessory price guide and Thos. de la Rue Illustrated Retail Price List Guide.

$220-280 MM

A white metal ashtray, with two matchbox holders, one embossed with laurel wreath and monogram "GBO", and decorative sides with embossed sporting accessories including tennis, golf, cricket and croquet.

7in (18cm) diam

$150-200 MM

A
B
C
D
E
F
G
H
I
J
K
L
M
N
O
P
Q
R
S
T
U
V
W
XYZ

An Azzedine Alaïa black taffeta gored dress.
51.5in (131cm) long

$300-500 S&T

A Balenciaga two-piece red skirt and top.
35in (89cm) long

$120-180 S&T

A 1960s Balmain yellow and black silk dress.
36.5in (93cm) long

$200-250 S&T

A 1970s Liz Berg for Bernie Bee Pucci-style gown.

$80-120 S&T

BIBA

◼ Set up by Barbara Hulanicki in 1964 in Kensington, London, the Biba boutiques defined the 'Swinging London' of the 1960s and early 1970s with a softer, more romantic feel than her contemporaries. Her 'slinky' figure-flattering look was particularly successful.

◼ Offering a complete look, including bags, hats and clothing at very inexpensive prices, Biba attracted a cult following until its closure in 1975. Its clothes are now highly sought after.

A Biba vintage floral gown.
52.75in (134cm) long

$270-330 S&T

A 1960s Biba plaid dress.
54.25in (138cm) long

$100-150 S&T

A rare 1960s Pierre Cardin couture space age green and black block dress.

Like André Courrèges, Pierre Cardin is renowned for his outer space inspired designs during the 1960s.

41.25in (105cm) long

A Byblos iridescent pink rain jacket.
23.75in (60cm) long

$120-180 S&T

A 1960s futuristic dress, possibly by Cardin.
57.5in (146cm) long

$1,000-1,500 S&T

An Ossie Clark elegant black dress, in crêpe tie with satin trim.
50in (127cm) long

$400-600 S&T

$700-1,000 S&T

An Ossie Clark black crêpe dress, with green trim.

$500-800   S&T

A rare Ossie Clark three-piece strawberry trouser suit, exhibited at the Ossie Clark Retrospective.

Jacket 17.25in (44cm) long

$1,200-1,800   S&T

A 1960s Ossie Clark cream floral dress, with Birtwell print.

57in (145cm) long

$500-700   S&T

An Ossie Clark romantic black and tan chiffon top.

22.5in (57cm) long

$300-500   S&T

OSSIE CLARK

- Born Raymond Clark in 1942 in Lancashire, England, Clark first studied building and art before moving on to the Royal College of Art, London, to study fashion. His first pieces, in partnership with Alice Pollack, hinted at accentuating female curves, which was to become his hallmark later in his career.

- In 1969 he married the fabric designer Celia Birtwell whose designs for beautiful dress fabrics included Art Deco and heavy floral motifs in a range of unusual colors, such as saffron, blues, prune and antique rose. Choice of fabric was also important, with chiffons, moss crêpes and satins being common.

- Clark and Birtwell's marriage was immortalised by David Hockney in the famous painting 'Mr & Mrs Clark with Percy', now in the Tate Modern, London.

- His wife's innovative fabric designs combined perfectly with his famed cutting skills and his style completely broke away from the square cut, mini shift dresses of the period to a more sensual and sinuous shapeliness that accentuated female curves. His popularity reached its height from 1964-1976. Ossie Clark pieces with prints by Birtwell are very desirable.

- In 1964, Clark traveled to the USA and met Bette Davis, Jimi Hendrix and Andy Warhol. He was inspired by the Op Art he saw there.

- From his boutique in London called 'Quorum', he dressed Elizabeth Taylor, Twiggy, Raquel Welch and Bianca Jagger on her wedding day to Mick Jagger.

- Never a skilled businessman, he went through divorce, depression and bankruptcy in quick succession in 1981 and during the 1980s and 1990s, he struggled in vain to relaunch himself. He was murdered by a former lover in 1996.

A rare Ossie Clark Art Deco floral blouse, rust and cream.

32.5in (83cm) long

$800-1,200   S&T

An early 1970s Ossie Clark oriental-style wrap.

39.25in (100cm) long

$100-150   S&T

A very rare late 1960s Ossie Clark velvet floral maxi skirt.

$500-700   S&T

A very rare Ossie Clark sample jacket, in green and black printed cotton.

8.75in (73cm) long

$700-1,000   S&T

A Courrèges ivory knit dress.

40.5in (103cm) long

$270-330   **S&T**

A Courrèges size 10 skirt and blouse, with cream and beige stripes.

$300-400   **S&T**

COURRÈGES

- André Courrèges was born in Pau, France in 1923. He studied fashion design before going on to work as an assistant to Cristobal Balenciaga from 1960-1961.
- His fashion house, the 'White' salon, was opened in 1961 and 1965 saw his 'Space' collection being shown. In 1967, he introduced three lines: 'Prototype' (made to measure), 'Couture Future' (expensive prêt a porter) and 'Hyperbole' (inexpensive prêt a porter).
- Outer space was a popular theme during the entire 1960s, culminating with Neil Armstrong landing on the moon in 1969. This was expressed in clothes of the time through ultra modern, non gender-specific futuristic uniforms. Today, this look is highly popular amongst collectors.
- Courrèges' style was based around mini-dresses, catsuits and two piece suits in a stiff and wrinkle free fabric that gave the wearer a clean and linear profile.
- In 1985, his business became part of the Japanese group 'Itokin'.

A Courrèges black and white dress and belt.

34.5in (88cm) long

$300-500   **S&T**

A Courrèges museum quality couture maxi skirt, with appliqué daisies.

40in (102cm) long

$2,200-2,800   **S&T**

A Courrèges couture green dress, unlabeled.

35in (89cm) long

$700-1,100   **S&T**

A Courrèges couture two-piece red trouser suit.

22.5in (57cm) long

$2,000-2,500   **S&T**

A Courrèges couture two-piece tan and white suit.

c1960

$1,000-1,500   **S&T**

A Courrèges white and blue dress.

2.5in (108cm) long

$400-600   **S&T**

A Courrèges couture green wool coat.

37in (94cm) long

$3,000-3,500   **S&T**

A Courrèges two-piece rust and cream tweed suit.

27.5in (70cm) long

$300-500   **S&T**

A Courrèges fuchsia jacket.
26in (66cm) long
$150-200   **S&T**

A Courrèges pink jacket.
31.5in (80cm) long
$200-300   **S&T**

A Courrèges brown jacket.
28.75in (73cm) long
$320-380   **S&T**

A Courrèges pink and white silk blouse.
$150-200   **S&T**

A Courrèges 1980s re-issue wet-look pink waistcoat.
21.5in (55cm) long
$300-500   **S&T**

A Courrèges wet-look turquoise jacket.
Although this futuristic material may look robust like other fabrics used by Courrèges, it is quite fragile and is easily damaged. Damage to these pieces will affect value and desirability.
21.5in (55cm) long
$500-700   **S&T**

A Christian Dior fuchsia suit.
Jacket 24.5in (62cm) long
$120-180   **S&T**

A Christian Dior Puc dress.
46.5in (118cm) long
$180-220   **S&T**

A Gina Fratini dress, some damage.
60in (152cm) long
$100-150   **S&T**

A Bill Gibb print turtleneck top.
28.25in (72cm) long
$120-180   **S&T**

A Bill Gibb black striped top.

$50-80   **S&T**

BILL GIBB

■ Gibb was born in Scotland in 1943 and studied at the St Martin's School of Art from 1962-1968.

■ Opening his first shop in 1975, he was inspired by the rich diversity of ethnic patterns from other cultures as well as by Scottish dress. His style is typified by layered clothing to fit and flatter the body, using contrasting materials, colors and patterns.

■ He worked with Kaffe Fassett on knitted garments and used the 'bee' logo as a signature.

■ Interest in his work declined during the recession of the 1970s, but he continued to work for a small group of private clients up until his death in 1988.

A Bill Gibb multi-print dress.

60in (150cm) long

$100-150   **S&T**

A 1960s Givenchy two-piece suit.

Jacket 23.5in (59cm) long

$180-220   **S&T**

A Nicole Groult peach-colored dress.

c1910

$1,800-2,200   **S&T**

A Hartnell aqua and pink sequin dress and jacket.

23.25in (59cm) long

$500-700   **S&T**

A Christian Lacroix yellow prêt-à-porter jacket and skirt.

17.75in (45cm) long

$200-300   **S&T**

A Liberty flow gown.

55in (140cm) long

$200-300   **S&T**

A Missoni two-piece print skirt and top.

Top 23.25in (59cm) long

$100-150   **S&T**

A rare Missoni dress, in blue, orange and white.

Milan-based Missoni is also well-known for knitted designs, including vertically striped sweaters.

$700-1,000   **S&T**

A Missoni orange and red dress with belt.

46in (117cm) long

$500-700   **S&T**

A Hanae Mori gown.

53in (135cm) long

$500-700   **S&T**

A rare Benny Ong blue and yellow two-piece crêpe suit.

26.25in (67cm) long

$300-500   **S&T**

A rare 1960s Alice Pollock two-piece grey trouser suit.

$270-330   **S&T**

An early Pucci size 10 dress and belt, printed with blue and green flowers.

43.75in (111cm) long

$400-600   **S&T**

A rare Jean Patou blue, leather trim coat and matching dress, (dress not shown).

Jean Patou (1880-1936) saw his heyday during the 1920s and is notable for being the first European designer to present his designs on American models. Designers including Marc Bohan, Karl Lagerfeld and Christian Lacroix continued his business and name.

43.25in (110cm) long

$1,200-1,800 (set)   **S&T**

A 1960s Emilio Pucci blouse and skirt.

skirt 21.5in (55cm) long

$400-600   **S&T**

A late 1960s Emilio Pucci size 10 pink dress.

39in (99cm) long

$300-500   **S&T**

A 1960s Pucci Saks 5th Avenue size 12 dress and belt.

47.25in (120cm) long

$300-500   **S&T**

An Emilio Pucci turquoise dress.

52.75in (134cm) long

$120-180   **S&T**

A CLOSER LOOK AT A PUCCI DRESS

This instantly recognisable use of complicated geometric design and bright colors are Pucci hallmarks. Pieces in this style are the most sought-after as they exemplify his style.

The 'T-shirt' or 'chemise' dress with a thin belt is one of his most used, and most popular, designs.

Genuine Pucci pieces bear the name 'Emilio' as part of the design. The word is very small, so look closely to ensure the piece is not a copy.

This dress was owned and worn by Marilyn Monroe, adding to it's value.

EMILIO PUCCI

- Born the Marchese Emilio Pucci di Barsento in 1914, he studied political science and shone as a First World War pilot.

- In 1947, he was discovered skiing in a suit of his own creation by a 'Harper's Bazaar' photographer. This tapered pant ski suit was soon introduced in America. His first women's wear collection was shown in 1949, and he opened a studio in Florence in the same year.

- His earliest pieces are characterised by solid colors or simple figural motifs, some typical of the 1950s. However, during the late 1950s and 1960s, his style changed and pieces were made in highly recognisable bright, psychedelic colors, most famously with sophisticated freeform or geometric psychedelic designs that covered the entire body.

- Fabric is typically silk or silk jersey, but during the late 1950s he worked on improving a figure-hugging stretch material. This became known as 'Emilioform' and was heavily used during the 1960s and 70s.

- His designs soon covered a wider range of items including dinner sets, ties, scarves, lingerie and towels. During the 1980s he enjoyed a revival of his style. After his death in 1992, his daughter carried on his name and work.

- During the 1990s his clothing was revisited again and is now fixed as being highly popular amongst collectors. In the late 1990s, Christie's and Sotheby's held fashion and costume auctions containing pieces by Pucci.

An Emilio Pucci long-sleeved mini dress, in silk with geometric abstract design in shades of blue and turquoise, with stitched "Emilio Pucci made in Italy" label to neck, separate cord tie belt and clear bead ends, owned and worn by Marilyn Monroe, with a letter of authenticity, dated April 23, 1998, from Eleanor "Bebe" Goddard.

$3,000-4,000   **CO**

A Pucci blue silk blouse.

27in (69cm) long

$120-180   **S&T**

A Pucci fuchsia shirt.

30in (77cm) long

$320-380   **S&T**

A Pucci red sweater.

25.5in (65cm) long

$220-280   **S&T**

A Pucci peach halter top.

9in (22cm) long

$50-80   **S&T**

A pair of 1960s Pucci pants, with red and purple designs on yellow.

41in (105cm) long

$350-400   **S&T**

A 1960s Pucci pink nylon long skirt.

37in (94cm) long

$320-380   **S&T**

A pair of Mary Quant red and white striped slacks and top.

46.75in (119cm) long

$200-300   **S&T**

A 1960s rare Mary Quant two-piece black and white striped slacks and top.

49.5in (126cm) long

$270-330   **S&T**

A 1950s Ric Roc red and white dress.

$70-100   **S&T**

A Sonia Rykel red and black knit dress.

41.25in (105cm) long

$220-280   **S&T**

An early 1970s three-piece Yves Saint Laurent outfit, including jersey, pants and necklace.

$1,000-1,500   **S&T**

A rare Yves Saint Laurent couture crème satin evening coat.

$1,200-1,800   **S&T**

A Diane Von Stonberg black and white gown and jacket.

Jacket 28in (71cm) long

$120-180   **S&T**

A jacket from a Valentino two-piece print suit.

19in (48cm) long

$100-150 (suit)   **S&T**

A Versace two-piece black, yellow and purple pants and top.

Top 17.75in (45cm) long

$350-400   **S&T**

A Vivienne Westwood Gold Label primrose angora bow dress, from 'Vive la cocotte', from Westwood's own archive.

97cm long

$400-600 **S&T**

A Vivienne Westwood tulip bow dress, from Pagan I collection, also from Westwood's own archive.

36.25in (92cm) long

$500-700 **S&T**

A Vivienne Westwood Sèvres porcelain print rain cape, from the Pagan V collection, also from Westwood's own archive.

42in (107cm) long

$300-500 **S&T**

A Vivienne Westwood two-piece suit.

Jacket 22.5in (57cm) long

$320-380 **S&T**

VIVIENNE WESTWOOD

- Westwood was born Vivienne Isabel Swire in 1941. She opened 'Let It Rock', her first boutique selling second hand clothes with her partner Malcolm McLaren in 1971 on the King's Road, London.

- The 1970s saw Westwood making headline news with the aggressive S&M, bondage and punk themed clothes, which were worn by The Sex Pistols.

- After the punk look had become too commercial, they released their first collection, 'Pirates', in 1981. This was followed by the 'Buffalo Girls' collection of 1982 which foresaw the 'grunge' look of the 1990s with its dirty colors and camouflage.

- Her solo career began in 1983 with her 'Witches' collection. Since then her hallmarks of unconventionality, theatricality and sexuality that allow her to shock, combined with an understanding of historical dress, have made her a global name in fashion design.

A Vivienne Westwood nautical jacket.

31in (79cm) long

$200-300 **S&T**

A pair of Vivienne Westwood purple pants.

39.35in (100cm) long

$100-150 **S&T**

A pair of Vivienne Westwood silver leather pants, slight tear to rear.

43in (109cm) long

$180-220 **S&T**

A 1960s collectable pair of Vivienne Westwood shorts.

12.5in (32cm) long

$100-150 **S&T**

A Vivienne Westwood brown fuzzy skirt.

20in (51cm) long

$270-330 **S&T**

A Vivienne Westwood body.

Westwood began using the now familiar orb motif for her clothing in 1987.

28in (71cm) long

$180-220 **S&T**

A grey and purple dress.
1910

$300-500 **S&T**

A 1920s devoré velvet dress, with maribou trim.

$500-800 **S&T**

A 1920s pink and grey beaded flapper dress.

$300-500 **S&T**

A 1920s Art Deco beaded dress, probably French.

$1,800-2,200 **S&T**

A 1930s brown and orange dress.

$100-150 **S&T**

A 1950s black and white floral dress, with swagged waist.

$80-120 **S&T**

A B C D E F G H I J K L M N O P Q R S T U V W XYZ

A 1950s black and white spotted prom dress, with crinoline.

$320-380 S&T

A 1950s cream and wool dress, with blue robe swirls.

$200-250 S&T

A 1950s blue and white puffball dress.

$270-330 S&T

A 1960s pink floral print dress.

$80-120 S&T

A 1960s flower print coat.

$70-100 S&T

A 1950s pink dress, with appliqué flower motif.

$100-150 S&T

A 1960s dress, with belt.

$80-120 S&T

A 1970s patterned dress.

$50-80 S&T

A very rare and touchingly handmade tunic, with pink embroidery, buttons, metal bits, and coins, possibly Afghan.

$1,000-1,500 S&T

A vintage Chinese robe, with black appliqué embroidered grape vines.

$400-600 S&T

A 1950s Hermes 'La Clé des Champs' pattern scarf, Jacquard silk with hand-rolled edges, designed and signed by F.R. Façonnet.

35in (89cm) wide

$200-250 REN

A Hermes 'Brides de Gala' pattern scarf, silk twill with hand-rolled edges, designed by the Hermes Studio (unsigned).

c1960 *35in (89cm) wide*

$120-180 REN

A 1960s silk scarf, with figural pattern, produced for the "21 Club" New York, maker unknown.

66in (167.5cm) long

$80-120 REN

A 1970s Hermes 'Les Bécanes' pattern scarf, silk twill with hand-rolled edges, designed by the Hermes Studio (unsigned).

35in (89cm) wide

$150-200 REN

A 1970s Hermes 'Grand Apparat' pattern scarf, silk twill with hand-rolled edges, designed and signed by Jacques Eudel.

35in (89cm) wide

$100-150 REN

A 1950s Hermes 'Chiens et Valets' pattern scarf, silk twill with hand-rolled edges, designed and signed by C.H. Hello.

35in (89cm) wide

$120-180 REN

A 1980s Hermes 'Grands Fonds' pattern scarf, silk twill with hand-rolled edges, designed by the Hermes Studio (unsigned).

35in (89cm) wide

$180-220 REN

A 1970s Hermes 'Harnais des Presidents' pattern scarf, silk twill with hand-rolled edges, designed by the Hermes Studio (unsigned).

35in (89cm) wide

$120-180 REN

A 1940s Jacqmar 'Swan Lake' pattern parachute silk scarf.

33in (84cm) wide

$80-120 REN

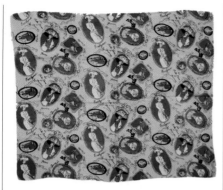

A 1940s Jacqmar 'Les Belles Dames' pattern rayon scarf.

34in (86.5cm) wide

$100-150　　　　REN

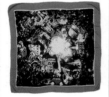

A 1940s Kaystyle 'Wartime' pattern rayon scarf, signed "London by Kaystyle".

33in (84cm) wide

$300-400　　REN

A 1970s Liberty's of London 'Paisley pattern' silk scarf.

26.5in (67.5cm) wide

$30-50　　REN

A 1940s synthetic fabric 'Sporting' pattern scarf, designed by Thirkell.

32in (81.5cm) wide

$40-60　　　　REN

A 1950s Jacqmar 'Geese' pattern silk scarf, designed by Peter Scott.

29in (73.5cm) wide

$50-80　　　　REN

A 1940s Jacqmar 'The Flower Seller' pattern rayon scarf.

1940s　　*29in (73.5cm) wide*

$80-120　　　REN

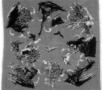

An Yves St. Laurent silk scarf.

c1970　　*35in (14cm) wide*

$80-120　　　REN

A Welsh Margetson & Co. Ltd 'Coronation Derby 1953 – Pinza' pattern scarf, from the series "Winners of the Derby since 1780".

1953　　*34in (86.5cm) wide*

$200-300　　REN

A 'Winston Churchill 80th Birthday' pattern silk scarf, designer's signature illegible.

1954　　*27in (68.5cm) wide*

$80-120　　　REN

An 'Empire Games 1958' pattern synthetic fabric scarf, maker unknown.

1958　　*25.5in (64.5cm) wide*

$20-30　　　REN

A 1950s 'Letters' pattern silk scarf, maker unknown.

35.5in (90cm) wide

$50-80　　　　REN

HANDBAGS

- The 'retro' trend of the past decade has seen a revival in use of handbags from previous decades. Collectors and specialist dealers have sprung up all over the world to service celebrities, fashion stylists, 'fashionistas' and collectors with uniquely stylish and highly individual handbags.

- The increase in informal occasions during the 1950s saw an explosion in 'light hearted', highly decorative handbags that used different materials such as plastic, brocade, straw, metal and raffia, embellished with sequins, hand-painted scenes and ribbons.

- Bags by named and notable designers are hotly sought after, as are early plastic bags from the 1930s-1950s. These are generally made in bright colors, from 'Catalin', a brightly colored form of Bakelite, or 'Lucite' a largely transparent plastic that is also often colored brightly or made to look like tortoiseshell. These bags are rigid, generally in the form of shaped boxes and can be decorated with metal strips, jewels or carved patterns.

- Before you buy a Lucite or early plastic bag, smell the interior – if it exudes a chemical smell, do not buy it as this marks the beginning of the material degrading resulting in a bag covered with tiny cracks. Look for names such as 'Rialto' or 'Willardy' and keep them away from heat or strong sunlight which will bring on disintegration.

An early 19thC figural beaded purse.

4in (10cm) wide

$150-200   **S&T**

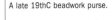

A late 19thC beadwork purse.

4.75in (12cm) wide

$100-150   **Men**

A beadwork purse, hand-worked on black velvet with flowers and the name Emily M. Hollister, back and front detail.

c1810   *9in (23cm) long*

$500-800   **RAA**

BEADWORK

- Beadwork is a form of embroidery where small glass beads are threaded onto silk thread and stitched to a fabric ground, or threaded onto wire, which is then shaped.

- It was popular during the 19th and 20th centuries for handbags and purses, but was first used in the 17th century for picture or mirror frames and small cabinets.

- The intricate nature of beadwork allows for sophisticated designs, some of which recorded specific dates or events.

- As colored glass beads are used, the color tends not to fade, meaning that bags most often retain their brilliance even after a century or more.

- Condition is important as it is difficult to repair beaded bags through replacing torn silk linings or sewing the tiny beads back on.

A Victorian beaded purse.

6in (15cm) wide

$200-250   **S&T**

A late 19thC beadwork purse, with blue and gold beads.

3.25in (8.5cm) wide

$80-120   **Men**

An antique beaded purse, with faux tortoiseshell clasp.

6in (15cm) wide

$100-150   **S&T**

A late 19th/early 20thC metal and beadwork purse.

c1900   *6in (15cm) wide*

$200-300   **Men**

A late 19thC beadwork purse.

5.5in (14cm) wide

$100-150   **Men**

An extremely rare French beaded black and floral vanity purse, with lipstick, powder and cigarette sections inside.

$500-700   **S&T**

A B C D E F G H I J K L M N O P Q R S T U V W XYZ

A beaded moth purse.

9in (23cm) long

$2,000-3,000 Rox

A 1940s black beaded purse, with flowers.

10.25in (26cm) wide

$200-300 S&T

A 1940s black beaded figural purse.

10in (25.5cm) wide

$500-700 Rox

A 1940s black beaded purse with rose design.

11in (28cm) wide

$320-380 Rox

A 1950s black beaded, jeweled purse, with poodle motif.

14.5in (37cm) wide

$200-250 SM

A 1950s black jersey jeweled and beaded tapestry purse.

7.5in (19cm) wide

$100-150 SM

A 1940s white beaded figural purse.

9in (23cm) wide

$500-600 Rox

A late 1950s Enid Collins beaded bucket bag, with butterfly motif.

13in (33cm) wide

$100-150 SM

A 1940s white beaded box purse.

7in (17.5cm) wide

$300-500 Rox

A 1950s black Lucite compartment purse.

$600-800 Rox

A 1950s red Lucite purse.

8.5in (21.5cm) wide

$2,000-2,500 Rox

A 1950s black purse with goldfish, wood, straw and Lucite.

11.5in (29cm) wide

$200-300   **Rox**

A 1950s yellow Lucite purse, with clear Lucite top.

9.5in (23.5cm) wide

$200-300   **SM**

A 1950s wooden box bag, with purple velvet grapes and Lucite handle, lined with brocade and ribbon, specially handmade by "Susan".

9.25in (23.5cm) wide

$100-150   **SM**

A strawberry wooden box bag, with hand-painted motif.

12.25in (31cm) wide

$70-100   **S&T**

A 1950s wooden octagonal bag, with butterfly découpage and Lucite handle.

7in (18cm) wide

$100-150   **SM**

A metal box bag.

8.75in (22cm) wide

$80-120   **S&T**

A 1950s white woven basket, with felt fruit baskets.

8.5in (22cm) wide

$100-150   **SM**

A 1950s handmade wooden happy-house bag.

10.5in (26.5cm) wide

$180-220   **SM**

A 1930s Bakelite purse.

5.5in (14cm) wide

$650-750   **Rox**

A 1920s brocade purse with white metal clasp.

6.75in (17cm) wide

$180-220   **Men**

A 1920s tapestry petit point purse, with enamel clasp.

9.5in (24cm) wide

$180-220   **Men**

A 1920s tapestry petit point purse.

7in (18cm) wide

$180-220   **Men**

A 19th/20thC Native American purse.

6in (15cm) wide

$300-400   **Rox**

A beautiful 19thC petit point purse, with gilt frame.

8in (21cm) wide

$200-300   **S&T**

A 19thC satin Turkish purse, made for the European market.

5in (12.5cm) wide

$180-220   **Men**

A 1930s tapestry purse, probably French.

9in (23cm) wide

$320-380   **S&T**

A 1950s Souré black leather purse, with 3D scenic tapestry work, New York.

15.25in (38.5cm) wide

$180-220   **SM**

An incredibly detailed Art Nouveau purse, with celluloid clasp.

c1900   *8.25in (21cm) wide*

$500-700   **S&T**

A 1950s tapestry bag.

10.75in (27cm) wide

$120-180   **S&T**

A rare vintage 'Fragonard' girl on swing vanity case.

4in (10cm) wide

$270-330   **S&T**

A 1950s poet bag, with 'La Maison du Poet' on the front.

11.5in (29cm) wide

$120-180   **S&T**

A 1950s Rialto purse.

Purses from the 1950s are characterised by having shorter handles.

$180-220   **Rox**

A needlepoint clutch bag, with ladies' legs motif.

16.5in (42cm) wide

$80-120   **S&T**

A highly collectable 1940s felt bag, with appliqué fruit.

13.25in (34cm) wide

$100-150   **S&T**

A strawberry tote bag.

11.75in (30cm) wide

$50-80   **S&T**

A 1930s silk and celluloid rose purse.
9in (23cm) wide

$800-1,000   **Rox**

A vintage purse, with gold lace.
6.75in (17cm) wide

$100-150   **S&T**

A vintage Gucci blue leather clutch bag, probably 1950s.
11in (28cm) wide

$120-180   **S&T**

A Judith Lieber bird bag, with two small birds inside.
6.75(17cm) wide

$1,000-1,500   **S&T**

JUDITH LIEBER

- Judith Lieber was born in 1921 to a Jewish family in Budapest, Hungary. After escaping capture during the Second World War, she met Gertson Lieber, an American GI in 1945 and married him a year later, moving to New York.

- She initially worked for other bag manufacturers and started her own business in 1963.

- Although she does make day bags, she is most renowned for her glittering and highly individual evening bags, many of which are covered in rhinestones or diamanté. These are known as 'minaudières', and her style is often imitated.

- All her bags are hand decorated and can take many weeks to create. They are popular with stars and First Ladies of America, with Jackie Kennedy, Hillary Clinton, Nancy Reagan and Joan Collins being amongst the illustrious owners.

- Her work is now highly sought after by collectors and the glamorous who use them. In 1997, the Victoria & Albert Museum in London added one of her bags to its collection and an exhibition of one lady's collection of 300 Lieber bags in New Orleans was visited by over 10,000 people.

A Judith Lieber-style penguin minaudière bag, with diamanté.
6.25in (16cm) high

$800-1,200   **S&T**

A Christian Dior hat, with appliqué daisies.
8.75in (22cm) wide

$80-120   **S&T**

A Norman Edwin hat, with blue, yellow and pink print.

$40-60   **S&T**

An Original Louise's Showcase pink hat.

8.75in (22cm) diam

$50-80 **S&T**

A Ranleigh green feather hat.

8.75in (22cm) wide

$70-100 **S&T**

A Schiaparelli fake fur hat, with diamanté trim.

11.75in (30cm) wide

$220-280 **S&T**

A Schiaparelli black fuzzy hat.

11.75in (30cm) wide

$200-300 **S&T**

A Schiaparelli blue-jeweled hat.

8.25in (21cm) wide

$320-380 **S&T**

ELSA SCHIAPARELLI

■ Elsa Schiaparelli (1890-1973) is considered one of the most influential designers of the 20th century and her inventive clothes, costume jewelry and hats are highly desirable amongst collectors.

■ Her name is also synonymous with a stunning shade of pink. Many of her designs were inspired by the Surrealist art movement, such as her famous 1937 shoe-shaped hat which was suggested by Salvador Dali.

An Eddi Stix and Fuller cherry hat.

7in (18cm) wide

$70-100 **S&T**

An Italian grey feather trim hat, handmade by Shirley Sverett.

7.75in (20cm) wide

$70-100 **S&T**

A pink hat, with woven ribbon.

11in (28cm) wide

$20-30 **S&T**

A 1960s orange fake fur hat.

9.75in (25cm) diam

$30-50 **S&T**

A blue and white striped hat, with orange trim.

11in (28cm) wide

$40-60 **S&T**

An Oriental cat hat.

8.25in (21cm) wide

$150-200 **S&T**

A 1950s Coty brushed gold compact and lipstick, with original cream powder instructions.

3.25in (8.5cm) wide

$50-80 **SM**

A 1920s enameled compact and cigarette case, by Chelsea Cigarettes.

Larger 3.25in (8.5cm) wide

$180-220 **SM**

A 1950s jeweled pocket lipstick and mirror.

2.5in (6.5cm) wide

$30-50 **SM**

A 1950s Mop compact, by Ansico.

2in (5cm) wide

$30-50 **SM**

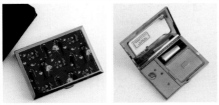

A 1950s Kissing Couples musical compact and lipstick by Thorens, plays 'The Night They Invented Champagne', original box.

4in (10cm) wide

$180-220 **SM**

A 1950s Dorset Fifth Avenue compact, lipstick and leather case.

6.75in (17cm) wide

$50-80 **SM**

A 1950s mirrored musical compact, with carved glass oriental scene, in the original box.

3in (7.5cm) wide

$100-150 **SM**

A pair of Balenciaga gold shoes.

9.75in (25cm) long

$80-120   **S&T**

A pair of Dolce and Gabbana green velvet shoes, with floral decoration.

12.25in (31cm) long

$300-400   **S&T**

A 1950s Johansen patterned shoe.

$70-100   **S&T**

A 1950s pair of Kitty Kelly leather and Lucite shoes, with yellow squiggles in the heel.

8in (22cm) long

$100-150   **SM**

A 1950s pair of blue leather stilettos, with a springalator, created for Kims.

The stiletto arrived on the fashion scene in 1952, although it is not clear who was responsible for its design.

Despite the fact that stilettos were often uncomfortable and dangerous to wear, and sometimes caused damage to floors, by the late 1950s they were highly fashionable, with Jayne Mansfield owning some 200 pairs.

Often seen as a sign of playful female aggression and sexuality, their popularity waned in the 1960s before returning in the late 1970s.

9.5in (24cm) long

$70-100   **SM**

A pair of Anne Klein pumps.

10.5in (27cm) long

$70-100   **S&T**

A pair of Herbert Levine asymmetrical blue suede stilettos.

11in (28cm) long

$70-100   **SM**

A pair of 1950s Nina flower pumps.

10.25in (26cm) long

$100-150   **S&T**

A pair of 1950s Pandora Footwear lilac devoré shoes.

9.75in (25cm) long

$100-150   **SM**

A pair of Randalls brown croc shoes.

11in (28cm) long

$180-220   **S&T**

A pair of Safinia Saks 5th Avenue shoes, in brown leather.

10.5in (27cm) long

$100-150   **S&T**

A pair of La Rose Jacksonville clear Lucite wedges made in USA.

This shoe uses Lucite, a plastic commonly used during the 1950s for decorative and fashionable handbags.

8.75in (22cm) long

$100-150   **SM**

A pair of Saks 5th Avenue gold shoes.

$50-80   **S&T**

A pair of 1940s grey cut-out platforms.

9.5in (24cm) long

$20-30   **S&T**

A 1940s pair of snakeskin ankle strap platforms, with utility mark.

9in (23cm) long

$100-150   **SM**

A pair of early 1950s black leather and suede pumps.

11in (28cm) long

$80-120   **S&T**

A pair of 1950s pumps.

11in (28cm) long

$50-80   **S&T**

A pair of 1950s beige lace pumps.

10.25in (26cm) long

$40-60   **S&T**

A pair of gold metallic boots.

7in (18cm) high

$80-120   **S&T**

A rare pair of 1960s Biba boots.

22.75in (58cm) high

$300-500   **S&T**

A pair of 1940s pink Lucite sunglasses.

5.25in (13.5cm) wide

$40-60   **SM**

A pair of 1950s blue tinted sunglasses, made in France.

5.5in (14cm) wide

$40-60   **SM**

A pair of 1950s Verres Filtrants cat's-eye and Lucite sunglasses, made in France.

5.5in (14cm) wide

$50-80   **SM**

A 1950s pair of plastic sunglasses, with stiffened cotton daisy trim.

5in (12.5cm) wide

$70-100   **SM**

A pair of original 1950s Ray-Bans sunglasses, with blue fleck coloring, made in USA.

5.5in (14cm) wide

$100-150   **SM**

A pair of early 1960s black sunglasses.

5.75in (14.5cm) wide

$40-60   **SM**

A pair of 1950s Doscar cat's-eye and diamanté sunglasses, with original tag, made in Italy.

6in (15cm) wide

$80-120   **SM**

A pair of late 1950s tortoiseshell plastic men's sunglasses, made in Italy.

5.75in (14.5cm) wide

$40-60   **CVS**

A 1940s hand-painted red palm tree tie.

$80-120   **CVS**

A 1940s hand-painted silk screened 3D 'Booby' tie.

Images of buxom or skimpily dressed ladies were favorite motifs during the late 1940s and 1950s and can be found on a wide range of objects.

1940s

$200-300   **CVS**

A late 1940s Salvador Dali tie, with candelabra motif.

$300-500   **CVS**

A B C D E F G H I J K L M N O P Q R S **T** U V W XYZ

A 1950s hand-painted 'butterfly' tie.

$40-60 CVS

A 1940s National Shirt Tops heart design silk tie.

$70-100 CVS

A King Kong tie, by Wembley.

$20-30 S&T

A Mickey Mouse tie.

$20-30 S&T

A Peanuts cartoon graphic tie, showing Charlie Brown and Snoopy.

$30-40 S&T

A musical jazz tie.

$20-30 S&T

A spaceship tie.

$20-30 S&T

A striped tie, with street scenes, made in Italy.

$20-30 S&T

A cartoon graphic tie, showing Disney characters including Bugs Bunny, Daffy Duck and Sylvester the Cat playing snooker.

'Humorous' ties depicting cartoon characters, were popular during the late 1980s and the early 1990s.

$20-30 S&T

A 1940s Swank sword tie-bar, with mother-of-pearl.

3.5in (9in) long

$30-40 CVS

A pair of Spotlight Sheers stockings, in off-black glamor sheer with a dark seam.

$30-50 SM

A pair of 1950s Missouri full-fashioned nylons, with a dark seam.

$40-60 SM

A 1930s packet of black rayon stockings, by Bluebird.

6.5in (16.5cm) wide

$20-30 SM

Three 1950s pin-up girl match boxes, made by the Superior Match Company, by the artist Petty.

2in (5cm) high

$10-15 each SM

A 1950s Gossard black lace and stretch all-in-one.

$80-120 SM

A 1950s Lady Marlene white all-in-one.

$50-80 SM

A 1950s Extasy matching blue lace-trimmed, suspender belt and bra, the bra with scalloped trimmed push-up cups, made in France.

$50-80 SM

FANS

- Fans date back some 3,000 years and were used as ceremonial tools, status symbols and fashion accessories. During the mid-18th century, they became popular amongst the upper classes but went into decline during the 1930s.

- Folding fans are the most common type and have a folding screen, known as a 'leaf', mounted on a series of folding 'sticks'. The front and back sticks are known as 'guard sticks' and are can be exquisitely decorated, being carved or beautifully inlaid with precious materials. Sticks can be made from wood, ivory, tortoiseshell, precious metals or Bakelite.

- Oriental fans often bear Eastern imagery such as pagodas and rustic scenes with and without figures and were made for export during the 18th and 19th centuries. Although they are not of as fine quality as the fans that the Chinese made for themselves, many are of excellent quality and are highly collectable.

- Look out for hand-painted fans from the 18th and 19th centuries, which are very desirable, particularly fans bearing unusual motifs such as hot air balloons, or specific scenes or famous events. Less expensive are advertising fans produced from the mid-19th century.

- Condition is important and splits to the leaf, broken sticks and staining affect value. Always take care when opening a fan, handle them as little as possible and avoid having them framed for display as light and heat will damage them.

A late 18thC fan, with decorated ivory sticks, the guards carved as figures.

11.75in (30cm) wide

$200-300 **Men**

A late 18thC fan, with painted scene entitled 'Rebecca at the well'.

11in (28cm) wide

$300-500 **Men**

A 19thC mother-of-pearl fan, painted on satin with romantic lady motif.

12.5in (31.5cm) wide

$320-380 **Men**

A 19thC gauze leaf fan, decorated with mischievous cherubs, with mother-of-pearl sticks, signed "L. S. Toudes".

12.5in (31.5cm) wide

$320-380 **Men**

A Victorian printed fan, decorated with scene of a gathering of ladies, with bone sticks.

10.5in (26.5cm) wide

$100-150 **Men**

A late 19th/early 20thC Japanese fan, the ivory guard sticks decorated with Shibayama, the semi-precious stones in the form of insects.

10.75in (27cm) wide

$320-380 **Men**

A late 19thC Cantonese lace fan, the leaf decorated with people wearing painted garments, with carved ivory sticks.

11in (28cm) wide

$300-500 Men

A 19thC black lace fan, decorated with birds and blossom, with mother-of-pearl sticks.

12.5in (31.5cm) wide

$320-380 Men

A 19thC black ebony fan, decorated with flowers.

12.75in (32.5cm) wide

$100-150 Men

A 1920s tortoiseshell and feather fan.

12.75in (32cm) wide

$100-150 Men

FIND OUT MORE...

The Fan Museum, 12 Crooms Hill, Greenwich, London SE10 8ER, England. www.fan-museum.org.

Helene Alexander, 'Fans', published by Shire Books, 1995.

Susan Mayor, 'The Letts Guide to Collecting Fans', Letts, 1991.

A 1920s ivory and red feather fan, with ivory sticks.

16in (41cm) wide

$100-150 Men

A 19thC mother-of-pearl fan, with Carrickmacross lace, the sticks in silver and gilt.

Lace fans were popular in Europe and the United States from the early 18th century until the early 20th century and are now a collectable field in their own right. Before the 18th century, all lace fans were produced from hand-woven lace, either 'needlelace' or 'bobbin' lace, with the finest examples being woven from silk. The high cost of manufacture made them the preserve of the wealthy and powerful. Machine-woven lace, such as 'Nottingham' or 'Swiss' lace, manufactured from the late 18th century onwards, made lace fans less costly. More of these fans survive than the delicate early versions which fetch high prices when found in good condition.

12.5in (31.5cm) wide

$320-380 Men

A 19thC black lace and mother-of-pearl fan.

11in (28cm) wide

$100-150 Men

LACE

- Prior to the late 18th century, lace was hand made from flaxen thread, silk, wool or cotton yarn. It was either stitched with a needle and thread (needlelace) or by twisting bobbins around pins that had been stuck into a stuffed pillow to outline the pattern (bobbin lace).
- Patterns included stylized animals, birds, foliate designs, floral patterns linked with scrolling designs and more. Needlelace patterns differ and there are many techniques – it is best to refer to an illustrated book to learn about them. 17th and 18th century lace is usually very expensive.
- During the 16th century, production centers sprang up in Italy (at Venice, Genoa and Milan), in Belgium (Brussels, Mechelen and Antwerp), in Spain and Portugal. France (Alençon, Argenton, Paris and Chantilly) and England (Honiton) developed centers during the 17th century. Most centers have carried on production to the present.
- Early lace was deemed a commodity and also displayed the wealth and influence of the wearer. This can be seen particularly in 16th and 17th century Dutch paintings.
- Machine-made lace, invented in the late 18th century, took off during the 19th century. It is much more affordable and can form excellent collections. Stitching is much more regular than hand-stitched lace.
- Check that modern lace has not been artificially aged in tea. Cleaning lace is best left to professionals, but can be achieved by washing gently in distilled water.

A mid-17thC Flemish lace, one of earliest and rarest laces.
56in (142cm) long

$700-1,000   **Men**

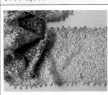

A pair of late 17thC point de France lace lappets.
53.5in (136cm) long

$400-600   **Men**

A pair of Brussels bobbin lace lappets.
c1725

$800-1,200   **Men**

An early to mid-18thC length of Milan bobbin lace.
143.75in (365cm) long

$400-600   **Men**

An 18thC length of Flemish bobbin lace.
151in (384cm) long

$800-1,200   **Men**

An 18thC point de Venise needlepoint.
50in (127cm) long

$500-800   **Men**

A length of Alençon needle point lace.
c1750   69.25in (176cm) long

$300-500   **Men**

A piece of 18thC lace.
48.75in (124cm) long

$300-500   **Men**

An very fine 18thC length of Binche bobbin lace.
76in (193cm) long

$400-600   **Men**

A 19thC length of Brussels duchesse lace.
63in (160cm) long

$180-220   **Men**

A piece of blonde silk lace.
c1800

$200-300   **Men**

A length of Binche lace.
55in (140cm) long

$300-500   **Men**

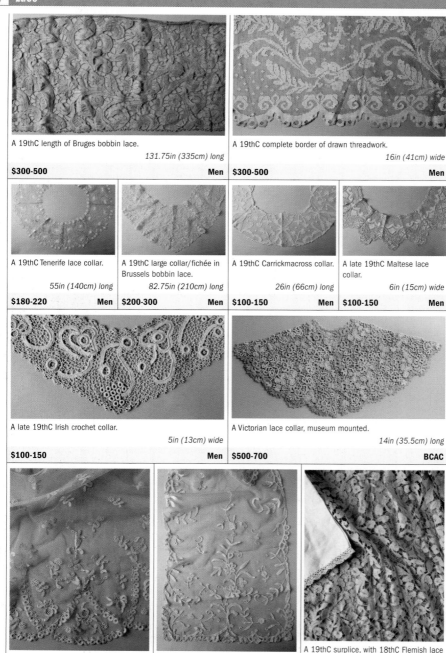

A 19thC length of Bruges bobbin lace.

131.75in (335cm) long

$300-500   **Men**

A 19thC complete border of drawn threadwork.

16in (41cm) wide

$300-500   **Men**

A 19thC Tenerife lace collar.

55in (140cm) long

$180-220   **Men**

A 19thC large collar/fichée in Brussels bobbin lace.

82.75in (210cm) long

$200-300   **Men**

A 19thC Carrickmacross collar.

26in (66cm) long

$100-150   **Men**

A late 19thC Maltese lace collar.

6in (15cm) wide

$100-150   **Men**

A late 19thC Irish crochet collar.

5in (13cm) wide

$100-150   **Men**

A Victorian lace collar, museum mounted.

14in (35.5cm) long

$500-700   **BCAC**

A 19thC large Honiton triangular shawl.

104.75in (266cm) long

$300-500   **Men**

A 19thC Honiton stole.

82.75 x 12.25in (210 x 31cm)

$180-220   **Men**

A 19thC surplice, with 18thC Flemish lace border.

31.5in (80cm) long

$400-600   **Men**

A 19thC lady's lace dressing jacket.

18.5in (47cm) long

$180-220 **Men**

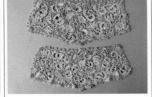

A late 19thC pair of Irish crochet lace cuffs.

10.5 x 4.75in (27 x 12cm) wide

$80-120 **Men**

A 19thC needlepoint cushion cover, with musicians and dancing figures.

40.25in (62cm) long

$300-500 **Men**

A 19thC decorative needlepoint panel, possibly for a cushion.

17.5in (44cm) diam

$180-220 **Men**

One of a set of six 19thC Normandy lace mats.

These mats encompass a mixture of embroidered and other lace with a needlepoint center, and as such they show a fine display of various techniques.

9in (23cm) diam

$100-150 (set) **Men**

An early 19thC large lawn handkerchief, with whitework, drawn threadwork and lace surrounding.

26.25in (67cm) wide

$200-300 **Men**

A 19thC handkerchief, with Valenciennes lace and drawn threadwork.

16.5in (42cm) wide

$100-150 **Men**

A late 19thC lawn handkerchief, with needlework border.

17in (43cm) wide

$100-150 **Men**

A late 18thC handkerchief, edged with lace.

17in (43cm) wide

$180-220 **Men**

A 19thC handkerchief, edged with fine Irish crochet.

13.25in (34cm) wide

$100-150 **Men**

A late 18thC lace handkerchief, embroidered with whitework.

26in (66cm) wide

$200-300 **Men**

A late 19thC lawn handkerchief, with border and insertion in Valenciennes lace.

13in (33cm) wide

$100-150 **Men**

An early 19thC lawn handkerchief, with drawn threadwork and lace border.

22.5in (57cm) wide

$100-150 **Men**

A 19thC lawn handkerchief, with whitework and surrendered Valenciennes lace.

15.25in (39cm) wide

$50-80 **Men**

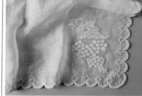

A late 18thC handkerchief, with whitework.

15.75 (40cm) wide

$200-300 **Men**

A 19thC handkerchief, with lawn Valenciennes lace.

14in (36cm) wide

$50-80 **Men**

A late 18thC baby's bonnet.

9.5in (24cm) wide

$200-300 **Men**

A late 18thC baby's bonnet.

11in (28cm) wide

$320-380 **Men**

A bonnet edged with lace, and with a lace insert.

c1800 *12.25in (31cm) wide*

$100-150 **Men**

A late 18thC baby's bonnet.

11in (28cm) wide

$50-80 **Men**

A lawn and Valenciennes lace baby gown.
c1880 *18.5in (47cm) long*

$80-120 **Men**

A 19thC broderie anglaise baby gown.

21.25in (54cm) long

$70-100 **Men**

A 19thC embroidered lawn baby coat, with large collar.

A coat is more desirable and unusual than a gown.

19.75in (50cm) long

$100-150 **Men**

A 19thC embroidered lawn child's pinafore, with lace and ribbon, opening at back.

20.5in (52cm) long

$100-150 **Men**

A 19thC baby's christening gown, with whitework.

43.7in (111cm) long

$180-220 **Men**

An infant's chemise, with lawn ruffles.

c1800 12.5in (32cm) long

$180-220 **Men**

An 18thC apron, with whitework embroidery.

41.25in (105cm) long

$200-300 **Men**

A Regency lace stole.

35in (89cm) wide

$200-300 **Men**

A needlework sampler, with rows of alphabet and verse above a building flanked by trees and bowls of strawberries, enclosed by bold flowers on a gauze ground, with the inscription "Louisiana, the daughter of John and Rachel Shrader, was born January 17, 1812, and worked this sampler in the year one thousand eight hundred and twenty five."

Louisiana Shrader was born in Louisville, Jefferson County, Kentucky, the daughter of Rachel Ross and John Shrader. She was married to Cullen Melone July 15, 1828 in Shelby County, Kentucky.

1825 21in (53.4cm) high

$10,000-15,000 **SI**

A needlework sampler, on a green linsey-woolsey ground, stitched in silk threads in shades of yellow, pink, blue, brown and beige, with rows of alphabet above inscription, "Ann Treadwell Green's Sampler, wrought in the 11th year of her age, December 1818," framed.

16in (41cm) wide

$5,000-8,000 **SI**

17th century woven silk panels such as these are highly desirable and fetch high prices at auction.

Usually referring to Biblical stories, they have an allegorical meaning and were often meant to educate. Additionally, some of the motifs used within the picture, such as the animals, have meanings in themselves that are related to the story.

Condition is vitally important with damage affecting value. Fading is common, with undamaged examples with the brightest colors fetching the highest prices. These panels were highly colored when made.

This panel tells the Biblical story of Abraham, Hagar and Ishmael. Abraham was married to Sara, but she bore him no children, so Sara gave her maid, Hagar, to Abraham so she could bear children for them. Hagar gave birth to Ishmael. God (usually represented by the sun) then made Sara pregnant and she bore Isaac. Ishmael mocked Isaac which displeased Sara who took her son away (right-hand scene) ordering her husband to banish Hagar and Ishmael, which he did (central scene), giving them a vase of water as they went into the desert. When the water was gone, Hagar cast Ishmael under bush (the left-hand scene) in despair. An angel appeared and provided a well of water so that they were saved. This scene is also found in 17th century paintings.

A sampler, stitched with a Long Island theme including a windmill, a colonial Dutchman and a family home.

This sampler needs cleaning. If it had been clean it would be worth three times as much.

1849

$400-600   **RAA**

A 17thC English linen and silk embroidered panel, depicting the story of Abraham, Hagar and Ishmael, executed in bold colors, in a tortoiseshell frame.

19.7in (50cm) high

$15,000-20,000   **FRE**

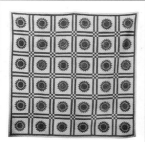

An American hand-sewn summer quilt, with cotton backing and pinwheel design, some deterioration.

6in (193cm) long

$70-100   **TWC**

An American hand-sewn summer quilt, with a large and colorful starburst centre, some stitches visible.

c1920   70in (178cm) wide

$70-100   **TWC**

Four Art Nouveau Arpad Basch silk panels, representing the four seasons.

15.5in (39cm) long

$300-500   **Men**

An American quilt.

1841

$300-500   **Men**

An 1920s double shawl, with two different patterns.

63in (160cm) wide

$300-500   **Men**

An American Shelton & Osborn, Birmingham, CT, rosewood coffin plane, with ivory and ebony inlay, very nice original as found condition with minor dents.

7.75in (19.5cm) long

$400-600　　　**TWC**

An American fine small cabinet maker's plane, maker unknown, probably made by "J.F.Helm" as marked by original owner and tool maker, with rosewood knob, excellent condition.

6in (15cm) long

$100-150　　　**TWC**

A mixed set of beech woodworking planes, by A. Mathieson & Son of Glasgow, Alex Marshall of Glasgow, Malloch of Perth, D Menzies and others; and various other woodworking tools.

$700-1,000　　　**L&T**

An American adjustable steel and iron woodwoker's plane, marked "R.H. Mitchell & Co. Hudson, N.Y.", marked "Evans, pat. Jan 28 1862 - Mar. 22 1864", some paint loss, surface rust.

1862　　10.5in (26.5cm) long

$150-200　　　**TWC**

An American early expandable ruler, marked "Charles B. Long Worcester Mass", with pattern "Apr. 25/26", brass trim, very good condition, specific use unknown.

24in (61cm) long

$1,000-1,500　　　**TWC**

An American "L.S. Starret" rule, with "C.S.Grannis" mounts with level, nice condition.

12in (30.5cm) long

$10-20　　　**TWC**

An American "Jordon" steel measure, marked "Germany", in millimetres and inches.

6.5in (16.5cm) long

$12-18　　　**TWC**

An American 19thC brass decorative beam trammel, set with steel points on mahogany bar.

6.5in (16.5cm) high

$300-400　　　**TWC**

An American maple scraper, used by cabinet makers to smooth wood.

c1830　　10in (25.5cm) long

$200-300　　　**RAA**

An American steel compass, marked　"P. Lowentraut - Newark, N.J." and stamped "J.F. Helm", minor surface rust.

8.5in (22cm) long

$20-30　　　**TWC**

An American turned wood device, with six wheels covered in black rubber.

8in (21cm) diam

$30-40　　　**TWC**

An American rosewood and brass gauge, marked "R. Helm", maker unknown, possibly made by owner, good condition.

7.5in (19cm) long

$40-60　　　**TWC**

An American primitive early bow saw, as found, worn condition.

c1850　　18in (45.5cm) long

$15-25　　　**TWC**

An American ash cabinet maker's mallet.

9in (23cm) long

$6-10　　　**TWC**

LEAD FIGURES

- Solid cast figures were popular during the 19thC. Look around the base of a figure as many manufacturers placed their marks and names there.
- Repainting affects value considerably – undamaged pieces in original colors have higher values. Modern paints are usually more opaque and have a different finish and touch. Never repaint a figure if the original paint shows wear as this will reduce the value.
- Repairs or conversions (where pieces, such as heads are replaced making a rare figure) usually cause lumps and require repainting so, with close inspection, can usually be spotted.
- New collectors should handle and see as many figures as possible to see original condition, colors, forms and which pieces comprise a correct set. Some collectors 'customised' figures with extra detail. This is also detrimental to value.
- Original boxes can almost double a value, especially if the box is in good condition with labels intact and little or no damage. If the box was inexpensively made or by a smaller maker, these are usually rarer as they were generally thrown away. Britains' boxes are more common.
- After World War I, the 1920s saw non-military subjects and characters being produced, such as Britains' famous 'Home Farm' series, zoo animals and footballers.
- Don't store lead figures in oak cases as the oak can secrete an acid which degrades lead. Damp also causes 'lead rot', which is irreversible.
- The 1950s, with the Coronation and the introduction of children's television, saw a massive resurgence of interest in lead figures, but plastic was becoming popular as it was inexpensive. Most companies moved to plastic from the mid-1950s onwards.

A boxed Britains' 1470 State Coach, comprising gold coronation coach containing the figures of King George VI holding the sceptre with Queen Elizabeth beside him, drawn by eight horses (four with riders) and with associated harness pieces, box good except for split corners at one end.

Horseman 3in (8cm) high

$150-200   DN

A selection of Britains' farm vehicles, comprising a farmer's gig with grey horse, a dairy cart with walking milkman and assorted churns (no horse), a roller with brown horse, and three four-furrow ploughs, unboxed.

$300-400   DN

A farm collection, mostly more-modern Britains', including Land Rover and horsebox, horse-drawn farm cart, two tractors and various items of machinery, and approximately 20 plastic horses, cows etc, unboxed.

$200-250   DN

A Britains' 44F Country Cottage, with a collection of lead garden items, the cottage of moulded composition cardboard, the garden items including a sundial, gate, walling and pillars, paving, lawn, flowerbeds and a quantity of flowers.

$800-900   DN

Three rare Britains' Mickey Mouse figures, from set 1645, comprising Minnie Mouse and Goofy and Pluto, some damage, all unboxed, and a tinplate flat figure of Mickey Mouse playing the concertina.

$350-450   DN

A Richard Courtenay figure of Sir Walter Raleigh, good, nose chipped, sword bent, paint chips.

$100-150   SI

A Richard Courtenay figure of Charles I, circular red base, signed "Made in England".

$80-120   SI

A Richard Courtenay figure of Nell Gwynne.

$100-150   SI

An early 20thC collection of 17 rare Heyde Arabs and Bedouins, including three seated smoking, three seated playing instruments and others, some flaking paint.

$400-450   **SI**

A Britains' set #1474 gilt Coronation Chair, two pieces with cushion.

1937

$80-120   **SI**

A set of 12 unusual Heyde tribesmen, each walking with circular and elongated shield, wearing striped loin cloths and carrying pole spears, some flaking paint.

$150-200   **SI**

A C.B.G. Mignot figure of a lady in waiting, wearing blue dress, in original box, box good.

$80-120   **SI**

A boxed set of Hornby engineering staff.

1.5in (4cm) high

$80-120   **WHP**

A C.B.G. Mignot figure of George Washington, with sword, in original box, chip to slightly bent sword.

$100-150   **SI**

A C. B. G. Mignot figure of Saladin, with wrong box, chips to hand and legs.

$100-150   **SI**

A John Hill & Co stagecoach, with driver and shotgun, together with two Britains' Indians, coach and horses.

John Hill & Co, often known as 'Johillco', produced figures in England from 1898-1959. Their figures often show less rigidity in pose and style than those by Britains'.

Coach and horses 6.75in (17cm) long

$60-80   **WHP**

A collection of eight assorted Mignot, German and other horses, comprising three Mignot, one Lucotte and four German horses, chips.

$100-150   **SI**

Two C.B.G. Mignot figures of Louis XVI, one as a boy, the other as an adult wearing a blue coat, both in original boxes.

$150-250   **SI**

A C.B.G. Mignot figure of Cardinal Richelieu on horseback, in original box, chips, box poor.

$150-250   **SI**

A Vertunni figure of Queen Elizabeth I.

$60-80 SI

A Vertunni figure of Catherine De Medicis #A-12, chip to head.

$45-55 SI

A Vertunni figure of Madame Du Barry #A-16.

$200-250 SI

A Vertunni figure of Empress Josephine, in Coronation robes.

$100-150 SI

A Vertunni figure of Marie Leczinka, with two ladies of the court, chips to pink robe.

$250-300 SI

A collection of four Vertunni figures, including Louis XIII, Francis I and others, bases repainted.

$150-200 SI

A collection of three Vertunni figures of personalities, including Heleise Selessi and two gentlemen in 19thC dress.

$400-500 SI

A collection of five Vertunni personality figures, including Conde, Henry II, Louis XI and Henry VIII, chips, the bases repainted.

$300-400 SI

A Vertunni figure of Charles VI, set #7, chipped nose.

$60-80 SI

A Vertunni figure of Louis XVI.

$120-180 SI

A Vertunni figure of Marie De Valois, wife of Henry IV.

$120-180 SI

A Vertunni figure of Catherine Parr, set #284, chips to face.

$80-120 SI

A Vertunni figure of Eleanor D'Aquitaine, chips to nose.

$120-180 SI

A large scale figure of George Washington, unknown maker, on a Heyde horse, some chips and scratches.

c1900-1912 4in (10cm) high

$150-200 SI

A Vertunni figure of Marie D'Anjou, wife of Charles VII, set #43, chip to hat.

$60-80 SI

A Vertunni figure of Louise De Lorraine, excellent condition except for chips to hand.

$80-120 SI

A 29-piece part circus/zoo set, comprising three clowns, a ringmaster, a lion tamer and others, various factory marks.

Largest 4.75in (12cm) high

$150-250 WHP

A large scale mounted Arab, possibly Heyde, cast in three separate pieces, chips.

3.75in (9.5cm) high

An unusual set of 23 English Robin Hood figures, unknown maker, with thick bases stamped, "England" and "M" numbers in pencil, together with two foot knights, three civilians and six knights, some off bases.

$300-400 SI

$150-200 SI

A collection of six assorted Ballada Napoleonic infantry figures, including a flag fearer, a grenadier, a drummer, a light infantry soldier and others.

$300-400 SI

Five Britains' Historical Series set #1664 Knights of Agincourt, comprising foot knights, in original box.

$300-400 SI

A Britains' part set #241 Chinese infantry, including two red jackets, one blue and green jacket, one figure repainted.

$150-250 SI

A Britains' set #5872 Valley Forge, in original box.

A pair of Britains' Collector's Series individual mounted figures, #8878 General Grant and #8877 General Lee in original boxes, boxes mint.

$60-80 SI

$25-35 SI

A Britains' set #276 US Cavalry, third version, three mounted on black horses and two mounted on brown, one leg broken, no box. *c1930*

$150-250 SI

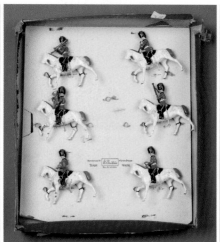

A Britains' part set band of 2nd Dragoons (Royal Scots Greys), six instrumentalists, in original box, chips to legs, lacks kettle drummer, box poor.

$200-300 SI

A collection of ten Britains' soldiers, including two fire fighters, two aviators, three 1930 bandsmen, one gunner set #28, two repainted squires, one figure has broken drumstick.

$150-200 SI

A collection of 12 Britains' Royal Air Force figures, comprising six set #2011 infantrymen, one WAAF in blue and five Infantry from set #1518, a few chips.

$150-200 SI

A Britains' Special Premier series set #8926 Thornycroft A.A.truck, created by Charles Briggs, with service detachment, the truck marked W.D., four personnel with paper labels, in original box, truck with two weak/bent supports, box good, one tear.

$150-200 SI

A Britains' set #9740 mobile 18in (46cm) heavy Howitzer, mounted for field service, in original box, some ammunition.

$250-350 SI

A Britains' set #2150 Centurion tank, a dark green model with aerials, tracks and revolving turret, with white United Nations Korean Conflict Star and chassis, in original box, a few chips.

c1957-1963

$550-650 SI

A rare early Britains' Ltd set#1643 Heavy Duty Underslung Lorry, with driver, anti-aircraft, gun #1522, and kneeling gunners, #1643 18 white wheels, with original illustrated box, a few chips.

$1,500-2,000 SI

A Britains' set #1725 Howitzer.

$150-250 SI

A Britains' set #1716 A.A. gun, together with a Saledo metal tank.

$30-40 SI

A Richard Courtenay Sieur William De Liniers, position XI, the base signed in black "Made in England by R. Courtenay".

A Richard Courtenay archer, the base signed "Made in England by R. Courtenay".

$550-650 SI

$1,200-1,800 SI

A large R. Cameron French Grenadier, by Ray Rubin, 1810 era, metal base, signed.

3.5in (9cm) high

$150-250 SI

An early Richard Courtenay Guy Sieur de Rochefort, position Z-8.

$1,200-1,800 SI

A Richard Courtenay Sieur W.M. de Courtenay, position Z5, moveable visor, signed, "Made in England by R. Courtenay".

$600-800 SI

A Richard Courtenay fallen knight, wounded by arrow, chips to left thigh and left shoulder.

$600-800 SI

A Richard Courtenay Sir Robert Holland, position H-2, the base signed, "Made in England by R. Courtenay", chip to nose.

$1,000-1,500 SI

A Richard Courtenay mounted Earl of Warwick, position H12, the base with hairline crack under right leg due to weight of figure.

$1,000-1,200 SI

A collection of four Richard Courtenay figures, including the Earl of Suffolk, K.G., position 19, base badly scratched, Prince Valiant, chips, Sir Miles Stapleton K.G., position 17, moveable sword, base chipped.

$550-650 SI

A collection of nine mounted Heyde American Revolution continental regulars, with black vests and blue neck facing.

$250-350 SI

A rare large-scale Richard Courtenay figure of Edward the Black Prince, the base signed "Made in England by R. Courtenay", chips to base and right elbow.

4.25in (10.5cm) high

$750-850 SI

A collection of 52 Heyde foot and mounted knights, including 21 foot knights with green bases, two knights on single green base in combat, nine knights running and charging with brown bases, six standing with arms overhead with brown bases, five mounted knights on galloping horses, one bugler, one standard bearer, seven banners on poles, some slightly damaged.

$550-650 SI

A collection of ten Heyde knights, with shields and spears, chips and some slightly damaged.

$100-150 SI

A Mignot Roman chariot and rider, the red chariot box ornamented with gilding, the horses at full gallop, with box, scratch to harness, box fair.

C.B.G. Mignot were founded in France in 1825 after taking over the historic Lucotte name and expanding the range enormously. Lucotte are recognised as being the first company to commercially produce three dimensional toy figures. Mignot are still producing solid cast toy soldiers today, and their past ranges are highly sought after.

$150-250 SI

A Mignot set #361/12 French Dragoons, nine marching at the slope, one drummer, one officer, retied in original box, box poor.

$250-350 SI

An Imrie/Risley French 5th Hussar, with Highland feather bonnet in hand, on wood base.

$60-80 SI

A Mignot Regiment of the Dauphine standard-bearer (1747), mounted on wood base in original box, re-glued to base, box poor.

$120-180 SI

An Imrie/Risley British Grenadier c1750, by Peter Blum, special figure made for a diorama at Trenton Barracks Museum, on wood base.

$150-200 SI

A Mignot General Lee figure, mounted, in original box, box fair.

$80-120 SI

A Minikin Norman Knight, after Richard Courtenay, in red, in original box, chip to leg.

$40-50 SI

A collection of eight assorted Mignot Standard bearers, including two Greeks (1917), two English Colonials, one Russian First Empire and others, a few chips, one repainted base.

$150-200 SI

A collection of eight assorted Mignot flag bearers, Armies of the World, all on foot, various regiments, one repainted base, chips.

$150-200 SI

A collection of five The Soldier Shop War of 1812 British Line Infantry, together with three additional flagbearers, three mismatched bases.

1988

$150-200 SI

A rare early Charles Stadden plaster mould British Scot Officer/Seaforth (1890-1900), sculpted and painted by Charles Stadden, on wood base, signed "Charles Stadden" on base in silver, some chips to legs and belt.

Figure 2.5in (6.5cm) high

$250-350 SI

A rare Charles Stadden 54mm super figure, 1914 British 11th Hussar Officer, the base with Charles Stadden stamp.

$600-800 SI

A Charles Stadden by Keith Whippler figure, Virginia Provincial Infantry Private 1755, on diorama base, signed "by Keith Whippler".

$55-65 SI

A Charles Stadden 1750 British Officer, on diorama base.

$150-200 SI

A large scale Stadden 1968 Drummer of the Coldstream Guards, on high oval base.

4in (10cm) high

$100-150 SI

A rare Warren set #41 U.S. Army scout car, with machine gunner, driver and seated soldier with rifle, white wheels, chips.

$1,500-2,000 SI

A group of Warren U.S. infantry figures, one U.S. standard bearer, one trumpeter, one flag bearer, one officer with sword raised and four marching troops, a few chips.

$1,200-1,800 SI

A World War II Recognition model 105 mm Howitzer, cast metal tank.

$120-180 SI

OTHER TOY FIGURES

- Elastolin was the name for a composition material used for toy figures by the German company Hausser between 1920 and the 1950s, when they converted to plastic. Elastolin products can be discerned from similar versions by their oval bases.
- 'Plastic' figures should not be considered unbreakable. Both age and the fact that the material was often mixed with chalk or kaolin to help the paint adhere can make them brittle and easy to damage.
- 1954 saw the introduction of Britains' first plastic figures – their 'Herald' range – which are considered to be the best moulded figures ever.

A Herald Set #790 Horse Guards Unbreakable models, comprising three mounted and three foot, tied in original illustrated box, one flag broken, box good.

c1950

$150-250 SI

A Herald Set #H7601 Cowboys and Indians Unbreakable models, comprising four cowboys and four Indians in active foot positions, tied in original box, box good to fair, age wear.

c1950

$150-250 SI

Four Elastolin, John Niblett & Co. and other figures, including three plastic figures including a 2.75in (7cm) Elastolin Norman knight on rearing horse, a mounted knight in Gothic armour and a foot knight (540 by Niblett), together with a silver figure of a Man-at-Arms by Plata De Ley.

$80-120 SI

A set of three Elastolin American Revolutionary band figures, including two drummers and another, chips.

1930s   *2.75in (7cm) high*

$100-150 SI

A large scale Elastolin American Flag Bearer.

7.25in (18.5cm) high

$150-200 SI

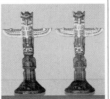

A set of three Elastolin totem poles , a few hairline cracks.

$400-500 (set) SI

A rare Elastolin figure of a condor, together with a turkey figure, wrong Elastolin box.

$150-200 SI

A rare composition Elastolin turtle.

$120-180 SI

A rare Elastolin figure of a bison, together with a small snail figure.

$120-180 SI

TOY TRAINS

- The first model trains were produced in the 1850s but were simple, heavy designs and not very realistic. It was not until the late 19thC that trains became more life-like and internal clockwork or steam-driven mechanisms were used.

- The German companies Marklin, Bing and Carette dominated the early years with good quality tinplate trains which were exported until World War I temporarily halted sales. Bing trains are lighter and have more realistic modeling than Marklin. Top quality pieces were hand painted but the majority had lithographed livery and decoration.

- Marklin introduced the concept of 'gauges' in 1891 at the Leipzig Toy Fair. The larger gauges of I, II and III were gradually replaced around 1910, due to a demand for smaller trains, by the smaller 0 gauge which itself was phased out in 1954. The even smaller 00 gauge was introduced in 1935. In 1948 the H0 gauge with better designed trains was introduced.

- By 1923 most British train companies had started to merge into four companies (LNER, GWR, SR and LMS) and manufacturers had to redesign liveries to match.

- Couplings between the locomotive and carriages help to date trains. Tin loops were used before 1904, hook couplings were used from c1904-c1913 and sliding drop link couplings thereafter.

- Plastic trains were introduced in the 1960s.

- Condition is important, with lost pieces and damage such as dents and wear to paintwork on early tinplate models seriously affecting value. Later examples should be in as fine condition as possible and sets or components with their original boxes will command a premium.

A Bing 0-gauge clockwork George the Fifth RN 2663, 4-4-0 and tender, well refinished with two-colour lining, three control levers to cab, central handle missing, minor wear to finish, distortion to cab roof.

$100-150   **W&W**

A Carette for Bassett Lowke clockwork 4-4-0 George the Fifth locomotive RN 2663, and six wheel tender finished overall in black with two-colour fine lining, with two-control rods to cab, minor wear to finish, some damage to cab.

Many of the trains sold by British company Bassett-Lowke (1899-1969) between 1900 and 1933 were supplied by the German companies Gebruder Bing and Carette. They also had their own factory, called George Winteringham, which they relied on after their relationships ended with Carette c1917 and Bing in 1933.

$250-350   **W&W**

A Bassett Lowke 'Duke of York' green clockwork O-gauge train. *c1927*

$300-400   **WoS**

A Bing 0-gauge 4-4-0 electric motored green RN 3422 locomotive, with litho-finish, some age wear to finish.

$150-200   **W&W**

A Hornby 0-gauge clockwork 4-4-0 no. two special tender locomotive, Yorkshire, RN 234, in LNER green livery with black running plate, LNER to tender sides, some repainting, tender reworked and refinished.

$200-250   **W&W**

A Hornby 0-gauge clockwork no. two tender locomotive, 4-4-0 with six wheel tender, refinished in green, with brass plate no. 2711 to cab sides, bolt together construction, minor wear, rust through to corner of tender, one driving wheel loose.

$300-400   **W&W**

A Hornby 0-gauge clockwork 2-6-0 Mogul and six wheel tender, based on Bassett Lowke mechanism with adapted body, valve gear, finished black with RN2867 to cab side, and associated six wheel tender finished LMS maroon, loco cab's coupling missing.

$300-400   **W&W**

A Leeds Model Co. 0-6-2 tank locomotive in LNER green livery, with black and white lining, LNER and RN 9356 to side tanks, applied Leeds label on underside of cab roof, electric motor good condition, overall minor wear and retouching.

$400-500   W&W

A Leeds Model Co 0-gauge 2-4-2 tank locomotive, refinished in LMS overall black with RN 10952, ex L&Y Railway Company, electric motored, minor wear.

$300-400   W&W

A Leeds Model Co 0-gauge 0-6-0 electric motored tank locomotive, in Southern green livery, RN 258, few minor chips.

$1,500-2,000   W&W

An 0-gauge assembled locomotive 4-4-2, in LNER green with RN 246 to tank, main body possibly Leeds, but with two-part chassis plate, minor wear overall.

$150-200   W&W

A GWR-style 0-gauge clockwork scratch-built tinplate 4-4-2 sloping boiler tank locomotive, finished in dark green, with no lining or transfers, handrails, brakepipes, with two control rods to cab, some overall wear.

$150-200   W&W

A Bing 0-gauge short precursor tank 4-4-0, in mid-brown LMS livery, RN 420, clockwork version, retouching to paintwork.

$200-250   W&W

HORNBY

■ Frank Hornby began manufacturing 0-gauge trains in 1920 as German imports became unpopular. Early trains were crude and sturdy, with clockwork mechanisms. By 1923 and particularly during the 1930s, they became more realistically modeled.

■ Hornby Dublo was introduced in 1938 to compete with Marklin's 00 gauge. Inexpensive clockwork Dublo version were produced until 1940 and are comparatively scarce and highly desirable today.

■ Lingering effects from World War II and the success of Dublo led to a serious decline in quality of 0-gauge trains. The range was redesigned in 1946 and was discontinued in 1969.

■ From 1953, trains displayed nationalised British Rail liveries, but these were dull. In 1957, the range was upgraded with great success. The introduction of plastic trains in 1960 proved to be too costly for Hornby who were taken over by Triang in 1964.

■ After 1964, production of Dublo passed to G&R Wrenn of Basildon, Essex, England. Triang saw its demise in 1971, but the Hornby name continued with the popular 'Hornby Railways', which has dominated 00 gauge ever since.

■ Increasing demand and nostalgia has extended collecting to later Triang pieces and 1970s and 80s 'Hornby Railways' sets. When assessing value look for complete sets, in excellent condition and boxed.

An 0-gauge clockwork scratch-built 4-4-2 LMS tank locomotive, finished in maroon, with lettering to side tanks, RN 701 to bunker sides, a metal chassis with mainly wood body and two control rods from rear of bunker, minor wear overall.

$200-250   W&W

A 1930s Hornby LMS train Tank locomotive, red clockwork, 0-gauge.

$80-120   WoS

A Trix Twin Railway 0.4.0 tender electric green loco, OO-gauge.

Until 1958, Trix Twin trains were produced by George Winteringham, the manufacturing arm of Bassett Lowke.

c1955

$80-120   WoS

A Hornby Dublo 'Duchess of Montrose' electric OO-gauge green locomotive .

c1956

$70-100 WoS

An East German Rokal loco and two timber wagons, electric and T-gauge.

c1955

$70-100 WoS

A Lionel 1668E grey electric train and tender, 20V, O-gauge.

c1930

$200-250 WoS

A Hornby Dublo 'Creppello' electric green diesel, OO-gauge.

c1962

$70-100 WoS

A Märklin S.B.B. electric RET 800 green locomotive, HO-gauge, with box.

c1956

$300-400 Wos

A Lionel O-Gauge locomotive, 'Santa Fe', no.2333-20, in silver and red with yellow trim, mint condition, with box.

1949   *13.25in (34cm) long*

$600-700 CR

A Lionel 027-Gauge loco and tender, the locomotive no. 2055 with smoke chamber and pellets, the tender no. 6026W with whistle, in original boxes, missing red jewel running light.

1953

$250-350 CR

An early Lionel O-Gauge tin green locomotive, no. 252 and observation car no. 604, enamel loss and pitting.

The US market was dominated by Lionel (1901-1969), New York, who bought the popular Ives company in 1928. Trains after World War I were mostly O-gauge, but Lionel introduced its own size called 'American Standard Gauge'. Other popular American companies included American Flyer (1907-1960s) and Carlisle & Finch (1896-1915).

$120-180 CR

An assembled Lionel 027-Gauge locomotive, 'Picatinny Arsenal', no. 42, along with box car no. 6454, cattle car no. 6656, double-dome tanker no. 6465, gondola car no. 6462, and caboose no. 6452, crack to one side.

1950s

$400-500 CR

A Märklin steam locomotive, no. 5747, 1-gauge with sound effects and three passenger wagons, two with serial no. 5.804, the other no. 5.805.

$1,200-1,800 TK

A Tri-Ang transcontinental blue electric train set, OO-gauge. *c1960*

$80-120   **WoS**

An O-gauge fine scale electric 4-4-0 and six wheel tender, entitled 'The Boat Train', of the SE & CR RN 740, finished in green lined livery with brass dome, heavy mainly brass construction, together with three built-up South Eastern Railway fine scale bogie coaches, cast compensating bogies and steel wheel sets, the whole train to represent a period boat train, minor wear.

$1,500-2,000   **W&W**

Two O-gauge LNER kit built coaches, the bodies varnished with teak finish, fully-glazed and with interior detail, cream wood roof to one and tinplate to the other, on cast bogies with metal wheels, minor wear.

17in (43cm) long

$100-150   **W&W**

A Bing O-gauge LNER saloon coach, in litho-print teak woodgrain effect with red and cream lining, with recessed vestibules with opening doors, white opening roof to reveal interior table and chair details, minor wear, roof refinished and coupling missing.

$150-200   **W&W**

A rare Leeds Model Co. O-gauge Nettle Sentinel Scammell Rail Car LNER, with all-wood construction with litho print paper detail overlays, electric motor bogie, die-cast Mansell-type wheels, minor wear over all.

$150-200   **W&W**

A Hornby Dublo 2-rail 'Start Set', OO-gauge, boxed. *c1964*

$200-250   **WoS**

Three O-gauge Hornby Metropolitan coaches, with litho tinplate wood grain finish, grey roofs, nut and bolt fixings to sole plates and bogies all finished in black, with tinplate and plastic wheels, one has "Fabrique en Angleterre" oval transfer to base, wear to finish.

$150-200   **W&W**

A rare Leeds Model Co. O-gauge SR Brighton Belle Pullman car 'Doris', in brown and cream livery with full lining and detailing on litho-print paper overlay on wood core, with two late-style bogies with plastic wheel sets, corridor connections and replacement brass buffers, minor wear.

$250-350   **W&W**

A Hornby Dublo Pullman coach, with OO-gauge, boxed.

c1962

$40-60   **WoS**

A Lionel Lines O-Gauge Pullman car, 'Madison' no.2627, in maroon, mint condition, with box.

1948-1949 15in (38cm) long

$550-650   **CR**

A Lionel Lines O-Gauge Pullman car, 'Manhattan' no.2628, in maroon, mint condition, with box.

1948-49 14.5in (37cm) long

$450-550 **CR**

Three O-gauge Leeds Model Co. articulated LNER coaches, the rake made up of three 1st/3rd composite non-corridor bodies finished in teak litho-print details with white tinplate roofs, standard bogies with die-cast wheels, some wear and repainting.

$120-180 **W&W**

A OO-gauge rake of three articulated coaches, in LNER livery, with litho-print teak paper detailing over wood with cream finished roofs in the style of LMC, all 3rd RN86703, 1st/3rd RN86701 and 3rd/Brake RN 86705, cast bogies with nickel silver wheels, minor wear.

$120-180 **W&W**

An American Flyer O-gauge 20V rolling stock, with two coaches, roofs repainted.

c1935

$300-400 **WoS**

A Bassett-Lowke catalog.

$20-30 **WoS**

A Hornby Dublo catalog.

$20-30 **WoS**

A Tri-Ang catalog.

$20-30 **WoS**

A Tri-Ang catalog.

$20-30 **WoS**

A Wrenn Railways catalog.

$20-30 **WoS**

A 1920s clockwork turntable, rare gauge 2 size, possibly Bing.

$50-80 **WoS**

Two Lionel train accessories, including Trestle Bridge no. 317 and 'The Whistling Station' no. 125, with original boxes.

$100-150 **CR**

TINPLATE

- The early 19th century saw toy makers turn away from wood and on to tinplate. New production methods meant it was cheaper and faster to produce.

- Tinplate toys are made from a stamped sheet of steel, plated with tin and then brightly colored. Toys made before 1895 were hand decorated and can show a very fine degree of detail, later ones were lithographed in color and are of comparatively lesser quality, but are still highly collectable.

- The second half of the 19th century saw many successful and prolific companies being set up, primarily in Germany, such as Marklin (1856), Gebruder Bing (1863) Ernst Planck (1866) and E.P. Lehmann (1881).

- Tinplate toys were made in the USA from the 1830s onwards, but not to the same extent as in Europe. The industry grew in the early 20th century, with prolific makers such as Louis Marx, who even opened a factory in England. Today, 19th century American tinplate toys are rare and much sought after.

- Many toys from the 1850s onwards were die-stamped 'penny toys', which were very simple cars, aircraft or boats with a simple flywheel or a push-along action. Their popularity peaked around 1905.

- German toys were not exported during wartime.

- Tinplate toys continued to be very popular until the 1930s, when die-cast toys superseded them, only to be followed in the mid 20th century by mass-produced, inexpensive plastic toys. Japan produced tin-plate toys from the 1920s onwards and their battery operated robots from the 1960s are very popular.

- Cars, trucks (including fire trucks) wind up or mechanical models, airplanes and particularly boats are very popular amongst collectors. As well as date, sophistication of design and any mechanical features, large sizes, bright colors and noted makers are all important factors to look for when collecting.

- Condition is imperative as when damaged, the surface is difficult to restore and poor restoration brings values down. Dents, splits and missing pieces will also affect value detrimentally. Packaging, especially from early toys, is hard to find and will augment values.

A clockwork Schuco streamlined car, orange and black body, missing key, excellent condition.

c1950

$250-350   **TK**

A clockwork Schuco 1010 Maybach streamlined car, working, missing key.

c1950

$250-350   **TK**

A clockwork Schuco streamlined toy car, missing key.

c1950

$250-350   **TK**

A clockwork Schuco Freilaufrenner 1250, steering front wheels, with automatic clutch, no key.

c1950

$150-250   **TK**

A clockwork red Schuco Fex 1111 toy car, distressed, with instruction leaflet.

c1950

$250-350   **TK**

A clockwork "Tipp & Co" toy car, rubber tires, steering front wheels.

c1950   *9in (23cm) long*

$100-150   **TK**

A Schuco Examinco 4001 driving school toy car, five gears, front wheel steering, no windscreen, steering wheel and key.

c1950

$350-450   **TK**

A Spanish Schuco Commando Auto 2000 streamlined toy car, with nickel parts, steering front wheels, with instructions and original box, no key.

c1950

$400-500   **TK**

SCHUCO

- Schuco was the trademark for the German company Schreyer & Co. who were founded in 1912.
- They are well known for their soft toys such as monkeys and teddy bears as well as for their clockwork toys.
- By comparison, their cars are often less expensive, with mechanical versions and well-known cars such as Donald Campbell's 'Bluebird' sitting at the top of the desirability stakes.
- The Schuco 'Akustico-Auto' was capable of making noises, using two separate clockwork mechanisms. It also could be fitted with a driver, 'Schuco Fritz', who had moveable arms and legs.

A Schuco Akustico 2002 toy car, with horn, two different clockworks, one distressed, steering front wheels, missing windshield and key, with instruction leaflet.

c1950

$250-350   TK

Three wind-up Schuco Micro Racers toy cars, one Mercedes 220, one VW-Käfer and one Porsche, made with original Schuco tools by Nutz, Germany, mint condition with original boxes.

1987

$250-300   TK

A Japanese Isetta tinplate clockwork bubble car.

7.5in (19cm) long

$250-300   CB

A Japanese Yonezowa tinplate MG car, friction-driven.

4.75in (12cm)

$55-65   CB

A 1930s Japanese tinplate clockwork tank.

4in (10cm)

$60-80   CB

An early tinplate lithographed racing car, with fly wheel propulsion, maker unknown, probably German, original finish with scratches.

c1910   4.75in (12cm) long

$300-400   TWC

A French Meccano Constructor motor car, with green body and wheels, yellow roof and wings, and white tires, marked "Meccano / France" at base of driver's side bonnet; no windscreen glass but generally fair condition, unboxed.

$300-400   DN

A post war Tri-Ang Minic Toys tinplate streamlined saloon.

5in (12.5cm)

$180-220   CB

A JEP ladder truck.

$800-1,200   BCAC

A TP fire engine.

$1,000-1,500   BCAC

A Burnett ladder truck.

$500-600 **BCAC**

An MMN fire truck.

$1,500-2,000 **BCAC**

A rare clockwork Baukastenauto Märklin truck, opening door, rubber tires, steered from driver's seat, original condition

c1930 *16.5in (42cm) long*

$1,500-2,000 **TK**

A tinplate Sutcliffe Racer 1 speedboat.

9.5in (24cm) long

$70-100 **CB**

A tinplate "United States" cruise liner.

15.5in (39.5cm) long

$650-750 **CB**

A rare musician clown, probably made by Distler, with a small musical box in the base, spring-operated, lithographed tin, in very good working condition.

Distler, of Nuremburg, Germany, is very well known for its tinplate cars, produced primarily during the 1920s and 1930s. The company was active between c.1900 and 1962.

c1950

$600-800 **TK**

A scarce Japanese Hadson tinplate friction-driven Greyhound bus.

13in (33cm) long

$500-600 **CB**

A Japanese tinplate San Francisco cable car, friction driven, boxed.

5in (19cm) long

$70-90 **CB**

A post war Japanese tinplate clockwork trombone playing clown.

9.25in (23.5cm) high

$350-450 **CB**

A Calypso Joe the Drummer tinplate wind-up toy, complete with original box, good condition.

4in (10cm) high

A West German tinplate part train set and terminal.

$40-60 **WHP**

$180-220 **CR**

A J Chein wind-up duck, in working order.
c1920-1930

$200-250 | **BCAC**

A 1920s French tinplate clockwork frog.
4.25in (10.5cm) high

$500-600 | **CB**

A very rare early version of a toy zeppelin, with two passenger cabins mounted directly under the airship.
c1912

$450-550 | **TK**

A Lehmann tin toy, 'The Performing Sea Lion'.
c1899

$300-400 | **TK**

A tinplate clockwork crocodile.
15in (38cm) long

$100-150 | **CB**

FIND OUT MORE...

David Pressland, 'The Art of the Tin Toy', published by Schiffer Publishing, 1992.

Jurgen Franzke, 'Tinplate Toys: From Schuco, Bing & Other Companies', published by Schiffer Publishing, 1997.

A CLOSER LOOK AT A TIN MERRY-GO-ROUND JUG

This complicated and attractive tin toy is highly unusual, and very well made. By winding up the mechanism, the airships revolve at speed and lift slightly, with their propellers twirling as they move through the air.

It has many protruding parts which could have become damaged or broken off, but on this example all parts are still in very good condition with bright colors.

Airships, or 'zeppelins', are an unusual vehicle to be used on a toy as they were only generally used as a mode of transport during the first few decades of the 20th century. Today, pieces and memorabilia related to airships are highly collectable.

Despite lacking a maker's name, it dates from before the First World War. This fact, the condition and the combination of hand-painted and lithographed parts makes it a desirable piece for collectors.

A rare Arnold Mac 700 tinplate clockwork motorcycle, black with green, cream and silver detailing, rider in period clothing will mechanically mount and dismount in between riding his machine, produced in the immediate post WWII period, very good condition for age and type, minor wear, complete with key and original instruction sheet.

$350-450 | **W&W**

A wind-up tin merry-go-round toy, with zeppelin-type air ships, French flag on top, unknown manufacturer, hand painted tin socket and lithographed airships, good working condition, extremely rare.
1910 *15.75in (40cm) high*

$1,200-1,500 | **TK**

DINKY TOYS

- Dinky Toys were manufactured by Meccano. The first toys were released in 1931 as accessories to Hornby train sets with the first cars (set 22) being released in 1934, both under the name 'Meccano's Model Miniatures'. Both ranges were very successful and by late 1934, the name had changed to 'Dinky Toys' and over 100 models were available.
- The earliest models were made of lead, but this soon changed to aluminum zinc which can be die cast better, with greater detail. The years from 1931 until 1941 are considered the 'golden age' of Dinky.
- The Second World War led to a decline and pause in production. Many pre-war toys did not survive in good condition. As such, pre-war Dinky toys in excellent condition are very highly sought after. Series 28 delivery vans and 25 series lorries are particularly desirable.
- After the war, Dinky reintroduced pre-war models, but there are differences. These include fatter wheels, drab colours and black finished base plates.
- The larger range of 'Dinky Supertoys' was introduced in 1947. In 1954, Dinky changed their numbering system from numbers with a letter suffix to a three digit code from 001-999. Models using this new numbering system sell for less.
- By 1963, the company was in financial trouble and in 1964 was bought out by Lines Bros, who made Triang products, in 1964. In late 1979, the Liverpool factory closed.
- Scratches, repainting and other damage seriously affects value.

A No. 501 Foden Dinky Diesel eight-wheeled wagon, with first-type brown cab and back, black chassis, silver side flash, brown ridged wheels, herringbone tyres, no hook, back with some corrosion, in buff box, split at one end.

$250-300   Vec

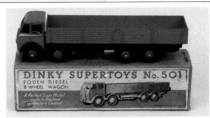

A rare US export No. 501 Dinky Foden eight-wheeled wagon, with first-type red cab and back, silver cab flash and black chassis, in early Supertoy box with red spot on end label.

The Dinky Foden 501 Diesel 8-Wheel Wagon, with the first type cab, was issued in various colours, but the rare US export only issue had a red cab and back, silver cab flash and black chassis. In mint condition it can be worth up to £4,000. The common UK version (above) is in mid-brown with silver flash and black chassis and in mint condition is worth up to £350.

$1,200-1,800   Vec

A Dinky Toys 504 Foden 14-ton tanker, first type cab and chassis, in red with silver flash to cab, fawn tank, red wheel hubs, boxed, some wear, vehicle in good condition, minor chipping, rusting to tank.

$400-500   W&W

A Dinky Toys 942 Foden 14-ton tanker "Regent", with red hubs, fair condition with paint chipping and wear, blue-stripped box.

$80-120   DN

A Dinky Toys 905 Foden flat bed truck with chains, boxed.

7.25in (18.5cm) long

$200-300   CB

A Dinky Toys 903 Foden flatbed truck with tailboard, dark blue cab and chassis, orange flatbed and light blue hubs, unboxed.

$120-180   DN

A Dinky Toys 959 Foden dump truck, red with silver chassis and yellow wheel hubs, complete with plough blade to front, boxed, minor wear, minor chips.

$450-550   W&W

Two Dinky Toys commercial vehicles, a 533 Leyland Comet Cement Wagon "Ferrocrete", unboxed and a 922 Big Bedford Lorry with maroon cab and chassis and fawn truck body.

$80-120   DN

A Dinky Toys 917 "Spratts" Guy van 917, with box.

5.25in (13.5cm)

$500-600 CB

A Dinky Toys 945 AEC Fuel tanker in Lucas Oil livery, green cab and tank with white decals, promotional model for Lucas Services in original Lucas bubble pack, age wear to pack.

$200-300 W&W

Five Dublo Dinky small vehicles: an 061 Ford Prefect in fawn with smooth grey wheels, box good; an 064 Austin Lorry in green with smooth grey wheels, box fair to good; an 068 Royal Mail Van with treaded grey wheels, box poor; an 062 Singer Roadster in orange with smooth grey wheels, unboxed; and another 064 Austin Lorry in green with treaded grey wheels, paint faded, unboxed.

$120-180 DN

Three Dublo Dinky commercial vehicles: an 066 Bedford Flat Truck in grey, no hook, unboxed, an 072 Bedford Articulated Flat Truck in yellow and red with grey wheels, small paint blelmish on trailer, box fair and an 070 AEC Mercury Tanker in Shell/BP livery with green cab, red tank and grey wheels, box fair.

$150-200 DN

A Dinky Toys 987 ABC TV mobile control room, in light blue and grey, with red flash, complete with camera and camera man, boxed, minor wear.

$200-300 W&W

A Dinky Toys 986 BBC TV roving eye vehicle, in standard green-grey livery, complete with cameraman, camera and aerial, boxed.

$120-180 W&W

A Dinky Toys Ambulance "ID19" Citroen, produced by the French factory, with box.

4.5in (11cm) long

$150-200 CB

A Dublo Dinky Toys 073 Land Rover and Horse Trailer, with green vehicle fitted with black ramp, complete with horse, box good.

$150-200 DN

Four assorted Dinky Toys cars, comprising a 38d Alvis in maroon with grey seats and black hubs, a 23d Auto-Union in silver with racing number 2 and no driver, a 230 (205) Talbot Lago in blue with yellow racing number 4 and uncommon yellow plastic hubs, and a similar but smaller French Dinky 23h Talbot Lago unboxed.

$150-200 (four) DN

A Dinky Toys 255 Mersey Tunnel Police van, with box, one end missing flap.

2.75in (7cm) long

$60-80 CB

A pre-war French-made Dinky Super Streamline Saloon, of 24e type but with no side window framing, possible repaint, unboxed.

$250-350 DN

Four early post-war Dinky Toys cars, including a 30b Rolls-Royce in fawn with black chassis, a 36f British Salmson Four Seater Sports in green with black chassis, and a 39a Packard Sedan in brown, unboxed.

$250-350 DN

Three Dinky toys, comprising: a 23e/221 Speed of the Wind racing car, playworn, unboxed; a 163 Bristol 450 Sports Coupé in green with racing number 27, box good; and a 481 Bedford van "Ovaltine", unboxed.

$120-180 DN

A Dinky Toys 289 Routemaster bus, with box.

4.75in (12cm)

$70-100 CB

A rare pre-war Dinkie Toys RML bus.

4in (10cm) long

$500-600 CB

A Dinky Toys Observation Coach.

4.5in (11cm) long

$40-60 CB

A rare Dinky Toys 749 Avro Vulcan, cast in aluminium; some roundel deterioration, unboxed.

Only 500 of these Vulcans were made, for export to Canada, the models being numbered 749 under the wing whereas 992 was used in the catalogue and on the box.

$1,500-2,000 DN

FIND OUT MORE...

John Ramsay, 'Ramsay's British Die-Cast Model Toys Catalogue', 9th edition, published by Swapmeet Publications, 2001.

Mike Richardson & Sue Richardson, 'The Great Book of Dinky Toys', published by New Cavendish Books, 2000.

A Dinky Toys prototype model in diecast of the Phantom II F-4K, painted in light grey, with hand-applied dark green camouflate, minor wear.

$250-350 W&W

A Dinky Toys prototype wooden model 671 Mk 1 Corvette high speed warship, painted in grey, cream and white with simple detailing but includes diecast metal rocket launcher to aft deck, some marking.

$200-300 W&W

A Dinky Toys Joe 90's car, together with two Sam's cars from the same TV series.

4in (10cm) long

$40-60 WHP

A Dinkie Toys 698 Gift Set Tank Transporter with tank, boxed, one corner frayed.

12in (30.5cm) long

$200-250 CB

A Dinky Toys die-cast Lady Penelope FAB1 Rolls Royce and Thunderbird 2.

5.75in (14.5cm) long

$80-120 WHP

A Dinky Supertoys Ruston Bucyrus Excavator, 975 red chassis, yellow cab and green jib. In original box with inner packaging and instructions, minor wear.

$120-180 W&W

CORGI TOYS

- Corgi Toys were made by Mettoy Limited, based in Swansea, Wales. Although Mettoy has its origins in the 1930s, Corgi toys were not introduced until the 1950s, and are still in production today.

- In 1950, Mettoy released a range of 'Entirely New Miniatures' as a forerunner to Corgi. In 1954 Marcel van Cleemput produced the first Corgi designs. The range was launched in July 1956.

- Corgi aimed to compete with Dinky's 'Supertoys' range, and its innovation over Dinky was that each toy had windows, a fact that was used in advertising slogans of the period.

- 1957 saw the first catalogue and 1959 saw other popular innovations such as suspension (known as 'Glidamatic') and trunks and doors that opened.

- Corgi produced highly successful models from many TV programs and films, primarily from the 1960s onwards, including cars from 'Batman', 'The Man from U.N.C.L.E.', James Bond films, 'Chitty Chitty Bang Bang' and 'Superman'.

- Versions are a key area for collectors. Some models were re-released and values differ depending on the version you own. A good example is the 1964 range of 'Corgi Classics' which ceased in 1969 after a factory fire and was re-released in 1985. Here, as with many variations, the later base plate has a different name, reading 'Special Edition'. Wheels are also important with some having flat 'WhizzWheels' rather than cast wheels.

- Variations are another key area to understand. Many models were produced in limited production runs, finished in different colors to the standard model, or with different elements such as differently colored components.

- Condition is vital, with scratches and repainting reducing the value seriously. The original box will always make a model more desirable, but the box must be in good condition too. If it is crushed, faded or has damaged cellophane, the value will be affected.

A Corgi Toys Mini-Cooper 249, black with deluxe wickerwork, with box.

2.75in (7cm) wide

$100-130 CB

A scarce Corgi Austin Mini van 450, metallic mid-green with red interior and silver grille, boxed, vehicle mint.

$80-100 W&W

A Corgi BMC Mini Cooper S 1967 Monte Carlo winner 339, red with white roof, RN 177, LBL 6D numberplates, complete with roof rack and spare wheels, in special box with paperwork, minor wear to label, car mint.

$70-90 W&W

A pale blue Corgi Toys Morris Mini-Minor.

2.75in (7cm) long

$30-40 CB

A scarce Corgi Toys Mercedes Benz 220 SE Coupé 230, black, with box.

4in (10cm) long

$100-130 CB

A Corgi Toys BMC Mini police van with tracker dog 448, with box, box missing one flap.

It is hard to find this car complete with the policeman and dog as they were often lost when played with due to their size.

Car 3in (7.5cm) long

$150-180 CB

A Corgi Toys Bentley Continental Sports Saloon 224, by H. J. Mulliner, black, some minor chips, tears along folds in box.

4.25in (11cm) long

$70-90 CB

A Corgi Toys Ford Mustang Fastback 2+2 competition model 325, with box.

3.75in (9.5cm) long

$80-100 CB

A Corgi Toys Le Dandy Coupé Henri Chapron body on Citroën D.S. chassis, burgundy, doors and trunk opens.

4in (10cm) long

$60-80 CB

An aqua blue Corgi Toys Citroën D.S., Monte Carlo Rally No. 75.

4in (10cm) long

$100-120 CB

A racing green Torgi Toys Bentley Le Mans 1927, soft top lifts up.

3.75in (9.5cm)

$30-40 CB

A Corgi Toys T.S. 9B Whizzwheels 153, with Italian finish, mint and boxed.

Box 6.5in (16.5cm) wide

$35-45 CB

A Corgi London Transport Routemaster double-decker bus, in the colours of the New South Wales Govt. Transport Dept., green, cream and dark brown, with Naturally Corgi Toys Corgi Classics adverts, boxed, with small paper slip.

$70-100 W&W

A scarce Corgi Toys London Route Master bus 469, mint with box.

Box 6in (15cm) wide

$40-50 CB

A Corgi Toys Circus Giraffe Transporter with giraffes 503, with box, flap torn, one taped.

3.75in (9.5cm) long

$100-150 CB

A Corgi Toys Chipperfields Circus Crane Truck 1121, with box, box taped at one corner.

5.5in (14cm) long

$150-200 CB

A Corgi Chipperfields Performing Poodles set 511, comprising a light blue and red Chevrolet Impala with bodywork conversion to carry dogs, complete with poodles and female figure on green stand, boxed, contents mint.

The diverse Chipperfield's Circus range was first released in 1960. Today, complete sets in boxes in excellent condition are highly sought after.

$120-180 W&W

A Corgi Prototype Tarzan gift set 36, a manufacturer's pre-production die-cast metal mock-up containing a green and white striped Land Rover and trailer with opening roof hatch, diorama background, with made-up box illustrated with stick-on lettering and decals, some age wear.

$225-275 W&W

A pre-production white metal Corgi Supermobile, finished in blue with decals.

This rare model was produced by the factory before the release of the toy. It has a small factory fault on the left hand arm, but is otherwise in near mint condition. Constructed from a white metal, it has silver-colored arms rather than red plastic arms as on the standard model. These facts make this a desirable model with a higher value standard models.

$375-425   **W&W**

A Corgi Toys "Man From Uncle" Oldsmobile Super 88.
4.25in (10.5cm) wide

$55-75   **CB**

A Corgi Magic Roundabout Citroën Dyane, with Dougal, Dylan and Bryan.
4.75in (12cm) long

$45-55   **WHP**

A Corgi Toys Chitty Chitty Bang Bang.
6in (15cm) long

$70-100   **WHP**

A Corgi Toys Batmobile with Batman and Robin 267, first issue with box.

Corgi has always enjoyed great success with its models produced from popular TV programs and films. The TV program 'Batman' starring Adam West is a good example.

The Batmobile was the first Batman model and was released in 1966. It came in a gloss or matt finish, with a red 'Batman' decal on the doors and an array of accessories including rockets.

Box 6in (15cm) wide

$625-675   **CB**

ROBOTS

■ The 1960s saw a deep fascination with outer space, reinforcing the popularity of robots. Collectors should look for battery powered robots from this period made from tin plate, particularly those by Japanese manufacturers. 'Remote control' robots from the 1980s are now also becoming popular amongst a new breed of collectors, but it will be some time before they begin to fetch the high prices commanded by those from the 1960s.

A battery-powered toy robot, with plastic body.
12.25in (31cm) high

$50-70   **TK**

A 1960s battery-powered toy robot.
11in (28cm) high

$250-300   **DH**

A rare Secret Weapon Space Scout toy robot, by SH Horikawa Toys, Japan, battery-operated.
c1960
8.75in (22cm) high

$1,000-1,500   **TK**

A Tomy Omnibot programmable or remote control robot.
c1984   14.in (36cm) long

$120-180   **HLJ**

A Tomy Omnibot Jr. remote control robot.
c1984   10.25in (26cm) long

$70-90   **HLJ**

An American cast-iron trolley bank, unmarked, with rolling wheels painted gold and embossed "Main Street", minor paint losses.

6.5in (16.5cm) wide

$250-300 **CRA**

A 1940s Pearson Page Jewsbury & Co. Lloyds Bank money box, in the shape of a book.

4.5in (11.5cm) high

$20-30 **DH**

A clock-work driven 'Santa', by Alps, Japan, with original box, moves arms, rocks from left to right and rings the bell.

10in (25.5cm) high

$300-400 **TK**

A 1930s Celluloid 'Happy' dwarf skittle, unmarked.

9in (23cm) high

$80-120 **BEJ**

An American composition 'Felix the Cat' figure.

c1930

$350-450 **Fra**

A battery-powered animated bear, by Alps, Japan, Cragstan Toy No.714, excellent working condition.

c1958 *8.25in (18.5cm) high*

$300-400 **TK**

A post-war English plastic clockwork Bo Peep and sheep.

$100-130 **CB**

A 'Jabba the Hutt' boxed action playset, from the Star Wars series.

$15-20 **WHP**

A Product Enterprises 'Talking Dalek', in white and gold plastic, designed by Stephen J. Walker.

c2001 *6.25in (16cm) high*

$40-50 **FFM**

A Product Enterprises 'Dalek Rolykin', designed by Stephen J. Walker.

From the 'Dr Who' TV series originally conceived by Terry Nation.

2000-02   *1.75in (4.5cm) high*

$6-9   **FFM**

A rare 1940s vintage hollow-hull schooner pond sailboat, of mahogany and other woods with painted hull, two tall masts, two sails and full spinnaker, brass fittings and movable rigging, tiller and rudder, complete with 48-star miniature American flag, in wooden table stand, some solder to tiller, rigging loose.

72in (183cm) high

$1,000-1,500   **CRA**

A model ship #29 "Falcon", in original box, box fair.

$80-120   **SI**

A 1940s Wilesco working steam engine, with horizontal cast-metal boiler, flywheel, and seven experiment accessories including electro-magnet, light, bell, battery unit, belt and pulley and more, the main unit mounted on metal base and attached to plywood, metal tag and "Made in England".

16in (40.5cm) wide

$550-650   **CRA**

Two 20thC painted cast-iron 'Overland Circus' Wagons, one with six musicians dressed in white, two outriders and driver, pulled by four white horses, a red Polar Bear Wagon with driver and two outriders, white horses, some new paint, missing bear, unmarked.

Larger 16in (40.5cm) wide

$250-350   **CRA**

A 1960s friction-powered 'X-Ray Space Pilot' toy gun, 'With Sparkling Barrel & Explosive Firing Noise', made in Japan.

Box 8.25in (21cm) wide

$120-180   **DH**

A 1950s friction-powered toy Rocket Racer.

6.75in (17cm) wide

$100-150   **DH**

A 'Captain Marvel Club Kit', by Fawcett, including envelope, induction letter, membership card, with pin, a secret message, an ad for various goodies and a secret message clipped from a comic book.

c1946

$250-350   **HC**

A Dubreq 'Rolf Harris Stylophone', signed by Rolf Harris.

c1971 Box 13in (33cm) wide

$70-100   **HLJ**

An MB 'Big Trak and Transport' programmable tank.

c1979   *23.5ins (60cm) long*

$120-180   **HLJ**

CHESS

- Most chess sets date from the 18th, 19th and 20thC. Sets from the 17thC do exist but these are extremely rare and very valuable. Most sets were made in India and China and exported to England.

- The 19thC saw the largest growth in chess set manufacture as the Industrial Revolution improved distribution and the growing middle class began to play this formerly 'aristocratic' game.

- Look for complete and original sets as missing or replaced pieces devalue a set. The exceptions are very rare incomplete sets which will retain a value as collectors often buy several incomplete examples of the same set to assemble a complete set.

- Cracked pieces devalue a set considerably, so examine all the pieces carefully. Pay special attention to ivory sets with stained or colored pieces, especially those in green or red, as the precise color is very difficult to match exactly when effecting a repair.

- 'Staunton' sets by Jaques of England are highly desirable and represent a collecting field of their own. Staunton sets were made in materials including wood and ivory from the 1940s and are still produced today. Most pieces are marked 'Jaques of London' but marks do vary depending on period. Boxes for Jaques sets usually have green labels, but yellow and red are also known.

- Chess boards are comparatively good value for money as, unlike today, sets were originally sold without boards. Demand amongst collectors is low as they usually focus on sets rather than boards.

An 18thC Burmese carved ivory figural set, one side stained dark red, the other side left natural, kings and queens as crouching deities, bishops as towers, knights on horseback, rooks as figures on elephants, pawns as crouching monkeys.

King 3.2in (8cm) high

$12,000-18,000   **FRE**

A late 18thC Russian walrus ivory Kholmogory set, the Christians versus the Turks, the Christians dressed as Roman soldiers, the Turks in national dress, kings seated on thrones, queens as viziers, bishops as elephants, knights as rearing horsemen, rooks as double-masted sailing ships, pawns as footsoldiers, the chessmen mounted on circular elephant ivory bases, one rook missing half a mast.

The set reflects Eastern influences with the use of viziers as queens and the use of elephants as bishops. As is usual with Russian sets, rooks are depicted as ships. Kholmogory sets are carved typically from walrus ivory.

King 3.5in (8.8cm) high

$10,000-15,000   **FRE**

An early 19thC Nepalese carved ivory figural set, one side stained red, the other side left natural, kings as deities seated on thrones, queens as viziers, bishops on elephants, knights as horsemen, rooks as pagodas, pawns as squatting soldiers.

King 3.2in (8cm) high

$10,000-15,000   **FRE**

An Indian Vizagapatam ivory playing set, one side stained a nut brown color, the other side left natural, kings with open galleried crowns incorporating a seated prince of alternate color, queens with foliate decoration and mounted kneeling viziers, bishops with curved foliate miters, knights as rearing horses, rooks as turrets mounted with standard bearers, again in an alternate color.

c1840   *King 5in (12.7cm) high*

$3,000-5,000   **FRE**

An early 19thC Russian carved mammoth ivory figural set, one side stained red, the other side left natural, kings wearing crowns, cloaks and holding orb and scepter, queens in Empire period dress and wearing tiaras, bishops with beards and wearing cross-surmounted caps, knights as Roman cavalry with shields, rooks as elephants bearing turrets and flags, the pawns as footsoldiers wearing Roman-style helmets, holding spears in their left hands and swords in their right.

King 4.2in (10.6cm) high

$12,000-18,000   **FRE**

An Indian Vizagapatam ivory playing set, one side stained dark brown, the other side left natural, kings with pierced galleries and foliate knops, queens with split feathered open crowns, bishops as pierced miters, knights as horses' heads, rooks as slender turrets raised on circular bases, pawns with decorated bulbous knops.

c1840   *King 5in (12.7cm) high*

$2,000-3,000   **FRE**

A Berhempore ivory 'East India (John) Company' figural set, the British East India Company versus native troops, one side with black-stained bases, the other side left natural, kings as elephants with howdahs, queens as elephants with open howdahs and parasols, bishops as camels, knights as horsemen, rooks as turrets with standard bearers, pawns as sepoys wearing pearls, and native troops, together with a framed certificate from Maskett-Beeson explaining the historical background to the set.

These sets reflect the extent of British colonialism, before the Indian Mutiny of 1857 led to the imposition of direct rule from the United Kingdom. One side represents the East India Company, while the other side are Indian native troops. The East Indian pawns are Indian-born sepoys in the uniform of the East India Company. Sets such as these were intended for display, rather than play.

c1840   *King 4in (10cm) high*

$15,000-20,000   **FRE**

A 19thC ivory chess set, of turned form, half stained in red, some damage.

King 4in (10cm) high

$1,500-2,000   **DN**

A Northern Chinese ivory figural set, the pieces in traditional dress, kings with swords, queens with robes, bishops with horsewhips, knights as warriors on horses, rooks as elephants, pawns as footsoldiers.

King 3.5in (8.8cm) high

$2,500-3,500   **FRE**

A 19thC Indian ivory chess set, the castle with flags, half stained in red, some damage.

King 4.7in (12cm) high

$1,200-1,800   **DN**

A 19thC Chinese carved ivory chess set, the castles with Union Jack flags, stained in red and green, some damage, lacking one pawn.

King 3.5in (9cm) high

$1,200-1,800   **DN**

A 19thC Cantonese export ivory 'Puzzleball' set, stained red and left natural, the pieces in traditional Chinese dress, kings and queens as Emperor and Empress, bishops as mandarins, knights as warriors on horseback, rooks as elephants, pawns as footsoldiers, together with a 19thC Cantonese Export japanned gilt-decorated chess board/box, the interior for backgammon.

King 5.2in (13.2cm) high

$1,000-1,500   **FRE**

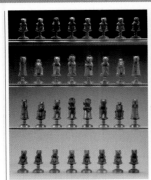

A 19thC Cantonese export ivory chess count set, one side stained red, the other side left natural, the pieces with chess symbols against a pierced and carved florally decorated ground.

1.5in (3.8cm) diam

$1,200-1,800 **FRE**

A 19thC Swiss pearwood 'Bear of Berne' figural set, one side in a darker wood, kings and queens wearing crowns and holding scepters, bishops with staffs, knights as bears carrying smaller bears on their backs, rooks as turrets with bears' heads looking out, pawns as squatting bears.

'Bear of Berne' sets appear to be scarce. The center for carving of this type was the area around Brienz in the Bernese, Switzerland.

King 3.5in (8cm) high

$5,000-8,000 **FRE**

A 19thC Cantonese export ivory 'Puzzleball' set, stained dark red and left natural, the pieces in traditional Chinese dress, the king and queen as Emperor and Empress, bishops as mandarins, knights as warriors on horseback, rooks as elephants with flags, pawns as warriors on horseback.

King 5.5in (13.9cm) high

$2,500-3,000 **FRE**

A 19thC English bone barleycorn playing set, stained red and left natural, kings and queens with petaled knops, bishops with split miters, knights as horses' heads, rooks as turrets with flags, some damage to stems.

King 4in (10cm) high

$600-1,000 **FRE**

A 19thC English ivory playing set, one side stained red, the other side left natural, the king and queen with multi-knopped stem, the bishops with bulbous split miters, knights as horses' heads, rooks as stepped turrets with carved brickwork decoration.

King 2.5in (64.5cm) high

$1,200-1,800 **FRE**

A 19thC Cantonese export ivory figural set, one side stained red, the other side left natural, the white king as King George III, the white queen as Queen Charlotte, bishops as mandarins, knights as warriors on horses with bows, rooks as elephants, pawns as footsoldiers with triangular shields.

King 4in (10.5cm) high

$1,500-2,000 **FRE**

A 19thC English ivory playing set, stained red and left natural, the pieces with multi-knopped stems, bishops with split miters, knights as horses' heads, rooks as turrets with flags.

King 3.5in (9cm) high

$500-800 **FRE**

A 19thC French bone Lyon set, one side stained black, the other side left natural.

King 3.75in (9.5cm) high

$1,500-2,000 **FRE**

A 19thC Jaques Staunton boxwood and ebony set, the white king stamped "Jaques London", in a wooden box with a sliding lid and a green label marked "Jaques & Son, London".

King 3.5in (9cm) high

$600-1,000 **FRE**

A 19thC Jaques Staunton ivory set, one side stained red, the other side left natural, the white king signed "Jaques London", in a Jaques Cartonpierre paper-mâché box, the underside with red label marked "Jaques London", together with a 19thC leather mounted folding board by Leuchars of London, the board with alternate tan and red squares, gilt-tooled borders, and signed "Leuchars...Piccadilly".

King 3.5in (9cm) high

$3,000-5,000 | FRE

A late 19thC Chinese ivory chess set, each piece carved with concentric balls, the bishops carved with masks, and two dice shakers half stained in red, some damage, lacking a bishop.

King 4in (11cm) high

$700-1,000 | DN

A late 19thC German cast iron figural set, in the Zimmerman style, Romans versus Gauls, the Roman side with black stained bases, the Gaulish side with brown colored patinated bases, kings and queens as generals and their consorts, bishops as standard bearers, knights as cavalry, rooks as campaign tents, pawns as footsoldiers, one pawn with damaged base.

King 2.5in (6.5cm) high

$600-1,000 | FRE

A late 19thC Ceylonese ivory and ebony figural set, the king and queen in the lotus position, the queen praying, bishops as turrets, knights as rearing horses wearing crowns, rooks as elephants heads, pawns as flower buds.

King 5.5in (14cm) high

$9,000-12,000 | FRE

An Indian Rajhasthan painted and lacquered ivory figural set, one side with a green colored background, the other side with a red background, kings as kneeling princes, queens as kneeling viziers, bishops as camel heads, knights as horses' heads, rooks as elephants' heads, pawns as seated footsoldiers, all the pieces with gilt decoration.

King 4.5in (11.5cm) high

$5,000-8,000 | FRE

A Chinese carved ivory chess set, each mounted on a concentric ball and round base, half stained in red, some damage, lacking a pawn.

King 5.5in (13.5cm) high

$300-400 | DN

A Jaques Staunton boxwood and ebony weighted set, both kings stamped "Jaques London", in a box with a green label marked "J. Jaques & Son Ltd, London, England", the box stamped "Made in England".

King 4in (10cm) high

$600-1,000 | FRE

An Indian ivory and sandalwood playing set, the pieces with circular foliate carved bases, kings and queens with open crowns, bishops with closed miters, knights as horses' heads, rooks as pagodas.

King 4in (10.5cm) high

$800-1,200 | FRE

A Mexican bone and wood mounted playing set, one side stained purple-brown, the other side in a lighter color.

King 5.5in (14cm) high

$300-400 | FRE

A hardstone bust set, one side an amber color, the other side opaque white, with an onyx board.

King 3.5in (9cm) high

$150-200 **FRE**

A 20thC Indian bone playing set, one side stained dark red, the other side left natural, kings with pierced crowns, queens with petaled knops and multi-faceted stems, bishops with tri-form knops, knights as horses' heads, rooks as castellated turrets on multi-faceted stems, pawns with multi-faceted knops.

King 6in (15cm) high

$400-600 **FRE**

A Soviet Olympiad plastic set, collector's edition, one side black, the other side white, the pieces with gilt bands around the stems, in a fitted plastic and velveteen lined board/box.

King 4in (10cm) high

$300-400 **FRE**

A Venetian Murano decorative glass figural set, one side predominantly white, the other side predominantly black, kings and queens wearing crowns, bishops wearing caps, knights as horses' heads, rooks as turrets, pawns with striped bases and stems.

King 7.5in (19cm) high

$1,800-2,200 **FRE**

A Japanese ivory figural set, one side stained nut brown, the other side left natural, the pieces in traditional Japanese costume, kings and queens in robes, bishops holding scrolls, knights as warriors on horseback, rooks as pagodas, pawns as Japanese footsoldiers holding staffs, in a fitted board/box.

c1950 *King 2.5in (6.5cm) high*

$1,000-1,500 **FRE**

A 20thC Indian bone set one side stained brown, the other side left natural, kings and queens with alternate colored knops, the bishops similar, knights as double-headed horses, pawns with alternate colored knops.

King 5.5in (14cm) high

$300-500 **FRE**

A Russian wooden doll Star Wars set, one side painted predominantly blue, the other side red, the pieces depicting the various Star Wars characters.

King 3.75in (9.5cm) high

$180-220 **FRE**

A 20thC Spanish Pulpit-style wooden set, one side in a lighter colored wood, the other side in a darker colored hardwood.

This set is a modern copy of the 18thC bone Spanish Pulpit sets. Debate continues as to the origin of these sets.

King 5in (13cm) high

$150-200 **FRE**

A 20thC Peruvian pottery figural set, one side predominantly red/brown, the other side a cream color, kings wearing helmets, queens with plaits, bishops as stags, knights as llamas, rooks as rusticated towers, pawns with pipes, with wooden board/box.

King 2.5in (6.5cm) high

$100-150 **FRE**

A 20thC American stained glass set, one side with white opaque glass, the other side with pale green glass, the pieces of abstract form and metal-mounted, kings and queens with copper 'crown' finials.

King 4.5in (11.5cm) high

$700-1,000 **FRE**

An Indian camel bone Americans versus Taliban figural set, the Taliban side stained black, the American side left natural, Americans with carved eagle motif, Taliban with crescent moon and star motif, knights as rearing horses, rooks as turrets.

King 4.5in (11.5cm) high

$300-500 **FRE**

A resin The Lord of the Rings figural set, by Dennis Fairweather, representing good versus evil, kings as Aragon and Sauron, queens as Lady Galadriel and Shelob, bishops as Treebeard, Gollum, Gandalf and Sarmuran the White, knights as Bilbo, Frodo and the Ring-Wraiths, rooks as Hobbit holes, Rivendell, the Dark Tower and the Mines of Moria, pawns as Hobbits and Orcs, together with an accompanying leaflet describing the characters in The Lord of the Rings.

King 7in (18cm) high

$600-1,000   **FRE**

A Chess Teacher of the Century board in honour of John Collins, from the players of the U S Amateur Chess Team Championship, February 1991, the wooden board has several plaques inscribed with the names of chess champions including: Robert Fischer, Robert Byrne, Donald Byrne and William Lombardy.

30in (75cm) wide

$300-500   **FRE**

Chess Memorabilia

A Dresden Meissen-style porcelain group depicting a lady and gentleman in 18thC dress playing chess.

5.5in (13.9cm) wide

$300-500   **FRE**

A 20thC Japanese ceramic group, depicting two gentleman in 18thC dress playing chess, one smoking a pipe.

7in (17.7cm) high

$100-150   **FRE**

A 20thC cold-painted bronze group, in the Vienna style and after Bergman, depicting two Arabs playing chess, seated on a carpet.

3.5in (8.8cm) wide

$400-600   **FRE**

Bill Jacklin (American, b. 1943), "The Chess Players" screenprint, signed, inscribed A/P and dated.

This print shows chess players in Washington Park Square, New York.

1987   *29in (73.6cm) wide*

$600-1,000   **FRE**

A collection of international chess tournament flags, including the Reykjavik International Chess Tournament 1986, Stofnad 1954, the Iceland Chess Safari 1985, and the Ethel B. Collins Memorial Chess Festival.

1995-1996.

$60-100   **FRE**

A chess tournament clock, by Linden, the twin dials mounted on a wooden block, with a push rod mechanism, together with an American chess clock, 'The Blitzer' and a hand-built ten-second chess timer by Edward Lasker, the timer in a wooden case.

8in (20.3cm) wide

$300-500   **FRE**

A Tomy Blip hand-held analogue game.
c1977 6.76in (17.5cm) wide

$30-50   HLJ

A Prinztronic Tournament 1V games system.
c1978 11.75in (30cm) wide

$50-80   HLJ

An Atari 2600 Video Computer System game console.
c1978   13.5in (34cm) wide

$80-120   HLJ

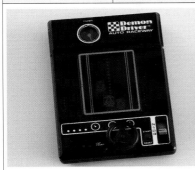

A Tomy Demon Driver hand-held analogue game.
c1978   5.5in (14cm) wide

$30-50   HLJ

COMPUTER GAMES

■ Computer games first arrived on the mass market around 1979 and grew rapidly in popularity during the 1980s. Early games can be characterized by the simple – but addictive – game 'Pong'.

■ Japan is considered to be the 'home' of the computer game. Many games were produced solely for the Japanese market and these are desirable as comparatively few are found outside Japan. However, it is important that these games contain little Japanese text so that it is easy to work out how to play them.

■ Collectors look for 'shoot 'em up' and 'beat 'em up' games. These are highly sought after by dedicated collectors as they tend to be the most popular types of game format.

■ Collectors should look out for highly sought after names including 'Neo-Geo', 'PC Engine' and 'Vectrex', all produced during the 1980s and 1990s. Sinclair products are also popular and constitute a collecting field of their own due to the wide range of models made and their innovative nature.

■ Games must be complete and in working order. The box and instructions add further value, especially with handheld models.

An Atari, Ultra Pong four-player game system.
c1978   10in (25.5cm) wide

$60-100   HLJ

A Videomaster Superscore game, with spy briefcase-style box.
c1978 13.5in (34cm) wide

$60-100   HLJ

A Grandstand Kevin Keegan's Match of the Day tabletop game.
c1979 4in (10.5cm) wide

$50-80   HLJ

A Tomy Stunt Bike hand-held analogue game.
c1978 8.75in (22.5cm) wide

$30-50   HLJ

A Kenner Star Wars Electronic Battle Command tabletop game.
c1979 8.25in (21cm) wide

$80-120   HLJ

A Tomy Desert Race hand-held clockwork game.
c1979   *5.75in (14.5cm) wide*

$15-25   HLJ

A Bambino Basketball tabletop game.
c1979   *7.5in (19.5cm) wide*

$40-60   HLJ

A Bambino Football tabletop game.
c1979   *7.5in (19.5cm) wide*

$40-60   HLJ

A Toytronic Racetrack hand-held game.
c1980   *3.5in (9cm) wide*

$30-50   HLJ

A Bambino Safari tabletop game.
c1980   *9.5in (24cm) wide*

$40-60   HLJ

A Sinclair ZX 81 home computer.
c1981   *6.25in (16cm) wide*

$60-100   HLJ

A CGL Grand Prix hand-held game.
c1981   *5in (13cm) wide*

$40-60   HLJ

A CGL Galaxy Twinvader tabletop game.
c1981   *6.5in (17cm) wide*

$30-50   HLJ

A Grandstand Astro Wars tabletop game.
c1981   *5.7in (14.5cm) wide*

$40-60   HLJ

A Tomy Lupin tabletop game.
c1981   *6in (15cm) wide*

$40-60   HLJ

A Grandstand Crazy Kong hand-held game.
c1981   *4in (10.5cm) wide*

$40-60   HLJ

A Grandstand Mini-Munchman hand-held game.
c1981   *4in (10.5cm) wide*

$30-50   HLJ

A Nintendo Fre FR-27 wide screen game and watch.
c1981   *4.25in (11.5cm) wide*

$60-100   HLJ

A Nintendo Popeye PP-23
wide screen game and watch.

c1981   *4.25in (11cm) wide*

$80-120   **HLJ**

A Sinclair ZX Spectrum Personal
Computer, with rubber keys.

c1982   *8.75in (22.5cm) wide*

$80-120   **HLJ**

A Grandstand BMX Flyer hand-
held game.

c1982   *6in (15cm) wide*

$40-60   **HLJ**

A Tomy Caveman tabletop
game.

c1982

$30-50   **HLJ**

A Tomy Thundering Turbo 3-D hand-held
game.

c1983   *5.5in (14cm) wide*

$30-50   **HLJ**

A Tomy Tron tabletop game, based on the
1982 Walt Disney movie.

c1982   *6in (15cm) wide*

$80-120   **HLJ**

A Nintendo Donkey Kong DK-52
multiscreen game and watch.

c1982   *4.25in (11.5cm) wide*

$40-60   **HLJ**

A silver Nintendo Fireman RC-04 game and watch.

c1980   *3.75in (9.5cm) wide*

$200-300   **HLJ**

A Nintendo Snoopy Tennis SP-30 wide screen game and watch.

c1982   *4.25in (11cm) wide*

$40-60   **HLJ**

A Nintendo Greenhouse GH-
54 multiscreen game and
watch.

c1982   *4.25in (11.5cm) wide*

$60-100   **HLJ**

A Nintendo Mickey & Donald
DM-53 multiscreen game and
watch.

c1982   *4.25in (11.5cm) wide*

$60-100   **HLJ**

A Nintendo Donkey Kong Jr.
DJ-101 new wide screen game
and watch.

c1982   *4.25in (11cm) wide*

$40-60   **HLJ**

A Nintendo Oil Panic OP-51
multiscreen game and watch.

c1982   *4.25in (11.5cm) wide*

$50-80   **HLJ**

An ORIC-1 home computer.

c1983   *10.75in (27.5cm) wide*

$80-120   **HLJ**

A CBSD Electronics Colecovision game console.

c1983   *14.5in (37cm) wide*

$100-150   **HLJ**

An Atari 800 XL home computer.

c1983   *15in (38cm) wide*

$80-120   **HLJ**

A Grandstand Pocket Scrambler hand-held game.

c1983   *6.7in (17cm) wide*

$40-60   **HLJ**

An MB Vectrex game system, with built in TV screen.

c1983   *9.5in (24cm) wide*

$200-300   **HLJ**

A CGL Junglar tabletop game, with pop up screen.

c1983   *6.5in (16.5cm) wide*

$50-80   **HLJ**

A Rosy Astro Attack tabletop game.

c1983   *7.5in (19cm) wide*

$40-60   **HLJ**

FIND OUT MORE...

'Electronic Plastic' edited by Jaro Gielens, Die Gestalte Verlag, 2001 ISBN: 3931126447, which covers handheld games only.

'The Ultimate History of Video Games: From Pong to Pokemon – The Story Behind the Craze That Touched Our Lives and Changed the World' by Steve L. Kent, Prima Publishing, 2001. ISBN: 0761536434

eBay (www.ebay.com) is recognised as being one of the best venues to buy and sell games, but also try www.gamesradar.com who have a special section for 'retro games'.

A Grandstand Firefox F-7 tabletop game.

c1983   *7.5in (19cm) wide*

$40-60   **HLJ**

A Ninetendo Mario Cement Factory ML-102 new wide screen game and watch.

c1983   *4.25in (11cm) wide*

$50-80   **HLJ**

A Grandstand Pocket Scramble hand-held game.

c1983   *3.75in (9cm) wide*

$40-60   **HLJ**

A Ninetendo Donkey Kong II JR-55 multiscreen game and watch.

c1983   *4.25in (11.5cm) wide*

$40-60   **HLJ**

A Nintendo Rain Shower LP-57 multiscreen game and watch.	A Nintendo Mario's Bomb's Away TB-94 panorama screen game and watch.	A Nintendo Donkey Kong Jr. CJ-93 panorama screen game and watch.	A Nintendo Mario Cement Factory CM-72 tabletop game and watch.
c1983 3.25in (8.5cm) wide	c1983 3.75in (9.5cm) wide	c1983 3.75in (9.5cm) wide	c1983 5in (13cm) wide
$100-150 HLJ	**$120-180** HLJ	**$120-180** HLJ	**$100-150** HLJ

A CLOSER LOOK AT A COMPUTER GAME

Nintendo is a renowned name still producing highly popular and innovative games and gaming systems today.

Hand-held games often had detachable battery covers – it is essential that they are present.

This 'Game & Watch' game is rare, complete and in excellent condition which means that the price is comparatively high.

The 'Game & watch' range is highly desirable for three reasons: the size of the games; the reputation of the manufacturer; and the size of the range.
Around 65 different versions were produced and rarer games can fetch comparatively high prices as collectors need them to complete the set.

A Nintendo Donkey Kong Circus MK-96 panorama screen game and watch.

c1984   3.75in (9.5cm) wide

$300-500   HLJ

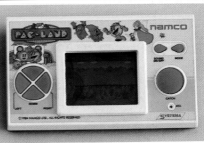

A Sinclair ZX Spectrum+ personal computer.	A Systema Pac-Land hand-held game.
c1984 12.5in (31.5cm) wide	c1984 5.25in (13.5cm) wide
$60-100 HLJ	**$30-50** HLJ

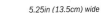

A Ninetendo Entertainment System Deluxe set, including R.O.B.
(Remote Operating Buddy).
c1985

$120-180   **HLJ**

An Atari 2600 game console.
This is a smaller version of the more common woodgrain model.
c1986   *15in (26.5cm) wide*

$60-100   **HLJ**

An Atari 7800 game console.
c1988   *11.5in (29cm) wide*

$60-100   **HLJ**

A Ninetendo Climber DR-106
new wide screen game and
watch.
c1988   *4.25in (11cm) wide*

$60-100   **HLJ**

A Ninetendo Super Mario Bros.
YM-105 new wide screen game
and watch.
c1988   *4.25in (11cm) wide*

£25-40   **HLJ**

A PC Engine game console.
c1987   *5.5in (14cm) wide*

$200-250   **HLJ**

A Ninetendo Balloon Fight BF-107 new wide screen game
and watch.
c1988   *4.25in (11cm) wide*

$100-150   **HLJ**

A PC Engine GT hand-held
portable game system.
c1990   *4in (10cm) wide*

$200-300   **HLJ**

A SNK Neo-Geo CD top-loader
console.
c1994   *10.5in (27cm) wide*

$200-300   **HLJ**

A Sega Multi-Mega (combined
Mega Drive-Mega CD) game
console.
c1994   *5in (12.5cm) wide*

$120-180   **HLJ**

An SNK Neo-Geo Pocket Color
portable game system.
c1999   *5in (13cm) wide*

$60-100   **HLJ**

An MB 'Pac Man' board-game.
c1982   Box 19in (48.5cm) wide
$20-25   HLJ

An MB 'Defender' board-game.
c1983   Box 19in (48.5cm) wide
$20-30   HLJ

An MB 'Donkey Kong' board-game.
c1983   Box 19in (48.5cm) wide
$20-30   HLJ

An MB 'Frogger' board-game.
c1983   Box 19in (48.5cm) wide
$20-25   HLJ

An MB 'ZAXXON' board-game.
c1983   Box 19in (48.5cm) wide
$20-30   HLJ

A Waddingtons 'Super Mario Bros' board-game
c1992   Box 15in (38cm) wide
$10-25   HLJ

An Astronauts jigsaw puzzle,
containing 20 pieces.

c1968   4.5in (11.5cm) high
$6-8   DH

An electronic 'American Flipper Coney Island' pinball game,
coin-operated for four players.

*Coney Island, Brooklyn, New York was considered to be the
world's largest and foremost amusement area during the first
half of the 20th Century. As well as a beach resort, it contained
three large amusement parks; Luna Park, Steeplechase and
Dreamland, all for the amusement of New Yorkers.*
                              63in (160cm) long
$200-300   TK

A pair of Regency lacquer card
trays, one decorated with a king
and queen, the other with the
word "GAME".
          4.5in (11.5cm) long
$150-200   **PSA**

A 'Centennial Presidential
Game' board-game, by
McLoughlin Bros., New York,
covering the first 100 years of
American Presidency, with a
deck of 54 cards, wood block
spinner and instructions, boxed.
1876
$1,200-1,800   TK

A rare 1930s Alfred Dunhill
bridge set, comprising four Royal
Doulton ashtrays and a Dunhill
Namiki maki-e lacquer bridge
pencil in a fitted case.

*This set is extremely rare and
typical of the high quality
items retailed by Alfred Dunhill
in the 1920s and 1930s.*
          Pencil 3in (8cm) high
$600-800   PC

A boxed Pelham puppet type SL "Ballet Girl", with original control bar and colored strings, generally good condition in good original first type yellow box with lid.

12.5in (32cm) high

$70-100 **DN**

A boxed Pelham puppet "Big Ears", early version with large wooden head, with black strings and original control bar, minor damage but generally good condition in good period but incorrect card box with red and blue label to the lid, marked Type LS "Gypsy".

11in (28cm) high

$600-1,000 **DN**

A boxed Pelham puppet type SL "Bom", Enid Blyton's toy soldier character with original control bar fitted with colored strings, moth hole in cap otherwise generally good condition, in poor type yellow box with lid, colors faded, lid split and torn.

13.5in (34cm) high

$300-400 **DN**

PELHAM PUPPETS

- Robert Pelham (1919-1980) founded 'Wonkey Toys Ltd' based in Marlborough, England in 1947. It was renamed 'Pelham Puppets Limited' a year later and underwent a number of name changes in subsequent years before being dissolved in 1997.

- An architect who enjoyed making toys during World War II, Pelham's first designs included a black girl called Chloe, Sandy McBoozle and Wonky Cowboy.

- In 1953, Pelham Puppets acquired the rights to manufacture Walt Disney characters. Pinocchio is one of the most produced characters ever, but the factory also made Mickey and Minnie Mouse, Donald Duck, Snow White and the Seven Dwarfs and Cinderella. Some characters, such as Mickey Mouse, were made in different variations over the years.

- Other well-known characters to have had their own Pelham Puppet include Andy Pandy, the Muppets, Peanuts, Thunderbirds, the Pink Panther and Muffin the Mule.

- Condition is very important as in its peak the company produced thousands of each character and many people have kept their puppets since childhood. Puppets that were not played with and do not have blemishes, scratches or worn clothes and retain their strings intact will be more desirable.

- As a general rule early puppets are more valuable than later ones. However, some of the rarest puppets are the later ones as relatively few of them were made.

- If the puppet has its original box, this will make it more desirable. It is possible to date a Pelham puppet from its box (if correctly matched):
  - 1947-1956 A brown box with a blue label followed by yellow box with a blue and red label.
  - 1956-1968 A yellow-lidded box for the first six years featuring the Mad Hatter from Alice in Wonderland. He was then replaced by a snake charmer character.
  - 1968-c.1970 A yellow box with a clear acetate window.
  - 1970-1986 A band of cardboard was added across the acetate window.
  - Late 1980s A red and yellow candy striped box.
  - Note: Some late production special collectors' characters had differently designed boxes.

A boxed Pelham Puppet type SM "Chef", with original control bar, in need of restringing, some signs of age and one half of mustache missing but otherwise in good collectable condition in poor original cardboard box with blue label to lid.

13.5in (34cm) high

$1,500-2,000 **DN**

A boxed Pelham puppet type SL "Gretel", with original control bar and colored strings, and complete with instruction sheet and 1966 club slip, very good condition in very good second type yellow box with lid.

12.5in (32cm) high

$50-80 DN

A boxed Pelham puppet type SS "Gypsy", with original control bar, colored strings and additional clothing, very good condition in very good original second type yellow box with lid.

11.75in (30cm) high

$40-60 DN

A boxed Pelham puppet type SS "Gypsy", with original control bar and colored strings, good condition in good original second type yellow box with lid.

12.25in (31cm) high

$40-60 DN

A boxed Pelham puppet type LL "Lulabelle", with colored strings, early version with bamboo limbs and rubber-ring lips, some paint loss but generally very good condition in fair to good original card box with blue label to the lid.

23.5in (60cm) high

$220-280 DN

A boxed Pelham puppet type SL "Merlin", dressed in blue robes and hat with original colored strings, complete with instruction sheet; moth damage to robes but in good condition in good original second type yellow box.

$300-400 DN

A boxed Pelham puppet type SL "Mickey Mouse", with original control bar and colored strings and complete with instruction sheet, excellent condition in good original second type yellow box with lid.

10.25in (26cm) high

$120-180 DN

A boxed Pelham puppet type SM "Macboozle", with original control bar and colored strings, good condition in fair to good original cardboard box with red and blue label to the lid.

13.5in (34cm) high

$60-100 DN

A boxed Pelham puppet "Muffin the Mule", early example with original control bar, good condition in fair to good original yellow-striped box.

6.75in (17cm) long

$320-380 DN

A boxed Pelham puppet type SL "Pinocchio", version with plastic legs, with original control bar and colored strings and complete with instruction sheet, excellent condition in good but incorrect second type yellow box with lid, marked for "Tyrolean Boy".

11.75in (30cm) high

$60-100 DN

AUTOMATA

■ The production of automata originates in the 18th century with clocks mounted with complicated mechanical figures. Commercial production began in the early 19th century and reached its apex between c1880-c1920.

■ Value is dependant on the originality and complexity of the mechanism and the condition of the head and costume, which should be original. Replacements and repair will reduce value, less so if done appropriately.

■ Makers from around Paris such as Roullet & Descamps (1832-1972), Vichy (1862-1905), Bontems (1840-1905) and Phalibois (c1850-c1910) are the most desirable names.

A papier-mâché musical bust of a black banjo player, by G. Vichy, on a wooden base, plays two tunes strumming his banjo and pauses to thumb his nose and stick out his tongue, re-dressed.

This example has dancing eyelids, which are a trademark of Vichy.

c1880   21.75in (55cm) high

$12,000-18,000   AMM

A fur-covered papier-mâché tiger automaton, by Roullet & Descamps, with later harness and inset glass eyes, the tiger crouches, roars and leaps with movement of the jaw and head.

c1875   20.75in (53cm) long

An original German wind-up bisque doll, attributed to Porzellanfabrik Rauenstein.

$1,000-1,500   DE

$2,200-2,800   AMM

A Japanese Kobi hand-operated automaton, made of carved and stained fruitwood.

Kobi toys are named after the Japanese port and were made as souvenir pieces for tourists. They are based on Japanese folktales and always have a grotesque element.

A papier-mâché 'The Acrobat' automaton, by G. Vichy, Paris, with clockwork mechanism, performs handstand and then lifts one hand off to two-air musical movement, all original.

It is rare to find a piece with all its original clothing.

c1880   31.5in (80cm) high

$30,000-40,000   AMM

A life-size flock-covered papier-mâché French bulldog automaton, with nodding head and bark and inset glass eyes, on wheels.

c1900   15in (38cm) high

$2,000-2,500   AMM

c1880   4in (10cm) high

$300-500   AMM

BISQUE DOLLS

- Look on the back of the bisque head above the nape of the neck to see the incised marking which shows the mold number, which helps identify the maker and period. Unmarked dolls can often be identified by their facial characteristics and form.

- The body should be original. Dolls made from different pieces have lesser values – a head is generally worth around 50% of the complete doll. Size is important with larger sizes being more valuable.

- Condition is important, with damage reducing value. Some factory defects or flaws are acceptable if not too conspicuous – bisque should be smooth and clean. Cracks decrease value – shining a strong light into a bisque head will reveal cracks, but always ask before carefully removing the wig to do this.

- Look for dolls with original clothing as these command a premium over redressed examples. However, dolls in original clothing are not common and appropriate clothing is acceptable as standard.

- As well as condition, the visual appeal and attractiveness of the doll affects the price. Dolls with the same mold number can even vary in price, with finer quality and more attractive painting being more valuable. Experience will generate an ability to spot a fine doll.

An Armand Marseille bisque-head doll, with sleeping blue glass eyes, four upper teeth, jointed composite body and woven wig, some original clothing, model number 390 61/2.

The 390 series, made from 1900 onwards, is the most commonly found doll by Armand Marseille. Collectors should look for examples with finer, less simplistic features.

3.5in (60cm) high

$200-250   **WHP**

An Armand Marseille baby, with five-piece body, mold 971.

c1915   *17in (43cm) high*

$500-800   **BEJ**

An Armand Marseille German child doll, mold 390.

c1890   *20in (50cm) high*

$500-800   **BEJ**

A marotte bisque shoulder-head doll, with inset blue glass eyes, open mouth, music box plays when doll is turned, wig missing, marked "370 A.M 10/OX. DEP".

c1920   *15in (38cm) high*

$400-500   **TK**

An Armand Marseille bisque socket-head baby, human hair wig and bent limb composition body, for George Borgfeldt, marked "G.327.B Germany A.12.M".

c1913   *19in (48cm) high*

$500-700   **TK**

An Armand Marseille Oriental bisque-head doll, with composition body, all original.

12in (30.5cm) high

$500-800   **DE**

An Armand Marseille black child doll, with three outfits, mold 390.

c1890   *11in (28cm) high*

$400-600   **BEJ**

ARMAND MARSEILLE

- Armand Marseille, based in Thuringia, Germany is one of the most prolific doll makers.

- They made bisque dolls from 1885 onwards after Armand Marseille and his son took over a porcelain factory. Production peaked from around 1900 to 1930.

- Their dolls are marked with 'A M' lettering amongst the German marks.

An Armand Marseille googly doll, all original, no. 323.

c1915   *10in (25.5cm) high*

$2,200-2,800   **BEJ**

SIMON & HALBIG

- Simon & Halbig, based in Grafenheim in Thuringia, Germany, were active from c1869 until c1930 and made many dolls heads for other companies including Kammer & Reinhardt and the French company, Jumeau.
- Their early dolls had fixed glass eyes, solid domed heads and closed mouths. Later dolls have open socket type heads with card pates and open mouths.
- Their dolls can be recognized by the 'S H' lettering as well as by mold number. In 1920, they were bought by Kammer & Reinhardt.

A Simon & Halbig character-face child doll, mold 531.

c1890   *18in (45.5cm) high*

$1,000-1,500   **BEJ**

A Simon & Halbig shoulder-head 'fortune teller' doll.

c1890   *8in (20cm) high*

$500-700   **BEJ**

An early 20thC Simon and Halbig 'Lady' doll, no. 1159.

12in (30.5cm) high

$800-1,200   **DE**

An early 1900s Simon and Halbig/Adolf Wislizenus toddler doll, all original.

$1,000-1,500   **DE**

A Simon & Halbig child doll, for Kämmer & Reinhardt.

c1890   *9in (23cm) high*

$500-800   **BEJ**

A Simon and Halbig girl doll, with bisque socket-head, brown mohair wig and papier mâché/wood ball-jointed body.

5.25 (64cm) high

$500-800   **TK**

A Simon & Halbig tiny child doll, in an Orkney chair.

c1890   *7in (17.5cm) high*

$400-600   **BEJ**

A Simon & Halbig character boy, with fully-jointed composition body, blond mohair wig, dressed in vintage clothes, includes "1908 Baseball Fan" pin, incised "S&H 150/2".

21in (53.5cm) high

$20,000-30,000   **Ber**

A S.F.B.J. Jumeau laughing toddler doll, no. 236.

$1,000-1,200   **DE**

S.F.B.J.

- The 'Societe Francaise de Fabrication de Bébés & Jouets' was a group of French doll makers who joined together to challenge the threatening German doll industry.
- They were based primarily at the Jumeau factory in France and were active from 1899-c1950. As they tried to control costs to produce less expensive dolls, quality was often compromised.
- Dolls tend to be slim, with high cut legs and composition or wooden bodies. Their character dolls, made from 1911 onwards, were more successful.

A S.F.B.J. Bébé, mold 301.

c1900   *18in (46cm) high*

$1,200-1,800   **BEJ**

A S.F.B.J. Bébé, mold 301, all original.

c1900

$2,000-2,500   **BEJ**

An early S.F.B.J. Bru-like mold doll, with high forehead, incised "Depose SFBJ9".

21in (53.5cm) high

$1,200-1,800   **DE**

JUMEAU

- Jumeau, based in France, were active from 1842-1899 and after releasing the first bébé, went on to produce portrait bébés from 1870 and 'Jumeau Triste', sad dolls, from c1880. The heads are marked clearly with the Jumeau name.
- Pierre Francois Jumeau created the first 'bébé' doll, an idealised version of a chubby young girl, in 1885. It was a departure from previous dolls which were shaped to look like slim ladies.
- Competition from less expensive dolls from Germany led to the decline of the company in its last decade.

A S.F.B.J. Bébé, with chair, mold 60.

c1900   12.5in (31.5cm) high

$700-1,000   **BEJ**

A S.F.B.J. Bébé, original outfit, mold 60.

c1900   12.5in (31.5cm) high

$700-1,000   **BEJ**

A Jumeau 'Portrait Fashion' doll, with pressed bisque socket-head on bisque shoulder plate, with blue paperweight eyes, closed mouth, pierced ears, original gusseted kid body, ivory net and lace dress, elaborate lace bonnet, chip to neck.

21in (53.5cm) high

$3,000-4,000   **Ber**

A Jumeau 'Tête' doll, with open mouth, original wig and cork pate, size 8, with red stamp on head.

19in (48.5cm) high

$2,500-3,500   **DE**

A Jumeau 'Tête' doll, with open mouth and creamy composition, size 9, red stamp on head.

21in (53.5cm) high

$3,000-4,000   **DE**

A Jumeau Bébé, size 8.	A Jumeau Bébé, in chemise, size 7.	A Jumeau Bébé, size 9.	A Gebrüder Heubach German schoolboy.
c1890 22in (56cm) high	c1890 18in (46cm) high	c1885 24in (61cm) high	c1900 16in (40.5cm) high
$2,000-2,500 BEJ	**$1,800-2,200** BEJ	**$3,000-4,000** BEJ	**$1,000-1,500** BEJ

A Gebrüder Heubach boy doll, with domed bisque socket-head, closed pouty mouth, intaglio eyes, blond molded hair and composition baby's body, probably marked "0 68 96 Germany", blue ink stamp "19" or "13" and another mark "27", slight repairs.

1912   8.5in (22cm) high

$800-1,000   TK

A Gebrüder Heubach pouty child, all original.

c1915   9.5in (24cm) high

$700-1,000   BEJ

A rare Heubach character child, with bisque socket-head and heavily molded hair, painted intaglio eyes, open mouth with two painted teeth, and fully-jointed composition body, plaid linen dress with lace and ribbon trim, wool cape, red silk shoes.

The character dolls produced by the Thuringian company Gebruder Heubach (c1840-1945) are highly sought after for their visual appeal. Much effort was devoted to the heads, with well-painted molded hair, rosy cheeks and extremely characterful faces. Their eyes were realistic with an indented pupil and an iris highlighted with a white dot.

19in (48.5cm) high

$20,000-30,000   Ber

An Ernest Heubach googly doll, all original.

$300-500   DE

A Kestner doll, with four upper teeth and mohair wig, with mâché/wood ball jointed body and red ink stamp "Germany 6", marked "L*made in Germany* 164".

28in (71cm) high

$800-1,200   TK

A Kestner doll, all-bisque on 'wrestler body', huge size.

c1885   *11in (28cm) high*

$3,000-5,000   **BEJ**

A Kestner Baby doll, with composition baby's body, bonnet marked "11".

1912   *13.75in (35cm) high*

$600-1,000   **TK**

A Kestner all-bisque googly doll, replaced legs.

7in (17.5cm) high

$250-350   **DE**

A German Max Oscar Arnold fashion doll, with shoulder-head and kid body.

c1890   *16in (40.5cm) high*

$700-1,000   **BEJ**

A French Belton doll, with Bru-like face, wooden body and straight wrists.

20in (51cm) high

$3,000-4,000   **DE**

A CLOSER LOOK AT A TWO-FACED DOLL

Bru Jeune & Cie (1866-1883) produced a number of very unusual and fine quality bébé dolls. These examples are much sought after, more so than those produced after 1899 when the company was taken over.

The 'two-faced' style was introduced by Jumeau and features a knob in the hair to turn the head round. The first face is crying, the second is smiling.

A very rare two-faced Bru doll, with bisque cup-and-saucer head on bisque shoulder plate and gusseted kid body with bisque hands, first face has blue-painted intaglio eyes with finely stroked lashes, the open-closed mouth with tiny painted teeth, original bonnet flips to reveal second face of a crying child with closed-screaming mouth, narrow-painted eyes, furrowed brows and appropriately tinted red face, marked No.4.

15in (38cm) high

$20,000-30,000   **Ber**

A Belton doll, with closed mouth, the body with molded red stockings, the swivel flange neck of early design.

9in (23cm) high

$300-500   **DE**

An Ettiene Denamur French Bébé.

c1885   *11.5in (29cm) high*

$2,000-3,000   **BEJ**

A Bru Jne. & Cie Fashion doll, Paris, with pale bisque socket-head on bisque shoulder plate, gusseted kid body, blue paperweight eyes, finely painted eyelashes and brows, closed smiling mouth, human hair wig, wearing ivory cotton pique dress, undergarments, leather shoes, picture hat with flocked flowers on brim, chest stamp, blue oval "Au Nain Bleu, CHAUVERE, 27 Boule Parvoire", damage to kid arms.

18in (46cm) high

$3,000-4,000 **Ber**

A French fashion doll, by Francois Gaultier, incised "S".

1880-90 *20in (51cm) high*

$3,000-4,000 **DE**

A German Goebal fly-on-nose character doll.

c1900 *14in (35.5cm) high*

$1,000-1,500 **BEJ**

A German Alt, Beck & Gottschalk shoulder-head lady, with kid body.

c1890 *21in (53cm) high*

$1,200-1,800 **BEJ**

A Kämmer & Reinhardt girl doll and doll bed, short human wig and composition body jointed at hip and shoulder.

c1930

$180-220 **TK**

A French Damerval Laffranchy Bébé, with walking body.

c1900 *15in (38cm) high*

$1,200-1,800 **BEJ**

A French Bébé Lanternier, with two original outfits.

c1900 *35in (89cm) high*

$5,000-8,000 **BEJ**

A French Charles Marcoux Bébé, in rocking chair.

c1890 *16in (23cm) high*

$1,200-1,800 **BEJ**

A Porzellanfrabrik Mengersgereuth baby.

c1915 *9in (23cm) high*

$300-500 **BEJ**

A Bébé Mothereau, blonde wig and original fully-jointed body, wears period embroidered cotton and crocheted dress, straw hat and original leather boots.

12in (30.5cm) high

$12,000-18,000 **Ber**

A rare pair of Rose O'Neill huggers.

3.25in (8.5cm) high

$320-380 **SFel**

A German Hertwig Rose O'Neill-type Kewpie, with half the box (not shown).

c1910

$1,000-1,500 **BEJ**

A Rose O'Neill kewpie doll, original skirt, mint condition.

4.5in (11.5cm)

$100-150   **DE**

A German Schoenau & Hoffmeister doll, riding a tricycle, wearing a lamb outfit.

c1910

$400-600   **BEJ**

A German Hertel Schwab & Co. baby, unmarked.

c1915

$1,000-1,500   **BEJ**

A German Bruno Schmidt boy doll.

c1915   17in (43cm) high

$1,000-1,500   **BEJ**

A CLOSER LOOK AT A THULLIER BÉBÉ DOLL

A. Thullier of Paris (1875-1893) are a highly sought after name. Their fine quality dolls fetch good prices when sold.

Her enchanting face, clothing and wig are all in excellent condition.

Her wig and clothing are original. She has not been redressed.

At 21 inches this is a very large doll. Dolls this size are not at all common.

She retains her original shoes, which match the doll and were marked by the maker.

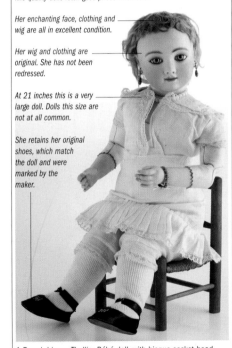

A French bisque Thullier Bébé doll, with bisque socket-head, gusseted kid body, bisque lower arms, blue paperweight eyes, pierced ears, closed mouth, original mohair wig and marked head and shoulder plate, originally marked shoes with butterfly rosettes, original chemise, mint condition, incised "A.9.T."

21in (53.5cm) high

$60,000-90,000   **Ber**

A Limoges bébé.

Several of the well known porcelain factories at Limoges produced a wide range of bébé dolls of differing qualities between c1897 and c1925.

c1910   19in (48cm) high

$800-1,200   **BEJ**

An unmarked all-bisque googly doll, with extra clothing, boxed.

c1910   6in (15cm) high

$700-1,000   **BEJ**

A Jules Steiner doll, fully-jointed composition body, red mohair wig, fixed blue glass eyes, painted brows and eyelashes, closed mouth and pierced ears, dressed in ivory cotton and lace dress, tan wool overcoat, underwear, socks, brown leather shoes and silk bonnet, marked "Le Petit Parisien, BEBE STEINER", incised "Figure C No. 2, J. Steiner BTE S.G.D.G, Paris".

19in (42.5cm) high

$4,000-6,000   **Ber**

A late 19thC bisque-head doll, with cloth body and open mouth, in contemporary sailor dress, possibly marked "Alma".

12.5in (32cm) high

$70-100   **WHP**

ANNALEE DOLLS

- In 1933, after leaving school, Barbara Annalee Davis created her first dolls, selling them as an extension of her hobby through the 'League of New Hampshire Craftsmen'. Many of the first dolls were puppets.

- During the 1940s she married Charles 'Chip' Thorndike and they set up an egg farm together. By the 1950s this business faltered and they took the decision to hire staff to concentrate on Annalee's doll production. Chip invented the wire frame that became the basis for the poseable or 'mobilitee' dolls known today.

- 1954 saw the first price list and photo catalog, which was followed by huge expansion during the 1960s, due to a large rise in popularity when dolls were sold in over 40 states. Despite many workers working from home, 1964 saw the opening of the first factory and also the introduction of bunnies to the range.

- 1973 saw the first bears being added to the range followed in 1978 by the first Hallowe'en mouse. In 1985, other characters were added, creating the Halloween range.

- In 1983 a museum and society were founded. Despite Annalee's recent death, the factory, museum and society continues to grow, as does interest in these historic dolls.

- Annalee dolls fall into many categories, but they center around the full gamut of human emotions, illustrating many human characters and also serve to celebrate seasonal holiday events such as Christmas, Valentine's Day and Hallowe'en.

- Annalee dolls are made from brightly colored fabrics, so should be kept out of strong light to prevent fading. Collectors should also ensure that pests such as moths are kept away from the dolls. Mothballs, or the more pleasantly smelling cedar, act as very good deterrents.

An Annalee 'Rabbit' doll, one of a limited edition.

1964   7in (18cm) high

$750-850   **MSC**

An Annalee 'Turtle' doll, one of a limited edition.

1968   7in (18cm) high

$550-650   **C&M**

An extremely rare late 50's Annalee 'Calypso Dancer' doll, one of a limited edition, signed by Annalee.

7in (18cm) high

$450-550   **MSC**

An Annalee 'Beach Girl' doll, one of a limited edition.

When new this doll was advertised as having "handmade boobs and buns".

1956   10in (25.4cm) high

$1,000-1,200   **MSC**

An Annalee patchwork clown doll, one of a limited edition. of 2742.

1981   18in (45.5cm) high

$80-120   **MSC**

A pair of Annalee 'Go-Go Dancer' dolls, man with rare green eyes, both from a limited edition.

1950   22in (55.8cm) high

$450-550 (each)   **MSC**

A pair of early Annalee 'Square dancer' dolls, from a limited edition.

1956   10in (25.4cm) high

$1,200-1,800   **MSC**

Left: An Annalee 'Doctor' doll.

1959   10in (25.4cm) high

$750-850   **CMS**

Right: An Annalee 'Nurse' doll.

1959   10in (25.4cm) high

$750-850   **CMS**

Left: An Annalee 'Footballer Mouse' doll, one of an edition of 5998.

The doll on the left is an updated version of the other.

1990   7in (18cm) high

$20-50   **MSC**

Right: One of an edition of 1545.

1950   7in (18cm) high

$40-70   **MSC**

An Annalee 'Lawyer Mouse' doll.

This early doll shows Annalee's attention to detail. The will in the mouse's hand is bound in blue paper, just as a real will would be.

1965   7in (18cm) high

$120-180   **MSC**

A one-of-a-kind Annalee 'Mermaid' doll.

7in (18cm) high

$450-550   **MSC**

An Annalee 'Photographer' doll, from a limited edition.

14in (35.5cm) high

$1,000-1,500   **MSC**

A one-of-a-kind Annalee 'Scottish Bear' doll, made for the Disneyworld Doll and Teddy Bear Convention.

1994   18 in (46cm) high

$2,000-2,500   **MSC**

An Annalee 'Sheriff' doll, from a limited edition.

1959   10in (25.4cm) high

$1,800-2,200   **MSC**

An Annalee 'Bank Robber' doll, from a limited edition.

1959   10in (25.4cm) high

$1,200-1,800   **MSC**

An Annalee 'Windsurfer Mouse' doll, one of an edition of 1762.

The figures on the sail represent Annalee's birthday, February 11, 1915.

1982   7in (18cm) high

$40-70   **MSC**

Left: An Annalee St Valentine's Day 'Be Mine Mouse' doll.

7in (18cm) high

$20-30   **MSC**

Right: A prototype Annalee St Valentine's Day 'Be Mine Mouse' doll.

Both dolls were prototypes, but only the one on the left went into production.

7in (18cm) high

$150-250   **MSC**

A pair of Annalee St Valentine's Day 'Fox' dolls.

Never put into production.

7in (18cm) high

$80-120 each   **MSC**

An Annalee St Patrick's Day 'Leprachaun' doll, from a limited edition of 199.

1974   7in (18cm) high

$500-600   **MSC**

An Annalee St Vaentine's Day 'Be Mine Panda Bear' doll.

Never put into production.

7in (18cm) high

$200-300   **MSC**

An Annalee St Patrick's Day 'Leprachaun' doll.

Never put into production.

7in (18cm) high

$80-120   **MSC**

An Annalee St Patrick's Day 'Leprachaun' doll.
7in (18cm) high

$15-25 **MSC**

Three Annalee 'Boy with Firecracker' dolls, from a limited edition of 1893.
These shows how the same doll had many different faces.
1984 *7in (17.5cm)*

$100-150 (each) **MSC**

An Annalee doll, 'Elephant'.
30in (76cm)

$500-600 **MSC**

An Annalee doll, 'Elephant'.
18in (45.7cm)

$300-400 **MSC**

An Annalee doll, 'Elephant', signed by Annalee.
1976 *10in (25.4cm)*

$450-550 **MSC**

A CLOSER LOOK AT AN ANNALEE DOLL

The hand painted faces of these pigs show the skill of the painters in using delicate brush strokes to create faces full of character.

Although pigs are not usually associated with Easter, the pair's cheerful gaze has a springlike feel.

The labels on the pigs' legs show that they are samples from Annalee's stock room.

A pair of Annalee 'Mother' and 'Father' Pigs, store room samples.
1979 *10in (25.5cm) long.*

$450-550 **MSC**

Left: An Annalee 'Colonial Drummer Boy' doll, from a limited edition of 402.
1976 *10in (25.5cm)*

$300-400 **MSC**

Right: An Annalee 'Colonial Drummer Boy' doll, from a limited edition of 4759.
1976 *18in (45.5cm)*

$200-250 **MSC**

An Annalee 'Fourth of July' doll, edition size unknown, cost $10 when new.
1957 *10in (25.5cm)*

$1,200-1,800 **MSC**

An Annalee 'Yankee Doodle Dandy' doll, one of limited edition 153.
1976 *18in (45.5cm)*

$220-280 **MSC**

Left: A pair of Annalee 'Colonial Mice' dolls, from a limited edition of 1527,
1976 *12in (30.5cm)*

$250-350 **MSC**

Right: of Annalee 'Colonial Mice' dolls.
7in (17.5cm) high

$150-250 **MSC**

Left: An Annalee doll, 'Uncle Sam', one of 245.
1976 *25in (63.5cm) high*

$700-800 **MSC**

Middle: An Annalee doll, 'Uncle Sam', one of 1095 made.
1976 *10in (25.5cm) high*

$200-300 **MSC**

Right: An Annalee doll, 'Uncle Sam', one of 245.
1976 *18in (45.5cm) high*

$450-550 **MSC**

An Annalee doll, 'Donkey'.
30in (76cm)

$500-600 **MSC**

An Annalee doll, 'Donkey', one of limited edition 285.
1976 *18in (45.5cm)*

$300-400 **MSC**

An Annalee doll, 'Donkey', one of limited edition 1202.
10in (25.5cm)

$100-200 **MSC**

An Annalee Fall Kid 'Playing with Leaves' doll.
1999 *7in (18cm) high*

$30-50 **MSC**

Left: An Annalee Trick or Treat Series doll, 'Trick or Treat Elf'.

1990   *7in (18cm) high*

$30-60   **MSC**

An Annalee Fall Kid 'Harvest' doll.

2000   *7in (18cm) high*

$30-60   **MSC**

Right: An Annalee Trick or Treat Series doll, 'Elf', from a limited edition.

1990   *5in (12.7cm) high*

$20-30   **MSC**

FIND OUT MORE...

The Annalee Doll Museum, Reservoir Road, Meredith, New Hampshire, U.S.A.. A museum founded by Annalee Davis containing a wealth of information and doll displays.

www.annalee.com – the home of Annalee dolls online with access to the current catalog and help researching retired dolls.

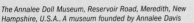

An Annalee Trick or Treat Series doll, 'Skeleton', from a limited edition of 5200.

1990   *7in (18cm) high*

$50-80   **MSC**

Three Annalee 'Hallowe'en' series pumpkins, large pumpkin from a limited edition of 2022, medium from an edition of 1198.

1987-1996

S $15-25 M,L $100-250 MSC

An early Annalee 'Santa' doll.

1956   *12in (30.4cm) high*

$1,000-1,500   **MSC**

Two Annalee Trick or Treat Series dolls.

1996-97

$25-50 each   **MSC**

A pair of Annalee Mr and Mrs Christmas dolls.

    3in (7.6cm) high

$50-100   **MSC**

A pair of Annalee 'Mr and Mrs Christmas' dolls.

2000   *18in (48cm) high*

$100-200   **MSC**

A pair of early 60s Annalee 'Mr and Mrs Christmas' dolls.

    7in (18cm) high

$80-120   **MSC**

A Lenci Maxette doll, with two tags near hem, mint condition.

Lenci was founded in Turin, Italy in 1918. Between 1920 and 1940, they produced a variety of sophisticated fabric dolls in elaborate costumes. The felt face is painted in a surprisingly expressive way. Clothes are usually brightly colored. Lenci dolls must be clean with bright clothes. Dirty faced or worn examples with faded or damaged clothing will be worth a third to a half of the price of a clean and bright example. Correct tags add a premium if present.

$200-300   **DE**

A Lenci 'Mascotte' doll, with rare costume, labeled.

$200-300   **DE**

An Italian Lenci 'Schoolboy' felt doll, all original.

c1930   *17in (43cm) high*

$550-750   **BEJ**

A 1930s Lenci mechanical store display mannequin, from Lord & Taylor with Lord & Taylor tag, all original.

$800-1,200   **DE**

A 1930s Nora Wellings black doll, with painted plush velvet face, flirty glass eyes and smiling mouth.

$80-120   **WHP**

A Nora Wellings 'Mountie' doll.

9.75in (25cm) high

$20-40   **WHP**

A 1930s Empire-marked 'Sailor', often mis-sold as a Nora Wellings doll.

8in (20cm) high

$20-40   **BEJ**

A 1950s Invicta 'Marine' doll.

9in (23cm) high

$15-25   **DH**

A rare early Setti 'St. Nicholas' doll, handmade and painted by artist John R. Wright.

18in (45.5cm) high

$1,800-2,200   **DE**

Left: An early Setti 'Farmer' doll, handmade and painted by John R. Wright.

19in (48.5cm) high

$1,200-1,800   **DE**

Right: An early Setti 'Farmer's Wife' doll, handmade and painted by John R. Wright.

18in (45.5cm) high

$1,000-1,500   **DE**

A large size Steiff 'Pucki', with tag and money bag.

$220-280   **DE**

A British made Dutch boy, labeled "Allwin".

c1930 18in (46cm) high

$200-300 BEJ

A rare Steiff 'Golfer' doll.

$80-120 DE

A Macauley Culkin 'Home Alone' figure, some original clothing.

c1988 19in (48cm) high

$6-9 WHP

One of a pair of 'Raggedy Ann' doll, in rare dress, all original, Georgene label.

'Raggedy Ann' was based on a story by the American Johnny Gruelle. Gruelle's publisher was the first to mass produce these dolls from 1918, but other companies such as Georgene Averill of New York (1876-1963) also produced variations.

$300-400 (pair) DE

A Philadelphia painted cloth doll, with gusseted shoulder and knee joints, well-molded features and stocking body.

22in (56cm) high

$3,000-4,000 Ber

A Käthe Kruse girl doll, with painted head, blonde human wig, swivel neck, cloth body and original red and white dress, slight rubbing to nose and left cheek.

Kathe Kruse of Germany made a very small range of cloth dolls between 1911 and 1956. Early dolls fetch a premium and can be recognised by having three hand-stitched pate seams on their heads.

c1953

$600-1,000 TK

Left: An American Izannah Walker cloth doll, with brown eyes, distinct mouth, brown painted short hair with wisps at sides, unmarked indicating early specimen.

Izannah Walker dolls are rare and like many early American cloth dolls, highly sought after. Based in Rhode Island, she patented her cloth dolls on November 4th 1873 with designs for oil painted features and stitched hands with separate thumbs. Later versions are marked with the patent date.

17in (43cm) high

$15,000-20,000 Ber

Right: A Columbian cloth doll, with hand-painted features, painted blue eyes and curly brown hair, wears ivory cotton dress and blue gingham checked bonnet over lace trimmed bonnet.

22in (56cm) high

$8,000-10,000 Ber

An Alabama 'Indestructible' baby, with signed body.

18.5in (47cm) high

$3,000-4,000 Ber

MARY HOYER

- Mary Hoyer of the 'Mary Hoyer Doll Mfg Co.' of Reading, PA, introduced her first doll in 1939. The first dolls did not bear marks, with composition being used until 1946 when the material changed to hard plastic.
- By the mid 1950s, Hoyer's dolls were being shipped all over the world. Markings read 'The Mary Hoyer Doll' or 'ORIGINAL Mary Hoyer Doll'.
- The production of marked hard plastic dolls ceased in 1960, and unmarked examples were made, but these soon ceased too. Production recommenced in 1990 with the 'Doll with the Magic Wand Collection', based on a story Hoyer had written in 1956.
- Vintage Hoyer dolls, made using original molds, but not produced by the factory can be found. They are of lower quality, often with poorer quality painting over a red body using paint that flakes easily. They are not marked.
- Condition is paramount – dolls must be clean, undamaged and wear unfaded, original, tagged clothes in excellent condition. Boxed examples command a premium.

A very rare 1930s early Mary Hoyer doll, with twist waist, unmarked.

This was one of her first dolls.

$200-300   **DE**

A vintage Mary Hoyer doll, with tagged outfit, original shoes and replaced wig.

$400-500   **DE**

A vintage Mary Hoyer 'Southern Belle' doll.

$400-600   **DE**

A 1950s Mary Hoyer doll, with rare platinum blonde hair, doll marked and outfit tagged.

$700-1,000   **DE**

A vintage Mary Hoyer doll, in hard plastic with tagged dress, marked on back, all original.

$300-500   **DE**

A 1950s vintage Mary Hoyer doll, with factory-made clothes and hat, original shoes and socks.

14in (35.5cm) high

$300-500   **DE**

A 1950s Mary Hoyer doll, with a rare hairstyle and red hair, no tag on gown, marked and boxed.

The box adds to the value. Without it, this doll would be worth £450-500.

$700-1,000   **DE**

A vintage Mary Hoyer 'Rollerskating' doll.

$300-500   **DE**

A vintage Mary Hoyer 'School Time' doll.

$500-700   **DE**

A vintage Mary Hoyer 'At The Beach' doll, all original.

$500-700   **DE**

A 1950s Mary Hoyer boy doll, with tagged shirt and pants, marked and boxed.

$700-1,000 **DE**

A 1950s vintage Mary Hoyer boy doll, with original clothes.

Boy dolls are hard to find.

$500-700 **DE**

PLASTIC DOLLS

■ To be collectible, plastic dolls need to be in perfect condition, with the body and face fresh and clean. The hair must be set in the original style – look for examples with rare styles and colours.

■ Damage, such as chewed hands and pulled hair or non-original parts will reduce the value considerably.

■ Clothes must be original, clean and unfaded. Boxed plastic dolls will command a premium. These dolls were mass produced, so only those in as perfect condition as possible will be desirable to collectors. Dolls by named mid-20th century makers are the most collected, so look for names such as Barbie, Sasha, Terri Lee and Vogue.

A blonde-haired blue-eyed Sasha doll.

17in (43cm) high

$100-150 **WHP**

A dark-haired brown-eyed Sasha doll, with some original clothing and original Sasha wrist tag.

17in (43cm) high

$220-280 **WHP**

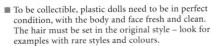

A brunette gingham 103 Sasha doll, in original clothing and box.

15.75in (40cm) high

$220-280 **WHP**

A Sasha boy, with brown hair and eyes, some original clothing and Sasha wrist tag.

17in (43cm) high

$150-200 **WHP**

An early 1950s Vogue Doll Company strung 'Ginny' doll, with tagged dress and later plastic Ginny shoes.

$300-500 **DE**

Two blonde-haired baby boy and girl Sasha dolls.

The girl doll is worth slightly more than the boy.

2.75in (32cm) high

$100-150 each **WHP**

A Cheryl Vogue Doll Company 'Ginny' doll.

c1953

$600-1,000 **DE**

An April Vogue Doll Company composition strung 'Ginny' doll, all original.

c1953

$600-1,000 **DE**

An early rare Vogue 'Toddler Cowboy' doll, with lasso and signed shoe, all original, mint condition.

$300-500 **DE**

Two 1950s Rosebud Kewpie dolls.

Taller 10.25in (15cm) high

$50-80 (price for two)

OACC

An Alexander 'Sonja Henie' composition doll, all original.

c1939   14in (35.5cm) high

$700-1,000

DE

An Alexander 'Dr. Allen Defoe' composition doll.

This is a rare model.

1937-1939 15in (38cm) high

$1,500-2,000

DE

A 1930s Arranbee 'Nancy' composition doll, with all original clothes.

12in (30.5cm) high

$200-300

DE

A 1940s DeWees Cochran 'Cindy' Latex composition doll, with original clothes.

DeWees Cochran made one of a kind dolls based on photos of children and had a line of three dolls: 'Barbara', 'Cindy', and 'Sue'.

16in (40.6cm) high

$700-1,000

DE

A 1930s Effanbee 'Patsy' composition doll, all original.

14in (35.5cm) high

$200-300

DE

A German Schilling Regency young man doll, with kid body, all original.

c1870   18in (46cm) high

$800-1,200

BEJ

A British Pierotti wax baby, with inserted hair.

c1890

7in (17.75in) high

$700-1,000

BEJ

A German Schilling child, in wax on papier-mâché.

c1880   11in (28cm) high

$800-1,200

BEJ

A large German Schilling glazed papier-mâché doll.

c1880   *33in (84cm) high*

$2,200-2,800   **BEJ**

An American Schoenhut girl, with molded painted brown hair, intaglio blue eyes, closed mouth, blue linen dress and original ivory leather shoes, model no. 102, stamped patented "JAN-17-11".

     16.5in (42cm) high

$3,000-5,000   **Ber**

A Schoenhut No.205 character doll, with early carved hair, original clothes and older repro shoes.

These wooden dolls were sold as indestructible. They were inexpensive when new and often show signs of wear.

     14in (35.5cm) high

$800-1,200   **DE**

A German Parian doll, with shoulder head, glass eyes, deep modeling to hair, black hairband and pierced ears.

     20in (51cm) high

$800-1,200   **DE**

A German china doll, signed "Germany", mint condition, with original body and clothes.

1890s

$120-180   **DE**

A German Parian head Scottish boy, all original.

c1880   *12.5in (32cm)*

$300-500   **BEJ**

A Dutch doll, in contemporary costume with hoof feet and blue eyes.

     11in (28cm) high

$30-50   **WHP**

A 19thC Dutch doll, with painted wooden face and blue eyes, some original clothing.

     12in (30cm) high

$15-20   **WHP**

A wax head doll, with blue glass eyes, some original clothing, possibly French.

c1870   *14in (36cm) high*

$40-60   **WHP**

A composition baby doll, with sleepy blue glass eyes, open mouth with two upper teeth and stuffed cloth body, marked "Germany".

     15in (38cm) high

$40-60   **WHP**

A 1920s mechanical black composition baby.

$100-150   **JPA**

A carved marble swaddling baby, in wooden black forest cradle, all original.

c1880 Cradle 5.5in (14cm) high

$300-400   **BEJ**

A doll, made from black lisle stockings, yarn hair, shoe button eyes, felt lips and calico dress.
c1910   *15.5in (39.5cm) high*

$220-280   RAA

A composition soft-bodied St. Trinian's girl, in original outfit.
c1920   *16in (40.5cm) high*

$300-500   BEJ

An early plastic googly-style doll, in original crêpe paper costume.
c1930   *7in (18cm) high*

$20-30   WHP

An early 1940s doll, all original.

$300-400   DE

A 1950s American 'Sweet Sue' character doll, all original.
15in (38cm) high

$100-150   DE

A group of three Gofun-head Chinese dancers.
c1890

$300-500   BEJ

A Japanese costume doll, with silk costume, Gofun-head, boxed, superior quality.
c1920   *14in (35cm) high*

$300-500   BEJ

An American 'Eloise' character doll, all original with label at right hip, designed by Bette Gould.
c1955

$300-400   DE

A Japanese Gofun-head man-doll, on stand.
6in (15cm) high

$180-220   BEJ

A pair of Edi walking Tyrolean figures with ball and thread mechanism.
c1940   *6in (15cm) high*

$50-80   WHP

A pair of 1920s Chinese plaster dolls, boxed, mint condition.
3in (7.5cm) high

$100-150   BEJ

A mid-20thC papier-mâché clown.
1940-50

$200-300 BCAC

A pair of 20thC German-made Dutch art dolls, all original outfits, unmarked.
10.5in (26.5cm) high

$300-500 BEJ

A pair of 20thC Swiss travel dolls.

$70-100 (pair) DE

Dolls' Clothes and Accessories

A 19thC muslin doll's dress, museum mounted.

$300-500 BCAC

A Victorian doll's dress, in leaf and flower print fabric, neck and arms finished with tatting.
1870-80

$500-800 BCAC

A fashion doll's three-piece outfit, to fit a 21in (53cm) doll.
c1890

$200-300 BEJ

A print and calico doll's quilt, mounted.

9.75in (25cm) long

$300-400 BCAC

A late 19thC mounted postage stamp doll's quilt, in pieced cotton.
6.75in (17cm) long

$300-400 BCAC

A late 19thC doll-sized tied quilt.

18in (46cm) long

$270-330 BCAC

A wooden doll's house bookcase, with wooden "books" on the shelves.

5.25in (13.5cm) high

$60-100 SFel

A Walterhausen doll's house bureau, with drop-down writing slope, good condition.

5.5in (14cm) high

$270-330 SFel

A rare 19thC Walterhausen doll's house desk.

4in (10cm) wide

$350-400 SFel

A doll's house chaise longue.

2.25in (5.5cm) long

$30-40 SFel

A 1930s dolls house painted wooden single bed with bed clothes.

4.25in (11cm) long

$150-200 SFel

A doll's house wooden armchair.

2in (5cm) high

$15-25 SFel

A pair of doll's house padded chairs (one shown).

2.75in (7cm) high

$30-50 SFel

A doll's house painted wooden crib.

2in (5cm) wide

$30-40 SFel

A 1930s doll's house sink.

3.25in (8cm) wide

$15-18 SFel

A hand-painted miniature vase, decorated with birds, with Japanese marks to base.

2in (5cm) high

$15-25 SFel

A 19thC German doll's house carved ivory gazebo, with a Stanhope lens set in the finial.

4.25in (10.5cm) high

$220-280 SFel

A hand-painted miniature vase, decorated with pagodas, with Japanese marks to base.

2in (5cm) high

$30-40   **SFel**

A miniature vase, with "New York Chinatown" on the side and "Made in Japan" on the base.

2.5in (6.5cm) high

$20-30   **SFel**

A miniature vase, marked "Made in Japan" on the base.

2.5in (6.5cm) high

$5-8   **SFel**

A doll's house turned ivory vase, with fabric flowers.

5.5in (14cm) high

$80-120   **SFel**

A doll's house mounted pheasant display.

1.75in (4.5cm) high

$15-25   **SFel**

A doll's house gilt-painted plastic jug.

2.5in (6cm) high

$80-120   **SFel**

A Limoges miniature coffee/tea set, marks to base.

c1910   *3.5in (9cm) wide*

$80-120   **SFel**

A doll's house carved ivory jardinière.

5in (12.5cm) high

$80-120   **SFel**

A doll's house oak longcase clock.

7.5in (18.5cm) high

$30-50   **SFel**

A mid-to late 19thC doll's house six-branch chandelier.

6in (15cm) high

$300-500   **SFel**

A doll's house globe on stand.

1.5in (4cm) high

$10-15   **SFel**

A terracotta bust of a man with a felt hat, smoking a pipe.

2.5in (6.5cm) high

$10-15   **SFel**

A 19thC doll's house frame, with inset engraving of Osbourne House.

3.25in (8cm) wide

$30-50 SFel

A Tri-Ang doll's house clothes mangle.

2.75in (7cm) high

$30-50 SFel

A doll's house sewing machine on stand.

c1900 *2.75in (7cm) high*

$100-150 SFel

A doll's house floor sweeper.

3in (7.5cm) high

$5-8 SFel

A painted tinplate step ladder.

2.25in (5.5cm) high

$12-18 SFel

A "Coronation" Smokers' Set, dated.

1911 *3in (7.5cm) wide*

$50-80 SFel

A Limoges doll's house foot bath, with gilt trim.

0.75in (2cm) long

$15-25 SFel

A doll's house metal coal shovel.

2.75in (5cm) long

$10-15 SFel

A ceramic doll's house bath.

2.25in (5.5cm) long

$12-18 SFel

A doll's house typewriter, painted green.

$30-50 SFel

A 1920s doll's house cloth "cook" doll, holding a knife and fork.

6.5in (16.5cm) high

$40-60 SFel

A 1920s doll's house cloth "maid" doll, holding a broom.

6.5in (16.5cm) high

$30-50 SFel

A CLOSER LOOK AT A TEDDY BEAR

Although unmarked, this bear shows many characteristics of early bears.

His snout is long – later bears made after World War II generally have shorter snouts.

His eyes are early 'boot buttons'. Glass was used after the late 1920s, with plastic being used from the 1950s onwards.

He is covered with mohair, later bears used a 'shinier' synthetic plush material.

His jointed arms are long and curved. Bears from the 1950s onwards usually have shorter arms.

An early 20thC teddy bear, the fully-jointed golden body stuffed with wood wool, with felt pads and black button eyes.

13in (33cm) high

$1,500-2,000   **DN**

A Steiff 'Zotty' bear, with bells in paw, original paper tag.

Zotty bears were introduced by Steiff in 1951. Their name comes from the German word 'zottig' which means 'shaggy'. These popular bears are characterized by their long shaggy mohair and open mouths.

12in (30.5cm) long

$250-300   **SI**

A Farnell bear, with long jointed arms and legs, humped back, and stitched claws.

J.K. Farnell were an early manufacturer of teddy bears in England. They were founded in 1840 and produced their first soft toys in the late 1890s.

c1912   *11in (28cm) high*

$800-1,200   **SFel**

A Steiff bear, with mohair plush.

Steiff made their first bear in 1902, and their bears grew in popularity from 1905 onwards. They are now highly collectable, with age and condition deciding value. The famous 'button in the ear', which changed in shape and colour over the years, and the overall form, help to date Steiff bears.

c1907   *17in (43cm) high*

$1,000-1,500   **BEJ**

A 1930s/40s teddy bear, probably by Chiltern, the fully-jointed golden plush body with fabric pads and glass eyes, small patch on left arm.

15.75in (40cm) high

$300-400   **DN**

A Steiff bear, with no button, in mint condition.

c1950   *11in (28cm) high*

$500-700   **BEJ**

An early British bear, maker unknown, with glass eyes.

c1915   *18in (46cm) high*

$500-700   **BEJ**

A 1920s teddy bear, the fully-jointed golden plush body with worn velvet pads and glass eyes, the body containing an inoperative musical movement.

18.5in (47cm) high

$300-400   **DN**

A 1930s Merrythought teddy bear, the fully-jointed golden plush body with fabric pads and glass eyes, printed maker's label to right foot.

15in (38cm) high

$350-400   **DN**

A 1930s German Hermann open-mouth teddy bear, with growler.

20in (50cm) high

A British aubergine-colored bear.

c1940   *15in (38cm) high*

A 1930s British Pedigree teddy, with label.

19in (48cm) high

$350-400   **BEJ**

A 1930s British Chad Valley teddy bear.

20in (50cm) high

$700-1,000   **BEJ**

$500-700   **BEJ**

$300-500   **BEJ**

A German bear, with round muzzle and growler.

c1950 18in (46cm) high

$500-700   **BEJ**

A British cubbie bear, with short limbs, maker unknown.

c1930   *14in (35.5cm) high*

$300-500   **BEJ**

A British glum bear cub, unmarked.

c1950   *11in (28cm) high*

$400-600   **BEJ**

A British Chiltern 'Hugmee' bear.

One of English company Chiltern's (1908-1967) most popular ranges was the Hugmee bear. It was introduced in 1923 and there were many different designs, including this one with its unusual unshaved muzzle. After the war Hugmees had shorter arms and legs to conserve materials. Chiltern bears typically have upturned paws.

c1930   *16in (40.5cm) high*

$700-1,000   **BEJ**

A British 'Monty' bear, with original outfit, maker unknown.

c1940

$300-500   **BEJ**

SOFT TOYS

- Steiff, better known for its teddy bears, is the earliest and most popular manufacturer of soft toys. Steiff's patent dates back to 1892, although the founder Margarete Steiff made small animal-shaped pin cushions as presents for friends before then.
- Although somewhat overshadowed by the success of the teddy bear, ranges grew in the early 20th century. Other makers such as Schuco and the English companies 'Merrythought' and 'Chad Valley' also moved into this market.
- The period from the 1920s – 1950 is the 'golden age' of collectable soft toys. Toys from the 1960s onwards, especially from the Far East, are less well made and were made in vast quantities.
- The material used, the type of eyes and the label all help with identification and dating. Clothed animals often date from during the war, when mohair was scarce and other fabrics were used.
- Cartoon and character toys are popular across markets and tend to fetch high prices. Pre-war Disney related toys are better quality.
- Collectors should look for toys in good, unworn condition. Retention of the label is important. Steiff is the most collectable name, but their small bugs, insects and more unusual 'creatures' have not yet found widespread favour with collectors, so tend to be less valuable.

An early Schuco clockwork somersaulting bear.

The German company Schuco are very well known for their tinplate toys and wind-up mechanisms. They produced ingenious small monkeys and bears containing perfume bottles or with clockwork mechanisms like this one.

4.75in (12cm) high

$300-500   **SFel**

FIND OUT MORE...

Puppenhaus Museum, Steineck-Foundation, Steinenvorstadt 1, 4051 Basle, Switzerland. www.puppenhausmuseum.ch. A collection of over 2,000 teddy bears, mostly dating from before 1950.

Sue Pearson, 'Bears', published by De Agostini Editions, 1995.

Pauline Cockrill, 'Teddy Bear Encyclopaedia', published by Dorling Kindersley, 2001.

A 1950s Steiff 'Peggy' penguin.

13in (33cm) high

$200-300   **DE**

A Steiff mohair lamb, in mint condition.

c1950   *11in (28cm) high*

$300-500   **BEJ**

A Steiff mohair cat, with green glass eyes.

Cats are popular subjects and soft toys by a range of manufacturers are commonly found.

6in (15cm) long

$80-120   **DE**

A Steiff 'Jumbo' mechanical, limited edition number 1927 of 4000.

1988-90

$200-300   **DE**

A Steiff 'Snobby' grey jointed poodle, with collar and original paper tag, button in ear.

5in (13cm) high

$120-180   **SI**

A Steiff 'Mimic Tessie' arm puppet, with original paper label and button in ear, some fading to tongue and ruff of mouth.

12.5in (5cm) high

$350-400   **SI**

A Steiff 'Gaty' hand puppet, with original paper label and button in ear, model number 317.

$150-200   **SI**

A Steiff rabbit, with original paper tag and button in ear, model number 2965/20.

8in (20cm) long

$300-400   **SI**

A Steiff 'Snobby' black poodle hand puppet, with original paper label and button in ear.

$220-280   **SI**

A Steiff 'Gaty' hand puppet, with original paper label and button in ear, model number 317.

$150-200   **SI**

A Merrythought 'Jerry' mouse, in velveteen, with label.

c1930   *9in (23cm) high*

$300-400   **BEJ**

A 1930s German mohair clockwork kitten.

6in (14cm) high

$300-400   **BEJ**

A 1950s British Merrythought piglet, with label.

9in (23cm) high

$120-180   **BEJ**

A pale blue plush lamb, boxed, unmarked.
c1930

$180-220   **BEJ**

A 1960s Chad Valley Golly, with felt eyes and plastic suede-effect mouth and teeth, typically dressed in yellow waistcoat, striped trousers and blue jacket, with printed label.

2.5in (62cm) high

$40-60   **DN**

A British Golly, unmarked.

c1930   *14in (34cm) high*

$80-120   **BEJ**

A 1970s Wendy Boston Basil Brush.

15.75in (40cm) high

$40-60   **WHP**

TREEN

■ Treen, meaning 'from the tree', is the descriptive term given to a huge range of items produced from turned or, more rarely, carved wood.

■ Produced since medieval times until the late 19th century, these small items had a variety of domestic uses in the home or on the farm.

■ Although treen was produced for such a long period, early pieces, which are usually very well modeled, are extremely scarce and command very high prices when found. The majority of pieces available to the collector will date from the 19th century.

■ Woods used are always tightly grained and robust, often with good colors. Recognizing a particular wood can be challenging.

■ Treen from the 17th century is characteristically made from yew, fruitwoods, beech, elm and chestnut. The 18th century saw the use of imported boxwood, maple and pine. By the second quarter of the 18th century, exotic hardwoods such as lignum vitae, ebony and mahogany had become popular.

■ Well modeled and finely formed pieces will always be popular, but pieces bearing dates, inscriptions and mottoes are also highly sought after.

■ Condition is important as all of these pieces were made to be used and can show wear. Damage will seriously affect values unless the piece is rare. Patination is also important.

A 19thC English treen spice turret, in sycamore.

5.75in (14.5cm) high

$100-150　　PC

A mid-19thC wooden chemist's jar.

7in (18cm) high

$40-60　　OACC

A late19thC pine butter marker, with thistle mold.

4.75in (6.5cm) high

$15-25　　PC

A Victorian olivewood string box.

c1860　　3.75in (9.5cm) high

$60-100　　MB

A 19thC English boxwood glove powdering flask.

6in (15cm) high

$50-80　　PC

A mid/late 19thC American turned wood finial, original finish.

13.5in (34.5cm) high

$20-30　　TWC

A 19thC English nutmeg grater, carved from a coquilla nut.

The coquilla nut comes from the South American Attalea funifera tree. In Europe, these nuts have been carved since the 18thC.

4.5in (11cm) high

$500-800　　PC

A butter pot, with excellent patination.

4in (10cm) diam

$40-60　　PC

An American boxwood ink sander, with pierced Star of David design.

c1810　　2.75in (7cm) high

$120-180　　RAA

A 19thC English fruitwood double-cup measure.

From the W.J. Shepherd Collection STO 206. Chemists and apothecaries used these measures to make soda water. They were not designed, as is often thought, as a cup to hold a duck or a hen's egg.

3.75in (9.5cm) high

$70-100　　PC

Two 19thC turned wood lamp stands.

7in (18cm) high

$500-700 SI

An 18thC American turned and incised burl mortar and pestle.

Provenance: The Society of the Cincinnati. The collection records state that the mortar and pestle were originally owned by Silas Kellogg, a Revolutionary War officer.

6.5in (17cm) high

$300-400 SI

An American tiger maple mandrill.

A tinsmith used this tool to make sized rings for bails and handles. This wood is highly desirable to collectors.

13.5in (34cm) high

$100-150 RAA

A pair of treen beakers, each clasped by a hand, carved from solid wood, one rim repaired.

7in (18cm) high

$400-600 GorL

A pair of 19thC turned walnut chambersticks.

9.5in (24.5cm) high

$350-400 OACC

FIND OUT MORE...

Edward Pinto, 'Treen and other Wooden Bygones: An Encyclopaedia and Social History', published by Bell, 1983.

Jonathan Levi & Robert Young, 'Treen for the Table: Wooden Objects Relating to Eating and Drinking', published by the Antique Collectors' Club, 1998.

A West Country thatcher's legget, used to pack the thatch tightly.

18in (46cm) long

$50-80 OACC

A wooden nutcracker.

Just as corkscrews have become collectable, nutcrackers are also becoming increasingly desirable and sought after. Although they are not as easily classified as corkscrews and many examples do not bear patents or makers' names, the variety available to collectors is huge, with many decorative examples, and they are still comparatively reasonably priced. This is almost certainly an area to watch for in the future.

7in (18cm) high

$80-120 OACC

A pair of 19thC mahogany book markers, each carved in the shape of a book, with gilded 'pages' and applied turned handles.

10.5in (26.5cm) long

$1,200-1,800 L&T

A Victorian truncheon, painted with crowned garter motto containing "PP" above initials "PW" and dated 1848, well worn.

17.5in (44.5cm) long

$60-100 W&W

An 17thC English carved oak bible box, the front with scoop decoration, the molded base carved with lunettes.

26in (65.5cm)

$1,000-1,500   **SI**

A silver piqué and moss agate oval box.

c1780   *4in (10cm) wide*

$300-500   **RdeR**

A painted "Wilber Force" anti-slave box, lined with tortoiseshell, showing a slave in chains.

c1759-1833   *3in (7.5cm) diam*

$600-800   **RdeR**

An 18thC Continental painted tortoiseshell box, probably French, rectangular with hinged cover, finely painted with 18thC figures in a landscape of classical architectural ruins.

3.5in (8.5cm) wide

$600-1,000   **SI**

One of a pair of George III crossbanded mahogany serpentine-front knife boxes, with herringbone borders, the hinged tops with engraved brass shield-shaped crests on ogee bracket feet, one with original fitted interior.

15in (38cm) high

$2,200-2,800   **CLV**

An 18thC enamel-on-copper circular box, probably French, the hinged cover finely painted with a boat wharf scene, the base painted with colorful floral sprays.

5in (12.5cm) diam

$300-500   **SI**

A late 18thC/early 19thC south Staffordshire green enamel patch box, the hinged cover painted with a Neo-classical building in a landscape and "Virtue is the greatest ornament of the fair", some damage and lacking the mirror.

1.5in (4cm)

$150-200   **DN**

Three late 18thC/early 19thC south Staffordshire enamel patch boxes, comprising one in yellow, the cover painted with an allegorical scene depicting an angel upon a cloud protecting a medallion of George III from arrows and "May no weapon form'd against him prosper, God save the King", one in pale blue, the cover painted with a dove and buildings and "As the dove so is my love", the other in royal blue, the cover "A present from Birmingham", all with chips and restoration.

Largest 2.5in (6cm) diam

$800-1,200   **DN**

A Victorian tortoiseshell rectangular pin box, plush-lined, lacks name plaque.

3.25in (8cm) wide

$100-150   **BAR**

A Regency blonde tortoiseshell casket, with dome top, paper-lined interior and on white glass bead feet, lacks thumb piece.

2.5in (6.5cm) wide

$120-180 **BAR**

An early 19thC tortoiseshell round box, with pique work scrolling borders, the cover with a monogram, chips and cracks.

3in (8cm)

$180-220 **DN**

An early 19thC miniature chest, mahogany-veneered with applied reeded edge above two short and three long drawers, fitted brass knob handles, on splay bracket feet.

8.75in (22.5cm) wide

$1,500-2,000 **WW**

An American early 19thC leather-covered dome top box, with bail handle, newspaper-covered interior, tooled leather with star and rotary designs, some loss to leather.

8.75in (22cm)

$120-180 **TWC**

An American Chippendale mahogany tea caddy, molded hinged lid with cast brass handle over conforming case with molded base, raised on bracket feet.

12.75in (32cm) wide

$220-280 **SI**

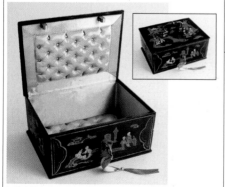

A 19thC black and gilt-decorated steel rectangular strong box, with loop handle and satin-lined interior, finely decorated with figures in landscapes.

8in (20.5cm) wide

$300-400 **LFA**

An American japanned and painted tin document box, probably New York State.

c1830

$1,000-1,500 **RAA**

An American basswood painters' box for painting materials.
c1830   *15in (38cm) long*

$1,000-1,500   **RAA**

A German pressed box, depicting Frederick the Great, tortoiseshell lined.
c1830   *3.25in (8cm) wide*

$220-300   **RdeR**

A 19thC inlaid mahogany and satinwood tea caddy, with fitted interior and ivory escutcheon, the brass pull engraved with the initials "L.A.A." and the letter "K", refinished.
12in (30.5cm) wide

$300-400   **SI**

An early Victorian mahogany and brass bound writing box, the hinged lid with a central cartouche, enclosing a fitted interior with leather inset slope above a side drawer and inset brass handles.
19.5in (49.5cm) wide

$300-500   **DN**

A Victorian tortoiseshell card case.
c1840   *4.25in (10.5cm) long*

$180-225   **MB**

A Victorian mother-of-pearl card case.
c1850   *4.25in (10.5cm) long*

$100-150   **MB**

A 19thC tortoiseshell small canted rectangular box, the hinged cover with silver banding.
2.5in (6.5cm)

$300-400   **DN**

A 19thC tortoiseshell and brass-strung small rectangular box, on turned ivory feet.
3.5in (6.5cm)

$100-150   **DN**

A 19thC mahogany box, the hinged lid enclosing four square section glass decanters and three stoppers with gilt decoration, some damage to decanters.
8.75in (22.5cm) high

$600-1,000   **DN**

A 19thC French faience box, rectangular with hinged cover, painted floral sprays on a white ground, signed "VP".
5.5in (14cm) wide

$200-300   **SI**

A Victorian crossbanded figured walnut rectangular box, the hinged cover with brass plaque engraved 'Gloves and Handkerchiefs'.

10.5in (26.5cm) high

$220-280 **CLV**

A late Victorian tortoiseshell and silver-mounted cigarette box, the hinged cover with a central monogram and shaped panels at the corners, Birmingham hallmarks for "A. & J. Zimmerman".

1900 *7.5in (19cm) wide*

$500-700 **DN**

A silver cigar box, with engine-turned decoration and pull out ashtray, on ball feet, London hallmarks.

The drawer is an extremely rare feature, making this box more valuable than other silver cigar/cigarette boxes.

1920 *6in (15cm) wide*

$800-1200 **Tag**

Two late 19thC French enameled brass rectangular boxes, the larger with a light blue ground, the cover painted with amorous couple, both with raised "jeweled" decoration.

9.5in (24cm)

$2,000-3,000 **SI**

A late Victorian silver gilt small circular box, the cover design by William Burges and made by Carl Krall, with plain surface except for the hinged cover engraved with "A Pelican in Piety" against a hatched silver ground, flanked by arched panels, four of which contain Lombardic script, with a "CK" punch to the base for the maker, "Krall" for the company and with London hallmarks.

In 'William Burges and the High Victorian Dream' by J. Mordaunt Crook, John Murry (publishers) Ltd, London 1981, illustration 209 we see the cover of a wafer box by Burges and part of a traveling communion set, probably made by Barkentin & Krall. The image on that cover is identical to this piece and is incidentally made by Carl Krall of that same company. Even though this piece was made 11 years after the death of Burges, the image on the cover is still considered to be by Burges.

1892

$1,500-2,000 **DN**

An early 20thC mahogany liqueur case, the fall front rectangular box with a mirrored lid, the case fitted to contain two cut glass decanters, a silver-plated shaker, a bitters bottle and six cut glass cordials.

14.25in (36.5cm) wide

$600-1,000 **SI**

A Piero Fornasetti wooden box, with alphabet motif.

c1953 *11.75in (30cm) long*

$350-400 **FM**

A French shagreen cigar box, with ivory trim to the lid.

c1940 *8in wide*

$1,000-1,500 **Tag**

An 18thC rectangular tea chest on bun feet, with later gilt and black lacquer decoration, the oak interior with divisions, a secret drawer to one side containing an early Victorian silver engraved caddy spoon, the bowl with a split.

10in (25.5cm)

$300-400   **WW**

A late 18thC rectangular tea chest, with canted corners, veneered in burr-yew within chain circlets, feather-banded inlaid stringing and fluting, the interior with two lidded compartments.

10.5in (26.75cm)

$1,800-2,200   **WW**

A George III mahogany fan inlaid double tea caddy.

c1800   *7.5in (19cm) wide*

$300-400   **MB**

A George III oval tea caddy, veneered in harewood with marquetry inlay of crossed bow and arrow within a floral garland, an open escutcheon, the hinged cover with a flowerhead panel.

4.5in (11.5cm) high

$1,000-1,500   **WW**

A Regency cube shape tea caddy, veneered in satinwood with oval fan inlay, checked stringing, the interior with a lid.

4.75in (12cm)

$400-600   **WW**

A Regency cube tea caddy, veneered in sycamore with painted penwork panels of Neo-classical figures and inlaid stringing.

5in (12.5cm) wide

$270-330   **WW**

A Victorian single canister rosewood tea caddy, with original bowl.

c1830   *7.25in (18.5cm) wide*

$200-300   **MB**

A 19thC ebony tea caddy, the sarcophagus shape mounted with ivory reel and bead bands and inlaid with flowers.

9.5in (24cm) wide

$220-280   **Chef**

A Victorian oval tea caddy, with a carved woven effect ivory body, an oval vacant cartouche with beaded edge, plated mounts and hinged cover with a ribbed bud finial, maker's mark Henry Wilkinson of Sheffield.

5.75in (14.5cm)

$800-1,200   **WW**

A Victorian tortoiseshell and mother-of-pearl tea caddy, of canted rectangular form, on bun feet.

4.25in (11cm) wide

$700-1,000   **DN**

A late Victorian oak tea chest, with plated metal mounts, handle and engraved hinged cover, with two lidded compartments, on brass baluster-turned feet.

8.5in (21.5cm)

$300-400   **WW**

A 19thC French novelty ebonized tea chest, no mixing bowl.

11.5in (29cm)

$270-330   **WW**

- The Black Forest is a mountainous region of Bavaria, Germany, and has been a popular European vacation destination for centuries. Most Black Forest carvings date from the mid 19th century onwards and were bought as souvenirs.

- Not all Black Forest items come from the eponymous Bavarian region. The title is applied to a style, with items being produced in Germany and Switzerland.

- As well as novelty items, cuckoo clocks are common, having been produced since the mid 18th century, as are larger items such as hall chairs and umbrella stands.

- Bears are the most common subjects, with dogs, birds, stags and other animals typical of the areas also being produced. Carvings are still being made, so collectors should look out for signs of age as modern examples only have a decorative value. Larger or functional pieces are very desirable.

A Swiss Black Forest bear, with moveable limbs.

c1860   8.75in (22cm) high

$180-220   **SS**

A Swiss Black Forest bear match holder.

c1860   5.5in (14cm) high

$200-300   **SS**

A late 19thC Black Forest carved wood smoker's compendium, modelled as a bear standing on its back legs, with a hinged head, the right arm raised supporting a leaf and branch quatreform top, with a brass ashtray, two lidded compartments, each with a bear and a third to the back.

34in (86.5cm) high

$4,000-6,000   **WW**

A Black Forest carved wood inkwell, modelled as a bear, feeding a cub from a bottle, the hinged head fitted with a glass well.

6.75in (17cm) high

$700-1,000   **WW**

A Black Forest carved wood inkwell, modelled as a sitting bear, with a hinged head fitted with a cut glass inkwell.

6.5in (16.5cm) high

$600-1,000   **WW**

A Black Forest carved wood model of a bear, and another, cracked.

13in (33cm) long

$1,000-1,500   **WW**

A Black Forest carved wood model of a bear, the base inscribed "St Moritz".

5.75in (14.5cm) high

$100-150   **WW**

A Black Forest carved wood model of a bear, with a thermometer.

5.25in (13.5cm) high

$100-150   **WW**

A Black Forest carved wood model of a bear, together with two similar models.

5.5in (14in) long

$100-150 **WW**

A 19thC Black Forest carved limewood figure group, depicting an eagle on a rocky outcrop, wings outstretched and holding its prey, a young deer.

17.25in (44cm) high

$1,200-1,800 **L&T**

A Black Forest carved wood model of a bear, seated behind a hollowed tree trunk, fitted with a brass liner.

5.5in (14cm) high

$120-180 **WW**

A Swiss Black Forest basket box.

c1860 *7.5in (19cm) wide*

$200-300 **SS**

A Swiss Black Forest inkwell, carved as birds and a nest on a leaf with acorns.

c1860 *11.5in (29cm) wide*

$300-400 **SS**

A Swiss Black Forest pot, carved as a fox beside a tree stump.

c1860 *3in (8cm) high*

$180-220 **SS**

A Black Forest clock, carved with two figures of St Bernard dogs on a base of entwined branches.

c1860 *23in (58cm) high*

$10,000-12,000 **SS**

A pair of Black Forest vases, each carved with figures of stags and deer standing under a tree.

c1860 *18.5in (47cm) high*

$6,000-7,000 **SS**

TREEN & BOXES

TUNBRIDGEWARE

- The majority of Tunbridgeware is produced using a technique, known as 'stickwork', of cutting slim rods of differently coloured wood into thin slices. These small 'tiles' are then applied to the surface of objects in an intricate mosaic pattern. Geometric borders surround floral, landscape or further geometric designs.
- Early pieces produced before the 19th century used traditional marquetry techniques, but 'stickwork' was faster and less expensive and dominated from the 1820s onwards.
- The most common objects found are boxes, picture frames, rulers and other small domestic objects. Larger pieces such as sewing or work tables are scarce and fetch high prices when offered for sale.
- It was made in and around the English spa town of Tunbridge Wells, often as souvenirs for visiting tourists.
- Although the technique dates back to the 17th century, most of the Tunbridgeware available to collectors dates from the mid- to late 19th century until around 1930.
- Tunbridgeware is difficult to repair so condition is important. Ensure tiles are not missing or that the surface is not warped or lifting. Wood colours were exploited by the makers, so look for good contrast and pleasing colours. Original labels or pieces marked with a maker's name will command a premium.
- Due to its complexity, it is not often faked, but German strapwork and Sorrento ware resemble Tunbridgeware and are often mistaken for it.

A Victorian inlaid rosewood Tunbridgeware box.
c1870   *3.75in (9.5cm) wide*
$100-150   **MB**

A Victorian rectangular Tunbridgeware box, the hinged cover with a panel of flowers.
4.5in (11cm) wide
$100-150   **LFA**

An inlaid rosewood Tunbridgeware needle box.
c1870   *2.5in (62cm) wide*
$80-120   **MB**

A Victorian square Tunbridgeware box, the cover with a spray of flowers and leaves.
2.75in (7cm) wide
$75-85   **LFA**

A square Tunbridgeware box, with geometric parquetry top.
3in (7.5cm)
$120-180   **GorL**

A small Victorian rectangular Tunbridgeware sewing box, the sliding cover with a pin cushion.
2in (7cm) wide
$100-150   **LFA**

A 19thC rectangular walnut and Tunbridgeware tea caddy, with flared base, the domed hinged lid enclosing two lidded compartments, on turned disc feet.
9.5in (24cm) wide
$150-250   **L&T**

A 19thC rosewood Tunbridgeware box, the cover with unusual tessera bird in a tree panel within Vandyke crossbanding.
2.5in (6.5cm) wide
$400-500   **B**

A 19thC rosewood Tunbridgeware box, with perspective cube top.
2.5in (6.5cm) wide
$70-80   **B**

A 19thC rosewood Tunbridgeware stamp box, printed Edward VII Penny Red.
1.75in (4.5cm) wide
$150-200   **B**

A 19thC oak Tunbridgeware stamp box, with mark of Royal Tunbridge Wells Ware, the top inlaid the with word 'Postage'.
3.5in (9cm) wide
$300-400   **B**

A 19thC Tunbridgeware stamp box, depicting the head of the young Queen Victoria.
1.5in (4cm) wide
$300-400   **B**

A 19thC Tunbridgeware rouge box, with tessera eight-pointed star.
1.75in (4.5cm) diam
$80-100   **B**

A 19thC Tunbridgeware pomade pot, with eight-pointed star.
1.75in (4.5cm) diam
$80-100   **B**

A 19thC cylindrical Tunbridgeware counter box, the threaded cover with eight-pointed star.
1.25in (3cm) diam

$80-100　　**B**

A 19thC cylindrical Tunbridgeware counter box, the threaded cover with eight-pointed star and Vandyke crossbanding.
1.25in (3cm) diam

$100-150　　**B**

A Victorian round Tunbridgeware box.

$40-60　　**LFA**

A Victorian small, round Tunbridgeware box.

$250-300　　**LFA**

An inlaid rosewood stickware Tunbridgeware sovereign box.
c1840　1.25in (3.2cm) diam

$70-100　　**MB**

Two 19thC Tunbridgeware napkin rings.

$100-150　　**B**

Left: A 19thC Tunbridgeware clothes brush, with perspective cube back.
6.5in (16.5cm) long

$70-100　　**B**

Centre: A 19thC Tunbridgeware clothes brush, the back with perspective cube and the handle with tessera flowers.
9.5in (24cm) long

$100-150　　**B**

Right: A 19thC Tunbridgeware clothes brush, with tessera floral back.
6.5in (16.5cm) long

$50-60　　**B**

A Victorian Tunbridgeware wedge-shaped menu holder.

$40-60　　**LFA**

A 19thC Tunbridgeware cribbage board, with half-square mosaic, restored condition.
9in (23cm) wide

$250-300　　**B**

A 19thC Tunbridgeware ebonised photograph frame, with tessera banding.
6.5in (16.5cm) wide

$250-300　　**B**

A 19thC rosewood Tunbridgeware paper knife, with tessera mosaic handle.

$80-120　　**B**

Left: A 19thC rosewood Tunbridgeware paper knife, with tessera mosaic handle and blond wood blade.
8in (20cm) long

$80-120　　**B**

Right: A 19thC rosewood Tunbridgeware paper knife, with tessera mosaic handle, with damage.
9.5in (24cm) long

$80-120　　**B**

FIND OUT MORE...

Brian Austen, 'Tunbridgeware and Related European Decorative Woodwares', Published by Trans-Atlantic Publications, 1989.

Tunbridge Wells Museum, Civic Centre, Mount Pleasant, Royal Tunbridge Wells, Kent TN1 1JN, England.
www.tunbridgewells.gov.uk/museum/

TREEN AND BOXES

MAUCHLINEWARE

- Mauchlineware is a form of souvenir ware including boxes and small domestic objects, such as sewing accessories. It would have been bought by 19th century tourists travelling around Scotland as a functional momento of their visit.

- It is usually made from the light wood of the sycamore and is characterised by a small 'decal' showing a local scene which is commonly applied as a transfer. Otherwise, surfaces are largely plain. Early pieces were hand painted or hand decorated with penwork, but these are comparatively scarce and fetch higher prices.

- It takes its name from the small Scottish town of Mauchline in Ayrshire, where it was produced primarily by W.A. Smith from the 1820s onwards. From the 1860s, it was also made in Lanark at the 'Caledonian Box Works' of Archibald Brown.

- Box production ceased in 1933, when the factory suffered a serious fire. Despite this, the range is highly diverse, so collectors may consider collecting a type, such as boxes or sewing accessories.

- The transfer scene and the entire piece are covered with layers of varnish meaning that they are usually intact, but collectors should beware scratched and dented pieces as these reduce the value considerably.

A Mauchlineware box, with a print of Gardens, Bournemouth.
4.25in (10.5cm) wide

$70-100　　　　　**OACC**

A Mauchlineware box, with a print of Lyndhurst.
5in (13cm) wide

$70-100　　　　　**OACC**

A Mauchlineware box, with a print of a Welsh market scene.
6.75in (17cm) wide

$120-180　　　　　**OACC**

A Mauchlineware glove box, with a print of Osbourne House in centre and Ventnor from the east and west on either side, catch broken but repairable.

Osborne House, on the Isle of Wight, was bought in 1845 by the Royal Family, but was not found to be large enough. Prince Albert embarked upon rebuilding the house in the style of an Italian villa and, upon its completion in 1851, it had grown enormously. Queen Victoria and Prince Albert enjoyed staying there greatly as it provided a fine escape from royal and public life, and Victoria spent much of her time there after Albert died. Victoria died there herself in January 1901.

9.75in (25cm) wide

$120-180　　　　　**OACC**

A Mauchlineware turned wood money box, with a print of Ravenscraig Castle, Dysart, with unusual turret design.
c1890　　3.25in (8cm) high

$40-60　　　　　**PC**

A barrel-shaped Mauchlineware money box, with a print of University College, Oxford.
3.25in (8cm)

$70-100　　　　　**OACC**

A circular Mauchlineware box, of George Square, Glasgow.

$50-80   OACC

A circular Mauchlineware box, with a print of Windsor Castle.

1.25in (3cm) diam

$70-100   OACC

A late 19thC Mauchlineware root snuff mull.

2.25in (5.5cm) wide

$500-800   PC

A late 19thC Mauchlineware skittle, with a print of Sandown Bay, Isle of Wight.

3.25in (8cm) high

$50-80   PC

Two Mauchlineware napkin rings, with a print of St Leonard's Church, Seaford, Lyndhurst.

$20-30 each   OACC

A Mauchlineware sycamore napkin ring, with a print of Wells Cathedral.

1880   *2in (5cm) diam*

$30-40   MB

A Mauchlineware egg timer, with a print of The Beach, Marblethorpe.

3.25in (8cm) high

$70-100   OACC

A CLOSER LOOK AT A FERNWARE BOX

Ferns were very popular during the late 19th century, where their leaf shape was used as a decorative motif on ceramics, glass, wood, metal and in architecture. Fernware is a form of Mauchlineware and was produced from around 1870.

There were several techniques for achieving this subtle effect. These included attaching fern leaves to the item and using them as a 'stencil', whilst dye was spattered over the piece. Some leaves were then removed and the piece was spattered with dye again. This would happen several times before the final leaf was removed, leaving the lightest color and almost an 'three dimensional' effect to the whole piece.

Other methods used paper printed with a fern pattern or transfers. Joins are usually easy to spot on the paper-covered objects.

Fernware has become increasingly popular amongst collectors recently with the size of the object, unusual shapes and condition being primary factors for collectors to consider when building a collection.

A late Victorian fernware box.

c1890   *3.5in (9cm) diam*

$70-100   OACC

A late Victorian fernware vesta case.

c1890   *1.25in (3cm) diam*

$50-80   OACC

FIND OUT MORE...

John Baker, Mauchline Ware and associated Scottish souvenir ware, Shire Books, Shire Album 140, 1985.

Princess Ira von Furstenberg, Tartanware: souvenirs from Scotland, Pavilion Books, 1996.

David Trachtenberg & Thomas Keith, The Collector's Guide to Mauchline Ware, Antique Collectors' Club, forthcoming.

Edward & Eva Pinto, Tunbridge and Scottish Souvenir Woodware, G.Bell & Sons, 1970.

TRIBAL ART

- Tribal art refers to the work of the Peoples of Africa, Oceania, South East Asia and the Americas. These traditional items were made for ceremonial and functional purposes, rather than as aesthetic objects. Every piece of tribal art, whether a mask, figure, currency, piece of jewelry or textile is a one-off.

- The climate and natural environment mean that a lot of very old primitive art has been destroyed. However, some of the most exquisite examples date from the late 19th and early 20th centuries.

- Generally speaking, tribal art is extremely difficult to date. Documented provenance with an object can help to ascertain an approximate age, and this will also add to the value. The pieces are often heavily patinated, making them look very old, but wear and usage will also have this effect. This does not affect the desirability. Tribal art is valued for its visual impact, cultural diversity and artistic expression.

- Unfortunately this area has been marred by an abundance of fakes. The surge in interest in tribal art in recent years has meant a huge increase in the number of imitations. However, the heavy patination and wear created by age and continued use is not easily replicated and a trained eye will be able to tell the difference. It is always advisable to visit a reputable dealer or auction house when buying tribal art.

An early 20thC Ingulia pig mask, with good patination.

12.25in (31cm) wide

$1,000-1,500   **GR**

An African Tshokwe mask, with oval face and coffee bean eyes, with scarification marks on cheeks, chin and forehead.

7.5in (19cm) high

$1,200-1,800   **GR**

A late 19th/early 20thC Ntoma Bambara mask, with detailed decoration covered by heavy patination.

This mask would originally have been applied with cowrie shells and iron rings.

12.5in (32cm) high

$3,000-4,000   **GR**

A Haya mask, from Tanzania, Africa.

10in (26cm) high

$650-750   **GR**

A Dan mask, with stylized protruding jaw, from the Ivory Coast, West Africa.

10in (26cm) high

$4,500-5,000   **GR**

A Baule tribe mask, with a well-formed naturalistic human face, a delicate pouting mouth, finely drawn T-shaped nose and eyebrows, almond-slit eyes delineated with white, the simple cross-hatched hair balances a white crescent moon, from the West Coast of Africa.

17.75in (45cm) high

$4,000-4,500   **GR**

An Agbogho Mmwo or white maiden mask, from the Igbo tribe, Central Nigeria.

This mask defines female beauty and was used in masquerades and festivals. It is rare to find these masks in such perfect condition, including original fringe decoration.

28.75in (73cm) high

$5,000-6,000   **GR**

An early 20thC Baule Kple Kple mask, of the Goli dance.

This is one of the most abstracted of African masks.

15.25in (39cm) high

$7,000-8,000   **GR**

A Chiwara headdress, with heavy patination, from the Bambara tribe, Mali.

15.75in (40cm) high

$2,000-2,500   **GR**

A very old Karli mask, showing Newan religious dualism between Hindu and Buddhist iconography.

15.75in (40cm) high

$800-1,000   **GR**

An Igorots Shaman's headdress, with monkey and snake skulls, possibly from the Longat or Kankani tribes in Northern Luzon, Phillippines.

11.5in (29cm) wide

$800-1,000   **GR**

An Indian tribal mask, depicting Ganesh, the Hindu elephant God.

31.5in (80cm) long

$700-1,000   **GR**

A 19thC tribal mask, depicting Ganesh, from Maharashtra district, India.

29.5in (75cm) long

$1,000-1,500   **GR**

An early 20thC Himalayan carved wood mask, with signs of kaolin, pitch and applied animal hair.

17in (43cm) high

$1,200-1,800   **GR**

A Sub-Himalayan mask, strong form with bold shapes and good patination.

11in (28cm) high

$800-1,000   **GR**

A Maprik Yam mask, in highly abstracted form, from Papua New Guinea.

Yam masks from the Maprik area of Papua New Guinea are used for ceremonial purposes during the yam harvest festival. The yams, which can grow up to 12ft (366cm) long, are decorated with these masks as well as flowers, fruit and leaves. The yams represent clan ancestor's spirits, and are believed to be present as seeing and hearing human beings. They are exchanged with traditional exchange partners. The partner with the biggest yam is said to have the most power.

18.5in (47cm) high

$500-600   **GR**

A Himalayan humanish mask, with red and white bands.

13in (33cm) high

$1,200-1,800   **GR**

An Indonesian mask, depicting a Mahabharata or Rama character.

7.75in (20cm) high

$300-400   **GR**

A fine Kalimantan mask, with original paintwork and fibre hair, Borneo.

14in (36cm) high

$4,000-4,500   **GR**

A Bahay or Modang Dayak tribe pig mask, used in planting ceremonies, from north east Kalimantan, Borneo.

10.25in (26cm) high

$4,000-4,500   **GR**

A Bahay or Modang Dayak tribe pig mask, used in planting ceremonies, north east Kalimantan, Borneo.

13.75 (35cm) high

$4,000-4,500   **GR**

An Ikenga carving of a warrior, from eastern of Nigeria.

13in (33cm) high

$500-600 GR

A Bon-po carving, possibly from the Himalayas or Nepal.

20in (51cm) high

$1,500-2,000 GR

An excavated bronze of a warrior, holding a shield, India.

6.75in (17cm) high

$1,200-1,800 GR

A Shiva deity bronze votive, India.

2.75in (7cm) high

$60-80 GR

A 17thC primitive bronze, depicting a cow, from Kanataka, India.

5.75in (14.5cm) high

$700-800 GR

A Khond tribe votive bronze, from India.

2in (5cm) high

$60-80 GR

A Khond tribe votive bronze, from India.

2.75in (7cm) high

$70-100 GR

A Khond tribe votive bronze, from India.

2in (5cm) high

$60-80 GR

A Khond tribe votive bronze, from India.

2.25in (6cm) high

$60-80 GR

A Khond tribe votive bronze, from India.

2.5in (6.5cm) high

$100-150 GR

A tribal bronze figure, depicting a three-headed shiva, from Sub-Himalayas, India.

7.5in (19cm) high

$600-700 GR

A pair of Ifugao rice gods, both male and female deities, the male with one hand to his chin, the female supporting her head with both hands, from the Philippines.

9in (23cm) high

$600-700 pair GR

An excavated iron torque, from Chad, West Africa.

11in (28cm) high

$800-1,200 GR

A m'bun status currency, in throwing knife form, from Gabon, Africa.

17in (43cm) high

$700-1,300 GR

Three metal pendants, in female image, from Taraba, Africa.

$250-300 each GR

Two Katanga crosses, from Africa.

9in (23cm) wide

$200-300 each GR

A fine Chamba tribe rattle, with two small and one large bell, from Nigeria.

9.5in (24cm) high

$350-450 GR

A Chamba rattle, with finely wrought detailing, from Nigeria.

22in (56cm) wide

$800-1,000 GR

A Senufo tribe pulley, from West Africa.

6.5in (16.5cm) high

$650-750 GR

A carved and painted wooden spoon, with a figure of a woman with elongated body, short strong legs, possibly Senufo tribe, from the Ivory Coast, West Africa.

18.5in (47cm) long

$400-500 GR

Three ceremonial spoons, from Timor.

Tallest 11.75in (30cm) long

$800-1,000 GR

A beautifully formed and eroded ceremonial ladder, from west Timor.

64.5in (164cm) high

$2,500-3,000 GR

An rare early 20thC iron lamp, decorated with birds and with heavy patination, from Yoruba, Africa.

$2,500-3,000 GR

A tribal cooking pot, from Africa.

6in (15cm) high

$200-300 GR

A Naga tribe necklace, made with glass beads and monkey bones, from the North Indian/Burmese border.
11.75in (30cm) diam

$200-300   **GR**

A Naga tribe necklace, made with conch shells.
11.75in (30cm) diam

$275-375   **GR**

A Naga tribe necklace, from the North Indian/Burmese border.
25in (64cm) long

$200-300   **GR**

A Naga tribe conch bead necklace, from Burma.
24.75in (63cm) diam

$1,000-1,200   **GR**

An excavated Naga tribe bronze bracelet.
3.5in (9cm) diam

$120-180   **GR**

An African ivory bracelet.
4in (10cm) diam

$500-600   **GR**

An ivory bracelet, from Yoruba, West Africa.
5in (13cm) wide

$275-375   **GR**

Two ivory rings, from South Sudan.
Largest 2in (5cm) long

L $120-180, R $250-300   GR

Three Ethiopian pendants.
Largest 3.75in (9.5cm) long

$120-180 each   **GR**

A necklace, from Misoram, India.
13.25in (34cm) diam

$60-100   **GR**

A brass tribal necklace.
16.5in (42cm) long

$1,000-1,200   **GR**

A Miris tribe necklace, with blue and orange beads, from Arunachal Pradesh, India.
17.25in (44cm) diam

$300-400   **GR**

An early 20thC abstract raffia panel.

These pieces were used as status currency by the chiefs and nobles of the Shoowa tribe in the Kuba Kingdom of Zaire.

$650-750 GR

An early 20thC abstract raffia panel.

22.5in (57cm) high

$800-900 GR

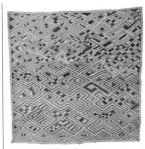

An early 20thC abstract raffia panel.

22.5in (57cm) high

$900-1,000 GR

An early 20thC abstract raffia panel.

21.25in (54cm) high

$800-900 GR

An early 20thC abstract raffia panel.

24.5in (62cm) high

$850-950 GR

An early 20thC abstract raffia panel.

24in (61cm) high

$800-900 GR

An early 20thC abstract raffia panel.

31.5in (80cm) high

$800-900 GR

An early 20thC abstract raffia panel.

23.25in (59cm) high

$850-950 GR

A red died ntshak, from the Bushong tribe in the Kuba Kingdom of Zaire.

Ntshak are dance skirts or ceremonial wraps worn by members of high status within the tribe.

36.25in (92cm) high

$800-900 GR

An early 20thC Nergede Kuba tribe panel, with appliquéd raffia status cloth.

38in (97cm) high

$800-900 GR

POCKET WATCHES

- The most common types of pocket watch are open-faced watches, followed by 'hunters' and 'half-hunters'. Movements differ depending on the period. During the 19th century, the two most popular mechanisms were the cylinder escapement and the more efficient lever-escapement, which dominated from the 1830s.
- By the 1870s an in-built winding mechanism was developed which meant that watches need not be wound with a key, as before.
- Collectors should ensure that the movement inside the watch matches the case and face. Movements are often signed and if they do not match, the value will be reduced. Pocket watches by noted manufacturers will fetch higher prices.
- Pocket watches with fine decoration, chronographs or extra dials showing moon phases, and calendars are more desirable. 14 carat gold pocket watches are American in origin.
- Lady's versions of pocket watches are smaller in overall size. Usually more ornately decorated than gentlemen's versions, they are often found hanging from a ribbon or short chain, mounted upside down so that they could be read easily when worn.
- The silver or gold chain that often accompanies a gentleman's pocket watch is known as an 'Albert' and they generally have an intrinsic value in themselves. The other end could hold useful accessories such as watch keys and pencils.

A 14K gold open-faced keyless pocket watch, by Waltham, the white enamel dial with Arabic numerals and seconds subsidiary, the 19-jewel movement signed "Riverside Waltham" no. 22070858, with gold cuvette, the case engraved with a monogram.

$150-200   **FRE**

A 14K gold open-faced keyless pocket watch, the dial signed "Tavannes Watch Co." with Arabic numerals and seconds subsidiary, the 15-jewel movement no. 251956, with base metal cuvette, the case with engine-turned decoration.

$300-400   **FRE**

A gold and enamel lady's open-faced fob watch, with cylinder escapement.

$200-250   **FRE**

A 14K gold open-faced octagonal pocket watch, by Waltham, the white enamel dial with Arabic numerals, one hand missing.

$150-200   **FRE**

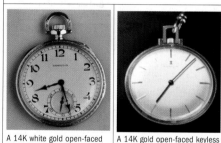

A 14K white gold open-faced keyless gentleman's pocket watch, by Hamilton, enamel dial with Roman numeral and seconds subsidiary, the 19-jewel movement no. 3051462 *1925*

$300-400   **FRE**

A 14K gold open-faced keyless pocket watch, by Waltham, gilt dial and Arabic numerals with seconds subsidiary, the 17-jewel movement no. 14123822, the case engraved with initials.

$150-200   **FRE**

A 14K gold hunter keyless pocket watch, by Waltham, the white enamel dial with Roman numerals and seconds subsidiary, the movement no. 8733290, with gold cuvette, the case engine-turned with milled bezel, incorporating an initialed cartouche.

$300-400   **FRE**

WALTHAM WATCH COMPANY

- The 'Waltham Watch Company' started as the 'Warren Mfg Co.' set up by Edward Howard, David Davis and Aaron Dennison in 1851. A factory was built at Waltham, Massachusetts in 1853, and the company name changed many times during the 1850s.
- After 1859, the name was changed finally to 'The American Waltham Watch Company' with pocket watches bearing the name 'Waltham' shortly afterwards.
- Many millions of inexpensive watches were produced by Waltham, who are credited with being the first mass-producer of watches in America.
- The company closed in 1957. Collectors particularly look for early 'Waltham' pocket watches bearing the names of the three original founders or 'Appleton, Tracey & Co.' used in the late 1850s. All pocket watches are marked with a serial number which accurately dates them.

A 14K gold hunter lady's fob watch, by Elgin, the white enamel dial with Arabic numerals and seconds subsidiary, the movement no. 16430097, with gold cuvette signed and dated, the case with engine-turned decoration.

1914

$150-200 FRE

A 14K gold hunter keyless pocket watch, by Waltham, the white enamel dial with Roman numerals and seconds subsidiary, the three-quarter plate movement no. 4978010, the gold cuvette signed and dated, in bright-cut engraved case.

1898

$200-250 FRE

A 14K gold hunter keyless pocket watch, by Waltham, the white enamel dial with Roman and Arabic numerals and seconds subsidiary, the movement no. 1498563, with gold cuvette, engine-turned oration, missing glass.

$250-300 FRE

A French silver pair cased pocket watch, with Danish hallmarks, the movement signed "Lepine à Paris", lacking outer case.

$300-500 FRE

An 18K gold and black enamel lady's fob watch, with white enamel dial, the case with engine-turned decoration and black enamel garter cartouche, one hand loose, glass badly cracked.

$150-200 FRE

A Swiss gold and enamel lady's fob watch, by L. Muonier, the white enamel dial with Roman and Arabic numerals, the Geneva bar escapement with mono-metallic balance, the back of the case ornately decorated with coloured enamel with a portrait of a lady.

$300-400 FRE

A gold and enamel lady's fob watch, by LeRoy à Paris, with signed gold cuvette, the enamel worn.

$300-400 FRE

A silver and enamel Art Deco lady's pendant fob watch, the white enamel dial with Roman numerals, triangular fan-shaped form, broken loop.

c1930

$120-180 FRE

A 14K gold pendant lady's fob watch, by G. Eckhardt, with gold lapel pin, with 10-jewel movement.

$200-250 FRE

A 10K gold and diamond set fob locket, with lion mask decoration.

$300-350 FRE

A Victorian silver and agate-inset gentleman's Albert chain, fitted with a pencil holder.

$200-250 FRE

WATCHES

WRISTWATCHES

- Watches were first worn on the wrist in the early 20th century. Early wristwatches look like small pocket watches with thick wire at the top and bottom to hold the strap. They are always circular in shape and have unsigned silvered or enamel dials and chrome, silver or gold cases. Despite their early date, they are generally of comparatively low value.

- It was not until the First World War that wristwatches began to become common when they were issued to servicemen. The style quickly took off and by the 1930s, wristwatches outnumbered pocket watches many times over.

- Watches from the 1920s and 1930s took a range of styles, with square, rectangular and octagonal case shapes being popular. Many matched the Art Deco stylings of the period. Automatic watches were developed around 1926 and became more reliable during the 1930s.

- The 1940s saw watch styles matching jewelery designs of the period. During the war, many noted manufacturers made standard issue watches for the armed forces which are characterised by robust steel construction, black dials and luminous numerals.

- The 1950s saw a move towards futuristic styling, with technical innovations including the first electric battery powered watch being developed by Hamilton Watch Co in 1957.

- Maker, complexity, materials and model can all add to the value, with sophisticated watches by renowned makers being the most desirable and valuable. Names to look for include Patek Philippe, Rolex, Cartier, Jaeger le Coultre and Audemars Piguet. Styling is also important and adds to desirability.

- Wristwatches with extra features such as calendars, chronographs and moon phases are highly sought after.

- Although quartz had been used for timepieces from the 1920s, it was not until the early 1970s that it was used for wristwatches.

A gentleman's 14ct gold wristwatch, by Hamilton, the dial with seconds subsidiary, 19-jewel movement no.M39777, no winder.

$300-400   FRE

A gentleman's 14ct gold automatic wristwatch, by Hamilton, the dial with center seconds sweep hands, and calendar aperture, no winder.

$500-600   FRE

A gentleman's 14ct gold Masterpiece wristwatch, by Hamilton, the dial with seconds subsidiary, the back inscribed and dated.
1971

$300-400   FRE

A gentleman's 14ct gold Thinline wristwatch, by Hamilton.

$150-200   FRE

A gentleman's 14ct gold Thin-O-Matic Masterpiece wristwatch, by Hamilton, the dial with center seconds sweep hand, the back of the case with presentation inscription and dated, lacks strap.

$200-250   FRE

A gentleman's 14ct white gold wristwatch, by Hamilton, the dial with seconds subsidiary, the chapter ring with Roman numerals, 19-jewel movement no. 2901879.

$1,000-1,500   FRE

A lady's 14ct gold dress watch, by Hamilton, with 17-jewel movement.

$70-100   FRE

A 14ct gold Omega watch, with engine-turned bezel and alligator band.

$250-300   FRE

A gentleman's 18ct gold wristwatch, by Omega, the dial with seconds subsidiary.

$300-350   FRE

A gentleman's 14ct gold wristwatch, by Omega, the dial with seconds subsidiary.

$250-300   FRE

A gentleman's 14ct gold wristwatch, by Omega, broken strap.

$400-450   FRE

A gentleman's gold and steel automatic Miester Constellation chronograph wristwatch, by Omega, the dial with center second sweep and calendar aperture, the 24-jewel movement no. 24757082.

$250-300   FRE

An 18ct yellow gold and stainless steel Rolex Prince.

Face 0.75in (2cm) wide

$6,000-6,500   WG

A CLOSER LOOK AT A ROLEX OYSTER

Rolex developed the world's first fully waterproof, dustproof and airtight watch case in 1926 and named it the 'Oyster'.

In 1927, it was successfully tested by Mercedes Gleitze, a young female swimmer as she swam across the English Channel.

A 1920s Rolex cushion Oyster, with original porcelain dial.

Face 1.25in (3cm) wide

$6,500-7,000   WG

A stainless steel Rolex Explorer, ref: 5504, with original lacquered dial.

c1959

$4,000-4,500   WG

A 1970s stainless steel Rolex Comex Sea Dweller, ref: 1665, with plastic face.

$15,000-18,000   WG

A stainless steel Rolex GMT Master, ref: 1675, with painted crown guard and dial with gold or gilt chapter ring.

c1961 1.5in (3.5cm) w

$3,500-4,000   WG

LONGINES

■ Longines was founded in 1832 at a watch making workshop in St Imier, Switzerland. The first factory was built at 'Es Longines' close to the town, hence the name. They used the 'winged hour glass' logo on many of their watches. Longines watches have sold very successfully, with a great many ranges being released. As such, they are currently very reasonably priced and make a good name to start a collection with.

A gentleman's 14K gold wristwatch, by Longines, the dial with seconds subsidiary, the 17-jewel movement no. 776829.

$400-500   FRE

A gentleman's 14ct gold wristwatch, by Longines, the dial with seconds subsidiary, the 17-jewel movement no. 8275833.

$200-250   FRE

A gentleman's 14ct gold wristwatch, by Longines, the dial with seconds subsidiary, the 17-jewel movement no. 8100554.

$400-500   FRE

A gentleman's 14ct gold wristwatch, by Longines, the dial with seconds subsidiary, lacking winder, band broken.

$150-200   FRE

A gentleman's 14ct gold wristwatch, by Longines, the dial with seconds subsidiary, the jewel movement no. 10113768, the back inscribed and dated. *1958*

$250-300 FRE

A platinum Breitling Navitimer 1461, no.8 from a limted edition of 25.

Face 1.5in (4cm) wide

$20,000-25,000 WG

A gentleman's alarm chronometer wristwatch, by Henri Giraux.

$200-250 FRE

A gentleman's 14K gold wristwatch, by Invicta, the dial with seconds subsidiary, 17-jewel movement.

$350-400 FRE

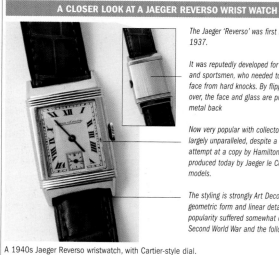

A CLOSER LOOK AT A JAEGER REVERSO WRIST WATCH

The Jaeger 'Reverso' was first introduced in 1937.

It was reputedly developed for polo players and sportsmen, who needed to protect the face from hard knocks. By flipping the watch over, the face and glass are protected by a metal back

Now very popular with collectors, it has been largely unparalleled, despite a short-lived attempt at a copy by Hamilton. It is still produced today by Jaeger le Coultre in various models.

The styling is strongly Art Deco, with a clean geometric form and linear details. Its popularity suffered somewhat during the Second World War and the following years.

A 1950s 18ct gold round International Watch Company dress watch, with calibre 83 movement and orginal dial.

Face 1.5in (3.5cm) wide

$1,500-2,000 WG

A 1940s Jaeger Reverso wristwatch, with Cartier-style dial.

Face 1in (2.5cm) wide

 WG

A 1950s Jaeger Le Coultre Automatic Memovox, with alarm, date and original tortoiseshell brown patina.

Face 1.5in (3.5cm) wide

$2,500-3,000 WG

A gentleman's 14ct gold wristwatch, by Movado, the dial with seconds subsidiary, the 15-jewel movement un-numbered, crack to glass.

$250-300 FRE

A 1950s 18ct gold rectangular Patek Philippe, ref: 2433, with original dial.

$5,500-6,500 WG

A 1940s Jaeger Reverso wristwatch caption note: **$4,500-5,500**

A gentleman's 14ct gold wristwatch, by Mathey Tissot, the dial with center seconds sweep hand, back of case inscribed and dated, no winder.

1965

$120-180 FRE

A late 1940s/early 1950s 18ct gold oversized round Vacheron & Constantin watch, with original engine-turned guillouche dial.

Face 1.5in (3.5cm) wide

$5,000-5,500 WG

A gentleman's 14ct gold Premiere wristwatch, by Waltham, the dial with subsidiary seconds, the 17-jewel movement no. 74807, the back of the case engraved and dated, the minute hand loose.

1942

$150-200 FRE

A gentleman's 14ct gold wristwatch, by Zodiac, the dial with subsidiary seconds, 17-jewel movement.

$120-180 FRE

Novelty Watches

A Swiss gentleman's 14ct gold wristwatch, the dial with one hand missing.

$400-500 FRE

A Budweiser promotional wristwatch, by Jay Ward Productions, depicting Anheuser-Busch Inc, Budweiser on center dial, with leather wristband, base metal bezel, stainless steel back, 12-jewel movement.

$60-80 FRE

An Energizer Bunny promotional wristwatch, by Hana Time, depicting the Energizer Brand Battery bunny on center dial with leather wristband, case movement, assembled in China from Swiss parts, Hong Kong case complete in sleeve with original warranty.

$12-18 FRE

A Nestlé Little Hans promotional wristwatch, by Rega Industries, Ltd., depicting Little Hans of Nestlé on center dial, eyes of character move in accordance with seconds, with leather wristband and complete with original shipping package and warranty.

c1972

$30-40 FRE

A 40th Anniversary Howdy Doody wristwatch, by NBC Inc and K.F.S Inc, depicting four profiles of Howdy Doody on the center dial, leather wristband in original sleeve case and with warranty.

$50-70 FRE

A Ronald McDonald promotional wristwatch, by American Watch Service, depicting Ronald on center dial, base metal bezel, stainless steel back, Swiss made, complete with original box and warranty.

McDonalds have recently expressed doubts about continuing to use Ronald McDonald as he is now seen as an 'outdated' character, no longer popular with children. If they decide to discontinue the clown, items showing him may increase in popularity.

c1974

$30-40 FRE

A Donald Duck wristwatch, by Bradley Time, Walt Disney Productions, precision Swiss movement, anti-magnetic, blue leather wristband, in original red case with warranty.

$40-60   FRE

A Dr. Seuss "The Cat in the Hat Time Teller" wristwatch, by Lafayette Watch Co., Swiss made and base metal, with depiction on center dial, red wristband, complete in original box.

c1972

$100-150   FRE

A Mickey and Minnie Mouse wristwatch, by Walt Disney Productions, depicting a spirited tennis match between Mickey and Minnie, base metal bezel, stainless steel back, and Swiss made, leather band.

$30-40   FRE

A Popeye the Sailorman "I Yam what I Yam" wristwatch, by Sheffeld Watch Corp., depicting Elzie Segar's comic strip character on center dial, fabric wristband, with warranty.

c1972

$30-40   FRE

A Porky Pig wristwatch, by Sheffeld Watch Corp., Swiss made and base metal, depicting the Loony Tunes classic character on center dial, leather wristband, complete warranty.

c1972

$30-40   FRE

A Scooby-Doo "Where Are You?" wristwatch, by NanRic Watch Co., base metal and Swiss made, depicting the famous canine sleuth on center yellow dial, in original box with warranty.

With the current trend of comic book characters being made into feature films, original memorabilia relating to the characters in question should become more highly sought after, providing the films succeed in capturing the public's imagination.

c1970

$250-300   FRE

A Sesame Street Big Bird wristwatch, by Bradley Time, depicting the well known Sesame Street character on the center dial, base metal and Swiss-made, red wristband, in original box with warranty.

c1977

$30-40   FRE

A Snoopy wristwatch, by United Features Syndicate, Swiss made and stainless steel back, depicting Snoopy from the Charles M. Schultz comic strip, complete in original box and warranty.

c1972

$30-40   FRE

A Superman wirstwatch, by Bradley Time, depicting Jerry Siegel's classic hero of Action Comics on center dial, fabric wristband, complete in original box.

c1973

$25-30   FRE

A Woody Woodpecker wristwatch, by Walter Lantz Productions, Inc., the convex center dial depicting Walter Lantz's Woody Woodpecker, waterproof and Swiss made, red wristband.
c1972

$30-40 FRE

A 1970s patriotic construction worker wristwatch, styled by Manfred, depicting male construction worker on center dial, diamond-tooled, base metal case, electronically timed, Swiss made, fabric patriotic wristband, in original box.

$45-55 FRE

A President George Herbert Walker Bush wristwatch, by Sanders & Co., the president seated on a Republican elephant, leather wristband, in original velvet box with original sales receipt.
c1990

$30-40 FRE

A "Clinton – Gore" Presidential campaign wristwatch, stainless steel back and metal case red leather wristband.
1992

$12-18 FRE

A President Bill Clinton wristwatch, depicting Clinton on center dial, leather wristband.

$18-22 FRE

A President Richard Nixon wristwatch, by Dirty Time Co., depicting "Dicky Nixon" diamond-tooled, electronically timed, base metal case, Swiss made, patriotic wristband, with warranty.

$120-180 FRE

An "I'm Not A Crook" Richard Nixon wristwatch, by Tru Time, a whimsical Nixon character on the center dial, stainless steel back, with red, white and blue fabric wristband.

$120-180 FRE

A "Keep the Spirit of '76" bicentennial gentleman's wristwatch, by Bradley Time, base metal case and Swiss movement, depicting George Washington and fellow comrades waving the American flag, in original box with warranty.
c1976

$30-40 FRE

An offical "Philadelphia '76'" Bicentennial commemorative timepiece, electronically timed, diamond-tooled, Swiss movement, wristband, with original sleeve case and sales receipt, wear to brass case.

$12-18 FRE

A President Ronald Reagan wristwatch, by Timely Creations, depicting Reagan seated on Republican elephant, base metal bezel, stainless steel back, on fabric wristband.
c1980

$12-18 FRE

A Statue of Liberty wristwatch, depicting the American flag and the Statue of Liberty, base metal, Swiss made, diamond-tooled, unbreakable mainspring, electronically timed, in original box with sales receipt.

$20-30 FRE

A 1970s "Uncle Sam" calendar watch, by Birmingham Watch Co., base metal bezel and stainless steel back, depicting Uncle Sam on center dial, patriotic fabric wristband, in original shipping package with warranty.

$30-40 FRE

A Ghostbusters wristwatch game, by Nelsonic.

c1990   8.75in (22cm) long

$20-25   HLJ

A official E.T. wristwatch, by Nelsonic, anti-magnetic and stainless steel back, depicting the extraterrestrial character on center dial, leather wristband, in original box.

c1982

$30-40   FRE

An official Star Wars wristwatch, by Bradley Time, depicting the droids R2-D2 and C-3PO on center dial, precision Swiss movement, electronically timed and anti-magnetc, navy wristband, complete in original box with warranty.

c1977

$50-70   FRE

A "Forever Elvis" commemorative wristwatch, by Precision Watch Company Inc, depicting Elvis on one of his national tours on center dial, with leather wristband, base metal back and Swiss made, complete in original box and with warranty.

$40-50   FRE

A "Keep Time with the Fonz" wristwatch, by Time Trends, depicting The Fonz from "Happy Days" TV series on center dial with simulated fabric wristband, complete in original box with warranty.

c1976

$25-30   FRE

A Jack and Jill "Digital Tell Time" wristwatch, by Sutton Time Ltd, Swiss made, depicting nursery rhyme children Jack and Jill on center dial, red leather wristband, in original box with warranty.

c1974

$250-300   FRE

The Evel Knievel wristwatch, by Bradley Time, depicting the motorcycle daredevil on center dial, with leather and star-studded wristband, anti-magnetic, electronically timed, precision Swiss movement, complete in box with warranty.

c1975

$100-150   FRE

A Lucky Las Vegas wristwatch, depicting the lucky dice of Las Vegas above a green gaming background on center dial, on leather wristband, electronically timed, base metal, Swiss manufactured, anti-magnetic.

$30-40   FRE

An original Laurel and Hardy wristwatch, by Dirty Time Company, depicting the comic legends on center dial, with red leather band, wear and corrosion to bezel.

$25-30   FRE

A wristwatch commemorating the lunar landing, by Fashion Time, leather wristband, Swiss made, and complete with original box and warranty.

c1972

$120-180   FRE

A humorous bearded doll watch.

$12-18   FRE

CORKSCREWS

- The first recorded mention of using a 'screw to remove a cork' was in 1681, but they had been known and used before then. The 19th century saw the 'golden age' of inventions with many patents for new designs being issued.

- The 'screw' is known as a 'worm' or 'helix' and can be made from shaped wire or cast in shape. The first turn often had sharp edges, known as 'cyphered' edges to help with penetration into the cork.

- Corkscrews fall into two main categories, 'straight pull', where the force to extract the cork comes from the user, and 'mechanical', where a mechanism helps draw out the cork. Mechanical versions and early or finely made straight pulls are generally more desirable.

- Corkscrews with unusual mechanisms, those made from precious materials and those marked with desirable makers' names will fetch the highest prices.

- It is worth considering condition. Collectors should ensure that the corkscrew works and is complete. Rust or other marks should be carefully cleaned off and moving parts gently oiled. Repairs will devalue a corkscrew, as will serious damage to the worm.

A mother-of-pearl and silver pocket corkscrew, by Samuel Pemberton.

There are many designs for these early corkscrews with silver, often ornate, sheaths. They were mainly made in Holland.

c1810   3.25in (8.5cm) long

$300-400   **CSA**

A peg and warm steel corkscrew.

2.5in (6cm) long

$120-180   **BS**

A pocket corkscrew, the casing made from a British Lee Enfield .303 rifle cartridge.

c1918

$20-30   **CSA**

A 1930s Schlitz Beer advertising corkscrew, with bell cap.

5in (12.5cm) long

$20-30   **CSA**

An American Williamson bell cap continuous action corkscrew.

c1910   7.5in (19cm) long

$40-60   **CSA**

A steel corkscrew, with finger grip.

c1900   6in (15cm) long

$80-120   **BS**

A 19thC steel corkscrew, with bone handle, replaced brush, crack in bone.

6in (15cm) long

$200-300   **BS**

Brushes were inset into handles from the late 18thC until the late 19thC. They were used to brush deposits off the label or bottle top.

The first corkscrew patent, in 1795, used a 'button' at the top of the worm which prevented the worm moving further into the cork and also helped to 'unstick' the cork.

A Henshall button-type corkscrew, with bone handle and brush.

c1830   6in (15.5cm) long

$70-100   **CSA**

A 1930s San Benito advertising corkscrew.

5in (12.5cm) long

$15-25   **CSA**

A stainless steel Valenzina corkscrew, 1949 registration.

$30-40   **CSA**

A German plastic Sieger 600 continuous action corkscrew.

c1960   4.5in (11.5cm) long

$15-18   CSA

A 1960s American chrome barman's tool, with spirit measure and can opener.

6in (15.5cm) long

$10-12   CSA

A pair of English 1930s carved pinewood figural corkscrews, carved as a fighting cat and Scottie dog.

Dog 5in (12.5cm) wide

$20-30   CSA

An American syrocowood "The Waiter" corkscrew.

Due to Prohibition, corkscrews had to be disguised. In this case, the head of the waiter lifts off and acts as the handle for the corkscrew.

A carved rosewood figural Chinaman corkscrew.

c1930   5in (12.5cm) high

$10-12   CSA

c1910   8in (20.5cm) high

$100-150   CSA

A German celluoid mermaid corkscrew, with metallic painted scales, marked "GES GESCHULTZ".

c1900   4.25in (10.5cm) long

$400-600   CSA

A German celluloid covered lady's legs folding corkscrew, with half-length stockings.

These whimsical corkscrews are very popular with collectors and are reminiscent of debauched nights spent watching the can-can dancers at the Moulin Rouge, Paris. they come in large and small sizes with a variety of coloured full or half stockings.

c1880-90 2.5in (6.5cm) long

$200-250   CSA

A German celluloid lady's legs folding corkscrew, with pink-striped stockings.

c1880-90 2.5in (6.5cm) long

$200-250   CSA

An English eight-tool folding bow corkscrew, with hoof pick, leather hole punch, gimlet, grooved helical worm corkscrew, spike, auger, screw driver and button hook, stamped "B.B. Wells West Strand".

c1820 Closed 2.75in (7cm) long

$100-150   CSA

A cast brass two-finger figural spider and fly corkscrew.

c1930   6.5in (16.5cm) long

$15-20   CSA

A 1920s steel corkscrew, with cast iron bottle opener.

5in (12.5cm) long

$40-60   BS

A bone-handled perfume corkscrew, for opening perfume bottles.

c1830   5in (12.5cm) long

$15-25   CSA

A 1950s brass set of scales bottle opener.

4.5in (11.5cm) long

$4-6   CSA

A 1950s Australian aluminum hand bottle opener, marked "Made in Australia".

6.75in (17cm) long

$4-6   CSA

A 1950s Canadian souvenir bottle opener, by Century, decorated with a family of bears in a mountainous landscape.

3.75in (9.5cm) long

$4-6   CSA

A 1950s brass Eiffel tower souvenir bottle opener.

4in (10cm) long

$4-6   CSA

A 1950s heavy cast brass double sided horses head bottle opener.

4in (10cm) long

$4-6   CSA

A 1950s Johnnie Walker spirit pourer.

5.75in (14.5cm) long

$10-15   CSA

A Greek souvenir bottle opener, with a classic head and "EPMH" on one side and diaphanous figure and a cartouche with a deer and "NA 1947".

c1947   3in (7.5cm) long

$10-12   CSA

A Booth's spirit pourer.

c1935   5.75in (14.5cm) long

$10-15   CSA

A 1950s wooden man in morning suit bottle opener, with articulated arms.

5in (12.5cm) long

$4-6   CSA

A 1940s King George IV whisky spirit pourer.

5in (12.5cm) long

$10-15   CSA

A 1950s Burdon Sherry spirit pourer.

4in (10cm) long

$6-9   CSA

A 1940s King George IV whisky spirit pourer.

5in (12.5cm) long

$10-15   CSA

A John Haig's whisky spirit pourer.

6.5in (16.5cm) long

$10-15   CSA

A 1960s Wade china Beefeater Gin cork.

$15-25   CSA

A 1960s pottery "Bob Cratchet" spirit pourer.

Bob Cratchet was a character in Charles Dickens' novel 'A Christmas Carol'.

$20-30   CSA

A 1950s Italian Alps novelty carved wood articulated cork, carved as a drinking man.

5in (12.5cm) high

$10-15   CSA

A 1950s Italian Alps novelty carved wood articulated cork, carved as a kissing couple.

5in (12.5cm) high

$15-18   CSA

Cocktail Shakers

A silver-plated cocktail shaker, with spot-hammered decoration, marked "AM 0990" on the base.

c1935   11.5in (29cm) high

$700-900   Tag

A silver-plated cocktail shaker, in the shape of a hand bell, with wooden handle.

c1935   11.5in (29cm) high

$500-800   Tag

A silver-plated cocktail shaker, with gilt details, with cocktail ingredients marked on the exterior.

This is a very popular design, where the user twists the silver plated sleeve until an inscribed arrow points at his chosen cocktail. The series of windows then displays the ingredients for that cocktail.

c1935   4.5in (11cm) high

$1,000-1,500   Tag

A silver-plated cocktail shaker, in the shape of a bowling pin, with wooden handle.

c1935   15.5in (39.5cm) high

$700-1,000   Tag

A Mixit cut glass and silver-plated cocktail shaker, the silver-plated lid with revolving cocktail menu, including Martini, White Lady, Kicking Horse and Bacchante.

c1935   9.5in (24cm)

$500-800   Tag

MURANO GLASS

The production of the many famous glassworks at Murano, near Venice, Italy, has always been popular, with many vintage pieces now becoming increasingly sought after. Although the factories at Murano continue to produce many high quality pieces, collectors should look for quality pieces from up and coming glassmakers, or pieces by established makers who may not yet be recognized.

A contemporary and unique Vittorio Ferro murano 'Murrine' vase, in blown glass, signed.

10.25in (26cm) high

$1,500-2,000   **FM**

A contemporary and unique Vittorio Ferro pale blue glass vase, signed.

$1,300-1,800   **FM**

VITTORIO FERRO

- Vittorio Ferro is part of a well known glass-making family. He started working at the renowned Fratelli Toso in Murano at the age of 14 and was promoted to glass master at 20.
- He studied under his uncles, the Zuffi brothers, and Professor Ansolo Zuga, and produced a great many of the designs at Fratelli Toso until its closure in 1981, when he was immediately offered a position as a Master at the de Majo glassworks.
- His passion lies in 'murrine', where many rectangles or circles of differently colored glass made from cut rods are gathered and fused together into a mosaic pattern and applied to the exterior of a clear glass vessel.
- He won the Borselle d'Oro prize in 1969 and the 'Altino' prize in 1993 and was included in a book on famous glass masters in 1994.
- He retired in 1994 and is now working at the Fratelli Pagnin workshop, directing production of his own creations using murrine and many other historic techniques.

A contemporary and unique Vittorio Ferro vase, in red and blue hand-blown glass.

11.25in (28.5cm) high

$1,300-1,800   **FM**

A contemporary and unique Vittorio Ferro polychrome vase, signed.

$1,300-1,800   **FM**

A contemporary and unique Vittorio Ferro yellow glass vase, signed.

10.25in (26cm) high

$1,750-2,250   **FM**

A contemporary handmade turquoise glass vase, designed by Riccardo Licata.

16.25in (41cm) high

$800-1,000   **FM**

A contemporary G. Michello blown glass vase.

9in (23cm) high

$800-1,000   **FM**

RICCARDO LICATA

- Born in Turin in 1929, Licata studied at the Liceo Artistico and the Accademia di Belle Arte and produced designs for numerous Murano glassmakers, who used blanks and painted mirrors.
- In 1952, he designed a popular range known as 'Aquarium' for Gino Cendese amongst many other commissions for various important glassmakers.
- From 1957, he was a professor at the 'Ecole des Beaux Arts' in Paris and also worked on projects including set designs and book illustrations.

A contemporary handmade blue glass vase, designed by Riccardo Licata.

16.25in (41cm) high

$800-1,000   **FM**

A contemporary glass piece 'Espanol vinas hez', by Soumero.

10.5in (27cm) high

$1,000-1,500   **FM**

A

Acid Etching A technique using acid to decorate glass to produce a matt or frosted appearance.

Albumen print Photographic paper is treated with egg white (albumen) to enable it to hold more light sensitive chemicals. After being exposed to a negative, the resulting image is richer with more tonal variation.

Ambrotype A glass negative plate treated with chemicals and mounted on a dark background to show the image.

Autographic A feature used by Kodak between 1914 and 1932 that allowed the user to 'write' directly onto the film, using a stylus via a hinged door on the back of the camera.

Applied Refers to a separate part that has been attached to an object, such as a handle.

B

Baluster A curved form with a bulbous body and a slender neck.

Bébé The French term for a doll that represents a baby rather than an adult.

Bisque A type of unglazed porcelain used for making dolls from c1860 to c1925.

Boards The hard covers of a book.

Brassing On plated items, where the plating has worn off to reveal the underlying base metal.

Broderie Anglaise Meaning 'English embroidery', white thread is embroidered onto a white cloth, used after the 1820s.

C

Cabochon A large, protruding, polished, but not faceted, stone.

Cameo Hardstone, coral or shell that has been carved in relief to show a design in a contrasting color.

Cameo glass Decorative glass made from two or more layers of differently colored glass, which are then carved or etched to reveal the color beneath.

Cartouche A framed panel, often in the shape of a shield or paper scroll, which can be inscribed.

Celadon A distinctive grey/green or blue/green glaze derived from iron and used to imitate jade in China for over 2,000 years.

Character doll A doll with a face that resembles a real child rather than an idealized one.

Charger A large plate or platter, often for display, but also for serving.

Cloisonne A decorative technique using small cells created by soldering thin strips of metal to an object which are then filled with colored enamels.

Clubhouse Signature A player's signature that was not actually signed by the player, but by one of his colleagues such as a batboy.

Composition A mixture including wood pulp, plaster and glue and used as a cheap alternative to bisque in the production of dolls' heads and bodies.

Compote A dish, usually on a stem or foot, to hold fruit for the dessert course.

Craze A network of fine cracks in the glaze caused by uneven shrinking during firing.

Cultured pearl A pearl formed when an irritant is artificially introduced to the mollusc.

D

Daguerrotype A 'positive' image photographed directly onto a metal plate which is then usually mounted into a decorative case. The first practical photography process and used from c1839 until the1850s.

Diecast Objects made by pouring molten metal into a closed metal die or mould.

Ding A very small dent in metal.

DQ Standing for 'diamond quilted', where a repeated pattern of diamond shapes cover the surface.

E

Earthenware A type of porous pottery that requires a glaze to make it waterproof.

Ebonized Wood that has been blackened with dye to resemble ebony.

Escapement The mechanical part of the clock or watch that regulates the transfer of energy from the weights or spring to the movement of the clock or watch

F

Faience Earthenware that is treated with an impervious tin glaze. Popular in France from the 16th century and reaching its peak during the 18th century.

Fairing A small porcelain figure made in Eastern Germany and given away as prizes or sold inexpensively at fairs. They usually have an amusing subject and title.

Ferrotype Similar to an ambrotype but black enameled tin, not glass, is used. The quality of the image is usually inferior to that of the ambrotype.

Finial A decorative knob at the end of a terminal, or on a lid.

Flatware The term for any type of cutlery.

Foliate Leaf and vine motifs.

G

Guilloché An engraved pattern of interlaced lines or other decorative motifs, sometimes enamelled over with translucent enamels.

IJKL

Inclusions Used to describe all types of small particles of decorative materials embedded in glass.

Iridescent A lustrous finish that subtly changes color depending on how light hits it. Often used to describe the finish on ceramics and glass.

Kutani Japanese porcelain made at Kutani, in the Kaga province of Japan, in the 17th and 18th centuries.

Lambrequins A shaped decoration derived from the hanging fringes on tents at a jousting competition. Used to describe similarly shaped borders on ceramics, silver and furniture.

MNO

Meiji A period in Japanese history dating from 1868-1912.

Mon A Japanese family crest. A common example is the 16 petal chrysanthemum flower.

M.O.P. Mother of pearl. The shiny and colored interior of some shells.

Netsuke A small toggle, usually carved from ivory or wood, used to secure pouches and boxes (known as sagemono) hung on cords through the belt of a kimono. They are most often carved as figures or animals.

Opalescent An opal-like, milky glass with subtle gradations of color between thinner more translucent areas and thicker, more opaque areas.

P

Paisley A soft woollen fabric with a stylized design based on pinecones.

Paste (Jewelry) A hard, bright glass cut the same way as a diamond and made and set to resemble one.

Patera An oval or circular decorative motif often with a fluted or floral center.

Penwork Black japanned items were decorated with white japanned patterns, with details and shading being applied using Indian ink and a pen. Popular in England during the 18th and 19th centuries.

Pique A decorative technique where small strips or studs of gold are inlaid onto ivory or tortoiseshell in a pattern and secured in place by heating.

Pontil A metal rod to which the glass vessel is attached when it is being worked. When it is removed it leaves a raised disc-shaped 'pontil mark'.

Pounce pot A small pot made of wood (treen), silver or ceramic. Found on inkwells or designed to stand alone, it held a gum dust that was sprinkled over parchment to prevent ink from spreading. Used until the late 18th century.

Pressed (Press Moulded) Ceramics formed by pressing clay into a mold. Pressed glass is made by pouring molten glass into a mold and pressing it with a plunger.

R

Reeded A type of decoration with thin raised, convex vertical lines. Derived from the decoration of classical columns.

Repoussé A French term for the raised, 'embossed', decoration on metals such as silver. The metal is forced into a form from one side causing it to bulge.

S

Satsuma Collective term for potteries on the island of Kyushu, Japan, which made items for export to the West. Their ware is typified by a clear, yellowish glaze, often decorated with colored figures and flowers and gilt decoration.

Sweet Spot The area of a baseball between the two curving lines of stitching where it is most desirable to find a player's autograph.

Stoneware A type of ceramic similar to earthenware and made of high-fired clay mixed with stone, such as feldspar, which makes it non-porous.

Suzuribako A Japanese writing box containing tools such as brushes, inkpots and ink slabs.

T

Tazza A shallow cup with a wide bowl, which is raised up on a single pedestal foot.

Tooled Collective description for a number of decorative techniques applied to a surface. Includes engraving, stamping, punching and incising.

Tsuba A Japanese sword guard. An often ornate disc placed between the blade and the handle to protect the hand from the blade.

V

Vermeil Gold-plated silver.

Vesta case A small case or box, usually made from silver, for carrying matches.

W

White metal Precious metal that is possibly silver, but not officially marked as such.

Whitework Decorative white embroidery on white fabric, usually cotton. Often said to be the forerunner of lace.

Y

Yellow metal Precious metal that is possibly gold, but not officially marked as such.

KEY TO ILLUSTRATIONS

EVERY COLLECTIBLE ILLUSTRATED in *Collectibles Price Guide 2003* by Judith Miller has a letter code which identifies the auction house or dealer who sold it. The list below is a key to these codes. In the list, auction houses are shown by the letter Ⓐ and dealers by the letter Ⓓ. Some items may have come from a private collection, in which case the code in the list is accompanied by the letter Ⓟ. Inclusion in this book in no way constitutes or implies a contract or a binding offer on the part of any of our contributors to supply

or sell the goods illustrated, or similar items, at the prices stated.

If you wish to have any item valued, it is advisable to contact the dealer or specialist in advance to check that they will carry out this service and whether there is a charge. While most dealers will be happy to help you with an enquiry, do remember that they are busy people. Telephone valuations are not possible. Please mention *Collectibles Price Guide 2003* by Judith Miller when making an enquiry.

ACM Ⓓ
Antiques of Cape May
Tel: 800 224 1687

AGI Ⓐ
Aurora Galleries International
30 Hackamore Lane, Suite 2, Bell Canyon, California 91307
Tel: 818 884 6468
Fax: 818 227 2941
vjc@auroragalleriesonline.com
www.auroragalleriesonline.com

AMM Ⓓ
Automatomania
Shop 124, Grays Antiques Market, 58 Davies Street, London W1K 5LP UK
Tel: 00 44 (0) 7495 5259
00 44 (0)7790 719097
www.automatomania.com

AnA Ⓓ
Ancient Art
85 The Vale, Southgate, London N14 6AT UK
Tel: 00 44 (0)20 8882 1509
Fax: 00 44 (0)20 8886 5235
ancient.art@btinternet.com
www.ancientart.co.uk

AS&S Ⓐ
Andrew Smith & Son Auctions
Hankin's Garage, 47 West Street, Alresford, Hampshire UK
Tel: 00 44 (0) 1962 842 841
Fax: 00 44 (0)1962 863 274
auctions@andrewsmithandson.
fsbusiness.co.uk

ATM Ⓓ
At the Movies
17 Fouberts Place, Carnaby, London W1F 7QD UK
Tel: 00 44 (0)20 7439 6336
Fax: 00 44 (0)20 7439 6355
info@atthemovies.co.uk
www.atthemovies.co.uk

B Ⓐ
Bracketts Fine Art Auctioneers
Auction Hall, The Pantiles, Tunbridge Wells, Kent TN2 5QL UK
Tel: 00 44 (0) 1892 544 500
Fax: 00 44 (0) 1892 515 191
sales@bfaa.co.uk
www.bfaa.co.uk

BA Ⓓ
Branksome Antiques
370 Poole Road, Branksome, Poole, Dorset BH12 1AW UK
Tel: 00 44 (0) 1202 763 324 /679 932
Fax: 00 44 (0) 1202 763 643

BAC Ⓓ
Burlwood Antique Center
Route 3, Meredith, NH 03253
Tel: 603 279 6387
rckhprant@aol.com
www.burlwood-antiques.com

BAR Ⓐ
Bristol Auction Rooms
St John's Place, Apsley Road, Clifton, Bristol BS8 2ST UK
Tel: 00 44 (0) 117 973 7201
Fax: 00 44 (0) 117 973 5671
info@bristolauctionrooms.co.uk
www.bristolauctionrooms.co.uk

BCAC Ⓓ
Bucks County Antique Center
Route 202, Lahaska PA 18931
Tel: 215 794 9180

BEJ Ⓓ
Bébés & Jouets
C/o Post Office, 165 Restalrig Road, Edinburgh EH7 6HW UK
Tel: 00 44 (0) 131 332 5650
bebesetjouets@u.genie.co.uk

Ber Ⓐ
Bertoia Auctions
2141 Demarco Drive, Vineland NJ 08360
Tel: 856 692 1881
Fax: 856 692 8697
bill@bertoiaauctions.com
www.bertoiaauctions.com

BG Ⓐ
Bob Gowland International Golf Auctions
The Stables, Claim Farm, Manley Road, Frodsham, Cheshire WA6 6HT UK
Tel/Fax:
00 44 (0) 1928 740 668
bob@internationalgolfauctions.com
www.internationalgolfauctions.com

Bib Ⓓ
Biblion
1/7 Davies Mews, London W1K 5AB UK
Tel: 00 44 (0) 20 7629 1374
Fax: 00 44 (0) 20 7493 7158
info@biblion.com
www.biblion.com

BonS Ⓐ
Bonhams, Sevenoaks
49 London Road, Sevenoaks, Kent TN13 1AR UK
Tel: 00 44 (0) 1732 740 310
Fax: 00 44 (0) 1732 741 842
info@bonhams.com
www.bonhams.com

BS Ⓓ
Below Stairs of Hungerford
103 High Street, Hungerford, Berkshire RG17 0NB UK
Tel: 00 44 (0) 1488 682 317
Fax: 00 44 (0) 1488 684 294
hofgartner@belowstairs.co.uk
www.belowstairs.co.uk

MSC Ⓟ
Mark Slavinsky Collection

CAA Ⓓ
Contemporary Applied Arts
2 Percy Street, London W1T 1DD UK
Tel: 00 44 (0) 20 7436 2344
Fax: 00 44 (0) 20 7436 2446
www.caa.org.uk

CA Ⓐ
Chiswick Auctions
1-5 Colville Road, London W3 8BL UK
Tel: 00 44 (0) 20 8992 4442
Fax: 00 44 (0) 20 8896 0541

CB Ⓓ
Colin Baddiel
Stand B25, Stand 351-3, Grays Antique Market, South Molton Lane, London W1Y 2LP UK
Tel: 00 44 (0) 20 7408 1239
Fax: 00 44 (0) 20 7493 9344

CHAA Ⓐ
Cowan's Historic
Americana Auctions
673 Wilmer Avenue,
Cincinnati, OH 45226
Tel: 513 871 1670
Fax: 513 871 8670
Info@HistoricAmericana.com
www.historicamericana.com

Chef Ⓐ
Cheffins
The Cambridge Saleroom,
2 Clifton Road, Cambridge
CB1 4BW UK
Tel: 00 44 (0) 1223 213 343
Fax: 00 44 (0) 1223 413 396
fine.art@cheffins.co.uk
www.cheffins.co.uk

Clv Ⓐ
Clevedon Salerooms
Herbert Road, Clevedon,
Bristol BS21 7ND UK
Tel: 00 44 (0) 1275 876 699
Fax: 00 44 (0) 1275 343 765
clevedon.salerooms@
cableinet.co.uk
www.clevedon-salerooms.com

CO Ⓐ
Cooper Owen
10 Denmark Street,
London, WC2H 8LS UK
Tel: 00 44 (0) 20 7240 4132
Fax: 00 44 (0) 20 7240 4339
info@cooperowen.com
www.cooperowen.com

ColC Ⓓ
Collectors Cameras
PO Box 16, Pinner,
Middlesex HA5 4HN UK
Tel: 00 44 (0) 20 8421 3537

CR Ⓐ
Craftsman Auctions
333 North Main Street,
Lambertville, NJ 08530
Tel: 609 397 9374
Fax: 609 397 9377
info@ragoarts.com
www.ragoarts.com

CRIS Ⓓ
Cristobal
26 Church Street,
London NW8 8EP UK
Tel/Fax: 00 44 (0) 20
7724 7230
steven@cristobal.co.uk
www.cristobal.co.uk

CS Ⓓ
Christopher Seidler
Stand G13, Grays Mews
Antiques Market, London
W1K 5AB UK
Tel: 00 44 (0) 20 7629 2851

CSA Ⓓ
Christopher Sykes Antiques
The Old Parsonage, Woburn,
Milton Keynes MK17 9QL UK
Tel: 00 44 (0) 1525 290
259/290 467
Fax: 00 44 (0) 1525 290 061
sykes.corkscrews@sykes-
corkscrews.co.uk
www.sykes-corkscrews.co.uk

CVS Ⓓ
Cad Van Swankster at The
Girl Can't Help It
Alfies Antique Market, Shop
G100 & G116, Ground Floor,
13-25 Church Street,
Marylebone, London
NW8 8DT UK
Tel: 00 44 (0) 20 7724 8984
Fax: 00 44 (0) 20 8809 3923

DAC Ⓓ
Dynamite Antiques &
Collectibles
Tel: 301 652 1140
bercovici@erols.com

DE Ⓓ
The Doll Express
P.O. Box 367, 1807 North
Reading Road, Reamstown,
PA 17567
Tel: 717 336 2414
Fax: 717 336 1262
thedollexpress@thedollexpress.
com
www.thedollexpress.com

DH Ⓓ
David Huxtable
11 & 12 The Lipka Arcade,
288 Westbourne Grove,
London W11 UK
Cell: 00 44 (0) 7710 132 200
david@huxtins.com
www.huxtins.com

DN Ⓓ
Dreweatt Neate
Donnington Priory Salerooms,
Donnington, Newbury,
Berkshire RG14 2JE UK
Tel: 00 44 (0) 1635 553 553
Fax: 00 44 (0) 1635 553 599
fineart@dreweatt-neate.co.uk
www.auctions.dreweatt-
neate.co.uk

DO Ⓓ
DODO
Alfies Antique Market, 1st floor
(F071,2 & 3), 13-25 Church
Street, Marylebone, London
NW8 8DT UK
Tel: 00 44 (0) 20 7706 1545

DRA Ⓐ
Rago Modern Auctions
333 North Main Street,
Lambertville, NJ 08530
Tel: 609 397 9374
Fax: 609 397 9377
info@ragoarts.com
www.ragoarts.com

Duk Ⓐ
Hy. Duke and Son
The Dorchester Fine Art
Salerooms, Weymouth Avenue,
Dorchester, Dorset
DT1 1QS UK
Tel: 00 44 0) 1305 265 080
Fax: 00 44 (0) 1305 260 101
enquiries@dukes-auctions.com
www.dukes-auctions.com

FA Ⓐ
Fraser's Autographs
399 The Strand, London
WC2R 0LX UK
Tel: 00 44 (0) 20 7836 9325
Sales@frasersautographs.co.uk
www.frasersautographs.com

FFA Ⓓ
Finesse Fine Art
Empool Cottage, West
Knighton, Dorset DT2 8PE UK
Tel: 00 44 (0) 1305 854 286
Fax: 00 44 (0) 1305 852 888
Cell: 00 44 (0) 7973 886
937
tony@finessefineart.com
www.finessefineart.com

FFM Ⓓ
Festival
136 South Ealing Road,
London W5 4QJ UK
Tel: 00 44 (0) 20 8840 9333
info@festival1951.co.uk

FLA Ⓓ
Fayne Landes Antiques
593 Hansell Road,
Wynnewood, PA 19096
Tel: 610 658 0566

FM Ⓓ
Francesca Martire
Stand F, 131-137, First Floor,
13-25 Alfies Antiques Market,
13 Church Street, London
NW8 0RH UK
Tel: 00 44 (0) 20 7723 1370
www.francescamartire.com

Fra Ⓓ
France Antique Toys
Tel: 631 754 1399

FRE Ⓐ
Freeman's
1808 Chestnut Street,
Philadelphia, PA 19103
Tel: 215 563 9275
Fax: 215 563 8236
info@freemansauction.com
www.freemansauction.com

G Ⓐ
Guernsey's Auctions
108 East 73rd Street, New
York, NY 10021
Tel: 212 794 2280
Fax: 212 744 3638
guernsey@guernseys.com
www.guernseys.com

GA Ⓓ
Gentry Antiques
c/o Rod & Line Shop,
Little Green Polperro,
Cornwall PL13 2RF UK
Tel: 00 44 (0) 7974 221 343
info@cornishwarecollector.co.uk
www.cornishwarecollector.co.uk

GG Ⓓ
Guest & Gray
1-7 Davies Mews,
London W1K 5AB UK
Tel: 00 44 (0) 20 7408 1252
Fax: 00 44 (0) 20 7499 1445
info@chinese-porcelain-
art.com
www.chinese-porcelain-
art.com

GorB Ⓐ
Gorringes
Terminus Road,
Bexhill-on-Sea, East Sussex
TN39 3LR UK
Tel: 00 44 (0) 1424 212 994
Fax: 00 44 (0) 1424 224 035
bexhill@gorringes.co.uk
www.gorringes.co.uk

GorL Ⓐ
Gorringes
15 North Street,
Lewes BN7 2PD UK
Tel: 00 44 (0) 1273 472 503
Fax: 00 44 (0) 1273 479
559
auctions@gorringes.co.uk
www.gorringes.co.uk

GR Ⓓ
Gordon Reece Galleries
16 Clifford Street,
London W1X 1RG UK
Tel: 00 44 (0) 20 7439 0007
Fax: 00 44 (0) 20 7437 5715
www.gordonreecegalleries.com

Gro Ⓓ
Mary Wise and
Grosvenor Antiques
Grosvenor Antiques, 27
Holland Street, London W8
4NA UK
Tel: 00 44 (0) 20 7937 8649
Fax: 00 44 (0) 20 7937 7179

GS Ⓓ
Goodwins Antiques Ltd
15 & 16 Queensferry Street,
Edinburgh EH2 4QW UK
Tel: 00 44 (0) 131 225 4717
Fax: 00 44 (0) 131 220 1412

H&G Ⓓ
Hope and Glory
131A Kensington Church
Street, London W8 7LP UK
Tel: 00 44 (0) 20 7727 8424

HA Ⓐ
Hunt Auctions
75 E. Uwchlan Ave. Suite 130,
Exton, PA 19341
Tel: 610 524 0822
Fax: 610 524 0826
info@huntauctions.com
www.huntsauctions.com

HamG Ⓐ
Hamptons
Baverstock House, 93 High
Street, Godalming, Surrey
GU7 1AL UK
Tel: 00 44 (0) 1483 423 567
Fax: 00 44 (0) 1483 426 392
fineart@hamptons-int.com
www.hamptons.co.uk

HC Ⓐ
Heritage Comics
Heritage Plaza, 100 Highland
Park Village, 2nd Floor, Dallas,
Texas 75205-2788
Tel: 800 872 6467 / 214
528 3500
Fax: 214 520 6968
www.heritagecomics.com

HLJ Ⓓ
Hugo Lee-Jones
Tel: 00 44 (0) 1227 375 375
Cell: 00 44 (0) 7941 187
2027
electroniccollectables@hotmail
.com

J&H Ⓐ
**Jacobs and Hunt Fine Art
Auctioneers**
26 Lavant Street, Petersfield,
Hampshire GU32 3EF UK
Tel: 00 44 (0)1730 233 933
Fax: 00 44 (0)1730 262 323
auctions@jacobsandhunt.co.uk
www.jacobsandhunt.co.uk

JBC Ⓟ
James Bridges Collection

JBS Ⓓ
John Bull Silver
139A New Bond Street,
London W1Y 9FB UK
Tel: 00 44 (0) 20 7629 1251
Fax: 00 44 (0) 20 7495 3001
elliot@jbsilverware.co.uk
www.jbsilverware.co.uk

JDJ Ⓓ
James D Julia Inc
PO Box 830, Fairfield,
Maine 04937
Tel: 207 453 7125
Fax: 207 453 2502
jjulia@juliaauctions.com
www.juliaauctions.com

JPA Ⓓ
Jessica Pack Antiques
Chapel Hill, North Carolina
Tel: 919 408 0406
jpantiqs1@aol.com

Koz Ⓓ
Bill and Rick Kozlowski
Tel: 215 997 2486

L&T Ⓐ
Lyon and Turnbull Ltd.
33 Broughton Place,
Edinburgh EH1 3RR UK
Tel: 00 44 (0) 131 557 8844
Fax: 00 44 (0) 131 557 8668
info@lyonandturnbull.com
www.lyonandturnbull.com

LB Ⓓ
Linda Bee
Grays in The Mews Antiques
Market, 1-7 Davies Mews,
London W1K 5AB UK
Tel/Fax: 00 44 (0) 20 7629
5921
Cell: 00 44 (0) 7956
276384

LC Ⓐ
**Lawrence's Fine Art
Auctioneers**
South Street, Crewkerne,
Somerset TA18 8AB uk
Tel: 00 44 (0) 1460 73041
Fax: 00 44 (0) 1460 74627
enquiries@lawrences.co.uk
www.lawrences.co.uk

LFA Ⓓ
Law Fine Art Ltd.
Firs Cottage, Church Lane,
Brimpton, Berkshire
RG7 4TJ UK
Tel: 00 44 (0) 118 971 0353
Fax: 00 44 (0) 118 971
3741
info@lawfineart.co.uk
www.lawfineart.co.uk

MA Ⓓ
Manic Attic
Stand SO11, Alfies Antiques
Market, 13 Church Street,
London NW8 8DT UK
Tel: 00 44 (0) 20 7723 6105
Fax: 00 44 (0) 20 7724
0999
manicattic@alfies.clara.net

MB Ⓓ
Mostly Boxes
93 High Street, Eton, Windsor,
Berkshire SL4 6AF UK
Tel: 00 44 (0) 1753 858 470
Fax: 00 44 (0) 1753 857
212

Men Ⓓ
**Mendes Antique Lace
and Textiles**
Flat 2, Wilbury Lawn, 44
Wilbury Road, Hove,
BN3 3PA UK
Tel: 00 44 (0) 1273 203 317
www.mendes.co.uk

MH Ⓓ
Mad Hatter Antiques
Unit 82, Admiral Vernon
Antique Market, 141-149
Portobello Rd, London
W11 UK
Tel: 00 44 (0) 20 7262 0487
Cell: 00 44 (0) 7931 956
705
madhatter.portobello@virgin.net

MHC Ⓟ
Mark Hill Collection
Cell: 00 44 (0) 7798 915
474
stylophile@btopenworld.com

MHT Ⓓ
Mum Had That
Tel: 00 44 (0) 1442 412 360
info@mumhadthat.com
www.mumhadthat.com

MM Ⓐ
Mullock Madeley
The Old Shippon, Wall-under-
Heywood, Church Stretton,
Shropshire, SY6 7DS UK
Tel: 00 44 (0) 1694 771 771
Fax: 00 44 (0) 1694 771 772
info@mullockmadeley.co.uk
www.mullock-madeley.co.uk

NBen Ⓓ
Nigel Benson
20th Century Glass, 58-60
Kensington Church Street,
London W8 4DB UK
Tel: 00 44 (0) 20 7938 1137
Fax: 00 44 (0) 20 7729 9875
Cell: 00 44 (0) 7971 859 848

OACC Ⓓ
**Otford Antiques and
Collectors Centre**
26-28 High Street, Otford,
Kent TN15 9DF UK
Tel: 00 44 (0) 1959 522 025
Fax: 00 44 (0) 1959 525 858
www.otfordantiques.co.uk

PB Ⓓ
Petersham Books
Unit 67, 56 Gloucester Rd,
Kensington, London
SW7 4UB UK
Tel/Fax: 00 44 (0) 20 7581
9147
ks@modernfirsts.co.uk
www.modernfirsts.co.uk

PC Ⓟ
Private Collection

PJC Ⓟ
Peter Jackson Collection

PR Ⓓ
Paul Reichwein
2321 Hershey Avenue, East
Petersburg, PA 17520
Tel: 717 569 7637
paulrdg@aol.com

PSA Ⓐ
Potteries Specialist Auctions
271 Waterloo Road, Cobridge,
Stoke-on-Trent ST6 3HR
Tel: 00 44 (0) 1782 286 622
Fax: 00 44 (0) 1782 213 777
enquiries@potteriesauctions.com
www.potteriesauctions.com

PSpA Ⓓ
Pantiles Spa Antiques
4-6 Union House, The
Pantiles, Tunbridge Wells TN4
8HE UK
Tel: 00 44 (0) 1892 541 377
Fax: 00 44 (0) 1435 865 660
psa.wells@btinternet.com
www.antiques-tun-wells-
kent.co.uk

PTA Ⓓ
Past-Tyme Antiques
Tel: 703 777 8555
pasttymeantiques@aol.com

QUAD Ⓓ
Quadrille
146 Portobello Rd, London
W11 2DZ UK

RAA Ⓓ
Axtell Antiques
1 River Street, Deposit, New
York 13754
Tel: 607 467 2353
Fax: 607 467 4316
rsaxtell@msn.com
www.axtellantiques.com

RB Ⓓ
Roger Bradbury
Church Street, Coltishall,
Norwich, Norfolk,
NR12 7DJ UK
Tel: 00 44 (0) 1603 737 444

RBL Ⓓ
Richard Ball Lighters
richard@lighter.co.uk

RdeR Ⓓ
Rogers de Rin
76 Royal Hospital Road,
Paradise Walk, Chelsea,
London SW3 4HN UK
Tel: 00 44 (0) 20 7352 9007
Fax: 00 44 (0) 20 7351 9407
rogersderin@rogersderin.co.uk
www.rogersderin.co.uk

Ren Ⓓ
Rennies
13 Rugby Street,
London WC1 3QT UK
Tel: 00 44 (0) 20 7405 0220
info@rennart.co.uk
www.rennart.co.uk

RG Ⓓ
Richard Gibbon
34/34a Islington Green,
London N1 8DU UK
Tel: 00 44 (0) 20 7354 2852
neljeweluk@aol.com

RH Ⓓ
Rick Hubbard Art Deco
3 Tee Court, Bell Street,
Romsey, Hampshire
SO51 8GY UK
Tel/Fax 00 44 (0) 1794 513 133
rick@rickhubbard-
artdeco.co.uk
www.rickhubbard-
artdeco.co.uk

Rox Ⓓ
Roxanne's
Tel: 888 750 8869 /
215 750 8868
gemfairy@aol.com

S&T Ⓓ
Steinberg and Tolkien
193 King's Road Chelsea,
London SW3 5ED UK
Tel: 00 44 (0) 20 7376 3660
Fax: 00 44 (0) 20 7376 3630

SCG Ⓓ
**Gallery 1930 –
Susie Cooper Gallery**
18 Church Street, Marylebone,
London NW8 8EP UK
Tel: 00 44 (0) 20 7723 1555
Fax: 00 44 (0) 20 7735 8309
gallery1930@aol.com
www.susiecooperceramics.com

SFel Ⓓ
Sandra Fellner
Grays Antiques Market, Davies
Street/Davies Mews/South
Molton Lane, London
W1Y 5AB UK
Tel: 00 44 (0) 20 8946 5613

SI Ⓐ
Sloans
4920 Wyaconda Road,
N Bethesda, MD 20852
Tel: 301 468 4911
Fax: 301 468 9182
www.sloansauction.com

SM Ⓓ
**Sparkle Moore at The Girl
Can't Help It**
Alfies Antique Market, Shop
G100 & G116, Ground Floor,
13-25 Church Street,
Marylebone, London NW8 8DT UK
Tel: 00 44 (0) 20 7724 8984
Fax: 00 44 (0) 20 8809 3923
Cell: 00 44 (0) 7958 515 614
sparkle.moore@virgin.net
www.sparklemoore.com

SN Ⓓ
Sue Norman at Antiquarius
Stand L4, Antiquarius, 135
King's Road, Chelsea, London
SW3 4PW UK
Tel: 00 44 (0) 20 7352 7217
Fax: 00 44 (0) 20 8870 4677
sue@sue-norman.demon.co.uk
www.sue-norman.demon.co.uk

SRA Ⓐ
Sheffield Railwayana
43 Little Norton Lane,
Sheffield S8 8GA UK
Tel/Fax: 00 44 (0) 114
274 5085
ian@sheffrail.freeserve.co.uk
www.sheffieldrailwayana.co.uk

SSc Ⓟ
Sue Scrivens Collection

SSp Ⓓ
Sylvie Spectrum
Stand 372, Grays Antiques
Market, 58 Davies Street,
London W1Y 2LB UK
Tel: 00 44 (0) 20 7629 3501
Fax: 00 44 (0) 20 8883
5030

Tag Ⓓ
Tagore Ltd
Stand 302, Grays Antiques
Market, 58 Davies Street,
London, W1Y 2LP UK
Tel: 00 44 (0) 20 7499 0158
Fax: 00 44 (0) 20 7499
0158

TK Ⓐ
Auction Team Köln
Postfach 50 11 19, Bonner
Str. 528-530, D-50971
Köln, Germany
Tel: 00 49 (0) 221 38 70 49
Fax: 00 49 (0) 221 37 48 78
Auction@Breker.com
www.Breker.com

TR Ⓓ
Terry Rodgers & Melody LLC
30 & 31 Manhattan Art and
Antiques Center, 1050 2nd
Avenue, New York, NY 10022
Tel: 212 758 3164
Fax: 212 935 6365

Trio Ⓓ
Trio
Stand L24, Grays Antiques
Market, 1-7 Davies Mews,
London W1Y 2LP UK
Tel: 00 44 (0) 20 7493 2736
Fax: 00 44 (0) 20 7493 9344
www.trio-london.fsnet.co.uk

TWC Ⓐ
T W Conroy
36 Oswego St,
Baldwinsville, NY 13027
Tel: 315 638 6434
Fax: 315 638 7039
www.twconroy.com

V Ⓓ
Ventisemo
Unit S001, Alfies Antique
Market, 13-25 Church Street,
Marylebone, London
NW8 8DT UK
Cell: 00 44 (0) 7767 498
766

VE Ⓓ
Vintage Eyeware
Tel: 917 721 6546
www.vintage-eyeware.com

Vec Ⓐ
Vectis Auctions Limited
Fleck Way, Thornaby, Stockton
on Tees TS17 9JZ UK
Tel: 00 44 (0) 1642 750 616
Fax: 00 44 (0) 1642 769 478
enquiries@vectis.co.uk
www.vectis.co.uk

W&W Ⓐ
Wallis and Wallis
West Steet Auction Galleries,
Lewes, East Sussex
BN7 2NJ UK
Tel: 00 44 (0) 1273 480 208
Fax: 00 44 (0) 1273 476 562
grb@wallisandwallis.co.uk
www.wallisandwallis.co.uk

WG Ⓓ
The Watch Gallery
129 Fulham Road, London,
SW3 6RT UK
Tel: 00 44 (0) 20 7581 3239
Fax: 00 44 (0) 20 7584 6497

WHP Ⓐ
WH Peacock
26 Newnham Street, Bedford
MK40 3JR UK
Tel: 00 44 (0) 1234 266 366
Fax: 00 44 (0) 1234 269 082
info@peacockauction.co.uk
www.peacockauction.co.uk

Wim Ⓓ
Wimpole Antiques
Stand 349, Grays Antiques
Market, 58, Davies St,
London, W1K 2LP UK
Tel: 00 44 (0) 20 7499 2889
Fax: 00 44 (0) 20 7493 9344

WO Ⓓ
Wiseman Originals
34 West Square, Lambeth,
London SE11 4SP UK
Tel: 00 44 (0) 20 7587 0747
Fax: 00 44 (0) 20 7793 8817
wisemanoriginals@compuserve
.com
www.wisemanoriginals.com

WoS Ⓓ
Wheels of Steel
Unit B10-11, Grays Mews
Antiques Market, 1/7 Davies
Mews, London W1Y 2LP UK
Tel: 00 44 (0) 20 7629 2813
Fax: 00 44 (0) 20 7493 9344
wheels-of-steel@grays.clara.net

WW Ⓐ
Woolley and Wallis
51-61 Castle Street, Salisbury,
Wiltshire SP1 3SU UK
Tel: 00 44 (0) 1722 424 500
Fax: 00 44 (0) 1722 424 508
enquiries@woolleyandwallis.co.uk
www.woolleyandwallis.co.uk

NOTE

If you wish to have any item valued, it is advisable to contact the dealer or specialist in advance to check that they will carry out this service and whether there is a charge. While most dealers will be happy to help you with an enquiry, do remember that they are busy people. Telephone valuations are not possible. Please mention *Collectibles Price Guide 2003* by Judith Miller when making an enquiry.

DIRECTORY OF SPECIALISTS

Specialist Dealers wishing to be listed in the next edition, space permitting, are requested to email info@thepriceguidecompany.com

ADVERTISING

Bill & Rick Kozlowski
Tel: 215 997 2486

The Nostalgia Factory
51 North Margin St
Boston, MA 02113
Tel: 617 720 2211
posters@nostalgia.com
www.nostalgia.com

Alice's Advertising Antiques
131 Allenwood Rd
Great Neck, NY 11023
Tel: 516 466 8954

AMERICANA

Richard Axtell Antiques
1 River St
Deposit, NY 13754
Tel: 607 467 2353
Fax: 607 467 4316
raxtell@msn.com
www.axtellantiques.com

Buck County Antique Center
Route 202
Lahaksa, PA 18931
Tel: 215 794 9180

Fields of Glory
55 York St
Gettysburg, PA 17325
Tel: 717 337 2837
foglory@cvn.net
www.fieldsofglory.com
(Civil War Items)

Olde Hope Antiques
P.O. Box 718
New Hope, PA 18938
Tel: 215 297 0200
Fax: 215 297 0300
info@oldhopeantiques.com
www.oldhopeantiques.com

The Splendid Peasant
Route 23 & Sheffield Rd
P.O. Box 536
South Egremont, MA 01258
Tel: 413 528 5755
folkart@splendidpeasant.com
www.splendidpeasant.com

ANTIQUITIES

Frank & Barbara Pollack
1214 Green Bay Rd
Highland Park, IL 60035
Tel: 847 433 2213
fpollack@compuserve.com

AUTOGRAPHS

Autographs of America
P.O. Box 461
Provo, UT 84603-0461
tanders3@autographsofamerica.com
www.autographsofamerica.com

Nate's Autograph Hound
10020 Raynor Road
Silver Spring, MD 20901
autohnd@access.digex.net

Platt Autographs
1040 Bayview Dr #428
Fort Lauderdale, FL 33306
Tel: 954 564 2002
ctplatt@ctplatt.com
www.ctplatt.com

AUTOMOBILIA

Dunbar's Gallery
76 Haven St
Milford, MA 01757-3821
Tel: 508 634 8697
Fax: 508 634 8698

BOOKS

Abeboo
www.abebooks.com

Aleph-Bet Books
218 Waters Edge
Valley Cottage, NY 10989
Tel: 914 268 7410
Fax: 914 268 5942
helen@alephbet.com
www.alephbet.com

Deer Park Books
609 Kent Rd, Route 7
Gaylordsville, CT 06755
Tel/Fax: 860 350 4140
deerparkbk@aol.com
www.abebooks.com/home

CAMERAS & PHOTOGRAPHICA

Bryan Ginns
2109 Cty Rte 21
Valatie, NY 12184-6001
Tel: 518 392 805
Fax: 518 392 7925
the3dman@aol.com
www.stereographica.com

The Camera Man
1614 Bethlehem Pike
Flourtown, PA 19031-2026
Tel/Fax: 215 233 4025

CANES

Tradewinds Antiques & Auctions
24 Magnolia Ave, P.O.Box 249
Manchester, MA 01944
Tel: 978 768 3327
Fax: 978 526 4085
taron@tiac.com
www.tradewindsantiques.com

CERAMICS

Blue & White Dinnerware
4800 Crestview Dr
Carmichael, CA 95609
Tel: 916 961 7406
thefourls@aol.com

Fayne Landes Antiques
593 Hansell Road
Wynnewood, PA 19096
Tel: 610 658 0566

The Perrault-Rago Gallery
65 Ferry Street
Lambertville, NJ 08530
Tel: 609 397 1802
www.ragoarts.com

The Royal Pair Antiques
12707 Hillcrest Dr
Longmont, CO 80501-1162
Tel: 303 772 2760
(Chintzware)

The World of Ceramics
208 Hemlock Dr
Neptune, NJ 07753
antique208@msn.com
(Cups & Saucers)

Greg Walsh
32 River View Lane
P.O. Box 747
Potsdam, NY 13676-0747
Tel: 315 265 9111
gwalsh@northnet.org
(Stoneware)

Happy Pastime
P.O. Box 1225
Ellicott City, MD 21041-1225
Tel: 410 203 1101
hpastime@bellatlantic.net
www.happypastime.com
(Figurines)

Ken Forster
5501 Seminary Road, Ste.
1311South Falls Church,
VA 22041
Tel: 703 379 1142
(Art Pottery)

Mellin's Antiques
P.O. Box 1115
Redding, CT 06875
Tel: 203 938 9538
remellin@aol.com

Mark & Marjorie Allen
6 Highland Drive
Amherst, NH 03031
mandmallen@antiquedelft.com
www.antiquedelft.com

Charles & Barbara Adams
289 Old Main St
South Yarmouth, MA 02664
Tel: 508 760 3290
adams_2430@msn.com

Stephanie Hull Winters
Classic Treasures
3232 Morgan Rd
Temple, GA 30179
Tel: 770 562 1332
swinters@bellsouth.net
(Art Pottery)

COMICS

Carl Bonasera
A1-American Comic Shops
3514 W. 95th St
Evergreen Park, IL 60642
Tel: 708 425 7555

The Comic Gallery
4224 Balboa Ave
San Diego, CA 92117
Tel: 619 483 4853

COSTUME JEWELRY

Roxanne's
Roxanne Stuart
Tel: 215 750 8868
gemfairy@aol.com

Terry Rodgers and Melody LLC
30 Manhattan Art & Antique
Center 1050 2nd Ave
New York, NY 10022
Tel: 212 758 3164
Fax: 212 935 6365
melodyjewelnyc@aol.com

EPHEMERA

Kitt Barry Ephemera
88 High St, Box S-I
Brattleboro, VT 05301
Tel: 802 254 3634
www.tradecards.com

Paper Pile
P.O. Box 337 San Anselmo,
CA 94970-0337
Tel: 415 454 5552
Fax: 415 454 2947
apaperpile@aol.com
www.paperpilecollectibles.com

Ruth A. Miller Knott
The Papereneur
2601 Kittias Highway
Ellensburg, WA 98926
Tel: 509 962 8840
Fax: 509 962 3609
ruthie@ellensburg.com

FIFTIES & SIXTIES
**Lois' Collectibles of Antique
Market III**, 413 W Main St
Saint Charles, IL 60174-1815
Tel: 630 377 5599
(Lady Head vases)

Steve Colby
Off The Deep End
712 East St
Frederick, MD 21701-5239
Tel: 301 698 9006
chilimon@offthedeepend.com
www.offthedeepend.com

FILM MEMORABILIA
STARticles
58 Stewart St, Studio 301
Toronto, Ontario, M5V 1H6
Tel: 416 504 8286
info@starticles.com
www.starticles.com

Norma's Jeans
3511 Turner Lane
Chevy Chase, MD
20815-2313
Tel: 301 652 4644
Fax: 301 907 0216

George Baker
CollectorsMart
P.O. Box 580466
Modesto, CA 95358
Tel; 290 537 5221
Fax: 209 531 0233
georgeb1@thevision.net
www.collectorsmart.com

GENERAL
Antiques of Cape May
Tel: 800 224 1687

Burlwood Antique Center
Route 3
Meredith, NH 03523
Tel: 603 279 6387
rckhprant@aol.com

GLASS
C. Lucille Britt
4305 W 78th St
Prairie Village, KS 66208
Tel: 913 642 3587

Past-Tyme Antiques
Tel: 703 777 8555
pasttymeantiques@aol.com

Jeff E. Purtell
P.O. Box 28
Amherst, NH 03031-0028
Tel: 603 673 4331
Fax: 603 673 1525
(Steuben)

Paul Reichwein
2321 Hershey Ave
East Petersburg PA 17520
Tel: 717 569 7637
paulrdg@aol.com

Paul Stamati Gallery
1050 2nd Ave
New York, NY 10022
Tel: 212 754 4533
Fax: 718 271 6958
mail@rene-lalique.com
www.rene-lalique.com

Suzman's Antiques
P.O. Box 301
Rehoboth, MA 02769
Tel: 508 252 5729
suzmanf@ride.ri.net

JEWELRY
Arthur Guy Kaplan
P.O. Box 1942
Baltimore, MD 21203
Tel: 410 752 2090

Tony Laughter
Perry's at SouthPark
SouthPark Mall
Charlotte, NC 28211
Tel: 704 364 1391

KITCHENALIA & HOUSEHOLD
Dynamite Antiques & Collectibles
Ellen Bercovici
Tel: 301 652 1140

MECHANICAL MUSIC
The Music Box Shop
7236 E 1st Ave
Scottsdale, AZ 85251
Tel: 602 945 0428
Fax: 602 200 9365
musicboxshop@home.com
www.themusicboxshop.com

Mechantiques
The Crescent Hotel
75 Prospect St
Eureka Springs, AR 72632
Tel: 501 253 9766
mroenigk@aol.com
www.mechantiques.com

METALWARE
Wyne & Phyllis Hilt
RR1, Haddam Neck, CT 06424
Tel: 860 267 2146

MEDICAL INSTRUMENTS
C. Keith Wilbur
The Doctor's Bag
397 Prospect St
Northampton, MA
01060-2047
Tel: 413 584 1440

Armbrook Antiques
531 Doub Rd
Lewisville, NC 27023
Tel: 336 945 9477
Fax: 336 945 9914
olestuff@armbrookantiques.com
www.armbrookantiques.com

Scientific Medical & Mechanical Antiques
P.O. Box 412
Taneytown, MD 21787
Tel: 301 447 2680
smma@americanartefacts.com
www.americanartefacts.com/smma

MILITARIA
Articles of War
358 Boulevard
Middletown, RI 02842
Tel: 401 846 8503
dutch5@ids.com

Stewart's Military Antiques
108 W. Main St
Mesa, AZ 85201
Tel: 602 834 4004

Terry Porter Fine Antique Arms
P.O. Box 59028
Mesquite, TX 75150
Tel: 214 679 7410
Fax: 972 681 8992
terry.porter@fineantiquearms.com
www.fineantiquearms.com

OPTICAL INSTRUMENTS
Vintage Eyeware
Tel: 917 721 6546
www.vintage-eyeware.com

ORIENTAL & ASIAN
Oriental Treasures Antiques
159 W. Kenzie Street
Chicago, IL 60610-4514
Tel: 773 761 2907
Fax: 773 761 0789

Gallery of Fine Netsuke
163 Third Ave, Ste 295
New York, NY 10003
Tel: 212 533 3666
mspindel@mindspring.com
www.spindel.com

**Oriental Antiques Shop
Miracle Ventures**
P.O. Box 75
Flushing, NY 11363
Tel/Fax: 718 225 1461

Sharon & Arno Ziesnitz
7835 Painted Daisy Dr
Springfield, VA 22152
Tel: 703 451 1033
Fax: 703 569 4221
ziesnitz@aol.com

PENS & WRITING EQUIPMENT
Fountain Pen Hospital
10 Warren Street
New York, NY 10007
Tel: 212 964 0580
info@fountainpenhospital.com
www.fountainpenhospital.com

Gary & Myrna Lehrer
16 Mulberry Rd
Woodbridge, CT 06525-1717
Tel: 203 389 5295
Fax: 203 389 4515

David Nishimura
Vintage Pens
P.O. Box 41452
Providence, RI 02940-1452
Tel: 401 351 7607
Fax: 401 351 1168
info@vintagepens.com
www.vintagepens.com

Sandra & L. 'Buck' van Tine
Lora's Memory Lane
13133 North Caroline St
Chillicothe, IL 61523-9115
Tel: 309 579 3040
Fax: 309 579 2696
lorasink@aol.com

Sam Fiorella
Pendemonium
15231 Larkspur Lane
Dumfries, VA 22026-2075
Tel: 703 670 8549
Fax: 703 670 3875
sam@pendemonium.com
www.pendemonium.com

PLASTICS
Dee Battle
9 Orange Blossom Trail
Yalaha, FL 34797
Tel: 352 324 3023

Malabar Enterprises
172 Bush Lane
Ithaca, NY 14850
Tel: 607 255 2905
Fax: 607 255 4179
asn6@cornell.edu

POSTERS
Poster America
138 West 18th St
New York, NY 10011-5403
Tel: 212 206 0499
Fax: 212 727 2495
pfair@dti.net
www.posterfair.com

Vintage Poster Works
P.O. Box 88
Pittford, NY 14534
Tel: 716 218 9483
Fax: 716 218 9035
debra@vintageposterworks.com
www.vintageposterworks.com

La Belle Epoque
11661 San Vincente, 3304
Los Angeles, CA 90049-5110
Tel: 310 442 0054
Fax: 310 826 6934
ktscicon@ix.netcom.com

MODERN PRINTS

Pace Prints
32 East 57th St, 3rd Floor
New York, NY 10021
Tel: 877 440 7223
Fax: 212 832 5162
www.paceprints.com

The Media Group
7510 W. Sunset Blvd, 553
Los Angeles, CA 90024
Tel: 323 661 3382
jfarrow@fineartsite.com
www.fineartsite.com

Artnet
www.artnet.com

ROCK & POP

Hein's Rare Collectibles
P.O. Box 179
Little Silver, NJ 07739-0179
Tel: 732 219 1988
Fax: 732 219 5940
(The Beatles)

Tod Hutchinson
P.O. Box 915
Griffith, IN 46319-0915
Tel: 219 923 8334
toddtcb@aol.com
(Elvis Presley)

PERFUME & SCENT BOTTLES

Oldies But Goldies
P.O. Box 217
Hankins, NY 12741-0217
Tel: 914 887 5272
oldgood@catskill.net
www.catskill.net/oldgood

Monsen & Baer Inc
P.O. Box 529
Vienna, VA 22183-0529
Tel: 703 938 2129
monsenbaer@erols.com

SCIENCE & TECHNOLOGY

George Glazer
28 East 2nd St
New York, NY 10021
Tel: 212 535 5706
Fax: 212 988 3992
worldglobe@aol.com
www.georgeglazer.com

Tesseract
Box 151
Hastings-on-Hudson, NY
10706
Tel: 914 478 2594
Fax: 914 478 5473
e-mail: coffeen@aol.com
www.etesseract.com

Bob Elsner
Heights Antiques
29 Clubhouse Lane Boynton
Beach, FL 33436-6056
Tel: 561 736 1362
Fax: 561 736 1914
rjelsner@aol.com
(Barometers)

The Olde Office
68-845 Perez Rd, Ste 30
Cathedral City, CA 92234
Tel: 760 346 8653
Fax: 760 346 6479
info@thisoldeoffice.com
www.thisoldeoffice.com

Jane Hertz
6731 Ashley Ct
Sarasota, FL 34241-9696
Tel: 941 925 0385
Fax: 941 925 0487
auction@breker.com
www.breker.com
(Cameras, Office & Technical
Equipment)

SILVER

Argentum –
The Leopard's Head
414 Jackson St, Ste 101
San Francisco, CA 94111
Tel: 415 296 7757
Fax: 415 296 7233
www.argentum-
theleopard.com

Gary Neiderkorn Silver
2005 Locust St
Philadelphia, PA 19103-5606
Tel/Fax: 215 567 2606

Lauren Stanley Gallery
300 E 51st St
New York, NY 10022
Tel: 212 888 6732
Fax: 212 486 2503
info@laurenstanley.com
www.laurenstanley.com

Jonathan Trace
P.O. Box 418, 31
Church Hill Road
Rifton, NY 12471
Tel: 914 658 7336

SMOKING

Richard Weinstein
International Vintage Lighter
Exchange 30 W. 57th St
New York, NY 10019
vinlighter@aol.com
www.vintagelighters.com

Ira Pilossof
Vintage Lighters Inc.
P.O. Box 1325
Fairlawn, NJ 07410-8325
Tel: 201 797 6595
vintageltr@aol.com

Mike Cassidy
1070 Bannock #400
Denver, CO 80204
Tel: 303 446 2726

Chuck Haley
Sherlock's
13926 Double Girth Ct
Matthews, NC 28105-4068
Tel: 704 847 5480
(Pipes)

SPACE MEMORABILIA

Gregg Linebaugh
AVD Services
P.O. Box 604
Glenn Dale, MD 20769
Tel: 301 249 3895

The Ultimate Space Place
P.O. Box 5411
Merritt Island, FL 32954
Tel: 407 454 4236
questions@thespaceplace.com
www.thespaceplace.com

SPORTING MEMORABILIA

Classic Rods & Tackle
P.O. Box 288
Ashley Falls, MA 01222
Tel: 413 229 7988

Larry Fritsch Cards Inc
735 Old Wassau Rd
P.O. Box 863
Stevens Point, WI 54481
Tel: 715 344 8687
Fax: 715 344 1778
larry@fritschcards.com
www.fritschcards.com
(Baseball Cards)

George Lewis
Golfiana
P.O. Box 291
Mamaroneck, NY 10543
Tel: 914 835 5100
Fax: 914 835 1715
george@golfiana.com
www.golfiana.com

Golf Collectibles
P.O. Box 165892
Irving, YX 75016
Tel: 972 594 7802
furjanic@directlink.net
www.folfforallages.com

The Hager Group
P.O. Box 952974
Lake Mary, FL 32795
Tel: 407 788 3865
(Trading Cards)

Hall's Nostalgia
21-25 Mystic St, P.O. Box 408
Arlington, MA 02174
Tel: 781 646 7757

Tom & Jill Kaczor
1550 Franklin Rd
Langhorne, PA 19047
Tel: 215 968 5776
Fax: 215 946 6056

Mike's Tackle Box
P.O. Box 5827
Bellingham, WA 98227
Tel: 360 734 7379
mike@mikestackle.com
www.mikestackle.com

TEXTILES & COSTUME

Colette Donovan
98 River Road
Merrimacport, MA 01860
Tel: 978 346 0614

Cora Ginsburg
19 East 74th St
New York, NY 10021
Tel: 212 744 1352

Fayne Landes Antiques
593 Hansell Road
Wynnewood, PA 19096
Tel: 610 658 0566
fayne@comcast.net

Sweethaven Lace
4681 Bloomfield Rd
Taylorsville, KY 40071
Tel: 502 477 8819
sfierbaugh@acm.org

Vintage Clothing Company
P.O. Box 20504
Keizer, OR 97307-0504
retrothreads@aol.com

Yesterday's Threads
206 Meadow St
Branford, CT 06405-3634
Tel: 203 481 6452
Fax: 203 483 7550

TOYS, GAMES & DOLLS

Barry Carter
Knightstown Antiques Mall
136 W. Carey St, Knightstown,
IN 46148-1111
Tel: 765 345 5665
bcarter@spitfire.net

France Antique Toys
Tel: 631 754 1399

Litwin Antiques
P.O. Box 5865
Trenton, NJ 08638-0865
Tel/Fax: 609 275 1427
(Chess)

Harry R. McKeon, Jr.
18 Rose Lane
Flourtown, PA 19031-1910
Tel: 215 233 4094
toyspost@aol.com
(Tin Toys)

The Doll Express
P.O. Box 367
Reamstown, PA 17567
Tel: 717 336 2414
www.thedollexpress.com

Jessica Pack Antiques
Chapel Hill
North Carolina
Tel: 919 408 0406
jpants1@aol.com

The Old Toy Soldier Home
977 S. Santa Fe, Ste 11
Vista, CA 92083
Tel: 760 758 5481
Fax: 760 758 5481
info@oldtoysoldierhome.com
www.oldtoysoldierhome.com

Treasure & Dolls
518 Indian Rocks Rd, N.
Belleair Bluffs, FL 33770
Tel: 727 584 7277
dolls@antiquedoll.com
www.antiquedoll.com

Trains & Things
106 East Front St
Traverse City, MI 49684
Tel: 616 947 1353
Fax: 616 947 1411
tctrains@traverse.net
www.tctrains.com

Marion Weis
Division St Antiques
P.O. Box 374
Buffalo, MN 55313-0374
Tel: 612 682 6453
(Teddy Bears & Toys)

TRIBAL

Hurst Gallery
53 Mount Auburn St
Cambridge, MA 02138
Tel: 617 491 6888
nhurst@compuserve.com
www.hurstgallery.com

**Marcy Burns American
Indian Arts**
P.O. Box 181
Glenside, PA 19038
Tel: 215 576 1559
mbindianart@home.com

Malter Galleries
17005 Ventura Blvd
Encino, CA 91316-4128
Tel: 818 784 7774
rarearts@earthlink,net
www.maltergalleries.com

Elliot & Grace Snyder
P.O. Box 598
South Egremont, MA 01258
Tel: 413 528 3581

WATCHES

**Finer Times Vintage
Timepieces**
P.O. Box 273020
Tampa, FL 33688
Tel: 813 963 5757
Fax: 813 960 5676
dontime@minspring.com
www.finertimes.com

Temes & Co.
338 N. Charles St
Baltimore, MD 21201
Tel: 410 347 7600
Fax: 410 685 3299

Texas Time
3076 Waunuta St
Newbury Park, CA 91320
Tel: 805 498 5644
Fax: 805 480 9514
paul@dock.net
www.texastime.com

WINE & DRINKING

Derek White
The Corkscrew Pages
769 Sumter Dr
Morrisville, PA 19067
Tel: 215 493 4143
Fax: 609 860 5380
dswhite@marketsource.com
www.taponline.com

Donald A. Bull
P.O. Box 596
Wirtz, VA 24184
Tel: 540 721 1128
Fax: 540 721 5468
corkscrue@aol.com

**Steve Visakay Cocktail
Shakers**
P.O. Box 1517 West Caldwell,
NJ 07007-1517
Tel: 914 352 5640
svisakay@aol.com

DIRECTORY OF AUCTIONEERS

Auctioneers who wish to be listed in this directory for our next edition, space permitting, are requested to email info@thepriceguidecompany.com

ALABAMA

Flomaton Antique Auctions
P.O. Box 1017
320 Palafox Street
Flomaton 36441
Tel: 334 296 3059
Fax: 334 296 3710

ARIZONA

Dan May & Associates
4110 N. Scottsdale Road
Scottsdale 85251
Tel: 602 941 4200

ARKANSAS

Ponders Auctions
1504 South Leslie
Stuttgart 72160
Tel: 501 673 6551

CALIFORNIA

Aurora Galleries International
30 Hackamore Lane, Suite 2
Bell Canyon, CA 91307
Tel: 818 884 6468
Fax: 818 227 2941
vjc@auroragalleriesonline.com
www.auroragalleriesonline.com

Butterfield & Butterfield
7601 Sunset Blvd
Los Angeles CA 90046
Tel: 323 850 7500
Fax: 323 850 5843
info@butterfields.com
www.butterfields.com

Butterfield & Butterfield
220 San Bruno Ave
San Francisco CA 94103
Tel: 415 861 7500
Fax: 415 861 8951
info@butterfields.com
www.butterfields.com

Clark Cierlak Fine Arts
14452 Ventura Blvd
Sherman Oaks 91423
Tel: 818 783 3052
Fax: 818 783 3162
clark@estateauctionservice.com
www.estateauctionservice.com

I.M. Chait Gallery
9330 Civic Center Drive
Beverly Hills CA 90210
Tel: 310 285 0182
Fax: 310 285 9740
imchait@aol.com
www.chait.com

Cuschieri's Auctioneers & Appraisers
863 Main Street
Redwood City CA 94063
Tel: 650 556 1793
Fax: 650 556 9805
info@cuschieris.com
www.cuschieris.com

eBay, Inc
2005 Hamilton Ave
Ste 350, San Jose CA 95125
Tel: 408 369 4839
www.ebay.com

L.H. Selman
123 Locust St
Santa Cruz
CA 95060
Tel: 800 538 0766
Fax: 408 427 0111
leselman@got.net
www.paperweight.com

Malter Galleries
17003 Ventura Blvd
Encino 91316
Tel: 818 784 7772
Fax: 818 784 4726
rarearts@earthlink.net
www.maltergalleries.com

Poster Connection Inc
43 Regency Drive
Clayton 94517
Tel: 925 673 3343
Fax: 925 673 3355
sales@posterconnection.com
www.posterconnection.com

Profiles in History
110 North Doheny Drive
Beverly Hills 90211
Tel: 310 859 7701
Fax: 310 859 3842
acquisitions@profilesinhistory.com
www.profilesinhistory.com

San Rafael Auction Gallery
634 Fifth Avenue
San Rafael CA 9490
Tel: 415 457 4488
Fax: 415 457 4899
srauction@aol.com
www.sanrafael-auction.com

Slawinski Auction Co.
6221 Graham Hill Road,
Suite C
Felton, CA 95018
Tel: 831 335 9000
Fax: 831 335 6933
antiques@slawinski.com
www.slawinski.com

CONNECTICUT

Alexander Autographs
100 Melrose Ave
Greenwich 06830
Tel: 203 622 8444
Fax: 203 622 8765
peter@alexautographs.com
www.alexautographs.com

Norman C. Heckler & Company
79 Bradford Corner Road
Woodstock Valley 0682
Tel: 860 974 1634
Fax: 860 974 2003
info@hecklerauction.com
www.hecklerauction.com

Lloyd Ralston Gallery
250 Long Beach Blvd
Stratford 016615
Tel: 203 386 9399
Fax: 203 386 9519
lrgallery@aol.com
www.lloydralstontoys.com

DELAWARE

Remember When Auctions Inc.
42 Sea Gull Rd
Swann Estates
Selbyville 19975
Tel: 302 436 8869
Fax: 302-436-6144
sales@history-attic.com
www.history-attic.com

WASHINGTON DC

Weschlers
909 E St NW Washington,
D.C. 20004
Tel: 202.628.1281
Fax: 202.628.2366
fineart@weschlers.com
www.weschlers.com

Sloans Auction Galleries
4920 Wyaconda Rd
N Bethseda 20852
Tel: 301 468 4911
Fax: 301 468 9182
sloans@sloansauctions.com
www.sloansauction.com

FLORIDA

Auctions Neapolitan
995 Central Avenue
Naples 34102
Tel: 941 262 7333
kathleen@auctionsneapolitan.com
www.auctionsneapolitan.com

Burchard Galleries
2528 30th Ave N
St Petersburg 33713
Tel: 727 821 11667
mail@burhcardgalleries.com
www.burchardgalleries.com

Dawson's
P.O. Box 646
Palm Beach 33480
Tel: 561 835 6930
Fax: 561 835 8464
info@dawsons.org
www.dawsons.org

Arthur James Galleries
615 E. Atlantic Ave
Delray Beach 33483
Tel: 561 278 2373
Fax: 561 278 7633
arjames@bellsouth.net
www.arthurjames.com

Kincaid Auction Company
3214 E Hwy 92
Lakeland 3381
Tel: 800 970 1977
kincaid@kincaid.com
www.kincaid.com

Sloan's Auction Galleries
8861 NW 19th Terace Ste
100 Miami 33172
Tel: 305 751 4770
sloans@sloansauction.com
www.sloansauction.com

GEORGIA

Great Gatsby's
5070 Peachtree Industrial
Blvd, Atlanta
Tel: 770 457 1905
Fax: 770-457-7250
internet@greatgatsbys.com
www.gatsbys.com

My Hart Auctions Inc
P.O. Box 2511
Cumming 30028
Tel: 770 888 9006
myhart@prodigy.net
www.myhart.net

IDAHO

The Coeur D'Alene Art Auction
P.O. Box 310
Hayden 83835
Tel: 208 772 9009
Fax: 208 772 8294
cdaartauction@cdaartauction.com
www.cdaartauction.com

INDIANA

**Curran Miller Auction &
Realty Inc**
4424 Vogel Rd, Ste 400
Evansville 47715
Tel: 812 474 6100
Fax: (812) 474-6110
cmar@curranmiller.com
www.curranmiller.com

Kruse International
5540 County Rd 11A
Auburn IN 46706
Tel: 800 968 4444
info@kruseinternational.com
www.kruse.com

Lawson Auction Service
923 Fourth Street
Columbus 47265
Tel: 812 372 2571
dlawson@lawson-auction.com
www.lawson-auction.com

Slater's Americana
5335 N. Tacoma Ave, Suite
24, Indianapolis 46220
Tel: 317 257 0863

Stout Auctions
529 State Road 28 East
Willamsport IN 47993
Tel: 765 764 6901
Fax: 765-764-1516
stoutauctions@hotmail.com
www.stoutauctions.com

ILLINOIS

Joy Luke
300 East Grove Street
Bloomington, Illinois 61701
Tel: 309 828 5533
Fax: 309 829 2266
robert@joyluke.com
www.joyluke.com

IOWA

Gene Harris Auctions
2035 18th Ave
Marshalltown 50158
Tel: 641 752 0600
ghaac@geneharrisauctions.com
www.geneharrisauctions.com

**Jackson's Auctioneers &
Appraisers**
2229 Lincoln St
Cedar Falls 50613
Tel: 319 277 2256
sandim@jacksonsauction.com
www.jacksonsauction.com

Tubaugh Auctions
1702 8th Ave
Belle Plaine IA 52208
Tel: 319 444 2413
www.tubaughauctions.com

KANSAS

**Manions International
Auction House**
P.O. Box 12214
Kansas City, Kansas 66112
Tel: 913 299 6692
Fax: 913 299 6792
collecting@manions.com
www.manions.com

CC Auctions
416 Court St, Clay Center
KS 67432
Tel: 785 632 6021
dhamilton@cc-auctions.com
www.cc-auctions.com

Spielman Auctions
2259 Homestead Rd
Lebo 66856
Tel: 316 256 6558

KENTUCKY

Hays & Associates Inc
120 South Spring Street
Louisville, KY 40206
kenhays@haysauction.com
www.haysauction.com

Steffens Historical Militaria
P.O. Box 280, Newport 41072
Tel: 859 431 4499
Fax: 859 431 3113
www.steffensmilitaria.com

LOUSIANA

**Morton M. Goldberg
Auction Galleries**
547 Baronne Street
New Orleans LA 70113
Tel: 504 592 2300
Fax: 504 592 2311

**New Orleans Auction
Galleries**
801 Magazine Street
New Orleans LA 70130
Tel: 504 566 1849
Fax: 504 566 1851
info@neworleansauction.com
www.neworleansauction.com

MARYLAND

DeCaro Auction Sales Inc.
117A Bay Street, Suite D
Easton, 21601
Tel: 410 820 4000
Fax: 410 820 4332
info@decaroauctions.com
www.decaroauctions.com

**Hantman's Auctioneers &
Appraisers**
P.O. Box 59366
Potomac, MD 20859
Tel: 301 770 3720
Fax: 301 770 4135
hantman@hantmans.com
www.hantmans.com

Isennock Auctions & Appraisals
Isennock Auction Services, Inc.
4106B Norrisville Road
White Hall, MD 21161
Phone 410-557-8052
Fax 410-692-6449
info@isennockauction.com
www.isennockauction.com

Sloans Auction Galleries
4920 Wyaconda Rd
N Bethseda 20852
Tel: 301 468 4911
Fax: 301 468 9182
slaons@sloansauctions.com
www.sloansauction.com

NORTH CAROLINA

Robert S. Brunk
Post Office Box 2135
Asheville 28802
Tel: 828 254 6846
Fax: 828 254 6545
auction@brunkauctions.com
www.brunkauctions.com

Historical Collectible Auctions
P.O. Box 975 Burlington 27215
Tel: 336 570 2803
bids4hca@aol.com
www.hcaauctions.com

SOUTH CAROLINA

Charlton Hall Galleries
912 Gervais St Columbia 29201
Tel: 803 799 5678
info@charltonhallgalleries.com
www.hcharltonhallgalleries.com

NORTH DAKOTA

**Curt D Johnson Auction
Company**
P.O. Box 135, Grand Forks 58201
Tel: 701 746 1378
merfeld@rrv.net
www.curtdjohnson.com

MAINE

Guyette & Schmidt
P.O. Box 522, West
Farmington, Maine 04992
Tel: 207 778 6256
Fax: 207 778 6501
decoys@guyetteandschmidt.com

**James D. Julia
Auctioneers Inc.**
P.O. Box 830, Fairfield
Maine 04937
Tel: 207 453 7125
Fax: 207 453 2502
jjulia@juliaauctions.com
www.juliaauctions.com

**Thomaston Place
Auction Galleries**
P.O. Box 300, 51 Atlantic
Highway, US Rt 1 Thomaston
ME 04861
Tel: 207 354 8141
Fax: 207 354 9523
barbara@kajav.com
www.thomastonauction.com

MASSACHUSETTS

Eldred's
P.O.Box 796, 1483 Route 6A
East Dennis, MA 02641
Tel: 508 385 3116
Fax: 508 385 7201
info@eldreds.com
www.eldreds.com

Grogan & Company
22 Harris St, Dedham
MA 02026
Tel: 800-823 1020
Fax: 781 461 9625
grogans@groganco.com
www.groganco.com

Simon D. Hill & Associates
420 Boston Turnpike
Shrewsbury 01545
Tel: 508 845 2400
Fax: 978 928 4129
simondhill@earthlink.net
www.simondhillauctions.com

Skinner Inc
The Heritage on the Garden
63 Park Plaza, Boston, MA 02116
Tel: 617-350-5400
Fax: 617-350-5429
info@skinnerinc.com
www.skinnerinc.com

Willis Henry Auctions
22 Main St, Marshfield, 02050
Tel: 781 834 7774
Fax: 781 826 3520
wha@willishenry.com
www.willishenry.com

MICHIGAN

DuMouchelles
408 East Jefferson Ave
Detroit 48226
Tel: 313 963 6255
Fax: 313 963 8199
info@dumouchelles.com
www.dumouchelles.com

MINNESOTA

Buffalo Bay Auction Co
5244 Quam Circle
Rogers 55374
Tel: 612 428 8480
buffalobayauction@hotmail.com
www.buffalobayauction.com

Rose Auction Galleries
2717 Lincoln Drive
Roseville MN 55113
Tel: 651 484 1415
Fax: 651 636 3431
auctions@rosegalleries.com
www.rosegalleries.com

MISSOURI

Ivey-Selkirk
7447 Forsyth Blvd
Saint Louis 63105
Tel: 314 726 5515
Fax: 314 726 9908
www.iveyselkirk.com

MONTANA

Allard Auctions Inc
P.O. Box 460 St Ignatius 59865
Tel: 406 745 0500
Fax: 406 745 0502
info@allardauctions.com
www.allardauctions.com

NEW HAMPSHIRE

Northeast Auctions
93 Pleasant St, Portmouth
03801-4504
Tel: 603 433 8400
Fax: 603 433 0415
www.northeastauctions.com

NEW JERSEY

Bertoia Auctions
2141 Demarco Dr.
Vineland 08360
Tel: 856 692 1881
Fax: 856 692 8697
bill@bertoiaauctions.com
www.bertoiaauctions.com

Craftsman Auctions
333 North Main St
Lambertville 08530
Tel: 609 397 9374
Fax: 609 397 9377
info@ragoarts.com
www.ragoarts.com

Dawson's
128 American Rd
Morris Plains 07950
Tel: 973 984 6900
Fax: 973 984 6956
info@dawsons.org
www.dawsons.org

Greg Manning Auctions Inc
775 Passaic Ave
West Caldwell 07006
Tel: 973 883 0004
Fax: 973 882 3499
info@gregmanning.com
www.gregmanning.com

Rago Modern Auctions LLP
333 North Main St
Lambertville 08530
Tel: 609 397 9374
Fax: 609 397 9377
info@ragoarts.com
www.ragoarts.com

NEW MEXICO

Parker-Braden Auctions
P.O. Box 1897 4303 National
Parks Highway, Carlsbad 88220
Tel: 505 885 4874
Fax: 505 885 4622
www.parkerbraden.com

NEW YORK

Christie's
20 Rockefeller Plaza
NY 10020
Tel: 212 636 2000
Fax: 212 636 2399
info@chrisites.com
www.christies.com

TW Conroy
36 Oswego St
Baldwinsville 13027
Tel: 315 638 6434
Fax: 315 638 7039
brad@twconroy.com
www.conroy.com

Samuel Cottone Auctions
15 Genesee St
Mount Morris 14510
Tel: 585 658 3119
Fax: 585 658 3152
scottone@rochester.rr.com
www.cottoneauctions.com

William Doyle Galleries
175 E. 87th St, NY 10128
Tel: 212 427 2730
Fax: 212 369 0892
info@doylenewyork.com
www.doylenewyork.com

Guernsey's Auctions
108 East 73rd St
New York 10021
Tel: 212 794 2280
Fax: 212 744 3638
auctions@guernseys.com
www.guernseys.com

**Phillips, De Pury &
Luxembourg**
23 West 57th St,
New York 10019
Tel: 212 940 1200
Fax: 212 688 1647
carole.bellidora@phillips-dpl.com
www.phillips-dpl.com

Sotheby's
1334 York Ave at 72nd St
New York 10021
Tel: 212 606 7000
Fax: 212 606 7107
info@sothebys.com
www.sothebys.com

Swann Galleries Inc
104 E. 25th St
New York 10010
Tel: 212 254 4710
Fax: 212 979 1017
swann@swanngalleries.com
www.swanngalleries.com

OHIO

Cowans Historic Americana
673 Wilmer Avenue
Cincinnati45226
Tel: 513 871 1670
Fax: 513 871 8670
info@historicamericana.com
www.historicamericana.com

DeFina Auctions
1591 State Route 45 Sth
Austinburg 44010
Tel: 440 275 6674
info@definaauctions.com
www.definaauctions.com

Garth's Auctions
2690 Stratford Rd, Box 369
Delaware 43015
Tel: 740 362 4771
Fax: 740 363 0164
info@garths.com
www.garths.com

PENNSYLVANIA

Alderfer Auction Gallery
501 Fairgrounds Rd
Hatfield 19440
Tel: 215 393 3000
info@alderferauction.com
www.alderferauction.com

Noel Barrett
P.O. Box 300,
Carversville 18913
Tel: 215 297 5109
toys@noelbarrett.com
www.noelbarrett.com

Dargate Auction Galleries
214 North Lexington
Pittsburgh 15208
Tel: 412 362 3558
info@dargate.com
www.dargate.com

Freeman's
1808 Chestnut Ave
Philadelphia 19103
Tel: 610 563 9275
info@freemansauction.com
www.freemansauction.com

Hunt Auctions
75 E. Uwchlan Ave, Suite 1
30 Exton 19341
Tel: 610 524 0822
Fax: 610 524 0826
info@huntauctions.com
www.huntauctions.com

Pook & Pook Inc
463 East Lancaster Ave
Downington 19335
Tel: 610 269 4040
Fax: 610 269 9274
info@pookandpook.com
www.pookandpook.com

Skinner's Auction Co.
170 Northampton St
Easton 18042
Tel: 610 330 6933
skinnauct@aol.com
www.skinnerauct.baweb.com

Stephenson's Auctions
1005 Industrial Blvd
Southampton 18966
Tel: 215 322 6182
info@stephensonsauction.com
www.stephensonsauction.com

RHODE ISLAND

WebWilson
P.O. Box 506,
Portsmouth 02871
Tel: 800 508 0022
hww@webwilson.com
www.webwilson.com

TENNESSEE

Berenice Denton Estates
4403 Murphy Road
Nashville 37209
Tel: 615 292 5765
lnichols66@home.com

Kimball M. Sterling Inc
125 W. Market St
Johnson City 37604
Tel: 423 928 1471
kimsold@tricon.net
www.sterlingsold.com

TEXAS

Austin Auctions
8414 Anderson Mill Rd
Austin 78729-4702
Tel: 512 258 5479
Fax: 512 219 7372
austinauction@cs.com
www.austinauction.com

Dallas Auction Gallery
1518 Socum St
Dallas 75207
Tel: 213 653 3900
Fax: 213 653 3912
info@dallasauctiongallery.com
www.dallasauctiongallery.com

Heritage Comics
Heritage Plaza
100 Highland Park Village,
2nd Floor, Dallas 75205-2788
Tel: 214 528 3500
Fax: 214 520 6968
jsmith@heritagecomics.com
www.heritagecomics.com

UTAH

America West Archives
P.O. Box 100, Cedar City
84721
Tel: 435 586 9497
awa@utah.net
www.americawestarchives.com

VERMONT

Eaton Auction Service
RR1 Box 333, Fairlee 05045
Tel: 802 333 9717

VIRGINIA

**Ken Farmer Auctions &
Estates**
105A Harrison St
Radford 24141
Tel: 540 639 0939
Fax: 540 639 1759
info@kfauctions.com
www.kfauctions.com

Phoebus Auction Gallery
14-16 E. Mellen St
Hampton 23663
Tel: 757 722 9210
Fax: 757 723 2280
bwelch@phoebusauction.com
www.phoebusauction.com

Signature House
407 Liberty Ave
Bridgeport, West Virginia
25330
Tel: 304 842 3386
Fax: 304 842 3001
systems@signaturehouse.net
www.signaturehouse.net

WISCONSIN
Krueger Auctions
P.O. Box 275
Iola 54945-0275
Tel: 715 445 3845

Schrager Auction Galleries
2915 North Sherman Blvd
P.O. Box 100043
Milwaukee 53210
Tel: 414 873 3738
Fax: 414 873 5229
askus@schragerauction.com
www.schragerauction.com

WYOMING
**Cody Old West Show
& Auction**
1215 Sheridan Ave
Cody 82414
Tel: 317 587 9014
Fax: 307 587 3979
oldwest@codyoldwest.com
www.codyoldwest.com

Manitou Gallery
1715 Carey Avenue
Cheyenne 82001
Tel: 307 635 7670
Fax: 307 778 3926
ptassi@aol.com

CLUBS AND SOCIETIES

ADVERTISING
**Antique Advertising Association
of America**
P.O. Box 1121
Morton Grove IL 60053.
Tel: 708 446 0904
www.pastimes.org

**Coca Cola Collectors Club
International**
P.O. Box 49166
Atlanta GA 30359-1166

**Tin Container Collectors
Association**
P.O. Box 440101 Aurora,
CO 80044

AMERICANA
Folk Art Society of America
P.O. Box 17041, Richmond, VA
23226-70

**American Political Items
Collectors**
P.O. Box 340339
San Antonio TX 8234-0339
http://www.collectors.org/apic

AUTOGRAPHS
**International Autograph
Collectors Club & Dealers'
Alliance**
4575 Sheridan St. Ste. 111
Hollywood FL 33021-3515
Tel: 561 736 8409
www.iacc-da.com

**Universal Autograph Collectors
Club**
P.O. Box 6181
Washington DC 20044
Tel: 202 332-7388
http://www.uacc.com

AUTOMOBILIA
Automobile Objets d'Art Club
252 N. 7th St. Allentown
PA 18102-4204
Tel: 610 432 3355
oldtoy@aol.com

BOOKS
**Antiquarian Bookseller's
Association of America**
20 West 44th St, 4th Floor
New York NY 10036
Tel: 212 944 8291
abaa@panix.com

CAMERAS
**American Society of
Camera Collectors**
7415 Reseda Blvd
Reseda CA 91335
Tel: 818 345-2660.

**American Photographic
Historical Society Inc.**
1150 Avenue of the Americas
New York NY 10036
Tel: 212 575 0483
gfine@monmouth.com

CERAMICS
**American Art Pottery
Association**
P.O. Box 834
Westport MA 02790-0697
postetal@aol.com
www.amartpot.com

American Ceramics Circle
520 16th St
Brooklyn NY 11215
Tel: 718 832 5446
nlester@earthlink.net

**American Cookie Jar
Association**
1600 Navajo Rd, Norman
OK 73026
davismj@ionet.net
www.cookiejarclub.com

Style 1900
David Rago
9 Main St.
Lambertville
NJ 08530

The Belleek Collectors Society
144 West Britannia Street
Taunton MA 02780
Tel: 508 824-6611
Fax: 508 822-7269.

Blue & White Pottery Club
224 12th Street N.W.
Cedar Rapids, Iowa 52405
Tel: 319 362-8116.

U.S. Chintz Collectors Club
PO Box 50888
Pasadena CA 91115
Tel: 626 441-4708
Fax: 626 441-4122
chintz4u@aol.com
http://www.chintznet.com

Clarice Cliff Collectors' Club
1 Foxtell Way, Chellaston
Derby, Derbyshire DE73 1PU UK
webmaster@claricecliff.com
www.claricecliff.com

**Dedham Pottery Collectors
Society**
248 Highland St.
Dedham MA 02026
Tel: 800 283-8070
dpcurator@aol.com

Goebel Networkers.
P.O. Box 396, Lemoyne,
PA 17043

Hummel Collectors Club
1261 University Dr., Yardley,
PA 19067-2857
Tel: 888 548 6635
Fax: 215 321 7367
http://www.hummels.com

**Roseville of The Past
Pottery Club**
P.O. Box 656 Clarcona, FL
32710-0656
Tel: 407 294 3980
Fax: 407 294 7836
rosepast@bellsouth.net
http://members.tripod.com/~ro
sepast/index.html

Royal Bayreuth Collectors Club
926 Essex Circle, Kalamazoo, MI
49008
Tel: 616 343-6066
judykazoo@aol.com

**Royal Doulton International
Collectors' Club**
700 Cottontail Lane,
Somerset, NJ 08873
Tel: 800 682-4462
Fax: 732 764-4974

Stangl & Fulper Club
P.O. Box 538, Flemington
NJ 08822
Tel: 908 995 2696
kenlove508@aol.com
www.stanglpottery.com

**American Stoneware
Collectors Society**
P.O. Box 281, Bay Head, NJ
08742
Tel: 732 899 8707

Susie Cooper Collectors Group
Panorama House, 18 Oaklea
Mews, Aycliffe Village, County
Durham DL5 6JP U.K.
www.susiecooper.co.uk

DISNEYANA
**National Fantasy Club For
Disneyana Collectors &
Enthusiasts**
P.O. Box 106, Irvine
CA 92713-9212
Tel: 714 731 4705
info@nffc.org
http://www.nffc.org

Walt Disney Collectors' Society
500 South Buena Vista St.
Burbank, CA 91521-8028
Tel: 800 932 5749

DOORSTOPS
Doorstop Collectors of America
2413 Madison Ave.
Vineland, NJ 08630.

EPHEMERA
Ephemera Society of America
P.O. Box 95
Cazenovia NY 13035-0095
Tel: 315 655-2810
Fax: 315 655-1078
info@ephemerasociety.org
http://www.epemerasociety.org

National Valentine Collectors Association
P.O. Box 1404,
Santa Ana, CA 92702
Tel: 714 547 1355

FIFTIES & SIXTIES
Head Hunters Newsletters.
P.O. Box 83H, Scarsdale, NY
10583.
Tel: 914 472 0200

FILM & TV MEMORABILIA
The Animation Art Guild
330 W. 45th St., Ste 9D
New York NY 10036-3864
Tel: 212 765 3030
theaagltd@aol.com

James Bond 007 Fan Club & Archive
The: P.O. Box 007, Surrey KT15 IDY, U.K.
Tel: 01483-756007

Lone Ranger Fan Club
19205 Seneca Ridge Court,
Gaithersburg, MD 20879-3135

GLASS
American Carnival Glass Association
9621 Springwater Lane
Miamisburg OH 45342.

Land of Sunshine Depression Glass Club
P.O. Box 560275
Orlando FL 32856-0275
Tel: 407 298 3355

Lalique Collectors Society
400 Veterans Blvd
Carlstadt NJ 07072-2704
Tel; 800 274 7825
info@lalique.com
www.lalique.com

Vaseline Glass Collectors
P.O. Box 125, Russellville,
MO 65074
vgci@hotmail.com
http://www.icnet.net/users/dav
epeterson/

JEWELRY
Cuff Link Society
PO Box 5700, Vernon Hills IL 60061.
Tel: 847 816 0035

Leaping Frog Antique Jewelry & Collectible Club
4841 Martin Luther King Blvd
Sacramento CA 95820-4932
Tel: 916 452 6728
pandora@cwia.com

Vintage Fashion & Costume Jewelry Club
P.O. Box 265, Glen Oaks
NY 11004-0265
Tel: 718 939 3095
vfcj@aol.com

KITCHENALIA
Kitchen Antiques & Collectibles News
4645 Laurel Ridge Dr.
Harrisburg, PA 17119

MECHANICAL MUSIC
Musical Box Society International
700 Walnut Hill Rd
Hockessin DE 19707
Tel: 302 239 5658
cotps@aol.com
http://www.mbsi.org

MILITARIA
Civil War Collectors & The American Militaria Exchange
5970 Toylor Ridge Dr.
West Chester OH 45069
Tel: 513 874 0483
rwmorgan@aol.com
www.civiwar-collectors.com

OPTICAL, MEDICAL, SCIENTIFIC & TECHNICAL
International Association of Calculator Collectors
PO Box 345
Tustin, CA 92781-0345
Tel: 714 730 6140
Fax: 714 730 6140
mrcalc@usa.net
http://www.geocities.com/silico
nvalley/park/7227/

ORIENTAL & ASIAN
International Chinese Snuff Bottle Society
2601 North Charles St
Baltimore MD 21218-4514
Tel: 410 467 9400
www.snuffbottle.org

International Netsuke Society
P.O. Box 161269, Altamonte
Springs, FL 32716-1269
Tel: 407 772 1906
odanuki@worldnet.att.net
http://www.netsuke.org/

PENS & WRITING
The Society of Inkwell Collectors
P.O. Box 324, Mossville IL
61552
Tel: 309 579 3040
director@soic.com
www.soic.com

Pen Collectors of America
P.O. Box 80
Redding Ridge CT 06876
www.pencollectors.com

PERFUME BOTTLES
International Perfume Bottle Association
396 Croton Rd., Wayne, PA
19087
Tel: 610-995-9051
jcabbott@bellatlantic.net
http://www.perfumebottles.org

ROCK N ROLL
Elvis Forever TCB Fan Club
P.O. Box 1066
Miami FL 33780-1066

Working Class Hero Beatles Club
3311 Niagara St
Pittsburgh PA 1213-4223

SMOKING
Cigarette Lighter Collectors Club
SPARK International
rainer.kytzia@hamburg.sc.philips.com
http://members.aol.com/intspark.

Pocket Lighter Preservation Guild & Historical Society, Inc.
PO Box 1054, Addison, IL
60101-8054
Tel: 708 543 9120

The Society for Clay Pipe Research
2 Combe Avenue, Portishead
Bristol BS20 6JR U.K.

SPORTING MEMORABILIA
Boxing & Pugilistica Collectors International
P.O. Box 83135
Portland OR 97283-0135
Tel: 502 286 3597

Golf Collectors Society
P.O. Box 24102
Cleveland OH 44124
Tel: 216 861 1615
kkuhl@aol.com
www.golfcollectors.com

National Fishing Lure Collectors Club
H.C. 33, Box 4012
Reeds Spring MO 65737
spurr@kingfisher.com

Society for American Baseball Research
812 Huron Rd E. 719
Cleveland OH 441155
info@sabr.org
www.sabr.org

SPACE MEMORABILIA
National Space Society
600 Pennsylvania Ave SE., Ste 201
Washington DC 20003-4316
Tel: 202 543 1900
nsshq@nss.org

TEXTILES & COSTUME
The Costume Society of America
55 Edgwater Dr., P.O. Box 73
Earleville MD 21919-0073
Tel: 410 275 1619
www.costumesocietyamerica.com

American Fan Collectors' Association
P.O. Box 5473
Sarasota FL 34277-5473
Tel: 817 267 9851
Fax: 817 267 0387International
Old Lacers
P.O. Box 554, Flanders NJ
07836
iolinc@aol.com

TOYS & DOLLS
Annalee Doll Society
P.O.Box 1137
Meredith NH 03253
Tel: 800 433-6557
Fax: 603 279-6659

The Antique Toy Collectors of America, Inc
C/o Carter, Ledyard & Milburn
Two Wall St - 13th Floor
New York, NY 10005

Chess Collectors' International
P.O. Box 166, Commack
NY 11725-0166
Tel: 516 543 1330
lichness@aol.com

Effanbee Doll Club
Tel: 888 272 2363
pacenet@pacenetinc.com
www.effnbeedolls.com

The Matchbox International Collectors Association
13a Lower Bridge Street,
Chester. CH1 1RS U.K.
http://www.matchboxclub.com

National Model Railroad Association
4121 Cromwell Rd
Chattanooga TN 37421
Tel: 423 892 2846
nmra@tttrains.com

Toy Soldier Collectors of America
5340 40th Ave N
Saint Petersburg FL 33709
Tel: 727 527 1430

United Federation of Doll Clubs
10920 N. Ambassador Dr.
Kansas City MO 64153
Tel: 816-891-7040
ufdc@aol.com

TREEN & BOXES
Mauchline Ware Collectors' Club
14 Blake Ter. SE, Cedar Rapids,
IA 52403
Tel: 319-362-2643
tknyc@earthlink.net

TRIBAL ART
The Antique Tribal Art Dealers Association
PO Box 620278, Woodside, CA
94062
Tel: 415 851 8670.
Fax: 415 851 3508.

WATCHES
Early American Watch Club
P.O. Box 81555
Wellesley Hills MA 02481-1333

National Association of Watch & Clock Collectors
514 Poplar St
Columbia PA 17512-2130
Tel: 717 684 8261
www.nawcc.org

WINE & DRINKING
International Correspondence of Corkscrew Addicts
670 Meadow Wood Road
Mississauga Ontario, L5J 2S6
Canada
Dugohuzo@aol.com
www.corkscrewnet.com/icca

Using the Internet

THE INTERNET HAS REVOLUTIONISED the trading of collectibles. Compared to a piece of furniture, most collectibles are easily defined, described and photographed. Shipping is also comparatively easy, due to average size and weight. Prices are also generally more affordable and accessible than for antiques and the internet has provided a cost-effective way of buying and selling, away from the overheads of shops and auction rooms. Many millions of collectibles are offered for sale and traded daily, with sites varying from global online marketplaces, such as eBay, to specialist dealers' websites.

When searching online, remember that some people may not know how to accurately describe their item. General category searches, although more time consuming, and even purposefully misspelling a name, can yield results. Also, if something looks too good to be true, it probably is. Using this book to get to know your market visually, so that you can tell the difference between a real bargain and something that sounds like one, is a good start.

As you will understand from buying this book, color photography is vital – look for online listings that include as many images as possible and check them carefully. Be aware that colors can appear differently, even between computer screens.

Always ask the vendor questions about the object, particularly regarding condition. If there is no image, or you want to see another aspect of the object – ask. Most sellers (private or trade) will want to realise the best price for their items, so they will be more than happy to help – if approached politely and sensibly.

As well as the 'e-hammer' price, you will probably have to pay additional transactional fees such as packing, shipping and possibly regional or national taxes. It is always best to ask for an estimate for these additional costs before leaving a bid. This will also help you tailor your bid because you will have an idea of the maximum price the item will cost if you are successful.

As well as the well-known online auction sites, such as eBay, there are a host of other online resources for buying and selling, such as fair and auction date listings.

Internet resources

icollector
www.icollector.com
customerservices@icollector.com
A free service which allows users to search selected auction house catalogues in Europe, the U.S.A and the United Kingdom. Through its unique connection with eBay, users can bid live into salerooms as auctions happens. Users can also leave absentee bids through the internet and search an archive of auction catalogs dating back to 1994.

invaluable.com
www.invaluable.com
sales@invaluable.com
A subscription service which allows users to search selected auction house catalogues from the United Kingdom and Europe. Also offers an extensive archive for appraisal uses.

The Antiques Trade Gazette
www.atg-online.com
The online version of the UK trade newspaper, comprising British auction and fair listings, news and events.

Appraisers' Association of America
www.appraisersassoc.com
A comprehensive American database allowing users to find an experienced appraiser for their item.

Maine Antiques Digest
www.maineantiquesdigest.com
The online version of America's trade newspaper including news, articles, fair and auction listings and more.

Auctionnet.com
www.auctionnet.com
Simple online resource listing over 500 websites related to auctions online.

AuctionBytes
www.auctionbytes.com
Auction resource with community forum, news, events, tips and a weekly newsletter.

Go Antiques/Antiqnet
www.goantiques.com
www.antiqnet.com
An online global aggregator for art, antiques and collectibles dealers who showcase their stock online, allowing users to browse and buy.

eBay
www.ebay.com
Undoubtedly the largest and most diverse of the online auction sites, allowing users to buy and sell in an online marketplace with over 40 million registered users. Collectors should also view eBay Live Auctions (www.ebayliveauctions.com) where traditional auctions are combined with realtime, online bidding allowing users to interact with the saleroom as the auction takes place.

Acknowledgments

DORLING KINDERSLEY would like to thank the following people for their assistance in producing this book: Philip Gilderdale, Caroline Hunt, Julian Gray, Kelly Meyer, Martin Dieguez and Scott Stickland.